The World That Never Was

A True Story of Dreamers, Schemers, Anarchists and Secret Agents

ALEX BUTTERWORTH

THE BODLEY HEAD
LONDON

FOR MATILDA AND THOMAS

Published by The Bodley Head 2010

2 4 6 8 10 9 7 5 3 1

First published in Great Britain in 2010 by
The Bodley Head
Random House, 20 Vauxhall Bridge Road,
London SW1V 2SA

www.bodleyhead.co.uk
www.rbooks.co.uk

Addresses for companies within The Random House Group Limited can be found at:
www.randomhouse.co.uk/offices.htm
The Random House Group Limited Reg. No. 954009

A CIP catalogue record for this book
is available from the British Library

ISBN 9780224078078

The Random House Group Limited supports The Forest Stewardship
Council (FSC), the leading international forest certification organisation. All our titles that are
printed on Greenpeace approved FSC certified paper carry the FSC logo. Our paper procurement
policy can be found at www.rbooks.co.uk/environment

Mixed Sources
Product group from well-managed
forests and other controlled sources
www.fsc.org Cert no. TT-COC-2139
© 1996 Forest Stewardship Council
FSC

Typeset in Dante MT by Palimpsest Book Production Limited,
Grangemouth, Stirlingshire

Printed and bound in Great Britain by
Clays Ltd, St Ives PLC

Contents

Introduction

In the early years of the twenty-first century, a British Home Secretary recommended that those wishing to understand what at that time was still termed the 'War on Terror' should look back to the 1890s. Parallels were widely drawn with the wave of bombings and assassinations that had swept Europe and America at the end of the nineteenth century, perpetrated by anarchists and nihilists for whom London and Switzerland had provided refuge. Then as now, it was remarked, disaffected young men from swollen immigrant communities had been radicalised by preachers of an extremist ideology and lured into violence. Some commentators wrote of 'Islamo-anarchism', while others remarked that Al-Zawahiri, the 'brains' of Al-Qaeda, had studied the revolutionary writings of the godfather of anarchism, Michael Bakunin.

The parallels were persuasive and the comparison of the new threat to western civilisation with one long since vanquished appeared almost comforting. Yet, such references are largely misleading when detached from any sense of the circumstances that moulded the revolutionaries of the nineteenth century, impelling them to seek an alternative and better future. When their world is viewed from the position they occupied at society's margins, whether by choice or ill fortune, an era named for its glittering surface as a belle époque or Gilded Age is thrown into stark relief. The effect is uncanny, for many features of that landscape do indeed echo those of our own times but in ways that should shame us as well as causing deeper disquiet.

The obscene discrepancies of wealth between the rich and the poor were painfully obvious in the last decades of the nineteenth century, existing cheek by jowl in cities such as London, but they are scarcely less troublesome now, and still more extreme in the global village. Back then, the industrial exploitation of labour and the greed of the few generated social injustice and economic instability; the unwillingness of politicians to confront malign corporate and financial powers led to disillusionment, even in purported democracies; and all was set against a background of economies staggering from crisis to crisis, uncertain how to tame a rampant, savage capitalism. Organised religion, discredited by science, flailed against its loss of authority, while others saw the greater spiritual threat in the nascent consumer culture and intrusiveness of advertising. Mass migration challenged the resilience of national cultures and created a strong cross-fertilised internationalism. Meanwhile, in a multi-polar world shaped by Great Power geopolitics, shifts in the balance of economic dynamism threatened peace, with alliances wrangled in the hope of averting or retarding the dance towards the precipice.

Extreme caution should be exercised in supposing that history ever even rhymes, let alone repeats itself. Nevertheless, the news headlines during the years that I have spent researching and writing this book have time and again left me with the impression that the intervening century has in some strange way folded back upon itself. We must sincerely hope that we too are not unknowingly caught up in such a deadly dance, and that the most extreme consequences of the flaws in that world are not to be repeated. Throughout the period in question a silent, secret clock-work of intrigue and manipulation was in operation to protect the status quo, just as it is today, yet then as now the risk of unforeseen consequences was not to be underestimated.

Framed by two revolutions, beginning with the Paris Commune of 1871 and ending with that staged by the Bolsheviks in October 1917, these are years tormented by the constant fear and possibility of violent upheaval. It was an age characterised by many contemporary social commentators as decadent or degenerate, a moment of crisis, perhaps even for the human species as a whole. The anarchists, seen as advocates of destruction and promulgators of terror, were often posited as the most shocking symptom of the malaise. The control, suppression and ultimate demonisation of their fiendish sect appeared to many a moral imperative, and was clearly as much a pleasure as a duty for many official defenders of law and order. For them 'anarchism' was a useful shorthand for the subversive threat posed by revolutionaries of all hues. Nor could the anarchists rely on the solidarity of their supposed brethren on the political left, to whom their liberal critique of state socialism was almost as intolerable as their socialist critique of capitalism was to those who wielded political power. With anarchism exposed to enemies on all sides, the violence perpetrated in its name by a few headstrong young men was more than enough to confirm the movement's pariah status in perpetuity.

It was a fate scarcely deserved by the leading ideologues of the movement, some of them figures of international standing as scientists, who
had vied with the dogmatic Marxists for the claim to champion a form
of 'scientific socialism'. Variously derided as utopian dreamers and reviled
as desperate conspirators, with hindsight they emerge instead as plausible visionaries. Even the social democratic heirs of their fiercest critics
would be hard pressed to deny that history has vindicated many of their
remedies: female emancipation with state support for the care and education of children, collective social security, sustainable communities with
power devolved as far as possible, with a federal United States of Europe
to prevent the continent-wide wars that they foretold. The human spirit
was to be celebrated against the dead hand of centralisation, and self-
fulfilment would be achieved through creative work rather than material
gain: the essence of the political agenda of 'well-being' now in vogue.
Even their espousal of autonomous federated communities as the basis
for a new form of society prefigures the ideas of localism and sustain-
ability that many believe must now be implemented to preserve the health
of the planet.

Peter Kropotkin's theory of Mutual Aid, which asserted an evolutionary
argument that cooperation rather than competition was the natural state
of human relations, has received support from recent discoveries in the
field of genetics. All that was required for mankind's best instincts to flourish,
he and his colleagues argued, was for the accreted institutions, hierarchies
and privileges that had corrupted society to be swept away; left to their
own devices, people would quickly and surely create a cooperative paradise. And yet it was this naïve optimism that left the movement so vulnerable to attack and manipulation.

Judged by the standards of political pragmatism, the position adopted
by Kropotkin and others was catastrophic on many counts. At a time
when many other socialist factions were busily marshalling their troops
and handing executive power to conspiratorial elites, anarchism eschewed
formal organisation or leadership of any sort, recoiling from coercion
and central control. By placing such deep faith in the individual conscience
and allowing validity to every honestly held opinion, consensus was
inevitably elusive, while the movement left itself defenceless, almost on
principle, against both malicious infiltration and co-option by those who
sought to use political idealism as a cover for criminal intent. And whilst
the anarchist philosophers' hopes that the social revolution might come
to pass with little or no bloodshed was doubtless sincere, it is hard to
excuse their failure to forestall the extremes of violence to which their

acolytes were driven by frustration at the absence of any popular appetite for a more creative apocalypse. A dangerous credulity, though, was not the exclusive preserve of those who awaited Utopia.

Faced with a world of increasing complexity and rapid change, a complacent bourgeoisie craved easy explanations of anything that challenged its easeful existence. In such circumstances, the phenomenon of the all-encompassing 'conspiracy theory' was able to take root. The fanciful notion of an internationally coordinated anarchist revolution of which the isolated attacks with bombs, knives and revolvers marked the first skirmishes was only one example. Others drew in the credulous masses with fantastical stories of Freemasonic satanism and megalomaniac supermen. It was a fictitious conspiracy that harnessed the rising tide of anti-Semitism, though, which would truly define the genre: *The Protocols of the Elders of Zion*. And although public opinion was not yet ready to embrace the simplest, most ruthless solutions to such a perceived threat, the contemporary debate over criminal anthropology and eugenics darkly foreshadowed what lay ahead. That such ideas were advanced from and encouraged by the political left, with the most humane intentions, is typical of the paradoxical nature of the period.

From out of the midst of a tangled knot of forgeries, provocation, black propaganda, misplaced idealism and twisted political allegiances the horrors of world war, totalitarianism and genocide that plagued the twentieth century would grow, having already set deep roots. Credible theses have been advanced that the origins of fascism lie in nineteenth-century anarchism, or that the French nationalism of the *fin de siècle*, which itself embraced elements from the radical left, may have been the progenitor of Nazism. My interest here, however, is merely to unpick the elaborate deceptions and intrigues generated by all sides, in an attempt to discern the confluence of factors that led to the first international 'War on Terror' and the consequences that flowed from it. For amidst a welter of alarmism and misdirection, a genuine conspiracy of sorts does lie buried, less cogent and universal than that described by the *Protocols*, despite them sharing a common author, but far-reaching nonetheless. And if there are valuable lessons to be learned from the period, the most imperative are perhaps to be discovered here, however uncomfortable they may be.

In exploring such a murky world, I have been unsurprised that the evidence has been elusive and the official paper trail often sparse. How welcome would be the reappearance of the suitcase, last seen in Paris during the 1930s, containing the private papers of Peter Rachkovsky, the head of Russia's foreign Okhrana and the fulcrum for so much of the intrigue in the period. How convenient if the files relating to the Okhrana's activities in London, and its relations with the American Pinkerton Agency, had not at some point been emptied; or, indeed, if the Belgian cabinet had forgotten to instruct that key police reports should disappear into secret dossiers, never to emerge again.

What has taken me aback, however, has been the tenacity with which the Metropolitan Police's Special Branch in London have sought to prevent access to their apparently limited records from the period: a number of ledgers, listing communications received from a wide range of sources. Along with the correspondence itself, for many years the ledgers themselves had been thought lost: pulped in the war effort, it was claimed, or destroyed by a bomb. Since their surprising reappearance in 2001, to be used as the basis of a doctoral thesis by a serving Special Branch officer, such access has not been replicated for other researchers, despite a Freedom of Information case I have pursued for several years. Following a ruling in favour of disclosure by the Information Commissioner and reprimands for the Metropolitan Police handling of the case, the police appeal to the Information Tribunal in 2009 resulted in the universal redaction of all names contained in the documents. The censored material raises as many questions as it answers.

Nevertheless, enough documentary evidence is available for a patient researcher to piece together a picture of this clandestine world of late nineteenth-century policing. The spiriting to America of the Okhrana's Paris archive following the revolution in Russia, unveiled at the Hoover Institute in the 1950s, has preserved a rich resource; so too have the archives of the Paris Prefecture of Police, whose basement contains box upon box of material, including agents' field reports, readily accessible to the public on request. Official documents jostle with a fascinating mass of material of more questionable reliability: reports from duplicitous informants, eager to prove themselves indispensible by passing off conjecture as fact; press coverage of false-flag police operations. And then there are the memoirs published by policemen and revolutionaries, all with an agenda to promote, or a desire to dramatise or justify their achievements.

The world that this book sets out to portray is one of slippery truths, where the key to success lies in the manipulation of popular opinion, where masters of deception weave webs of such complexity that they will ultimately trap themselves, and a clinical paranoiac offers some of the most perspicacious testimony. I have chosen to represent it in a mode that emphasises narrative over analysis, and in order to capture something of the subjective experience of those involved, at times I have taken the protagonists at their own estimation, recounting stories that they told about themselves as fact. For the fullest exploration of those decisions, as well as for additional material relating to certain areas covered, the reader should look to the online notes that accompany this book: those published here offer only minimal citation.

Works of literature that are more ostensibly fictional, or offer a creative interpretation of the period in some other form, are presented more critically. Radical politics and cultural bohemia frequently rubbed shoulders, each in search of new truths and on a quest to reshape reality, and the art and literature of the period are uncommonly revealing about both the life of that milieu, and the ideas that informed it. The fantastical genre of 'anticipatory' fiction, then so popular, at first articulated the promise of technological progress to which the anarchists looked for the foundations of a utopian future, but latterly evoked the destructive horrors of which anarchism was thought capable. Similarly, the social realist novels of the day offer an unequalled insight into the hardship and injustices of everyday life, and occasionally open windows too into the underworld of intrigue.

Chimerical though the notions of an international conspiracy largely were, the geographical scope of the anarchist movement and activities of the associated revolutionaries was truly global. Rarely at rest for long, the group of protagonists with whom the book is particularly concerned were time and again dispersed by exile, deportation or flight, travelling to make a stand wherever the prospects of insurrection appeared most auspicious. Their interweaving paths are tracked across five continents, while the communities in St Petersburg, Paris, London and elsewhere where they occasionally coalesced, for congresses or in search of refuge, are more closely explored. Equal attention, though, is given to the police officials who hang on the anarchists' tails, or else lurk in the shadows with dubious intent. The book's overall progression is chronological, though the reader should be aware that consecutive chapters often overlap in time to keep pace with the disparate lives of their subjects. Individuals and themes may disappear into the background for some time, but their strands of story are more likely to resurface.

Russia, although a relative backwater for anarchism, figures prominently as a disseminator of terrorism and focus of revolutionary zeal. Paradoxically, Spain and Germany, hotbeds of anarchism and socialism, remain largely offstage except where events there impinge on the story elsewhere: more discrete in their national movements, they each warrant books to themselves, of which kind many exist. At crucial junctures in my story, much original research is deployed. Elsewhere, the panorama described is largely a work of synthesis, and I am therefore grateful to all those on whose specialist research I have drawn, especially where it is yet to be published.

To the Victorian public, proud of their national tradition of liberal policing and of Britain as a beacon of tolerance, the very idea of a political police carried the stigma of foreign despotism. In the nineteenth century, Britain's elected politicians would never have dared venture anything resembling the kind of legislation that recent years have seen passed with barely a blink of the public eye, to threaten civil liberties that have for generations been taken for granted. That changing times demand changing laws is hard to dispute, but if new powers are to be conceded it is essential that we be ever more vigilant in guarding against their abuse. Likewise, if our political leaders are allowed blithely to insist that 'history' should be their judge, then we should at least be in no doubt that the historians of the future will have access to the material necessary to hold those leaders to account for any deceptions they may have practised. Histories bearing an official sanction, of the kind that appeal to today's security services, are not a satisfactory alternative. This book is a pebble cast on the other side of the scales.

Prologue

This Thing of Darkness

Paris, 1908

In the eyes of the world, the group that assembled daily in Boris Savinkov's spartan Paris apartment in October 1908 would have represented the most formidable concentration of terrorists history had yet seen. The sixty-six-year-old Peter Kropotkin, a descendant of the Rurik dynasty of early tsars, may have appeared unthreatening, with his twinkling eyes, bushy white beard, paunch and distinguished, bald dome of a head, but some suspected him of having incited the 1901 assassination of McKinley, the American president. With him sat his Russian contemporaries, the revolutionaries Vera Figner and German Lopatin, who had only recently emerged from the terrible Schlüsselburg fortress, against whose vast walls they had listened to the freezing waters of the River Neva and Lake Ladoga lap ceaselessly for twenty years. Locked in solitary confinement, in cells designed to prevent any communication, they were there as leaders of the organisation that had assassinated Tsar Alexander II in 1881. And among the younger generation, scattered around the room, there were others who could count grand dukes, government ministers and police chiefs among their many victims. But whatever the suspicions at the French Sûreté, Scotland Yard or the Fontanka headquarters of the Russian Okhrana, whose agents loitered in the street outside, their purpose on this occasion was not to conspire, but to uncover the conspiracies of others.

Kropotkin, Lopatin and Figner – an exalted trio in the revolutionary pantheon – had been summoned to form a Jury of Honour, for a trial convened by the central committee of the Socialist Revolutionary Party of Russia. Their task was to determine the truth or otherwise of an extraordinary accusation made by one of their number: that the movement's most idolised hero, Evno Azef, was in fact in the pay of the Okhrana, and responsible for a shocking series of deceptions and betrayals.

Commissioned for the weight of authority and experience that they could bring to bear in a case of unprecedented sensitivity, it was hoped that their status would ensure that, whatever the verdict, it would be beyond challenge.

It was a necessary precaution, for in this looking-glass trial, staffed exclusively by notorious lawbreakers, one thing above all was topsy-turvy. Vladimir Burtsev, the revolutionary movement's self-appointed counter-intelligence expert, who had levelled the original accusation of treachery, had become the accused. Okhrana ruses to seed dissent in the revolutionary movement were all too common, and after his defamatory allegations concerning the legendary Azef, the Jury of Honour needed to settle the matter once and for all.

So it was that, for three weeks, the distinguished jurors sat behind a table and listened as the neat, intense figure of Vladimir Burtsev, with his light goatee beard and steel-rimmed spectacles, earnestly explained how the revolutionary they all knew as the 'Frenchman' or 'Fat One' at the same time figured on the Okhrana payroll as 'Vinogradov', 'Kapustin', 'Philipovsky' and 'Raskin'. *Their* Azef had bound his comrades in a cult of self-sacrifice by his sheer charisma, relished the destruction of the tsar's allies and fantasised about remote-control electrochemical bombs and flying machines that could deliver terror ever more effectively. The Okhrana's Azef had set his comrades up for mass arrest by the political police in raids that stretched from the forests of Finland to the centre of Moscow, then celebrated at orgies laid on by his secret-police handler in a private room of the luxurious Malyi Iaroslavets restaurant. A St Petersburg apartment was, Burtsev alleged, reserved exclusively for the fortnightly meetings at which Raskin-Azef and the head of the Okhrana coordinated their priorities. This Azef thought nothing of murdering comrades, or betraying them for execution, to cover his tracks. And his heinous treachery was tinged with the macabre: once, on being shown the head of an unknown suicide bomber preserved in a jar of vodka by his police handler, he had appeared to relish identifying it as that of 'Admiral' Kudryavtsev, a rival from the Maximalist faction of terrorists.

As those in the courtroom listened to Burtsev's allegations, an instinct for psychic self-protection closed their minds. To the veteran revolutionaries Azef was a potent avenger of past wrongs, while the younger generation had allowed themselves to become emotionally enslaved to their mentor's mystique. For either group to entertain the possibility that Azef might be a traitor was to peer into an abyss. How, they demanded, could Burtsev possibly prove such an absurdity? That very day, Savinkov told the court, he was awaiting news of Tsar Nicholas' assassination on board the new naval cruiser *Rurik* during its maiden voyage, according to a plan formulated by Azef. What comparable proof of his own commitment to the cause could Burtsev offer? Was the truth not, in fact, that it was Burtsev himself who had been turned by the Okhrana and assigned to destabilise their organisation? Why, others pressed, did Burtsev refuse to name his witnesses, if they actually existed, unless they were of such questionable reliability as to make protecting their anonymity a safer strategy for him to pursue? Vera Figner, whose long imprisonment had done nothing to soften her pitiless dark eyes, snarled at Burtsev that once his infamy was confirmed he would have no choice but to make good on his promise to blow out his own brains.

Under such pressure, Burtsev played his trump card. Shortly before the Jury of Honour had convened, he confided, feeling their rapt attention, he had tracked down the ex-chief of the Russian political police, Alexei Lopukhin, to Cologne. Discreetly, he had followed him on to a train, hesitating until they were under steam before he entered his compartment. Lopukhin might have been expected to flinch at the appearance of a possible assassin, and curse the loss of the protection he had enjoyed when in police service: the armed guard of crack agents and the locked carriages and shuttered windows. Instead, encountering one of his enemies on neutral territory, he treated him like an honoured foe. At Burtsev's suggestion, the pair settled down to a guessing game: he would hazard a description of the police department's foremost secret agent, and Lopukhin would confirm only whether his surmise was correct . . .

As Burtsev concluded his compelling tale, German Lopatin groaned. 'What's the use of talking?' he said. 'It's all clear now.' Azef had refused to attend the trial, arguing that a sense of affront prevented him from being present in the courtroom to clear his name. His punishment was therefore decided *in absentia*. A villa would be rented with a tunnel that led to a cave just across the Italian border where the traitor could be hanged without diplomatic repercussions. Realising that the man he had trusted above all others had played him for a fool, Savinkov bayed loudest for blood.

*

Until Burtsev had delivered his bombshell, only the elderly Kropotkin had been resolute in his support of his thesis. There was a personal sympathy, certainly, for Burtsev who, like his own younger self, had managed to escape from the tsarist police in the most dramatic fashion. And Kropotkin may have remembered too how, over thirty years before, he had spent many hours trying to convince a sceptical German Lopatin, now his co-juror, of his own credibility: that his aristocratic background should not stand in the way of his joining the revolutionaries. Most of all, though, he possessed a hard-earned understanding of the bottomless depths that the chiefs of the Russian political police would plumb in their scheming. In the course of his career as one of anarchism's greatest theorists and leading activists, he had repeatedly seen idealistic men and women across the world fall prey to the wiles of agents provocateurs. Kropotkin had come to believe where persistent charges of spying and provocation were made by a number of individuals over a period of time, that the smoke nearly always signalled fire.

Stepping out into the rue La Fontaine, after the agreement of Azef's sentence, careless of the watchful eyes that swivelled towards him over upturned collars and twitching newspapers, Kropotkin would have felt a mixture of relief and dismay: that the traitor had been unmasked, but that the struggle to which he had devoted his life had engendered such a creature. The exposure of Azef was surely to be celebrated for the light it shed into the diabolical realm of shadows where he had dwelt: a world in which the boundaries of reality and invention were blurred. Kropotkin had many regrets about anarchism's long drift into the use of terror tactics, and must have been tempted to blame the intrigues and provocations of the secret police, and imagine the cancer excised. And yet, in many ways, Evno Azef embodied the central paradox of the political philosophy that Kropotkin had done so much to develop and promulgate. Simple in his brute appetites, yet dizzyingly adept as a conspirator, Azef's unusual blend of attributes shaped him into a phenomenon of a sort that no one involved in the revolutionary struggle had adequately foreseen.

Anarchism's ultimate aim was to usher in a society of perfect beings; a heaven on earth in which harmonious coexistence was achieved without coercion or the impositions of distant authority, but rather arose out of each individual's enlightened recognition of their mutual respect and dependency. Such a world, Kropotkin believed, would flourish naturally once the age-old cages of commerce, hierarchy and oppression that stunted and distorted human nature were torn down. Until then an anarchist programme of education could usefully preserve a generation from such taint, and prepare it to claim mankind's birthright in full. There were those, however, who acted on the impulse to hasten the advent of that paradise, or else out of vengeance or frustration, taking only their own vaunted conscience as their guide.

Though consistent with anarchism's idealistic tenets, such a creed was a recipe for disaster in a flawed society whose injustices already drove men to insanity and crime. For when the movement's ideological leaders refused on principle to disown murder, violent theft or even paid collaboration with the police, if it helped feed a starving mouth or might advance the cause, the scope for the malicious manipulation of susceptible minds was boundless.

The world was far from what Kropotkin had dreamed it might become, but was there no hope for the future? Adjoining Savinkov's apartment block in rue La Fontaine stood the architect Guimard's newly constructed art nouveau masterpiece, Castel Béranger. In the sinuous, organic forms of its gated entrance – in the mysterious leaves and tendrils of its decorative wrought iron, that curled up from the ground like smoke, then whiplashed back – ideas central to his political creed had been distilled into a compelling visual form: individualism challenged uniformity, while progress vanquished convention. And yet the Paris in which he had spent the last three weeks – a belle époque city of exclusive pleasures and spasmodic street violence – fell far short of the aspirations expressed in its architecture.

The filigree ironwork that vaulted the new Grand Palais, the crowds that issued periodically from the stations of the recently tunnelled Métro, and the soaring pylon of the Eiffel Tower eloquently expressed the great era of change that had passed since Kropotkin's first visit to the city three decades before. But there was scant evidence that the human ingenuity expended on the technological advances of the age had been matched by developments in the political and social spheres. While the years had mellowed the elegant masonry in which Baron Haussmann, Emperor Napoleon III's prefect of the Seine, had rebuilt Paris in the 1860s, the crushing bourgeois values of self-interest and conformity celebrated in his mass-produced blocks still held sway. Fear of a rising Germany had ten years earlier driven the French Republic into a shameful alliance with despotic Russia, and more recently it had become a full and eager signatory to the draconian St Petersburg protocol on international anti-anarchist police cooperation. Worst of all, it was old radical associates of Kropotkin's like Georges Clemenceau, prime minister for the past two years, who bore much of the responsibility for betraying the principles on which the Third Republic had been founded.

Kropotkin nevertheless retained an unshakeable faith that the rebirth of society was imminent. Perhaps in tacit acknowledgement of his part in allowing the creation of monsters like Azef, he would devote his last years to the culminating project of his life: a work of moral philosophy for the dawning age of social revolution. That future, Kropotkin was quite certain, would be born in war and strife. A renewal of hostilities between Germany and France, which had threatened repeatedly during the three decades and more since Bismarck's armies had besieged Paris, would at long last precipitate a fight for justice against the forces of re-action. It would come soon – next week, perhaps, or the week after – and its challenges could only be met if the lessons of past failures had been fully addressed. Those who remained of his generation, who had lived through those failures, must point the way.

He would have thought of them often during his time in Paris: the men and women of the Commune, who for eight extraordinary weeks of insurrection during the spring of 1871 had risen up to create their own autonomous government in the city. Some of them, now dead of old age, had become Kropotkin's closest friends: the geographer Elisée Reclus, who had been captured during the Communards' first, disastrous sortie against the Versaillais forces intent on crushing their social experiment; Louise Michel, the Red Virgin, who had still been there at the doomed defence of the Issy fortress, and throughout the Communards' tragic, fighting retreat across the city.

It had been stories of the Paris Commune that had helped inspire Kropotkin to leave behind his life as a leading light of Russia's scientific Establishment and devote himself to the revolutionary cause. Ten years after first hearing the wistful recollections of Communard exiles, drinking in a Swiss tavern in the immediate aftermath of defeat, he had written them down. 'I will never forget', one had said, 'those delightful moments of deliverance. How I came down from my supper chamber in the Latin Quarter to join that immense open-air club which filled the boulevards from one end of Paris to the other. Everyone talked about public affairs; all mere personal preoccupations were forgotten; no more thought of buying or selling; all felt ready to advance towards the future.' Both Reclus and Michel had died in 1905, the year when revolution had finally touched Russia, only to end before it could begin, but that optimism remained alive.

In his obituary of Reclus, Kropotkin had paid tribute to the role played by his fellow geographer during the 1870 Siege of Paris, when he had served as an assistant to the great balloonist Nadar, whose daring aeronauts ferried messages out of the city and over the Prussian lines. Had his cerebral, reticent old friend really been one of those fearless men who floated aloft in the balloons, braving the Prussian sharpshooters? Had Reclus looked down across Paris from a vantage point higher than that from the tower, that was then not yet even a glimmer in Eiffel's eye, and dreamed of what the world might be? It mattered so much from where you saw things, and what you wanted to see. For fiction could so easily be confused with truth, and truth relegated to the realm of fiction.

I

A Distant Horizon

Paris, 1870

A blizzard was blowing when Elisée Reclus arrived in London in the winter of 1851 and took lodgings in a modest garret, shared with his older brother, Elie. Yet it was the search for shelter of a very different kind that had brought the twenty-year-old pastor's son to the British capital: a haven where he could engage in political debate, free of censorship or persecution.

Having abandoned his theological training when the great wave of revolutions had swept Europe in 1848, Reclus had occupied himself in its aftermath with a new course of studies under the radical geographer Carl Ritter in Berlin. On his return to France after graduation, Reclus found himself in a country braced for renewed political turbulence, as Bonaparte's nephew Louis-Napoleon edged towards the *coup d'état* that would overturn the infant Second Republic and elevate him from the presidency to the imperial throne. Reclus decided to go to London. And if he had any doubts about his decision to leave France again so soon, they were quickly dispelled when he was repeatedly stopped by the police, stationed along the roads to the Channel, and interrogated as to the purpose of his journey.

From the famed Italian socialist Mazzini, to the little-known German political journalist Karl Marx, London alone offered reliable asylum to the political renegades of the Continent. Although 7,000 had fled there after the turmoil of 1848, there was little sign of Britain's hospitality diminishing; freedom fighter Joseph Kossuth's arrival only a few weeks before Reclus, after the revolutionary had been ousted by Russia from the presidency of Hungary, had been greeted by cheering crowds. Reclus, who increasingly counted himself a fellow traveller, could venture out without fear to public lectures by such exiled luminaries as Louis Blanc and the Russian Alexander Herzen, or to rub shoulders with the Freemasons of the Loge of Philadelphes, who were pledged to reverse Napoleon's usurpation of power. Yet amidst the excitement of open debate, it was Reclus' visits to a showman's marvel in Leicester Square that left the strongest impression on him.

Sixty feet in diameter and named after Queen Victoria's geographer, Wyld's Globe offered tourists the chance to stand on a central staircase that ran from pole to pole, and gaze up at the contoured map of the world that covered its inner surface. 'Here a country looks like an immense cabbage-leaf, flattened out, half green and half decayed, with an immense caterpillar crawling right over it in the shape of a chain of mountains,' reported Punch. 'There a country resembles an old piece of jagged leather hung up against the wall to dry, with large holes, that have been moth-eaten out of it.' Whatever the globe's aesthetic shortcomings, crowds were drawn by the chance to wonder at the glorious extent of the British Empire, or identify the provenance of the many luxuries with which global trade provided them. Reclus saw the construction rather differently. Tutored in Ritter's holistic vision of the natural world, and inspired by his pioneering work on the relationship between mankind and its environment, his thoughts were animated instead by the globe's potential as an instrument of humanitarian instruction.

Growing up in the countryside of the Gironde, one of fourteen children, Reclus had been forbidden by his strict and self-denying father from wandering in the fields around their home, lest his fascination with nature distract his younger siblings from their devotions. The vision that Wyld's Globe now afforded Reclus, of a world open to curiosity and enquiry, more than vindicated his conversion from the cast-iron certainties of the Church to the empirical values of science. One inheritance from his father that Reclus had embraced, though, was the desire to evangelise. Recalling proposals for a great spherical 'Temple to Nature and Reason' made by the visionary architect Etienne-Louis Boullée at the height of Robespierre's influence during the French Revolution, Reclus began to dream of building an edifice vaster still. It would celebrate a world stripped of such artificial impositions as national borders, and symbolise one in which race, class and property no longer divided mankind.

In its review of Wyld's Globe, Punch had commented on how the positioning of the central iron staircase, which impeded a panoramic view, demonstrated 'how one half of the Globe doesn't know what the other half is doing'. Several months in London had greatly enhanced Reclus' understanding of contemporary currents in socialist thought, but his practical ignorance of the world demanded redress. Departing England in the continued company of Elie, his scientific purpose was to discover those laws of nature that, throughout history, could explain the relationship between the physical environment and the beliefs, institutions and languages on which human society was founded. Above all, though, the journey that would take him halfway around the world over the coming years was to be one of political self-discovery.

At every stage of his travels, Reclus encountered the bitter reality of the division between powerful and oppressed, and the wilful ignorance that sustained it: an Irish farm whose emerald green pastures were used to fatten cattle for export to the English market while famine racked the country; African slaves, torn from their homes and worked like beasts for profit on the plantations of Louisiana; even the rivalries of the supposed free-thinkers in Panama with whom he entered a doomed collaboration in communal living. Yet in the solidarity of the oppressed he detected a glimmer of hope. The displaced Choctaw tribe, on whose ancestral lands the Reclus brothers set up home on first arriving in America, had sent a large donation to the starving Irish, remembering their own suffering on the 'Trail of Tears' to the reservation. Equally, the campaign for the abolition of slavery affirmed the survival of a human decency amidst the corrupt capitalism that was visible all around them in America. 'Every negro, every white who protests in exalted voice in favour of the rights of man, every word, every line in all the South affirms that man is the brother to man,' Elisée reassured his brother.

Having long since repudiated religious dogma, Reclus embraced the alternative, secular article of faith found in the enlightenment philosophy of Rousseau which had inspired the prime movers of the French Revolution of 1789. Man was innately perfectible, he asserted, not fallen for some long-dead ancestor's sin; nor was he to be saved by divine intervention, but by his own hunger for justice and equality. Schooled by Elie in the new utopian socialism of Saint-Simon, Charles Fourier and Joseph-Pierre Proudhon, it seemed to Reclus that the old revolutionary doctrines of the previous century merely needed to be recast in new terms.

The France to which Reclus finally returned in 1857 proved even less receptive to radical politics than that which he had abruptly left six years earlier. When Louis-Napoleon had seized power and proclaimed himself emperor as Napoleon III, the move had been presented as a just response to efforts by vested monarchical interests to stymie his supposedly popular policies of paternalistic socialism by refusing to alter the constitution to allow him a second presidential term. Once installed as emperor, however, he had held back from implementing his progressive vision, on the grounds that 'liberty has never helped to found a lasting political edifice, it can only crown that edifice once time has consolidated it.'

Not until 1864 did Napoleon's success in seducing the bourgeoisie, by way of their bulging purses and swelling national self-confidence, create a climate conducive for him to begin the risky transition from autocratic rule to a democratic, liberal empire. In a bold gamble, the prohibition on strikes was lifted and the draconian restrictions on the press eased, but after more than a decade of repression, the radical factions had little appetite for what they perceived as half measures. Every concession Napoleon III granted, it seemed, merely released another outburst of resentment, or provided a further opportunity for plotting against his regime. Nothing better illustrated the emperor's predicament than his decision to sponsor sixty representatives of France's workers to attend a conference of their international peers that was to be held in London during the Universal Exposition of 1862, an event that carried considerable significance in an age when a nation's status was defined by technological change, commercial innovation and the fruits of expanding empire. The relationships they formed led directly to a strong French involvement two years later in the foundation of the International Association of Working Men, which encompassed a wide range of revolutionary socialist views, and whose statement of principles Karl Marx would draft.

Elisée Reclus might have felt the occasional twinge of unspoken sympathy for the emperor, as he too tried in vain to realise his ideals on the impossible middle ground of moderation and reform. At a time when Jules Verne had coined a new genre of 'science fiction' and was writing a series of books 'that would describe the world, known and unknown, and the great scientific achievements of the age', Reclus' scientific insights and literary talent commanded great interest. The prestigious *Revue des Deux Mondes* was delighted to take his scientific articles, while Verne's own publisher, the masterful Jules Hetzel, made bestsellers of his more popular works of geography. No such success, however, attended Reclus' attempts to chart his own map of Utopia, as he and Elie poured their political energies into developing a series of mutual organisations.

The brothers began their project by establishing Paris' first food co-operative, on principles similar to those pioneered at Rochdale in England some years earlier. Next, infuriated by the failings of the Crédit Mobilier, a supposedly socialist bank that pandered to bourgeois prejudices in its granting of loans, the brothers formed La Société du Crédit au Travail to offer workers a better deal. Then, finally, they founded a journal,

L'Association, to propagate their ideas. The aim, Elisée wrote, was 'to contribute to a promotion of the relations between the republican bourgeoisie of goodwill, and the world of the workers'. Each project failed, in turn, for lack of popular involvement. Even those friends that Reclus had made in the radical clubs of Batignolles and Belleville, the heartland of Red Paris, were reluctant to explore the viability of alternative economic models that depended on such 'goodwill', preferring simply to prepare for confrontation. Disillusioned, Reclus joined their ranks, and by 1867 had become a close associate of such prominent French members of the International as Benoît Malon. He even undertook to translate Marx's *Das Kapital* into French: a pressing concern to its author, who wished to 'counter the false views in which Proudhon buried them, with his idealised lower middle classes'.

In the early summer of that year, Napoleon III welcomed the world to Paris for a Universal Exposition of his own. On the surface it was a triumph of optimistic modernity. Those visitors able to afford the entry price could wander through an enchanted world where extraordinary feats of European engineering were demonstrated within a stone's throw of stalls staffed by tribesmen from the depths of French colonial Africa or the remotest islands of Polynesia, and could witness the autopsy of a freshly unwrapped Egyptian mummy or inspect the model homes and ideal villages that Napoleon had designed for workers in the iron foundries of Le Creusot. Beneath the vast glass dome of the main pavilion, every important field of human endeavour was celebrated, while night after night in the Tuileries Gardens, hordes of ball-goers spun to the new waltz tunes of Johann Strauss the Younger.

Beneath the fairy-tale twinkle of tens of thousands of electric bulbs, however, lay a darker truth. Travellers arriving by train to wander the vaulted glass galleries of the exhibition halls, or promenade through Haussmann's new boulevards, could easily forget that the tracks of the railways and the iron substructure of housing and exhibition spaces alike had originated in the strike-ridden foundries at Le Creusot. And when they looked at examples of ideal workers' houses, they chose to ignore the reality that occupancy was offered only as a reward for those workers who toed the line. The radicals of the Red districts, though, were not so easily misled. Expelled from the city centre to make way for Haussmann's grand new urban scheme, they seethed with resentment, seeing in Napoleon's proposed welfare provisions for new mothers and injured workers projects proof that the emperor lacked either the will or the hard political support to implement in full.

Nor was it only in the realm of social reform that the Expo exhibited the overconfidence of the Second Empire. The crowds in the Champs-de-Mars who inspected the impressive scale model of the submarine *Le Plongeur*, and watched demonstrations of the secret *mitrailleuse* machine gun, spitting fire from concealment in a tent, were comforted that France possessed the ingenuity to protect her status as the Continent's pre-eminent military power. They admired with misguided equanimity the steel bulk of the enormous Krupps cannon sent to represent Prussia, Europe's rising power. And when the hot-air balloon *Géant*, owned by the satirical caricaturist and pioneering photographer and aeronaut Nadar, or the *Impérial*, Napoleon's state-commissioned balloon, carried tourists up for a bird's-eye panorama of the exhibition, few remarked on the stinking gas leaks that made their ascent so laborious, any more than they had concerned themselves over *Le Plongeur*'s failed tests of seaworthiness. Rather, they covered their noses and imagined themselves pioneering passengers on what Henry Giffard, the other aerostatic impresario at the Expo, brazenly touted as a journey to the first station of a Paris–Moon Railway.

Yet whilst the technological sensations on display appeared to promise a future of brilliant accomplishments, one dramatic incident two months into the Exposition came far closer to revealing what the immediate future would hold. Nine years had passed since the bomb attack on Napoleon III by Felice Orsini had left eight people dead and 156 bystanders injured. During recent months, however, first Tsar Alexander II of Russia and then Chancellor Bismarck of Prussia had narrowly escaped assassination at the hands of the young radicals Dmitri Karakozov and Ferdinand Cohen Blind. That both King Wilhelm and Tsar Alexander were to visit the Expo at the same time and appear alongside Napoleon III for a military parade at Longchamp racecourse should have seen the French police at their most vigilant. Somehow, though, a young Pole by the name of Boleslaw Berezowski, seeking vengeance for the brutal repression of a revolt in his Russian-occupied homeland, took his place in the crowd and discharged a pistol at the tsar, only narrowly missing his target.

The event represented the coincidence of the two great threats that faced Napoleon, and would trouble the Continent for decades to come. For it was from the Red clubs of Batignolles that Berezowski had emerged to make his attempt on the tsar's life, one of many foreign revolutionaries who swelled the ranks of the indigenous radicals, and fired their imaginations with tales of political uprisings. And it was France's desire to redress a prospective imbalance of power in Europe that suffered as a consequence of his attack.

Industrialisation in the German states was rampant, their birth rate growing even faster than France's declined, and their production of coal – the key energy source of the age – was approaching that of France and Belgium combined, with no slowdown in sight. Whilst little love was lost between the tsar and the parvenu Bonaparte, whose ancestor had once entered Moscow as conqueror, France courted Russian friendship as a much-needed counterweight to the growing power across the Rhine. Now, though, Napoleon III had failed adequately to protect his guest from attack. In an attempt to redeem the situation, the French emperor turned to the tsar, who was flecked with the blood of the horse that the bullet had struck. 'Sir, we have been under fire together; now we are brothers-in-arms.' Alexander's brusque response saw any small chance of an alliance disappear almost before the smoke of the assassin's pistol.

The three years following the Exposition saw the emperor's authority at home further eroded and the opposition to his regime mount as republicans of all colours increasingly made common cause. A disastrous intervention in Mexico, where France installed a puppet king only to abandon him in the face of a powerful insurgency, was compounded by a messy victory for French auxiliaries over an Italian nationalist force led by Garibaldi, whose attempt to liberate Rome from the deeply reactionary Pope Pius IX enjoyed the approval of the French left. Sensing Napoleon's weakness, the republican press in Paris tested his powers of censorship with growing audacity until, in January 1870, journalistic activism crossed from the page on to the streets.

The occasion was the funeral of Victor Noir, a journalist with the radical *La Marseillaise*, who had been shot dead by the emperor's cousin, Pierre Bonaparte, in murky circumstances, having visited him regarding a challenge to a duel. Up to 200,000 republicans joined the procession, which briefly threatened to become violent before fizzling out for lack of clear leadership. The arrest and imprisonment of the ringleaders bought Napoleon III time, but a month later another journalist from the newspaper, the glamorous and flamboyant Gustave Flourens, attempted to stage an insurrection in Belleville. On that occasion, the weapons issued to his troops proved to be mere replicas, stolen from the props room of the local theatre, but a full performance seemed certain to follow the dress rehearsal before long. Having tried repression, conciliation and reform over many years, the only option left to Napoleon was the fallback of every struggling leader: the distraction of war.

*

When the Spanish throne fell vacant in the early summer of 1870, Bismarck baited the trap, proposing a Prussian candidate in what was both an affront to French pride and a tacit threat of encirclement. After the French ambassador to Prussia importuned the vacationing King Wilhelm during his morning promenade in the spa town of Bad Ems to express Napoleon's outrage, Bismarck leaked to the press the king's version of the encounter, carefully edited to impugn France's breach of diplomatic etiquette. It was the eve of the 14 July celebration of Bastille Day in France and his timing was perfect. With leisure to debate the insolence of Prussia, and wine coursing hotly through their veins, the French buoyed Napoleon III up and along on a wave of chauvinism. A pope who within days would declare himself infallible gave his blessing, and the emperor declared war on Prussia.

'A Berlin! A Berlin!' resounded the cries of the Paris crowds on 19 July, and among the voices were those of many republicans, who later preferred to deny it, or else to claim that they had welcomed France's aggression only as a prelude to revolution. Inconveniently, though, the archetypal bumbling Teuton pilloried by French popular culture failed to materialise on the battlefield. Instead France was wrong-footed by its own incautious rush to war: its railway system had been too busy introducing its hedonistic citizens to the pleasure of seaside holidays to prepare proper mobilisation plans as Prussia had done; its artillerymen were untrained to operate the army's secret wonder-weapon, the *mitrailleuse*, and its regiments were optimistically given maps of Germany but none of France. The result was chaos when, engaged by a well-organised and highly manoeuvrable enemy, the French armies were forced to retreat.

Only six weeks later, the emperor found himself leading the last stand of the Army of Châlons, outside the citadel of Sedan. Nearly 20,000 French soldiers had already been killed in the attempted breakout and a similar number captured, with over 100,000 now encircled. According to the loyalist press, Napoleon rode before the ramparts to rally the defenders; in reality he was dosed with opiates, and courting a bullet to end the agony of his gallstones that France's military shame exacerbated. The courage he showed the following day, 2 September, was of a greater kind, when his acceptance of the need for surrender to save further futile loss of life led to his own capture and exile.

Despite the military defeat, Napoleon's opponents in Paris received the news with elation. 'We shook off the empire as though it had been a nightmare,' wrote Juliette Adam, the feminist and journalist, as those imprisoned for political crimes were freed and borne aloft on the shoulders of the crowd. Amid rapturous scenes at the Hôtel de Ville, on 4 September Léon Gambetta appeared at a window to proclaim a republic to the packed square below, the names of prospective members of the new Government of National Defence confirmed by popular acclamation. Outspoken critics of the old regime, lawyers who had campaigned against its injustices in particular, received key roles, with Gambetta himself appointed as interior minister. Descending to the crowd that thronged the steps outside, Jules Favre, the new minister for foreign affairs, embraced the most radical figures present, among them students to whom he taught politics and science at night school, calling them 'my children' in a gesture of the inclusiveness with which he and his colleagues meant to govern. The harmony did not last long.

France had achieved the creation of a new republic, which all on the left had devoutly craved, but as the armies of general Moltke closed in to encircle the capital, the question of what that republic should aspire to be was thrust to the fore. Informed of developments in Paris, King Wilhelm fretted that France's new government might somehow conjure a *levée en masse*. He was old enough to remember tales from his childhood of how, in 1793, just such a popular army had risen to drive out the forces of the First Coalition, Prussia's among them, when they attempted to suppress the original French Revolution. The mirror image of those thoughts now preoccupied the more extreme radicals who saw, in an embattled France, fertile ground from which a true social revolution might grow, reversing the setbacks of the past eighty years.

Although reluctant to strengthen the extremists' hand, the new government agreed to throw open recruitment to the National Guard to all able-bodied men of military age. Elisée Reclus was among the 350,000 volunteers who would enlist in the weeks that followed, but he at least was under no illusion that the Guard alone would be able to raise the siege. That would require the reserve Army of the Loire to be marshalled to liberate the capital. With this in mind, Gambetta was chosen for an audacious mission: to leave the encircled city by balloon for Tours, from where he would rally the counter-attack. It was a venture in which there was a promising role for Reclus, who had recently written to Félix Nadar, now head of emergency aerostatic operations, to offer his services as 'an aspiring aeronaut . . . and something of a meteorologist'.

Whilst the preceding month had been warm and breezy, the September nights starry over Paris, now that the survival of the newborn republic hung in the balance, the windmills on the slopes of Montmartre had suddenly stopped turning. On 6 October 1870, an accurate forecast of the easterly winds that could carry Gambetta safely across the Prussian lines was of vital importance. Elsewhere in the city that day, Gustave Flourens, the political firebrand from *La Marseillaise*, led a demonstration that demanded the restoration of the municipal government of Paris, banned during the Second Empire. The marchers' cries of '*Vive la Commune!*' recalled the insurrectionary government of 1792. That evening, though, in the place Saint-Pierre, revolutionary fervour was set aside and all thoughts anxiously fixed on the present, as sailors paid out the tethering ropes of a meteorological balloon that rose slowly into the misty sky.

Other novice aeronauts who rode up into the Paris sky in the weeks that followed would recount how, as the horizon curved with increasing altitude, they experienced a revelatory oneness with the 'pantheistic "Great Whole"'. The globe was already long established as a potent symbol of the deep brotherhood of man for Reclus, a committed advocate of the fledgling International League of Peace and Liberty, whose congresses called for a United States of Europe as a solution to the hazard posed by feuding dynasties and a precursor to a federal republic that would span the world. Strikingly tall, gaunt and bearded, forty years of asceticism had sculpted him into the image of a medieval saint, and he had the temperament and kind but penetrating gaze to match. Yet his days of religious devotion had long since given way to a faith only in a new and just social order. As he peered down from the balloon, between taking measurements of air pressure, the view below would have revealed to him a future fraught with difficulties.

Away to the south-east, Paris lay spread out below in all its glory, Haussmann's great radial boulevards arrowing out to the suburbs, evidence of France's defeat and not far beyond. Along the roads that extended towards the forty miles of walls that girdled the city, lines of yellow tents marked where the reserve battalions of the French army were encamped, mingling with those defeated units that had fallen back on the capital following the recent debacle in Alsace. Meanwhile, in the Bois de Boulogne – laid out by Haussmann as a great, green public space – evidence of the siege was everywhere. Hardly a tree remained standing amidst a stubble of stumps, while the grass was cropped by a flock of 250 sheep brought into Paris in a wholly inadequate gesture towards self-sufficiency.

From time to time, close to the perimeter of Paris, a dark droplet of troops would coalesce and trickle out in formation through the city's gates to relieve the garrison in one or other of the fourteen great fortresses that comprised the capital's outermost line of defence. Every such

movement drew heavy fire from German rifles and cannon. For outside
the embrace of the ramparts, 200,000 conscripts from Prussia and the
North German Confederation sat warming themselves beside braziers,
ready to starve the City of Light into submission.

*

From his headquarters at Versailles, Colonel Wilhelm Stieber, secret
councillor to Bismarck's government and head of military intelligence
for the North German Confederation, could have watched the speck of
the tethered meteorological balloon with a degree of equanimity, confident
that the dice were increasingly loaded against any aeronautic politician foolish
enough to attempt an escape.

For more than a week, Stieber's agents had been close to choking
the last lines of communication in and out of Paris. They had tapped
and then cut a telegraph cable laid secretly in the waterways between
Paris and Tours as the Prussian armies approached; meanwhile, all
possible sites of signal exchange with the semaphore stations on the
Arc de Triomphe, the Panthéon and the roof of the newly built Opéra
were under tight surveillance. To interdict the return flights of hundreds
of homing pigeons that had been exchanged between Paris and the
provinces prior to hostilities, Stieber had equipped the army with trained
falcons. And as for the decrepit balloons that occasionally limped out
of the city with no hope of return, delivery was expected any day of a
new wagon-mounted gun from Krupps, with a trajectory high enough
to send whatever small store of the gas-filled leviathans remained in
Paris plummeting to the earth in flames. But sealing the city off from
the world was only the start of Stieber's strategy.

Stieber had first applied his talents to military intelligence during Prussia's
rapid victory over Austria in 1866, but it was in the clandestine struggle
against revolutionary elements that he had made his name. Amply
rewarded for his nefarious efforts, he could boast the unique honour of
having served concurrently as a leading figure in the political police of
both Prussia and Russia and, even as he masterminded the intelligence
campaign against France for Bismarck, he remained a senior security
adviser to the tsar. The key to his success, in conventional war as in the
fight against subversion, lay in a simple truth: that by controlling the flow
of information, he could shape reality to his own design. It was a lesson
he had learned long before and whose application he had been refining
ever since.

Though Stieber would not have known it, his path and that of the geographer in the balloon had run strangely parallel. Some years the senior of Elisée Reclus, when Stieber was dispatched to London in 1851 by the Prussian police, he already had several notable successes under his belt as a deep-cover agent, first during the bloody suppression of an uprising by Silesian weavers in 1844, then six years later in Paris, when his intrigues at the heart of the Communist League had destroyed the organisation from within. The former escapade had led the police president to dub him a 'degenerate subject', but the latter had won him the admiration of the Prussian minister of the interior, Ferdinand von Westphalen, who promptly handpicked him for the delicate mission in England. Its ostensible purpose was the protection of precious objects loaned to the Great Exhibition of that year; the real aim, though, was to discover evidence for the prosecution of Karl Marx, who had married the minister's own half-sister and dragged her into shameful and penurious exile.

Posing as Herr Dr Schmidt, journalist and physician, Stieber had quickly inveigled his way into the Marx family's home in Soho. His reports back to Berlin were full of blood and thunder as they attempted to frame Marx and his colleagues as conspirators in a planned campaign of assassination that would usher in a general European revolution. However, his claim that 'the murder of princes is formally taught and discussed' failed to persuade a British government whose distaste for foreign spies outweighed that for their victims. Worse for Stieber, Marx deftly outflanked his campaign of provocation, writing to the *Spectator* to denounce the attempt to lure him into a conspiracy. 'We need not add that these persons found no chance of making dupes of us', he concluded. Determined to have the last word, Stieber would counter that, on the contrary, Marx had fallen for his medical disguise so completely as to ask his trusted guest to treat his haemorrhoids. Subsequent fabrications by Stieber saw the grudge between the two men deepen into a lifelong vendetta.

Always sailing too close to the wind, Stieber had eventually been dismissed from the Prussian secret police for abuses of power, but the scurrilous charges levelled at him by the press seemed only to excite suitors for his services. Installed as manager of the Kroll restaurant and Opera House in Berlin's Tiergarten, a sinecure obtained through the good offices of influential friends, Stieber one night received an invitation from the Russian Embassy that would propel him into the secret realm of realpolitik. That it was a pivotal moment in his career is apparent from his excitedly embellished account of his ensuing journey across Berlin, concealed in a laundry basket, to avoid detection by a mob still thirsty for his blood. Having helped unpack him, the young Arthur von Mohrenheim, a consular attaché, hired him on the spot. After only a short time in St Petersburg, his recruit had transformed his basic intelligence-gathering role into one of effective control over Russia's entire foreign intelligence service. So impressed was the Prussian ambassador there, Otto von Bismarck, that when appointed president in 1863, he took Stieber back with him to Berlin to serve as director of the very police force which, only a few years earlier, had hung him out to dry.

Stieber's continued involvement with Russia created inevitable conflicts of interest. He would provide indispensable advice and intelligence to the tsar for many years to come in his struggle against sedition, but from this time on his ultimate loyalty would always be to Prussia, or rather to Bismarck and his vision of a strong and unified German state. No lover of socialists and revolutionaries, it was always a pleasure for Stieber when their persecution was his clear imperative. But when, as occasionally happened, the greater benefit for Bismarck lay in their manipulation, he was quite prepared to do whatever was required, regardless of his other freelance loyalties.

Such, it appears, was the situation in 1867, when Alexander II asked Stieber to contrive for him a seemingly chance meeting with Napoleon III. Fearing that it was cooperation against Prussia that the tsar wished to discuss, according to his own account, Stieber instead worked to keep France and Russia at loggerheads. Among the most valuable resources he possessed was a burgeoning index-card register of subversives, containing information extracted from police and underworld contacts, including at least one from the Batignolles district of Paris. Stieber claimed to have consulted this informant immediately upon arriving for the 1867 Expo on Tsar Alexander's train, and that it was he who provided the advance warning of Berezowski's assassination plans.

Tall tales were a speciality of Stieber's and his memoirs recount them compellingly, but the ability to manipulate or even rescript the seemingly inevitable course of events in the real world was also an essential aspect of his extraordinary talent for intrigue. The *mise en scène* in his recollections of the parade at Longchamp is superbly facetious: the glittering silver cuirasses and polished bayonets of 40,000 French soldiers, lined up to witness the unveiling of the *mitrailleuse*. And then, when the moment arrives to prevent the assassination, technology and cavalry elan are shown to be equally futile beside Prussian good sense: it takes only a well-aimed elbow by Stieber to jog Berezowski's arm as he steps from the crowd with a double-barrelled pistol, and so deflect a bullet meant for the tsar. Discrepancies between Stieber's account and that of other first-hand witnesses are of little consequence. His version might have been true or false, his informant real or not; he might have had no foreknowledge of Berezowski's attack, or arranged for it to be provoked. All that mattered, finally, for Stieber, was the larger message: that for all its pride and pomp, France could not be relied upon when it came to matters of life or death.

Surveying Paris in the distance that misty October evening in 1870, Stieber could reflect that he had served Bismarck well. France had been provoked to war by the doctored 'Ems Telegram', that bore all the hallmarks of Stieber's cunning, and now, in her hour of greatest need, Alexander II refused to be drawn by the envoys of the Government of National Defence into offering assistance. With a supposed tally of 36,000 agents under his control in the occupied territory, and a base in the pleasant park-city of Versailles, whose monarchist population appeared for the moment to hate the Parisian republic even more than they did the Teutonic invader, the Prussian spymaster could now indulge in a subtler and more finessed form of intrigue.

Already he had rewritten the details of Napoleon's defeat at Sedan for propaganda purposes, inventing a scene in which Napoleon was seized while struggling to fire a jammed *mitrailleuse* at the approaching enemy. Facile in its symbolism, the account expressed a still unsatisfied desire for France's utter humiliation. Stieber was astute enough, however, to realise that Bismarck's plans for German unification were not necessarily best served by a straightforward victory; France must rather be weakened for a generation, divided and impoverished. He would have been pleased to see that in the ranks of her new republican rulers, there were already signs of dissent, ripe for exploitation.

*

With a favourable weather forecast, eleven o'clock on 7 October marked Gambetta's moment of destiny. The bulging eye of which caricaturists were so fond stared anxiously as he held the lip of the gondola of the *Armand-Barbes* with a tightening grip, his usually florid face blanching at the prospect of flight. '*Lâchez tout!*' shouted the pilot, the mooring ropes were cast off and the crowd gathered in place Saint-Pierre cheered as France's putative saviour raced into the sky, accompanied by a second balloon, the *George Sand*, carrying sympathetic American arms dealers.

Both behemoths then dipped alarmingly, descending towards the Prussian lines from where a barrage of shots was heard. The hearts of those watching from Paris dropped with them, before rising again as the gas warmed and Gambetta soared away.

At Gambetta's moment of apotheosis, however, those republicans in the crowd of a racist disposition doubted whether he could truly be trusted, influenced by repeated, knowing references in the combative and scurrilous *La Lanterne* to his 'Jewish nose' and resemblance to a 'Polish Jew'. And had they looked for a lead to the reaction of their long-standing hero, Victor Hugo, easily identifiable in the crowd by the kepi that he had worn since the fall of Napoleon had allowed his return from exile, they would have seen standing next to him the very editor responsible for the insidious slanders, the marquis de Rochefort-Luçay.

A tall figure, whose dark, pointed beard, high cheekbones and inimitable brush of wild hair created an appearance somewhere between Mephistopheles and Don Quixote, Rochefort was a contrarian to his fingertips and, more than that, an inveterate egotist. Both he and Hugo waved off the balloons, but Rochefort did so with gritted teeth. For whilst Gambetta was supposedly an ally, who had gifted Rochefort his own unused seat in the Chamber of Deputies little more than a year earlier, Rochefort seethed with resentment at the prospect of his benefactor being greeted in Tours as a 'Messiah fallen from the sky', convinced no doubt that he could have played the part with more panache than the grocer's son from Cahors. Even the graze that Gambetta's hand received from a Prussian sharpshooter's bullet irked him: a veteran duellist of notorious cowardice, he knew only too well how effectively, by conceding a flesh wound, one could win sympathy even in defeat.

Had Rochefort sincerely wanted the honour of the balloon flight, it might conceivably have been his, since Gambetta, though always a promising candidate, had been chosen only by default after his cabinet colleagues had cavilled at the risks. Yet just as Rochefort was adept at eluding death at the hands of one of his enraged challengers, despite his dauntless audacity in print, he had also revealed himself to be equally good at absenting himself whenever real danger threatened. What now troubled Rochefort most was a growing but unspoken anxiety that his own lack of nerve would forever prevent him claiming the demagogic leadership of the radical left: a position that alone, for all his vaunted egalitarianism, might have freed him from the compromises he found so painful.

Until recently, Rochefort's political future had looked so promising.

Every Saturday morning during 1868, subject only to intermittent bans that the government would have liked to make permanent, the orange-red ink from the cover of *La Lanterne* had bled on to the hands of well over 100,000 eager readers, who were happy to flaunt their complicity with its virulent republicanism. Then, he had preferred exile to silence, fleeing Paris for Brussels, from where he had smuggled the weekly editions into France while enjoying the hospitality of Hugo, who adopted him as 'another son'. And when, at the time of the 1869 elections to the republican Chamber of Deputies, Elisée Reclus had written to a friend that 'those who have the most resolution, the most love of progress and justice, those whom the government detests the most' must vote for 'the most revolutionary' candidate on the ballot, it had been Henri Rochefort to whom he was referring.

The funeral of Victor Noir the previous January, though, had revealed the cowardice that flawed Rochefort's character. Having stoked up the marchers to a high pitch of militancy with his rhetoric, at the very moment when the crowd was slavering for Napoleon's deposition, Rochefort had gone missing. Hunger had made him faint, the radical marquis claimed. In his absence, the mob's ardour had cooled and the insurrectionary moment passed. The debacle had sent his credibility tumbling. Without the proof of resolute action, erstwhile friends asked, did his satirical journalism and revolutionary pronouncements amount to anything more than a safety valve for popular exasperation, dissipating pressure rather than bringing it to a head? Even a spell in prison, from where he was liberated by the jubilant crowds on the day of the republic's birth, failed to restore his reputation.

Following Gambetta's departure to Tours, the gulf between Rochefort and hard-line colleagues such as Gustave Flourens, Paschal Grousset and Benoît Malon from his old paper, *La Marseillaise*, seemed set to widen further. For whilst they remained free to challenge the Government of National Defence with more radical visions of a new society, Rochefort could not resist the offer of a place as the token radical on its twelve-man executive, tied in to collective responsibility as a minister without portfolio. As a deputy, in 1869, Rochefort had campaigned for universal conscription to the French army. Now, though, his arguments that Paris should resist to the end found little favour with colleagues in the executive who hoped for an accommodation with the Germans. Meanwhile, fearing mob rule, the government equipped the burgeoning National Guard with only the most antiquated weapons. Rochefort was torn: stay and compromise, or rebel. To take the former option, he insisted to old friends among the radicals, required his descent 'to all but the most impenetrable cellars of my conscience'. And yet, for the moment, he decided to retain his position.

In the midst of the brewing storm, Rochefort's responsibilities as president of the Barricades Commission at least afforded him the chance to rehabilitate his reputation for leadership while proving that he 'was not given by nature and temperament to systematic opposition'. Throwing his energies into the practical work of organising Paris' civil defences, he signed the appeal, posted around Paris, for every home to prepare two bags of earth for the barricades that would provide a last line of resistance against any Prussian assault. Meanwhile, bottom drawers and overwrought minds were ransacked in search of national salvation. 'Hardly a day passed', Rochefort recorded, 'without seven or eight Archimedes coming in to propose some infallible means of destroying the besieging army in one blow.' A giant hammer could be lifted by balloons and dropped on the Prussian lines, suggested one proposal, another that lions from the zoo be set loose against the enemy. Most of the ideas received were rather less practical, but the republic offered a broad church for scientific talent: the commission for designing a super-explosive for use against the Prussians went to the man responsible for the bomb with which Orsini had failed to kill Napoleon III.

The highest priority was still the maintenance of robust communication with the outside world. Recollecting his first, hated job at the Department of Patents a year before, Rochefort may have regretted dismissing too hastily the myriad proposals for balloon guidance mechanisms that had then crossed his desk. In the absence of any great leap forward in the years since, it seemed that the most outlandish suggestions were now to be encouraged with funding. Pigeons equipped with whistles to deter Stieber's falcons proved especially effective, the pellicles strapped to their legs carrying photographically reduced letters. Each delivery kept a team of hunched copyists busy for several days, transcribing from a megascope projection. Even the eccentric Jules Allix's twenty-year-old notion of a communications system based on 'sympathetic snails' – pairs of molluscs rendered telepathic over huge distances by the exchange of fluid during mating, whose synchronised movement could communicate letter codes – saw a brief revival of interest.

Like the endless hours that the National Guard spent in drill, however, such displacement activities could keep the radicals of Paris occupied only for so long. As suspicion mounted that the government was preparing to sell out the country, the talk in Batignolles and Belleville became as feverish as the inventors' imaginings, and demonstrations more frequent and more heated: as long as Gambetta's Army of the Loire was awaited, the true patriots of the left, it was argued, deserved their chance to claim victory where the armies of the empire had failed. Trapped in a political no-man's-land, Rochefort was finally presented with a way out of his predicament on 26 October, when the commander-in-chief of the republic, General Trochu, confided in him that the fortress city of Metz, which alone had stood unconquered in the path of the Prussian advance for the previous month, was about to surrender. What was more, he was told, Jules Favre and Adolphe Thiers, the government's leading doves, had already entered into secret negotiations with Prussia.

Burning with indignation at having been kept in the dark for so long, Rochefort turned to Victor Hugo for advice. 'Don't remain any longer with a party of men who deceive everybody, yourself included' affirmed the novelist, but for Rochefort simply to submit a letter of resignation would have gone against his scheming nature. Instead, he leaked Trochu's secret disclosure to Flourens, with only an empty promise that it would go no further as a fig leaf for his mischief-making. The next day, news of the fall of Metz was splashed across the headlines. Frayed nerves finally gave way, and crowds burned the newspapers in public, while the headstrong commander of the fortress of Saint-Denis, inflamed to insubordination, launched a surprise attack on a salient that the army had previously abandoned as indefensible. Paris went wild for a glimmer of solace but speedy victory turned to even more sudden defeat as the Prussian guns opened fire on the jubilant French troops. Then, just as the city thought it could bear no further disappointment, rumours began to circulate of the armistice negotiations.

In a heavy drizzle, angry crowds converged on the Hôtel de Ville, steaming sulphurously under their umbrellas. While the drums and trumpets of the National Guard sounded, Flourens seized his chance. Dressed in a theatrical uniform from his service in the Cretan uprising against the Turks three years earlier, scimitar swinging by his side, he arrived at the flashpoint with his personal retinue of devoted sharpshooters, several hundred strong. Conciliatory officials invited him in to the council room to discuss the situation, but once there he leaped on to the great table to assert his will, carelessly shredding the baize surface with his spurs while he spat out denunciations of government treachery. In scenes more worthy of a second-rate farce than an attempted *coup d'état*, the standoff lasted late into the night, by when the Hôtel de Ville was packed with 8,000 Guardsmen, the air fetid with their nervous sweat. Not until three o'clock in the morning was a settlement brokered by Edmond Adam, the prefect of police: municipal elections would be staged within eight days, with immunity from reprisals for the insurgents. Two days later, though, the government reneged, arresting some leading radicals and driving more underground, where they would regroup with an even sharper sense of righteousness and entitlement.

Commentators in the Parisian press mistakenly agreed that, with the 'Red threat' exposed as impotent, the danger had passed. More pragmatic minds merely hoped that the arrival of the army from Tours might stymie the threat of revolution and save the republic. In Versailles, however, Colonel Stieber was doing everything in his power to ensure that both were proved wrong.

*

For all Stieber's boastful letters to his wife claiming that six aeronauts had been seized in a day – more, in fact, than were captured during the entire siege – the Krupps anti-balloon gun had scored few hits. Meanwhile, new balloons continued to float off the production lines under the vast vaulted roofs of the Gare du Nord and Gare d'Orléans. Seamstresses worked overtime along platforms from which the trains had nowhere to run, to produce vessels blessed with the names of Rationalism's heroes: Kepler, Galileo, Newton and Lavoisier. But by forcing Nadar to switch to night launches, Stieber's strategy of targeting the balloons proved a decisive factor in the conclusion of the war.

Midnight was close to striking when the *Ville d'Orléans* took off into a cold fog, carrying essential information to the Loire army. Not until daybreak did the crashing waves of the North Sea down below alert its crew to their navigational error. Having cast all excess weight overboard, including the mailbags, they finally made land in Norway after a record-shattering journey of more than 1,000 miles, tumbling into thick snow when their basket became entangled in pine trees. Amazingly, the key message concerning the movements of the two armies, from inside and outside Paris, was caught in fishermen's nets and finally forwarded to Tours, only to arrive too late. Without the key information, it had been impossible to coordinate the French attack and the Army of the Loire were forced back in disarray, while the 100,000 troops who crossed a pontoon bridge over the River Marne from Paris were decimated when they encountered the strongest sector of the encircling Prussian front line.

The North German Confederation had demonstrated to the dissenting southern states that it could hold together far beyond the first thrilling rush of war, and attention now returned to preparations for the official unification of the German Empire.

Short of a humiliating surrender, the Government of National Defence had no more answers to offer, nor many remaining concessions to pacify the radicals. As the frosts of a harsh winter ate into the resolve of those in the capital, and even the middle-class population was reduced to eating rats or, for the lucky few, exotic cuts from the animals in the zoological garden, the fault lines in Parisian society widened. In the revolutionary clubs, growing crowds gathered night after night to listen to Rochefort or Flourens press for ever greater freedoms for the people. Half starved and frozen, grief-stricken for the infants who had died on a diet of cloudy water masquerading as milk, those attending warmed themselves with the wine that was the only consumable which Paris had left in abundance, and swore that all their suffering should not be in vain. Meanwhile the Montmartre women's group, chaired by the revolutionary virago Louise Michel, thrashed out details of long-mooted social projects that made the prospect of a better world seem tantalisingly close to souls in desperate need of some source of hope.

Then, on 27 December, the city was suddenly shaken by the onset of a thunderous bombardment. From the Châtillon Heights, the newest Krupps cannon, *Grande Valérie*, rained down shells of an unprecedented calibre, each weighing 119 pounds. One by one, the outer ring of forts – Issy, Vanves, Montrouge – were pounded into submission, and the capital braced itself for a direct onslaught. General Moltke recorded the shift in tactics in chillingly abstract terms: 'An elevation of thirty degrees,' he observed, 'by a peculiar contrivance, sent the shot into the heart of the city.' The first shell to land smashed into the home of Madame Montgolfier, whose father and uncle had made the pioneering balloon flights that had so thrilled rational France in the years before the Revolution of the previous century; before long, the Panthéon and Salpêtrière hospital, the pride of Paris, were targeted directly. Placards appeared across the city: 'Make way for the people! Make way for the Commune!'

Two weeks into the bombardment, King Wilhelm of Prussia was crowned kaiser of a united Germany in Louis XIV's Hall of Mirrors at Versailles. Military dress boots clattered across the polished floors under the protective eye of Colonel Stieber, who had secured the palace against a mass assassination attempt by French partisans to avenge the grotesque affront. In fact, the patriots of Paris were too busy with other matters.

Returning to his residence that evening, the secret councillor received gratifying news from his spies. Even as the new Germany celebrated its victory, the first shots had been exchanged between the troops of the regular army and the radical battalions of the National Guard during a confrontation around the Hôtel de Ville. By the end of the month an armistice was agreed, subject only to ratification by a new National Assembly.

Elected to the Assembly, Elisée Reclus was clear, if hopelessly idealistic, about his duty: 'Orléanists, legitimists, simple patriotic bourgeois have said to us: dream now, guide us, triumph for us, and we shall see what happens! Let us accept the dream, and if we carry out our mandate, if we save France, as we are asked to do, then the republic will be secured and we shall have the pleasure of beginning for our children an era of progress, justice, and well-being.' Arriving in Bordeaux, where the Assembly was to sit, the scales fell rapidly from his eyes as the 'morally perilous' nature of the venture on which he had embarked revealed itself. Elected by the whole of France, the body was republican in name only, and overwhelmingly monarchist, Catholic and conservative in complexion; less than a fifth of the 768 delegates were genuine republicans, barely one in forty a radical. By choosing as its leader the seventy-three-year-old Adolphe Thiers, the strongest proponent of the armistice in the Government of National Defence, the Assembly signalled its intolerance of anyone who advocated continued resistance.

Despite Rochefort's presence on the Assembly's executive, even his attempts to plead for the protection of 'a young and tottering republic against the clerical element that menaced it' were barracked into inaudibility. Reacting to near certain defeat by developing a case of almost asphyxiating erysipelas, his resignation this time was prompt, followed by an extended rest cure in the Atlantic resort of Arcachon. Gambetta opted to spend his conveniently timed convalescence in Spain.

That the stresses of the previous months should have made both ill is hardly surprising, but their absence was also politic, allowing them to remain temporarily above the fray as Paris and metropolitan France reacted with inevitable anger to the Assembly's perceived betrayal of the national interest. Even the normally buoyant Reclus struggled to disguise his despondency. 'Now that everything is lost,' he wrote to Nadar, 'we must begin life over again, as though, waking from a 1,000-year sleep, we realise that everything is there for us to gain: homeland, liberty, dignity, honour . . .' A similar sense of determination led his more extreme associates in Paris, and those of Rochefort, to start preparing in earnest for a revolutionary year zero.

When the German army marched through the capital on its victory parade, it can have derived little pleasure from the experience. Crowds of Parisians watched its progress in lowering silence, while any innkeepers who might have thought to sell the enemy a drink were deterred by the threat of a beating. Nevertheless, the guerrilla attacks that Stieber feared had failed to materialise: having dragged the hundreds of cannon, bought for their use by public subscription, to the safety of the Red districts, the National Guard were keeping their powder dry. And whilst great pyres were lit to fumigate the place de l'Etoile after the Germans had passed through, they did nothing to dispel the germs of civil war.

2

Communards

Paris, 1871

Louise Michel wiled away the early hours of 18 March 1871 at the sentry post on the rue des Rosiers in Montmartre, drinking coffee with the National Guardsmen stationed there. A teacher by profession, with her own school in the rue Oudot that she ran on progressive principles, her political views had made her an increasingly prominent feature of the radical landscape of Paris. As comfortable now among political extremists and citizen soldiers as in the classroom, she rarely missed the chance to preach the social revolution. This time, though, it may have been the prospect of the funeral later in the day for Victor Hugo's son that kept her awake.

The months of the siege had provided ample cause for mourning, but the thirty-six-year-old Michel's deep affection for the great writer and republican lent her grief that day a special poignancy, for since she and Hugo had first met twenty years earlier, they had developed an intimacy that transcended his usual philandering habits. The 'N' in Hugo's diaries beside her name suggests that they had, at least, been naked together, but for Michel, their relationship was above all a meeting of poetic souls. To the novelist she was his 'Enjolras', so named after the heroic student revolutionary in Les Misérables, and perhaps in teasing reference to her strong and somewhat masculine features; she addressed him simply as 'Master'. Only he, she felt, could truly appreciate her 'exalted temperament' and the mystical imaginings that filled her mind and her verse: of ravening wolves, boiling oceans, revolution and martyrdom.

As well as being confidant and mentor, Hugo was also the dependable protector that she desperately needed, as the illegitimate daughter of the heir to a family of provincial gentry now making a name for herself as one of the most outspoken radicals in Paris. For Michel had an uncanny ability to place herself at the centre of historic events, where the danger was greatest. She had been among those embraced by Jules Favre, her old night-school instructor, on the steps of the Hôtel de Ville after the proclamation of the republic the previous September; when she had returned there in January, rifle in hand, to join in the firefight between the Breton army regulars defending the building and Flourens' brigade of insurrectionary sharpshooters, it had taken Hugo's intervention to secure her release from custody. The escapade had been the most violent manifestation to date of the rumbling resistance of radical Paris to the authority of the National Assembly, and had demonstrated a seriousness of intent that the government could not afford to ignore. Now Michel was about to find herself caught up in the decisive showdown.

It was three o'clock in the morning when the soldiers of the 88th regiment of the line, loyal to the Assembly, marched up the winding road towards Montmartre, their tramp muffled by ground left soft after a recent fall of snow. A Guardsman named Turpin, taking his turn on sentry duty, peered through the thick fog, before challenging their approach. Suddenly, a crack of gunfire rang out in the dark and he slumped to the ground. Rushing to assist the wounded man, with a characteristic disregard for her own safety, Michel was instantly apprehended by the troops of General Lecomte.

One of fourteen operations launched simultaneously across the city under cover of night, Lecomte's objective was the artillery park on the Buttes Chaumont, where the National Guard had, following the peace agreement with Germany, secured half of the cannon bought by public subscription during the siege. While dragging them to safety, the Guardsmen had sung the 'Marseillaise', and the guns, pointing towards Versailles, where the Assembly was now based, represented a practical symbol of their independence. Their confiscation would deliver a crippling blow to the National Guard, whose shadowy central committee had in recent weeks begun to assert itself as an alternative power in the city. In Michel's eyes, Lecomte's mission exposed the government's wholehearted contempt for the disproportionate sacrifice that the capital's poor had endured in the national cause, but more than that its timing, on the day of the funeral of Hugo's son, struck her as a deep personal affront. For it was under Hugo's patronage that the campaign to buy the cannon had been conducted.

Intoxicated with indignation, hands bloody from her attempts to staunch Turpin's wound, by her own account Michel eluded her captors and made a run for it. Down the cobbled streets of Montmartre to raise the alarm she careered, past the creaking windmills that crowded the upper slopes of the hill. The denizens of Montmartre were slow to wake despite the vehemence of her cries and not until almost eight o'clock did a sizeable crowd gather, by which time the captured guns should have been long gone. In fact, they were still there, an administrative oversight having delayed the arrival of the horse-drawn limbers needed to carry the artillery away.

From atop the Buttes, the beat of the tocsins could be heard in the streets below; 'All that miserable sound,' Louise Michel marvelled, 'produced by a pair of sinewy wrists clutching a pair of fragile sticks.' Then up the hill the mob surged, women in the lead, draping themselves over the cannon, challenging the soldiers of the 88th to open fire. A tense stand-off ensued, during which the mayor of Montmartre, Georges Clemenceau, a trained doctor, pleaded with Lecomte to be allowed to move Turpin to his surgery for treatment. The general refused. With discipline among his tired and hungry men rapidly breaking down, as they accepted breakfast from motherly hands and stronger refreshment from the National Guard, it was a fatal mistake. In an attempt to assert order, Lecomte ordered his men to stand clear and fire. No one moved. Fix bayonets! For a moment, nothing; then his own soldiers turned on the general, hauling him from his horse. Amidst scenes of jubilation, rifle butts were tossed skywards and fraternisation turned to desertion. From the big guns themselves, a salvo of three blanks was fired, and the scenes at the Buttes were repeated at the smaller artillery compounds across the city.

After facing the famously loyal Breton soldiers holed up inside the Hôtel de Ville two months earlier, Michel had asserted her faith that 'One day you'll join us, you brigands, for you can't be bought.' For a blissful moment that March morning it seemed that the dreamed-of day had at last arrived, and that a peaceful revolution might be under way. Such hopes barely lasted into the afternoon, as festering resentments were given murderous vent, and the tensions between radicalism and reaction that had long troubled French political life finally revealed themselves in a mutual desire for outright confrontation to settle matters once and for all.

The first violence occurred where the debacle of the guns had itself begun, in Montmartre. Clemenceau had instructed that General Lecomte should be taken, for his own protection, to the Chateau-Rouge dance hall, one of the bohemian pleasure palaces for which the area was famous. Overruling him, Théophile Ferré, the young deputy mayor, ordered Lecomte's transfer back to the guardhouse in the rue des Rosiers. Barely five feet tall, Ferré's bespectacled air of fastidiousness belied a ruthless streak echoing that of the Jacobins who had perpetrated the Terror in 1793, when ideological purity had been pursued by means of the guillotine. Though he was sixteen years her junior, Louise Michel was infatuated with him. Entering the spirit of the wild carnival breaking out around her, she joined the horde that followed Lecomte's journey back, only to be met, unexpectedly, by a second mob arriving from place Pigalle with General Clement Thomas, the loathed ex-chief of the National Guard, as its captive.

The mood of mockery quickly turned into a clamour for retribution. Forcing open the doors of the guardhouse, the mob poured in and drove the two captive generals into the walled garden of the building to face its rough justice. Powerless to intervene, Clemenceau witnessed the terrible scene. 'All were shrieking like wild beasts without realising what they were doing,' he would write. 'I observed then that pathological phenomenon which might be called bloodlust.' General Thomas was the first to die, staggering to stay on his feet, cursing his assailants, until riddled by bullets; Lecomte was dispatched with a single shot to the back. Of the rifles fired, most belonged to his own mutinous troops. The identity of those who then desecrated the corpses is less certain.

Sated or sickened by its own violence, the mob quickly ebbed away, leaving the rue des Rosiers in eerie silence. The other, lesser prisoners were immediately released, with Ferré claiming that he wished to avoid 'cowardice and pointless cruelty'; Michel later insisted that she had only demanded that the dead men be kept prisoner, without any intent to do them injury. But it was already too late for either scruples or denials to carry any weight or serve any purpose. For the time being, no authority remained in Paris to judge their crimes.

Senior officials at the Hôtel de Ville and those ministries still based in Paris had begun their evacuation to Versailles early in the afternoon, while events were still unfolding in Montmartre. Not long after, Adolphe Thiers himself, chairman of the executive and de facto head of the interim government, had made his escape, riding out to his new capital at the head of a great column of troops, who had been ordered by General Vinoy to withdraw en masse from their barracks in the city. Jules Ferry, the mayor of Paris, had to sweat out his fate for a few hours before following them in ignominious style. But their departure had been neither a rout nor flight, suggesting a premeditated strategy in case the confiscation of the cannon provoked resistance, and their disdain for the disrespectful crowds that lined the streets boded ill for how they might avenge their humiliation on the people of Paris.

By dusk the central committee of the National Guard was in full control of the city. The gas flares usually reserved for the celebration of military triumphs were lit to illuminate the facade of the Hôtel de Ville, celebrating the first time since 1793 that Paris as a whole had been subject to insurrectionary rule. Yet as Benoît Malon, the leader of the International in Batignolles, would ruefully reflect, for all their bellicose posturing of the previous months, 'Never had a revolution taken the revolutionaries more by surprise.'

The mood of the Montmartre vigilance committee that night was reflective, its young members pondering, perhaps, whether a revolution born in such brutality might not be fated to end in like manner. Louise Michel's veins alone still coursed with adrenaline. Like a child eager for approval, she proposed to set out directly for Versailles, where she planned to assassinate Thiers in the supposed safety of his palace and 'provoke such terror that the reaction against us would be stopped dead.' It took the combined efforts of Ferré and his young friend Raoul Rigault, usually the most extreme voices in the group, to dissuade Michel from an action that would surely have been suicidal. Yet her instinctive sense that swift action was needed to press the advantage would soon be confirmed by the advice of General Duval, who demanded an immediate sortie of the National Guard to catch the Versaillais government on its heels. That his warnings went unheeded was perhaps the greatest error made by the insurrectionists.

Determined to erase the memory of the generals' murder, the central committee of the National Guard instead set out to demonstrate its legitimacy as a responsible and effective civic government. Even while the roadblocks thrown up around the city to impede the removal of the guns were being dismantled, it was announced that municipal elections, suspended for almost two decades under Napoleon III, would be held within a fortnight. When the results were returned, the left had a fat majority of sixty-four seats. Though war and the subsequent tensions had driven many bourgeois families from the city, the turnout was still a good two thirds of what it had been for the Assembly elections, making it difficult for Thiers, try as he might, to declare the result invalid. The correspondent for *The Times* in London was right to discern in the vote 'the dangerous sentiment of Democracy'.

On 28 March, the 'Paris Commune' was officially declared, 'in the name of the people,' in a benign spectacle staged outside the Hôtel de Ville, with red flags flapping in the wind and red sashes worn with pride. That the representatives of the city, whose election had restored to Paris after a long absence the same administrative rights enjoyed by 'communes' of villages, towns and cities throughout France, should have chosen to adopt a similar corporate appellation was unsurprising. An already nervous bourgeoisie, however, would have received the news with profound unease, for it had been 'the Commune' of Paris that had deposed Louis XVI in 1792, and that had wielded substantial power behind the scenes throughout the Terror, growing ever more monstrous in its whims. Nevertheless, for many the ceremony was to be cherished as a rare cause for jubilation.

'What a day!' proclaimed Jules Valles, editor of *Le Cri du Peuple*. 'That clear, warm sun that gilds the gun-muzzles, that scent of flowers, the flutter of flags, the murmur of passing revolution . . . Whatever may happen, if we are to be again vanquished and die tomorrow, our generation is consoled! We are repaid for twenty years of anxiety.' Michel celebrated the occasion by leading a procession that bedecked the statue representing Strasbourg in the place de la Concorde with swags of flowers, and left a tricolour propped in the crook of its arm in a pledge of the Commune's commitment to the integrity of France that the Assembly had traded away for the benefit of the affluent few, by ceding Alsace and Lorraine to Germany.

Popular expectations were sky-high, buoyed up on a sense of empowerment. 'We are not rogues and thieves, we are the people, nothing more, and nothing is above us,' one young craftsman wrote to his family in the country, assuring them of his safety and warning them against the lies of the reactionary press. He then went on to list the Communards' aspirations: 'We do not want looting or theft, we do not want pomp and ceremony. Here is what we want and nothing else. A united and indivisible republic; the separation of Church and State; free and compulsory education by lay teachers; the abolition of all permanent armies and every citizen to bear arms, but in his own district, that is, as the National Guard.' Across France, revolutionary communes were declared in Lyons and Marseilles, Toulouse and Le Creusot, Saint-Etienne, Limoges, Perpignan and Cette. Viewed from Paris, the country appeared to be ablaze with revolutionary fervour.

Yet victory would not be quite so easy to achieve. Even in the capital there were pockets of reaction to be found, with the newly formed 'Friends of Order' offering a standard to which those who feared the Commune could rally. And the Commune ignored at its peril the guiding hand of Thiers, who had orchestrated the 'Friends' as an early part of his far larger strategy to take back the capital and rid France for good of the troublemaking radicals.

*

In Versailles, Thiers watched and waited, presiding over the affairs of the Assembly with an air of lawyerly predation, his cropped head and thick neck swivelling within the high, starched collars he favoured, his hooked nose befitting his owl-like nature. The weeks preceding the debacle over the cannon had seen Chancellor Bismarck and other foreign leaders urge Thiers to confront his enemies on the left. Evoking a conspiracy hatched in London, that had supposedly cast its net across France and which, if unchecked, might spread far beyond its borders, their aim was the extirpation of the International, led by Karl Marx and Friedrich Engels. That the German pair's influence over how the 'desperate folly' of the Commune unfolded was quite negligible was disregarded by Europe's forces of reaction. Colonel Stieber and the Prussian leadership may have vacated Versailles, leaving many tens of thousands of German soldiers to garrison France until the agreed reparations were paid in full, but Thiers, installed in the same offices, needed little encouragement to act resolutely from a shared hatred of socialist sedition.

Some would later suggest that Thiers had conceived the attempt to seize the guns as a ruse to draw the sting out of the revolution, pointing as evidence to the notorious unreliability of the regiment handed the job and the failure of the limbers to materialise. Either way, he had a long-cherished plan available to exploit its failure, following the government's withdrawal from Paris. During 1848, when wildfire uprisings had spread across Europe, he had been France's prime minister, advising King Louis-Philippe on how to stamp out radicalism: the fourteen fortresses surrounding Paris, including Mont-Valérien, had been built under his supervision with, some said, half an eye on implementing just such a strategy of internal control. He would now pursue the very policy he had recommended in vain back then: playing for time, to allow the army to regroup outside the capital, he would then launch a massed attack on Paris that would silence radicalism for a generation to come. Nothing, though, was a foregone conclusion.

Had the leaders of the Commune realised the true fragility of Thiers' position, both political and military, General Duval's argument for a swift and decisive attack out of Paris might have received a more positive hearing. For Thiers' very legitimacy, like that of the National Assembly as a whole, was fading by the day, with hard-line monarchist representatives sniffing for any signs of weakness that might allow them to usurp power. Even the crack battalions filled with 'the flower of French chivalry' that Thiers claimed to have at his disposal were a chimera, comprising no more than the 12,000-strong residue of the regular army, a force vastly outnumbered by the National Guard in Paris. And most troublesome of all for Thiers' strategy was the fact that, in the rush to withdraw loyalist units from Paris, the key fortress of Mont-Valérien that loomed over the road out to Versailles had been unintentionally abandoned to the rebels.

To capitalise on the challenging circumstances that prevailed, Thiers required all the considerable cunning he could muster. Desperately needing time for the army to rebuild, he deftly confided to the press that he expected the city to be back under the rule of the Assembly within three weeks. Meanwhile, protracted talks with the Communards, carried out through proxies, allowed him to pose as a peacemaker. By indulging the hopes of conciliation still harboured by those who had found them-selves Communards more by accident than design, he delayed for the moment any military offensive from the capital.

Meanwhile, Thiers set about harnessing the defeated French army to his will by manipulating its impugned sense of martial honour. The Communards flattered themselves that they were the true defenders of the republic, who alone had held out when the rest of France buckled. To counter the perception of their diehard patriotism, Thiers labelled them as treacherous fanatics whose subversion of the state was to blame for the fall of France and the loss of Alsace and Lorraine: they were 'communists' not 'Communards', the Paris administration's choice of name twisted to conjure the phantasm of global conspiracy against which the Catholic Church so vehemently inveighed, as a heretical pestilence that threatened civilisation. Eliminate the communists, Thiers seemed to wink at the troops, and your own, unfairly tarnished reputation will be restored.

In their naïve enthusiasm, the insurrectionists played into his hands. Publishing a letter from a general at Prussian headquarters to the new government in Paris, Paschal Grousset, a firebrand journalist, colleague of Rochefort and now the Commune's minister for foreign affairs, care-lessly translated as 'friendly' the general's far vaguer assurance that 'peaceful' relations existed between Germany and the Commune. It was all grist to a Versailles propaganda mill that was busy grinding out rumours, including one that detailed how the Prussians had stood on the terraces of their billets around the city and laughingly watched through telescopes the events of 18 March unfold, while military bands played a jaunty accompaniment to the folly of the French.

Meanwhile, resentment of the Commune was further fermented by the cost to the National Assembly, in money and pride, of the predica-ment in which it now found itself. Lacking access to the National Bank of France, there were humiliating delays in paying the indemnity due to Germany. 'Paris has given us the right to prefer France to her,' Thiers had announced after the killing of generals Lecomte and Thomas, and *la France profonde* now rallied to his cause.

After a fortnight's hiatus, on Palm Sunday, 2 April, the supporters of the Versaillais government were finally given something to cheer when its guns opened up with a brief bombardment of the suburb of Courbevoie. 'Thank God!' Thiers confided to his diary, 'civil war has begun.' His Catholic and monarchist opponents would have been gratified that the deity's shadow fell heavily over the first clash of arms. '*Vive le roi!*' shouted the Zouaves as they charged and broke the Communard lines; only six months earlier they had been serving in the international regiment that protected Pope Pius IX as he strong-armed a fractious Vatican Council into declaring him infallible in all matters of faith and morality. The atheistic Communards may not have considered themselves to have much in common with the Protestant Huguenots massacred 300 years earlier in the French Wars of Religion, but in the weeks and years to come they would discover a growing affinity with their heretical forebears.

*

Despite the initial rout of the Commune's forces, optimism in Paris was undimmed. The previous two weeks had seen so many changes. Labourers and artisans had emerged from the sumps of poverty into which Baron Haussmann's social zoning of the city had penned them, blinking into the bright light of freedom and self-rule. Their 'descents' into the affluent heart of the city revealed to many a world of opulence and luxury that previously they had seen, at best, from afar. A small contribution to a fund for recent war widows bought them admission to the Tuileries Palace, the one-time home of emperors, with its acres of gilding, while they could sample the refined musical fare on offer at the new Opéra entirely gratis. Surrounded by the conspicuous pleasures and privileges of the bourgeoisie and aristocracy, yet with no cause now to be daunted by rank, Parisians greeted each other as '*citoyen*' and '*citoyenne*'.

'We are free,' proclaimed Louise Michel, 'able to look back without unduly imitating '93 and forward without fear of the unknown.' They were bold words but her hopes were not without foundation. Idealistic decrees had begun to pour from the Hôtel de Ville. Gambling was banned to save the poor from themselves, the Church disestablished, and a three-year moratorium declared on debt. It was only the beginning of what would become an extensive programme of legislation, yet immediately the virtuous example of the Commune seemed to begin trickling down. As the spring sun shone, observers claiming impartiality recorded that, in the absence of envy and oppression, crime spontaneously ceased. Only cynics whispered that the explanation lay in the abductions of troublesome elements by the Commune police under cover of night, or else suggested sarcastically that the criminals no longer had time to break the law, now that they themselves were in power.

It was a holiday mood, too, that infused the tens of thousands of the National Guard who mustered in the squares and parks of western Paris before dawn on 3 April, ready to march on Versailles. Some blithely likened the atmosphere to that of a picnic party setting out for the country, and hopes were high that by nightfall they would have secured the heights of the Châtillon plateau and control of the road to Versailles, barely a dozen miles further on. Elisée Reclus was there, as was his brother Elie, posted to different regiments. Leading the central tine of the trident of three columns was the flamboyant Flourens, his blond locks floating in the wind, the heroic role he had so long imagined finally his to command. Such was the abounding optimism that no one had thought to deploy the big guns that had seemed so precious to their defenders in Montmartre only a fortnight before.

'*Vive la République!*' cried the first Versaillais battalion to engage the National Guard on the right flank, as if in fraternal greeting. The Communard troops felt vindicated in their hopes and lowered their rifles as the seemingly congenial foe advanced from cover. Once at bayonet's length, however, the Versaillais jerked back into an offensive posture. '*Vive la République* is all well and good,' they barked, 'but now surrender!' Beaten by a ruse, the credulous men of the Guard were bound together at the wrists, five and six abreast, and made to submit to a gauntlet of sticks and curses by the bourgeois inhabitants of Versailles as they were led through the town towards an uncertain fate. The absurd hopes that had allowed the Commune troops to become so fatally trusting was less damaging, however, than the Commune's complete failure in military intelligence concerning Mont-Valérien, the fort abandoned by the Assembly's troops in their rush to withdraw from Paris but whose massive gates had subsequently been left invitingly open by the National Guard entrusted with its defence.

Undaunted by the setbacks on his right flank, Flourens had ridden on, the romantic spirit of the Commune embodied. Intent on punching through to Versailles, his column followed the straightest route, directly under the fortress' imposing walls. Were he and his generals ignorant of its reoccupation by the enemy, some days earlier, or did men whose previous campaigns had been fought at second hand, in bars and revolutionary clubs, merely underestimate the significance of its loss? Holding fire until the head of the column had passed, the fort's cannon and *mitrailleuses* then roared out, ripping into the ranks of the National Guard at close range. Within minutes, scores of bodies lay shattered in the fort's lines of fire, with many hundred more untried recruits limping or carried back towards the city. When the Versaillais cavalry rode in to finish the job, what remained behind of the straggling column was too disorientated to mount any effective resistance. It was not yet midday.

Taking shelter at an inn, Flourens allowed himself a brief rest, but awoke to find himself surrounded. The witty intellectual and eloquent rabble-rouser must finally have realised how utterly different a real-life revolution was to the stage-play antics in which he had indulged a year before, using weapons from a theatre's props store. Immune to the charms of 'Florence', a Versaillais gendarme serving under Boulanger strode forward, raising his sabre, and cleaved the vaudeville general's handsome head in two.

Alone now, on the left flank of the attack, General Duval showed what might be achieved if the National Guard was marshalled with a degree of professionalism. His men, Elisée Reclus among them, managed to fight their way up on to the Châtillon plateau. But lack of logistical foresight meant a night without cover or rations, and in the morning Duval had no choice but to order his men to lay down their weapons. Herded along in a pathetic column of the defeated, Reclus witnessed those of his comrades who had deserted the regular army to join the Guard lined up for summary execution. Duval himself was dragged out from the 'miserable scum' and gunned down, to the jeering of the victors, in front of a sign advertising 'Duval, Horticulturalist'.

'Never had the beautiful city, the city of revolutions, appeared more lovely to me,' Reclus would remember, the panorama of Paris before him as he gazed down from the pathetic column of the defeated, only for a Versaillais officer to interrupt his reverie. 'You see your Paris! Well, soon there will not be a stone left standing!' Further on Reclus might have watched local women prodding the brains that spilled from Flourens' split head with their umbrellas. After such experiences, not even the most idealistic believer in the perfectibility of man could fail to comprehend the visceral passions that had riven French society, nor the depth and intensity of the hatreds that had taken root.

Only days before the National Guard had marched out, the artist Daumier had made a drawing that envisioned the apocalypse that might engulf Paris in almost mystical terms. 'Death disguised as a shepherd playing his pan pipes among the flowers of a water meadow beside the Seine, every flower a skull' was how Jules Verne described Daumier's picture, published in the magazine *Charivari*. Already, the image seemed horribly prescient and if the credulity, unprofessionalism and lack of organisation demonstrated by the National Guard's catastrophic sortie proved representative of the Commune as a whole, further tragedy was inevitable. As long as the opportunity remained to them, however, the Communards would allow themselves to dream.

During the hard winter of the siege, Louise Michel had been a vocal advocate of the immediate needs of the poor, as well as of their wider aspirations, petitioning the mayors of the arrondissements to assist with food for the starving and help meet the educational needs of the young. Clemenceau had responded to her pleas as best he could in Montmartre, and in Belleville it was Benoît Malon who had answered her call, a figure familiar to Michel from visits before the war to the Paris offices of the International on the rue de la Cordonnerie, where it seemed to her that the narrow, dusty staircase led to 'the temple of a free and peaceful world'.

If Bismarck and Thiers truly believed the International to be a tight-knit and disciplined conspiratorial network, they could not have been more wrong. When attending its founding conference in London seven years earlier, Malon had, he would insist somewhat disingenuously, known of Karl Marx merely as 'a German professor'. Whilst Marx and Engels had imposed their will on the organisation in the years since, the French section had yet to be converted to their ideological dogmatism. 'I frequent all the parties, democratic, radical, Proudhonian, positivist, phalansterist, collectivist . . . Fourierist cooperations, etc. . . . I see everywhere men of good faith and that teaches me to be tolerant,' Malon had written of his pre-war position. Despite Marx endorsing Leo Franckel and the young Elizaveta Dmitrieva as his two emissaries to the Commune, while he stayed in London to nurse a conveniently recurring kidney complaint, the same pragmatic ecumenicalism now applied to the Commune's attempts to mould a new and ideal society in microcosm.

Malon's own sympathies lay with the federalism of the Russian Bakunin, Marx's rival for influence over the International, but it was the older anti-authoritarian theories of the Frenchman Pierre-Joseph Proudhon with which the experiment in social revolution now initiated in Paris was most strongly stamped. On 16 April, reviving the legacy of the Ateliers Nationaux of 1848, all workshops that had been abandoned or stood unused were taken into national ownership. The initiative provided the basis for a federalised, cooperative model of industrial organisation, and less than a fortnight later the system of fines imposed on workers as a means of unjust social control was abolished. Franckel's efforts to secure a prohibition on night baking, which had entailed notoriously inhumane working conditions, provided Marx with a rare success.

For all Louise Michel's admiration for the late Proudhon, however, she could hardly condone his conservative and some said misogynistic views on the role of women. For whilst the deliverance of the working men of France appeared to be at hand, Michel was adamant that for the social revolution to be truly radical, women would have to win their portion of liberty too; not only for reasons of justice and equality, but because it was they whose experience of oppression taught them the extent of what was required. 'Men are like monarchs, softened by their constant power' had been the sermon preached at the women's clubs in which she had been so active over the winter. To break through the final barrier of male tyranny she would embrace whatever alliance was necessary, even with one of Marx's envoys.

The relationship between Michel and the twenty-year-old Elizaveta Dmitrieva contained more obvious grounds for rivalry than cooperation. Dmitrieva was as spirited and inspiring as Michel, but half her age and far more conventionally beautiful. Like Michel, who had worn the black of mourning ever since the funeral of Victor Noir, Dmitrieva too dressed to be noticed, in a black velvet riding habit with a red silk scarf slung around her neck. And whereas the romantic life of the Red Virgin always seemed tinged with obsession, the Russian flaunted the kind of carefree attitude to romantic passion that Michel must have envied. But their common background of illegitimacy bonded them, and in the newly formed Union des Femmes they found a vehicle for the social change to which they both aspired. The combined pressure they brought to bear on the Commune's legislature quickly produced policies that would constitute the Commune's most humane achievements, many of them more than a century ahead of their time.

A guarantee that unmarried widows would receive the same pension as those who had been married was adopted on 10 April; a week later a law was passed banning discrimination against illegitimate children, while a groundbreaking commitment to equal pay for women would follow. Yet even then the battle would only be half won, with education the key to further success. For if the new society were to allow women to participate fully, it would need not only to alleviate their present burdens, but assist them in the essential task of raising the enlightened citizens of the future. 'Politically,' Michel would write, 'my goal is the universal republic, which is to be achieved through the development of the highest facilities of each individual, the eradication of evil thoughts through proper education, the profound comprehension of human dignity.'

Michel was not alone in seeking to redress the skewed and inadequate syllabus of France's Catholic schools: the Freemasons had been prominent in recent years as campaigners for reform. Nevertheless, the methods she advocated, based on ideas innovated with the 200 children taught in her own school, must have seemed somewhat esoteric: the use of a pedagogic language that children could naturally understand, of easily legible visual aids and of learning through play. And yet the programme for universal state education that she submitted to the Commune found influential advocates, with Edouard Vaillant, the commissioner for education, shepherding through legislation for compulsory free schooling until the age of twelve, together with provision for children of nursery age that would allow their mothers to train for work. Only the ideal society being forged in Paris in the spring of 1871, with its uncertain future, could afford to countenance ideas so far ahead of their time.

Across the Channel, the Commune struck many commentators as a fascinating social experiment. With Samuel Butler delivering *Erewhon* to his publisher on 1 May, and *The Coming Race* by the bestselling Edward Bulwer-Lytton evoking an extraordinary future world in which genetic difference had replaced class divisions as the defining feature of society, the theme of Utopias – and their dystopian flip sides – was in the air. On the Commune's espousal of federalism, British opinion was divided over whether it offered a taste of the future or retreat into the past. *The Times* considered curious the Commune's 'wish to imitate the small Italian republics or the French communes, at the moment when other nations are grouping together and condensing in order to club their forces and their interests', while the positivist philosopher Frederick Harrison argued that 'the idea of the gradual dissolution of nations into more similar aggregates and truer political union is the idea of the future.' In light of the Commune's social achievements, however, the educationalist and social critic Matthew Arnold felt bound to concede 'that all the seriousness, clear-mindedness and settled purpose is hitherto on the side of the Reds.'

The Commune's proclamation of 19 April that 'The Communal Revolution . . . inaugurates a new political era, experimental, positive, scientific' chimed too with the insistence of the English biologist Thomas Huxley, 'Darwin's bulldog', that the Pope's latest syllabus of acceptable knowledge was meaningless, since power was now vested in science. But the arts too were accorded a privileged role in the Commune's vision of society, with a central committee of forty-seven practitioners appointed, some without their permission or approval, to promote the cultural life of Paris. The salon was re-established and museums thrown open to the public, while Elisée Reclus' brother Elie, who unlike his sibling had avoided capture during the Flourens sortie, took over the supervision of libraries. 'Paris is a true paradise!' the painter Courbet swooned on 30 April, 'no nonsense, no exaction of any kind, no arguments! Everything in Paris rolls along like clockwork. If only it could stay like this forever. In short it is a beautiful dream!' Distracted by their ideals, however, the Communards were sleepwalking to disaster.

The portents were already unsettling. Four days before Courbet recorded his sense of wonderment, a long procession of Freemasons had marched out to the Paris ramparts, wearing their secret insignia in public for the first time, and carrying a white banner that bore the legend 'Love One Another'. The leadership of both the Commune and the Versailles government counted Masons among their number, but Thiers had repeatedly responded with scorn to attempts by the Paris Lodges to act as disinterested peace-brokers. Ever since the French Revolution, Catholics had been expressly forbidden to join Masonic lodges, and Masons had been placed next to communists in the list of those held to be anathema; by his attitude, Thiers had aligned himself with their paranoid vision of a French society steeped in conspiracy and polarised beyond repair. Standing braced against the wind along the ramparts, their aprons and pennants flying, the Masons had bravely presented Versailles with a final challenge to respect their neutrality, but sharpshooters picked them off like the fairground ducks on which Louise Michel had practised her marksmanship.

Wistfulness was a recurring sentiment in letters and diaries of the time, while the strains of 'Le Temps de Cerises' that drifted out of clubs and cafés, or were whistled by workers on their awestruck promenades through the city, provided the mood music. 'I will always love cherry-blossom time, and the love that I keep in my heart' went its nostalgic refrain, its story that of a beautiful woman won and lost, set to a melody that tugged the heartstrings. It had been a strange anthem for a spring-time filled with hope and elation, but as the days lengthened towards summer, it assumed a bittersweet relevance. For whilst not consciously despairing or defeatist, it began to seem as though those Communards who persisted in laying the foundations for an ideal society were, in reality, storing up happy memories for the hard times which, they secretly suspected, lay ahead.

As the last hopes of reconciliation ebbed away, so did the Commune's more moderate leadership. Its original leaders were ground down by physical and nervous exhaustion after weeks of catching naps on hard benches as they worked through endless nights, struggling to change the world by mere strength of will. Military and political leaders had been drafted in and then dismissed, or had resigned in short order, having tried and failed to assert control over a society for whom the abandonment of deference and rejection of all authority was an article of faith. Now, with a dangerous power vacuum developing, the most extreme Jacobin elements were only too eager to step into the breach.

As a teenager Raoul Rigault had spied on the Prefecture of Police through a telescope, imagining what he might achieve were he prefect. Two days after the abortive seizure of the guns, still aged only twenty-five, he had achieved his ambition. His rule since then had been ruthless. In the ten days following his installation, over 400 men and women had been arrested as suspected traitors and whilst more than half were soon released, rumours circulated of arbitrary punishments meted out to ideo-logical opponents and of a certain lasciviousness in his treatment of women in custody. But it was his imprisonment of the Archbishop of Paris and other religious figures that had cemented his reputation. Held hostage both against any repeat of the Versaillais' brutality following their defeat of Flourens' army, and as a bargaining chip for the release of Auguste Blanqui, their lives had so far been spared. But as Henri Rochefort remarked of Rigault, 'He was exactly the sort of fellow to say, "I'm very fond of you, but circumstances unfortunately compel me to have you shot. I am, therefore, going to do so!"'

On 27 April, Rigault was promoted to *procureur* of a newly instituted Revolutionary Tribunal. With the announcement of a committee of public safety the following day, the Jacobins were in the ascendant, and grim memories of 1793 and the reign of Revolutionary Terror came flooding back. The Paris guillotine had been destroyed by crowds on 6 April, but no one doubted that there were now even more efficacious means avail-able for the state to rid itself of its enemies, and it was feared that the 'new political era, experimental, positive, scientific' might produce a new form of terrorism all its own.

In a further echo of the glorious days of the French Revolution, anti-clericalism ran rife. Across the city, churches and nunneries were raided, floors dug up and walls pulled down in search of evidence of crimes and moral corruption. In the convent at Picpus, three aristocratic madwomen were discovered in a shed, where they had spent the last nine years locked away to save their families from shame in a clear case of abuse, while magistrates were summoned to investigate infanticide after bones found in the crypt of Saint-Lazare were thought to belong to the illegitimate children of the nuns. A naturalist who ventured that they were more likely animal bones, mixed with the mortar for structural strengthening, barely escaped a lynching. Under the guise of rationalism, the flight of reason became increasingly widespread.

Though generally supportive of the Commune, Rochefort had maintained a careful journalistic detachment from its politics. Now, though, he wrote vehemently against Prefect Rigault, referring especially to the nauseating glee with which the clerks referred to the hostages as his 'private prisoners', arguing the need for a dictator to counterbalance the Jacobin's growing concentration of power. His preferred candidate, a year younger even than Rigault, was General Rossel, who had recently been elevated to commander-in-chief of the Commune's forces, following the dismissal of his predecessor for casting doubt on their chances of victory against the Versaillais. 'These people have good reason for fighting; they fight that their children may be less puny, less scrofulous, and less full of failings' Rossel announced; but only 6,000 men of the 200 regiments of the National Guard responded to his summons to defend the city from imminent attack, and on 8 May he resigned and went into hiding.

Rigault and his friends, among them Louise Michel, seized their opportunity and appointed Charles Delescluze, the much-imprisoned veteran of '48, to lead the coming battle. 'Enough of militarism!' he declared, 'No more general staffs with badges of rank and gold braid at every seam! Make way for the people, for the fighters with bare arms! The hour of revolutionary warfare has struck!' Dressed like a remnant of a bygone age, his health ruined by consumption, Delescluze was an oddly fitting figurehead for what the Commune had become as its moment of destiny approached.

Fifty dawns had come and gone since Louise Michel had raised the alarm in Montmartre, but none can yet have seemed more ominous than that which broke over the fortress of Issy on 5 May. Visiting as a journalist for the Commune's *Journal officiel*, Clemenceau described the scenes of ruined masonry, smashed by German Krupps guns and now blasted by ten Versaillais shells a minute, and noted the bodies of the 500 soldiers killed by their own countrymen, stored in a makeshift morgue in the cellars. The focus of his piece, though, was his friend Michel, ambulance woman turned virago, who four days earlier had rallied the troops to retake the key salient at the Clamart rail station, and was now keeping watch alone as the enemy earthworks came ever closer. 'In order not to be killed herself, she killed others and I have never seen her to be more calm' reported Clemenceau. 'How she escaped being killed a hundred times over before my eyes, I'll never know. And I only watched her for an hour.' It was morale-boosting stuff, but if the propaganda exaggerated her courage, then Michel was more than happy to live the lie.

'It's not heroism, I assure you,' she wrote to Victor Hugo, 'I just love danger! Perhaps that's the savage in me.' The role of Enjolras, in which Hugo had cast her in their playful communications, now fitted like a glove, and Michel seemed ubiquitous. From service on the front line as a member of the National Guard she rushed to chair meetings of the revolutionary clubs and vigilance committees, then on to a hospital to tend the wounded. Nothing could sap her 'exalted' spirit so long as new schools such as one that would teach industrial arts to girls continued to be opened, or whilst she could play her part in redistributive justice, levying a tax on the convent of St Bernard to help pay for the care of the injured. But while she soldiered on, others sought distraction from their impending doom.

When the shells had begun to fall on 1 May, softening up the city for the assault, public performances continued to draw audiences. There was even an appetite for operas with what seemed like morale-sapping themes, though the success of *Le Prophète*, Meyerbeer's dramatic account of the crushing of the Anabaptist insurrection in sixteenth-century Munster, might simply have been due to the ice ballet choreographed with dancers on roller skates that was introduced to lighten the tone. 'This grandeur, this tranquillity, this blindness in an assembly of men already menaced by 100,000 *chassepots*, is one of the most stupefying facts ever given to a historian to record' wrote the twenty-one-year-old Gaston Da Costa, Rigault's secretary from the Prefecture of Police.

Da Costa's reaction to the complacency was to climb on to the roof of Thiers' town house, urging on the crowd that accompanied him to loot its contents and burn it to the ground. The next day, 16 May, it was the Vendôme Column that was targeted, crowds filling the square to witness the demolition of the great monument that Napoleon had erected in celebration of his victory in the Battle of Austerlitz. 'We wanted it all' remarked Courbet, who as head of the arts commission would be blamed for inciting the vandalism. For three hours that afternoon they hacked and sawed and pulled on ropes until the column toppled. Laid out on manure straw, its verdigris mass provided a spectacular backdrop for photographs, in which Communards arranged themselves in formal rows, as though attending some bourgeois festivity. Few there would live long enough to have their picture taken again. 'This colossal symbol of the Grand Army – how fragile it was, how empty and miserable! It seemed to have been devoured from the middle by a multitude of rats, like France itself, their glory tarnished' was how one survivor remembered the grand act of destruction.

For the previous week, the enemy from Versailles had been advancing, overwhelming the forts and fighting their way across the Bois de Boulogne. The Communards may have disparaged the enemy troops as lackeys of the rich and powerful, but the release by Bismarck of over 200,000 prisoners of war had made them a formidable opponent. The failings in military discipline were all on the Commune's side, where too many of those who had revelled in their new freedoms now spurned Delescluze's rallying call to 'save the country, though possibly now only behind the barricades' in favour of further symbolic gestures of retribution.

As the Versaillais pressed forward, the Tuileries Palace, the Hôtel de Ville, the Palais de Justice and the prefecture all went up in flames, along with dozens of other public buildings. In the case of the Tuileries, the central dome of the Salle des Maréchaux was blown up with gunpowder less than forty-eight hours after the last Sunday concert in the gardens had attracted an audience of 1,500. The Communards' explanation, that the arson was strategically necessary to slow the advance of the Versaillais, was plausible only in rare instances.

Day after day the enemy pressed on, fighting from street to street, flanking the barricades thrown up in their path, charging through alleys and courtyards, or sledgehammering their way through the internal walls of apartment blocks to emerge and shoot down their defenders from behind. It was a bewildering battlefield even for veterans, let alone those experiencing war for the first time. National Guard reinforcements would arrive to find themselves in the eerie stillness of a killing ground from which the battle had moved on, their dead comrades left propped against the walls under a drifting pall of gunpowder smoke. And when saboteurs were blamed for the explosion of the avenue Rapp arsenal that cost 200 lives, fear spread in Communard Paris that the enemy was already in their midst.

*

As dawn broke on 23 May, Louise Michel was back in Montmartre where the adventure had begun, awaiting an assault more ferocious by far than when General Lecomte had come for the guns. In the quiet of the night, amid the perfume of early summer, she picked flowers for the dead, and must have wondered whether she would join them before the day's end. There were scarcely a hundred Guardsmen to defend the Buttes, while in the previous six weeks the cannon in the artillery park had been allowed to rust beyond use. Once again descending the hill to summon help, Michel found herself caught up in the fighting in the streets below. Before she could return, the hill had fallen. The captured National Guard were marched directly to the garden of the rue des Rosiers guardhouse where the generals had been killed, one of the many liquidation centres that were springing up across the city, and massacred.

East along the boulevard de Clichy the Commune fighters were pushed back. A fierce resistance was mounted in place Blanche, where a battalion formed from the Union des Femmes and led by Michel's friend, Natalie Lemel, was said to have been in the thick of it; women whose loved ones had died and had nothing left to lose, they fought with abandon. Falling back, Michel passed General Dombrowski, the Polish commander of the Right Bank, who shouted that all was lost; the next moment a bullet knocked him dead from his horse. His comrades improvised a shroud out of blue silk sheets they found in the nearby home of Baron Haussmann, whose urban redesign with its long straight boulevards was proving so useful to the Versaillais army's manoeuvres.

'I proclaim war without truce or mercy upon these assassins,' the Versaillais commander General Gallifet had warned more than a month earlier. It was the women of the Commune above all who were demonised by the Catholic country boys of Thiers' army, the sexual revolution that had taken place an unwelcome challenge to their conventional sense of masculine prerogatives. At Chateau d'Eau, among the last of the barricades to fall three days later, the female defenders would be stripped and brutalised before being slaughtered. Michel, captured at some point along the way, miraculously managed to avoid their fate, but with every misstep by the Commune's defenders, any hope of quarter receded.

During the weeks since Rigault had taken them hostage, the Archbishop of Paris and his fellow prisoners had remained untouched, despite mounting Communard losses. Now, finally, Rigault's self-restraint cracked. Ferré, his recent successor as prefect of police, signed the death warrant for the archbishop, who had generously written of his persecutors that 'the world judged them to be worse than they really were'; Rigault himself commanded the firing squad at Saint-Pelagie prison. Though he and the archbishop had been bitterly at odds during the recent Vatican Council, Pius IX would condemn his murderers as 'devils risen up from hell bringing the inferno to the streets of Paris', and the Versaillais treated them accordingly. The harshest persecution of all, though, was reserved for the *pétroleuses*, crones rumoured to have set Paris ablaze in a diabolical hysteria, in what rapidly came to resemble a witch hunt.

'I am known to be cruel, but I am even crueller than you can imagine,' Gallifet snarled at a column of prisoners containing Michel. She sang a mocking tune in reply, but once more seemed strangely invulnerable, amid scenes that became more hellish by the hour. Among the general population, any suspects found with powder-blackened hands or shoulders bruised from the recoil of rifles were selected for summary execution, while the general himself picked out others to die simply for their ugliness. Somewhere among the carnage, Rigault was killed by a shot to the head, his body dumped in a gutter among the piles of corpses.

'All around us fall from the skies, like black rain, little fragments of burned paper; the records and the accounts of France,' wrote the novelist Edmond de Goncourt, reminded of the ash that had smothered Pompeii. For others the agony of the city brought to mind 'a great ship in distress, furiously firing off its maroons'. From the boulevard Voltaire, the last small remnant of the Commune's soldiers retreated, but with almost nowhere left to go. Turning, they saw their leader Delescluze climb the barricade and offer himself to the enemy's rifles, silhouetted against the sunset. 'Forgive me for departing before you,' he had scribbled to his sister, 'but I no longer feel I possess the courage to submit to another defeat, after so many others.' The report of the shots that felled him would have merged into the ambient noise of killing that filled the balmy, sun-soaked evening.

Mostly it was the whirr of the *mitrailleuses* doling out deadly punishment: 'an expeditious contrivance', said *The Times*, that 'standing a hundred yards off, mows them down like grass'. In the Red neighbourhoods its distant sound blended with that of flies that buzzed over the makeshift mortuaries, gorging on the spilled blood. A few score men, the final defenders of a society that believed that 'property is theft', would hold out for one more night in the Père Lachaise cemetery, sheltering behind the tombs and gravestones, on plots bought and owned by their occupants 'in perpetuity'. The following morning they were coralled over the crest of the hill towards the rear wall, against which they would be butchered. And yet the Semaine Sanglante, or Bloody Week, still had several days to run. 'No half measures this time. Europe will thank us when it's over,' a priest in Versailles reassured a friend.

'Childhood, individual liberty, the rights of man – nothing was respected. It was a mighty letting loose of every sort of clerical fury – a St Bartholomew to the sixth power,' Rochefort would later record of the Semaine Sanglante, recalling the terrible massacre of Huguenots by Catholics 300 years earlier. He underestimated by half. The death toll of the 1793 Terror too was overshadowed, as was its rate of execution. Then, only 2,500 had been guillotined in eighteen months; in a single week of 1871, ten times that number or more died from bullets sprayed by the *mitrailleuses*. The Paris municipality paid for the burial of 17,000 Communards, but the bodies of many more disappeared into the fabric of the city, buried haphazardly beneath the overturned barricades, in the Parc Montceau, or in the chalk mines under the Buttes Chaumont, the pleasure garden gifted to the working class four years earlier, where now the tunnels were dynamited to conceal the dead.

Rochefort himself was arrested on a train outside Paris, attempting to escape via a route operated by the Masons that had previously spirited Elie Reclus to safety. He had been betrayed, it was said, by Paschal Grousset, one of the Jacobins with whom he had verbally crossed swords. Louise Michel's route out of Paris was guaranteed, as a member of one of the columns of prisoners a quarter of a mile long that bled out of the city towards the army base on Satory Plain, now a concentration camp. 'We walked and walked,' she would recall, 'lulled by the rhythmic beat of the horses' hooves, through a night lit by irregular flashes of light . . . We were marching into the unknown . . .'

3

From Prince to Anarchist

Russia and Switzerland, 1871–1874

In 1871, Prince Peter Kropotkin, one of Russia's most eminent young scientists, reached a watershed, his growing awareness of social injustice leading him to question whether he could remain a part of the Establishment. During the previous decade he had led expeditions by the Imperial Russian Geographical Society into Asia and beyond the Arctic Circle, travels that informed his groundbreaking reconstruction of the geological changes that had reshaped the earth during the glacial period. Now, when offered the post of its secretary, he declined. In the face of the widespread human suffering that he had witnessed in the course of his life, the honour struck him as an empty vanity. 'What right had I to these higher joys,' he reasoned, 'when all around me was nothing but misery and the struggle for a mouldy bit of bread?'

For more than ten years, after the 'Saviour' tsar, Alexander II, had first granted the serfs their freedom then backtracked on a slew of other reforms that might have made the gesture meaningful, the youth of Russia had postured as nihilists. During that time, Kropotkin and his older brother, Alexander, had remained focused on the theoretical challenges of effecting social change. In 1871, however, a female friend of Alexander's wife had crystallised Kropotkin's dilemma. Sofia Nikolaevna Lavrova was a graduate of the Alarchinsky courses, which from 1869 had offered women in Russia a non-degree programme of higher education. She was now studying in Switzerland and, during a trip back home to Russia for the summer, became a regular visitor to Kropotkin's apartment in St Petersburg, charming him with her intellect and challenging him over his lack of political engagement. When their friendship prompted the political Third Section of the police to search his rooms for smuggled seditious literature, Kropotkin was torn between outrage at the intrusion and contentment from finally being deemed worthy of their attention. When the withdrawal of government funding for his next Arctic expedition was withdrawn, he had the excuse for which he had been waiting: he would visit Sofia in Zurich and use his time in Switzerland to take stock.

Until only a few years earlier, the final stage of the journey would have been arduous, travelling by coach along the military roads that Napoleon had laid across the Alpine passes, before concluding his journey with a rapid descent on the far side of the mountain range by sledge: 'like being precipitated downstairs in a portmanteau' according to one English traveller of the time. A Fell railway had offered a questionable improvement in 1868, its locomotive heaving soot-blackened carriages over the Saint-Cenis route by means of a cogged ratchet on a notched rail; by the time Kropotkin set off in February 1872, Alfred Nobel's dynamite had blasted a route clear through the mountains to the promised land beyond. A man used to challenging travel, he would nevertheless have appreciated what it meant to live in an era of remarkable technological progress.

A decade earlier, Kropotkin had graduated from the Academy of the Corps of Pages with the highest distinction and a choice of the most prestigious military commissions. To the shock of the imperial court and his family, he had enrolled instead in a regiment of Cossacks stationed in the depths of Siberia, deliberately cutting himself adrift from his privileged background. His hectoring father was apoplectic: all the military discipline he had imparted to his son, all the gifts of rifles and sentry boxes, had failed to inspire Peter to better his own rather undistinguished army career. It did not help that his late wife, whose memory Peter's stepmother had done everything she could to erase, had herself been a Cossack, with all that fiery tradition of independence. Peter's rectitudinous cousin, Dmitri, then serving as Tsar Alexander II's aide-de-camp, had tried to intervene, urging him to stay and pursue the glittering opportunities that awaited him in St Petersburg. Even the tsar himself had taken an interest, insisting that his erstwhile page de chambre explain his eccentric decision in person. On being told by Kropotkin that he hoped travel might afford him insights into how society could be improved, Alexander II had appeared overwhelmed with world-weariness. Kropotkin would later conclude that the tsar was already predicting defeat in the great programme of reforms that he had set in motion only months before. Fortunately, however, the young Peter was owed a favour. When mysterious fires had swept through the adminstrative district of St Petersburg, the initiative Kropotkin had shown in raising the alarm had saved much of the old wooden city from devastation. He chose the Siberian posting as his reward.

The twenty-year-old Kropotkin took with him to Siberia a smouldering disdain for all arbitrary authority. As children on the family's
feudal estate in Nikolskoe, deprived of their dead mother's tender atten-
tions, Peter and his brother Alexander had considered themselves fortunate to enjoy 'among the servants, that atmosphere of love which children
must have around them'. But it was the kindness and fellow feeling of
the oppressed. Little had changed for the serfs since the days of Ivan
the Terrible, and to Kropotkin's father and his ilk, they remained mere
property: 'souls' to be traded without regard to ties of blood or affection and ruthlessly exploited. Not even death could free them from their
bondage, as the teenaged Kropotkin would have learned when helping
his tutor translate Gogol's *Dead Souls*: in the vicious world it satirised,
beatings were liberally administered, and those serfs punished by being
sent into the army as cannon fodder, where the floggings were still
crueller, and those who expired under the whip would have the remaining
quota of lashes administered on their corpse. 'Leave me alone,' one of
his father's serfs had snapped when Kropotkin tried to comfort him after
a whipping at the local barracks, 'When you grow up, you think that
you won't be exactly the same?' The rebuke stung the young prince and,
as a cadet, a display of intolerance for unjust authority, of the kind that
permeated society from top to bottom, had landed him in solitary
confinement for six weeks on a diet of bread and water: a foretaste of
what was to come.

Kropotkin's journey to Irkutsk in 1862 offered an education he would
not forget. It took him past endless scenes of human suffering: a living
hell of a kind he could never before have conceived. In the labour camps
of the east, convicts mined gold waist-deep in freezing water, or quar-
ried salt with frostbitten hands for the few short weeks that they could
expect to survive the appalling conditions: to be sent there was a death
sentence. As fast as they expired, others replaced them, transported
from occupied Poland in their thousands, and in soaring numbers after
the Polish rebellion of 1863 was ruthlessly suppressed. Kropotkin was
relieved to discover that there were at least humane, even liberal men
serving among his colleagues in the regiment, though it soon became
obvious that they were very far from representative of the imperial
administration as a whole.

Shortly after Kropotkin's arrival, his commanding officer General Kukel,
who had taken the new recruit under his wing, was removed and disciplined for wilful negligence, having allowed Michael Bakunin, the lionised
revolutionary, to escape and plague the regime with his plotting from

abroad. Eager to avoid Kukel's hard-line successor, Kropotkin volunteered to oversee a convoy of barges along the River Amur, a 'new world' ceded to Russia by China only a few years before. But the job served only to deepen his disillusionment. When a storm wrecked the convoy, Kropotkin undertook a breakneck mercy mission back to St Petersburg – by means of sled, horse and train – to demand assistance from the capital. Funds were forthcoming, but soon squandered on personal luxuries by the local officers responsible for the purchase of rescue tugboats.

Promotion brought Kropotkin further dismal insights into the canker of corruption and callous self-interest that infected the Russian Empire. Having secured an appointment as secretary of the prison reform committee, the condition of the Siberian transit camps had horrified him, but his recommendations were disregarded, leaving him no alternative but to resign. Beneath the casual brutality and venal incompetence that confronted him at every turn, in the exploitation of the workers Kropotkin had started to perceive an underlying dynamic that was more pernicious still: the harsh imperatives of Western capitalism, as it rapidly colonised a Russian economy built on the robust and flexible foundation of the village *mir*. 'This is where one can gaze every day to one's heart's content upon the enslavement of the worker by capital,' he wrote to his brother Alexander following a visit to the Lena gold mines, 'and at the great law of the reduction in reward with the increase in work.'

Years later, Kropotkin made an even bolder claim in his *Memoirs of a Revolutionary*. 'I may say now, that in Siberia I lost all faith in state discipline. I was prepared to become an anarchist.' The sight of hungry peasants handing crusts to prisoners more famished than themselves, the 'semi-communistic brotherly organisation' of the political prisoners, and the non-hierarchical structure of the indigenous tribes of Asia all seemed evidence that altruism, mutuality and cooperation were the true bedrock of a well-functioning human society. Meanwhile, his experience of military command, in the most adverse conditions, reinforced the belief that collective effort lies at the heart of all successful social enterprises, while the best leadership inspires rather than directs.

During the latter years of the 1860s, as vested interests at court seized upon any pretext to roll back the reformist agenda initiated by the tsar, Alexander Kropotkin was the more active of the brothers in opposing the tsarist regime, while Peter continued to enjoy many fringe benefits from membership of the Russian elite. Geography rather than politics claimed most of his attention, on expeditions that filled the state's coffers: charting new routes to the gold fields to increase their profitability helped

win him a gold medal from the Imperial Society. When the hazardous
dynamiting of cliffs for the construction of one road prompted a revolt
by the Polish slave gangs, leading to the execution of five of their number,
Kropotkin was sickened. Nevertheless, he found it hard to renounce the
joy of scientific discovery that his work afforded him: 'the sudden birth
of a generalisation, illuminating the mind after a long period of research',
such as he felt on apprehending how geological folding had formed the
Asiatic mountain ranges. And his glittering career promised many more
such moments.

In years to come, Kropotkin applied these same powers of analytical
and synthetic thought to the question of how to create the ideal human
society, and the form it should take, dismissing any 'study of nature
without man [as] the last tribute paid by modern scientists to their previous
scholastic education'. For the moment, though, he salved his conscience
by compiling a comprehensive guide to the soils and topography of Russia,
to assist the peasants in their productive cultivation of the land. It was a
token gesture of solidarity with the twenty million or more serfs, whose
predicament had only worsened under the ill-considered terms of their
recent emancipation.

The greatest threat to the peasants' economic independence, however,
came not from any shortcomings in their husbandry of the land but from
the rapacious attitude of their former masters, whose greed had not been
satisfied by compensation with government bonds. Once released from
the tacit contract of mutual obligation that had provided the foundation
for centuries of feudalism, Russia's landowners embraced the capitalist
ethos of the market with a rough passion, while continuing to pocket
the government's cash. Rents were doubled, land reclaimed for the slightest
infraction on the part of its new owners, and every effort made to claw
back property through the landed class' domination of local government.
Still tied to their village communities, unable to afford better land elsewhere, those serfs who had been freed looked back on their indentured
days with more than a little nostalgia.

Under intense lobbying by vested interests and the grinding pressure
of a deeply conservative culture, Alexander II's bold plans had crumbled faster even than Napoleon III's progressive social schemes had in
France. With unrest brewing among large elements of society, ambitious reforms to the army, judiciary and the education system were all
reversed: schools, maternity facilities and homes for injured workers
were either closed or else never opened, and censorship was reimposed.
The second wave of emancipation, which many hoped would prove

more thorough and genuine than the first, broke and lost its force before
it reached land. And following the attempt by the young radical Dmitri
Karakozov to assassinate the tsar in 1866, hardliners had the perfect
excuse to reassert themselves at court, accelerating the drift towards
repression; ineptitude and a lack of resources were the only brake on
the conservative backlash.

The educated youth of Russia felt the collapse of the reforms as both
a moral outrage and a personal disaster, restricting as it did their own
intellectual and political freedoms, while exposing the hypocrisy of their
parents' generation. Seeing how their fathers shamelessly mouthed idealistic platitudes while continuing to act as petty autocrats, they had adopted
an attitude of excoriating candour, in defiance of all the hollow proprieties of social convention. Where they could be acquired, the writings
of foreign authors and philosophers were read and discussed in search of
possible solutions to the extreme injustices of a sclerotic society, a process
stymied by the tsarist censor's restrictions on books and papers that
contained the faintest hint of sedition. Among home-grown writers, the
St Petersburg novelist Nicholas Chernyshevsky developed a huge
following: 'there have been three great men in the world,' wrote one
prominent young firebrand at the time, 'Jesus Christ, Paul the Apostle,
and Chernyshevsky.'

Chernyshevsky's character Rakhmetov in his 1863 novel *What is to be
Done?*, written in the Peter and Paul fortress while he was imprisoned on
charges of sedition, was seized upon as the very model of a revolutionary.
A university dropout who renounces wealth, God and all the mores of a
moribund civilisation, Rakhmetov pledges himself to a life of extreme asceticism, without wine, women or cooked meat and with a bed of nails on
which to prove his powers of will and endurance; science and socialism are
the sole object of his devotion, and cigars his only pleasure. That
Chernyshevsky had intended the characterisation as a critique of the follies
of youth did nothing to deter young people from aping Rakhmetov's
manners and demeanour, any more than Ivan Turgenev's satirical intention
when creating Bazarov in *Fathers and Sons* discouraged them from adopting
the label of 'nihilist' coined by the author. The nihilists were easy to identify: with shoulder-length hair, bushy beards, red shirts and knee boots for
the men, bobbed hair and dark, unstructured clothes for the women, and
a unisex fashion for blue-tinted glasses, walking staves and smoking endless
cigarettes, they stood out a mile. When it came to policing them, however,
and censoring their reading or the course of their education, the reversals
in the reform programme had left one crucial loophole.

Since 1861, male Russian citizens had enjoyed far greater travel rights: a passport and official permission to leave the country were still required, but their acquisition was usually a formality. The consequence was burgeoning émigré communities, especially in Switzerland, that had long been bolt-holes for dissidents of all hues. It was not merely the chance to applaud revolutionary sentiments that brought the younger sections of the audience to their feet at every performance of Rossini's *William Tell* in the St Petersburg opera house; they were applauding the example set by Switzerland's legendary liberator in resisting oppression.

In the aftermath of the Europe-wide upheavals of 1848, the Swiss authorities had briefly bowed to international pressure, handing over a number of political refugees to their own governments. Since then, though, trust had gradually returned, with Zurich and Geneva now a cacophony of foreign voices, and only the lurking presence of spies to remind the political refugees of their troubles back home. Unsurprisingly, Switzerland had become the most fecund source of the banned works of literature, history or philosophy that were smuggled into Russia to feed its more enquiring minds. But from the late 1860s cities like Zurich also held a less cerebral attraction for male émigrés, being home to an unusual concentration of passionately idealistic young women.

Medicine was a favoured subject for student radicals, offering an opportunity to alleviate suffering – of the individual, if not of society as a whole – and the pride of having embraced a truly rationalist vocation. For young women, the thought that their parents might be shocked by the notion of their cosseted daughters dissecting cadavers in anatomy lessons may well have held its own appeal. But there were many practical obstacles to be overcome. In 1864, the St Petersburg Medical-Surgical Academy excluded women, and they were subsequently banned from taking the final exams necessary for a medical degree in any institution in the country. The result was a continuing exodus to Switzerland, where a medical diploma could be obtained.

Domineering fathers who withheld their permission were outflanked by means of marriages of convenience with male friends, which combined cunning with the frisson of moral transgression. Those impressionable youths who had read Chernyshevsky possibly considered the role of cuckold an honourable one: taking his feminist and free-love principles to an extreme, the author himself insisted on remaining faithful to his wife, despite her attempts to contrive affairs for him, while goading her into taking numerous lovers herself. It was said that on one occasion he had even continued scribbling away while she took her pleasure with a Polish émigré in an alcove of the same room. For the male friends and tutors who agreed to marry the aspiring female doctors, however, separate bedrooms were usually considered a sufficient sacrifice.

The earnest young women of the émigré colony were nevertheless uncompromising in their expectations, and not least of the men who wooed them. Whilst the privileged male youth of Russia might dabble in socialism and empathise with the peasantry at arm's length, without necessarily causing undue damage to their career, for their female counterparts the success or failure of the reformist enterprise had huge personal ramifications. Accepting the case for sublimating their feminist agenda in the cause of a wider 'social revolution', they were determined to instil in their male colleagues a shared sense of determination, and a commitment to the cause that demanded almost monastic austerity.

Vera Figner vividly captured the earnest atmosphere of this radical milieu. Years later, when she wrote her memoirs, she could still remember her arrival in a dreary, drizzly Zurich, and the drab view of tiled roofs from the window of her room. Having married to secure freedom to travel, and then sold her wedding gifts to cover the cost of several years' study abroad, not even the severe temptation (for a tomboyish country girl) of a lake teeming with Switzerland's famously sweet-fleshed fish, the fera and gravenche, could distract her. 'I won't even go fishing!' she primly assured her diary, 'No! There'll be no fishing or boating! There'll be nothing but lectures and textbooks!'

Studious attendance on the courses soon forged strong bonds between her female companions – Auntie, Wolfie, Shark and Hussar, as they called themselves – who encouraged each other's awakening political awareness. Thirteen of the women formed a discussion and study circle, on the model of those then flourishing in Russia, and named it after the Fritsche boarding house where most of them lodged. 'Mesdames – all of Europe is watching you!' the chairwoman – most often Lydia Figner, Vera's sister – would declare, grandiosely paraphrasing Napoleon Bonaparte. The full pathos of some of the subjects they thrashed out could not have been predicted at the time: of the group who engaged with the question of 'Suicide and Psychosis', tsarist persecution would later impel five to take their own lives.

When the Swiss hosts expressed concern over the young women's supposedly lax attitudes, the opportunity was seized upon to practise their developing powers of rhetoric. The vicious rumours of sexual orgies – the usual slanders used throughout history to undermine independent women and radicals – were most likely promulgated by the network of Third Section spies that Wilhelm Stieber established in Switzerland some years before his involvement in the Siege of Paris. In reality, the darkest secret of their gatherings was their addiction to an expensive import from the Orient, which crippled their finances and blunted their dynamism: tea. When it came to sex, by contrast, the women may have appeared to embrace Chernyshevsky's free-love ethos, but their creed of renunciation far outweighed any tendency to libertinage.

Kropotkin was not alone in being lured to Switzerland by the prudish, caffeine-addled temptresses of Zurich, but he was among the most pure-hearted. Week after week he worked through the night in the socialist library that Sofia Lavrova had established with her room-mate, gorging on the theoretical literature of which he had for years been starved. By day, he sampled the melting pot of revolutionary and utopian ideas that the different exile traditions had created in the city, until his desire for further knowledge outstripped even his fascination with Sofia. Eager to further his education, it was not long before Kropotkin packed his bags for Geneva, for centuries a centre of religious as well as political dissent and now the scene of a simmering dispute between the followers of Karl Marx and Michael Bakunin.

*

When Michael Bakunin had visited London in 1865 as a fugitive from Siberia, Karl Marx remarked with barbed generosity that he was 'one of the few people improved by prison'. Since then the relationship between the two men had deteriorated to an extravagant degree. Marx, busy insinuating his way into the leadership of the newly founded International Working Men's Association and intent on making it a vehicle for the dissemination of his own theories, was adamant that a hot-headed Slavic rival like Bakunin should not be allowed to challenge his monopoly of influence. In this he had the support of his friend and financial supporter Engels, whose skill as a propagandist was a huge asset to his cause. Bakunin, meanwhile, though born into an aristocratic family with extensive estates, possessed an impressive if rather over-inflated reputation as a revolutionary whose mettle had been tested on the barricades of 1848, with an exciting story to tell of his escape from prison in Siberia, and racial prejudices that even exceeded Marx's own. What he lacked, however, after years of enforced absence in Siberia, was a formal organisation to sustain his self-image as the high priest of socialism.

During the second half of the 1860s Bakunin had gained a tenuous foothold in the International, brokering alliances with other radical groups whose grand titles belied their infinitesimally small membership. But with Marx increasingly intolerant of Bakunin's presence, the battle lines between them were drawn: Bakunin's doctrine of federalism and grass-roots activism on one side, Marx's vision of a centralised authority guiding the workers towards the coming revolution on the other. Bakunin would doubtless have put it more simply: freedom and autonomy against authority and repression.

The bitterness between the two men and their supporters had grown in intensity since the outbreak of the Franco-Prussian War. Bakunin's early and abortive attempt to inspire the creation of a federal, revolutionary France by his declaration, in October 1870, of a commune in Lyons had prompted Marx to comment that 'At first everything went well but those asses, Bakunin and Clusuret, arrived at Lyons and spoiled everything.' And yet, despite the paucity of Marxists among the leading figures of the Commune and his initial opposition to the Paris insurrection, it was Marx who had contrived to emerge, in the summer of 1871, as the perceived mastermind of the international revolutionary movement and all its actions.

After listening to Engels present a summary account of the Commune's origins to the executive committee of the International in late March 1871, Marx had been content to accept the commission to write a longer address on the subject. Surfacing only to repudiate the most egregious slanders against him, Marx had kept his head down for the duration, digesting every scrap of information to emerge from Paris. Only when the Bloody Week was drawing to a close had he read On the Civil War in France to the central committee in London. Quickly and widely disseminated, it presented a powerful first draft of history to counter the Versaillais lies.

'Working men's Paris, with its Commune, will be for ever celebrated as the glorious harbinger of the new society,' boasted his opportunistic obsequy, and Marx was gleeful when his address was mistaken as something akin to a general's valediction to his brave but defeated troops, that promised a counter-attack across an even wider front. 'I have the honour to be at this moment the best calumniated and most menaced man of London,' he wrote to a German benefactor, 'which really does one good after twenty years' idyll in my den.' But while the prestige that accrued to Marx may have encouraged him to face down Bakunin once and for all, it was a sensational murder case in Russia that provided him with the ammunition to assert his ascendancy over the International.

*

Sergei Nechaev had arrived on Bakunin's doorstep in March 1869 like some irresistible Lucifer: young, handsome, bright and charismatic, with a matchless pedigree in the political underground. He was, he claimed, a collaborator in the 'Secret Revolutionary Committee' – the inner core of the 'European Revolutionary Committee' set up by an associate of the tsar's would-be assassin, Karakozov – and codenamed simply 'Hell'. Having been arrested in St Petersburg, he was on the run. And lest anyone should doubt the sincerity of his commitment, he was dedicated to a life of fanatical asceticism.

Bakunin was wholly enchanted. For years, his bravura assertion that Russia was ripe for spontaneous revolution had rested on nothing but wishful thinking; now here was the son of a serf, a factory worker who had clawed his way up by dint of will and intellect, come to vindicate his claims with the most compelling personal testimony, and bearing fiery tidings that their time had come. If Bakunin wanted an acolyte, though, Nechaev was not going to be an easy conquest. The twenty-year-old made clear that he was seeking not a mentor but an equal, whose sponsorship could burnish the lustrous aura he already possessed. Bakunin agreed, and a potent but misbegotten manifesto soon emerged from their collaboration.

When presenting his ideas, the manifesto had long been Bakunin's preferred form, the assertive nature of such documents punching through the tedium of the essay, their titles claiming 'secrecy' and promising deliciously occult insights. *The Revolutionary Catechism* was no exception, but for its new-found vigour and razor-sharp edge; Nechaev's nihilist influence led Bakunin's zeal to new extremes. 'We devote ourselves exclusively to the annihilation of the existing social system. To build it up is not our task but the task of those that come after us,' asserted one of its more restrained statements, while others advocated terroristic murder outright. The document gifted Bakunin's enemies the opportunity to caricature his theories as advocating senseless violence. When Nechaev returned to Russia with the aim of preparing a full-scale revolution for 19 February 1870, his actions seemed to prove their case.

Travelling in disguise between St Petersburg and Moscow, with a certificate from Bakunin declaring him to be 'an accredited representative of the Russian section of the World Revolutionary Alliance No. 2771', Nechaev set about creating his own cell-based organisation called the People's Revenge (Narodnaya Rasprava). Members were expected to adhere to the imperatives of the *Catechism*: 'The revolutionary is a dedicated man. He has no personal interest, no business, no emotions, no attachments, no property, not even a name . . . In his innermost depths he has broken all ties with the social order, not only in words but in actual fact'. Most importantly, however, they were required to submit themselves unquestioningly to Nechaev's will and the instructions he conveyed to them from the central committee.

When a member of the St Petersburg cell, Ivanov by name, astutely questioned the very existence of this secret committee, Nechaev decided to eliminate the threat to his authority. Each of Ivanov's colleagues was to take a hand in his murder to demonstrate their absolute commitment to the cause. Nechaev had already acquired the habit of incriminating students in order that their punishment by the authorities should radicalise them, and this was the next logical step. Following the macabre farce of Ivanov's killing, Nechaev had succeeded in escaping back to Switzerland before the crime was discovered, but had been tried and convicted *in absentia* in 1871 and was, at the time of Kropotkin's visit, fighting extradition.

That Nechaev had all along been a terrible liability was now obvious to Bakunin yet still he could not bring himself entirely to disown his protégé. 'No one has done me, and deliberately done me, so much harm as he,' Bakunin would write, and yet he maintained a correspondence with Nechaev. It was a fatal error, both for the future of revolutionary socialism and, more immediately, for Bakunin's reputation.

Accusations concerning the pair's ongoing conspiratorial activities were collected by Utin, the leader of the Marxist faction in Geneva, or else fabricated. For his pains, Marx rewarded Utin with recognition of his group as an official splinter of the International in Switzerland. He then convened a meeting of his cabal at the Blue Posts pub in Soho for what he termed the London Congress of the International. The challenge of travel in post-Commune Europe prevented many delegates from attending, while the émigré Communards in London, who had begun to distrust Marx's egotism and challenge his dominance within the organisation, were excluded on the grounds that they might be French police spies. Having eliminated all sources of disagreement, the congress did Marx's bidding: Nechaev was indicted and Bakunin thoroughly smeared as an accessory to and beneficiary of his violent crimes. The German Marxist Wilhelm Liebknecht topped off the character assassination by labelling Bakunin as a tsarist agent, paid to undermine the International.

The feud between Marx and Bakunin now spilled over into open warfare. Convening a congress of its own in the Swiss village of Saint-Imier in late

1871, the Jurassian Federation – the anti-authoritarian core of Bakunin's support, which had been founded in the Swiss canton of the Jura a year before – denounced the London event as a partisan farrago. Some delegates countered Liebknecht's charge by asserting that it was Marx himself who was the spy, hired by Bismarck. In fact, Bakunin sincerely saw strong similarities between the two autocratic Prussians, while the new Germany itself seemed to him the very embodiment of the modern nation state: one 'based on the pseudo-sovereignty of the people in sham popular assemblies' while exploiting them for the 'benefit of capital concentrated in a very small number of hands'. Writing his pamphlet *Statism and Anarchy* in 1873, Bakunin presciently identified in Bismarck's Germany the roots of a kaiserism and militarism that would generate something monstrous. Where his judgement carried less moral weight, however, was in his accusations of anti-Semitism.

Hypocritically, Bakunin insisted that he was 'neither the enemy nor the detractor of the Jew', while denouncing 'this whole Jewish world which constitutes a single exploiting sect', and 'reign[s] despotically in commerce and banking.' Having become the victim of its machinations, Bakunin now decried the London Congress of the International as 'a dire conspiracy of German and Russian Jews' who were 'fanatically devoted to their dictator-Messiah Marx'. From a man who possessed both strong conspiratorial and millenarian tendencies himself, his words sounded like a bitter and vicious howl of envy. Such anti-Semitic sentiments, however, were far from unusual, and would only become more vehement and widespread with the passage of time.

*

Once in Geneva, it took Kropotkin a certain amount of trial and error to discover his natural political allies. Home to the city's branch of the International, the Masonic Temple Unique was an obvious first port of call for someone of his background and socialist inclinations. In Russia, Freemasonry had for a century provided a haven for, in Bakunin's words, 'the choicest minds and most ardent hearts' from among the gentry, where they could nurture their social conscience. But whilst it had been Masons who were imprisoned in Schlüsselburg for their radicalism under Catherine the Great, the fire had long since gone out. 'A jabbering old intriguer . . . useless and worthless, sometimes malevolent and always ridiculous,' was Bakunin's verdict of Italian Freemasonry when he had tried to co-opt it to the revolutionary cause, and Kropotkin could only concur. And whilst Kropotkin admired the enthusiasm of the workers attending the classes run by the International, 'the trust they put in it, the love with which they spoke of it, the sacrifices they made for it' seemed to him wholly misguided. Dominated by the followers of Marx, its meetings struck him as fatuous: a display of intellectual vanity that bamboozled those who deserved better.

Preferring the company of the workers to that of the Marxists from the International, Kropotkin, 'with a glass of sour wine . . . sat long into the evening at some table in the hall among the workers, and soon became friendly with some of them, particularly with one stonemason who had deserted France after the Commune.' The stonemason, like many hundreds of Communards who had flooded into Switzerland in the wake of the Bloody Week, had little left to do but reminisce.

Tales of the utopian dreams that had briefly flickered into life in Paris the previous spring touched Kropotkin with inspiring visions of a future in which society might be comprehensively refashioned. The contrast between this spirit of optimism and the power-hungry machinations of the local Marxists shocked Kropotkin – in particular, reports of how Utin was conniving to get an influential Geneva lawyer elected to the local government by suppressing workers' plans for strikes – and brought a moment of revelation. 'I lived through it after one of the meetings at the Temple Unique,' he recollected in his memoirs, 'when I felt more acutely than ever before how cowardly are the educated men who refuse to put their education, their knowledge, their energy at the service of those who are so much in need of that education and that energy.' If his friends and acquaintances in Zurich, most of them supporters of Bakunin, had left him in any doubt of where he should look for a political ideal that still burned hot, the Communard workers in Geneva set him firmly on the right path. The final stage of his journey of self-discovery led him to the Jura, where Bakunin had his strongest following.

The industry that had made the Jura so hospitable to federalist, anti-authoritarian politics – the dawning 'anarchist' movement – owed its origins, ironically, to the autocratic instincts of a radical who had preceded Marx by three and a half centuries. As part of Jean Calvin's programme of moral reforms, the wearing of jewels had been banned in 1541, driving the city's goldsmiths into a new trade that would employ their miniaturist skills towards a utilitarian rather than sumptuary end: watchmaking. By the end of the century, Geneva boasted the first watchmaker's guild in the world, and the success of the industry during the following hundred years led its practitioners to spread out from the saturated confines of the city along the Jura mountain range. Over time, villages set amid the meadows of the Jura became home to specialist workshops that worked in a process of cooperative manufacture, each contributing distinct parts of the mechanisms. This innovative division of labour helped make the region a centre of precision horology, with the Grand Council of Neuchâtel founding an observatory in 1858 to provide a chronometric service, and the initiation of the Jura's famous time-keeping competitions. Accuracy to within one second a day was the minimal requirement for all products, with prizes for the watches that best withstood a range of environmental factors. Little can the winners – Edouard Heuer with his workshop in Saint-Imier, and Georges Piaget in nearby La Côte-aux-Fées – have guessed the glamour and prestige that before long their names would represent.

The luxury enjoyed by those who bought their products, however, was not reflected in the lives of the majority of watchmakers. Working within a scientific context, and with high demands made of their skill by the intricate engineering, they were nevertheless part of a community that was intellectually alive and receptive to new political ideas. Already living on the poverty line and now threatened by the mass-production processes being developed in the United States, those working on a small scale from their homes were ready recruits to a movement that drew inspiration from their own autonomous society. Content in its isolation and self-sufficiency, how glorious it would be, the Jurassian Federation argued, if its example could only convert the world.

Kropotkin's way into Jurassian society was through James Guillaume, a young teacher from the Jura town of Le Locle and Bakunin's trusted lieutenant. The young ladies of the Fritsche circle had met Guillaume at the congress of the anti-authoritarian International at the village of Saint-Imier in the autumn of 1871 but any initial introduction they provided was not effective. At first Guillaume received Kropotkin frostily, being overwhelmed by his many responsibilities as an editor of the movement's newspaper. It was only when Kropotkin volunteered to help in the task that he received a warm handshake. In return for his work, he would be introduced to the community of watchmakers and learn all he wished about the federation. Kropotkin felt that he had found his spiritual home, and was determined to adopt a trade that would allow him to remain, after his twenty-eight-day travel permit had expired.

The months that Kropotkin spent in the Jura exposed him to yet more stories of the Paris insurrection of spring 1871. Among the illustrious

Communards who had sought refuge there was Benoît Malon, ex-mayor of the Batignolles district, now working as a basket maker in Neuchâtel and also assisting Guillaume with his newspaper. Malon's stories of the Commune brought the dream to life for Kropotkin in a way that the testimony of the Geneva exiles had failed to do. They also reinforced the true horror of the Commune's suppression. Kropotkin recalled how 'the lips of Malon trembled and tears trickled from his eyes' when he recollected the tragic slaying during Bloody Week of thousands of young men who had rallied to the radical cause. Trawling the international press to better understand the disaster in Paris, Kropotkin was 'seized by a dark despair'.

It was while Kropotkin was staying in the Jura that Elisée Reclus too finally reached Switzerland, arriving on 14 March. After months of imprisonment, his sentence of transportation had finally been commuted to ten years' exile thanks to the good offices of the American ambassador to France, an admirer of his four-volume geological history *The Earth*. The experience had left him traumatised: 'I felt around me the impenetrable wall of hate, the aversion of the entire world to the Commune and the Communards,' he wrote. But in Switzerland he could at last begin the slow process of recovery.

There is no record that the two great geographers met in 1872, though had they done so, the grey-faced, haunted survivor of the prison barges with the faint aura of holiness would surely have made a strong impression on Kropotkin. It would be three decades before Reclus agreed to set down in writing his thoughts on the Commune, but he had resolutely upheld the prisoners' oath to defend it. He later recollected how, on his first day in Switzerland, he gently converted an old woman from her horrified prejudices about the insurrection in Paris to a warm respect for its aims. Bakunin, who had some years earlier turned his back on Reclus, having erroneously suspected him of sympathising with Marx, could not help but be reconciled to him. 'There is the model of a man,' the old Russian is reported to have said, 'so pure, noble, simple, modest, self-forgetting . . . a valuable, very earnest, very sincere friend and completely one of ours.' In light of Bakunin's own uncertain temperament, even his slight criticism that Reclus was 'perhaps not so completely the devil of a fellow, as might be desired' might be taken as a recommendation.

Kropotkin found it harder to gain Bakunin's attention. Though he longed for an audience with the great man, no invitation was forthcoming – this despite Kropotkin's passionate belief that his was the right side of the socialist schism. At a time when even Bakunin's most fervent acolytes were beginning to question his judgement, Kropotkin was unreserved in his admiration for the old man's achievements. In particular, the failed expedition that Bakunin had led in 1870 to establish a commune in Lyons – which Marx had brusquely dismissed – struck Kropotkin as 'the first case in recent years, if I am not mistaken, of a serious protest against a war from the side of the population.'

Kropotkin did not need Guillaume to shower him with evidence of Marx's monstrous egotism and the simmering vindictiveness of Engels; his experiences in Geneva were enough. He was repelled by Marx's extraordinary belief that he was owed the gratitude of the Communards for 'having saved their honour' in writing *The Civil War in France*, and by Engels' vicious slander of a Communard exile in London by the name of Adolphe Smith who had protested about the high-handed behaviour of the Marxists in the International.

Most of all, Kropotkin distrusted Marx's claim to have discovered in the nebulous realm of economics a science of human society. Marx and Engels could rant at Bakunin and his followers as 'babblers of nonsense' who had 'no idea of social revolution . . . only its political phrases; [for whom] its economic conditions have no meaning', and whose theories were 'Schoolboyish rot!' However, the question remained: beneath all the spurious historical analysis and baroque argumentation, was Marx's hope that the state would ultimately 'wither away' really any more hard-headed than Bakunin's expectation of a spontaneous revolution by the peasantry? The Marxists may have bandied about 'utopian' as a term of disparagement, but the vestiges of metaphysical thought were endemic to socialist theory. Surely what mattered most, Kropotkin realised, was the practical means by which society was moved in the right direction. And in Bakunin's writings – even the shockingly violent *Catechism* – there was a genuine attempt to answer the question of how it was possible to be both truly democratic and act decisively by embracing collective responsibility and rigorous discipline.

Kropotkin waited for weeks in the hope of an invitation to visit Bakunin at home in Locarno. Neither the evenings he had shared with Bakunin's wife and his old gaoler General Kukel in Siberia, nor Bakunin's friendship with Sofia Lavrova's flatmate Natalia Smetskaya seemed to help. Was the delay down to Bakunin's precoccupation with his work on *Statism and Anarchy*, or with the Nechaev affair, Kropotkin must have wondered, or was the explanation to be found in the imminent return to Russia of Bakunin's wife and children and, in light of his declining health, their possible last parting? Eventually, Guillaume informed Kropotkin that Bakunin would not be able to see him. He was under too much strain in dealing with the schism. Instead Kropotkin should abandon his plan to learn a trade – a waste of his talents, and a position in which, as a foreign prince, he would struggle to gain acceptance – and return to Russia without delay, where he would be of more use to the cause.

So it was that the man destined to become Bakunin's ideological heir never did crunch across the butts of cigarettes and cigars that littered the floor of Bakunin's study to meet his intellectual mentor. Not until years later did Guillaume divulge that Bakunin had, in fact, disregarded Peter Kropotkin as being, like his brother Alexander, a follower of the more cautious and gradualist ideas of Peter Lavrov, who urged the intellectuals of Russia to teach as well as follow the peasantry. It was perhaps inevitable that Bakunin should shun a fellow aristocrat. In flight from his own privileged origins, and questioning more than ever his right to lead the people while not being of them, even Bakunin's ill-judged embrace of the 'authentic' Nechaev had not taught him to see beyond the guilt he felt for his aristocratic birth.

Perhaps, though, the fruitless wait was not so arduous or lonely for Kropotkin. It seems that the 'Fritsche' girls had developed a taste for the pastoral beauty of the Jura and took to spending their spring vacations there. And the Jurassic landscape, which had already given its name to a whole age in the earth's development, would have provided the geographer in him with abundant opportunities for observation at a time when he was working out his theory about the ice caps that had once covered northern Europe.

Three months after arriving in Zurich, and two months after the Russian authorities had expected him home, Kropotkin set off on a circuitous journey back to St Petersburg: first to Belgium, bypassing Paris and the suspicious eyes of post-Commune France, then doubling back to Vienna, before heading to Warsaw, and finally back to Cracow. Somewhere along the way he collected a large cache of banned literature; before crossing the Russian border, he stopped to arrange a smuggling operation that would carry it and future material into the country under the noses of the tsarist police. Having crossed the line of legality, nothing would be the same again for Prince Kropotkin. Years earlier, aged twelve, he had abandoned the use of his title, but only now was he ready to renounce the last ties to his past life and the security that his privileged status had always afforded him.

4

Around the World in 280 Days

New Caledonia to Switzerland, 1873–1875

Henri Rochefort felt seasick from almost the moment he set foot on the frigate *Virginie*. Only a few dozen metres into his four-month ocean journey and he was already retching: not the mere queasiness of a sensitive stomach first encountering rough waters, but hearty vomiting that would continue for days on end until he was bringing up only bile. Among the five men with whom he shared his cage in the cargo hold, and the twenty-one women in the enclosure opposite, there were those who remembered quite well the sudden illness that had felled him during the Noir funeral demonstration three years earlier, and the eye infection that kept him away from Paris, recuperating, in the prelude to the Commune. Forced to listen to Rochefort's groans night and day, they must have wondered whether he was not in fact suffering a nervous reaction to the turbulent circumstances of his embarkation.

The period since Rochefort's capture in the dying days of the Commune had held horrors and humiliations far worse than he had experienced during previous spells in prison in the Second Empire. Arraigned before the military tribunal, the charges had threatened his dignity as much as his freedom: not grand accusations of treason or conspiracy that he might have batted aside with a rhetorical flourish, but demeaning insinuations that he had stolen artworks from the Louvre and bronzes from Thiers' ransacked home. And when it came to his inflammatory journalism, the fact that Rochefort had cunningly continued to propose hypothetical violence to his readership whilst dismissing the awful notion at the same time cut little ice. 'You turned this government to ridicule in your articles,' inveighed the president of the tribunal, enthroned beneath a vast painted crucifixion scene, 'and you know that in France ridicule kills.'

Brutal and exemplary sentences were being handed down unstintingly: twenty-five of the Commune's leaders and fiercest proponents, including

Ferré and General Rossel, were shot at Satory military camp in short order. Influential friends were concerned that Rochefort might suffer a similar fate, or that his name might at least slip on to the lengthening lists of lesser miscreants due for deportation to France's distant penal colonies in South America or the Pacific. The price of clemency, they ascertained, would be Rochefort's acceptance of humiliation. When Edmond Adam, hero of the 1870 stand-off at the Hôtel de Ville, testified that his ex-colleague was merely a 'fantasist who lacked prudence', Rochefort had sat in chastened silence; when summoned to the dock, he bore himself with a meekness that few would have recognised. His lawyer, Albert Joly, even persuaded him to compose a compromisingly abject letter pleading with Gambetta to secure his release. The strategy of self-abasement appeared to work and the threat of transportation lifted, though Rochefort is unlikely to have felt much gratitude as he sat shackled atop a stinking mattress, as a Black Maria juddered its way to the prison fortress of La Rochelle.

Imagining himself the romantic heir of the Calvinist rebels three centuries earlier, who had held out there against an interminable Catholic siege, Rochefort enjoyed sufficient freedom in prison to start work on a novel, buying off the antagonism of inmates with abundant gifts of contra-band tobacco. Even after his transfer a year later to the slightly less congenial conditions of Fort Boyard between Île d'Aix and Île d'Oléron, he had watched unperturbed as the frigates *Danae* and then *Guerrière* steamed away over the horizon, carrying his old comrades to the penal colonies. The worst that fate might have in store, solicitous friends assured him, was a brief spell in an apartment on the prison island of Sainte-Marguerite followed by early release. But then, on 23 May 1873, the hard-line General MacMahon, ex-commander of a French army whose officers found it easier to blame the Communards for the country's defeat than their own shortcomings, became president of the republic.

Rochefort, it was announced, would join the final consignment of Communards to be shipped to New Caledonia. His friends were horri-fied. What of the compassionate considerations that had weighed upon the original judges: his weak health, and the children he would be leaving as virtual orphans, following the death of their mother, a servant whom Rochefort had finally married while in prison? Victor Hugo took up the cudgels, arguing that transportation exceeded the court's terms: 'By it, the punishment is commuted into a sentence of death!'

No one who had seen the pitiful hulk of the *Virginie*, languishing on mudflats off the Atlantic coast, could have doubted the legitimacy of

Hugo's concern. The long line of sea-salts who declined to captain the ship may well have suspected that President MacMahon considered a deep-water grave to be the most convenient end for her undesirable cargo. Destined to be sold as firewood at the end of the journey, the ship's minimal refit allowed only just enough time for the Communards' last appeals to prove futile. Finally accepting his hazardous fate, Rochefort signed the papers appointing Juliette Adam – outspoken feminist, wife to Edmond Adam, and Rochefort's own ex-lover – as guardian to his children, and instructing the sale of his property for their benefit. The anxiety he felt at his predicament as he clambered on board was enough to have turned even a strong stomach queasy.

*

The first Rochefort knew of Louise Michel's presence on the *Virginie* were the jokes she cracked across the narrow corridor that divided their cages. 'Look at the pretty wedding trousseau MacMahon has sent me,' she had offered by way of introduction, posing her gangly, angular body in the regulation navy-issue clothes with which the prisoners had been supplied. Rochefort, of course, knew of the Red Virgin by repute. He could hardly have avoided the tall tales of her courage during the dying days of the Commune and had read, in prison, Victor Hugo's poem in celebration of her metamorphosis into the 'terrible and superhuman' figure of Virgo Major. He was glad of her company.

On the face of it, Rochefort and Lousie Michel had little in common. Rochefort was a philandering aristocrat, a potentially bitter reminder to Michel of her own father, with whom he shared a predatory taste for servant girls. Moreover, in contrast to the marquis' supplicatory contrition before the tribunal's authority, Michel had been unflinching in her resolve. 'Since it appears that any heart which beats for liberty has only one right, and that is to a piece of lead, I ask you for my share,' she had declared, calling the judges' bluff, while threatening that 'if you permit me to live, I shall never cease to cry for vengeance.' From Rochefort's perspective, in turn, Michel might have seemed the revolutionary counterpart of those deluded Joans of Arc whose appearance across France as putative saviours in the face of the Prussian invasion had attracted his scorn. Nevertheless, in the close confines of the *Virginie*, they discovered a complicity that went beyond the terrible oath of loyalty and vengeance that the imprisoned Communards had sworn. When Rochefort was moved to a private cabin for the sake of his health, and served seven-course dinners from the officers' table, Michel did not join in the sniping of those who suspected favouritism due to his Freemasonic connections. And when Michel gave up her own warm clothes and shoes to other prisoners, Rochefort passed on a pair of felt boots supplied by the captain, claiming that they had been given to him by his daughter, but were too small.

Without steam engines to assist the *Virginie* when she was becalmed, the journey was long enough for a firm friendship to form, even before unforeseen revisions to the planned route. The ship had only just left port when the French admiralty issued the captain with orders to steer clear of the waters around Dakar, lest she be intercepted by a revolutionary fleet from the Spanish port of Cartagena, where insurrectionists had declared a republic. The ship's lookouts scoured the horizon for sight of the old red and yellow pennant of Spain with the royal crest ripped out, and a lengthy detour was charted by way of the Canary Islands. In reality, however, whilst Elisée Reclus, in Switzerland, might dream that a revolutionary Mediterranean federation had risen to assume the mantle of the Commune, by the time the *Virginie* had set sail Cartagena was already under intense siege by monarchist forces, and about to fall.

The hysterical propaganda that had enveloped the Commune had left nervous officials susceptible to even the most improbable scares. Just a few weeks earlier, the military governor of Marseilles had assembled a hundred-strong posse of mariners to hunt down a school of killer sharks that proved to be wholly imaginary. The source of the misleading intelligence was letters purporting to be from local fishermen but in reality forged by a disgruntled cub journalist on the local paper. It was a first coup in the career of Gabriel Jogand-Pages, as he was then known, on his way to becoming the greatest hoaxer of his era. For decades to come he would expose with mounting ruthlessness the true depths of prejudice and credulity that was rotting French society from the core.

As the *Virginie* charted her slow and creaking course south through the Atlantic, other monsters preyed on the minds of the passengers. In 1857, a ship called the *Castilian* had spotted a terrifying creature in those very waters, while four years later the French naval frigate *Alection* had barely escaped the clutches of a giant squid. Then, in 1866, there were repeated sightings, of a pulsing, phosphorescent object beneath the waves, far longer than any whale. By 1873, such accounts had become entrenched in the popular mind through the fictional filter of Jules Verne's *Twenty Thousand Leagues Under the Sea*, which had first been published in the run-up to the Franco-Prussian War: the phosphorescent tube was explained as the submarine *Nautilus*, with the squid cast as its mortal enemy.

Verne's glorious anti-hero, Captain Nemo, held an obvious attraction for the Communards. A brooding champion of freedom and science, he salvaged the treasure of sunken wrecks to fund national liberation movements, and crowned his scientific engagement by recognising the imperative of social revolution. 'The earth does not want new continents,' he opined, 'but new men.' And quite apart from the inclusion in the book's second edition of line drawings by newspaper artists who so recently had illustrated the tragedy of the war and the Commune, Verne's novel contained veiled references to contemporary radical politics. Components of the *Nautilus* had been fabricated at the Le Creusot steelworks and Cails & Co. in Paris, the two main centres of recent socialist unrest, while only the delicate diplomatic situation between France and Russia at the time of the book's composition had prevented Verne from making explicit Nemo's background as a Polish patriot whose young family had died under Russian occupation. The fictional captain may have brought to mind comrades from the Commune like Dombrowski or Wroblewski, his fellow Polish commander in the doomed defence of Paris against the Versaillais. It was his sheer force of will, however, as a traceless 'Nobody' hell-bent on vengeance – 'monstrous or sublime, which time could never weaken' – that would have resonated most powerfully with the book's Communard readers. That, together with the fate of the *Nautilus*, sent tumbling to the seabed by the giant squid in the book's final scene, another sunken dream.

So potent and uncannily predictive did the symbolism of *Twenty Thousand Leagues Under the Sea* seem to those left reeling by the Commune's fall and its pitiless aftermath that later, as the dates and details of the book's publication faded from memory, rumours even began to circulate that the work's true creator was none other than Louise Michel herself, paid 200 francs by Verne for a first draft inspired by the *Virginie*'s crossing to New Caledonia. In reality, Michel's only personal connection to the underwater tale was the membrane between her toes that she had inherited from her father and which she displayed to Rochefort on board the *Virginie*; perhaps to reassure him that in her web-footed company he could not drown, or else to illustrate the Darwinism she had learned at night school.

In later years Rochefort would talk of the kindnesses of 'his lady neighbour of the starboard side' but Michel herself was not easy to help, constantly accepting charity, only to give it away. So it was that the felt boots that Rochefort had hoped would protect her from the frost-coated deck were soon warming feet that Michel considered to be needier than her own. According to Michel's autobiography, however, she treasured far more the intellectual insights with which Rochefort furnished her on the journey: an introduction to 'anarchism' that would inform the remaining thirty-five years of her political life.

Which ideas, though, did Michel mean to encompass, in her some-what anachronistic application of a term yet to be properly defined in 1873? Doubtless, she would already have encountered the theories of the leading French exponents of the anti-authoritarian, communistic tradi-tion among friends in the Montmartre clubs. But if not Proudhon or Fourier, perhaps it was the federalist principles of Bakunin that were so thrillingly novel to her when expounded by Rochefort, or else the older example of Gracchus Babeuf, a progenitor of anarchism from the days of the first French Revolution. It might even have been the ancient tradition – that reached from before Jesus Christ, through the Gnostics and Anabaptist sects – which Rochefort used to hook in to Michel's mystical inclinations, though there is little to suggest that he was a man who took the long view.

One old, Enlightenment theme, at least, that seems certain to have arisen in their discussions was that of the 'noble savage'. Charges of 'savagery', sometimes 'cannibalistic', had flown in all directions during France's recent upheavals: against those who had waged war on Prussia, only then to cry foul; against the murderous mob in Montmartre; and the troops who perpetrated the massacres of the Bloody Week. But for the deportees to New Caledonia, home to the aboriginal Kanaks, the question assumed a stark, new relevance. In purging French society of its regressive strain by a policy of transportation, the pseudo-republic of the early 1870s believed that it had definitively reclaimed the high ground of civilised behaviour, on which national moral regeneration might be founded. For those romantic souls who persisted in cherishing both the ideals of social revolution and a faith in noble savagery, the message of their punishment was clear: taste the brute laws of nature in the Antipodes, and then decide whether you were right to reject the solaces of pater-nalistic government. And once converted, if they chose to act as unofficial agents of French colonialism during their exile among the native Kanaks, then so much the better.

*

The *Virginie* cast anchor in Nouméa harbour on 10 December 1873, four months to the day after leaving Orléron, having made up time since rounding the Horn. After countless days in the vast emptiness of the Pacific Ocean, even those passengers due to begin a sentence of hard labour must have felt some relief at stepping ashore. But as the new arrivals were separated out into three categories of convict and led off to their respective grades of punishment, New Caledonia quickly revealed itself to be among the harshest of colonial territories.

Two hundred miles from tip to tip and twenty-five or so across, the long, thin strip of the main island is surrounded by coral reefs and distinguished by two mountain peaks that rise from a ridge running most of its length. First occupied by France in 1853, its geographical features served to demarcate the island's various communities. North of the larger mountain lay the area to which the indigenous Kanaks were now mostly restricted, their population already plummeting from an original 100,000 due to a range of nefarious French practices (though not yet halfway to the mere one in ten who would be left at the end of the century). On Nou Island, out in the ocean to the east, the harshest regime of all awaited those transported as violent criminals, who were clapped into manacles to drag out their sentence of 'double chains', under threat of further dire punishments for recalcitrance. For those 'Deported to a fortified place', the Ducos peninsula near Nouméa, the island's capital, offered a marginally less arduous environment, and it was thence that Rochefort and Michel were first taken, the latter in transit to the Île des Pins, fifty miles off the southern tip of the main island, which was home to those for whom deportation alone was deemed sufficient hardship.

Eager crowds of Communard exiles from the earlier convict ships, promised that their families would one day be able to join them, had gathered to welcome the new arrivals. Their hopes were swiftly dashed when they saw no sign of their relatives. Rochefort and Michel, too, experienced a sinking of the spirits. After they absorbed the immediate shock of finding such a concentration of notorious radicals so far from home – among the non-Communard prisoners, was the tsar's would-be assassin from 1867, Berezowsky – they would have noticed the emaciated faces of ragged creatures who had all but given up on life in the fourteen months since their arrival.

Rochefort was grateful to be delivered from the pathetic scene as Olivier Pain and Paschal Grousset intervened to usher him towards their huts, which they had newly extended to offer their old journalistic colleague temporary accommodation. If, as credible rumours in France suggested, it had indeed been Grousset who had tipped off the Versaillais authorities about Rochefort's planned escape from Paris in the dying days of the Commune, then this hospitality was the least he could offer by way of amends.

Michel, reunited with her bosom friend from the barricades, Natalie Lemel, was also drawn into life on the Ducos peninsula, where she wisely insisted on staying despite demands from the administration that she be moved on. The sketches she made here are deceptively picturesque, almost Arcadian, with the huts of the small prisoner communities grouped around a central fire and cooking area, implying the kind of simple conviviality enjoyed by native tribes the world over. By day, the convicts followed the custom of the Kanaks: fishing for lampreys and hunting the island's kangaroos, though the physical gulf between the sickly, clumsy Communards and the strong and graceful natives, with their traditional Stone Age methods, was all too obvious. By night, especially in the high summer of December and January, the Europeans escaped the clouds of mosquitoes by retreating to the basalt rocks by the sea and the shelter of nets.

The reality, unfiltered by idealising draughtsmanship, was less comfortable. The Communards' solidarity with their fellow men only went so far, a fact noted by Rochefort as he pottered about in his regulation straw hat and ungainly moccasins, with sailor's culottes exposing his spindly calves. During his days as a newspaper editor, Rochefort had become known to the Arabs as 'the good man' for his advocacy of the rights of the North African peoples who had participated in the South Oranian insurrection against French rule; and yet on New Caledonia he found himself almost alone in treating the Algerian Arab prisoners with comradely respect. Although victims themselves, the heroes of the Commune were only too ready to vent their frustrations on the Africans in displays of vicious disdain that would eventually take a more deadly form in their dealings with the Kanaks.

Then there were the cases of 'fatal nostalgia'. Although it did not suit the resolute tone of Rochefort's later accounts to discuss it, he must have found it awful to watch as, one by one, his fellow prisoners succumbed to the condition. Though not recognised by the colony's doctors, who preferred to record anaemia or dysentery as the causes of death, terminal grief was all too real for those who had been transported. Its favourite victims were the heartbroken fathers of small children, but 251 Communard prisoners were said to have been afflicted during the first three years, with the eight-month lapse between sending and receiving letters home making the torture of homesickness a perpetual feature of New Caledonian life. Some simply wandered off into the forest to die, others wasted away, like the Communard

Passedouet, who, watched by Rochefort, sat endlessly rocking and intoning 'Proudhon, Proudhon'.

Survival depended on maintaining one's morale. While awaiting transportation, Louise Michel had secured permission from the French Geographical society to serve as its correspondent in New Caledonia. The society perhaps hoped that she would supply observations on the nickel deposits that had been discovered there a few years earlier and for which state companies had begun to mine. Michel, however, chose to disregard the public demands of the society's president that members embrace 'besides a scientific end, a political and commercial object', and busied herself with gentler plans to experiment with the cultivation of papayas and record Kanak folklore. Meanwhile, to vent her fury at those who now ruled France, on the 28th of every month, without fail, she wrote a letter of remonstration to 'la Commission dite des Graces' that had failed to commute the execution of her beloved Ferré on that day in November 1871.

Rochefort would later insist that he had shown even greater foresight than Michel, researching, even during the Prussian siege, the geography of New Caledonia in case one day he should be called to escape from it. In fact, rather than initiating an escape plan Rochefort was fortunate to be allowed to join Pain's and Grousset's existing scheme. At huge risk, the pair had been scouting opportunities for several months, concealing themselves at the entrance to the harbour from where they tried to hail passing ships. What Rochefort brought to the project was the cash that could open the reluctant ears of the ships' masters, and the English captain of a coal supply ship called the PCE – the Peace, Comfort and Ease – was soon recruited. Whilst Rochefort underwent a training regime of nocturnal bathing expeditions to accustom his eyes to the dark nights and toughen his muscles, three Freemasons among the six prospective fugitives persuaded key guards to turn a blind eye.

By chance, the date chosen for the escape was 18 March 1874, the third anniversary of the confrontation over the Montmartre cannon that had precipitated the Commune. The previous evening, the prisoners had been forced by an approaching storm to seek cover in their huts. Rochefort slept badly; woken in the early hours by a friendly black chicken, he seized upon it as an auspicious sign. When he, Pain and Grousset reached the shore, however, the swollen seascape that stretched out before them was of the kind Michel celebrated in her wild, romantic verse, but which evinced from Rochefort nothing but dread. Recognising that the chance might not come again, all three launched themselves into the heaving darkness. At the appointed rock, the other members of the escape party hauled them out of the water and, before long, a launch appeared to carry them to the *PCE*. With a 1,000-mile voyage to Australia, they had ample opportunity to celebrate their freedom.

*

The long and circuitous journey back to Europe began well with a hearty welcome in the Australian port of Newcastle. 'It is enough for [England] that men who struggle for freedom flee to her for refuge, and the protection of her powerful arm will be at once thrown around them,' declared the local newspaper, while the celebrity status accorded them by the press in general afforded the fugitives a first inkling of how the outside world was perceiving the Commune as France's 'third revolution'. The holiday mood persisted as they set out on a route similar to that taken by Bakunin thirteen years earlier on his escape from Siberia, via South East Asia, with Rochefort using a visit to Fiji and Honolulu to cram his luggage with tribal art. In San Francisco, however, the solidarity of the group began to fracture. Taking umbrage at claims by Grousset that he was reneging on his promise to pay their passage home, Rochefort ignored the eagerness of the city's socialists to feast their heroes, and the press to hold interviews, and hid himself away. Only two days after arriving, he and Olivier Pain were gone, leaving behind their four companions to accept the lavish plaudits of the city's well-wishers, together with a £165 collection that, in the absence of Rochefort's financial help, would eventually cover their Atlantic passage.

The America that Rochefort travelled through was one whose press was not uniformly indulgent to his escapes. In a country still coming to terms with its own vastly more destructive civil war, the Commune had received a huge amount of coverage, most of it hostile. Even the moderate *Harper's Weekly* inveighed against the supposed savagery of the Commune's 'cruel and unreasonable' women, asserting that it would prefer to find itself at the mercy of a horde of Red Indians; while even the more sympathetic *Nation* swallowed the lie that the transportation of Communards was 'for their mental and moral health'. Versaillais propaganda had flooded across the Atlantic, finding a sympathetic hearing in a nation whose propertied classes feared the likelihood of social strife closer to home.

The threat had never been more real. Ever since the 1830s, immigrant labour from the poorer areas of Europe had been lured to the New World of opportunity by promises of good jobs and land for free. The chance to begin afresh appealed powerfully to those who had suffered most from the injustices inflicted by the Old World's arbitrary authorities. Wave after wave of determined poor had entered the country, to be ruthlessly exploited by established industrialists, only for those who clawed their way up to some small position of power to oppress the new ethnic groups who followed them. It was a brutal and ugly system, yet hugely productive of wealth. Now, though, the monstrous, accelerating engine of unregulated capitalism appeared to have stalled, and the society it had sustained looked likely to collapse into chaos.

In September 1873 the inconceivable had happened when the great railway entrepreneur Jay Gould went bankrupt, a victim of his own corruption, triggering an economic collapse that, within weeks, had plunged the country into a depression. With unemployment soaring and wages plummeting, the Commune appeared to offer the burgeoning ranks of America's social malcontents a dangerous example. The *New York Times* predicted a time when the immigrant 'socialists of the cities would combine to strike at the wealth heaped up around them' and the 'native American' would respond with arms to the 'rebellion against property', just as he had to the 'rebellion against freedom' that sparked the Civil War. During that winter, tens of thousands had turned to the International in search of support and representation, and there was widespread fear that a mere spark might 'spread abroad the anarchy and ruin of the French Commune'. Warnings received by the New York police were terrifyingly unambiguous: plans were in hand for a paramilitary organisation of 1,600 men modelled on the National Guard whose battalions had occupied Paris. The great demonstration in Tompkins Square of January 1874, brutally suppressed by nightstick-wielding mounted police, was only a first skirmish. All New York needed, four months later, was the arrival of France's most polemical propagandist.

Having passed through Salt Lake City and Omaha, it was while Rochefort's train was halted at Chicago station that the press finally caught up with him. The proposition borne by Mr O'Kelly from the *New York Herald* was a generous one: a fat fee, and a two-page spread guaranteed over two days in return for exclusive rights to Rochefort's first article about the Commune and life in New Caledonia. The chance to set the record straight, free of censorship and with no concessions required to the prejudices of his readership, attractive in itself, was made irresistible by an undertaking that an edition would be distributed in France, regardless of any possible negative reaction there. While Olivier Pain visited Niagara Falls, Rochefort worked through the night scribbling more than two thousand lines of impassioned prose.

Concerned that Rochefort should not be distracted by invitations to receptions and dinners, and doubtless to hike the value of his exclusive rights, the *Herald*'s editor arranged for Rochefort to be taken off the train as it approached New York and conveyed the last few miles of his journey from the outskirts in a covered carriage. Such was the tumultuous reception of the first instalment of his article on 31 May, however, that not even the discretion of the Central Hotel on Broadway could seclude him from the besieging crowds, and he was obliged to retire briefly to the New York countryside in search of peace in which to prepare his speech for the promised public meetings.

The first lecture, delivered to a highly distinguished audience of several hundred in the New York Academy of Music, moved many who heard it to tears at the plight of the Communards and the fate of the Commune. One reference to the Kanaks claimed the last word on the subject of savagery: 'We send them missionaries,' he opined acerbically in a line he would repeat, 'while it is they who should send us their political leaders.' Further dates were added to a lecture tour that already included Boston and Philadelphia, but then, quite unexpectedly, Rochefort announced that he was to return to Europe.

His own explanation was homesickness, an ailment familiar to the exiled Communards of America: men like Edmond Levraud, who wrote of 'the disgust and the hatred I feel for this rotten race . . . [where] everyone is corrupt and degraded.' But Rochefort's sentimentality and fastidiousness were as nothing compared to his journalistic instinct for the scoop. Grousset suggested that Rochefort had intentionally tricked his companions in order to steal a competitive lead in selling his account to the press back home: Rochefort's booking of the last berth on the next Atlantic steamer coincided with news that his article had boosted sales of the *Herald* in Europe fivefold. Alternatively, a peremptory warning from those who feared the incendiary effect of his eloquence may have convinced him to leave.

*

Rochefort's travels of the previous 280 days had taken him almost 30,000 miles. As an achievement it could not rival that of the Bostonian radical and railway magnate George Francis Train, who four years earlier had managed a global circumnavigation in only seventy days, before heading off to France to try to claim the leadership of the Marseilles commune; nor that of Verne's fictional hero Phileas Fogg, who had scraped in just under the eighty-day limit stipulated by his Reform Club bet in 1873. But considering the extraordinary circumstances under which it was undertaken, and the enforced sojourn of several months in New Caledonia, his adventure surely outshone the Cook's Tour of 1872, whose well-heeled clients had boasted at every step of their 220-day itinerary in frequent dispatches to *The Times* of London. One last hazard lay ahead when, after nine days on board, Rochefort decided to land at Queenstown in Ireland. Finding that the Catholic country had little sympathy for a man tarred with the Commune's killing of the clergy, he was lucky to escape being lynched by a priest-led mob. London, however, promised a warmer reception altogether.

Of all France's neighbours, Britain had probably received more refugees from the Commune than any other country. While the fires still raged in Paris, Prime Minister Gladstone had signalled Britain's hospitality by declaring that there would be no extradition of those fleeing political persecution, despite pressure from certain quarters of the press. For decades it had been a central tenet of British liberalism that where social unrest was widespread, abroad at least, the causes were better dealt with by concessions that repression. Whilst Lord Elcho argued in Parliament that an exception be made for 'the authors of what can only be regarded by the civilised world as the greatest crime on record', initially, at least, there was strong sympathy in the country for the Communards and no little distaste for their persecutors.

Hypocrisy characterised the attitude adopted towards the refugees by the Versailles government, which vehemently complained that Britain was sheltering subversive criminals, yet made no effort to close the French ports. When Gladstone's government responded that the immigrants imposed a heavy social burden, there even followed an insouciant French offer to hand a subsidy to those departing. Up to 1,500 Communards arrived, their dependants raising the total number close to the 4,500 who had been punitively transported. Some arrived at Dover in chains, abandoned there for the local workhouse to feed before setting them off on the tramp to London, unshod, on blood-caked feet. Not until late 1872 had the stream of vagrants eased, by when the charitable system was overflowing and the capital's parks were littered nightly with French families sleeping rough.

Through a mixture of self-help and public benevolence, by the time of Rochefort's arrival the Communards had begun to put down roots.

For the most part they congregated in the rookeries of St Giles or Saffron Hill, or else the marginally better slums around Charlotte Street, north of Soho, that became an expatriate Belleville or Montmartre-in-miniature. From a top floor in Newman Passage, a cooperative *marmite* fed several hundred a day, while small tailors' and cobblers' workshops began to market the craft skills of which Paris found itself suddenly deprived. Keeping the Communards at arm's length, most middle-class British bene-factors preferred to channel their donations through the Positivist Society. Others shamelessly submitted their requirements, as if to an employment agency: for every £100 from an MP, or £5 from a cautious housekeeper, there was a request from a brothel owner in search of willing seventeen-year-olds, or a 'pinching housewife' offering £1 a year for a cut-price maid-of-all-work. Compassion fatigue soon set in, and suspicion displaced pity.

Although the British government declined to pass on surveillance reports to their Continental counterparts, such dossiers were neverthe-less compiled, with the Communards subject to frequent night raids by the Metropolitan Police. Inhabiting the dystopian metropolis depicted in Gustave Doré's *London: A Pilgrimage* of 1872, or Thomson's epic 1874 poem 'City of Dreadful Night', morale among the London émigrés suffered, and paranoia took hold. News of the escape of the New Caledonia fugi-tives provided a welcome boost, and Rochefort's arrival in London, just in advance of Grousset, was a rare opportunity for festivity. His decision to decline the invitation to a banquet held in honour of the escapees on the grounds that it might appear 'incendiary and saturnalian' sounded a misjudged note, however, that was at once pious, high-handed and cowardly. It seemed to confirm what his detractors had alleged: that he was an egotistical dilettante, a mere contrarian whose radicalism was superficial and self-serving. 'Rochefort is not a revolutionary,' a police informer claimed to have been told by the journalist Félix Pyat, 'he is a boy who stands next to the revolution in order to advance himself, but he has none of its principles; he has only hatred of governments.' Despite being Rochefort's most venomous rival, and a possible police agent, Pyat's character observations were rarely less than astute.

Rochefort's revival of *La Lanterne* in London, and his spirited if thwarted attempts to have it smuggled into France using techniques developed during the Prussian siege for the pigeon post, do not suggest a man who planned to retire his pen from the polemical struggle. But social standing mattered to the marquis, who was stung to discover that Madame Tussaud's waxworks museum had moved his statue from the company of France's elite to the Chamber of Horrors. Having excited the interest of the high-society hostess Madame Olga Novikoff, neither he nor Grousset were in any position to decline invitations to her cosmopolitan soirées at Claridge's that were attended by such luminaries as Gladstone, Matthew Arnold and the newspaper editor W. T. Stead. In her role as an arch tsarist propagandist and occasional Russian police agent, however, Novikoff always played a long game, and it is tempting to imagine that her cultivation of Rochefort was no exception.

*

During the few months that Rochefort remained in London, he monitored events in France closely in the fervent hope of a general amnesty that would allow the convicted Communards to return home. It was not to be. France had plunged into collective amnesia, and memories of the Commune and of those diverse characters associated with it had been hastily brushed under the carpet. Tourists continued to visit Paris as they might the ruins of Pompeii, to witness the archaeology of catastrophe, but the City of Light was already rising from the ashes. Observing the flowers that had begun to grow among the ruins of Paris, the patron of the Café Guerbois in Montmartre, a favourite haunt of the Impressionist artists, remarked that 'Inanimate matter, no more than men, is not made to suffer protracted grief.' He perfectly expressed the mood of the times. The artist Monet, recently returned from England where he had spent the war, enjoyed glittering success for the first time in his career with paintings informed by a similar sentiment. His famous views of the riverbanks at Argenteuil and Asnières give no hint of the fierce fighting that had taken place there, focusing instead on scenes of middle-class leisure, while the Parc Monceau, one of the bloodiest butcher's yards of the Versaillais execution squads, is depicted drowning in blossom.

Those seeking to lose themselves further in the Catholic and bourgeois mythology being laid down by the Third Republic need only have wandered up through the narrow, twisting streets of Montmartre, inhabited now only by widows and grieving mothers, to where the foundations were being laid for the most strident symbol of what that ideal republic had become. The decision to build the Sacré-Coeur marked an incontrovertible reassertion of Catholic France's dominance over its capital city. Designed in a neo-Romanesque style intended to evoke the churches of the pious, peasant south, its bleached dome would, its architects planned, loom above the city, a purifying presence. When it was revealed that the site purchased for its erection in 1875 included the very garden where the generals Lecomte and Thomas has been killed on the first day of the Communard insurrection, the Catholic *Bulletin du Voeu* expressed disingenuous surprise at the coincidence. Oriels of sunlight breaking from behind clouds over Montmartre had demonstrated divine approval of the site, declared the newly installed Archbishop Guibert, but the true reason for the choice was clear: to expiate the crimes of the Church's enemies, on ground made sacred by those martyred in the Catholic cause.

The Catholic Church was again ascendant, flush with new state subsidies and with its educational function, of which it had been stripped by the first act of the republican government, now restored by MacMahon's government. It was confident too, unequivocally damning the Commune as 'the work of Satan' at the ceremony to lay the first stone of the Sacré-Coeur's choir. There was clearly no place in this France for Henri Rochefort, the Mephistophelian polemicist whose deference-defying journalism many blamed for the country's descent into nihilist chaos. Even Gambetta appeared to turn his back on his erstwhile ally, arguing, not unreasonably, that the country was not ready for his return. And if Rochefort were tempted to test the vigilance of the country's security arrangements with a clandestine foray across the border, his expedition would have been short-lived. For in the previous three years, five million pages from the prefecture's archive of criminal records, destroyed by Raoul Rigault in the Commune's dying days, had been painstakingly reconstructed by cross-referencing with those of every court, tribunal and prison in France.

For his next haven, Rochefort chose Switzerland, from where the smugglers' routes to Paris were less well guarded than those across the Channel, allowing him to maintain distribution of *La Lanterne*. Not long after his arrival, however, he sat for a portrait by Courbet, who had escaped back to his native region of the Jura, on the Swiss side of the frontier, only to be declared liable by the French government for the 320,000-franc bill to rebuild the Vendôme Column. It was a chastening experience. Courbet's still lifes of the time expressed a soul locked into trauma, struggling to free itself but numbed in the attempt. Trout lie glassy-eyed, the hooks caught in their mouths and the fishing line tugging tortuously from out of frame, their blood dripping on stones that recall the slippery red cobbles of the Paris killing fields.

Invited by Courbet to view his portrait, Rochefort revealed a rare glimpse of self-loathing, recoiling from what he saw as the image of a Portuguese diamond merchant: shallow, mercenary and self-regarding.

Trapped among the dispossessed and embittered, it would not be easy for Rochefort to reconcile himself to his own company.

★

For Louise Michel, left to languish in New Caledonia, Rochefort's escape had made life far harder, with the imposition of a new regime whose severity would have been unrecognisable to the fugitives. The slightest infraction of the rules was punished with a spell in the sweltering cells, while the only work by which the deportees could now earn subsistence wages was on the chain gangs. The days of night swims, fishing and hunting were over, and while the 'harmonious cooperation' of the Kanaks in the face of ever more demeaning colonial oppression continued to encourage Louise Michel's belief in the perfectibility of man and society, any residual hopes of building a Rousseauist Utopia on the island crumbled away. Money orders from Georges Clemenceau and letters from Victor Hugo kept her spirits up, along with wholly impractical plans for an escape by raft, but the prurient interest shown by both her fellow Communards and the authorities in her ménage with Natalie Lemel soured her existence. Michel resisted attempts to separate them, insisting as always that her only passion was for the revolution, but the malicious rumour that they were lovers eventually led to an acrimonious split between the two women.

The Nouméa of 1876 was a far cry from the titular *Mysterious Island* of Jules Verne's new masterpiece, whose five fugitives are escaping not to America but from Confederate captivity in the Civil War, and by balloon rather than ship. Driven out into the Pacific by a storm, they land on a seemingly enchanted, uninhabited island where strange forces assist them in gradually reconstructing the sum of civilisation's knowledge. The novel's revelation that the guiding hand behind the marooned soldiers' achievements belongs to Captain Nemo, who survived the *Nautilus'* cataclysmic underwater battle and is in hiding on the island, is surely all Verne's own. But in its sympathy for those cut off by fate from their homeland, and its strangely inverted echoes of the Communards' experiences of exile, the influence of Paschal Grousset, who would collaborate on Verne's next book, may already be discernible. And for all the rancour between the fellow fugitives from New Caledonia, even Rochefort might have found some solace in the novel's optimistic vision of human resourcefulness, and a consoling echo of his own isolation in that of the proud Nemo.

5

To the People

On 22 March 1874, as the humming wires of the telegraph cables carried news of Rochefort's audacious escape from New Caledonia around the world, St Petersburg awoke to startling news of its own. The previous evening, Prince Peter Kropotkin had been taken into custody by the infamous Third Section of the police while on his way home from the Geographical Society after delivering a long-awaited lecture expounding his new theories about the Ice Age in Siberia. St Petersburg society was stunned, its salons feverish with rumour and outrage. Apparently Kropotkin had been tricked into responding when an undercover police agent, feigning distress, called to him by the code name 'Borodin'. Now he was being held at police headquarters, awaiting interrogation about his suspected involvement in the city's foremost subversive organisation, the Chaikovsky Circle.

A few weeks earlier, nearly all those members of the Chaikovsky Circle still at liberty had escaped south from St Petersburg in the hope of inciting a popular uprising. Kropotkin alone had insisted on remaining in the capital as part of a desperate recruiting drive intended to rebuild the underground networks that the police were busy uprooting. The plan had been that Kropotkin would join the others at the crucial moment of rebellion, but his obstinate confidence that his apparent respectability would protect him from arrest had proved pitifully misplaced.

Still wearing the formal dress required by the Geographical Society at its public events, Kropotkin was led into the Third Section's headquarters in the Summer Garden, up several flights of stairs and past endless pairs of guards, to the suite of cells on the top floor. While other detainees had often been left to stew, sometimes for months, before they were interrogated, at four o'clock in the morning, three days later, Kropotkin was dragged to the hot seat. Bleary-eyed, he refused to divulge anything but his name and a smattering of irrelevant detail and was soon transferred to solitary confinement in the notorious Peter and Paul fortress. His cell was in the old artillery embrasure of the Trubetskoy tower, whose walls had been padded to prevent the tapped communication that kept the other inmates sane. It was a chilling end to an adventure that had begun with so much hope.

*

The Chaikovsky Circle had its origins in the socialist library that a young Mark Natanson had created for his fellow students at the Medical-Surgical Academy in 1869, so that they might read and discuss banned works of political theory from abroad and censored Russian literature. Not until 1871, however, had the circle coalesced into something close to its final form. That summer, mathematics student Nicholas Chaikovsky graduated into a world rocked by the events of the Paris Commune. To meet the urgent need for a safe space in which the most daring young freethinkers of St Petersburg could take stock and look ahead, he arranged a retreat in the village of Kusheliovka, a few miles upstream from the city on the River Neva. Devoting themseles to study, those present fully embraced the circle's ethos of earnest commitment and austerity.

As well as Chaikovsky himself and Mark Natanson, the group included German Lopatin, a member of the general council of the International and a young veteran of conspiracy, Sofia Perovskaya, the estranged daughter of the ex-Governor General of the capital, and two sisters by the name of Kornilova. Their course of reading and discussion was sustained on a monotonous diet of soup and horse-flesh meatballs, varied only when they resolved to sacrifice the puppies who played under their balcony, 'so that in the name of the struggle against prejudice we might try dog'. That summer also provided most with their first taste of Third Section tactics when the students were first raided and then, despite the absence of incriminating evidence, hauled in for intensive questioning and photographed for the police records.

The attention of the authorities was not easy to shake off and the arrest of Natanson the following February brought home to members the seriousness of the risks. The less resolute soon withdrew, concerned that being implicated in such an enterprise would cause irreparable damage to their academic careers. Behind them, though, they left a determined core of activists, eager to carve their mark on Russian history.

*

Beside the Paris Commune, the other event that had marked the year 1871 for radical thinkers was the trial *in absentia* of Bakunin's dangerously charismatic protégé Nechaev, whose belief in the role of violence in maintaining discipline within his revolutionary groupuscule had led to the brutal murder of Ivanov. In reaction to this, the tight-knit Chaikovsky Circle adopted a firm policy of rational persuasion and set out to propagate further groups on the model of their own. Rejecting the strict hierarchy that Nechaev had espoused, the circles were to be characterised by equality and transparency, in which each member could be trusted to play their part. A national organisation for the publication and distribution of affordable editions of banned texts was rapidly established, the professionalism of which was said to have shamed the legitimate book trade. Seminal works, the most illicit of them printed in Switzerland and smuggled into the country, became available to readers for the first time: familiar names like Chernyshevsky, Dmitri Pisarev and Peter Lavrov, but also revolutionary French texts from the eighteenth century, as well as books by Marx (the translation of whose *Das Kapital* Lopatin initiated), Herbert Spencer, J. S. Mill and, perhaps most inspiringly of all, Charles Darwin.

It had long been a corrosive paradox of Russian intellectual life that a fierce passion for imaginative science among many in the educated sections of society was matched by indifference, or even outward hostility on the part of the authorities. Ever since Catherine the Great had failed to invest in Ivan Polzunov's refinement of the steam engine for the gold-mining industry in favour of the tried and tested British model, Russia's discoverers and inventors had struggled for lack of encouragement. Whilst groundbreaking research continued to thrive in the country's chemistry, engineering and medical faculties, society rarely saw the practical benefits.

The military ministry was the solitary exception, in the intermittent support it gave to aeronautical and rocket technology. Indeed, the previous twenty-five years had seen striking proposals emerge for balloon guidance systems such as might well have altered the outcome of the Franco-Prussian War, had they been available to the besieged Parisians. Whilst the ministry backed Alexander Mozhaisky's development of a prototype aeroplane during the early 1870s, even the successful flight of a scale model could not sustain its interest for long. Scant attention was paid either to the invention, some years before Edison's success, of the filament light bulb by Alexander Lodygin, as the curious by-product of his work on helicopter design.

Ironically, the very lack of any Russian tradition of implementing such innovations afforded great freedom to the empire's most enquiring minds, which were left untramelled by the practical requirements of production. Every conceptual breakthrough, however, appeared only to feed the growing tension between the claims of progressive thought, which challenged convention and pushed the boundaries of knowledge, and a moribund regime intent on holding the line. It was a tension symptomatic of that between reform and conservatism with which tsarist society as a whole was riven.

Throughout the 1860s, the positivist philosophy of Auguste Comte – a 'religion of humanity' whose central article of faith was the potential of scientific enquiry to reveal solutions to society's problems – had become a touchstone for progressive Russians. These were 'civilised' men, as the exiled political theorist Lavrov termed them, *intelligentnyi* and *kul'turnyi*, who understood Pisarev's imperative to test both scientific knowledge and atrophying cultural convention to the point of destruction. In a letter to the tsar, Comte even offered his scientific system as an audacious means for Russia to bypass the interim phase of democratic rule and head straight for a new dispensation based on the religion of humanity, but his proposal went unanswered. Instead, the tsarist regime became ever less tolerant: practitioners of science were no longer to be considered irrelevant bores, but as possible threats to the state. At a moment rich in scientific promise – from Dmitri Mendeleev's classification of the elements by their chemical properties in his Periodic Table of 1869, to Viacheslav Manassein's overlooked discovery of the properties of penicillin two years later – the censor's blue pencil regularly filleted *Znanie*, Russia's first popular scientific journal, of any taint of positivism.

Inevitably, a climate stifling of imaginative playfulness and emotional release was to prove dangerously counterproductive for those who wished to maintain the status quo. In those rare cases when utopian science fiction was written and published in Russia – such as Prince Odoevsky's novels *The Year 4338* and *The Town with No Name* – it was earnest in its preoccupations: concerned less with the extravagant possibilities of space travel and underwater exploration that so fascinated French and British authors, than with the new world that might be realised in the here and now by social renewal. Even the utopian section of Chernyshevsky's *What is to be Done?*, 'Vera Pavlovna's Fourth Dream' – by far the most notable example of utopianism from Russian literature of the period – alludes to futuristic architecture and food production only as background detail for its vision of a society made perfect by free love, socialism and the disappearance of religion.

By the beginning of the 1870s, though, the ground was shifting. A new generation of radicals was coming to the fore who insisted that there was 'more out there than the social sciences, that the anatomy of a frog won't get you very far, that there are other important questions, that there is history, social progress . . .' Alongside the elevated political and historical tracts that formed their staple reading, the high-minded youth of Russia developed an appetite for intrepid stories of adventure – by Fenimore Cooper and, especially, Verne – and they craved intellectual heroes who were similarly single-minded.

Before 1871, Darwin had been known in Russia merely as a disciple of Lamarck, who held that inheritance was subject to only limited environmental influence. The publication of *The Descent of Man* gave him a distinct and compelling reputation of his own, as a scientist whose daring new ideas might, by extrapolation, help unravel the whole tightly wound mythology of Russian hierarchy, in which the tsar's position was guaranteed by divine will and the instinctual deference of the masses. For if evolution discounted the Genesis story, then the rationale of Adam's fall and Christ's promise of redemption surely came tumbling down, dragging with it any claim to authority for God's intermediaries on earth. Moreover, Darwinism confirmed mankind's shared birthright, while Thomas Huxley and others tenaciously teased out the social significance of 'the survival of the fittest'; the political and economic subtext was not lost on those determined to work deep change in Russian society.

When an anxious Alexander Kropotkin wrote to his brother Peter in 1872 that he feared himself to be under police surveillance, he drew comfort from the imminent appearance in Russia of translations of Darwin's most recent work. 'Those nice children', he wrote facetiously of the tsarist goverment, 'simply don't comprehend that it is more dangerous than a hundred A. Kropotkins.' Ex-followers of Nechaev, abandoning terrorism for the subtler challenge that evolutionary theory posed to religious and state authority, lost none of their passion in the transition, 'Every one of us would have gone to the scaffold and would have laid down his life for Moleschott or Darwin.' The positivist efforts of Karl Marx to anatomise the social condition, diagnose its ailments and prescribe a cure were yet to make anything like such a deep impression.

*

Following Natanson's arrest and imprisonment in February 1872, Nicholas Chaikovsky emerged as a calm influence to which the circle's members

looked in the midst of the ideological ferment that engulfed them. Even
the heavy-handed policemen who had detained the pioneers in their raid
on the Kusheliovka summer colony in 1871 appear to have recognised
something exceptional in him: while the other suspects were subjected
to prolonged grilling, he had been left in peace to study for his university exams. Taking the lead in the circle's endless correspondence with
bookshops, libraries and their new sister groups, the circle became closely
identified with him. All members should fund the cause to the utmost
of their ability, he determined, while themselves maintaining a habit of
frugality in order to encourage self-discipline, and foster solidarity with
the privations of the Russian peasantry. When the book-trading business
found itself in urgent need of capital, one of the Kornilova sisters even
went so far as to marry a fellow 'Chaikovskyist' with the express aim of
extracting a generous dowry from her father, an affuent merchant, to
augment the regular contributions that she and her sisters made from
their allowances.

For a while, difficult decisions were taken by Chaikovsky almost unilat-
erally, but such a style of leadership was so at odds with the group's
guiding principles that it could not last. One applicant to the circle, who
on failing to receive the unanimous agreement of members necessary
for admission had turned informer for the Third Section, evoked their
devoted and egalitarian beliefs with surprising generosity. 'There are no
"juniors" and "elders" among them, all are equal, everyone acts according
to the circumstances, unaffected by the wishes of others, though the
manner of their actions does reflect a mood of resolute unity, as they are
always following a common aim.' In reality, by mid-1872 that unity was
becoming increasingly fragile, and even after the departure of members
who favoured a more direct form of action, the whispered debate over
future policy continued.

Into this simmering uncertainty stepped the dashing figure of Sergei
Kravchinsky. Intense and solitary by disposition, when he joined the
Mikhailovskoe Artillery Academy as a cadet he already spoke four
languages and, having honed his revolutionary credentials since adoles-
cence, possessed a grasp of radical ideas far in advance of his years.
Strikingly handsome, with a rich mane of brown hair and the beginnings
of a fulsome beard, he was remembered by one contemporary, Shishko,
as 'an exceptionally serious and even sombre young man, [with] a bit of
a stoop, a large forehead and sharp features'. The strongest impression
that the nineteen-year-old Kravchinsky had made on Shishko, though,
was during a summer camp in the forest near Lake Duderhof, when,

addressing a clandestine gathering of cadets on the imperative of revolution, his oratory had taken flight. Invoking the great and expeditious
changes wrought by the French Revolution, compared to which the
endless examples from history of concessions from above appeared meagre
and easily reversible, Kravchinsky's seditious ideas left his audience shaken
and intoxicated.

Weeks after his barnstorming performance the restless Kravchinsky
had abruptly abandoned his studies for an unglamorous posting to
Kharkov, a provincial backwater turned railway boom town. Fellow junior
officers remembered how his room was stripped of all furniture except
a stool, so that nothing should distract from his reading, which he
continued even while walking around the barracks. If the other soldiers
viewed such eccentricities with some suspicion, their respect for his burly
frame and innate acumen in military matters deterred mockery. He was
a man over whom women would swoon and men hover in the hope that
something of his aura might rub off on them.

Kravchinsky's admission at this time into the Chaikovsky Circle, un-
opposed and at the first attempt, was hardly surprising: he had already
demonstrated a ready talent for the circle's main business, having smuggled illicit pamphlets on his own initiative for some time. His knowledge
of the French Revolution also struck a chord with members, who self-
consciously modelled themselves on Danton, Desmoulins and the
Girondists of the 1790s. The welcome he received was in marked contrast
to the group's more circumspect reaction a few weeks later when Dmitri
Klements put forward the name of Prince Kropotkin for membership.

The thirty-year-old Kropotkin appeared, at first, an antiquated anomaly
to a group that was bound in most cases by connections from school and
college days, but there was more to their resistance than this. German
Lopatin did not mince his words. 'What prince do you have now? Perhaps
he wishes to amuse himself beneath the mask of democracy,' he argued,
'but later he will become a dignitary and cause us to be hanged.' Eventually,
Kropotkin was elected thanks to the testimony of the recently released
Sofia Perovskaya that he was reliable and 'completely young in spirit';
but whilst those who had suspected him of a hidden agenda mistook its
nature, they were not altogether misguided. Lev Tikhomirov probably
came closest to the truth when he recognised in Kropotkin an intellectual impatience with his colleagues: 'A revolutionary to the core [he was]
already at that time an anarchist, [while] anarchism for us was still entirely
new.' Even Kravchinsky lagged behind Kropotkin in this respect, for despite
his later profession to have been an anarchist at this point, his erroneous

claim that 'in 1870 the whole of advanced Russia was anarchist' suggests a certain ideological confusion.

Few in the circle would have disagreed with Kravchinsky's proselytising atheism, and most would have thrilled to Bakunin's claim that the traditional Russian village community, the *mir*, would be in the vanguard of the eventual revolution, 'freed from the oppressive tutelage of the state to become an ideal form of anarchical government, by all with the consent of all.' For most young Russians, however, faced with the realities of a tight tsarist security apparatus and the atrophied popular instinct for justice, any question of a revolution within their own lifetime appeared, for the moment, delusional. Replying to his brother's musings on the subject some years earlier, Alexander Kropotkin had expressed what remained the majority view among the country's dissidents: 'Of course I would rush to a social revolution; I would go to the barricades . . . But as for the success of the revolution, I wouldn't hope for much; it would be too early I'm sure, and they would defeat us.' Semi-clandestine visits to Russia by prominent figures from the Commune in the aftermath of the debacle of 1871 had briefly bolstered the extremist case, with Klements later reflecting that events in Paris had sparked 'a new era in the development of the revolutionary deed in Russia'. Yet the conspicuous pathos of the defeated Communards' predicament underlined the futility of insurrection, if launched prematurely. The fate of Marx's envoy to the Commune Elizaveta Dmitrieff, arrested on her return home from Paris and sent to suffer a slow death in Siberia, offered the bitterest reminder of the price to be paid for such sedition.

Kropotkin's admission had nevertheless galvanised debate within the twenty-strong circle over the nature and scope of the change that Russia required. Still, though, the majority held that it should be political only, rather than a more general upheaval in the structure of society, and must be achieved by constitutional means. Martin Langans, a leading member of the circle's sister organisation in the south of Russia, would offer an eloquent expression of the limit of their hopes: 'Back then,' he wrote, 'we believed that the state, like any powerful weapon, could both create happiness for mankind and oppress it, and that the mechanics lay in the creation of circumstances under which the abuse of power would become impossible.'

A visceral hatred for the tsar had yet to take hold, with the group directing its ire against those reactionary officials who were perceived to mislead and misinterpret him. On the one occasion when a member proposed assassinating Alexander II, the entire circle rounded on him, threatening to obstruct his intentions using whatever physical means necessary. And yet to those persuaded by Bakunin's analysis of Russia's predicament, any delay seemed certain only to weaken their position and play into their enemies' hands. While they hesitated, the advance of European capitalism and industry would continue to seduce the peasant from his loyalty to the land and erode the traditions of communistic solidarity, offering the distant prospect of individualistic self-advancement whilst plunging workers into even worse living conditions than before.

For all his admiration of the circle and its members, Kropotkin refused to cede on the key principle of collective action, and tried every ruse to win the majority around to his view. Initially declining to surrender his personal wealth to the communal coffers, he made certain that no one could mistake his stance for avarice or self-interest. It was 'because I am saving it for a more important time,' he told them. 'Later, when it becomes necessary to arm the workers in order to destroy the bourgeoisie, then no one will give a kopeck.' Staking his fragile credibility with the circle on this sensitive issue, he went on to reaffirm his commitment to the collective ideal, forcing his cautious colleagues' hand by volunteering for a task that entailed utter submission to the group's will.

The new role that Kropotkin proposed for himself would have meant severing all ties with the group, to plunge back into the life of the imperial court that he so despised. Only, this time, he would be there with something close to treachery in mind. 'I will agitate among the higher courtiers, I will try to unite them, if possible, into some form of organisation,' he promised the circle, who were eager for constitutional reform. To establish a radical cell so close to the heart of tsarist power, where reactionary forces were in the ascendant, risked almost certain arrest. But imprisonment was not the greatest sacrifice Kropotkin was prepared to make on behalf of 'such a collection of morally superior men and women': as a man who had renounced his title and his lineage, the denial of his true sympathies that such a deep-cover operation entailed would have amounted to a double torment. Fortunately for Kropotkin, his brinksmanship paid off: the question of policy was revisited to find more common ground.

On one subject all could agree: it was from the benighted common people of Russia – the *narod*, peasants and factory workers – that the pressure for change must come. For Chaikovsky, the greatest mistakes made during the reforms of the early 1860s stemmed from a lack of consultation with the people whom they affected, who might have anticipated the catastrophic consequences the tsar's advisers failed to foresee.

Some of the young idealists of the circle heeded Bakunin's advice that they should seek to merge with and learn from the people whilst inciting them to revolution. Most, however, preferred the lesson of Lavrov's *Historical Letters* of 1868: that as members of the intelligentsia they had a moral duty to lead the peasantry to enlightenment. Collectively, the Chaikovskyists decided to follow the latter's advice, 'breaking all ties with the past, leaving parents, friends, studies, social position, and dedicating oneself to the service of the masses.' It was to be a great, noble, bracingly self-effacing adventure.

The precocious Sofia Perovskaya had already set a fine example the previous year, when she had lived alongside the peasantry for several months while administering to them inoculations against smallpox. Now Chaikovsky, Kropotkin and Kravchinsky were among the first to venture out, testing the water with visits to local factories. It was an uphill struggle. Often they delivered the same lecture to the same audience, twice in quick succession, to be sure that they had understood. But while Kravchinsky was greeted with 'encores' for his rousing, demotic style, few were able to grasp the meaning of Kropotkin's rarified prose.

By the summer of 1873, the early trickle of radicals had surged into a torrent of many hundreds, their numbers swollen by the return of scores of young women from Switzerland, most trailing male admirers in their wake and with a moral point to prove. The government could scarcely have encouraged domestic disturbance more effectively than by its ill-considered and untimely threat to bar any medical students who stayed in Switzerland from ever graduating in Russia. And the government's dissemination of vicious propaganda claiming that the women were using their medical knowledge to abort the babies conceived of their promiscuity had fuelled their outrage. Like the original group of Chaikovskyists, once back in Russia the women of the Fritsche Circle also targeted factory workers as being 'more highly developed mentally' and therefore more receptive to their message.

Nevertheless, the tactics of the *narodniki* were fraught with hazards, and though well intentioned, the campaign 'to the people' was propelled by intellectual arrogance and class guilt, as Chaikovsky's later testimony admitted: 'We believed that history itself had laid upon us the mission to open up to the *narod* some truth that only we knew, and thereby . . . deliver the *narod* from all the suffering and humiliation that it bore for the sake of our education and our culture.' Time and again, the exuberance of privileged youth collided with the hard realities of work and poverty, producing consequences that were heavy with black comedy and pathos. With their motto of 'All for the people, and nothing for ourselves', the *narodniki* descended on unsuspecting factories and peasant communities in groups of three or four, yet few had any hard skills to offer in exchange for the food they took from the hungry mouths of their hosts' families. One gaggle of teenaged girls who earnestly resolved to acquire a trade in St Petersburg before departing typified the pervasive naïvety: 'Their faces are young, serious, decided and clear', reported one contemporary observer. 'They talk little because there is no time. And what is there to talk about? Everything has been decided. Everything is as clear as day.'

Nor were the privileged Chaikovskyists any longer immune to the indignities of proletariat justice. Bored by a lecture that Klements was delivering, one metalworker at a munitions factory reached round from behind to smear him with axle grease. Kropotkin decried the affront to his friend as symptomatic of the self-interested elitism that he had witnessed previously among the more complacent of the Swiss watchmakers. His own failure to find the right words to win over the ill-educated masses had left him smarting. Even when he turned his hand to written propaganda, in the form of a historical novella, Tikhomirov had to step in as ghostwriter to untangle the ideological knottiness of Kropotkin's prose.

Undoubtedly, some *narodniki* were better suited to their chosen task than others. A subscriber to the 'great man' theory of history, Kravchinsky's choice of a back-breaking job as a sawyer, and his physical strength and determination, apparently made such a strong impression on the peasants that it prised open their minds to his propaganda. Tikhomirov offered an equally upbeat assessment of his own dynamic contribution as a teacher: a more fitting and hard-headed choice of role than many. 'I would give an arithmetic problem to one; while he was solving it I would explain the alphabet to another. Then I would assign a lesson to one who could read, then explain a map to others.' Yet Tikhomirov's diligence in responding to his pupils' questions drew him into dangerous territory. Asked by his chemistry students about the will-o'-the-wisps and wood goblins that filled the fields and forests, he and his colleagues were perfectly unguarded in explaining away such features of rural folklore as phosphoric miasmas and magic-lantern effects; but what appeared to such confirmed rationalists as a virtuous debunking of superstition, was tantamount to an attack on the essential credulity of the masses on which the entire social system depended.

Even at the time of the supposedly liberalising reforms of 1862, an edict had brusquely outlawed the teaching of workers as 'likely to undermine faith in the Christian religion and in the institution of private property, and to incite the working classes to revolt.' To a Third Section grappling with an ever more complex society – one in which the emancipation of the serfs was accompanied by the growth of independent professions and a growing intelligentsia – the underlying principle remained crucial to their maintenance of social order. Since Karakozov's attempt to kill the tsar in 1866, an anxious and uncertain Alexander II had fallen deeper under the influence of a reactionary cabal at court, and the actions of the *narodniki* were bound to provoke a forceful response.

'They ruled by fear,' Kropotkin would write of this hard-line faction, led by Shuvalov and his ally Trepov, and advised by the manipulative Prussian counter-subversive, Colonel Stieber. The tsar himself was the prime target of their alarmism, and was soon in thrall to their exaggerated reports of 'the spectre of revolution about to break out in St Petersburg'. Even once it became clear that their concerted campaign of repression had backfired, following the decision to recall the female medical students from Switzerland, draconian tactics continued to be advanced as the only way out of a worsening predicament.

At first the arrests were haphazard, carried out by Third Section officers following a vague scent and lucky enough to stumble upon radicals clumsily disguised in their ersatz peasant costumes, or else to receive tip-offs from locals exasperated by the hectoring tone of their uninvited guests. The hopes of the *narodniki* that the economic slump of two years earlier, and the hardship that it had caused to subsistence farmers, might have broken the peasantry's deep loyalty to the tsar as their mystical leader proved misplaced. With time, plus a thousand Tikhomirovs and Kravchinskys to offer enlightenment, the peasants might perhaps have been cured of their superstitious awe of authority; as it was, radicals across all of Russia's thirty-seven provinces soon discovered that they had walked into a picturesque trap. More often than not it was *they* who were seen as the enemy, and the tsar's agents as the peasants' protectors.

The youthful elite of the country was picked up by the cartload and hauled into indefinite detention. Some were indeed committed activists, many others simply friends along for the ride and the country air, or merely unlucky acquaintances. But as the Third Section sifted through their haul of prisoners, patterns and connections began to emerge that made possible a further stage of more methodical and carefully targeted police action. Colonel Stieber's recent reforms of the Third Section had been designed to prepare it to confront and disrupt continent-wide networks of diehard, professional revolutionaries; the present campaign of persecution against untried men and women who were barely out of their teens was like shooting fish in a barrel.

Sofia Perovskaya was among those seized in the first St Petersburg raid late in the summer of 1873, Tikhomirov in one of the many that followed during that November. Piece by piece the movement in the capital, blamed for the ineffectual rabble-rousing, was dismantled. The exact numbers of those rounded up are elusive. Count Pahlen, the minister of justice, wrote of 612 being taken into custody in the course of the year, of which nearly a quarter were women. Others estimated the total, including those seized the following year, to be as high as 4,000, Pahlen's supposedly comprehensive figure representing rather the number who would be kept in detention for at least two years without trial. 'It was as though a disease had swept through a certain social stratum,' Vera Figner would remember. 'Everyone had lost a friend or relative.' Chaikovsky fled the city, along with Klements, Kravchinsky and the others; only Kropotkin, fatefully, remained behind.

As the radical movement buckled, the ideologues of reaction cranked up their rhetoric, encouraging the police to carry on relentlessly with the persecution. The contribution of Fyodor Dostoevsky at this time was insidious. A quarter-century before, the novelist had himself been under sentence of death for sedition and reprieved only at the very last moment. During his penal service in the army, however, he had come to revile the idols of his youth with the kind of excoriating scorn that only those for whom religion had filled an existential void can muster. Writing to Tsarevitch Alexander in 1873, he presented his work on *The Possessed* as a process of empathetic enquiry: 'to pose the question, and, as clearly as possible, to give an answer to it in the form of a novel: In what ways in our transitional and strange contemporary society is the emergence possible not just of Nechaev, but of Nechaevs, and in what way may it happen that these Nechaevs eventually gather for themselves Nechaevists?'

Whilst the literary merit of Dostoevsky's work is beyond question, his alarmist preoccupation was unjustified and arguably irresponsible. Nechaev was imprisoned in the dreaded Alexeyevsky Ravelin prison, a triangular moated tower, slightly removed from the Peter and Paul fortress and entirely isolated from the world at large; unlikely ever to re-enter society, the revelations during his trial had lost him all support and his doctrine of murderous conspiracy stood discredited. Nothing short of the most brutal suppression of dissent now seemed likely to drive the youth movement towards violent tactics, at least in any significant numbers. And yet it was just this kind of brutal suppression that

Dostoevsky's purportedly 'realist' writing risked encouraging in the members of a court that suffered from a congenital predisposition to fear the worst and to act accordingly. Nor was Dostoevsky alone in his distaste for the youth of Russia. As tutor to the tsarevitch, his friend Constantine Pobedonostsev, future head of the Orthodox synod, was busy inculcating the heir to the imperial throne with his own reactionary beliefs.

Meanwhile, at St Petersburg University the fervently expressed views of the brilliant new professor of physiology, Elie Cyon, and his harsh marking of papers which exhibited too great an attraction to positivism's political side, were provoking students attending his lectures to pelt him with eggs and gherkins. Thriving on the antagonism of an audience filled with radicals whose arrest and interrogation he craved, Cyon once even interrupted a lecture on the medical use of the cardiograph to venomously taunt them with the machine's alternative application: as a detector of lies and hypocrisy. Provocation of a different sort would, before long, become a consistent feature of the Russian police. Insofar as the young radicals' commitment to the positivist cause was tantamount to a religious calling, however, Cyon's accusations of blasphemous hubris held some water.

In an atmosphere heightened by grief and anger, pseudo-religious sentiments permeated the minds of even the most zealous atheists. 'They went out as bearers of a revelation rather than political propagandists,' Kravchinsky would recall, adding that 'Men were trying not just to reach a certain practical end, but also to satisfy a deeply felt duty, an aspiration for moral perfection.' Mere proximity to the movement's secret printing presses filled him 'with the subdued feeling of a worshipper entering a church', and as the *narodniki* huddled together with their hosts in smoky peasant huts, solemnly discussing politics late into the night, revolutionary hymns would spontaneously be sung. 'One couldn't help recalling scenes of the first centuries of Christianity,' admitted Kravchinsky, his thoughts as much about those absent in prison, as those active in the field. As had happened during the Paris Commune, the radical movement in Russia was already laying the foundations of a martyrology: one that Kravchinsky, the arch-propagandist, hoped might counter the self-righteous pieties of its Orthodox enemies.

Maintaining morale became ever more important. More by accident than design, the initial efforts of those who 'went to the people' had indeed scored an important symbolic point, by demonstrating the solidarity of what seemed like an entire generation against oppression in all its forms: whether by family, state, class or tradition. Yet such had been the pressure of the youthful energy released that the campaign had snow-balled out of control, losing discipline and focus.

As his friends were picked off one by one, Kropotkin seethed with frustration. Having elicited an invitation to draft a manifesto for the circle, he returned to the question of revolution that so vexed the Chaikovskyists, apparently with an agenda to railroad colleagues who were absent among the peasants or in prison, into adopting a more robust policy to counter the depredations of the police. Brushing aside the adamant assertions of other Chaikovskyists that they were not anarchists, but rather social democrats, populists or even democratic republicans, his document *Why We Must Concern Ourselves with the Structure of a Future Society* asserted that 'there is not the slightest doubt that among different socialists of the most varied shades there exists a rather complete agreement in their ideals'. Moreover, the vision it offered – of a federal society in which all benefited from advanced education and all participated in 'useful labour' – was premised on the notion that any lasting change in society must be revolutionary and would involve toppling the tsarist regime by force.

While in Switzerland, Kropotkin had wrestled with his conscience over the bloodshed that would inevitably accompany any revolution, and concluded that a popular rising in Russia could be justified. To succeed, however, it would need to be far greater in scope and organisation than the Paris Commune, and the inauspicious circumstances then prevailing could not be allowed to delay the job of preparation. 'By acquiring arms one can develop arsenals, and the troops will stand with the people,' he promised and, during the winter of 1873, set about plotting the creation of armed peasant bands, *druzhiny*, who even in failure would 'imprint their revolutionary action upon the minds and hearts with their blood'.

Although the draft of Kropotkin's manifesto was never presented to the Chaikovskyists for their approval, and never likely to receive it, when a copy fell into the hands of Third Section agents it was seized upon as powerfully incriminating evidence for their most extravagant claims against the circle. Kropotkin was not a figure whom the authorities could easily dismiss as a mere adolescent troublemaker: only a short time before, the Geographical Society had again offered him an official position. Once his secret identity as the revolutionary 'Borodin' was confirmed, however, arrest was inevitable, and yet for all Kropotkin's intellectual achievements, at the crucial moment his carelessness severely compromised the movement: a letter found by agents searching his apartment provided the key to deciphering the movement's coded communications, and exposed many of its members to persecution.

Stalwart silence whilst in the Peter and Paul fortress could now save only Kropotkin's self-respect, and yet nearly two years later, police records show that Kropotkin was still honouring the Chaikovskyists' pact of secrecy. By then, however, weakening health was threatening him with martyrdom in its fullest sense.

*

Alone in his freezing cell, cramped with rheumatism and wheezing with respiratory problems, the pressure on Kropotkin had been intense. Scores of prisoners had already succumbed to the terrible conditions in which they were forced to live. When a solicitous visit by the tsar's brother, Grand Prince Nicholas, failed to extract a statement of regret and renunciation from Kropotkin, the authorities appeared quite content that Peter Kropotkin should be next. 'Bring me a doctor's certificate that your brother will die in ten days and only then will I free him,' the procurator replied, with seeming relish, to pleas for clemency on his behalf by his sister-in-law, whose husband Alexander had himself been arrested while Peter was in prison, and sentenced to ten years' exile in Siberia on the flimsiest of pretexts. Kropotkin's predicament seemed equally hopeless, and the unproven claims by Nicholas Fodorov a few years earlier, that soon he would be able to resurrect the dead, provided scant comfort. Eventually, though, science did intervene in the form of the chief physician of the military hospital, who insisted that Kropotkin be transferred to his care for a period of convalescence.

Acting on Kropotkin's smuggled suggestions, a plan was drawn up by Dr Orest Veimar, a friend of Kravchinsky and an independent-minded sympathiser with the Chaikovsky group. The looser security measures in force at the prison infirmary in the northern suburbs of St Petersburg were probed and tested: the daily delivery of firewood noted, inside assistance procured, and a top-floor flat overlooking the exercise yard was rented. From there a violinist would signal the all clear as part of a complex system of communication. A prizewinning racehorse called Varvar, or Barbarian, was bought by the doctor and harnessed to the getaway carriage, and the other cabs in the vicinity hired to hinder the police pursuit.

As the day in late June earmarked for his escape approached, Kropotkin received a message, concealed inside a pocket watch, confirming his imminent rescue. Then, at the last moment, calamity struck: a run on red balloons had stripped St Petersburg's toyshops of a key element in the gaolbreakers' signalling system. A few days later, they arrived better equipped.

Those present recounted their memories of the sequence of events as a compelling montage: the bunch of red balloons drifting up over the wall of the prison infirmary, Kropotkin raising his prisoner's cap to indicate his readiness, then casting off his cumbersome coat for the 300-yard dash to the perimeter of the courtyard; the guards distracted by conjuring tricks performed by Kropotkin's accomplices, caught momentarily unawares. The fugitive then leaped into a waiting carriage, which rocked and threatened to overturn as it rounded a sharp corner at speed; from the barrels of the guards in the receding background puffs of smoke exploded harmlessly. And all was set to the strains of a wild mazurka that floated out from the violin played in a window high above the scene. Then the final shot: the anarchist prince, tapping a top hat firmly down on his head by way of disguise.

Discrepancies between the the participants' accounts of the evening that followed perhaps suggest a degree of embellishment, or else testify to the intensity of the celebrations, first in a private room in Donon's famous restaurant, and then a well-stocked dacha on the road out towards Finland. After so many tragic failures, the presence among the outlaws of Kropotkin, his face pale and drawn, almost unrecognisable after shaving his fulsome beard to conceal his identity, represented a much-needed success. Little can any of them have guessed, however, that his escape would mark the start of many decades of exile.

Travelling undercover from St Petersburg to Finland, then on by ship more openly to the Swedish capital, Christiana, now Oslo, Kropotkin finally arrived in Hull in June 1876. It was with a profound sense of relief that he saw the fluttering Union Jack, 'under which so many Russian, Italian, French and Hungarian refugees have found asylum'. For a restless Kropotkin, however, the search for congenial company and a secure environment in which to develop his dangerous ideas had only just begun.

6

Forward!

America and Back, 1874–1878

Just as the defeat had dispersed Communard fugitives around the world, so the persecution of the *narodniki* by the tsarist authorities now began to create a diaspora of Russian radicals. For most, the move abroad was impelled by a simple instinct for self-preservation, while revolutionary evangelism was the motive for others. In the case of Nicholas Chaikovsky, however, his arrival in New York in late 1875, with his heavily pregnant wife, had a quite different explanation. For whilst the other members of the circle that bore his name were still risking arrest in their struggle to galvanise the peasant masses, Chaikovsky had succumbed to a growing sense of alienation from precisely the 'adventurism of the intelligentsia' that he himself had done so much to foster in the preceding years.

Plunged into a maelstrom of spiritual self-doubt, Chaikovsky had experienced an epiphany whilst passing through the provincial town of Oryol in the spring of 1874, when he had chanced to meet Alexander Malinkov, the charismatic leader of a religious cult. 'In every man there is a divine element,' Malinkov taught. 'It is sufficient to appeal to it, to find the God in man, for no coercion to be necessary. God will settle everything in people's souls and everyone will become just and kind.' Amidst the growing attrition that surrounded the populist project, Chaikovsky found deep consolation in the message.

Chaikovsky's old associates had greeted news of his conversion with incredulity. How, they asked, could he have been won over by such a charlatan, whose son announced to visitors that 'Daddy is God', and who had once been a favourite student of the reviled Pobedonostsev? Conveniently they failed to remember how often Malinkov had challenged his tutor. When Chaikovsky made the mistake of inviting fellow members of the sect to shelter overnight in a safe house belonging to the circle, the radicals present had made their feelings known by keeping the pacifistic 'Godmen' awake deep into the early hours with bitter accusations. Chaikovsky, though, was adamant, in both his new-found faith and his determination to emigrate.

Messianic ideas had long flourished in Russia and, consciously or otherwise, had informed many of the socialistic theories to emerge from its political philosophers. Even Lavrov's popularism was premised on the idea that the soul of the peasant, the *muzhik*, contained the germ of social salvation, and that a hidden, mystical force inherent to the peasant community would one day rise and sweep away bourgeois complacency, bringing renewal to the whole of mankind. Similarly, the young missionaries 'to the people' regularly held up the United States as a model for the freedom and social justice to which Russia could aspire: a country with no tsar, but rather a president elected by and representative of the people themselves. In the years since the Civil War, the intelligentsia's fascination with America had seen any number of schemes and companies set up to assist with emigration, with pioneers dispatched to help populate new communities.

No such preparation had paved the way for Chaikovsky, however, and having travelled to America ahead of Malinkov's main party of fifteen, it fell to him, in New York, to determine their final destination. There was no shortage of existing communes that the sect might have joined: ready-made, if flawed, Utopias that included Josiah Warren's Modern Times on Long Island, Noyes' Oneida in New York State, the Fourierist Reunion in Missouri, or the Shakers at Sonyea, to name only the most prominent of several hundred then active. However, it was to a small colony called Cedar Vale, established near Wichita in Kansas, that Chaikovsky was drawn by an open invitation from its founder, a Russian calling himself William Frey, for newcomers to join him in 'the great laboratory of all ideas and aspirations that agitate against the contemporary world'.

In prospect, Chaikovsky would have found much about Frey with which to identify. Born William Giers, a mathematical prodigy like Chaikovsky himself, he had excelled first at the Artillery School in St Petersburg and then in the army. But Giers' professional life had exposed him to the suffering of the masses, and their dispiriting political inertia had plunged him into a state of suicidal despair. Rejecting a promotion to serve as Surveyor General of Turkestan, he had preferred to set sail for a new life, having adopted his new surname while passing through Germany to denote a devotion to freedom. 'We want persons who are kind, tolerant, and earnestly devoted to communism as the best means of benefiting the human race,' he had written of his colony, in the letter published by Peter Lavrov's newspaper *Forward!* He even warned potential recruits that 'they must be actuated by principles, and not merely selfish purposes'. The proposition must have struck any self-regarding idealist as irresistible, but there were reasons too for Chaikovsky to have hesitated.

While breaking his journey in London, Chaikovsky had been warmly received by Lavrov, whose purpose in publishing *Forward!* was to keep his readership informed about labour struggles internationally, including those with which the more industrialised regions of America were racked, and the picture it painted of the country on which Chaikovsky had set his sights was quite at odds with Frey's vision of rolling prairies and opportunity. 'Ship after ship departs from Europe bearing with it people who are filled to excess with sufferings in the Old World and who naïvely expect to find a different life in the New World,' Lavrov wrote, warning that 'The naïvety of these people is excellently made use of by clever swindlers.' Moreover, he explained, the time was at hand when the workers in America must fight their exploiters, and it was surely no place for idle social experimentation.

It was advice worth heeding, but all too easy for the imperturbable Chaikovsky to disregard as serving Lavrov's personal agenda that political change at home should be the primary duty of any Russians contemplating emigration. Chaikovsky's discovery that the atmosphere of growing intrigue and persecution he had found so intolerable in St Petersburg pervaded even émigré life in London must have made him uneasy too, and the steamer waiting in Liverpool docks all the more appealing. For whilst Lavrov himself was unaware that the sizeable private donation that sustained his newspaper was actually paid by the Third Section, the activities of its less subtle agents in Britain were all too obvious, as they used bribery and blackmail to stiffen Scotland Yard's somewhat desultory efforts at keeping the Russian community under surveillance.

On the long journey from New York to Cedar Vale with his wife and co-religionists, Chaikovsky would have ample opportunity to reflect on the wisdom or otherwise of his decision and to revise his rose-tinted view of America. During the previous decade, sums that were almost inconceivable had been spent on the expansion of the country's railroads, netting vast fortunes for the entrepreneurs who had driven their development far beyond any immediate need. In the process, tens of thousands of indigenous peoples had been displaced from their land, and huge numbers of railway workers had suffered injury or death, not to mention the attrition on those toiling without safety provision in the mines and foundries that fed the railroad with its raw materials. The risks to the brakemen were all too obvious as they clambered over moving carriages to set the brakes, or whipped out their fingers as the buffers of rolling stock clanged heavily together for manual coupling. Had Chaikovsky known in full the miserable terms of their employment, half starved and lacking legal protection of any kind, he might have thought the freed serfs of Russia almost fortunate by comparison.

Every stage of the journey brought new and alarming insights, but nowhere more so than the town of Wichita, at whose newly built station the Russian family and their fellow 'Godmen' finally alighted. 'Leave your revolvers at police headquarters and get a check,' read the sign that greeted them, but the sound of six-shooters being fired at flies on saloon walls spoke of a certain laxity in the enforcement of this rule. Wichita was booming. Rail links to the eastern cities and a steamboat connection to New Orleans saw to that, along with the influx of cash that came from the jangling-spurred cowboys who delivered herds of longhorn cattle for shipment along the Chisholm trail from Texas. In the six years since it had been founded, Wichita had already acquired close to 3,000 regular inhabitants, outstripping its once larger neighbours, and the building plots on its grid plan of 140 streets were rapidly starting to fill. Bars occupied a disproportionate number, though the Masons had already secured a prominent position for their hall.

Arriving as they did in the final weeks of 1875, Chaikovsky and his companions would have been just in time to witness the dregs of the wild carnival that engulfed the town between June and December. For a few days the population of Wichita swelled to twice its normal size with seasonal traders bringing with them an influx of gamblers and whores. Brass bands blared from the doors and windows of saloons every hour of the day and night, while Deputy Sheriff Wyatt Earp attempted to keep order. 'Near Brimstone' was how one journalist head-lined his report on Wichita, and Chaikovsky is unlikely to have lingered long.

If he had wondered what Lavrov meant when he wrote of the 'swindlers' who awaited naïve immigrants to America, Chaikovsky would by now have had a range of candidates, from the exploitative railroad bosses to the local card sharps. Perhaps, though, as the train had chugged through Missouri, he would have also reflected more closely on the letter Frey had written to *Forward!*: 'To veto the reproduction of undesirable children . . . grossly sensuous . . . gratification of his own senses': the phrases that leaped out were troubling indications of a dogmatism regarding the physical life of the commune. Might Lavrov's warning have been alluding to a swindler of a different kind altogether, who played on one's hopes of a promised land of freedom in the Midwest, but delivered only another kind of servitude?

Undaunted, Chaikovsky crossed the verdant plains outside Wichita with high hopes, approaching the 'Happy Valley' in which Cedar Vale lay. Nor, after the final forty-mile trek, did the place disappoint, at least at first sight: a pleasant community of seventy farms and twenty schoolhouses spread across rolling prairie, its people hard-working and peaceable. However, when William and Mary Frey – thin and feverish, shivering in threadbare old Unionist overcoats and smiling a slightly too eager greeting – emerged from a ramshackle building, the travellers must have felt more like a rescue party happening upon marooned sailors than hopeful recruits to a thriving social experiment. Perhaps, for a moment, Chaikovsky experienced a first twinge of the bitter homesickness described by a previous Cedar Vale colonist in his book *The Prairie and the Pioneers*, and the longing that he and his Russian cohabitants felt 'to be under our own poor grey sky, surrounded by naked and cold plains and forests!'

*

Letters from the author of the Prairie memoir, Grigori Machtet, to Mary Frey, once frequent, had become less so of late. The reason, though, would have become plain to the colony when editions of *Forward!* containing Machtet's recent contributions finally reached Cedar Vale. It was as if he and Chaikovsky had exchanged places, though the world of radical St Petersburg into which Machtet had immersed himself on his return from America seemed already to have progressed several steps further towards political upheaval in the short time since Chaikovsky had left.

When the reactionary professor Elie Cyon had roused his students to riot a year or two earlier, forcing the closure of the university for several months, the tsar had simply dispatched the outspoken academic to Paris as a privy councillor, and the tension had been defused. Recent protests, however, had incurred a more extreme and confrontational response, and none more so than the funeral of Pavel Chernyshev. A medical student who had been arrested in error, he had subsequently died from tuberculosis due to the appalling conditions in which he was held. While crowds chanted an elegiac verse hastily composed by Machtet, Chernyshev's open coffin was processed around sites symbolic of the tsar's infamous penal system: courts, police headquarters and prisons.

In the past, the tsarist administration had paid lip service, at least, to the basic dignities of political prisoners, but the time for such indulgence was now past. On direct instructions from the tsar, the words 'an honourable fighter for a sacred cause' were excised from the dead man's grave. 'A great judgement day' was coming, his outraged mourners proclaimed in re-action, when the thin crowds to whom they usually proselytised would 'be transformed into tens, even hundreds, of thousands, who, with weapons in hand, will go out into the square to judge the executioners, torturers, robber barons and exploitative landowners.' The authorities, however, moved swiftly to ensure that the cataclysm would be indefinitely postponed, with the Third Section stepping up its repression.

Having struggled against mounting odds to maintain the Chaikovskyists' links with the peasantry, frustration now drove Sergei Kravchinsky to join the exodus of fugitive dissidents. His first stop was Paris, as it had been for Chaikovsky, but his final destination was to be not some spurious heaven on earth but a war zone: Bosnia and Herzegovina, where the imposition of onerous taxes by the Ottoman Empire had provoked a popular revolt in which he meant to hone his skills as a militant revolutionary. While the tsar's generals hung back, hamstrung by factional wrangling over the geopolitical complexities of engagement in the Balkans, Kravchinsky would plunge in, sensing an opportunity to seed a socialist future in lands liberated from Turkish misrule.

Departing Paris in August 1876 with Klements as his sole companion, Kravchinsky crossed from northern Italy into war-torn Bosnia, where his military training promptly earned him the command of a rebel division's artillery: a single cannon. His excitement was to be short-lived, however. Marooned in a landscape of suffering, rendered toxic by a cycle of massacres perpetrated by Ottoman irregulars against the Bosniacs and avenged by them on the Turkish population, Kravchinsky felt the futility of his predicament deeply. Before long his pride would take a further battering: confronted by a steep hill, the rebels had no choice but to bury their cannon, while a puffed Kravchinsky – who had been famed among the bookish Chaikovsky Circle for his outstanding physical prowess and hardiness – had to be carried piggyback over the ridge by his commanding officer.

Contradictory messages filled his letters to Russia and his reports to Lavrov. In one letter he summons colleagues to the fight, then declares that 'I won't start calling comrades over from Russia until I have been convinced with my own eyes. I've become very sceptical.' The Bosniacs are 'a brave, decisive and cunning people', but the insurgents 'a gang of ordinary bandits'. 'There isn't even the faintest whiff of socialism here,' he claims, shortly before opining to another correspondent that 'You could lead socialist propaganda here wonderfully.' The contradictions suggest a man unsure of how best to brazen out the terrible reality of his disappointment, yet all too alive to the risks of defeatism. The candid appraisal of the liberation movement he has promised to *Forward!* cannot be delivered, he admits, until 'it's all over, because it would be counter-productive to tell the whole truth now. It has to be inflated for the sake of politics.'

Insofar as Kravchinsky's intention in Bosnia had been to convince those he had left behind in Russia that 'we have to take up, not the pen, but the knife', he had failed. His adventure ended with a brief spell in a deafeningly noisy and brutal Turkish gaol, about which he remained silent until many years later. The one saving grace, however, had been the friendships formed with members of the Italian contingent, among them the sons of the legendary Garibaldi, who like him had seen in the Balkan liberation struggle the perfect testing ground for revolutionary action.

While the insurgency of the nationalist Risorgimento remained a touchstone for Europe's revolutionaries, however, the new imperative since the watershed of 1871 was to promote the creed of internationalist socialism. 'It was on the cadaver of the Commune – fecund in its ruins – that we pledged ourselves to the struggle between the old spirit and the new,' wrote one member of the Italian movement, 'and it was from the blood of the slain Communards that the omens were drawn.' Foremost among the promulgators of this inspiring vision was the twenty-four-year-old Errico Malatesta, and whilst he had no personal experience of the Paris uprising to offer, he provided Kravchinsky with a living link to Bakunin, who had otherwise passed beyond reach.

From the furthest reaches of the Russian Empire in Asia to the southernmost point of Europe, where African and Latin blood mingled, the 1860s and 70s seemed to breed revolutionaries in a recognisably similar mould. The son of a propertied factory owner, Malatesta's early childhood had been blighted by respiratory illnesses that led doctors to predict his early death and left him vulnerable to infections throughout his life. Sickness, though, had not subdued a stubborn, contrarian streak that, subjected to the 'cretinising and corrupting' dogma of a religious boarding school in Naples, bred a spirit of resistance. A confirmed atheist and anti-authoritarian by the age of fourteen, only his youth saved him from prosecution for a disrespectful letter written to the new king of Italy,

Victor Emmanuel II. Next came medical studies, a characteristic first step for guilt-stricken young humanitarians on the road to political activism, the flamboyance of which, in Malatesta's case, led to his expulsion from the course and flight from Italy in search of a mentor. Having crossed the freezing St Gotthard Pass at the coldest time of the year, he arrived at Bakunin's home in Switzerland penniless and with a fever running so high that the Russian felt obliged to watch over his sickbed in person: he could hardly have made a more dramatic first impression.

Defeat in the struggle for control of the International in 1873 had seen the revolutionary fervour that had sustained Bakunin through countless doomed uprisings and secret societies begin to ebb. Exhausted by the ceaseless machinations of Marx and Engels and the calumnies they poured upon him, disappointed by a world where repression had become 'a new science taught systematically to lieutenants in military schools of all nations', Bakunin had grown weary of pushing 'the rock of Sisyphus against the reaction that is triumphant everywhere'. Regardless of the realities, Malatesta's devotion was absolute. 'It was impossible for a youth to have contact with [Bakunin] without feeling himself inflamed by a sacred fire, without seeing his own horizons broadened, without feeling himself a knight of a noble cause,' he wrote, and took up arms as the old man's paladin, travelling to Spain under the code name 'Beniamino'. In 1874, he prepared an insurrection in Bologna intended to reinstate Bakunin as the revolutionary hero that he had once been. 'I am convinced that the time of grand theoretical discourse, written or spoken, is past,' the Russian had declared. 'It is no longer time for ideas but for deeds and acts.'

It must have taken a wilful blindness, by this point, not to recognise Bakunin for the corrupt husk he now was, but Malatesta was not alone in his credulity. With a certain rheumy-eyed regret for the life of aristocratic ease that he had left behind in Russia decades earlier, Bakunin was squandering more than merely his energy in the spendthrift pursuit of an old man's folly: the refurbishment of the grand house and estate of La Baronata, on a hill overlooking Lake Locarno, the cost of which had absorbed nearly the entire sizeable inheritance of Bakunin's eager acolyte, Carlo Cafiero. It took the young Italian's belated realisation that hiring picturesque milkmaids and excavating an artificial lake was not wholly essential to the creation of a revolutionary headquarters before he finally staunched his indulgence of the old rogue.

If only to raise the spirits of their bombastic icon, and without any genuine prospect of success, the young Bakuninists had nevertheless proceeded with the Bologna plan. Unless from a sense of obligation, it is hard to explain Bakunin's own half-hearted participation except as a craving for the kind of heroic death that could obscure the embarrassment of the Baronata fiasco and extricate him from his responsibilities to his young family. Yet when the insurrection failed to take hold, he had been grateful to elude the Italian Carabinieri, even at the price of further crushing indignity: the notorious scourge of organised religion was reduced to shaving off his locks and donning a priest's robe to disguise his identity, while comrades had to push his capacious posterior through the door of a waiting coach.

Undaunted, Malatesta had followed up the Bologna debacle with a similarly doomed attempt to incite insurrection in Puglia, where only five of the several hundred expected activists actually materialised. Emerging from prison with his appetite for revolutionary adventure still unabated, the summer of 1875 had seen him on a mission to Spain to stage the prison break of an anarchist who proved infuriatingly reluctant to be liberated, before he returned to join the Masonic lodge in Naples, repeating Bakunin's mistake of a decade earlier by thinking that he could transform it into an instrument of revolutionary organisation. After such embarrassing disappointments, anyone less single-minded than the tight-framed, tousle-haired and alarmingly moustachioed Malatesta might have been chastened: instead, perfectly undeterred, he plunged headlong into the ideological quicksand of Bosnia.

By the same count, Kravchinsky should have noted Malatesta's unblemished record of failed insurrections and given him a wide berth. Had Kravchinsky been able to meet Bakunin for himself, while travelling through Switzerland on his way to the Balkans, perhaps his curiosity would have been satisfied, but only a few days previously age and ill health had finally claimed the sixty-two-year-old revolutionary. In Malatesta, Kravchinsky had found a surrogate who carried the conviction needed to help restore his battered faith in the possibility of a beneficent revolution. 'We must make unceasing attempts, even if we are beaten and completely routed, one, two, ten times, even twenty times,' Malatesta might have told his new friend, repeating words of encouragement written by Bakunin to another *narodnik* two years previously; 'but if on the twenty-first time, the people support us by taking part in our revolution, we shall have been paid for all the sacrifices we will have endured.'

With Malatesta's first mention of an arms cache in Puglia, left buried from two years earlier, and of a new scheme to mount an insurrection near Naples, all Kravchinsky's previous plans and promises were instantly forgotten.

*

'We had planned to go to Montenegro together, before he had the whim of going to Italy instead,' the earnest young Klements wrote plaintively from Berne, complaining about Kravchinsky, whom he nicknamed the 'Bluebird' dreamer. As Chaikovsky read the letter, the icy wind howling through the ramshackle walnut-wood walls that the 'Godmen' had thrown together for shelter at Cedar Vale, his baby wailing from the cold, his sympathy is likely to have been fleeting. His own predicament offered enough misery of its own, though whether the physical demands of life in Kansas or its communal nature was more taxing, he would probably have been hard put to say.

'They have neither pilots nor lighthouses,' had been how Frey described the ideal colonists he sought to recruit, since 'everything is unexplored, everything must be discovered anew'. The 'second-rate prairie' on which Frey had chosen to stake out his plots yielded little to the incompetent husbandry of the colonists, however, who lacked even the skill to milk their cow, let alone produce the cheese or butter that might have made more appetising the ascetic diet of unleavened bread prescribed by the vegetarian Frey. The material challenges the group faced, however, were at least equalled by the emotional torment they suffered.

Though a modest lifestyle was accepted as part and parcel of the struggle for a new social order, the newcomers baulked at Frey's evangelical imperative to 'break yourself' in order to release the true communist within, and vigorously resisted when he urged them to renounce clothes. Mealtimes were a trial too, with anyone late to the table forbidden to eat, even if delayed by urgent community business, while the other families winced as Frey subjected his daughter to daunting tests of mathematical prowess and punished her failure with a dowsing of cold water. Maybe he considered such treatment physically beneficial, as well as character building: with quinine unaffordable, a bath of rainwater was also the proposed cure for Chaikovsky's malaria on one occasion.

'This slow, constant mockery of man's moral liberty' was the overriding impression that would stay with Chaikovsky, who must have dearly wished that before leaving Europe he had thought to consult Elisée Reclus' travelogue of 1861, *Voyage à la Sierra-Nevada de Sainte-Marthe*. A bible for those seeking to establish communes in America (despite Reclus' antagonism to such social experiments), it warned of the perverse tendency of utopian communities to constrain rather than encourage liberty, and their susceptibility to petty tyrants. Reclus had no time either for the utopian theories of Charles Fourier, with his wild promises and bizarre symbolism, according to which two crops at least should have flourished in Cedar Vale: the cauliflowers of free love, and the cabbages whose leaves represented illicit liaisons.

That Frey had decided to create his own colony may have been due to his prudish distaste for the sexual antics he and Mary had encountered elsewhere. Their first taste of cooperative life, in New York, had ended when 'hungry debauchees' with an appetite for promiscuity had swamped the commune, and discomfort at the libertarian ethos at Reunion had similarly prompted their departure. Whether Mary agreed with his view that they had escaped 'the most discordant and hellish life that could be imagined', however, is an open question. As a radiant young bride, eight years earlier, she would have been entitled to expect great things of marriage to a well-connected and highly respected scientist. Even after settling in America, the prospect of being free to pursue her own ambitions as a doctor would have made the hardships endurable. Since then, though, Frey's neglect of his wife's romantic and libidinous needs had led her to search for satisfaction outside the marriage.

Grigori Machtet may not have been the first to fill the gap in Mary's heart and bed, but after his return to Russia, she had struck out desperately for independence, her brief visit to Chicago in search of a baby to adopt turning into a year's absence. When necessity finally forced her back to Cedar Vale she had maintained her habit of free-loving, conceiving a child by her next young Russian paramour. Despite belonging to that generation of Russian radicals which had held Chernyshevsky's writings as gospel truth, Frey's jealousy seems to have bitten deep, and in his ever more pedantic enforcement of the community's rules he may well have been sublimating the frustration he felt at the loss of control over his personal life. With his original partners in the foundation of Cedar Vale long gone, few of its subsequent residents were psychologically strong enough to withstand the Wednesday meetings that he still found so 'electric, thrilling, [and] beneficent': mutual criticism followed by enforced public confession may have been intended to clear the air, but the effect was rarely restorative.

The commune's manifesto had been full of fine sentiments: 'For the cause that lacks assistance, For the wrong that needs resistance, For the future in the distance, And the good that we can do,' it pledged. Its journal had once recorded such sentiments as being 'like sailors throwing the baggage overboard to save the life . . . in order to get something to live on', but entries had already ceased by the time of Chaikovsky's arrival. Since then, the reality of their shipwrecked existence had become painfully apparent to everyone: it was the colonists themselves who lacked assistance, and Frey who needed resisting, while the ideal future to which they aspired lay so far over the horizon as to be quite fantastical. By late 1876, Chaikovsky and a chastened Malinkov had moved their families to a second shack just across the river from Frey's own: 'With what shame one recalls many episodes of this life,' the leader of the 'Godmen' later wrote.

Chaikovsky bridled at the grim fascination with which the other residents of Cedar Vale watched their social experiment failing, and when the Kansas authorities launched a formal investigation into the commune's supposed immorality, the humiliation became too much. To extricate himself, though, was no easy matter. Chaikovsky had staked everything on Cedar Vale and was penniless. Reluctantly leaving his wife and child behind, he set off on foot in the hope of earning the price of their escape.

*

While Chaikovsky shivered through the icy American winter and spring of 1877, Kravchinsky basked in the balmy Mediterranean climate of Naples, where he had arrived from Bosnia late the previous year. Posing as a consumptive, Abram Rubliov, he had at first attracted little attention among the other northern Europeans there for their health, during what was then the peak tourist season. Only the attentive care he received from a pair of fetching young Russian ladies prompted malicious rumours of a *ménage à trois* at 77 Strada Vendagliere. Far more than Italian morality was at risk, however, for one of Kravchinsky's companions was Olympia Kutuzov, the radical activist who had married Carlo Cafiero a couple of years earlier, while the other, Natalia Smetskaya, was the ex-room-mate of Kropotkin's Zurich friend Sofia Lavrova, now in flight from punitive exile to Siberia. And the work that preoccupied him was the composition of a pioneering manual of guerrilla warfare.

Meanwhile, Malatesta devoted himself to practical preparations, convinced that the time was ripe for yet another attempt at insurrection. Although socialist in name, the national government had been elected on the suffrage of barely one in fifty of the population, and was dependent for its survival on support from the very propertied classes whose inept management of the land had caused widespread economic damage. Moreover, whilst ideologically at odds with the Catholic Church, and demonised by the intemperate Pope Pius IX, both shared a common enemy that was subject to ever more ruthless government persecution: the communists and, above all, the anarchists, whose numbers the police estimated to be in the tens of thousands nationwide, with Naples second only to Florence as a centre of support.

Faced with organised resistance to its half-hearted reforms in the 1860s, the Italian authorities had cast their opponents as 'brigands': a linguistic sleight of hand that had since earned a spurious scientific legitimacy from a young doctor called Cesare Lombroso. Like Malatesta, he too had been drawn to medical studies by his social conscience, and also shared a commitment to the education of the peasantry, the redistribution of land and a strong anticlericalism. One dull December morning in 1870, however, while examining the skull of Vilhella, Italy's most famous recent outlaw, 'a vast plain under a flaming sky' had revealed itself to him: the beautifully simple, if horribly mistaken apprehension that the criminal was 'an atavistic being who reproduces in his person the ferocious instincts of primitive humanity and the inferior animals'.

His notion of the inherently 'delinquent man' struck a blow against Catholic ideas of 'sinfulness', but at the same time challenged the fundamental tenet of revolutionary socialism: that man was perfectible. And whilst offering the nascent science of anthropometry a compelling vision of a subspecies whose 'facial asymmetry, irregular teeth, large jaws, dark facial hair, [and] twisted noses' could be measured and graded with calipers, it also opened the door to political repression and racial subjugation. For what, after all, were the doomed and stunted creatures of his imagination, if not genetic detritus, upon whose eradication mankind's highest development depended?

Malatesta could not have disagreed more. Following his late master's dictum that 'Popular revolution is born from the merging of the revolt of the brigand with that of the peasant', for him, the uneducated outlaw was to be celebrated as an avenging force of nature and recruited to the political struggle. It was with this belief that he and his friends focused their efforts on the Matese massif, a mountainous region several miles inland from Naples. During the winter of 1877 and into spring, they tramped repeatedly several thousand feet up to the icy massif, still deep in snow and home to packs of wolves, to build what they believed to be a strong relationship with the natives of the region: a population proud of their warrior ancestry and indomitable independence. For this they had the assistance of Salvatore Farina to thank, a veteran of Garibaldi's campaigns whose knowledge of the local dialect opened doors, and whose enthusiastic reading of the locals' reactions to their presence further emboldened them.

Attuned by Bakunin's constant urging of caution about informants, however, Malatesta had caught the scent of betrayal and Farina's sudden disappearance confirmed his fears. The action, scheduled to begin on 5 May, would be brought forward by a month, regardless of the wintry conditions that still prevailed in the mountains. It was not enough to outwit the authorities in Naples though, who had kept the revolutionaries under surveillance since January. Police spies noted every arrival and departure from the hilltop village of San Lupo, where Malatesta made his base camp, and before long the Carabinieri took up concealed positions around the Taverna Jacobelli, where the weapons from the Puglia cache were being stockpiled, and waited for the moment to strike.

Kravchinsky and his Russian companions had good reason in April to want to strike out against authority, as news came through of the recent mass persecutions of their friends in St Petersburg. Already, though, their contribution had fallen short. The funding of the adventure by a Russian heiress, who was rumoured to have named marriage to Kropotkin as the sole price of her support, had never materialised: the reality was simply that Natalia Smetskaya had been looking for a husband, to meet the conditions of a bequest. Far worse frustration was to follow. Returning to San Lupo from a visit to Naples, the day before the expedition was due to begin, Kravchinsky was intercepted at the nearby Solopaco station by armed police. There had been a shoot-out, a *carabiniere* had been killed, and Malatesta and Cafiero, together with only ten followers and a hastily arranged mule train, had escaped up into the mountains. Kravchinsky himself, however, was going nowhere.

Detained for interrogation in Benevento under the wittily improvised pseudonym 'Nobel', Kravchinsky may have kept his spirits up by imagining his friends carrying out a glorious tour of the Matese towns and villages, a great army of righteous peasants rising in their wake. In reality, though, such an outcome had never been likely, and the seizure of a copy of Kravchinsky's own guerrilla manual at the time of his arrest may have worsened their predicament, convincing the authorities to commit greater resources to snuffing out the band's activities. Twelve thousand troops were mobilised for the hunt, intimidating the peasantry into spurning their would-be liberators, and cutting off towns to starve them out.

The best that Malatesta could hope for in the circumstances was to impress

the peasantry he encountered with the zeal and honour of the revolutionaries. Passing through the villages of Gallo and Letino, his paltry band
indemnified the custodians of the municipal archives before making a bonfire
of their tax and property records. Without Farina to translate their words
into local dialect, however, their rousing speeches fell flat, and Cafiero was
reduced to the simplest rhetorical formula: 'If you want to, do something,'
he shouted in exasperation at the warily mute peasants, 'If not, then go
fuck yourselves.' Yet the group persisted in their ideals: each morning the
leadership passed to a new member of the party, approximating anarchist
principles of dispersed authority, and even when half starved after a forty-
eight-hour march they declined to eat a solitary goat out of pity for the
herdsman. But after five long days, the game was finally up. Trapped in a
farmhouse, they watched the troops close in. The powder from their guns
drenched beyond salvation, Malatesta and his friends surrendered.

During the months of his imprisonment Kravchinsky immersed
himself in the prison community of artisans, tradesmen, ex-Garibaldean
insurrectionaries and professional intellectuals from across the country,
learning Italian and Spanish, but struggling to keep boredom at bay.
Writing to Kropotkin, he reluctantly pleaded for 'domestic and personal
news' in place of the 'political argument' that caused letters to inmates
to be confiscated, though he appears to have had no trouble acquiring
copies of Marx and other socialist writers for his edification. Kravchinsky
must have feared that it would be a long time before he would be able
to put into practice the lessons he had learned. Even the astonishing
amnesty for political prisoners announced after the death of King Victor
Emmanuel on 9 January 1878 seemed unlikely to include the Matese
insurrectionists. At last, though, after many anxious hours of uncertainty, the heavy doors of the prison creaked open and Kravchinsky,
Malatesta and six companions emerged into the cold, crisp light of the
New Year.

Penniless and ill-shod, Kravchinsky set off to walk the 400 miles up
the Italian peninsula to Switzerland. As a parting gift, his fellow prisoners
had pressed upon him an Italian dagger, and as he strode on, pondering
the injustices inflicted on the youth and peasantry of Russia, his thoughts
must have dwelt on its stiletto blade and the deep mark it might carve
on the psyche of their persecutors.

*

Chaikovsky had done his walking during the summer of Kravchinsky's
imprisonment, and could hardly have chosen a worse time to be on the

tramp. The spring of 1877 had seen heavy rains turn the roads of Kansas to a quagmire, after which prairie fires had swept the Chisholm Trail in the unseasonally harsh heat of early summer. Elsewhere in the country, though, it was not merely the weather that was proving tempestuous as the press predictions of an American commune during Rochefort's visit three years earlier seemed set to be proved right.

After three years of recession, there appeared to be no end in sight to the plight of America's workers, victims of the great industrialists' rapacity: the willingness of their ruthless companies to cut wages to below starvation levels, and then halve them again, before knocking a dime off their shareholders' profits. Worse, the causes of the economic collapse lay in the robber barons' own greed: the overexpansion of their railroads and associated enterprises which had led to desperate price-cutting wars. 'Capital has changed liberty into serfdom, and we must fight or die,' asserted a labourer in St Louis, and one slogan reverberated across demonstrations, and was whispered conspiratorially in workers' hovels: that it was 'better to die fighting than work starving'.

Setting out equipped with nothing but $10, a Russian chemistry degree and 'a dilettante knowledge of carpentry', every step of Chaikovsky's three-week, 420-mile journey in search of work took him closer to Philadelphia. It was thence that Marx had attempted to transplant the International to save it from Bakunin in 1874, and there that it had quickly expired, only to take on a new life during the Centennial Exhibition of the Industry of All Nations the previous year, 1876, as the Working Men's Party of the United States. Of more immediate relevance to Chaikovsky, however, Philadelphia was also home to the railway companies that lay at the heart of the spreading storm. No one in the eastern states needed the telephonic apparatus that Alexander Bell had demonstrated at the exhibition to warn them of the violence: the bush telegraph of railwaymen conveyed the information only too clearly.

Chaikovsky had presumably left Cedar Vale before news filtered through of the first downing of tools by railroad workers on the Baltimore & Ohio line on 16 July, and the shooting dead of a striker by militiamen that followed it. He must already have been on his way by the time he heard about the troop shipments from Philadelphia to proletarian Pittsburgh where a new civil war seemed to be brewing, this time on class lines. The strike action would soon spread to over 80,000 workers nationwide. The wonder is that Chaikovsky did not turn in his tracks, but perhaps he felt somehow complicit; after all, the support and sympathy shown towards the strikers in the small towns through which he passed –

by free labourers, farmers and tradesmen, and even their sheriffs – was the stuff of which his St Petersburg circle had dreamed.

Newly inaugurated as president of the United States, Rutherford B. Hayes, however, was a world apart from the ideal holder of that office that the Chaikovskyists had described to the peasants. The bulk of his votes had come from working men, and his opposition to any unprecedented deployment of federal troops in a labour dispute was a matter of record. But while the election's outcome had hung in the balance, with contested results in Florida and elsewhere, it was the head of the Pennsylvania Railway who had chaired the special electoral commission, and it had been while travelling in a private company rail carriage that Hayes had finally celebrated its ruling in his favour. Then and since, he and half his cabinet had sold their souls to the railroad bosses, who had all but dictated the appointment of his secretary of war.

Hayes' resistance to his multi-millionaire puppeteers quickly crumbled. Troops were redeployed from South Carolina, Virginia and even Dakota to put down the strikers. From supervising resettled 'redskins', soldiers turned their attention to suppressing socialist reds, and from guaranteeing the new-won rights of blacks to denying the basic economic rights of working men of all colours. Thousands more troops were made ready, with the navy shipping men to Washington to secure the capital against rioters. In light of the scruples shown by regular officers, however, even this was deemed insufficient: mercenaries would be required to complete the job, and they would be supplied by the Pinkerton Agency.

Back in the late 1830s, the young Scot, Allan Pinkerton, had been among the leading firebrands of the Chartist movement, when mass support for its reformist challenge to the British Establishment posed a genuine threat of revolution, and shared friends in common with Marx and Engels. Under threat of deportation to Botany Bay he had fled to the United States, and in an extreme volte-face turned his insider's understanding of subversive organisations into a thriving business. Having established a name for himself during the Civil War as a Unionist spymaster, in peacetime his company's freelance operatives had earned their spurs chasing down Jesse James, then by infiltrating the Mollie Maguires: an Irish labour organisation notorious for its murderous bully-boy tactics against strike-breakers, mining company officials and any non-Irish immigrants who threatened their ascendancy. Pinkerton's exposure and extirpation of the Mollies in the first half of the 1870s had in short order sent union membership tumbling from 300,000 to barely a sixth of that number.

Like its clients, the detective agency suffered during the recession, but

Pinkerton had 'The Larches' to pay for: his fortress-like country house built with timber shipped specially from Scotland, from whose central cupola-topped tower guards equipped with binoculars watched for approaching assassins, and beneath which a secret escape tunnel ran. Safe behind its defences, Pinkerton surveyed the conflict racking the country with a keen professional interest. 'It was everywhere, it was nowhere. It was as if the surrounding seas had swept in upon the land from every quarter, or some sudden central volcano had . . . belched forth burning rivers that coursed in every direction,' he wrote, calculating his profit. The storm, however, subsided almost as quickly as it had gathered: the posting of army detachments along all the trunk lines, under the command of General Getty, broke the strikers' will, and almost all had returned to work by 1 August. For Pinkerton, though, this was only the beginning.

Using undercover investigators, the agency produced an unequivocal judgement: 'the strikes were the result of the communistic spirit spread through the ranks of railroad employees by communistic leaders and their teachings.' Middle-class fear and outrage was stoked, while the police, militia and army attacks that had provoked mob violence were speedily forgotten and the railroad bosses exonerated. The strikers were stigmatised with that cruellest of labels: they were 'un-American' socialists unworthy of the care or protection of the law in the Land of the Free. They lacked due respect for property or the hard-won wealth of men like the steel magnate Andrew Carnegie, who had pulled himself up by the bootstraps. Newspapers drew comparisons with France's Commune and suggested 'making salutary examples of all who have been taken red-handed in riot and bloodshed, just short of the bloody vindictiveness shown by the Versaillais in 1871.' In the absence of photographs of the events, the illustrated press now commissioned draughtsmen, who had previously lampooned the robber barons as lacking even the social conscience of the European monarchs, to produce images of infernal destruction and diabolic strikers.

*

After twenty-three days journeying through an embryonic civil war, Chaikovsky's fragile nerves were close to breaking. Having seen the viciousness of American class conflict he craved a speedy return home, but events in Russia rendered any such hopes futile. Pyrrhic victories in the war against Turkey had inflated nationalistic fervour, while the persecution of Chaikovsky's old friends and colleagues became ever more harsh. Up to four years on from their arrest, hundreds were still held awaiting trial in overcrowded conditions, and treated with growing contempt by their gaolers. And any illusions Chaikovsky harboured that his absence in America might prevent charges being laid against him would have been dispelled by news of the fate of Grigori Machtet, sentenced to exile in Siberia for his role in setting up a training camp for agitators.

Toiling as a hired-hand carpenter in the shipyards of Chester, near Philadelphia, Chaikovsky clung to the wreckage of his faith as the twelve-hour shifts under beady-eyed supervision brought him close to a state of complete breakdown. 'Religion is rising,' he persisted in claiming, 'and so I shall seek it no matter where, even in the most outworn and dying Christianity.' The utopian community of Harmonists near Pittsburgh, who saw in the Great Strike 'the beginning of the harvest-time spoken of in scripture', offered one possible haven, but on the suggestion of a fellow Russian he instead joined the Shakers at Sonyea. As time and rest healed his mental wounds, however, he recoiled from their submission to Christian doctrine, feeling that they should have been searching instead for 'the presence of divinity in themselves': the only sure foundation, he now held, for successful communistic life. Frey wrote to him, warning of the risks of political engagement – 'The building of the barricades and the beating of drums will drown out your voice. The people will simply not listen to you' – but the new-found solicitude of the Cedar Vale tyrant could not draw him back.

With the arrival of a subscription by friends in Russia to cover his family's travel expenses, Chaikovsky made directly for New York City, where his wife and daughters awaited him. Next came a ship for Liverpool. France and Switzerland lay ahead. By the time he arrived there, Kravchinsky would finally have staked his unsavoury claim to fame.

7

Propaganda by Deed

Switzerland, 1876–1879

For Europe's revolutionaries, Switzerland was a second home, but in the summer of 1876 it was visited too by those whose interest lay more in mankind's past than in its future. Only twenty miles along the shore of Lac Leman from Elisée Reclus' home in Clarens, and nearer still to Geneva, a Roman city was said to have been discovered, submerged beneath the water. Tourists from as far afield as Scandinavia and Poland descended, classicists and amateur antiquarians, and entrepreneurial locals rowed them out to where the city supposedly lay, pouring oil on the water's surface to create a window through which they might peer. There was a street corner, the experts gasped, and there, on the lake's deep bed, the statue of a horse. Learned papers verified the marvel, explaining the lost city's position with half-baked reference to the latest geological theories. It was, of course, a brilliant hoax. The young radical Jogand-Pages, whose last major coup had been convincing the French navy to chase imaginary sharks off the coast of Marseilles, had once again toyed with public credulity. And once again he had escaped undetected.

A pioneering theorist of tectonic shift, Elisée Reclus would have given the archaeologists' fanciful explanations short shrift, though he was probably too busy to notice. His vast project, *Universal Geography*, conceived and planned during his long incarceration in the prison barges at Trébéron, was in its early stages; every continent and country on earth would be examined, every great river and mountain range, all with reference to the human populations that had shaped and been shaped by them: the work of a lifetime. Not content with this undertaking, Reclus had also been refining his vision of an ideal society, and how it might be achieved. He had arrived in Switzerland in 1872, half broken by imprisonment, but now he was regaining his strength.

Reports sent back to Paris by agents of the French police stationed in Switzerland, including the sharp-eyed informant Oscar Testut, trace a growing vehemence in Reclus' political engagement. Early in 1874, Reclus' 'shadows' had seen little cause for concern in this 'very learned man, [who is] hard-working, with regular habits, but very much a dreamer, bizarre, obstinate in his ideas and with a belief in the realisation of universal brotherhood'. Within weeks, however, Reclus' second wife had died in childbirth on Valentine's Day, and the balance of his interests shifted. Craving distraction from grief and less constrained by family responsibilities, he now embraced the revolutionary cause with such ardour that, by 1877, his activities among the émigré plotters were being closely observed. 'Since his arrival in Switzerland,' another agent opined, somewhat overexcitedly, 'he has not ceased to give the most active assistance to every intrigue of the revolutionary party.'

That same year, the agents noted the return to Switzerland of another geographer, Peter Kropotkin, drawn back to the Jura by a hunger for passionate political companionship. But though their shared intellectual interests might have recommended Kropotkin to Reclus as a soulmate, the pair immediately found themselves rivals in an émigré community that was traumatised by the failure of the Commune, and increasingly polarised as to the best way forward. Bakunin's death in the summer of 1876 had left the anti-authoritarian wing of the International rudderless. Now, as its members gathered at socialist congresses across Europe, new leaders and fresh ideas were called for. Questions that had previously been of mere style and emphasis became a matter of genuine substance, epitomised by the disputatious search for an appropriate name by which to distinguish the movement, and to which adherents could rally.

Reclus, whose graveside eulogy for Bakunin had positioned him as a reliable bearer of the torch, had seized the ideological initiative that spring, proudly declaring himself an 'anarchist' during the anniversary reunion for the Commune at Lausanne. His statement echoed that by Italian delegates at a recent congress in Florence, who had embraced the theory of anarchist communism: common ownership of the means of production and distribution, but with every individual entitled to a share according to his needs. But what did Reclus intend the word to identify? In the original Greek, it meant simply 'without a ruler', and both Proudhon and Bakunin had borrowed casually in this regard. Concern was expressed in the émigré community, however, about its popular currency as a term of abuse for those whose actions created dangerous disorder. During the French Revolution, after all, the dictatorial Directorate had disparaged its enemies as proponents of 'anarchism'. James Guillaume, editor of the Jura Federation's newspaper and the man who had first introduced Kropotkin to the ideas of Bakunin, complained that the term contained 'worrying ambiguities . . . without indicating any positive theory' by way of counterbalance, and that its adoption would risk 'regrettable misunderstandings'.

In assuming the title of 'anarchist', however, Reclus was intentionally embracing the negative connotations with which the term was freighted. His own experience of the Commune's defeat had left him horrified and humiliated, and he longed to shake potential supporters of the anti-authoritarian movement out of their apathy. Attracting notoriety seemed an effective means to this end. Beyond this, though, he envisaged a revolution in pedagogy to generate the necessary groundswell in popular support, whereby children would be saved from the authoritarian tendencies of bourgeois education, and instead inculcated at the earliest and most receptive age with an appreciation of the virtues of true freedom. Though Elisée Reclus habitualy used his second rather than first forename, Jean-Jacques, it was the pioneering educational theories of his namesake, Rousseau – who like Reclus had been an exile from France, and who had lived only a few miles along the lake a hundred years earlier – that underpinned his thinking.

Kropotkin, by contrast, was insistently espousing a fierce anti-intellectualism that may have reflected his own guilty conscience over the educational privileges he had enjoyed. According to his fundamentalist vision at the time, educational advancement alone was a distraction: a pure anarchist society could only be produced by a spontaneous and instinctual revolution of the peasant masses, whose current state was, he erroneously insisted, like that of a volcano ready to erupt. Even the new international campaign for a weekly day of rest and leisure – intended to provide workers with the opportunity to expand their minds and strengthen their bodies through culture, sport and contemplation – appears to have left him cold. It was a stance that put him squarely in the camp of Guillaume and his 'Jurassians' of the north, in clear opposition to the southern 'Genevans' who were looking to Reclus for leadership. Kropotkin's faith in such a revolution was, however, severely shaken in the spring of 1877 by the failure of Malatesta's peasant revolt in the Matese mountains.

At the Berne Congress of Bakuninists in 1876, Guillaume and the Jurassians had enthusiastically adopted Malatesta's and Cafiero's proposal for a policy of 'insurrectionary deeds' as the most effective means of promoting 'the principles of socialism', and a fortnight later, the French socialist Paul Brousse had even coined the striking phrase 'propaganda by deed' to express this new strategy. 'Everyone has taken sides for or against,' Brousse had once written of the Commune. 'Two months of fighting have done more than twenty-three years of propaganda', and the same logic was now simply to be applied elsewhere. But whilst there was near unanimity among socialists when it came to celebrating the glorious failure of 1871, the Matese debacle would not be treated so indulgently. Reclus' old Communard friend, Benoît Malon, even charged that 'to act in such a manner must be downright insane. No one will question how much harm these parasites of labour masquerading as internationalists have done.'

Nevertheless, the notion of 'propaganda by deed' was taking hold as a means for revolutionaries, who felt increasingly marginalised and persecuted, to advance their cause. By 1878, when events in Russia turned towards violence, Kropotkin would be caught in the bind of lauding the assassins who were targeting the tsar's government, whilst perhaps hoping that the anarchists' own call to action would elicit a response that eschewed the purely terroristic in favour of something more insurrectional.

*

The trigger for the attack that launched the wave of violence that swept over the tsarist regime had been a lapse in social etiquette. When General Trepov of the Third Section had visited the Peter and Paul fortress on a tour of inspection, Bogoliubov, one of the young radicals imprisoned there, had failed to acknowledge him with due deference. In contravention of all the unspoken rules of Russian society, which demanded that a veneer of civilised respect should be maintained between those of the better classes regardless of circumstances, Trepov had reacted by ordering Bogoliubov to be publicly beaten. Outrage among the radicals at his humiliation was extreme and widespread, but it was Vera Zasulich, amorously involved with Bogoliubov before his arrest and herself a veteran already of several years in prison and internal exile, who nominated herself his avenger.

Zasulich had waited just long enough to avoid prejudicing the Trial of the 193, at which many of the young radicals arrested in recent years were finally to be judged. Then, within a day of a verdict being delivered that dismissed the charges against the mass of defendants, she had acted. Calmly awaiting her scheduled appointment with the chief of the Third Section, upon entering his office Zasulich, her hand trembling, had discharged her pistol at point-blank range. Trepov, though wounded, survived, but a bloodier sequel was not long in coming. Moved by Zasulich's courage, Kravchinsky was perhaps also relieved about her poor aim. He might still claim the footnote in the history books for which he had so earnestly prepared, as the first assassin of a high-ranking tsarist official.

Arriving in Switzerland from Italy, carrying the stiletto dagger given to him as a parting gift by his fellow prisoners, Kravchinsky had remained there for only a few weeks before setting off back to Russia, where a St Petersburg jury had just acquitted Zasulich, despite overwhelming evidence against her. Encouraged by the popularity of the verdict, on 4 August Kravchinsky approached General Mezentsev, the chief of police, as he was walking in a St Petersburg park, drew the stiletto from a rolled newspaper, and stabbed him dead. A carriage pulled by Dr Veimar's champion black trotter, Varvar, which had already given sterling service during Kropotkin's escape from prison, allowed the assassin and his accomplice to make a clean getaway. The shocking boldness of the attack was not lost on the public, nor the extent of the conspiratorial networks that must be active in St Petersburg for it to have been possible.

'A Death for a Death,' proclaimed the pamphlet already rolling off the secret presses, and in his memoir, published only a few years after the event, Kravchinsky would write that the assassination had ushered in the era of the ravening, moral superman. 'The terrorist is noble, irresistibly fascinating, for he combines in himself the two sublimates of human grandeur: the martyr and the hero. From the day he swears in the depths of his heart to free the people and the country, he knows he is consecrated to death . . . And already he sees that enemy falter, become confused, cling desperately to the wildest means, which can only hasten his end.'

As brutal gestures of Slavic resolve, the attacks provoked widespread exultation among the exile community in Switzerland, and their perpetrators were lionised. When Zasulich returned to Geneva, smuggled out by Klements after avoiding rearrest for several weeks by means of concealment in an apartment over Dr Veimar's orthopaedic clinic in St Petersburg, Henri Rochefort himself was on hand to offer assistance. Having fed and housed her, however, the French anarchists revealed an ulterior motive: arrangements were already under way for her to travel to Paris, where it was planned that her celebrity status would draw a crowd of several thousand well-wishers, who might then be manipulated into a confrontation with the police.

The anarchists of western Europe longed to gild their own abortive endeavours through association with their accomplished Russian colleagues, but Zasulich was reluctant to be drawn into their game. Remaining in Switzerland, she followed Klements' example, filling her days with long mountain walks; the arrival of news of a friend's execution or other sorrow from the motherland meant a day on paths not listed in the Baedeker guide, with only the occasional goatherd or lowing, bell-tolling cow for company. Before long, though, the mood would be temporarily lightened by Kravchinsky's reappearance, still wearing the Napoleonic beard and grand style of the fictitious Georgian Prince Vladimir Ivanovich Jandierov that he had been using as his disguise in St Petersburg, ever since the assassination of Mezentsev. Ignoring the risk of arrest, Kravchinsky had been determined to stay in hiding in Russia. It had taken trickery on the part of his colleagues to persuade him that he would be of greater use to them abroad, where his wife had given birth to a premature baby who had since died.

'Just sometimes, when reminiscing, he philosophises about love with us and teaches Vera and me the wise rules of coquetterie, by which you can make someone fall helplessly in love with you,' wrote the other woman with whom Kravchinsky shared the mountain chalet. Yet, even the mountains could not distract Vera Zasulich from the true path for long, and within a couple of years of her arrival in Switzerland she would be immersed in the discussions that led to the foundation of the first Russian group with an explicitly Marxist agenda, the Emancipation of Labour; Kravchinsky, though more circumspect about such affiliations, continued to share her sympathies. But the fact that members of the Russian movement had distinct priorities of their own was no reason for the anarchists in the West to despair: not when the dramatic impact of the new Russian tactics was being felt too by the rulers of their own countries.

Perhaps inspired by the violent Russian spring and summer of 1878, a spate of assassination attempts closer to home now supplied the multinational exiles gathered in Switzerland with fresh inspiration. At the beginning of May, a young tinsmith with anarchist connections, Emil Hoedel, fired a pistol somewhat haphazardly at Kaiser Wilhelm as his carriage travelled along Unter den Linden in Berlin. Hoedel's motivation appears to have been a thirst for personal fame as much as idealism, but an apartment overlooking the same grand boulevard had been rented by Dr Karl Nobiling, an intellectual loner with a background in the minor German gentry and a more coherent sense of purpose: the decapitation of the social hierarchy as a prelude to revolution. Only a month after

Hoedel's attack, Nobiling aimed a shotgun at the kaiser's head and discharged both barrels, leaving Wilhelm clinging to life, his face and arms lacerated by twenty-eight pieces of lead. Within the same year, Spain and Italy experienced failed attempts on their new young kings: Alfonso XII and Umberto I. Both were acts of class war, and in the latter case, the actions of the would-be assassin, Giovanni Passannante, demonstrated an almost ritualistic fervour: approaching the king's open carriage as it passed through Naples, he had lunged at him with a dagger drawn from the folds of a flag on which were the words 'Long Live the International Republic'.

Faced with such acts, even Switzerland had to reconsider its tolerance of revolutionaries. In the aftermath of the revolutions of 1848, Prussia had mobilised its troops on the Swiss border, insisting that the Swiss government render up those fugitives to whom it had granted political asylum. Germany's methods of persuasion in 1878 were subtler, though with the threat of harsher measures implicit, up to and including military action against its small neighbour. Switzerland needed a sacrificial victim. When Paul Brousse rashly used the December edition of his newspaper *L'Avant-Garde* to argue that it was the overly scrupulous methods employed by Nobiling and Passannante that had caused them to fail, when they should simply have thrown bombs at their targets without any care for the accompanying courtiers, the Swiss authorities were quick to act. His imprisonment and, latterly, expulsion were offered up to propitiate their angry neighbours.

In Germany itself, the crackdown was severe. The kaiser had survived the attack, but while rumours of his death were still circulating Chancellor Bismarck seized the national emergency he had long sought as a pretext for a draconian crackdown on Germany's socialists. Martial law was declared, and the city garrisoned, with the Tempelhof field converted to an army encampment. Censorship was introduced, with upwards of 1,000 books and periodicals outlawed; 1,500 suspects were arrested and others forced to flee abroad. Laws were speedily passed to suppress the burgeoning Social Democratic Party, which already boasted five million members. Stripped of parliamentary immunity, Johann Most, one of its most vociferous members, was given twenty-four hours to leave the country, prompting his ignominious rush to Hamburg, and thence to London.

*

In comparison to the term 'anarchist', the phrase 'propaganda by deed' may initially have struck those who heard it as somewhat functional, but

the events of 1878 had quickly lent it the character of a sinister euphem-
ism. The blithe heroism it seemed to imply now began to appear more
like a violent conspiracy to commit the terrorist outrages with which
anarchism would soon become all but synonymous in the public mind.
From exile, Johann Most would be at the forefront of those calling for
vengeance against the oppressive powers of state and capital.

Although four years younger than Kropotkin, Most too was more
closely associated with a slightly earlier radical generation than many of
Bakunin's other political heirs. Moreover, having been won over to
Marxism during a visit to a workers' festival in La Chaux-de-Fonds in
1874, he was perhaps still best known at this time as a populariser of
Marx's philosophy. His earlier experiences, however, suggest a man for
whom the anti-authoritarian International would always have offered a
more natural home, and reveal the psychological seeds of his violent
passion.

'Evils lurks deep in the breast of the child, but the whip drives it out,'
Most's father would reassure his young son after administering frequent
and ferocious beatings. Both the psychological and the physical scars of
his mistreatment were enduring. Crude surgery to excise an abscess on
the boy's cheek and jaw – itself the result of a punitive spell spent sleeping
in a freezing storeroom – left half his face grotesquely twisted, and Most
soon discovered in the injustices of society an insistent echo of those
who had blighted his own childhood. 'I wanted neither to lead "the good
life",' wrote Most of his young self, 'nor to earn a livelihood in the usual
sense. I had to do what I did because in my brain an obsession pounded:
The Revolution must happen!'

Thwarted in his ambition to be an actor by his facial disfigurement,
Most grew a thick beard and transferred his aptitude for melodrama on
to the political stage. As a prominent socialist in Vienna in the late 1860s,
his rabble-rousing address to a mass demonstration on the eve of a general
strike had incurred a sensational charge of high treason. 'If you judge
such constructive criminality and such justifiable malefaction and such
reasonable transgression wrong, then punish me,' Most declaimed to the
courtroom: the gavel banged out a sentence of five years, but he was
soon amnestied and deported. There followed a series of picaresque
adventures as he wrong-footed the Prussian police time and again, his
preaching of class war finally winning him election to the Reichstag and,
with it, immunity from prosecution. It was a privilege he tested to the
full during the war against France in 1870 and its aftermath, urging his
supporters to replace the bunting that festooned the industrial town of

Chemnitz in celebration of the Prussian victory at Sedan with tax receipts, and openly acclaiming the Commune. Bringing the same instinct for confrontation to the congresses of 1876 and 1877 in Switzerland, he was soon recognised as one of the most vociferous proponents of propaganda by deed: a linchpin, the police services of Europe mistakenly thought, of a tightly coordinated international conspiracy.

There was certainly a pattern of connections for suspicious eyes to discover, if they so chose. Kravchinsky's period of residence in Naples seemed to connect the murder of Mezentsev and the attack on Umberto I; Kropotkin's influence during his travels to Spain linked the attempt on the life of Alfonso XII to Switzerland; Rochefort, though the outsider in Swiss circles, provided a direct link to the Commune; whilst Most was fingered as the link to Nobiling's attack on the kaiser. Then, sometime between the end of 1878 and beginning of 1879, that other great impresario of anarchism, Errico Malatesta, reappeared in the Jura. Having fled to the Levant following his release from gaol in Italy, his expressions of solidarity with opponents of western colonialism whom he had befriended there, appeared to extend the scope of the imagined conspiracy far to the east.

Malatesta's first port of call on his travels had been Alexandria, where an anarchist group was already active by 1877, but he was impressed no less by the growing strength and dynamism of the Egyptian nationalist movement. Pillaged by Europe since time immemorial, the parlous state of Egypt's economy had become evident in 1875, when the Khedive's bankruptcy had forced him to sell his shares in the Suez Canal – the country's most precious strategic resource – to the British government of Disraeli, for the paltry sum of £4 million. In 1879 the European Commission would officially declare Egypt insolvent, but before then mutinous rumblings in the army had already signalled the depths of a problem that went beyond mere finance, to the very heart of Egyptian identity.

It was to the Italy of the early days of Garibaldi's Risorgimento that the new generation of Egyptian leaders turned in search of a model for their own endeavours. And although derelict as a revolutionary force in Europe, Freemasonry also provided for Egyptians with a crucible for political debate and organisation: the radical reformist Jamal al-Din al-Afghani, Latif Bey Salim (who would lead the army rebels in February 1879) and even the Khedive's heir apparent, Tawfiq, were all members of one secret lodge. Whether for his anarchist evangelising or his contacts with the ideologues of nationalism, the Egyptian authorities were sufficiently alarmed by

Malatesta's presence – and, in particular, his call for a demonstration outside the Italian consular building in support of the failed assassin Passannante – to order his immediate arrest and then bundle him aboard a French ship bound for Beirut. From there, Syria was his first choice of destination, then Turkey and finally his native Italy, but repeated refusals to allow him ashore forced his weary return to Geneva via Marseilles.

Malatesta's arrival could not have been less welcome to the Swiss Sûreté, which was clamping down on any of its guests who incited violence abroad. But it wasn't only the Establishment to whom he proved a headache. Kropotkin too may have been momentarily discomforted by the addition of a new element to the complex expatriate mix, just at the moment when external circumstances promised to effect a conciliation between himself and Reclus.

*

With the excuse of pressing deadlines for the annual delivery of the latest volume of his *Universal Geography*, Reclus was able to remain aloof from much of the sectarian wrangling that marred the late 1870s. He could instead adjust his own position in response to events, conveniently free from any immediate obligation to publicly account for himself. A saga-cious presence in the wings, he would perfect this persona over the rest of his long life. At some point during 1877, for example, the firebrand Most left his one and only meeting with the geographer convinced that 'Elisée Reclus I count as one of the greatest inspirers since I became an anarchist.' Yet, at the time, Reclus was adamant in opposing the violent action that Most had begun to espouse. Likewise, in the spring of 1878, Kravchinsky had been only too pleased to serve as a messenger, carrying important papers from James Guillaume to Reclus, despite knowing full well their recipient's views concerning attacks of the kind he was plan-ning against Mezentsev.

It seemed, for a while, that only Kropotkin would prove immune to Reclus' wisdom and charm. Yet such were the pressures bearing down on the nascent anarchist movement by late 1878 that even when Reclus published a stinging rebuke to Kropotkin concerning the Russian's pref-erence for dramatic, egotistical gestures over a gradualist, altruistic policy founded on education – expressed in the deeply humane article 'The Future of Our Children' – the slight was soon forgiven lest it jeopardise the pursuit of their common interests.

On one issue, above all, the geographers' rigorous grounding in empirical method brought Kropotkin and Reclus together in shared indignation: the conceited claims made by Marx and Engels to be the standard-bearers of 'scientific socialism', even while they slurred their rivals' ideas as empty utopianism. In a letter to Guillaume, Kropotkin delivered his verdict on Marx's great work with a succinct sneer: '*Kapital*', he wrote, 'is a marvellous revolutionary pamphlet but its scientific significance is nil.' Marx's reliance on the universal dialectical pattern that Hegel had conceived for the purpose of explaining the historical process in metaphysical terms, served only 'to repeat what the utopian socialists had said so well before him'. It was, Kropotkin asserted, not the anarchists who were guilty of wishful thinking, but those who claimed that the contradictions of bourgeois society would inevitably produce socialism: a dangerously fatalistic notion that appealed to the proletariat even as it sapped their will to strive for the revolution. 'The political authority of the state dies out,' Engels wrote. 'Man, at last the master of his own form of social organisation, becomes at the same time the lord over Nature, his own master': it seemed to Kropotkin a hateful doctrine of passivity, premised on a pseudo-religious promise of deliverance.

What was worse, the theories of Darwin that were so precious to adherents of the positivist tradition were all too readily abused by followers of Marx: forced to yield up analogies from nature to support the idea that out of class conflict, society would evolve into a perfect form. From Europe to America, the bones that were being dug out of the earth were making Darwinian ideas of evolution a hot topic. The year following the Universal Socialist Congress at Ghent in April 1877, an entire herd of iguanodons would be discovered by miners at the nearby St Barbara colliery at Bernissart. They were a time capsule from the Middle Cretaceous period, thirty or forty specimens in all, suspended in a sink-hole of Wealdian clay, together with the smaller fauna of 125 million years past: unprecedented proof, if any further was needed, of Darwin's theories.

The most obvious challenge to 'evolutionary socialism' came from the political right. In 1878, a Bismarckian nationalist called Ernst Haeckel, who in his professional capacity as a biologist was preoccupied with the deterioration of the Teutonic race, found himself wondering 'what in the world the doctrine of descent has got to do with socialism: the two theories are as compatible as fire and water'. Socialism 'demands equal rights, equal duties, equal possessions, equal enjoyments for every citizen alike', while evolutionary theory argues 'in exact opposition to this, that the realisation of the demand is a pure impossibility . . . [since] neither rights nor duties, neither possessions nor enjoyments have been equal for all alike nor ever can be.' The only answer Marx could offer was a metaphysical faith in the dialectic mechanism, whereby contradictions latent in the most recent, capitalist manifestation of that community would see to it that matters did eventually change.

Some years would pass before Kropotkin's thoughts on the subject settled into a coherent form, but as early as the mid-1860s he had begun to formulate a hypothesis informed by personal observations in Siberia of how the cooperative behaviour of animals appeared to be a key factor in a species' success. Meanwhile Reclus, doubtless inspired by his recent friendship with Kropotkin, presented in 1880 his own political observations on the subject in the pamphlet *Evolution and Revolution*. 'Will not the evolution which is taking place in the minds of the workers', Reclus wrote, 'necessarily bring about a revolution; unless, indeed, the defenders of privilege yield with a good grace to the pressure from below?' That same evolutionary process in popular consciousness would, if receptive young minds were properly tutored, ensure too that justice and equality prevailed in the new society that would follow.

While some sought in evolutionary theory a scientific justification for their dreams of human perfectibility, however, others recognised that its eruption into the political and social realm risked terrible consequences. Even before Cesare Lombroso had presented his first ideas on criminal anthropometry or Francis Galton coined the notion of eugenics, at either end of the 1870s, such concerns had permeated the fantastical fiction of two of France's and England's most popular novelists. In *The Coming Race*, published in 1871, Edward Bulwer-Lytton had astutely identified the fundamental tensions latent within 'scientific' socialism. The utopian world inhabited by his perfect beings, the Vril-ya, was exposed as something closer to a dystopia when its price was fully accounted: the slower and more brutish breed of *Untermenschen* left languishing in perfection's wake, and the suppression of individualism, such that 'a thousand of the best and most philosophical of human beings . . . would either die of ennui, or attempt some revolution.' Although written in a somewhat allegorical style, Jules Verne's *The Begum's Millions* of 1878 addressed similar questions within a more contemporary frame.

Reworked by an initially reluctant Verne from a first draft by none other than Paschal Grousset, the ex-foreign minister of the Commune and Rochefort's fellow escapee from New Caledonia, it inevitably struck a chord with the anarchists. Its two protagonists, the megalomanic

Professor Schultze and Dr Sarrasin, a specialist in the new field of hygiene, found neighbouring colonies in the American Midwest, that fabulous land of 'infinite possibilities' and false promises. In Frankville, Sarrasin's concern is the holistic health of the community, whilst the Stahlstadt of Schultze, author of *Why are all Frenchmen Stricken in Different Degrees with Hereditary Degeneration?*, is a militaristic city whose super-gun menaces its neighbour. 'Germany can break up by too much force and concentration, France can quietly reconstitute itself by more freedom,' was how its publisher, Herzel, explained the central theme, and neither Kropotkin nor Reclus would have disagreed.

The inexorable rise of Bismarck's mighty Germany seemed to them, as it had to Bakunin, strangely of a kind with the bullying and overbearing brand of Teutonic socialism propounded by Marx and Engels. Threats such as that made at the Ghent Congress by Wilhelm Liebknecht, leader of the Social Democrats and friend of Engels, against a leading anarchist compatriot then resident in Switzerland – that 'If you dare to come to Germany to attack our organisation we will use every means to annihilate you' – only compounded the impression. For all the hatred and distrust that existed between Bismarck and Marx, the projects of both were centralising and dogmatic, and the anarchists' hope was that, as their fortunes had risen together, so too they would fall, co-dependent to the end.

*

In 1879, staying at Reclus' house in Clarens, Kropotkin and his host collaborated closely, and together founded a newspaper, *Le Révolté*. It was a meeting of minds that proved productive on all fronts, the Russian offering the benefit of his specialist knowledge of Siberia as the Frenchman composed the sixth volume of his *Universal Geography*, while calm study and conversation allowed Kropotkin to work out 'the foundations of all that I wrote later on'. Their discussions sparkled, the advantage flowing without rancour from one to the other, generating fresh perspectives on tired subjects. Told that the two ideals of anarchism and communism howled in pain at being paired, Cafiero had shortly before observed that 'these two terms, being synonyms of liberty and equality, are the two necessary and indivisible terms of the revolution'. Not the least achievement of Reclus and Kropotkin at this time was to trace a path towards their reconciliation.

Government would be abolished, in favour of a free federation of producers and consumers; property would be distributed by need rather than the contribution of labour; and for the moment, rather than demanding improved wages and working conditions, trade unions should militate for the abolition of the wage system altogether. If Malatesta begrudged Kropotkin and Reclus their ascendancy as the anarchists' ideological guides, by the time he left Switzerland in the summer of 1879 – rather than accept a fine and imprisonment after his arrest near Lugano on the night of 12 June – he had to acknowledge how effective they had been in focusing minds.

In the course of the give and take of argument, it appears that a transformation also occurred in Reclus' stance towards the legitimacy of violence as a tactic, as he engaged with the hard moral choices implicit in a commitment to revolution. Having conceded some months earlier that if existing society was governed by force, the anarchists were justified in using force in response, in December 1878 he went further, writing in pained terms to a female correspondent that 'in order to give birth to the new society of peace, joy and love, it is necessary that young people not be afraid to die'. Galvanised, perhaps, by the personal resolve that Kropotkin had displayed in November when he publicly congratulated the assassins of the governor of Kharkov, Kropotkin's own cousin Dmitri, Reclus was finally released from the state of frozen circumspection in which his cruel experience of the Commune had left him. The painful duty of the conscientious man to embrace transgression was confronted head-on. 'In society today you cannot be considered as an honest man by everybody. Either you are a robber, assassin and firebrand with the oppressors, the happy and pot-bellied, or you are a robber, an assassin and a firebrand with the oppressed, the exploited, the suffering and the underfed. It is up to you, you indecisive and frightened man, to choose.'

The implications of that choice, however, were becoming increasingly stark. From the quiet shores of Lake Geneva, Reclus and Kropotkin would have heard the distant echo of explosions up in the mountains, as engineers blasted a route for railways or roads. Until recently, the use of dynamite had been a hazardous business. Nobel's own brother had died for a moment's carelessness, and at the factory at Ardeer in Scotland where dynamite was produced, the supervisor balanced on a one-legged stool, lest a moment of sleepy inattention lead to disaster. As geographers, Reclus and Kropotkin could have expatiated confidently on the kieselguhr used to stabilise the dynamite: a porous, friable clay composed of tiny, fossilised crustacea. It is doubtful, however, that they yet grasped quite so well the implications for 'propaganda by deed' of Nobel's recent innovation, gelignite. Stable, powerful and portable, it could be slipped all too easily into portmanteaux or else concealed beneath coats.

8

Spies and Tsaricides

Russia, 1878–1880

There was nothing in Peter Rachkovsky's career before 1879 to augur his destiny as the greatest spymaster of his age, who would inherit the mantle of Colonel Stieber. Born in the Ukraine, the son of a humble postmaster and a nobleman's daughter, both Polish Catholics, Rachkovsky's lack of a family fortune obliged him to make his own way in life, and aged sixteen, in 1869, he had joined the Civil Service. Beginning as clerk in the Odessa mayor's office, he was shunted through various minor secretarial posts in provincial administrations until, by 1875, he had finally clawed his way up to secretary in the office for peasant affairs. Along the way, however, lay the wreck of his failed marriage to Ksenia Sherle, from whom Rachkovsky had separated when the tedium of the life that he could offer had driven her to take lovers. An energetic man with higher expectations than his wife had appreciated, he responded by embarking on a course of legal studies that quickly led to a position as a prosecutor in the ministry of justice, and a posting to the frozen northern extremes of Archangel.

Quite what happened next, or rather why it happened, is hard to divine. Having shown no previous sign of the kind of angst that drove so many of his contemporaries into anti-tsarist activity, Rachkovsky perversely chose the very moment when he had finally gained a professional foothold to reveal a liberal streak. Dismissed on 23 September 1878, under pressure from hard-line local reactionaries enraged by his lenient attitude to the exiles, after only eighteen months his new career lay in tatters. But whilst his detractors must have sneered at the grand farewell arranged for him by the exiles, Rachkovsky already understood how a parting gift of letters from those very radicals, recommending him to the political dissidents in St Petersburg, could be turned to greater profit than any number of degrees or Civil Service commendations.

Effortlessly sliding into the capital's shady demi-monde, between
middle-class legitimacy and the revolutionary underworld, Rachkovsky
grew ever more slippery, and his intentions increasingly opaque. For where
did his loyalties lie when, during that winter, he worked as a tutor in the
household of Major General Kakhanov of the Third Section or, the
following April, secured the editorship of the newspaper *The Russian Jew?*
Were his purposes sincere, or was he insinuating himself into the trust
of either the police or the revolutionaries, on behalf of the other, with
mischief in mind? 'Tall, brown hair, big black moustache: dense and
drooping; long and fat nose, black eyes, pale face . . . Wears a grey over-
coat, a hard black hat; walks with a cane or umbrella. Intellectual face,'
stated the description of him handed out to police surveillance agents.
That he was being watched might simply have been a ruse to keep his
recruitment secret from all but those in the Third Section with the highest
clearance.

Short of the paunch and neat pointed beard he subsequently acquired,
the arch-intriguer of later years is already recognisable, of whom it would
be said that 'his slightly too ingratiating manner and his suave way of
speaking – made one think of a great feline carefully concealing its claws.'
For the moment, though, Rachkovsky was not yet the capricious master
but still the plaything of others, whose dangerous games would come
close to destroying him. Hauled in for interrogation by the Third Section
in the spring of 1879, over his association with a certain Semionovsky
who was suspected of concealing the assassin Kravchinsky, Rachkovsky
was obliged to declare his true allegiance once and for all. He would, he
confirmed, render the police whatever services they asked of him; his
offer was gratefully accepted, and he was directed to infiltrate the People's
Will without delay.

In only a few months, concurrent with Rachkovsky establishing himself
in St Petersburg, the People's Will organisation, or Narodnaya Volya,
had come to dominate the radical landscape in Russia, although its
numbers remained intentionally small. With its immediate roots in
the uncompromising 'Troglodyte' or 'Death and Freedom' faction of the
populist movement, most of its prime movers were familiar names from
the Chaikovsky Circle: men and women who had remained in Russia
during the worst of the persecution, and become radicalised by the
punishments inflicted on their comrades. For Lev Tikhomirov, the traumatic memory of Bogoliubov's vicious beating was compounded by the
knowledge that humiliation had since sent the poor man mad, while

others had witnessed naïve students, detained without charge while 'going to the people', locked in cages and then hung over the latrines until they passed out from the fumes. The toll of political prisoners who had died from neglect or mistreatment already approached seventy.

Among the populists who had risen rapidly through the depleted ranks of their local cells, many had come to recognise that a new level of ruthlessness and professionalism was required if anything resembling social justice was to be secured. Zhelyabov was one such, the son of serfs, who as a child had witnessed his aunt dragged away by the bailiff to be raped by the local landowner, and had enrolled in the radical movement following one of his frequent and groundless arrests. Frustrated by the failure of past efforts to force concessions from the tsar, Zhelyabov already concluded that 'History moves too slowly. It needs a push. Otherwise the whole nation will be rotten and gone to seed before the liberals get anything done.' And then there was the scientist Kibalchich, who as a student of physiology under Elie Cyon had rioted in 1874 against his professor's reactionary influence in the university, and for the crime of lending a prohibited book to a peasant had subsequently spent three years in prison, pending the pronouncement of his two-month sentence. Now a fully fledged militant, his fascination with rocket design was put on ice, while he devoted himself to the construction and testing of terrorist bombs in his home laboratory.

The aspiration that the rest of society might join the radicals in demanding change had reached its high watermark at the beginning of 1878, when the Trial of the 193 ended in acquittal for a large majority of the defendants, many of whom had been held for several years. The impudent Myshkin, who had railed in court against 'a farce . . . worse than a farce . . . worse than a brothel where girls sell their bodies to earn a living', received a sentence, though, of ten years' hard labour. In St Petersburg a heady atmosphere engulfed those who had been freed: 'People thronged their apartments from morning to night. It was an interrupted revolutionary club, where ninety to a hundred visitors attended in a day; friends brought with them strangers who wished to shake hands with those whom they had looked upon as buried alive.' Yet almost immediately the steel door of repression had again swung shut: extrajudicial measures were introduced to excise any leniency from the system, and a number of those acquitted were nevertheless sent into internal exile on the tsar's prerogative; jury trials were abandoned, with hearings moved from civil to military courts, and the investigative procedures of the Third Section sharpened.

The freelance, uncoordinated nature of a series of attacks in spring 1879 only invited further repression. Kropotkin's cousin, Dmitri, had been the first victim, shot in February; two months later, on 2 April, it was Tsar Alexander II himself who was in the firing line. Ambushed while walking in the grounds of the Winter Palace, the tsar frantically dodged five bullets and was saved only by the presence of mind of a loyal peasant who nudged the assassin's elbow. The hanging that followed was among fifteen executions for politically motivated crimes that year, including one as punishment for purely propagandist activities. Gone were the traditional Russian scruples about the sanctity of human life, which made it so difficult to recruit to the post of public executioner that one man covered all the European provinces. Now the job was often left to amateurs, fortified with vodka to the point of oblivion, and grotesquely clumsy: ill-tied nooses sent condemned men sprawling to the ground, only for them to be strung up again until the task was accomplished.

Observing the huddles of political prisoners waiting under guard to be led out of the city on the first stage of their long march to Siberia, even radicals previously inhibited about the use of violence were forced to reassess their position. The security of the movement had always warranted extreme sanctions against traitors: the euphemistic 'withdrawal from circulation'. The appearance in court of one informant from Kiev, who had been been repeatedly stabbed and left for dead, his face dissolved by the application of lime, offered an even more powerful warning than the note left with him: 'This is what happens to spies.' Logic dictated that such defensive measures should be applied equally to those who controlled the informants, but implied terrible ramifications. 'If you decide to kill a spy, why shouldn't you punish the policeman who encourages his base profession and who profits from his information by making more arrests?' was how Kravchinsky presented the argument, 'or even the chief of police who directs the whole thing? Finally and inevitably comes the tsar himself, whose power spurred the whole gang into action.'

It was this question that the leaders of the radical movement were summoned to debate in the forest of Voronezh in June 1879. Determined to stage a coup against any in the movement who resisted their terroristic agenda, the 'Troglodytes' had convened for a preliminary meeting, to plan strategy, in the nearby spa town of Lipetsk, in whose mineral waters no fish could survive. Whilst grimacing aristocrats downed their restorative draughts, Zhelyabov plotted with his extremist colleagues to administer a bitter and deadly medicine of his own. In readiness for the life ahead, he had already separated from his wife and young family to avoid their being persecuted for his future deeds, while his earlier fascination with the explosive charges used by the fishing fleet in Kiev to bring stunned shoals floating to the surface, hinted at what he had in mind.

By the time the members of the more moderate Land and Liberty faction of populists arrived at the designated clearing in the Voronezh forest, the trap was truly set. When the moderate Georgi Plekhanov leaned nonchalantly back on a tree to mockingly read out an article arguing the legitimacy of terrorism, he expected most of those present to endorse his abhorrence of such sentiments. Their silence left him nonplussed: 'In that case, gentlemen, I have nothing more to say,' was all he could muster. His colleagues were ready to cast aside the fundamental principle of non-violence which had guided the movement ever since the end of Nechaev's short and brutal career nine years earlier, although many still cavilled at Tikhomirov's argument for the formation of an organisational elite to coordinate a new strategy that would punch through to political power.

'It was my belief', one of the young women present would recollect, 'that the revolutionary idea could be a life-giving force only when it was the antithesis of all coercion – state, social and even personal coercion, tsarist and Jacobin alike. Of course it was possible for a narrow group of ambitious men to replace one form of coercion by another. But neither the people nor educated society would follow them consciously, and only a conscious movement can impart new principles to public life.' The fear was that they might recreate just those circumstances that had seen the decay of the French Revolution into dictatorship.

For a hard core, however, including Kibalchich and Vera Figner, Tikhomirov's recommendations were compelling. Some months would pass before the schism in the Russian radical movement would crystallise, but the Voronezh conference marked the fateful moment when hope gave way to anger. That their extremist policy had been necessitated precisely by their failure to inspire the 'people' to rise up was conveniently overlooked as they named their splinter organisation the People's Will.

In the more innocent age that was now drawing to a close, the radicals had referred to the feared agents of the Third Section, whose unofficial uniform made them quite easily identifiable, as 'the pea green overcoats'. Now, though, as the struggle shifted into the world of conspiracy, both sides were developing a more sophisticated approach to concealment and infiltration. The populist heirs of the Chaikovsky Circle had already scored a remarkable intelligence coup by placing a mole at the very heart of the tsarist security service. It had taken Nicholas Kletochnikov, a young graduate, considerable time and tenacity to acquire his post as confidential clerk to the investigation department of the Third Section: first he had insinuated himself into the maternal affection of his reactionary landlady, next convinced her that he shared her political views; only then had she felt inspired to recommend him for recruitment. Although Peter Rachkovsky did not yet know it, the police headquarters were severely compromised and a single misplaced word could blow his cover.

Rachkovsky's successes as a police spy had been swift and significant. Once the recommendations of the Archangel radicals had paved his way to acceptance by the People's Will, he had promptly betrayed the very friend about whom the police had first interrogated him, and soon after had exposed the previously unsuspected Tikhomirov as the pseudonymous 'Tigrich', whose identification was a Third Section priority. But as each new arrest narrowed the field of possible traitors in The People's Will, his associates were becoming suspicious. In the end, Rachkovsky's own incaution gave the game away.

To gain credibility in his undercover role, Rachkovsky had acted as a decoy on behalf of the radicals, donning a wanted-man's coat to distract the police while the real subject of their surveillance caught a train for Odessa using a forged passport. Unable to resist sharing his amusement at the ruse with his Third Section colleagues, Rachkovsky had chosen the People's Will plant Kletochnikov as his confidant; as Kletochnikov had by this time been awarded the Order of St Stanislas, perhaps Rachkovsky felt his loyalty was beyond question. The next edition of the *Narodnaya volya* newspaper exposed Rachkovsky's treachery. Spirited away to Vilnius under police protection, he was lucky to escape with his life. Never again would he take anyone at face value.

Temporarily, Kletochnikov's colleagues in the People's Will had the advantage, armed with a steady flow of privileged information about their opponents' plans and state of knowledge, and when necessary with invaluable tip-offs.

*

The 13,000 miles of railway track that had been laid in the preceding decade, financed for the tsar by loans from Western capitalists, must have appeared a terrible affront to the People's Will, whose members

prided themselves on standing in the vanguard of science and enlightenment. A piece of autocratic sleight of hand, it stole their progressive
thunder, dressing cold-hearted reaction in the stuff of forward-looking
optimism. For despite representing a practical statement of control and
confidence, the expanding railway network was experienced by the tsar's
subjects as a monumental act of generosity that embraced them all. By
striking the tyrant down as he raced along these sleek new tracks, using
state-of-the art explosives, the People's Will could symbolically reclaim
their rightful place as heirs to the future, while laying bare the tsar's
hubris and vulnerability. In expectation of the tsar's return from the imperial family's winter vacation at the Black Sea resort of Yalta, the decision
was taken to mine the railway network simultaneously at three points,
hundreds of miles apart, covering the most likely permutations in the
tsar's itinerary.

Targeting the first possible route, Vera Figner was dispatched to employ
her female wiles to assist one of the radicals in securing a job with the
railway company near Odessa. The sob story she told concerned a man-
servant in St Petersburg who was being sent south in search of fresh air
for his consumptive wife. It was an approach fraught with risks, and Figner
barely escaped an interview with her first mark, Baron Ungern-Sternberg,
with her honour intact; as the governor of the region, the Baltic aristocrat had assumed that her approach implied recognition of his seigneurial
rights. Dusting herself off, Figner next aimed lower, enthralling the local
railway master with the sleek velvet and swaying peacock plumes of her
outfit. Frolenko, the movement's master of disguise, fresh from springing
three revolutionaries from prison by posing as their gaoler, was chosen to
take the part of the railway guard and plant the bombs.

Leading the second team, Zhelyabov posed as an industrialist looking
to set up a tannery in Alexandrovsk, near the railway boom town of
Kharkov. His target was a section of track on the Simferopol–St Petersburg
line, the tsar's most direct route home, along which police patrols passed
every three or four hours. Nerves of steel and a high level of concentration were required, and the mere presence of the zealous, charismatic
Zhelyabov helped maintain the group's morale: 'He was a man who
compelled attention at first glance,' wrote one of his colleagues; 'he spoke
quietly, in a low full bass, with determination and conviction, on the necessity of terror.' Women succumbed readily to his charms, but in the heroine
of the third team, Sofia Perovskaya, he met his match: while she tamed
his philandering ways, he won her over from a distrust of men, rooted in
hatred for her tyrannical father.

The third route seemed the least likely, as it would require the tsar to divert his journey to Moscow, but Perovskaya and her comrades were not deterred. From the small house they had purchased near the railway line, only a couple of miles out from the Moscow terminus, a fifty-yard-tunnel had to be dug before the middle of November. The men worked in shifts, arriving before daybreak and continuing until the early hours. For weeks on end they edged forward: the bookish Morozov, wilting under the physical effort; the conceited Grigori Goldenburg, at whose hand Dmitri Kropotkin had died, and who insisted on being at the fore-front of any action; and Lev Hartmann, one of those freed from prison by Frolenko and since co-opted to the executive committee of the People's Will. Four others helped too, taking their turn at digging. They advanced a scant four yards each day, inserting props that sagged under the weight of the earth overhead and continually bailing out the water that seeped in, threatening to flood the tunnel. The wet sandy soil they excavated while wedged into the tunnel on their hands and knees, with scarcely room to wield their tools, was scattered as discreetly as possible over the yard outside. Piles of it filled the rooms of the house and its outbuild-ings, which smelled like a grave. The possibility of collapse loomed large as the tunnel passed beneath a muddy track; even the reinforced props creaked and bowed whenever a laden water cart passed overhead, and the sappers carried poison to ensure a speedy death should they be entombed.

While the men tunnelled, Perovskaya sat cradling a pistol, ready to fire at a bottle of nitroglycerine and blow them all up should the alarm be rung on the upper floor to warn of approaching police. Incidental problems were resolved with a quick wit: clever procrastination when an old resident arrived to retrieve her possessions from the soil-filled shed; a superstitious rant to deter neighbours who came rushing to extin-guish a fire; the invocation of a cat with an inexhaustible appetite to explain the quantities of provisions observed entering the house. When a gendarme and local surveyor arrived to assess a mortgage application made by the group to fund the purchase of a drill, Perovskaya's sangfroid saw them through. And day by arduous day, the intermittent thunder and clack of train wheels sounded out the diggers' growing proximity to the line, and the approaching moment when their work would be tested.

Then disaster struck. Dispatched to collect a case of dynamite and meet Kibalchich so that the scientist and bomb-making expert could advise him in its use, Goldenburg was arrested; after a mix-up over their rendezvous, Kibalchich arrived just in time to see him dragged away. Fresh explosives were sourced, but then, at the last moment, the Moscow electricians who had promised to provide Hartmann with the battery needed to detonate the charge haggled over the price. Lacking access to ready cash, Hartmann handed over his engraved gold watch: lavish overpayment and an incriminating error that would nearly cost him dear.

At last, though, everything was set. The three groups waited in feverish anticipation to know which route the tsar would take. At the last minute news came through. Fearing seasickness in rough weather, the tsar had decided against the Odessa route. If Zhelyabov failed, it would be down to the Moscow unit.

It was the night of 19 November 1879. Reeling from lack of sleep, having for months been leading the double life of aspiring businessman and local personality by day and ruthless terrorist by night, Zhelyabov could do no more. Heavy rain had flooded the depression between the high railway embankment and the position from which he would stake out the passing train, leaving him and his collaborators drenched and shivering as they buried their bombs and laid the wires. But as he watched the first decoy train pass and awaited the arrival of the second, as advised by spies in Simferopol, he must have felt confident that his moment of glory was fast approaching. Calmly he counted: one, two, three carriages, then the fourth. Was that the tsar at the window? Timing it perfectly, he pressed the lever. Nothing, save the sound of the train rolling on, uninterrupted. The bomb had failed to detonate.

On the outskirts of Moscow, Hartmann had dismissed the rest of the team: he and Sofia Perovskaya would stay on alone, two respectable citizens in their home, to all appearances: she with the honour of giving the signal, he to fire the charge that would kill the tsar. 'Price of flour two rubles, our price four' read the coded telegram that had arrived earlier, locating their target. Deep into the evening they too waited, as Zhelyabov had done a few hours before, allowing the first train to pass. But this time, as the fourth carriage of the second train drew level, the detonator was triggered. A deafening explosion of earth and the wrenching of steel. Then sudden pandemonium. It was a ghastly scene. Amidst the wreckage of the fourth carriage, sticky red ooze covered everything; only after the initial shock subsided and the sweet smell of preserved fruit began to pervade the air did onlookers realise that it was merely a bloodbath of jam, being shipped from the Crimea to supply the pantries of the imperial palaces. The tsar had changed trains just before his departure and had already arrived safely in Moscow.

*

Alexander II's relief would be short-lived. In February, a devastating explosion tore through the Winter Palace, killing eleven soldiers who were standing guard and injuring fifty others. Only his decision to extend a meeting elsewhere in the building with Alexander of Battenberg, the new puppet king of Bulgaria, saved him. The dining hall in which they were to have met was destroyed by a blast from the kitchens below, where a lone People's Will bomber had planted dynamite that he had brought in stick by stick over several weeks, under cover of his job as a carpenter. The terrorists' deadly game could not be allowed to continue, but how to stop it?

Differences over security policy divided the Russian elite, drawing out latent suspicions and personal resentments among those closest to the tsar. To restore the people's faith in the tsar as their friend and protector, liberal reforms were proposed most ardently by Alexander's mistress, Catherine Dolgorukaya. Pregnant with the fourth of his illegitimate children, with secret apartments reserved for her use in the royal palaces, the failing health of the tsarina made Dolgorukaya's position a strong one. But for the hardliners grouped around the tsarevitch and his mentor, Constantine Pobedonostsev, newly appointed as chief procurator of the Orthodox synod, the solution lay in ever more draconian repression to crush all seditious elements that threatened the status quo. And they were in do doubt about where the greatest danger lay.

After the Turkish War had ended ingloriously for Russia, and the terms of the Berlin Treaty had damaged her national interest, the novelist Dostoevsky had written of the British prime minister, Disraeli, as a tarantula who 'used the Turks to crucify Slav brothers in the Balkans'. The military intervention he had ordered was not the self-interested act of a Great Power, but one facet of a greater Jewish conspiracy. Reflecting on the state of Russia in a letter to Dostoevsky, Pobedonostsev saw its tentacles closer to home too. 'The Yids', he ranted, 'have invaded everything, but the spirit of the times works in their favour. They are at the root of the Social Democratic movement and tsaricide. They control the press and the stock market . . . They formulate the principles of contemporary science, which tends to dissociate itself from Christianity.' Anti-Semitic measures should, both men clearly believed, be central to the tsar's political agenda.

The chosen instrument of their hard-line policy was to be Count Loris-Melikov, whose capture of the city of Kars had been a rare high point in the recent war. Since succeeding the assassinated Dmitri Kropotkin as Governor General of Kharkov he had demonstrated a welcome ruthlessness, winning over even those who saw him as an Armenian parvenu. His advocates were stunned, however, when having been appointed chief of the Supreme Administrative Commission, he adopted a decidedly liberal slate of policies that aimed to tackle the causes of discontent as much as its consequences. It marked a major shift from the attitude that had prevailed previously, when members of the Kharkov *zemstvo*, the people's representatives, were sent to Siberia for petitioning the tsar to 'grant his own faithful servants what he had granted the Bulgars': a constitutional settlement. Nor was Loris-Melikov deterred from pursuing the tsar's new 'civilising mission' when, only days after his appointment, an assassin's bullet glanced harmlessly off the cuirass he wore beneath his regular uniform, and lodged in the fur collar of his coat.

Initially, at least, the strategy appeared to bear fruit. The executive of the People's Will promptly called off two bomb attacks against the tsar, including one for which a hundredweight of explosives had already been positioned in the Catherine Canal in St Petersburg, and indicated that a permanent ceasefire could be secured by concessions on constitutional reform. But whilst Loris-Melikov embarked on a series of consultations with interested parties, the People's Will were offered no place in the dialogue, and their fragile faith in his good intentions began to break down. The high price of trusting the authorities was soon amply illustrated by the Third Section's unscrupulous manipulation of the captured Goldenburg. Placed in a cell with a turncoat radical, to soften him up, he succumbed to his interrogators' persuasive assurances that only the threat of continued violence was preventing reforms. Those comrades whose names he divulged were promptly rounded up. Realising he had been duped, Goldenburg committed suicide.

When the Trial of the Sixteen in October 1880 resulted in the execution of three members of the People's Will for conspiracy, their friends resolved that it was no longer enough merely to have demonstrated the seriousness of their intent: they must achieve their threatened objective. The vote for the renewal of hostilities, pitilessly forced through by the group's female members, came at a moment of heightened vulnerability for the tsar. Loris-Melikov's bold initiative to disband the Third Section, and so bring an end to its counterproductive heavy-handedness, had inevitable consequences for the security of the tsar, while the secrecy surrounding his relationship with his mistress compounded the problem. When the ageing Wilhelm Stieber had passed on advance intelligence about the Winter Palace bomb plot from his spies in Geneva, for example, it was concern that Catherine Dolgorukova's residence in the Winter Palace should not be revealed that had led the tsar to refuse a search of his private quarters. After she became Alexander's wife as the 'Princess Yurievskaya' within a month of the tsarina's death in June 1880, she would attempt to safeguard his life, wheedling for him to take a winter holiday in Cairo, to be followed by his abdication; but her efforts were in vain.

The combat unit of the People's Will had learned the lessons of its failed attacks on the tsar's train, spread across locations several hundred miles apart, and now focused its attention on a shorter route: that of Alexander's weekly Sunday excursion from the Winter Palace to his riding school at the Mikhaylovsky manege. A cheese shop was rented on the Malaya Sadovaya, and in the biting cold of early January 1881 a tight-knit team that included Zhelyabov, Vladimir Degaev and Alexander Barannikov set about digging a tunnel from its cellar in order to mine the road. A backup squad would wait by the roadside with hand-held grenades, and Zhelyabov would loiter alone with a concealed dagger, ready to deliver the *coup de grâce* if all else failed.

The tunnelling tested their resources to the limit. The frozen ground made it hard and heavy work, and the old problem of how to dispose of the soil was solved by filling empty cheese barrels. With scant funds to provide stock that would allow the 'shopkeeper' to play his role, the barrels at least filled out the storeroom; when a surprise police inspection noticed liquid from the melting earth seeping from between the staves, it was plausibly explained as spilled sour cream. But still they were edgy. When Barannikov was apprehended, the knowledge that they would all be exposed to immediate arrest if he broke under interrogation drove morale even lower.

Then, one day at the end of January 1881, a letter smuggled out of the Peter and Paul fortress was delivered to Vera Figner: a voice from the past that carried an almost mythic force. In the eight years since Sergei Nechaev's capture and incarceration in the Alexeyevsky Ravelin, shackled in solitary confinement on the tsar's express instructions, little had been heard of him. Some assumed that he had been left to die, after striking a police general who had visited Nechaev's cell to recruit him as a spy. Now it was clear that not only had he survived but had retained enough of his guile to capture the sympathy of all the prison guards, and establish communication through one of them with the outside world.

The first request Nechaev sent Figner to pass on to the executive committee of the People's Will was that a team be assigned to break him out of prison. On learning that the resources committed to the assassination plot made this impossible, 'The Eagle', as he named himself, nimbly assumed a more selfless and flattering tone: though awed by their boldness, he would like to offer the benefit of his tactical expertise. Zhelyabov, he suggested, should assume the position of 'Revolutionary Dictator' once the established political order was overturned. But first, he said, they must 'Kill the tsar!'

When Nechaev's orchestration of the murder of his rival Ivanov had come to light back in 1870, many young radicals had been willing to give him the benefit of the doubt and exonerate his crime as a fine example of ruthless necessity in a greater cause. For those populists who had themselves now abandoned the moral scruples that had guided their action during the intervening years, something like their original assessment of Nechaev again pertained. 'There remained only an intelligence that had retained its lucidity in spite of years of imprisonment, and a will that punishment had failed to break,' Figner would later enthuse of her new correspondent. His smuggled approval was a decisive factor, perhaps, in light of the new shocks that the terrorists would face as the moment for action approached. For on Friday, 27 February (Old Style), only two days before the date scheduled for the attack, Zhelyabov was arrested, betrayed by a colleague who had turned informant to save his own life when awaiting trial the previous autumn.

With the entire project thrown into jeopardy, an emergency meeting of the core conspirators was called for three o'clock on the Saturday afternoon. As Sofia Perovskaya minuted the meeting's urgent resolutions, starting with the recovery of the bomb-making material from her lover Zhelyabov's apartment, she must have known that success in their enterprise would surely now mean execution for him. The self-control she showed inspired the others to hold their nerve. In Vera Figner's apartment, hours later, she and Kibalchich settled down to a long, tense night of bomb-making, while Perovskaya slept, emotionally exhausted.

It was hazardous work for tired eyes and shaky hands: cutting to size empty kerosene canisters, before filling them with nitroglycerine to create the impact grenades which Kibalchich had devoted his recent energies to perfecting. One slip and the entire building would have been rubble; wisely, Kibalchich set aside his trademark top hat, lest it fall disastrously

from his head. By daybreak, four neat canisters sat on the table, ready
for delivery to the home of Gesia Gelfman, where the designated bomb-
throwers had convened. When Figner got there, she was unimpressed to
find Frolenko – who was to light the mine's fuse – shovelling into his
mouth a breakfast of bread and salami, washed down with wine. 'To do
what I have to do, I must be in complete control of my faculties,' he
retorted, continuing with what seemed likely to be his last meal. The
diary of another accomplice, Grinevitsky, makes plain the bombers'
suicidal intent: 'I or another will strike the decisive blow . . . He will die,
and with him, us, his enemies and murderers.'

Ever since Goldenburg had named Zhelyabov as the prime mover of the
assassination plots, he had topped the 'Wanted' lists. News of his arrest
came as a great relief to the tsar, who had not spent consecutive nights
in the same bed for many weeks, to confound the imminent attempts on
his life that anonymous letters regularly threatened. Throughout that
time Alexander II had shown courage of a kind for which few at the time
gave him credit, determined as he was to fulfil his 'civilising mission' and
redeem his legacy as the Saviour Tsar: 'to see Russia set on her peaceful
path of progress and prosperity'. With his nemesis now in custody, he
had surely approached his crucial meeting with Loris-Melikov that
Saturday with a new lightness of spirit. For once, he may even have
allowed himself a reprieve from checking faces in the passing crowd
against the police album containing photographs of those known to want
him dead.

The following morning, when the tsar's entourage pulled out of the
palace and on to the icy streets of St Petersrbug, it took an unusual route,
to the home of Grand Duchess Catherine. It was a courtesy visit, at which
Alexander would explain to his elderly aunt the groundbreaking package
of constitutional reforms that he had agreed with Loris-Melikov the day
before, and whose announcement was imminent. The detour taken by
the imperial party reduced, at a stroke, the intended three-pronged ambush
by the People's Will assassins to a single point.

Loitering on either side of the road that ran beside the Catherine Canal,
the four appointed bomb-throwers must have felt that the bombs
concealed beneath their coats rendered them agonisingly conspicuous.
Yet by half-past one, when Sofia Perovskaya lifted her handkerchief in
warning, and the first horses of the tsar's Cossack bodyguard appeared,
nobody had raised the alarm, nor even paid them the faintest attention.

Nicholas Rysakov was the first to step forward and launch his grenade;

a momentary glimpse of Alexander as he passed was burned into Rysakov's retina by the blinding light of the explosion that followed a second later, catching the company of guards that followed. Undamaged, but for a few splinters, the imperial sleigh slowed to a halt a few dozen yards further on. From that moment, accounts differ. The loyalist press would later report how the tsar had stepped out and walked calmly back to survey the damage and offer what solace he could to those who lay injured on the road: soldiers with shrapnel wounds, some fatal, and a young boy who would not make it alive to hospital. If these accounts were accurate, it was a brave but disastrous decision.

Approaching the small group clustered around Alexander, Grinevitsky raised the second canister over his head and dashed it down between himself and his target. The blast consumed them both, and left the Tsar of all the Russias crumpled on the ground. His legs shattered, he tried to crawl, hands clawing the compacted snow as his entrails spilled out through a ragged hole ripped through dress uniform and stomach. So pathetic a sight did he present that one of the other assassins instinctively made to help him, only to be pushed back by guards.

His death, less than an hour later, was reported throughout the capitals of Europe before the end of the day. Almost as quickly, his planned programme of reforms was buried as the forces of reaction set about implementing long-cherished plans for repression. Whose purposes the rabid voice of the unseen Nechaev had best served is a matter of opinion: the nihilists may have finally made their point, but the result was to return the initiative to the reactionaries, with Pobedonostsev's protégé in line to assume the throne as Alexander III. Either way, by the end of the following year Nechaev's voice was silenced once and for all. The official record would state tuberculosis as the cause of death. However, the aptitude for dissimulation later shown by the reactionary cabal, and by its security chiefs above all, makes it is almost possible to imagine that the letter-writing Nechaev of 1881 never existed at all.

'We trust that no personal bitterness will cause you to forget your duty or to cease to wish to know the truth,' Lev Tikhomirov told the new tsar in the manifesto promptly published by the People's Will. 'We too have cause for bitterness. You have lost a father. We have lost fathers, brothers, wives, children, and our dearest friends. We are prepared to suppress our personal feelings if the good of Russia demands it; and we expect the same of you . . .' It was a bold negotiating tactic, not to say impertinent, and one doomed to failure.

9

Inconvenient Guests

Paris, 1879–1881

The rumbustious political life of France had been temporarily muted by the trauma of the war of 1870 and the revolutionary Commune that followed in 1871. Any trace of the radical ideals out of which the Third Republic had been born, as the Prussian armies closed in on Paris, had been all but erased during the presidency of MacMahon in the years that followed. Even moderate republicans had been sidelined, or else, when electoral success forced their inclusion in government, the slightest challenge to Catholic or conservative interests had seen them dismissed. In early 1879, though, MacMahon retired from office short of his seven-year term, having staked his credibility on a failed campaign to bolster the conservative vote. Nine years after the Third Republic had first been declared, and four years since its legality had been confirmed, the leadership of France was finally delivered into genuinely republican hands.

Installed as prefect of police soon afterwards, the thirty-nine-year-old Louis Andrieux epitomised the hard-headed pragmatism of the incoming administration. A lawyer by training, as a young procurator in 1871 he had backed the suppression of the Lyons commune, and since his election as a republican deputy in 1875 had won influential allies, including Léon Gambetta, the aeronautical politician of the Siege of Paris, for his deft understanding of the need to ensure social stability in a period of political transition. By a remarkable effort of collective will, the country had long since paid off its war reparation, far ahead of schedule, and appeared set on a course of national renewal. Yet as Andrieux took stock of his new responsibilities in the field of law and order, he was all too aware of the dangers and challenges that bubbled away just below the surface.

Against the economic odds, French commerce was thriving, whilst the resumption of Haussmann's vastly ambitious building plans for the boulevards of Paris signalled a boom in the construction industry. The night-time streets of the capital glowed with gas lighting, electricity flowed increasingly freely, and the Post Office operated an efficient pneumatic mail system, propelling letters to their recipients within the hour; for those still more impatient to communicate a message, the telephone offered a somewhat limited alternative. In the eyes of the world, too, the Universal Exposition of 1878 had proved that France had regained her confidence and *joie de vivre*, with the Moorish flamboyance of the Trocadéro Palace providing a striking addition to a city more usually bound by strict neoclassical discipline.

With national pride restored, however, the ghosts of the past, stranded in the purgatory of New Caledonia or the French émigré colonies abroad, forced their way back on to the agenda. At the Exposition itself, visitors could clamber, forty at a time, inside one exhibit that seemed to offer a silent rebuke to the unjust treatment of the Communards: the giant iron head of the Statue of Liberty. Designed by the sculptor Bartholdi, engineered by Gustave Eiffel and financed by bold entrepreneurialism, the statue was to be donated to the American people on the centenary of their Declaration of Independence. But among the thousands who attended a benefit opera by Gounod or bought a miniature replica of the sculpture, or the millions who played the 'Liberty' lottery to help pay for the gift, a proportion must have marvelled at the irony of celebrating America's revolutionaries, when France continued to deny its own their freedom.

Writing from Switzerland at the time, Henri Rochefort had coined the term 'opportunism' to disparage those timid republicans who procrastinated over the issue, fearful that if they were to address the question of an amnesty for the Communards, the monarchist parties might use their liberalism against them. 'The Opportunist', he argued, 'is that sensible candidate who, deeply affected by the woes of the civil war and full of solicitude for the families which it deprived of support, declares that he is in favour of an amnesty, but that he shall refrain from voting for it until *the opportune time* . . . *At the opportune time* is a term of parliamentary slang which means Never!'

The reporter for the committee of deputies, it had been Louis Andrieux himself who finally signed off in 1879 on an agreement for the return of those guilty only of political rather than criminal acts, and so deemed less dangerous to the state. As a succession of ships – the *Creuze*, the *Var*, the *Picardie*, the *Calvados* and the *Loire* – carried the Communards home, however, his new role as prefect of police seemed ever more a poisoned chalice. Walking among the crowds on the evening of the first Communards' return from exile, and listening to the speeches delivered by the pitiful straggle of broken convicts, their self-justificatory message, which sought to revise the official version of history, made Andrieux profoundly uneasy. It had been murders by the Versaillais army that had sparked any retributive acts of violence that the Commune of 1871 might have performed, they insisted, and more vengeance was due.

In the impoverished slums that Emile Zola had so shockingly evoked in his novel *L'Assommoir*, two years earlier, there were many ready to listen to such rabble-rousing. To oversee the Communards' peaceful re-integration into French society and prevent them becoming a catalyst for popular discontent would require every inch of Andrieux's skill as a schemer. Yet as the new prefect took stock of his job, familiarising himself with the workings of his domain, the case from the archives that particularly caught his attention was of an altogether more glamorous nature.

Dating from twenty or so years earlier, it involved his forerunner as prefect, Monsieur Lagrange, and the beautiful courtesan La Floriana, one-time mistress of the tsar. Having been deported from St Petersburg for some undisclosed offence, La Floriana had settled in London and fallen in with France's most dangerous revolutionaries. Lagrange had inter-vened. Contriving to take a seat next to her at the opera, he had intro-duced himself as a rich provincial merchant, and seduced her over dinner into believing that he wished to finance a conspiracy to assassinate Napoleon III. It was agreed that a miniaturised bomb would be constructed, small enough to be concealed in a lorgnette case. The risks were worthwhile, Lagrange had thought, for the insights that might be gained, but having been tipped off about his subterfuge, La Floriana had provided only false information, before absconding with 40,000 francs of the prefecture's money.

The case notes should have constituted a cautionary tale. The lesson that Andrieux chose to learn, however, was not that the dangers of provo-cation inevitably outweighed the potential benefits, but simply that Lagrange had been too easily duped. He, by contrast, was determined to be more cunning. By good fortune, the pragmatic deftness with which he responded to his first major challenge as prefect, involving a Russian émigré of a rather different kind, suggested that he might indeed have grounds for such self-assurance.

It was the gold watch, in exchange for which Lev Hartmann had finally persuaded the Moscow electricians to part with the battery needed for the People's Will attack on the tsar's train, that proved the terrorist's undoing. Within weeks of the failed bombing, the executive committee of the organisation had spirited Hartmann out of Russia on a steamship bound for Constantinople, insisting, as it had with Kravchinsky previously, that someone with so much to offer was of more use agitating among the émigrés abroad than rotting in Siberian exile. Even before Hartmann had time to establish himself among the Russian student doctors, scientists and engineers of the rue des Lyonnais, however, the detectives of the Third Section had caught up with him, having assiduously traced the battery back to its suppliers, then the watch to the woman who had bought it for Hartmann, and finally Hartmann himself to Paris.

The intense pressure brought to bear by Russia on the French government to allow Hartmann's extradition placed Andrieux in the eye of the storm. The outcome, though, was not obvious. The two countries were by tradition ideological foes, the opposed principles of tsarist autocracy and republicanism affording scant common ground. Faced with increasingly undiplomatic demands from Prince Orlov, the Russian ambassador, Andrieux appears to have had little inclination to acquiesce, despite a barrage of penal-code citations and precedential arguments for Hartmann's provisional arrest. Although seen as dashing by some in France, the black silk patch worn by Orlov over the eye he had lost while fighting the Turks made it only too easy to cast him as an avatar of a piratical despotism who should be resisted at all costs.

The soul of the Third Republic was already tarnished, however, and political pragmatism demanded that other considerations, both domestic and geopolitical, be weighed in the balance. Foremost of these was continued concern about the rising power of the united Germany. Whilst France had largely succeeded in putting the Commune out of mind for some years, the country was perennially torn between fear of Germany and resentment over its appropriation of Alsace and Lorraine: in 1875, cavalry horses were even bought in preparation for an imminent renewal of hostilities. France needed an ally, and Russia's concern over their shared neighbour made her a promising, if unlikely candidate for the role. Secret meetings between generals Boisdeffre and Obruchov, contrived by Elie Cyon, had so far failed to produce concrete results. Andrieux's domain of policing, however, appeared to offer a promising platform on which to build collaboration between the two countries, which would replace the strong links forged by Stieber between the political police forces in St Petersburg and Berlin.

A further factor in Andrieux's calculations was the impact that the terroristic methods being pioneered in the east might have closer to home, if they inspired France's own revolutionaries to similar feats. For most people in France the horrors of 1871 had bred not moral indignation at the crude strategies of power, but a kind of quiescence: an unquestioning contentment with the easy pleasures of bourgeois life, for as long as they lasted. That this complacency might be disturbed and the ball of history set rolling again was a source of dread to those in authority. In the aftermath of the Winter Palace bombing, French press reports of 6,000 troops being drafted into St Petersburg to reinforce the garrison stirred uncomfortable memories.

On 25 February 1880, Andrieux succumbed to pressure from above and abroad to take action. Whilst promenading with friends along the Champs-Elysées, the man purporting to be 'Edward Mayer of Berlin' was identified as Hartmann by means of photographs that the Russian Embassy had provided, and arrested. The Russian agent in his group was not required to break his cover. Victor Hugo and Georges Clemenceau, among others, complained vocally about the arrest, while Kropotkin, in Switzerland, organised a campaign against Hartmann's extradition. Recognising the hypocrisy of which he had been guilty, Andrieux is likely to have been stung most, however, by Hartmann's appeal to France's conscience. 'The Republic government has amnestied 1,000 Communards,' the renegade argued. 'Can they then deliver to Russia a political émigré who has come to France to seek asylum?'

The humiliating predicament prompted some French commentators to wish that Hartmann was England's problem rather than theirs, at a time when the British Empire was already entangled with Russia in the Second Afghan War, and therefore had little to lose. Deciding to act as an agent of destiny, Andrieux deftly made the switch, before anyone could argue, and personally escorted his prisoner to the port of Dieppe, where he handed him a ticket for the boat train to London. 'I had hoped to find protection and security of the kind that was always to be found in France, as in all free states for political émigrés, but I was badly deceived in my hope,' Hartmann would reflect, but the prefect's pragmatism had almost certainly saved him from execution, had he been sent back to Russia.

The tsar withdrew Prince Orlov from Paris in protest at the subterfuge, but only for a few weeks. Despite marking a setback in the slowly developing trust between France and Russia it was an acceptable outcome for what had become a seemingly intractable problem. By the time the ambassador returned to his duties, it was once again the Communards who were Andrieux's main preoccupation.

An early warning of the problems that lay ahead came on 24 May 1880, the ninth anniversary of the massacres of Bloody Week, after the prefect had sanctioned a demonstration at the Mur des Fédérés in Père Lachaise cemetery. It was the wrong decision. Violence erupted on the streets, the police were required to use brutal tactics in its suppression; Andrieux became a scapegoat for the council of ministers, yet hung on to his position. Of equal concern to the prefect, however, may have been the challenge to a duel that he received from Henri Rochefort, who was enraged by the sabre wounds that his son had suffered during the melee. Although still an exile in Switzerland, Rochefort's imminent return seemed probable as part of the phased amnesty of the Communards, and he was notorious for his duplicitous swordplay, having once skewered an opponent's knee, supposedly by accident, *after* the fight's conclusion. Andrieux was probably even more alarmed, however, by the resurgent political irrationalism and volatility that Rochefort represented and his utter lack of compunction in manipulating circumstances to his own ends.

The crowd of 200,000 that gathered outside the Gare de Lyon to greet Rochefort on his glorious return to Paris that July, standing on one another's shoulders and breaking the windows of the station to get a better view, appeared to testify to his immense popularity. That a promoter hired by Rochefort had persuaded them to attend would have been scant reassurance to the prefect, and the marquis' ingratiatingly demotic interviews are likely to have sent a shiver down Andrieux's spine. 'One is bourgeois out of sentiment, not by birth,' Rochefort told one newspaper interviewer. 'When one sincerely marches under the same flag against the enemy, social classifications disappear.' At least Andrieux's suspicion of Rochefort's morals and motives was shared by many of the marquis' erstwhile Communard colleagues, and a similar sentiment also found its way into the two dramatic paintings of *The Escape of Rochefort* that Edouard Manet executed at the time.

Manet's intention had been to exhibit the final painting in the Salon of 1881, but prolonged exposure to his sitter may have caused the artist, who had witnessed the aftermath of Bloody Week, to revise his ideas. In Manet's first attempt at the painting, Rochefort sits erect in elegant attire at the helm of a small boat in wide and rough seas off New Caledonia, neither seasick nor staggering to keep his balance, and there is the unmistakable hint of mockery of a man who cannot or should not be taken seriously at his own heroic estimation. In a second version, the image represented is further cropped to remove the horizon, creating a vision of terrible, turbulent alienation: of a figure adrift from all the certainties of dry land, of religion and social hierarchy, just as Rochefort argued that life should be. What violent and egotistical extremes might not such a man embrace, the painting seemed to demand.

It was a different kind of egotism, ostensibly self-denying though just as dangerous, that Louise Michel presented on arriving in France four months later. That she should be the last of the Communards to accept the amnesty, having refused offers of special treatment for years until the last of every one of her comrades was freed, told its own story. Where Rochefort had tried to milk the moment by being the first home, the turnout then had matched neither the size nor sincerity of the crowds that now greeted the Red Virgin, their exuberance at the station surpassing that for Rochefort's return, and threatening chaos around the barriers that Andrieux had thrown up. And while Michel's address showed magnanimity – 'We want no more bloody vengeance; the shame of these men will suffice' – there was also evidence of an undiminished zeal that must have further unnerved the prefect: 'Long live the social revolution!' she declared, then concluded, more ominously, 'Long live the nihilists!'

Her words sounded like a declaration of intent, and a letter she had written to Karl Marx shortly before leaving New Caledonia, chastising him for his armchair generalship, seemed to indicate the uncompromising activism she had in mind. Andrieux, it was clear, would need all the operational expertise he could muster to keep the threat of sedition under control, yet he failed to grasp the potential of the tools of physiological profiling being innovated under his nose by the young obsessive, Alphonse Bertillon. 'You have no scientific qualifications, and you produce an incomprehensible report which you cannot explain,' he told Bertillon, and withdrew support for his new-fangled ideas. Instead, he fell back on the kinds of methods that had cost his predecessor so dear in the La Floriana case, and used the prefecture's money to fund a new anarchist newspaper, *La Révolution sociale*.

Fortunately for Andrieux, whatever instinct Louise Michel may once have had for sniffing out police chicanery had been blunted by seven years on a desert island. Before making any important decisions, Michel would have been wise to reacclimatise to a country much changed in her absence, not least for women. For since the heady days of female emancipation during the Commune, every inch of political ground ceded had been clawed back; one interior minister of the 1870s had even banned meetings on the 'Female Question' out of simple distaste for the kind of women they would attract. Instead, impatient to assert her presence, Michel swallowed whole the account of the supposed anarchist sympathiser, Egide Serreaux, that he wished to invest a part of the fortune he had made in the pharmaceuticals business in the new publication, and readily agreed to become its star columnist.

It was like laying a telephone line direct to the heart of every anarchist conspiracy, Andrieux would delight in recollecting. When Michel's close associate, Sénéchal, expressed the opinion that 'There are a certain number of heads whose disappearance in France would singularly facilitate the solution of the social question', the cabinet was immediately informed. But whilst Michel had the greater popular support, before long a more insidious challenge emanated from Rochefort to threaten some of Andrieux's closest political friends. What was more, Rochefort's other activities seemed to make concrete the threats of international solidarity among the enemies of the state to which Michel had merely alluded.

Despite Gambetta's frequent kindnesses to him, not least his assistance when the military tribunal held Rochefort's life in the balance, Rochefort had come to loathe his old friend. Perhaps he didn't like feeling a sense of obligation. Certainly when Gambetta's brilliant political and journalistic protégé, Joseph Reinarch, took it upon himself to accuse Rochefort of ingratitude, the polemicist went on the attack. Using his newspaper *L'Intransigeant*, he inveighed against Gambetta for his willingness to reconcile himself to the spurious Third Republic, and poured scorn on the lawyer, Alfred Joly, hired by Gambetta on Rochefort's behalf in 1872, for the ineptitude with which he had defended him against transportation. The war of words escalated, Joly and Reinarch making public a letter written by Rochefort from prison. Its pathetic pleading for leniency undermined all his past claims of steadfastness in the face of persecution. His pride dented, and his journalistic armoury empty, Rochefort reached for the crude but potent weapon of anti-Semitism, publicly addressing Gambetta through Reinarch, both of them being Jewish, in vicious terms: 'I send you sufficient expectorations in the face to admit of your honourable master receiving some of them.'

It was an astute if cynical move which tapped into a rich vein of French prejudice against Jews, and in particular, at the time, against Jewish bankers and their suspiciously clever financial practices. Having helped underwrite the Suez Canal a decade before, Jewish money was now paying for the continued remodelling of Paris, and there were those who worried that the Jewish appetite to invest and control knew no end. 'These dogs, [of whom] there are too many at present in Rome, we hear them howling in the streets, and they are disturbing us in all places,' the late Pope Pius IX had written in 1870, blaming the Jews in part for the withdrawal of French protection that had forced him to retreat into the Vatican City. Increasing numbers of French nationalists and Catholics agreed and in 1878 a bank, La Société de l'Union Générale, was established to counter the Jewish monopoly of loans. The myth of an international Jewish conspiracy had begun to take root, with all the old reactionary bugbears of Freemasonry and socialism mixed in. Rochefort would quickly acquire a taste for the demagogic popularity that the preaching of anti-Semitism could confer, but not before it had placed him in a somewhat paradoxical predicament.

Louis Andrieux must have observed the consequences of Rochefort's campaign with some distaste, if only for the tragic suicide of Albert Joly it caused, his reputation destroyed in the crossfire. It was barely two years since Joly's brother Maurice, author of *The Dialogues between Machiavelli and Montesquieu in Hell*, that had satirised the intrigues and ambition of Napoleon III, had also died by his own hand. Amidst the shock surrounding the assassination of Tsar Alexander II, however, it must have been with near disbelief that Andrieux read Rochefort's article in *L'Intransigeant* in which he proudly boasted of having received a letter from a Russian in Geneva, signed only 'D', inviting him to be the first to hear the full truth about the assassination. For whilst alarming reports flooded in from French police agents that Rochefort 'has gone to conspire with the nihilists', the popular impression being propagated by the Russian government was that the murderous conspiracy had a strongly Jewish flavour. Then again, Rochefort had never been known for principled consistency.

Despite assurances from the informant 'Hervé' that Rochefort had known 'D' for a couple of years and was simply touting a journalistic scoop, Andrieux must have feared that his visit to Switzerland signified something more sinister. Even 'Droz', usually among the more level-headed police assets, reported proposals for the creation of a 'European revolutionary party', insisting that among those nihilists who had been frequent visitors to Rochefort's Geneva apartment, the details of the tsar's assassination were well known in advance. Most alarmingly of all, however, he warned that 'Alexander III will be no safer, and be assured that further blows will follow in Italy, Germany and Paris.'

Primed to swoop, it was frustrating for Andrieux when even his expensive infiltration of the Paris anarchists delivered merely reports of bluster, and none of incriminating action. 'Imitate the nihilists, and I shall be at your head,' Michel urged her comrades on 13 May 1881, in explicit contradiction of the eschewal of violence in her homecoming speech. 'On the ruins of a rotten society . . . we will establish a new social world.' Anarchist braggards talked of destroying the Palais Bourbon, the restored seat of the National Assembly, though no one volunteered for the hazardous task of planting the dynamite. Softer targets were then mooted – the Elysée Palace, the ministry of the interior, the Bank of France, even the Prefecture of Police itself – but still nothing definite. Andrieux was growing impatient: 'it was necessary that the act was accomplished for repression to be possible', he later admitted. Finally, his agent provocateur coaxed the anarchists to choose a victim: they would strike at Monsieur Adolphe Thiers, the nemesis of the Commune.

The prefect's officers were already waiting in the shadows of the Saint-Germain district as the terrorists approached the stately figure of Thiers, who sat stock still and oblivious. Silently, in the moonlight, the conspirators unwrapped a sardine tin stuffed with gun cotton from its protective handkerchief, rested it on the old man's shoulder and lit the fuse. A flash, a bang, and the police emerged to make their arrests. But the damage was minimal: a smudge of carbon. Thiers himself had died four years earlier, and the bronze statue that the terrorists had targeted to make their statement withstood the blast. Such was the futility of the attack that the authorities decided not even to bring charges: an early, disregarded warning of how provocation could backfire.

There was, however, the consolation for Andrieux of a tip-off about the forthcoming London Congress at which all the leading anarchists would be present, and which would provide the prefect with a great opportunity for mischief-making. 'In three months,' Droz wrote, 'the congress which will take place in London will give you the secret of this vast organisation, but until then I can only urge you to engage a great deal of surveillance, because it is fascinating to see how the revolutionary spirit has become exalted . . .'

10

Voices in the Fog

England and France, 1881–1883

Aboard the *John Helder*, the last shipment of amnestied Communards from New Caledonia were in high spirits as they passed through the Channel in early November 1880, on their way to disembark in London. The fog awaiting them in the Thames Estuary, however, was so dense that even men whose families had navigated the river for generations refused to pilot the sightless ships to dock. Stranded vessels sounded their horns eerily though the smothering whiteness, and captains fretted over their cargoes, the produce of Britain's wide empire – Indian tea, exotic fruits from Africa and Caribbean cotton. It was something altogether rarer, though, that was sought by the French émigrés who had chartered pleasure launches and fishing boats and bobbed out through the mist. Denizens of the Charlotte Street colony of ex-Communards and the slums of Saffron Hill, they had spent long years in exile, but now they discerned a glimmer of hope. '*Bonhomme, bonhomme, il est temps que tu te reveilles*' they chanted, 'Good fellow, it's time for you to wake,' and through the fog Louise Michel replied in kind, her sun-wizened face barely visible over the ghostly gunwale that loomed above them.

It was an old Communard song, though it might have struck a chord with the exiles and political émigrés of other nationalities who had congregated in London: Russians, Germans, Italians, even the odd Belgian and Spaniard. For on arriving in the world's great entrepôt, most soon sank into the depressed and somnolent state that prevailed among those who had been resident there for some time, the political activities to which they clung producing more noise than light. There were exceptions, of course. And among the many foreigners then enjoying Britain's hospitality, none took greater advantage of the liberties it afforded than the German socialist Johann Most.

It had been shortly after his expulsion from Germany in 1878 that Most had founded the newspaper *Freiheit* in London, to 'hurl', as he put it, 'a thunderbolt at that miserable state of affairs' created by Bismarck's suppression of the socialists. At the time Marx had dismissed Most as a weathercock, while Engels had gleefully predicted that his publication would last no more than six months. Yet with its calls for a 'revolution of the spirit' the paper had thrived, consistently outwitting attempts by the German police to infiltrate its distribution network: each edition was published under a different title to avoid censorship and smuggled into Germany inside mattresses exported by a factory in Hull. Most's audacity and outspokenness had made him something of a celebrity in Britain, not to say a tourist attraction. When the Belgian interior minister, Vandervelde, was in London, it was to observe the German firebrand in action that Sir Howard Vincent of the Metropolitan Police took him, the pair having disguised themselves to blend in with an audience that roared its approval of Most's attack on the iniquities of society and his pitiless solutions.

Their expedition was representative, in many respects, of the transformation in the methods and outlook of the British police that was then under way, as well as the factors that made it necessary. Vincent had spent time both in Russia, researching its military organisations, and with the French police in Paris, in his capacity as an unofficial assistant commissioner responsible for the creation of a central investigation department. He brought a new perspective to Scotland Yard, which had previously viewed its counterparts abroad with a certain liberal disdain. The reform of the old corrupt British detective branch had been necessitated precisely because of the opportunities afforded by its collaboration with the Belgian police for racketeering: the operation of private surveillance services by officers, and their sale of alcohol to brothels. Now, though, a growing recognition of the international menace of political subversion provided a new imperative for cross-border cooperation, and the adoption of new methods of working.

Despite the recruitment of German-speaking detectives by Vincent's deputy, Adolphus Williamson, however, the British government was finally forced to take action against Most not by reports from its own officers, but by intelligence received from foreign agents. A 'virulent philippic', was how a French agent named 'Star' described the speech Most delivered to a rally in mid-March 1881, celebrating the assassination of the tsar. But whilst the Home Secretary, Harcourt, agreed that Most had preached 'the most atrocious doctrines', he insisted that he could do nothing without an 'authentic record' of what had been said.

To many, both in London and abroad, such a circumspect response was unacceptable. Bismarck was furious. Despite having allowed Most to slip through his grasp three years earlier, he now wrote in person to the British government, while his ambassador intervened directly with Queen Victoria, who added her voice to that of the Russian propagandist Madame Novikoff in urging the first prosecution in British history for a statement made in support of a crime committed abroad. Even the British public, which normally prided itself on supporting the liberal principle of freedom of speech, especially when under threat by foreign despots, was temporarily persuaded to view the old enemy, Russia, in a more sympathetic light. 'The old Russia with the Siberian mines in the background was completely obscured for a time by the much more attractive figure of young Muscovy shedding its heart's blood in the Balkans,' the influential editor of the *Pall Mall Gazette*, W. T. Stead, would later recollect. He had himself ruthlessly exploited the heroic death of Novikoff's brother in Bosnia to help shift public opinion in favour of Russia; both he and Gladstone were regular attendees at Novikoff's salon.

Ultimately, though, it was probably domestic security considerations that precipitated Most's arrest. Following a Fenian attack on an infantry barracks in Lancashire in January 1881, the bombing campaign by those desiring Irish independence had continued with an attempt to blow up the Mansion House in London using 'infernal machines' imported from America in cement barrels. Three months later, with Gladstone's government in the process of petitioning the United States for the extradition of those responsible for the bombs' manufacture, it was considered politic for Britain to show itself amenable to similar requests from abroad. Johann Most, usually represented as the vulpine predator, was to be offered up as a sacrificial lamb on the altar of political convenience.

Most's own paper provided the requisite 'authentic record' of the incriminating speech, by publishing an article expressing the same views, and he was duly arrested. Whether by a quirk of court scheduling, or a clever contrivance to link terrorism and anarchism in the public mind, his trial coincided with the July congress of international revolutionaries of which agent 'Droz' had warned Andrieux some months before. The coincidence that the revolutionaries' conference room above a public house in Charrington Street, Euston, was next door to one booked for a meeting of Fenians must have simplified the surveillance operations of the British police.

*

The tense relationship between the neighbouring groups of insurrectionists did not augur well for the smooth running of what the congress organiser, the Communard Gustave Brocher, had advertised as 'the school of human dignity, the amphitheatre where one vivisects a rotten society and dissects the corpse of misery, the laboratory of the social revolution'. Only a few weeks earlier, the Catholic Fenians had clashed violently with the atheistic anarchists over an allegedly blasphemous banner the anarchists had been carrying during a Hyde Park demonstration against British rule in Ireland. The ructions within the Anarchist Congress threatened to be far more disruptive, however, caused as they were, in large part, by the participation of police spies. Having infiltrated the proceedings, the aim of such agents was to ensure that the image the congress presented to the world at large should be of a 'laboratory' dedicated solely to the development of explosives and terror tactics. It was as Kropotkin had feared. 'Let us go to London,' he had written with a scathing facetiousness to a colleague some months earlier, 'Let us cut a pathetic figure in the eyes of Europe.' Despite Malatesta's reassurances that he was overstating the problem, Kropotkin's misgivings about the advisability of the congress, and the scope for humiliating discord that it offered, seemed set to be borne out.

In the event, Kropotkin agreed to attend, playing along with the fiction by which delegates represented cities and countries from across the world, though most had only a tenuous link to the place in question. Chaikovsky joined him. Malatesta appeared as the delegate from Constantinople and Egypt, where he had participated in the fight against the colonialist British, as well as Turin, the Marches, Tuscany, Naples, Marseilles and Geneva. Taking time off from the ice-cream vending business that he had established since arriving in England a couple of months before, following his expulsion from Switzerland and France, he was accompanied by the Italians Merlino and Carlo Cafiero. John Neve, Most's publisher and right-hand man, was among the forty-five delegates, as were Frank Kitz and Joseph Lane from England; Madame LeCompte from Boston reported back to the *Paterson Labor Standard*, which was widely read by the émigré French and Italian factory workers in New Jersey. Louise Michel came too, back in London after her fleeting visit in the fog, as the delegate from the city of Reims. Also from France was Prefect Andrieux's plant, the provocative newspaper proprietor Serreaux, ready to exploit any fault lines that opened up.

The previous October, in Clarens, Kropotkin and Reclus had worked hard together to prepare a secret agenda for the congress that would emphasise the need to bring about the total destruction of all existing institutions before a genuine social revolution could take root. It was a triumph of hope over experience. Both believed that, after years in the wilderness, anarchism's day was fast approaching: that whilst hard evidence of a society in crisis was not yet to hand, the scent of trouble and opportunity was unmistakable. The moment must not be missed. And yet when Brocher was approached with their proposals, he showed infuriatingly little sense of urgency, merely asking whether it was 'really necessary to fix in advance the terms of a vote that might not take place?' The principles of anti-authoritarianism, it seemed, would govern the running of the congress as well as the content of the debates.

Malatesta's own behaviour in the weeks preceding the arrival of the international contingent hardly helped establish a mood of harmony: he had challenged his lover's adoptive brother Giuseppe Zanardelli to a duel for his vicious attempts to undermine the anarchists at the Ghent Congress four years earlier. But in the hothouse of the Charrington Street pub, differences quickly multiplied and the old resentments resurfaced. Blanquists from France, Germany and Belgium pressed their simplistic arguments for immediate revolution; Most's acolytes, Neve and Joseph Peukert, self-styled leader of the Autonomie group, wrangled in the background over their relative seniority during his imprisonment; while those with a lingering respect for Marx were ready to put their oar in, eager as ever to assert control over anything that might resemble a revival of the First International. While no minutes were taken of the congress, with even its delegates kept officially anonymous, the focus of the heated debates can be gauged from Malatesta's record of his own contributions.

Attempting to seize the initiative, Malatesta appealed to those 'who have no faith in legal methods and no wish to participate in political life, who want to fight with the greatest haste against those who oppress, and to take by force that which is denied by force'; there was no place for 'innocent utopianists' who favoured union with other socialist factions. He was not alone in recognising that victory would not come without struggle and sacrifice. 'Death by rifle: is it less terrible than death by explosion,' read a bullish letter from the anarchist miners of Belgium, whose friends had recently been shot by soldiers. Cafiero's manifesto would doubtless also have been heard: 'The bomb is too feeble to destroy the autocratic colossuses. Kill the property owners at the same time, prepare the peasant risings.' Serreaux's work was being done for him.

Although not intrinsically opposed to violence in a just cause, Kropotkin viewed such bloodlust as something like a mania, and there were others too who would have sought to temper the rush to terror tactics.

Underlying even Malatesta's bellicose rhetoric, however, was the frustrated concern, expressed to delegates, that 'we are fast approaching the point where a party must act or dissolve and where, if it is neither victor nor vanquished, it will die of corruption.' And whilst Kropotkin may have struggled to communicate the subtlety of his and Reclus' ideas amid the welter of opinionated debate, he did somehow manoeuvre the congress around the most dangerous pitfalls.

On the ethical underpinning of anarchism, Kropotkin talked down Serreaux's demands that any mention of 'morality' be excised: 'Morality is to be understood in the sense that today's society is founded on immorality; the abolition of immorality, through any means, will inaugurate morality', he insisted on recording. But that did not imply any softening of anarchism's militant stance, as he had made clear in a pamphlet published only two months earlier. 'Acts of illegal protest, of revolt, of vengeance' perpetrated by 'lonely sentinels', may well be necessary, he had concluded, while as part of a wider strategy of popular agitation they might even advance rather than set back the cause of revolution, since 'by actions which compel general attention, the new idea seeps into people's minds and wins converts'. As to the paradox of leadership in an anti-authoritarian movement, while the hierarchical character of the People's Will displeased Kropotkin, Reclus had persuaded him of the advantages of small conspiratorial groups over pure collective action.

It was no accident, however, that the real business of the congress was ultimately settled in camera. While many delegates may have been emotionally inclined to fall in with his absolute advocacy of extremism, Serreaux had clearly sensed the suspicions of Kropotkin and Malatesta about his true identity, and had attempted to allay them by taking the pair to visit his venerable aunt in her long-established London home. Malatesta, however, recognised in the aunt's house furniture from a second-hand shop that he regularly passed, confirming the agent's subterfuge. Cunning rather than confrontation was deemed the wisest response, and mixed into the congress' final resolutions – the reaffirmation of the policy of 'propaganda by deed' in a moderated form, and the agreement to learn the handling of chemicals, for purposes of self-defence and revolutionary warfare rather than terrorist aggression – were concessions to Serreaux that could be quickly discarded.

The proposed creation of a central bureau of information, supposedly to channel communications and give focus to the movement's disparate activities, would provide the authorities with a convenient junction at which to intercept intelligence on anarchist plans, while allowing them to give substance to the notion of an international conspiracy whose tentacles reached around the globe. It was everything Andrieux must have dreamed of. After discussing its organisation with Lev Hartmann, however, Malatesta let the idea wither from neglect. 'It is not by an International League, with endless letters read by the police, that the conspiracy will be mounted,' of that he was certain, 'it will be mounted by isolated groups.'

The loss did not matter to Andrieux personally, however, who had resigned as prefect of police within a week of the congress concluding. Political interference and the removal of the prefect's independent power were the reasons cited, but his real concern may have been what might be revealed about his operational methods, once subject to political scrutiny.

On one subject, at least, the congress had been able to agree whole-heartedly: the injustice of Johann Most's trial. The English delegates in particular saw it as their duty to rally to his defence, inspired, perhaps, by Most's counsel, who claimed to have taken on the case in order to ensure that English rather than Russian law prevailed. Standing on the steps of the Old Bailey, when the congress was not in session, they peddled copies of *Freiheit*. Meanwhile, public meetings at the Mile End Waste provided delegates with an opportunity to let off steam, after hours cooped in a small and smoky room. Their efforts had no influence on the outcome, though. The jury's guilty verdict was delivered promptly, having needed little discussion, and its pleas for clemency in the sentencing, out of sympathy for all Most had suffered abroad, were just as quickly disregarded. In light of the Establishment's opprobrium of Most, the maximum sentence was a foregone conclusion. Condemned to two years' hard labour, the unfortunate Most was dragged off to pick oakum in the medieval conditions of Clerkenwell gaol: forced to split tarred rope down to its fibres, with bleeding finger-nails, for ten hours a day.

If the aim of his prosecution had indeed been to influence the American policy on the extradition of Fenians, it failed: a week after the verdict, the State Department refused Britain's request point blank, leaving Gladstone to personally pursue other, less orthodox methods of counter-terrorism. Among the last letters that Allan Pinkerton would write on behalf of his agency, before it passed into his sons' hands following his death a year later, was one to the British prime minister, pitching for work in the delicate matter of disrupting the Fenian's fund-raising in the

United States. Unsurprisingly, it was not only the European democracies who were prepared to deal with the Pinkertons: before long the tsarist police would be among the agency's clients.

*

It had been a significant achievement for so many anarchists to convene in London from so many distant countries, even while the aftershocks of the tsar's murder continued to reverberate. For those more rootless émigrés among the delegates who stayed on for some weeks after the congress, as Kropotkin did to address several public meetings, the risks entailed in their visit to the British capital grew. When the time came for them to leave, the climate across the Continent had become significantly more hostile to political troublemakers, and their destination a matter of doubt. In the more sensationalist French press, whose reports fed off propaganda out of Russia and the fears of its own population, the 'nihilists' who had killed the tsar were firmly conflated with native anarchists. In Switzerland, as Malatesta could have warned Kropotkin, a new intolerance was abroad. Yet it was nevertheless to Switzerland, through France, that he now travelled, drawn back by the presence of his young wife of two years, Sofia, whose medical studies tied her to Geneva.

Even since March, Russian pressure had been building on Switzerland to expel its anti-tsarist refugees, the threatened sanctions severe and escalating: diplomatic relations would be broken off, Swiss citizens expelled from St Petersburg and prohibitive tariffs imposed on trade. Failure to cede, it was implied, would ultimately incur the same penalty as had loomed after the revolutions of 1848: annexation by Germany, only this time with Russian acquiescence. A small country, Switzerland was in no position to resist, and there were few fugitives whose presence was more likely to rile Russia than Kropotkin's. Barely had he arrived when a theoretical article published by him in *Le Révolté* concerning the tsar's assassination was seized upon as a pretext for his detention and expulsion. Dissuaded by friends from the suicidal madness of returning to Russia, where no one could be trusted and he would soon be betrayed, Kropotkin found himself adrift.

Events in France that autumn fuelled fears that a home-grown campaign of terror was imminent, when a young weaver called Florian murdered a middle-aged doctor, mistaking him for a politician; despite having no ostensible anarchist affiliations, he cited the ideology as justification for his act. The febrile atmosphere was exacerbated by growing political instability when Léon Gambetta, on beginning his first and long-awaited ministry that November, staked his political career on a policy of electoral reform, in a quest to end the factionalism that racked France's political life. When financial fears surrounding the viability of the Catholic Union Générale bank were added to the mix, the situation seemed highly volatile. In other circumstances, Kropotkin would surely have stayed to reap the revolutionary benefits when, within days of the New Year dawning, the bank crashed and Gambetta fell from office. As it was, the warning of a threat to his life by a secret society of diehard tsarist partisans, communicated to him through back channels by a high-ranking source in the Russian government, forced his return to London just before Christmas.

Though the threat was apparently real, the plot against Kropotkin might have sprung direct from the pages of an adventure story, and surely made for good telling during the festive season, as the émigrés moved between the Patriotic Club and celebrations with the old English radicals in Clerkenwell, and one another's homes. The tsarist assassins meant to avenge the late tsar and defend the new by hiring a 'consummate swordsman' who would kill Kropotkin in a duel; Rochefort was to be similarly challenged, and if the strategy was successful then further swashbuckling assassinations were to follow, with Hartmann next on the hit list.

Hartmann would, at least, have been able to counter Kropotkin's party piece with a compelling tale of his own, concerning the Italian spies who dogged him and Malatesta during their studies in chemistry and mineralogy in the British Museum. But any laughter their stories evinced, nervous or otherwise, would have been tinged with sadness at the condition of one of their fellow guests. The aggressive paranoia that Kropotkin had detected in Cafiero during their dealings earlier in the year had begun to manifest itself in a peculiar new symptom: he was 'haunted by the notion that he might be enjoying more than his fair share of sunlight'. It was a tragic, if strangely appropriate ailment to afflict the anarchist aristocrat who had devoted years of strain and suffering to the cause, and one that marked the beginning of a slow and pitiful decline into insanity.

Against this sombre backdrop, and despite the sympathetic minds he encountered in Britain, Kropotkin could not help feeling enervated by the country's political stolidity, just as he had done on his first arrival. Two decades before, his compatriot and ideological forebear Alexander Herzen had called life in London 'as boring as that of worms in a cheese'. It was a sentiment that Kropotkin now echoed and acted upon, rashly announcing 'Better a French prison than this grave.' His wish would be answered all too soon.

*

Having left his story of the assassin-duellist in the safe hands of the British press, by way of insurance, Kropotkin next made directly for the epicentre of social conflict in France: the strike-bound second city of France, industrial Lyons, in whose recession-hit mines and silk factories workers had risen up in protest at their working conditions. Louise Michel, who had addressed the local silk workers on a number of occasions in 1881 and 1882, described their campaign as 'a savage revolt against management and church oppression', which had as its target the symbols of Church power: in night-time raids, crosses were stolen from religious sites and thrown down wells or otherwise desecrated. However, the wild, carnivalesque atmosphere had soon turned into something darker and more dangerous as the Black Band, as they became known, appeared to turn its ire on individuals.

Threatening letters to leading figures in Montceau-les-Mines were followed by physical attacks. The campaign of violence reached its highest pitch on 22 October 1882, with a bomb thrown into the Bellecour theatre in Lyons, fatally wounding one of its staff. It was a turning point in public perception of the strikers, who despite having had little contact with local anarchists were seen as terroristic conspirators. Cyvoct, an anarchist, was accused of the bomb-throwing but fled to Belgium before he could be apprehended, while claims that the bomb itself had been donated by the nihilists of Geneva further fed the myth of an international revolutionary party.

Interviewed by *L'Express* newspaper, Sophie Bardina, the 'Auntie' of the old Fritsche group of female medical students, tried to make clear the distinction: 'Yes, we are anarchists,' she said of the Russians who had recently killed the tsar, 'but, for us, anarchy does not signify disorder, but harmony in all social relations; for us, anarchy is nothing but the negation of oppressions which stifle the development of free societies.' Despite the scrupulous semantics of Reclus' definition that 'All revolutionary acts are by their very nature anarchical, whatever the power which seeks to profit from them', neither he nor Kropotkin, both of whom were in Thonon at the time of the Bellecour bombing, appeared eager to dissociate themselves from the violence. After the shooting dead of a minor industrialist in the French transportation hub of Roanne by a disgruntled ex-employee in the spring of 1882, *Le Révolté* incautiously hailed the act as a laudable example of 'propaganda by deed', while Kropotkin's speeches to the Lyons strikers would be eagerly seized upon as evidence of incitement.

It was against the backdrop of the ongoing strikes that Emile Zola wrote *Germinal*. Set twenty years earlier in the fictional northern coal town of 'Montsou', its hyper-realist depiction of the landscape around the ravenous maw of the La Voreux coal mine, and its vision of poverty making animals of men, carry powerful echoes of the strikes of August 1882. The novel is interesting too, for the fictional portrait it paints of the Russian anarchist Souvarine: a cerebral, sensitive but outspoken opponent of the protagonist's Marxist 'balderdash', whose semi-detached advocacy of the need to tear down the old world and start afresh dripfeeds the violence that rages around him. Bakunin is usually thought the model, though the characterisation is perhaps closer to a demonic version of Kropotkin: indeed Souvarine's fondness for his pet rabbit echoes Kropotkin's passion for the species as 'the symbol of perdurability [that] stood out against selection'.

Whilst not culpable of the kind of gargantuan act of destructiveness ultimately carried out by Zola's Souvarine, Kropotkin found himself squarely in the frame for encouraging the violence of the current strikers. Following the arrests of close associates, he came under intense surveillance, pending the authorities' decision on how to deal with such a high-profile offender. 'Flocks, literally flocks of Russian spies besieged the house,' he wrote, 'seeking admission under all possible pretexts, or simply tramping in pairs, trios, and quartets in front of the house.'

With his wife's sick brother to nurse, and their new baby daughter to attend to, it was a testing, nervous time for Kropotkin, whose family was living in straitened circumstances. In the space of a few hours, however, overnight on 21 December 1882, matters were resolved in the saddest fashion when the death of his brother-in-law was followed, at dawn, by Kropotkin's arrest. His friends rallied round: Reclus immediately offered to give himself up to the authorities, in the hope that it would shame those persecuting his friend. In the prevailing climate, though, even Reclus' intellectual status counted for little. With Switzerland slipping ever further towards political and moral intolerance, he had also recently come close to expulsion for the scandalous indecency of allowing his two daughters to marry their sweethearts with neither priest nor mayor in attendance.

Kropotkin's long, tightly controlled speech to the Lyons court was a masterpiece of anarchist oratory: 'We want liberty, that is to say that we reclaim for every human being the right and the means to do as he pleases, and not to do what he does not like; to satisfy fully all his needs, with no other limit than the impossibilities of nature and respect for the equal needs of his neighbours . . . we believe that capital, the common inheritance of all humanity, since the fruit of collaboration of past and present generations, must be at the disposal of all.' And when cross-examined he challenged the loose logic employed by the prosecution, setting a precedent of witty sidestepping for future anarchists on trial. The verdict and heavy sentence, though, had been widely predicted. Most of the sixty-five other anarchists with whom he shared the dock were imprisoned for six months or a year, on the spurious grounds of membership of the defunct International. Kropotkin was condemned to a full five years, incurred a 2,000-franc fine and was placed under official surveillance for a further decade. The tsar could scarcely have hoped for a harsher punishment had he dictated it himself.

Neither a grand petition from 'English savants', inscribed in fine calligraphy, and bristling with the names of professors, editors and luminaries of the Royal Societies, urging that Kropotkin's intellectual importance warranted special treatment, nor the intervention of Victor Hugo, made any impression on the procurator general or the minister of the interior. The French authorities looked to Andalucia, where their Spanish counterparts were busy suppressing rural insurrections coordinated by what they took to calling La Mano Negra, the Black Hand, purely on the basis of the imprint of an ink-stained hand found on a wall near the scene of one crime. 'At a time when anarchism is on the march, we can see no reason to grant mercy,' they concluded, remarking snidely that the special treatment that Kropotkin received in Clairvaux prison, thanks to donations from well-wishers, had already aroused the resentment of his fellow inmates.

The next of the congress delegates to find themselves back behind bars was Louise Michel. After spending ten days in prison in January 1883 for commemorating the anniversary of Blanqui's death, she spent the rest of the year working tirelessly to help the amnestied Communards, even returning to London to try to raise funds for a Paris soup kitchen. Accepting all invitations to speak at meetings, she frequently had to disappoint audiences when she was accidentally double- or triple-booked. 'The cause of the revolution is not served by pointless murder', she told one packed hall, but was uncompromising in her threat that 'If they import the Russian system to fight us, we'll have the courage of the

Russians to detroy it!' Shouts of 'Long live dynamite!' punctuated her speeches, and her pledge to march henceforth behind the black flag of mourning rather than the red of revolution did nothing to reassure the police.

It was under the black flag that she and Emile Pouget led a demonstration in March to the politically sensitive site of Les Invalides, the resting place of Bonaparte's sarcophagus, where Michel offered an impassioned defence of the people's right to bread. Roused by her speech, the marchers became a mob, ransacking the bakeries of l'esplanade des Invalides and rue de Sèvres, before heading off towards the Elysée Palace. Alive to how bread riots could presage revolution, the police speedily intervened, but apprehending Michel herself proved far from straightforward. For three weeks one of the most closely watched figures in the country simply disappeared. Posters bearing her iconic features were circulated internationally, with false sightings reported as far apart as London and Geneva. Then, out of the blue, Michel simply presented herself for arrest at her local Paris police station. Having all the while been holed up in a nearby flat, tending her sick mother, she revelled in having made fools of the prefecture.

'We amnestied the Communards: look where that's got us' complained *Le Figaro*, and was relieved when the error was to some extent rectified, in a sentence for Michel of six years in prison and a further ten under surveillance. Other more moderate publications, however, feared that the severity of the sentence might prove counterproductive, with even one normally hostile journalist going so far as to comment that 'Two more judgements like those, and the anarchist party might become a reality.' In fact, while Louise Michel served her time in Saint-Lazare, other factors would decide the matter.

II

The Holy Brotherhood

Russia and Paris, 1881–1885

Retribution against those who plotted the tsar's death in 1881 had been swift, coming while St Petersburg was still draped in the black crepe of mourning, and Alexander II's heir sheltered behind the counter-mining fortifications of the palace at Gatchina. Having shown their ineptitude in failing to prevent the attack, Russia's newly reorganised police department conducted the round-ups with striking efficiency. Rysakov, who had thrown the first bomb, broke under interrogation, and using information he provided, the police soon tracked down the leading plotters and apprehended them amid a flurry of shoot-outs and suicides. On 26 March 1881, seven of the conspirators were put on trial and, a week later, condemned to death. Many fled abroad and by the middle of May, Vera Figner alone of the executive committee remained at liberty in Russia. Thirty-six conspirators would appear in court, eighteen were condemned to death, five executed and the rest sent to prison for a total of 500 years.

The new tsar was adamant that there should be no commutation of sentences, nor the slightest display of mercy. Sofia Perovskaya was hanged alongside her lover Zhelyabov on the Semyonovsky parade ground, a placard naming them as regicides around their necks. Rysakov was one of the three others who died the same day, spurned by his comrades for his treachery; Kibalchich another, his tragic struggle having failed, not only for the social justice which the tsar had appeared to impede, but for the right to intellectual self-fulfilment too. Having spent his last days scrawling plans for directional rocket engines, the specialism he had neglected while at liberty, Kibalchich had entrusted a document describing his vision of an aeronautic machine to the chief of the gendarmerie. His final wish was merely that his scientific peers confirm the practicality of his design – a first step towards space travel – so that he might 'meet death calmly, knowing that my idea shall not die with me but will benefit the human race for which I am willing to sacrifice my life'. But as the trapdoor opened beneath his feet, his ideas had already begun to gather dust in the archives of the police department. Its director had concluded that 'To give this to scientists for consideration now would hardly be expedient since it could only encourage wanton talk.' Scientific genius and terrorism were disquieting bedfellows.

Alone among the main conspirators in being Jewish, only Gesia Gelfman was spared the noose, on account of her pregnancy. On top of her life sentence, her punishment was to have her child taken from her the moment it was born for an Orthodox Christian upbringing, and shortly after she died of grief. That the authorities considered her much-publicised involvement in the attack insufficient incitement to racially motived revenge was demonstrated by the description that was circulated of another of the conspirators, not as a typical Slav, as he had been referred to in the immediate aftermath of the assassination attack, but an 'Oriental [with a] hooked nose'. For some, it seemed, the desire to galvanise anti-Semitic sentiment was of at least equal importance to identifying and catching the assassins.

Alexander III's mentor Pobedonostsev was perfectly sincere in his belief that the Jews were a 'great ulcer' eating away at Russia: at once a threat to its spiritual and racial purity and the secret force behind any foreign diplomacy that threatened the national interest. In his ideal world, the five million Jews already restricted to the Pale of Settlement in the west of the country would be reduced by two thirds, half of whom would die and half emigrate, with the remaining third converted to Orthodoxy.

On 15 April 1881, Orthodox Easter, the first pogrom had broken out. Surprisingly, no firm evidence has ever come to light that the attacks on Russia's Jews had been incited from above. Pobedonostsev, procurator of the Orthodox synod, would have understood all too well, though, how the conflation of the murdered tsar with Christ, the paschal lamb sacrificed by the Jews, might fuel the avengers' anger. Two hundred and fifty separate outbreaks of violence followed in the next two years, the pogroms spreading, as if spontaneously, along the recently laid railways, leaving dozens dead, hundreds more badly beaten and Jewish property in ruins. The migration of seasonal workers, rather than any more sinister agency, is the preferred explanation. However, there was an uncanny uniformity to the attacks, with victims knowing that when the pogrom arrived, a three-day carnival of terror and humiliation was in store.

*

The origins of the supposedly secret society that was formed as the elite's response to the assassination of the tsar are unclear. Intriguingly, though, the chief of the south-western railway, Sergei Witte, was later keen to claim the germ of the idea as his own. Having written to his uncle General Fedeev in the immediate aftermath of the tsar's assassination, proposing that loyalists should combat the terrorists using their own methods, he was summoned to meet the commander of the emperor's bodyguards, Count Vorontsov-Dashkov, and Count Peter Shuvalov, the ex-head of the disbanded Third Section, who there and then instructed him to swear an oath of allegiance 'to the society formed on the basis of my letter.' If it is true that the Holy Brotherhood was established with such speed, it makes it implausible that it was anything other than a long-cherished project for which a pretext had been found. The retired Colonel Stieber, a long-time ally of Shuvalov, now nearing the end of his life, would surely have nodded his grizzled head in approval.

Credulous as to the existence of a vast, international terrorist network, comprising myriad small self-sufficient cells in order to inhibit enemy penetration, the progenitors of the Holy Brotherhood structured their own organisation on the same model, with an added dash of the Masonic occult. At the apex of the Brotherhood stood a five-strong council of elders, each the designated contact for a subsidiary group of five, and so on, down to the sixth and eighth tiers of more than 3,000 cells, boasting such assertive or esoteric names as Talmud, Success or Genius. 'I dedicate myself entirely to the protection of His Majesty the emperor and to the persecution of sedition which casts shame on the name of Russia,' swore initiates, including the composer Peter Tchaikovsky: 'Brother number 6, Assistance.' They then received a macabre symbol of membership: a gold disc enamelled with the image of St Alexander Nevsky, his legs shattered as those of Alexander II had been by the fatal bomb.

Members of the Holy Brotherhood must have been intoxicated by its promise of state-sanctioned conspiracy but the confidence instilled by the supposed fraternal support of twenty thousand kindred spirits, the unseen members of nearly 4,000 cells, was wholly illusory. That the Brotherhood numbered scarcely more than 700, even at its peak, most of who were drawn from the idle rich of St Petersburg, including many members of the city's Yacht Club, was one secret it guarded with particular care. Nevertheless, lavishly funded by state and private donations, the Brotherhood launched a torrent of initiatives, mostly illegal and ill-judged, that were in reality little more than the superannuated adolescent fantasies of men who should have known better. There was the swashbuckling plan to challenge both Kropotkin and Rochefort to duels, that the former denounced to the press in London, and another to dispatch femmes fatales to marry and then eliminate such troublesome figures as Lev Hartmann. And then there was the revolutionary journal it founded in Switzerland to disseminate provocative falsehoods, brazenly titled *Pravda*, or 'Truth'. The inclusion of an article advocating the eradication of the landowning class, but specifically urging activists to blow up their cattle with explosives as an initial practical step towards revolution, however, took nobody in. Only the blue pencil of the censor shielded the Brotherhood from satire; the French Sûreté, however, felt no compunction about describing it as 'a complete joke', and it was not alone in finding its activities abroad to be a serious nuisance.

Within a short time, prominent figures of all persuasions were recoiling at the organisation's notoriety. 'The agents of the Brotherhood are compromising us everywhere,' complained the interior minister, Count Ignatiev, to Pobedonostev, who himself wrote to the tsar to disown any association with the failing project. How the ousted Loris-Melikov viewed its activities was best illustrated by his willingness to use the exiled Peter Lavrov as a conduit for the secret warning he passed to Kropotkin of the Brotherhood's murderous intentions. At a hazardous time for the new tsar's government, when clarity of message was essential, the Brotherhood was fostering chaos and confusion. Mindful of how the aristocratic and officer-class profile of the Brotherhood's membership resembled that of the groups which had cultivated troublesome court intrigues against past tsars, Pobedonostsev settled on drastic action and chose the fast-rising Lieutenant General Grigori Sudeikin as the ideal man to bring the dangerous farce of the Brotherhood to an end, appointing him to the new position of inspector of the secret police.

A slim and elegantly bewhiskered thirty-five-year-old of good breeding, with a scintillating, subtle mind and a ruthless dedication to his job, Grigori Sudeikin was said by some to have his eyes on the highest political prizes. His ticket to the top, the destruction of the Brotherhood, became a personal obsession: 'The revolutionaries are people, they have ideals,' he wrote, 'but this lot are a mob! A mob under protection! They are annoying me no end.' With a keen grasp of the black arts, he ruthlessly identified the back channels that the Brotherhood had opened for negotiation with the terrorists as the salient point for his attack. All that was needed to seal its fate, Sudeikin realised, was to exaggerate the degree of collusion, and so he arranged the forging of a document that purported to originate from the executive committee of the People's Will, discussing its coordination of strategy with the Brotherhood. Within weeks, recruitment to the Brotherhood was indefinitely suspended, and before long the organisation withered; certain members, however, may have internalised its principles.

Among the Brothers who were left searching for new fields in which to employ their morally dubious talents was Peter Rachkovsky. Since his exposure as a police infiltration agent in early 1880, he had drifted from assignment to assignment on the north-western periphery of the Russian Empire, first in Vilnius, then Cracow. His career stalling, due to his superiors' concern that he might be recognised, the advent of the Holy Brotherhood had offered Rachkovsky a timely opportunity, and he had promptly asked permission to return to Moscow and enrol. Quick-witted and calculating, he would have relished the Brotherhood's cavalier attitude to the law when plotting its intrigues, while the slosh of the millions of rubles in the Brotherhood's coffers would have appealed to his mercenary side and reaffirmed his fading belief in the personal profit he might derive from his chosen trade. There had been useful contacts to be made too, including perhaps Matvei Golovinsky, who would prove accomplished at contriving fraudulent evidence of heinous Jewish conspiracies. What Rachkovsky really needed, however, was a mentor to ease his professional advancement.

Colonel Sudeikin had been watching and assessing Rachkovsky for some time prior to May 1882, when he finally decided to overlook Rachkovsky's poor judgement in joining the Brotherhood and approached him with an offer of employment in the St Petersburg Okhrana. Rachkovsky accepted and it was not long before he had risen to become Sudeikin's invaluable lieutenant, a position that put him on a higher career trajectory than he could possibly have realised.

Determined to infiltrate the ranks of the People's Will that Vera Figner was striving to rebuild, Sudeikin needed informants. It was to this end that in late 1882 he targeted Captain Sergei Degaev, a recent recruit to the executive committee of the People's Will from among the disillusioned officers of the naval base at Kronstadt, whose character flaws of egotism and vanity suggested him as a likely candidate for 'turning'. Tracked down to Odessa, on leads supplied by his captured brother, Degaev was arrested in a raid on the underground printing workshop that he had been assigned to establish there. Flattered by Sudeikin's attention and the discussion of how they might help each other achieve their ambitions, Degaev became a paid agent of the Okhrana. What followed, however, would provide Rachkovsky with a masterclass in the subtleties and, ultimately, the fatal risks of psychological manipulation.

Exploiting the trust placed in him by the leading exiles in Switzerland, Degaev caused havoc among his colleagues, luring them into Okhrana traps and gathering information to assist Sudeikin in his raids. Vera Figner, the leading figure of the movement, was betrayed to Sudeikin in short order, arrested on re-entering Russia and handed a life sentence. Tikhomirov was more circumspect, however, refusing to take Degaev's story at face value. Doubts remained even when Degaev revealed the identity of a prominent police informant in the ranks of the People's Will, an asset deemed expendable by Sudeikin if his exposure bought his new agent's credibility.

Under interrogation by his colleagues on the executive committee of the People's Will, Degaev broke down and revealed his treachery, pleading for forgiveness. The request was granted but at the price of a deadly penance: he must murder Sudeikin. Degaev appeared genuinely discombobulated: torn between envy and duty, loyalty and ambition, from this point on his actions appeared to be calculated solely by short-term personal advantage. As such, Degaev acceded willingly, at first, to Sudeikin's suggestion that he act as an agent provocateur in inciting the assassination of two key figures of the reactionary Establishment, Grand Prince Vladimir and the interior minister, Count Dmitri Tolstoy. It was a devious plot meant to elevate the frustrated policeman to a ministerial post, while cutting the ground from beneath the feet of Degaev's critics in the People's Will, and he dearly wanted to believe that it might work. It was with great reluctance, therefore, that in December 1883 Degaev finally gave in to pressure and fulfilled his promise to the executive committee.

A gruesome scene would have confronted Rachkovsky in the apartment to which Degaev had lured his mentor the day before. Shortly after Sudeikin's arrival, two People's Will accomplices had emerged from hiding: one had fired the pistol shot that entered his abdominal cavity and burst the tissue of his liver, another had repeatedly bludgeoned his skull with a crowbar. The agents of the Okhrana did not take long to identify the main culprit and put his associates under surveillance, but Degaev had gone to ground and it took until the end of the year for them to catch his scent, when his wife was sighted in Paris. Immediately, Rachkovsky was dispatched to locate Madame Degaev and track down Sergei himself.

*

As the thirty-two-year-old Peter Rachkovsky closed the carriage door behind him on a cold, bleak St Petersburg and settled into his seat for the long journey to the west, he must have felt a certain sense of satisfaction. The Russian Embassy in Paris had been told to cooperate with him for the period of his inquiries, and he had been sanctioned to conduct the investigation according to his own initiative. It was the opportunity of a lifetime. When he stepped out on to the platform of Gare du Nord in Paris two days later, where censers puffed out smoke to fumigate the germs of the cholera epidemic that was sweeping the southern part of the Continent, he was surely resolved to make his mark in the world's most glamorous metropolis.

The Imperial Russian Embassy on the rue de Grenelle would have made a grand impression as Rachkovsky crunched across the gravel of its courtyard and under the broad glass canopy that sheltered its entrance. But in the two rooms of the wing occupied by the Okhrana's foreign agency, the director of the Paris bureau, Peter Korvin-Krukovsky, was running a shockingly ineffectual operation. A minor wordsmith with connections in the French literary world, whose personal fame rested on his co-authorship with Alexandre Dumas of the 1877 play *Les Davicheffs*, Korvin-Krukovsky had originally been employed by the Russian government to help soften French press attitudes towards Alexander III at the time of his coronation. How this stopgap public-relations officer had since been so over-promoted was a mystery to everyone and a source of ongoing interest, both professional and prurient, for the surveillance agents of the Sûreté. The complexity of his romantic life alone was sufficient to explain any inattention to his job: having married Stella Colas, star of the Odéon theatre, he had since moved in with her sister, who happened to be the ex-mistress of his own brother-in-law, Baron de Foelckersahmb. But even the need to counter the runaway success of Victorien Sardou's new revenge drama, *Fedora* – with Sarah Bernhardt returning to the Paris stage to play a heroine inspired by Figner and Perovskaya – could not justify his continued dabbling in theatre.

The prefecture's 'Agent Arnold', keeping watch over Korvin-Krukovsky's activities, struggled to conceal his contempt for the dilettante's affectations. Of greater interest to his superiors, though, were observations concerning the huge sums of money paid monthly into his bank account by figures linked to the Orléanist claimant to the French throne. As far back as the autumn of 1881, the Sûreté had noted the apparent use of agents provocateurs by the Russians in Paris. Such intrigues might be overlooked as long as they were confined to flushing out the remnants of the People's Will among the émigré community, but became intolerable if they intruded into the volatile domestic politics of France. At a time when the previously unknown League of French Nihilists was boasting in a leaked manifesto of its secret three-year campaign to poison hundreds of bourgeois families, that certainly now appeared the case.

In April 1884, the end of Prince Orlov's tenure at the embassy provided the occasion for Korvin-Krukovsky's recall on the pretext of financial laxity. The new Russian ambassador to France was Baron de Mohrenheim, the very man who, as a lowly consular attaché in Berlin nearly thirty years earlier, had arranged for Wilhelm Stieber to be smuggled across the city in a laundry basket and offered a job working for the Russians. Now an austere senior statesman with cropped grey hair and a waxed moustache, de Mohrenheim enjoyed the lasting favour of Alexander III for having facilitated his courtship of the Danish Princess Dagmar, now the tsar's wife, during his posting to Copenhagen in the 1870s, and yet he remained acutely aware of his vulnerability to the vagaries of court politics. Now that Stieber had quit the stage, de Mohrenheim was eager to recruit a new spymaster to take up the baton, and Rachkovsky appeared a promising candidate: one sufficiently independent of any faction, yet adept at feigning friendship and allegiance wherever necessary.

In the heady atmosphere of bohemian Paris in the 1880s, myriad rival sects flourished that cut across the clearly demarcated battle lines of reaction and revolution in the Russian émigré community. To understand their agendas, even to insinuate oneself into their trust, was to gain a powerful advantage in the deadly and secret games being played out. The contacts that Rachkovsky could draw upon from his time in the Holy Brotherhood stood him in good stead.

His 'Trojan Horse' appears to have been a young woman by the name of Yuliana Glinka, the granddaughter of a colonel whose Masonic affiliations had led to his arrest for involvement in the Decembrists' plot of 1825 against Tsar Nicholas I. Glinka had inherited her forebear's fascination with mysticism along with his taste for conspiracy. Recommended by a high-ranking family friend, she plunged into the city's occult subculture as Rachkovsky's proxy. In this she was helped no end by the sponsorship of Juliette Adam, the feminist wife of an ex-prefect of police and senator, who had been the doyenne of literary-political Paris for the best part of two decades, and was now editor of the influential *Nouvelle Revue*. It was perhaps no coincidence that three years earlier, when visiting St Petersburg, Adam had dined in the homes of some of the most generous funders of the Holy Brotherhood.

By the end of 1884, when Glinka's lover arrived from Russia, she was fully immersed in a demi-monde of dizzying complexity. Madame Blavatsky, who Glinka now numbered among her friends, was the cousin of Sergei Witte, and her works were published in Russia by the arch-nationalist journalist and ideologue Mikhail Katkov; Adam was in correspondence with Louise Michel, through whom she had sent clothes to the prisoners in New Caledonia, and was a friend of Henri Rochefort, who some even suggested had been her erstwhile lover in the 1860s, and the father of her child. Endless permutations of intrigue opened up to Rachkovsky, and when Ambassador de Mohrenheim's own contacts were factored in, the possibilities became even more elaborate. Of particular note, in this respect, was Alexandre Saint-Yves d'Alveydre, the French occultist, whose marriage to the Danish Countess Keller, a close friend of the new tsarina, had made him the favoured guru of the Russian court.

D'Alveydre was an evangelist of 'synarchy', a political philosophy conceived explicity to counter the anarchist threat of revolution, advocating a strict, caste-like social hierarchy and transcendent authority as the path to the new society. It was an aim that he tried to realise through his personal friendships with the crowned heads of Europe. And as with Blavatsky, who was, it has been suggested, recruited on to the Okhrana payroll at this time, he brought with him into Rachkovsky's orbit a coterie of devotees: men like Gérard Encausse, a physician then working with hypnosis in Charcot's psychiatric experiments at the Salpêtrière hospital, who was temporarily in thrall to d'Alveydre's reactionary teachings. Inevitably, however, rivals too lurked in the Parisian shadows, the most prominent being Elie Cyon, or 'de Cyon' as the ex-professor of physiology now called himself, the aristocratic prefix intended to add lustre to his honorary position as a privy councillor to the tsar. But while de Cyon had already staked his place as an international deal-broker, the novelist Turgenev, for one, considered him a 'great scoundrel', and his reactionary views had led to the rejection of his application for a chair at the Sorbonne.

Rachkovsky's priority, however, was to make himself indispensable to any in St Petersburg who doubted his abilities, which above all meant the new director of police, Vyacheslav von Plehve, who was soon to become deputy minister of the interior. When de Mohrenheim had the temerity to prompt Rachkovsky, over a tip-off claiming that Alexander II's widow was plotting with the émigrés and funding their activities, Rachkovsky's response to his interference was stinging. If the Princess Yurievskaya were channelling money to the group, he tartly replied, he would certainly have heard of it. There were solid grounds for his growing confidence. German Lopatin, elected as leader of the meagre remnants of the People's Will that were still at liberty, at a meeting of the executive in Paris early in 1884, had been apprehended in St Petersburg before the year was out, having just returned from France with an incriminating list of those who might rebuild the movement; Tikhomirov, the other key figure in exile, was 'surrounded by shipwrecked men, the debris of every imaginable circle and grouping', his psychological state becoming ever more fragile.

Nevertheless, Rachkovsky was far from complacent. Writing to Fragnon, the recently appointed chief of the Sûreté, he explained his strategy: 'I am endeavouring to demoralise [the émigrés] politically, to inject discord among revolutionary forces, to weaken them, and at the same time to suppress every revolutionary act at its source.' It was an attitude which paid professional dividends when, late in 1884, Police Councillor Sergei Zvoliansky, who had been sent to assess progress at the Paris *agentura* and smooth its relations with the French government, reported back that Rachkovsky should be given the time and space to build up his team without interruption or interference.

Since its inception, the Paris Okhrana had depended on the assistance, official and unofficial, of the French Sûreté, the investigative arm of the prefecture of police. Indeed its first detectives, known as the Barlet Brigade after their leader, Alexandre Barlet, had been hired from the ranks of the Sûreté's ex-officers. The Sûreté was, however, an unreliable organisation, staffed by those on punitive redeployment from elsewhere in the French police service and prone to leaks; staff were even known to moonlight for *La Lanterne*, writing articles attacking their own colleagues. The very ease with which Sûreté files found their way on to Rachkovsky's desk must have alarmed him, while the poor quality of much of the intelligence would have sounded a further warning. And on those occasions when Rachkovsky went to meet the incumbent prefect of police, Gustave Mace, in person, the tiny waiting room that visitors had to share with prostitutes and drunkards – sometimes squeezed in beside the hereditary state executioner, Louis Deibler – must have left a poor impression. The Paris Okhrana clearly needed fresh blood.

In developing his own stable of operatives, Rachkovsky learned from the mistakes that had cost Sudeikin his life. Even the security of the *agentura*'s offices was reinforced, with the addition of a second locking door and bars on the windows; the three clerical assistants and code-breakers who worked behind these fortifications were of proven loyalty, while a member of the Barlet Brigade, Riant, was bribed to spy on his colleagues. When it came to the kind of clandestine and provocative operations in which Rachkovsky would specialise – in particular those requiring deep-cover agents – it was impossible to exercise too much caution: he knew only too well how prolonged periods immersed in deception and betrayal could eat away at a man's psyche and corrode his loyalty.

It was Police Councillor Zvoliansky who had initiated the recruitment of Abraham Hekkelman to the Paris bureau, suggesting to Rachkovsky that 'he could be one of our most useful agents'. Amongst those in the know, Hekkelman's sangfroid was legendary, having consistently turned the tables on any colleague in the People's Will who had accused him of being an informant: even his old university friend, Burtsev, had been tricked into leaping to his defence, in the face of compelling evidence of his guilt. No exception would be made, however, to Rachkovsky's fastidious vetting of recruits and Hekkelman underwent four days of intense probing and indoctrination. Debriefed over and over again about past examples of carelessness in both Russia and Switzerland, his psychological resilience was tested and tempered. The intensive process paid off, its primary product an operative of steely ruthlessness who was impervious to suspicion and, as a by-product, a relationship was forged between agent and controller of constantly affirmative intimacy that would make both men rich and powerful.

Hekkelman must have recognised straight away that something special could come out of the promised partnership. When approached by Zvoliansky, he had demanded 1,000 francs a month and a posting to Paris, with all its fleshly delights. Rachkovsky persuaded him to work for less than a third of that sum, and to immediately return to Switzerland under cover, this time as 'Landesen', a name borrowed from an influential Latvian family. But there were benefits to sweeten the pill: direct access to the dossiers Rachkovsky had already compiled on those émigrés Hekkelman would encounter, and a well-financed cover story, setting him up as the son of affluent parents. Landesen's fictitious private income, drawn as necessary from the Okhrana coffers and available to fund whatever schemes he dreamed up to entrap his targets, was a sleight of hand typical of Rachkovsky.

For once, the Paris Okhrana chief could write in something like good faith to Fragnon in 1885 that 'all my internal agents are of deep conviction and . . . receive no salary but to enable them to live and proceed actively among the émigrés, never on a lucrative basis!' For Rachkovsky to make any further claim to virtue or honesty, however, would have been wholly disingenuous: prominent among his early initiatives were provocations designed to lure credulous émigrés into the most heinous crimes of which they may never have otherwise conceived.

The burden of responsibilities that Rachkovsky had assumed since coming to Paris made it hardly surprising that his original objective slipped through the net. As the ship returning the failed colony-builder William Frey to London in the autumn of 1884 crossed the Atlantic, it might have passed the one carrying a disguised Sergei Degaev in the opposite direction. And by early 1885, when the tsar handed the tsarina her first fabulously jewelled Easter egg, wrought by his favourite French goldsmith Peter Carl Fabergé, Degaev was already making a new life for himself in America. Reborn as Alexander Pell, he would in time become head of the mathematics department at the University of South Dakota. He would never return to Russia.

Frey, having established a business in London selling tooth-breaking wholewheat rusks, and with it a tiny cult following, did go back to his homeland on a brief trip that spring, that involved two notable encounters. The first was with the novelist Leo Tolstoy, converted some years earlier by another ex-resident of Cedar Vale to a life lived according to the literal interpretation of Christ's Sermon on the Mount – a religious form of anarchism – since when he had been regularly harassed and censored by the police. 'Yes, my friend . . . you are quite right. Thanks, thanks for your wise and honest words!' the author of *War and Peace* and *Anna Karenina* told his sage visitor, having listened to him speak for some time. The utopian insight Frey had offered? The suitability of fruit and nuts to the human diet.

Frey's second, more fleeting encounter was with a brilliant young zoology student who attended a lecture by Frey. Neither Alexander Ilyich Ulyanov, nor his younger brother Vladimir Ilyich, would have any truck with vegetarianism, but in the years to come first one, and then the other – under the *nom de guerre* 'Lenin' – became the most deadly of all the tsar's enemies.

12

A Great New Tide

England, 1881–1885

The year 1881, noted one British observer, 'marked the oncoming of a great new tide of human life over the western world . . . It was a fascinating and enthusiastic period . . . The socialist and anarchist propaganda, the feminist and suffrage upheaval, the huge trade-union growth, the theosophic movement, the new currents in the theatrical, music and artistic worlds, the torrent even of change in the religious world – all constituted so many streams and headwaters converging, as it were, to a great river.'

The words were those of thirty-seven-year-old Edward Carpenter who, after a decade of committed grass-roots engagement with the education of the working man, could claim a closer affinity with those making waves across the Continent than most Englishmen. In 1871 he had abandoned his life as a curate to visit Paris in the terrible aftermath of the Bloody Week, and had been arrested on the outskirts and interrogated by Stieber's police on suspicion of being a Communard refugee. By the time he returned to France two years later, for a rest cure on the Riviera, he had settled on a new vocation: to 'somehow go and make life with the mass of the people and the manual workers'. It was the same impulse that was then sending the Chaikovsky Circle on their campaign 'to the people'.

Although the Cambridge graduate did not face anything like the same hazards as his Russian peers in his work as a lecturer for Cambridge University's Extension Scheme, his frequent tours of northern industrial towns arguably afforded him a more effective education in the 'rude unaccommodating life below'. Unlike the majority of Russian peasants, the workers he taught were enthusiastic for the insights he could offer into materialism, Darwin's evolutionary theories or Beethoven's life and works, and responsive when he challenged them with the notion that 'Science has strode into the slumbering camp of religion and stands full armed in the midst. Some even brought their own makeshift telescopes to his lectures on astronomy, 'a curious subject in these towns where seldom a star could be seen'.

Carpenter's gruelling exposure to working-class poverty and hardship sharpened his sense of social injustice, while a growing consciousness of his own sexuality lent a powerful personal impetus to his political develop- ment. As much as Paris' status as a centre of social revolution, it was the promise of experimentation with male lovers that appealed: he visited occa- sionally 'to see if by any means I might make a discovery there!' He would soon realise that the answer was to be found closer to home, and that 'my ideal of love is a powerful, strongly built man, of my own age or rather younger – preferably of the working class . . . not be too glib or refined.'

In Sheffield, Carpenter joined the nearby community that had recently been founded by John Ruskin's St George's Guild, to pursue his creed that 'there is no wealth but life'; its failure to meet Carpenter's expectations did not stop him from embracing other experiments in living. A vegetarian, he welcomed the foundation of the anti-vivisection movement, along with a society to promulgate the virtues of a meat-free diet; having dispensed with his dress clothes in favour of a more fustian style, he would surely have been intrigued by the arrival in England of the tight-fitting, rough woollen clothes inspired by the writings of the German hygienist Dr Jaeger with their bold claims to let the body and the spirit breathe. Fascinated by eastern mysticism, he initially kept an open mind too towards the theosophical beliefs being propounded by Madame Blavatsky and the current of enquiry into psychic phenomena and spiritualism. All were symptoms of a new, enquiring age.

Around Easter 1883, Carpenter set about creating his own miniature Utopia on a smallholding at Millthorpe in the Derbyshire countryside, funded by a generous inheritance from his father: over £20,000 of shares in the Pennsylvania Railroad, which had been at the heart of the strikes and violent clashes of 1877, of which he promptly divested himself. But as the year progressed, with the tide in the Thames surging and the sky tinted red from the August eruption of Krakatoa on the far side of the world, Carpenter felt drawn towards a more practical and outward-looking engage- ment with the socialism about which he had begun to lecture to the workers of Sheffield. And so it was that October of that year saw him crossing Westminster Bridge Road, in the shadow of the Houses of Parliament, to enlist in the cause.

*

Compared to the grandeur of Pugin's great Gothic palace in Westminster, the basement venue for the meetings of the Democratic

Federation were far from salubrious. By the light of a couple of candles, propped in tin sconces, Carpenter encountered what seemed like a 'group of conspirators', but both the atmosphere of earnest debate and the considered bearing of the leading members of the movement's executive council reassured him that he was in the right place. Chairing the meeting with a proprietorial air was the federation's founder, Henry Hyndman, a recent candidate for Parliament as an independent Tory, now turned socialist, whose proselytising political work *England for All*, including one chapter neatly summarising the economic theories of *Das Kapital*, had attracted Carpenter's attention and helped him crystallise 'the mass of floating impressions, sentiments, ideals, etc. in my mind'.

The crotchety Marx, approaching death, had taken exception to Hyndman's interpretation of his theory of 'surplus value', while Engels remained intent on pressing charges of plagiarism against his rival populariser. For those who had struggled with the density of *Das Kapital*, however, Hyndman offered ready access to ideas that quickened their outrage and galvanised their activism, with the promise of social revolution and 'genuine communism' before the decade was out. 'The well-to-do should provide for the poor certain advantages whether they like to do so or not,' stated his audaciously titled essay 'Dawn of a Revolutionary Epoch', handed out to pioneering members at the federation's inaugural meeting in 1881. Such a doctrine of paternalistic compulsion was not to every member's taste, any more than were Hyndman's authoritarian tendencies, but in this embryonic phase in British socialism all could subscribe to the basic sentiment.

That was the position taken by William Morris, a recent recruit who had promptly been appointed treasurer of the federation, and whose burly presence and acknowledged status as a poet, artist and entrepreneur presented Hyndman with the only meaningful challenge to his primacy. 'I was struck by Morris' fine face, his earnestness, the half-searching, half-dreaming look of his eyes, and his plain and comely dress,' wrote one member, and there was certainly much to recommend a man whom others described as having the brusque and direct manner of a sea captain, instilling calm and confidence in his crew. For the moment, Morris denied any interest in leadership, and sincerely insisted that he had much to learn about socialism before contemplating any such responsibility. But prolonged disenchantment with the capitalist system had left him with a passionate longing for revolution, beside which Hyndman's rhetoric rang somewhat hollow. 'I think myself that no rose water will cure us,' Morris had pronounced five years earlier in reaction to Matthew Arnold's proposal to outlaw inheritance. 'Disaster & misfortune of all kinds, I think will be the only things that will breed a remedy: in short nothing can be done till all rich men are made poor by common consent.'

If Carpenter's identity as a sexual outsider gave him a clearer perspective on the iniquities of society, then Morris' position as a craftsman and artistic producer, and his awareness of the anachronistic nature of his practice and vision, had led him to an even more absolute position. In line with John Ruskin's philosophy, he believed that the pernicious effect of the division of labour deprived the worker of the spiritual benefits of real creative investment in his tasks. 'Art cannot have a real life and growth under the present system of commercialisation and profit-mongering,' he wrote in a letter to a federation colleague in late 1883, while telling his own daughter that 'art has been handcuffed by it, and will die out of civilisation if the system lasts'. The central position that Morris accorded to human creative fulfilment in his ideal society raised such statements above mere artistic pieties; they underwrote a passionate engagement with the most pressing debates of the day, and a growing commitment to 'the necessity of attacking systems grown corrupt'.

The challenges of degeneration and decadence were laid out in alarming fashion during 1883 by a flurry of publications in France, Germany and Britain; their shared thesis being that a dangerous pathology gripped industrialised society that was manifest too in the aesthetic of heightened artifice increasingly adopted by avant-garde culture. But whilst there was a certain consonance between Morris' diagnosis and that of the evolutionary biologist Ray Lankester, who asserted that 'Degeneration may be defined as a gradual change of the structure in which the organism becomes adapted to less varied and less complex conditions of life', he would have recoiled from the conclusions that many drew. The most acute symptoms of the decay that was gnawing at the very foundations of civilisation were to be found, they suggested, in the burgeoning underclass, whose existence was a necessary and permanent by-product of efficient capitalism. Following Henry Maudsley's assertion in *Body and Will* that human evolution, like that of the nauplius barnacle, was on the brink of going into reverse, Francis Galton capped a lifetime of research into heredity by giving a name to his favoured solution to the problem: eugenicism.

Even if mankind might no longer be capable of scaling the heights of perfection, Galton argued, well-intentioned science could at least assist those specimens best suited to the uphill struggle of maintaining the current status of the species. For without a programme of selective breeding, the risk was that 'those whose race we especially want to have would leave few descendants, while those whose race we want to be quit of, would crowd the vacant space with progeny.' Of course, for Galton, there was the humane consideration too: that by neutering the parents he could save the unborn children of the poor and indigent from a lifetime of suffering.

It had been the absence of struggle in the nauplius barnacle's carefree existence that had led to its degeneracy, according to Maudsley, and Morris was determined not to allow the same fate to befall the English working man. Morris was circumspect regarding the claim made by Engels following Marx's recent death that 'Just as Darwin discovered the law of evolution of organic nature, so Marx discovered the law of evolution of human history', but in no doubt that it was 'upon the struggles due to this [class] conflict [that] all progress has hitherto depended'. Degeneracy was most apparent to him not in the slum-dwellers and factory workers, fighting for survival, but among the middle class, whose tastes and appetites required the corruption of 'imagination to extravagance, nature to sick nightmare fancies . . . workmanlike considerate skill . . . to commercial trickery sustained by laborious botching'. It was there that the morbid signs could best be discerned of an old world trapped in terminal decline, and of a new one straining but unable to be born.

As such, it fell to men like Morris and Carpenter, middle-class renegades with all the insights that their background afforded them, to awaken the world to the danger, prevent the spread of the contagion, and illuminate the possibility of a better future. Morris' fiery commitment might have been enough to daunt Carpenter, with his somewhat retiring ways and aptitude for composing yearning poetry in a Whitmanesque mode. The contents of his recent slim volume, *Towards Democracy*, were certainly a far cry from the chivalric lays and heroic Norse epics that had hitherto inspired Morris' verse. But each contributed as best he could, and Morris was more than happy to bank Carpenter's generous contribution towards the founding of the federation's newspaper, *Justice*, first proposed to Hyndman by Kropotkin two years earlier, when the two had met at the time of the London Congress.

The reward Carpenter took away from that first meeting in Westminster was of the sort captured by Morris' pen in 'The Pilgrims of Hope', a poem that transposed the excitement of the federation's early days on to that experienced by an English volunteer in the Commune:

'And lo! I was one of the band.
And now the streets seem gay and the high stars glittering bright;
And for me, I sing amongst them, for my heart is full and light.
I see the deeds to be done and the day to come on the earth . . .
I was born once long ago: I am born again tonight.

Morris too had been grateful for Hyndman's distillation of Marxist theory, having grappled with *Das Kapital* and found the economic sections particularly taxing. His socialism arose rather from his moral perspective on society than from economic pragmatism, and the policies he embraced were inspired by outrage at the injustices he saw and read about in the world around him. Having previously recoiled from the logical conclusions to which his developing beliefs led him, Morris felt such fury over the prosecution of Johann Most for freely expressing his mortal hatred of the assassinated tsar that it loosed his inhibitions; he had declared the condemnation of Most to penal servitude to be an open invitation for men of conscience to abandon all but revolutionary politics. It was a book by one of the Russians who had actually plotted and carried out assassination attacks, however, that provided Morris with what one of his old friends described as the 'inciting cause' of his intractable stance: *Underground Russia*, by the pseudonymous 'Stepniak', meaning 'man of the steppes'.

'The terrorist is noble, irresistibly fascinating, for he combines in himself the two sublimates of human grandeur: the martyr and the hero,' its author pronounced. 'From the day he swears in the depths of his heart to free the people and the country, he knows he is consecrated to death . . . And already he sees that enemy falter, become confused, cling desperately to the wildest means, which can only hasten his end.' The French police would persist for two years in supposing Lev Hartmann to be 'Stepniak'. In fact, *Underground Russia*'s evocation of the joys and fears of conspiratorial life in St Petersburg under the watch of the brutal Third Section – and of the strains and stresses of chasing the ideal of constitutional democracy by whatever means necessary in the teeth of ruthless suppression – was the work of Kravchinsky.

Holed up in Geneva, with the Swiss authorities slowly buckling under pressure for his extradition, Kravchinsky had for some time been keeping a close eye on London as a possible alternative base for his operations. In 1880, Hartmann had called for help with his proselytising mission in England and Chaikovsky, taking Kropotkin's advice that 'the goal is to influence the opinion of western Europe and through it the governments', had responded by moving to the English capital. Since then, Chaikovsky had supplied his old friend with tempting insights into the liberal character of the English. '[John Bull] is a strong person, very strong, and I confess that I like him very much for that reason . . . he does not like anyone to try to convince him of anything,' he wrote in 1882. Observing from a distance, it was clear to Kravchinsky from the surprisingly positive reception of his book the following year that London would make a congenial new home, as long as he could conceal his true identity. For only that May, Britain had been outraged when Fenian 'Invincibles' had stabbed to death Lord Frederick Cavendish, the newly appointed chief secretary to Ireland, and his undersecretary, in Dublin's Phoenix Park, in an attack that some thought was inspired by that of Mezentsev four years earlier.

'I think such a book ought to open people's eyes a bit here & do good,' was Morris' verdict on *Underground Russia*. He first met Kravchinsky – now universally known as Stepniak, his old identity completely set aside – in July 1883, soon after the Russian's arrival in London, and was impressed to find him more the humane radical than the guerrilla leader; a man capacious in his thinking, and generous in his interests. Their very physicality was consonant: Morris, with his shaggy mane of hair, having the 'same consciousness of strength, absence of fear, and capacity for great instinctive action' as a lion, Kravchinsky a brawny but kind-hearted bear, who prompted one English acquaintance to remark that 'I never met an artist who was so amiable and so gentle in his judgements.' The similarity of their literary personalities chimed too, as they reached for new modes through which to explore and make accessible the burden of political aspiration that weighed heavy on both, intuiting how fiction – sensationalist or utopian – could both shape and reflect the emerging ideologies of the age. Straightforward and candid men, neither had much truck with the kind of fads and factionalism that later prompted Kravchinsky's dismissive comment that 'In London, you must understand, "isms" have a curious tendency to segregation.' Yet in some respects their instinctive friendship resulted in a strange transference of political perspectives.

By the time he reached England, Kravchinsky had already begun to distance himself from outright support for terrorism. 'The terrorists will be the first to throw down their deadly weapons, and take up the most humane, and the most powerful of all, those of free speech addressed to free men,' he had promised his readers, and memories of his youthful study of Henry Thomas Buckle's great unfinished *History of Civilisation in England* informed his hopes for his homeland's future development. Used to an oppressive despotism, the sheer relief of living in a functioning democracy, however flawed, drew him towards reformist liberalism more quickly than he could have expected. Morris, meanwhile, felt newly 'bound to act for the destruction of the system which seems to me mere oppression and obstruction; such a system can only be destroyed, it seems to me, by the united discontent of numbers.'

As to how to bring about that groundswell of popular support, Morris could draw upon the dynamic example of a small number of native activists, with the carter Joseph Lane and tailor Frank Kitz to the fore. During the boom years, as the British middle class prospered and capitalism crushed all in its path, Lane and Kitz had resolutely conserved the ideas of Chartism and then introduced those of socialism, first through the Manhood Suffrage League, which Kitz had founded in 1875, and more recently through the Labour Emancipation League. Kitz himself may have been half-German and fluent in the language, and have spent his youth gazing at illustrations of the French Revolution pinned to his bedroom wall, but it was the lost rights of the freeborn Englishman that both lamented: a Cockaigne of Anglo-Saxon justice and democracy, rather than bloody social revolution as formulated across the Channel. And it was with this Utopia as their touchstone that they organised public meetings around London, week in, week out, year after year, under the banner of the Manhood Suffrage League.

The Tory defeat in 1880 had raised hopes among many that Gladstone's new Liberal government would champion the cause of social justice, but despite moves to extend the franchise and provide universal primary education, many had been left disillusioned by the Coercion Act, and its suspension of civil rights in Ireland. Inspired by 'the propagandist zeal of foreign workmen' whom Kitz credited with the true genesis of the socialist movement in England, and having made common cause where possible with the Fenians, he and Lane began to generate interest and a growing following. From a base in the East End at the Stratford Dialectical and Radical Club, whose members had drifted from their secularist origins to outright socialism, the tireless Lane's recipe was simple: 'Take a room, pay a quarter's rent in advance then arrange a list of lecturers . . . then paste up bills in the streets all round . . . and [having] got a few members get them to take it over and manage it as a branch.' With Lane running two or three such operations at a time himself, the organisation's spread was rapid.

The street corners of impoverished London also provided Morris with the environment in which he was most at ease, evangelising from his soapbox like a Christian preacher. 'He bears the fiery cross,' observed his old friend, the artist Edward Burne-Jones, somewhat despairingly. Yet Morris, like many of the most radical of the English socialists, was instinctively averse to to the idea of anarchism, with its potent connotations of transcendence and its embryonic martyrology. There may have been some concern over how he might lose support among the general public by associating himself with something so notoriously foreign; after all, the federation's newspaper *Justice* had immediately been branded by its enemies as an 'incendiary . . . [work] by the hands of atheists and anarchists'. Andreas Scheu, his effective lieutenant in the federation, who had witnessed the ultimately pointless chaos caused by Johann Most's rabble-rousing in Vienna a decade earlier, was certainly in a state of perpetual exasperation with his fellow émigrés for 'passing bloodthirsty resolutions at the anarchist club under the leadership of tried agents provocateurs'. The influence of Kravchinsky may have been felt too, murmuring disparagingly about 'toy revolutionaries' when the anarchists who harangued the crowd in Hyde Park hailed him as a kindred spirit. Even Joseph Lane would complain at the imputation that the clubs he ran were anarchist 'just because we charged no entrance fee and no monthly contributions but [carry] out the doctrine "from everybody according to their ability".'

However, it is hard to see where either Lane or Morris, with their federated organisation of clubs, anti-parliamentary attitude, distaste for authority and belief in revolution, differed from anarchism's central tenets. And in such essays as Reclus' 'Ouvrier, prends la machine!', with its loathing of artifice, suburbs and spiritual deracination, and medievalist longing, there was surely much for Morris to approve. 'An end to frippery then!' Reclus had declared. 'An end to dolls' clothes! We shall go back to the work of the fields and regain our strength and gaiety, seek out the joy of life again, the impressions of nature that we have forgotten in the dark mills of the suburbs. That is how a free people will think. It was the Alpine pastures, not the arquebus, that gave the Swiss of the Middle Ages their freedom from kings and lords.' And whilst Morris was adamant in distinguishing himself from the 'anarchists', the difference between his view of revolution and that of Kropotkin or Reclus was a mere matter of nuance. For though he believed that violent upheaval might be avoided by middle-class acquiescence to the demands of socialism, he saw no realistic prospect of any such resolution.

Morris had to contend, though, with an increasing demonisation in Britain of the revolutionary impulse. Henry Maudsley, the evolutionary psychologist, had clarified the contemporary threat to civilisation by reference to the French Revolution, which he termed 'an awful example of how silently the great social forces mature, how they explode at last in volcanic fury, if too much or too long repressed'. For him, the greatest danger lay in giving concessions that were too generous. Charles Fairfield's alarmist novel of 1884, *The Socialist Revolution of 1888*, concurred, leaving its readers in no uncertainty about where responsibility for the predicted turmoil would lie. The novel evoked a society in which 'many desperate characters, including thousands of foreign anarchists, were abroad... preaching the duty of personal vengeance upon the middle and upper classes, and the nationalisation of women as well as of land.' Published in the wake of a Fenian bombing campaign that had struck at not only Scotland Yard and the Carlton Club, but the Underground trains in which ordinary citizens travelled, even the book's grossest exaggerations acquired a sheen of credibility.

In fact the threat may have been smaller than those responsible for its policing liked to maintain: before Scotland Yard had called in the contractors to clear away the debris of the Fenian bomb, the Metropolitan Police's internal journal, *Moonshine*, had managed to laugh off the Fenian threat by reference to the ease with which the perpetrators had been tracked down. Nevertheless, extraordinary measures were taken to reassure the British public. In an unprecedented invasion of intellectual privacy, police agents now proposed to scour ticket records from the British Museum Library for evidence of suspicious interests. Elisée Reclus, writing in the *London Contemporary Review* in May 1884, talked of 'devil raising' by the black propagandists and provocateurs deployed by the police. He may well have been right.

A bombing campaign was the last thing on the minds of those members of the Democratic Federation whose growing antipathy to Hyndman's dominance led them to coalesce into a libertarian faction. Their immediate anxiety concerned rumours of a plan to field candidates in the forthcoming parliamentary elections, and his overt jingoism in support of General Gordon's expedition to subdue Egypt. Whilst the former notion appalled all those who deemed representative government to be a fraud to perpetuate Establishment authority, the latter especially riled Morris, for whom Britain's colonial wars epitomised all that was worst about its exploitative commercial culture: the repression of the weak, abroad as at home, to prop up an economy that was faltering, as the second wave of the Industrial Revolution gave Britain's foreign competitors a novel advantage.

In the summer of 1884, Hyndman's ambition finally caused him to make a fatal strategic blunder, when he urged Joseph Lane to attend the federation's conference that August, eager for the mass of supporters he might bring with him. Moving swiftly, Morris outflanked him, inviting Lane to his home in Hammersmith where he persuaded him to help draft a new manifesto for the organisation, which would be renamed the *Social Democratic Federation*: a three-hour day of essential work would be promised for all, made possible by the common ownership of the means of production. When Hyndman refused to concede, a tense stand-off ensued. Approached by Marx's daughter Eleanor for advice, Engels backed Morris, despite having previously scorned him as an 'artist-enthusiast but untalented politician'. Morris, though, was reluctant to precipitate the circumstances that would oblige him to accept the leadership; it was with deep unease that he remembered how intoxicating was the sense of power he had felt, four months earlier, on finding himself unexpectedly at the head of a 4,000-strong procession to Marx's grave in Highgate Cemetery, on the anniversary of the Commune's declaration.

In December 1884, Morris headed for Edward Carpenter's home at Millthorpe in Derbyshire, 'a refuge from all our mean squabbles'. Reclus had recently reproved those who sought to withdraw from the struggles of the world, and before long Morris would address Carpenter in similar terms. Watching Carpenter's ease among the Sheffield factory workers, or in his small market garden, and envying the fact that his younger friend had put behind him the hierarchical prejudices of his middle-class upbringing, Morris must have doubted again his suitability for leadership of a movement whose commitment to equality he valued above all.

'I cannot stand all this, it is not what I mean by socialism either in aims or in means,' he wrote at the time, wrestling with his conscience, 'I want a real revolution, a real change in society: society a great organic mass of well-regulated forces used for the bringing about of a happy life for all.' Carpenter may well have steeled his friend's nerve with the thought that 'it seems to be admitted now on all hands that the social condition of this country is about as bad as it can be', and weighed the arguments for the necessity of a 'fierce parturition struggle' to see the new world born. And whilst Carpenter still felt bound by his original loyalty to Hyndman, it is clear that he already tacitly recognised the problem of egotism in a man who believed 'that it would be for him as chairman of [a committee of public safety] to guide the ship of the state into the calm haven of socialism.'

Morris returned to London fortified for the showdown. On 27 December, Hyndman was heavily defeated in a vote of the executive committee, and Morris led out the victorious dissenters. A new organisation was formed, the Socialist League, and according to Carpenter 'there was a widespread belief that [it] was going to knit up all the United Kingdom in one bond of a new life'. The first edition of the league's new organ, *Commonweal*, seemed to promise something more far-reaching still, with greetings from the Russians Peter Lavrov and Tikhomirov, and an early article from Kravchinsky offering a Russian perspective that resonated with Morris' undertaking as editor, 'To awaken the sluggish, to strengthen the waverers, to instruct the seekers after truth.'

That Kravchinsky was being granted a platform for his propaganda in London – the *Commonweal* being one of several publications that was taking his articles – was provoking in St Petersburg 'an extremely sore feeling . . . in the highest circles'. Olga Novikoff strove to counter his popularity, shamelessly exploiting sympathy for her martyred brother, Nicholas Kireev, who had given his life in the cause of Balkan liberty; having fought there himself, Kravchinsky must have felt doubly aggrieved that it became a cause célèbre. For the moment, though, he was safe in Britain, one of those nihilists whom it was unthinkable to throw back into the clutches of his hosts' autocratic enemy: 'Imagine the consequences in England', a recent Home Secretary had reasoned, 'if such a man was a Kossuth or a Garibaldi.' While Kravchinsky was a prophet abroad, however, Morris was one in his own land; for him, the years of Establishment opprobrium were only just beginning.

'It is good to feel the coming storm' Morris wrote, as the growth of the reactionary Primrose League and other such organisations seemed to signal a refusal on the part of the ruling elite and the middle class to concede or compromise. Less than four years had passed since Morris decided to join the federation, when he had read More's *Utopia* and Butler's *Erewhon* out loud to his family and guests. Now, congregations in the churches of the East End listened rapt to socialist hymns written by Morris himself, and dreamed of an ideal future of their own fashioning:

> Come hither lads, and hearken, for a tale there is to tell,
> Of the wonderful days a'coming when all shall be better than well
> And the tale shall be told of a country, a land in the midst of the sea,
> And folk shall call it England in the days that are going to be.

13

The Making of the Martyrs

London and Chicago, 1883–1887

'The king-killer is here for speeches and other radical mischief,' the *Chicago Times* proclaimed on Christmas Day 1882, warning its readers against Johann Most. His fingers sore from the hard labour of picking oakum, his eyes slowly readjusting to daylight after eighteen months in the gloom of Clerkenwell prison, Most had arrived in New York a week earlier, and despite a rough crossing of the Atlantic had immediately thrown himself into an ambitious lecture tour. His violent gospel of resistance drew eager audiences. For Most had a rich vein of discontent to mine among those workers who had lived through the recent depression and were now bracing themselves as the economy again began to founder, and among the tens of thousands of immigrants who poured into America every year, only to have their dreams broken on the brutal reality of industrial exploitation.

Seven years earlier, William H. Vanderbilt had received a $90 million inheritance from his father, a New York railroad magnate; that he had doubled his fortune since then was symptomatic of a society riven by obscene discrepancies in wealth. The period had seen the value of factory output rise exponentially, with 300 per cent increases in most years, as industrialists ambitious to secure monopolies had gambled carelessly with the jobs of their woefully underpaid workers, safe in the knowledge that they could sack them without compunction at the first sign of a downturn. 'Slavery is not dead, though its grossest form be gone' preached Henry George; 'The essence of slavery consists in taking from a man all the fruits of his labor except a bare living, and of how many thousands miscalled free is this the lot?'

Since 1879, the cruellest blows had fallen on those workers brought up in a tradition of craftsmanship, whose skills were abruptly rendered obsolete by the advent of mechanisation: coopers who had served long apprenticeships, only for machines to crank out barrels in a quarter of the time, or cigar rollers who could generate barely a quarter of the profit of a factory-line process. The social cost was enormous. Cigar workshops had offered a model of labour solidarity and of self advancement, appointing one of their number to read informative texts out loud while the others worked; now their representatives were reduced to crude scaremongering. 'More than half the smallpox patients in Riverside Hospital were inmates of tenement houses where cigars are made,' advised the *Paterson Labor Standard*; 'This ought to be a warning to persons who smoke non-union cigars.'

The New Jersey town of Paterson, where immigrant artisans from the highly politicised silk-manufacturing areas around Lyons in France and in north-west Italy had helped recreate the industry on American soil, proved especially receptive to Most's brand of socialism. 'Swiss workers coming to Paterson think it a paradise,' warned the *Standard*, 'soon they will realise it is a purgatory, and that their cheap labour will make it a hell.' And while it carried advertisements for the latest silk suits in the Paris style, and was wisely circumspect in its views concerning the attempt on President Garfield's life in 1881, the 'Best Family Newspaper in New Jersey' was not blind to the iniquities of the 'silk kings', nor to the more extreme position held by some in the community. Indeed, in the spring before Most's arrival, it was pleased to announce an instructive lecture entitled 'Dynamite and Freedom', to be delivered on the anniversary of Tsar Alexander II's assassination by 'Prof. Mezeroff, the Russian scientist who speaks like an educated Irishman'.

Nowhere on his travels, however, either in Europe or in the United States, can Most have encountered such a developed socialist movement or such determined activism as on the shores of Lake Michigan. While the workers in the Chicago industries were among the most exploited in the country, the last great year of strikes had revealed the depth of their solidarity. In 1877, on the anniversary of the Paris Commune, upwards of 40,000 had converged on the Exposition building to celebrate the 'Dawn of Liberty', and their unity had been maintained in the years since, with the annual event growing ever more elaborate, to include gymnastic displays, recitations and musical and dramatic performances.

Testimony to the participants' unshakeable optimism can be found in the plot of the play *The Nihilists*, performed in 1882, whose fourth act deviated from the historical account of the tsar's assassination by allowing the conspirators to escape while being transported to Siberia. The cast itself, unsurprisingly, provided a fertile recruiting ground for Most, with the ferociously theatrical style of his speech-making appealing to at least two of its members, the shopkeeper August Spies and salesman Oscar Neebe. Indeed, so taken with the notorious firebrand was yet another German from Chicago, Michael Schwab, that he joined Most as a warm-up act for his exhausting programme of 200 speeches in six months, during 1883.

The efficacy of dynamite and the bombing of police stations were recurring themes of their lectures, as Most glossed the idea of 'propaganda by deed' with his own terroristic interpretation. Yet for all the enthusiasm with which audiences received his bombast, Most seemed better able to provoke than to lead: a man of words rather than action; a cowardly braggard, according to some. While the flow of ships to and from Europe facilitated the smuggling of *Freiheit* and allowed Most to imagine that, based in New York, he presided over operations by his proxies in Europe, any hope that his American exile would be the short-lived prologue to a triumphal return seemed increasingly delusional. Although agents of the Imperial German Police continued to file compelling reports about his translation of Nechaev's *The Revolutionary Catechism* and the job he took in a dynamite factory in order to gain a first-hand knowledge of explosives, the ideas about which he only talked and wrote were being put into practice in Chicago.

For some time, police headquarters in Berlin had been preoccupied with the vast underground army of terrorists that Most's lieutenant, Johann Neve, was said to be organising on his behalf in Germany and around its borders, with the help of the Belgian Victor Dave. Alleged to number 7,000 members divided between eighty cells, it supposedly possessed a stockpile of bombs and poisoned daggers. But despite Neve's dedicated efforts, the threat from this 'army' was vastly overestimated. It would, in any case, be ruthlessly eradicated during 1884, when a further crackdown followed the failure of August Reinsdorf's spectacular attempt to blow up the kaiser, the crown prince and Chancellor Bismarck during the unveiling of a vast statue of Germania on the ridge of the Niederwald high above the River Rhine.

In Chicago, by contrast, the socialist militia was already a reality. The Lehr-und-Wehr Verein, or Society for Education and Defense, had been formed during the upheavals of 1877 to counter intimidation by paramilitary outfits in the pay of the bosses, and was now some 1,500 strong, grouped under nationality with names such as the Bohemian Sharpshooters. When Reinsdorf was sentenced to death, moreover, it was one of his old protégés, Louis Lingg, now living in Chicago, and not

Most, who would lead the tributes, addressing a working population that had always proved unwilling to concede their rights or their livelihoods without a fight, yet was now facing the loss of tens of thousands of jobs. Left to catch up as best he could, Most dedicated his autobiography to Reinsdorf as 'a tribute of esteem'. 'Let us never forget', he wrote in characteristic style, 'that the revolutionists of modern times can enter into the society of free and equal men only over ruins and ashes, over blood and dead bodies.' To effect his vision in a foreign land, though, Most would need new allies.

Despite the willingness of the American socialist movement to confront capitalism on the picket line, it had hitherto shown notable restraint in seeking to revive the ideals of the American republic without recourse to the revolutionary methods espoused by its European comrades. By 1883, however, the blatant injustices of a society under plutocratic rule had led to mounting despair that the ballot box could ever bring about meaningful reform, causing many socialists to seek an alternative in anarchism. Less than a month after the Niederwald incident, Most took his place on the speakers' platform when the American Federation of the Working People's Association met in Pittsburgh to thrash out a new policy. His observation that America's capitalists had exploited their workers more in twenty-five years than had Europe's monarchs in 200 stiffened their resolve, but among the more familiar faces it was Albert Parsons, an ex-colonel in the Texas militia and now one of Chicago's leading socialists, whose ideas lent American radicalism a new, patriotic dimension.

Back in 1877, Parsons had implicitly linked the socialist cause of liberating the workers with that of the abolition of slavery, framing the strikers as a 'Grand Army of Salvation' after the Grand Army of the Republic from the Civil War. The intervening years, however, had taught him harsh lessons about the corrupt nature of power, not least when he had been hauled off the street in Chicago and thrown before a conclave of the city's business elite in the cellars of the labyrinthine Rookery, the makeshift police headquarters. These men had warned him off in the crudest terms. Far from being deterred by their intimidation, though, Parsons renounced his previously moderate position after witnessing votes being rigged in a local election. Invoking historical precedent once again in his address to the federation, this time he looked further back, to the insurrectionary example of America's fight for independence. 'By force our ancestors liberated themselves from political oppression, by force their children will have to liberate themselves from economic oppression,' Parsons reminded the delegates. "'It is, therefore, your right; it is your duty," says Jefferson; to arms!'

Assisted by Spies, Most drafted the *Pittsburgh Manifesto*, setting down the principles agreed upon by the federation, and printing presses spun off hundreds of thousands of copies in English, German and French, for distribution. For all his egotism, Most had wisely decided to make common cause with Parsons and the others. 'A new era in America's labour movement has begun,' crowed *Freiheit*, 'The word is ALL ABOARD!' But what political species were the adherents to this new political configuration, and how should they be identified: as radical patriots, revolutionary socialists, or anarchists?

Inevitably, perhaps, it was the mainstream newspapers that would have the final say. During the 1870s, while the Commune was the greatest bugbear of the right, 'communist' had been the preferred term of disparagement for the socialists, but since around the time of the tsar's assassination, as a consequence of the usual legerdemain, 'anarchist' had become common, as an effective trigger for rousing middle-class ire and anxiety. As early as 1881, Parsons had written of how 'the capitalistic press began to stigmatise us as anarchists, and to denounce us as enemies to all law and government'. Quite apart from the undiscerning application of the term 'anarchist' to socialists whose sympathies lay with Marx, the development of a very different kind of individualistic American 'anarchism' by Benjamin Tucker made the label problematic even when used to refer to men like Spies and Schwab, who were inspired by the European tradition. Parsons, though, whilst conciliatory towards the diverse branches of socialism, accepted the inevitable: 'That name which was at first imputed to us as a dishonor, we came to cherish and defend with pride.'

Even before the Pittsburgh Congress, the more extreme Chicago socialists had embraced anarchist ideas. After it their revolutionary ambitions only expanded, fed by the publication in the summer of 1885 of Most's booklet, *The Science of Revolutionary Warfare*, whose detailed exposition of terroristic solutions was based on esoteric knowledge he had acquired while working for the munitions manufacturer. 'Rescue mankind through blood, iron, poison and dynamite,' he urged his readers: policemen could be done away with using dipped daggers and dosed cakes; dignitaries killed by grenades rolled under banqueting tables; miniaturised bombs enclosed in letters. Some months earlier, though, Spies' and Neebe's Chicago-based newspaper the *Alarm* had already been providing a steady stream of incendiary advice: 'One man armed with a dynamite bomb is equal to one regiment of militia, when it is used at the right time and place,' advised an edition from October 1884, while only a few weeks later another offered the view that 'In giving dynamite to the down-trodden millions of the globe, science has done its best work.' The same issue contained instructions for how to make a rudimentary pipe bomb for use against 'the rich loafers who live by the sweat of other people's brows'.

Faced with such threatening rhetoric, the businessmen of Chicago were inevitably shaken by the rapid radicalisation of their workers. Nearly 100,000 copies of the *Alarm* were printed in ten months between 1884 and 1885, most of which would have been handed from reader to reader, in homes or in such red clubs as the four-storey Florus Hall, to which bundles of the paper were delivered daily. Despite its recent expansion, Chicago's police force found itself overstretched in keeping the anarchists under surveillance, having to cover not only the indoor meetings but also picnics in the countryside, where dynamite demonstrations provided an added attraction. Of greater concern than the size of the police force, however, was the reliability of its leadership, at least to such leading indus-trialists as Cyrus McCormick Jnr, the new Princeton-educated manager of the family's vast Harvesting Machine Company works in the south-west of the city, then planning to cut costs by wage reductions and mass layoffs. A disgraceful even-handedness had recently been noticed in the city's police officers. The ascendancy of Captain John Bonfield, a failed businessman himself before he had joined the force, offered some reas-surance but the ruthlessness that he promised was yet to be tested *in extremis*.

McCormick had quickly made clear his managerial intentions by summoning the industrialists' most trusted friend the Pinkertons, who had their headquarters in the city. The agency's hard-boiled mercenaries garrisoned the McCormick Harvesting works, defending its periphery from incursions and guaranteeing the safety of strike-breakers shipped in from other states. With even the moderate Parsons claiming a core of 2,000 active anarchists in Chicago by the spring of 1885, and a hinterland of 10,000 supporters, the risk of escalation was only too obvious. It was heightened in December 1884 when the Pinkertons' role was extended to include the infiltration of anarchist meetings. Inevitably, the agency had a vested interest in exaggerating the threat it reported for its own commercial benefit, or even in provoking the kind of clashes that its clients dreaded. Alarmism cranked up the political temperature of the city, with both sides hardening their stance. It seemed ever more likely that the ghosts of civil war and revolution to which Parsons so often alluded would soon take solid form.

*

On Thanksgiving Day 1884, and again at Christmas a year later, Chicago's most affluent families were brought face to face with those on whose grinding efforts their comfortable existence rested. Down the millionaire's row of Prairie Avenue, past mansions decked out for the holidays, the anarchists paraded bearing the black banner of mourning and starvation, chanting and abusing the unearned privilege of those inside. They were the same benighted individuals who, when attending the annual Commune celebrations, had been described by the *Chicago Tribune* as being what might be found should one 'skim the purlieus . . . drain the bohemian socialist slums'. During a winter of mass unemployment, the same paper now urged farmers with land in the immediate environs of the city to poison their crops lest scavengers, left unfed by soup kitchens swamped by demand, steal crops from their fields. Whatever civil society had previously existed in Chicago no longer deserved to be dignified with the name.

For seven years, since his first election as Chicago's mayor in 1879, Carter Harrison had tried to treat his constituents, rich and poor, with an even hand, respecting the cosmopolitan make-up of the city, and even appointing socialists to his administration. In April 1885, when pressed by Cyrus McCormick to provide still more police to enforce the strike-breaking, he had chosen instead to support the labour movement's call for an arbitrated settlement. Captain Bonfield had first tested the mayor's authority three months later, when he led his men into action against a transportation strike: requisitioning a streetcar to drive through the crowds of protesters, policemen had swung their batons with abandon as they passed the strikers, cracking heads and breaking morale. But whilst the industrial action came to a swift end, the attitude of the city's anarchists stiffened in reaction, and the wafer-thin majority with which Carter Harrison was re-elected saw his authority wane. The first signs of a developing power vacuum in the city appeared. Union representatives began talking of their members 'buying $12 guns and playing soldiers', and the old socialist militias were said to be stepping up their training. With news that the industrialists were giving over their warehouses as drill grounds for their own clerks, the long-standing fears of bloody confrontation appeared to be coming to a head.

Through the long, hard winter of 1885, the air of militancy intensified, with the anarchist newspapers publishing ever more bellicose statements in favour of dynamite, 'the proletariat's artillery', and even a letter purporting to have been sent by an army officer from Alcatraz Island, offering illustrated guidance on street-fighting tactics. The *Tribune,* in turn, demanded 'A Regular Army Garrison for Chicago', but had to be satisfied with the 300-strong police guard posted under Bonfield to enforce a lockout at the McCormick works, with orders that seemed conceived to provoke clashes with the strikers. Within weeks the ensuing violence led to the gunning down of four strikers. In April 1886, seven more were killed by police bullets in nearby East St Louis, and Chicago's *Arbeiter-Zeitung* was reporting that the forces of law and order were readying themselves for a fight on May Day: 'The capitalists are thirsting for the blood of workingmen.'

The battle would be precipitated, it was thought, by concerted demands for a watershed in labour relations. For many years, workers had campaigned for a mandatory eight-hour day, to counter the relentless demands of their employers. Recognising the importance of a single cause around which protest could coalesce, Albert Parsons had been collaborating with the Knights of Labor and other organisations for the past three years to press the case. Set against the reality of hundred-hour weeks in some industries, however, the campaign's true purpose had always seemed more symbolic than achievable: to assert the respect and humane consideration that the working class deserved. Then at the beginning of 1886, a new intransigence entered the campaign, and the sense of possibility was further encouraged by Mayor Harrison's decision in April to grant the new working terms, wholesale, to Chicago's public employees. Finally, Parsons was able to convince Chicago's hard-line anarchists of the benefit of joining the bandwagon, if only to be in a better position to direct it.

The depth of the anger and alarm felt by the likes of Cyrus McCormick at the prospect of such solidarity across the working population should not be underestimated: the 71 per cent increase in profits since he had taken over could not be sustained in such circumstances. 'To arm is not hard. Buy these,' Herr Most told a meeting in New York's Germania Gardens, holding aloft a rifle, 'steal revolvers, make bombs, and when you have enough, rise and seize what is yours. Take the city by force and the capitalists by the throat.' The news that Most was due to be in Chicago on 1 May must have sent a shiver through the ranks of the city's businessmen, who hastily pledged $2,000 to arm the police with a Gatling gun, America's very own version of the *mitrailleuses* that had mown down the Communards fifteen years earlier.

When May Day arrived, of the 300,000 men who downed tools across the United States, a full fifth of them were in Chicago. Yet the day passed off without major incident. Steeled as they were for a showdown, McCormick, his colleagues and Captain Bonfield surely felt a certain sense of anticlimax, mixed with relief. Yet if their strategy had simply been to crush the demonstrators once the swell of popular support for the workers had subsided, they showed scant patience. It was only two days later, on 3 May, as Spies addressed a crowd gathered outside the McCormick works, that the rattle of rifle fire echoed out, as Bonfield's men intervened against pickets who were preventing strike-breakers from entering the gates. There was one fatality. Outraged, Spies rushed to the print room of his newspaper and, in the heat of the moment, set about compositing a call for vengeance: 'If you are men, if you are the sons of grandsires who have shed their blood to free you, then you will rise in your might, Hercules, and destroy the hideous monster that seeks to destroy you. To arms, we call you. To arms!'

A light drizzle was slanting down on the night of 4 May 1886, when Mayor Harrison arrived in Chicago's Haymarket Square to reassure himself that the demonstration he had authorised was passing off in good order. The city was on edge, but having satisfied himself as to the 'tame' character of the gathering, Harrison left at around half-past seven, advising the police to stand down. Ignoring the mayor's instructions, Bonfield merely withdrew with his men to positions of concealment in side streets nearby. Throughout the evening a steady flow of informants and plain-clothes policemen shuttled between the demonstration and Bonfield's post, relaying updates on the speeches, right until the moment when the last speaker, Samuel Fielden, mounted the wagon that was being used as a podium. 'Defend yourselves, your lives, your futures,' he urged those anarchists who remained. 'Throttle it, kill it, stab it, do everything you can to wound it,' was his recommended treatment of the law and its protectors, who even as he spoke were lining up, 180 strong in rows four deep, just out of sight.

It was 10.30 when Bonfield ordered his formation to advance. The worsening weather had thinned the crowd gathered near the corner of Desplaines Street, from 3,000 at its peak to a hard core of a few hundred. 'We are peaceable,' protested Fielden, somewhat disingenuously, as the captain ordered the meeting to disperse. The moments that followed would ever afterwards define anarchism in America, and arguably socialism as a whole. A few who glanced upwards saw the glowing fuse of the bomb as it arced through the air above them into the uniformed ranks; most only registered what had happened after the noise of the explosion had passed and the air had cleared of debris, leaving the cries of the dead and dying. One policeman was killed immediately, six more were fatally injured; fifty others wounded.

Accounts carried by the scattering crowds varied greatly, setting off wild rumours that soon ticked along the telegraph wires. Law-abiding citizens of Chicago, hearing reports that hundreds of policemen had died, formed defence groups in the expectation of imminent civil war, while apocryphal stories that the bomb had been followed by salvos of anarchist gunfire into the ranks of the police led them to believe that an insurrection had already broken out.

The police department itself was divided over how to respond. While Police Chief Ebersold tried to reassure the public, convinced that his priority must be to prevent panic, his junior officers set about under-mining his strategy by stoking the pervasive sense of fear. Bonfield having played his part, Captain Schaak now took the lead in championing the reactionary cause. Seventy anarchist suspects were rounded up in short measure and brutally interrogated, without access to water or legal repre-sentation. Witnesses were bribed, informants retained, reports forged, guns and bombs planted in the anarchist headquarters. Schaak was the sledgehammer of those with a wider anti-socialist and xenophobic agenda, as those around him at the time would later reveal. 'He saw more anar-chists than hell could hold,' wrote one eye-witness to his excesses; 'in the end, there was no society, however innocent or even laudable, among the foreign-born population that was not to his mind engaged in devilry.' Nevertheless, Schaak's tall tales of secret conspiracies were swallowed without question by most of Chicago's middle class, who preferred to blame Mayor Harrison's policies for giving comfort and encouragement to the anarchists, than question who had really thrown the bomb, and on whose orders.

Spies, Neebe, Lingg, Fielden and Schwab were among the eight men charged for the attack, though few of them had been present in the Haymarket, or could be linked to the event. Since they were the city's leading anarchist speakers and journalists, their removal struck the move-ment a critical blow. Albert Parsons, having gone into hiding, voluntarily turned himself in, in the hope that his presence in the dock would allay the risk of the trial making scapegoats of the immigrants. The man suspected of throwing the bomb, Schnaubelt, had fled, never to reappear.

If Johann Most had visited Chicago for May Day, he had made a quick getaway, but was nevertheless indicted by a grand jury. When eventually arrested, he was humiliated in front of fifty policemen who watched as he was photographed, familiarising themselves with his features for future reference and shouting out threats that 'If you show your teeth, or open your yap, we'll shoot you down like a dog.' Ironically, had Most not kept a certain distance between himself and Parsons, whose policies he still considered too moderate, he would almost certainly have joined those who now stood trial.

The atmosphere in which the eight Chicago anarchists appeared in the dock resembled that of a witch-hunt, and the prosecuting state attorney made no pretence as to the purely political and exemplary nature of the judgement that would be passed. 'Law is on trial. Anarchy is on trial. These men have been selected, picked out by the grand jury, and indicted because they were leaders. They are no more guilty than the thousands who follow them. Gentlemen of the jury: convict these men, make examples of them, hang them and you save our institutions, our society.' The gentlemen, and the judge, duly obliged, sentencing five to the death penalty and three to a life term of hard labour.

In Britain, as throughout Europe, the Haymarket debacle galvanised both extremes of the political spectrum. While those on the left rallied to the accused during the trial and afterwards, collecting petitions and addressing public meetings, the Tory press inveighed against the defendants, in a displaced expression of the loathing it felt for the immigrant and native socialists closer to home. For William Morris, the event exposed at a stroke the hypocrisy surrounding the vaunted ideal of Anglo-Saxon liberal democracy, on both sides of the Atlantic. 'Will you think the example of America too trite?' he asked an audience of moderate Fabians, challenging their willingness to operate within existing political structures. 'Anyhow consider it! A country with universal suffrage, no king, no House of Lords, no privilege as you fondly think; only a little standing army, chiefly used for the murder of red-skins; a democracy after your model; and with all that, a society corrupt to the core, and at this moment engaged in suppressing freedom with just the same reckless brutality and blind ignorance as the Tsar of all the Russias uses.'

After visiting the condemned men in prison, Marx's daughter Eleanor returned to England on the eve of their execution to report the belief, common among the working men of Chicago, that the true guilt for the bomb-throwing lay with a police agent. Subsequent investigations never

settled the matter, though the corruption in the Chicago police and judiciary at the time was eventually laid bare and officially acknowledged.
Foreign powers also had a hand in manipulating the aftermath of the
Haymarket Affair, however, and the possibility of their prior involvement
in provoking the bombing cannot be discounted; certainly, the most vociferous calls for vengeance came from a certain Heinrich Danmeyere, a
deep-cover agent of the Imperial German Police.

It may well have been Danmeyere too who, in the guise of an American-
based inventor known as 'Meyer', played a supporting role in a police
plot of 1887 to entrap Most's accomplice Johann Neve. The bait offered
was a new terror weapon he had supposedly devised, called the 'scorpion': a poisoned needle resembling that which Jules Allix had proposed
during the Siege of Paris as an effective means for Frenchwomen to kill
Prussians. The key figure in the plan was a certain Theodore Reuss: one
of the more flamboyant émigrés in London, where – on behalf of the
Imperial Police – he had been making mischief among the socialists for
the past couple of years, repeatedly evading exposure.

*

Even before the London Anarchist Congress, when the French spy
Serreaux had required such careful handling and Malatesta had almost
fought a duel with his lover's brother Giuseppe Zanardelli over attempts
to discredit the movement, there had been considerable unease about
police infiltration of the émigré communities in Britain. When Theodore
Reuss joined the Socialist League in 1885, the sincerity of his conversion
should immediately have been in doubt: a Wagnerian tenor who claimed
to have taken a lead role in the world premiere of *Parsifal* at Bayreuth
and to have re-founded the mystical Order of the Illuminati in Munich,
his shared interest in medievalism with William Morris was insufficient
by way of explanation. As it was, however, neither his decision to enrol
under the pseudonym of Charles Theodore, nor the generosity with
which he funded the league's propagandist activities at a level far beyond
his ostensible means, appear to have caused any initial suspicion.

Within a few months, however, with Reuss installed as 'Lessons
Secretary' for the League, coaching recent arrivals in the English language
and cultivating the most extreme of them, his more cautious colleagues
intuited a troublesome presence, and when he convened a conference to
propose that an international centre should coordinate the league's activities, veteran delegates surely recalled Serreaux's ruse in 1881. Perhaps
when Eleanor Marx lamented the vulgarity of the songs Reuss chose for

a recital, or a German colleague contradicted the verdict of the music critics by declaring Reuss to have 'a harsh voice', they were giving vent to a deeper-seated but unspoken unease. While the German émigrés could deal with traitors ruthlessly – a spy who had revealed details of the operation to smuggle *Freiheit* to the Continent had been 'accidentally' shot during a picnic on Hampstead Heath – for the moment a lack of evidence against Reuss saved him from a similar fate.

Those who doubted Reuss' integrity would soon regret their scruples. Insinuating himself into the trust of Joseph Peukert, who had established the Autonomie group as a means of distancing himself from Most's influence, Reuss cultivated the tensions between Peukert and his rivals, in particular Neve's Belgian assistant Victor Dave. Before long each was accusing the other of being a police spy. On a secret visit to the Continent by Dave, the ease with which Reuss was able to address letters to him raised further suspicions that he was in league with the police. These appeared to be confirmed when Dave tested Reuss by providing him alone with information about an imaginary visit to Berlin by Neve, to which police in the city responded. Peukert merely accused Dave of attempting to frame Reuss, and the mutual recrimination continued.

It was now that the agent provocateur Meyer offered Peukert the 'scorpion' as a means by which he could regain Neve's esteem, and when Neve agreed to meet in Belgium, Reuss eagerly tagged along. 'Now I've got him,' crowed Kruger, the director of the Berlin police, certain that 'this time he would not escape my grasp.' But the elusive Neve failed to appear, and the police agents to whom Reuss had signalled his movements returned empty-handed. Then, two days before Reuss was due back in London to perform in a concert, Neve offered to meet him alone.

The rendezvous was arranged for Luttich station. The minutes dragged by in the waiting room, the appointed time came and went, and just as Reuss was about to leave, the door creaked open and Neve entered. He had no real interest in secret weapons; only in reprimanding Reuss for his malicious slanders of Dave. 'You are a man without character,' Neve sneered, before making a cautious exit. Leaning on the bar, watching in the mirror, the only other man present was Kruger's agent, who had got a good enough view of Neve's reflection to be able to circulate a description.

At the meeting arranged by Reuss a fortnight later in the Autonomie Club in London to debate the expulsion of Dave, the accused read out a letter from Neve detailing how he was now under surveillance. A month later Neve was snatched in Belgium, bundled over the border and thrown into a German prison from which he would never emerge, abandoned to scratch out the days until his death a decade later. Having served his purpose, Reuss was lucky to escape merely with expulsion from the Socialist League; a shredded document from a meeting in May 1887, now held together by many strips of Sellotape, testifies to the red heat at which tempers ran. Confrontations between the Metropolitan Police and league members, including Morris, during mass demonstrations at Dod Street in the East End and Trafalgar Square, had left even the British socialists with little tolerance for traitors or turncoats.

Now that Neve had been eliminated, almost the only trace that remained in Europe of Johann Most's revolutionary ambitions took fictional form: while plotting *The Princess Casamassima* in 1886 Henry James struggled to accommodate Most's demonic personality, in the end deciding to share his unappealing attributes between three characters: a bookbinder, a chemist and a professional German revolutionary. In November 1887, though, America provided the world with an iconic image that for some provided a counterpoint to the diabolical reputation that anarchism was acquiring: that of four gowned men on a gallows, below ropes noosed ready to stretch their sacrificial necks – the Haymarket martyrs.

The actual scene was witnessed by 200 spectators seated in the high, narrow execution chamber at 11.30 on the morning of 11 November. Of the five men sentenced to an exemplary death, Lingg had already cheated the hangman by biting down on an explosive cartridge smuggled into his prison cell, only to die in prolonged agony. The remaining four awaited their fate; while Parsons stood with a semblance of calm, Spies spoke through the hood that had been placed over his head. 'There will be a time when our silence will be more powerful than the voices you strangle today,' he began, but before he could finish the trapdoor crashed open beneath him.

14

Decadence and Degeneration

'The city and its inhabitants strike me as uncanny,' a young Sigmund Freud wrote home from Paris in late 1885, during his visit to observe the experimental work that the neurologist Jean-Martin Charcot was conducting with hysterics at the Salpêtrière hospital. 'The people seem to me to be of a different species from ourselves; I feel they are possessed of a thousand demons.' Parisians were given, he believed, to 'physical epidemics, historical mass convulsions'. And if France's century-long history of revolution did not offer justification enough for Freud's thesis, the tumultuous events that had taken place in the French capital the previous May would have confirmed his impression.

For almost three decades, Victor Hugo, the towering figure of the republican left, had woven a mythology of heroic resistance to injustice in which he played the leading role. Even as his powers as a novelist declined, his privileged position in French society, latterly as a senator, had allowed him to remain a solitary if somewhat ineffectual voice of opposition to the rulers of the Third Republic during the Communards' exile. His death on 22 May 1885, two days short of the fourteenth anniversary of the Bloody Week, left his thousands of admirers bereft and disorientated. 'The Panthéon is handed over to its original and legal purpose. Victor Hugo's body shall be carried to it for burial', the Chamber of Deputies declared, hopeful that the honour might encourage a dignified and orderly laying to rest. Instead, a spirit of crazed carnival was released in the city that, for the bourgeoisie, echoed with their nightmare imaginings of a recrudescent Commune.

The strangely heightened mood of the city was first apparent in Père Lachaise cemetery, where the annual commemoration for those slaughtered there in 1871 coincided with the period of mourning. Confrontation with police had become a regular feature of the occasion, but this time its ferocity left several radicals dead, and over seventy others injured. When rumours spread that the anarchists meant to channel the emotion around Hugo's funeral into a popular uprising, three army regiments were drafted in, at significant expense, to accompany the cortège. As it was, the true melodrama on the route to the Panthéon had been scripted by the author himself, in specific instructions that his body should be carried in a pauper's hearse. Never averse to a sentimental *coup de théâtre*, the paradox of a state funeral stripped of all the usual trappings tipped Hugo's public straight from solemnity into the wild abandon of his wake. With the brothels closed for the day, the parks and boulevards hosted scenes of debauchery decried as 'Babylonian' by Hugo's enemies in the Catholic press. But it was not only the whores who offered to celebrate this most priapic of authors with open arms; 'How many women gave themselves to lovers, to strangers, with a burning fury to become mothers of immortals!' marvelled one spectator of the night's revels.

Behind the bars of the Saint-Lazare prison, Louise Michel paid tribute to her mentor, Hugo, in characteristically stormy verse. Her second major bereavement of the year, following the death in January of her beloved mother, Hugo's death inspired poetry that seethed at the butchery of the defeated Communards, and the terrible weeks that those who escaped the immediate slaughter had spent in the concentration camp at Satory. This wasn't, however, the only writing that Michel's incarceration had inspired. Throughout the two years she spent in Saint-Lazare, her pen provided a consistent safety valve for her frustrated idealism and the resulting rage. In overwrought novels written in Vernian vein, she explored the possible futures of mankind. *Les Microbes humaines* offered a robust riposte to those who applied the new language of virology to the slum-dwelling underclass, promising the emergence of a new race that would carry forward the ideals of the social revolution; *L'Ere nouvelle* conjured a vision of nature's power harnessed for the common good, with whirlpools directed to drive tunnels through mountains, and submarines colonising undersea continents. Then, quite suddenly, in the January after Hugo's death, the new government of Charles de Freycinet, whose cabinet included four radicals, made an immediate demonstration of its reformist intentions by pardoning both Michel and Kropotkin.

The unexpected move, and Kropotkin's release in particular, provoked international outrage. 'I have never had ill feelings towards France, for which I have always felt great sympathy,' Tsar Alexander III told the departing ambassador General Félix Appert in January 1886, after Appert had been expelled from Russia in protest, 'but your government is no

longer the republic, it is the Commune!' Appert, who had headed the
military tribunal that judged the Communards at Versailles, may well
have sympathised with Russia's decision to announce its withdrawal from
the forthcoming centenary celebrations of the Revolution. Yet the conse-
quent *froideur* between the two nations once again set back hopes of
cooperation in confronting the power of Bismarck's Germany. The
delivery of any future alliance, it was clear, would require a cunning and
resourceful midwife.

Typically Michel had stood on principle when news of her release came
through and reacted to the interior minister's order – 'Extreme urgency
Stop Liberate Louise Michel immediately Stop' – by refusing to leave her
cell. Since there had been no pardon for either her colleague Emile Pouget
or the strikers from Montceau-les-Mines, Michel insisted, she could not
accept privileged treatment. Increasingly desperate messages were
exchanged between the prison and the ministry of the interior in search
of a solution until, Michel would later claim, her pity for the painfully
perplexed gaoler finally persuaded her to go.

The political climate she discovered outside the prison walls was much
changed. Continuing arrests and trials in Lyons and the suppression of
the émigré population in Switzerland had transformed Paris into the
new heartland of a strengthening French anarchist movement. Groups
clustered in the old Communard areas to the north and east of Paris –
Belleville, Ménilmontant and Batignolles – with others scattered across
the city and its suburbs. But it was in Montmartre that radical sentiment
was to be found in its most concentrated form, with clubs on nearly
every corner in the maze of streets that clung to the hillside, and the
new bohemian bars and cabarets as congenial neighbours. 'If there is a
thing to be mocked, a convention to be outraged, an idol to be destroyed,
Montmartre will find the way,' wrote one observer of the bohemian
demi-mondc.

Nowhere epitomised the bonfire of deference better than the great
cabaret Le Chat Noir, founded in 1881. Outside, bouncers dressed parod-
ically in the uniform of the Pope's Swiss Guard saw off the gangs of
youths that roamed the area; inside was a topsy-turvy world of misrule.
Waiters were dressed in the regalia of members of the Académie française,
and the patron, Rodolphe Salis, accompanied visitors to their seats with
mocking servility, while in the murals behind them, the skeletal figure
of Death led a troupe of Pierrot clowns in a *danse macabre*.

Fuelled by wine, consumption of which soared during the 1880s, and
the mind-altering absinthe for which France had acquired a taste during

the years when the phylloxera virus had decimated the country's vines, the denizens of Montmartre seemed to inhabit a permanent party. From the Hydropathes to Les Incohérents, the Hirsutes to the Zutistes, myriad groups of revellers and entertainers proclaimed their proud devotion to the sybaritic cause. They found a welcoming home in the newly deregulated cafés, many of which were owned and run by refugees from Alsace and Lorraine, after they had been ceded to Germany following the war. The refugees had nothing to live on but profits from long hours of opening and a dipsomaniac clientele. On the once bucolic slopes of Montmartre, only the nascent sect of Naturiens held true to the pastoral ideal. Self-righteous vegetarians whose extreme ecological conscientiousness had grown out of a Proudhonist anarchism, the Naturiens eschewed all the fruits of progress, protested at the noxious smoke and effluent of factories, and longed for a return to a state of subsistence.

Louise Michel, who had little truck with either the frivolity of the cabaret or the triviality of the proto-ecologists, reserved her greatest disgust for the church of Sacré-Coeur, a work in progress that loomed from the top of the hill as 'an insult to our consciences'. At least the anarchists of Montmartre could appease themselves with the thought that, eleven years after the first stone was laid, the walls had only just begun to peep above the scaffolding, while unexpected modifications to the design had added close to 500,000 francs to its cost. It was just such profligacy and poor management in the civic sphere, all too often accompanied by an undertow of corruption, that had begun to rouse even the docile citizens of the Third Republic to indignation. Such discontent afforded the anarchist movement a rare opportunity to reach out and embrace a new section of society. However, the chances of this happening appeared dim while the movement remained so partial to factionalism that the proudest announcement made by one congress, meeting at Cette on the Mediterranean coast, was that 'We are anarchists because we can't agree.'

'Take away Louise Michel and her party would collapse,' wrote *Le Figaro* in a backhanded compliment. 'She is far and away the most interesting figure of the Third Republic.' Tirelessly she toured the clubs in the years after her release, always passionate in her outrage, but increasingly anxious to persuade her audiences that the disparate strands of the radical left should rediscover the solidarity they had shown at the time of her arrest. Her approach won few friends. Barbed comments from erstwhile colleagues, and their vicious innuendoes of collusion with the police, now augmented the usual loathing directed at Michel by moderates and reactionaries. Beyond the doors of the anarchist clubs, however, the alienation that underwrote much of the movement's appeal was finding new and purposeful expression in the artistic field, where the desire to destroy and renew assumed tangible form.

The French Establishment might scrutinise and disparage the radical left as morally and even medically degenerate, but as the editor of *Le Décadent*, Anatole Baju, made clear, the suspicion was perfectly mutual; the school from which his publication took its title had 'burst forth in a time of decadence, not to march to the beat of that time but "against the grain", in opposition to its time'. Two years earlier, Joris-Karl Huysmans had published his stories alongside Kropotkin's essays in a short-lived publication called the *Revue Indépendant*, founded by Félix Fénéon, a tall, lean and dandified twenty-three-year-old. Since then Huysmans had won notoriety for the elegant evisceration of the corruption and banality of the contemporary world in his novel *A Rebours*, which charted its protagonist's withdrawal into a world of absolute artifice. Now the writer was a leading contributor to Baju's magazine, together with Laurent Tailhade, Mallarmé, Rimbaud and Verlaine. And when Louise Michel lectured a gathering of decadent writers in Montmartre that 'Anarchists, just like decadents, want the end of the old world . . . Decadents are creating an anarchy of style', it was in its pages that Verlaine returned the compliment in the form of a paean dedicated to the Red Virgin, with the refrain *'Louise Michel est très bien.'*

It was not only in the avant-garde salons, however, that Michel found encouraging signs of creative destruction, but among the most downtrodden and deprived in society. As a writer and poet she understood the power of words to liberate or subjugate, and in prison had relished hearing the argot of the prostitutes with whom she lived, whose improvised words 'mixed up together like writhing monsters and yet sometimes assuming charming shapes, for slang is living language. Its imagery either touchingly innocent, or violently bloody.' Predictably, the criminal anthropologist Lombroso adduced such private languages, with their primal rhythms and squawking, rumbling use of onomatopoeia, as evidence of atavism: 'They speak differently because they feel differently; they speak as savages because they are true savages in the midst of our brilliant European civilisation.' To Michel, however, the energy of argot offered simple proof that 'there are geniuses among the people who speak slang, they're artists and creators', and that its challenge to bourgeois proprieties was of no less value than the more self-conscious efforts of the Decadents.

Among Félix Fénéon's most notable discoveries of the period, as the journalistic champion of avant-garde art, were two young painters who, in their daring experiments with colour and brushwork, were pushing the earlier experiments of Monet and his fellow Impressionists to startling new levels of control and refinement. Having first met in 1884 as exhibitors at the Salon des Indépendants, Georges Seurat and Paul Signac had become familiar faces in Le Chat Noir, which was within spitting distance of their studios next door to one another on the boulevard de Clichy. They were habitués of the decadent literary circles and, in Signac's case especially, sympathisers with the anarchist cause and admirers of its leading theorists, though their work was not yet overtly political. Both artists were concerned, above all, with the attempt to confer on nature 'an authentic reality' through their development of a method they called *la division* – the pointillist application of discrete touches of paint, inspired by the researches of the colour theorist Michel Chevreul. Nevertheless, the style they innovated made possible a revelatory critique of society of a kind that Kropotkin can scarcely have imagined when calling upon artists, in his 1885 book *Paroles d'un révolté*, to create an 'aesthetic socialism'.

Seurat's *A Sunday Afternoon on the Island of La Grande Jatte*, displayed at the last Impressionist exhibition in May 1886, was the product of four years of preparation, as he edged his way through a multitude of sketches and oil studies towards a *mise en scène* in which nearly fifty figures stand in a frozen evocation of the bourgeoisie at leisure. There is nothing in the painting to suggest social upheaval. Seurat's gaze is averted from the tawdry bars and dance halls that covered La Grande Jatte at the time, and the factories on the far banks of the Seine, just as his Impressionist precursors had turned their eyes from the effects of Prussian shelling when they painted the same location a decade earlier. Human forms dressed in the height of contemporary fashion are freed from time in the grid-like fixity of a classical frieze, their life a world apart from the vitality and hardship of Montmartre. The result, however, is unnerving: the optical mixing of the tiny points of colour creates a strange and luminous evocation of a sterile society, blind to itself and trapped within a straitjacket of artifice. Intentionally or not, in its own quiet way the painting offers a critique of the belle époque as devastating as Huysmans' *A Rebours*, with its closing sentiment 'So, crumble away society! Perish old world!'

It was a no less innovative, if more obviously acerbic, examination of the contemporary social malaise that could be seen at Le Chat Noir on those nights when the projection apparatus invented by the cartoonist Caran d'Ache lit up a shadow play of images drawn by Alfred Robida. A guidebook illustrator by trade, Robida's true genius lay in the narrow field of satirical futurology. In the panoramas and vignettes of Paris depicted in his book *The Twentieth Century*, the city has one foot in the mundaneness of contemporary bourgeois life, the other in the furthest corners of an imagination stranger even than that of Jules Verne. And yet preparations for war lurk in nearly every picture. While the skies teem with airship taxis, and genteel bus passengers listen to music pumped through pipes into headphones, barricades and gun emplacements intimate imminent international conflict and civil strife. It was an astute extrapolation of the flaws of the Third Republic, peopled by a complacent bourgeoisie lulled by luxury and leisure, whose anxiety that war or revolution might not be far away would render them highly susceptible to unscrupulous manipulation.

*

'Two thousand men who smoke, drink and chat, and seven or eight hundred women who laugh, drink, smoke, and offer the greatest gaity in the world,' marvelled one Russian aristocrat after his first visit to the Folies-Bergère. It was a world in which Peter Rachkovsky had made himself at home, a spider at the heart of his expanding web of spies and informants, alert for the slightest sign of weakness or insecurity that he might exploit, yet utterly insouciant. 'Nothing in his appearance reveals his sinister affairs,' one acquaintance of the time would recall. 'Fat, restless, always with an ever-present smile on his lips, he made me think of some genial fellow on an excursion.' The perfect disguise in a city where, it was observed, 'pleasure is a social necessity'. It is all too easy to imagine Rachkovsky sweet-talking international dignitaries at such nightspots, between indulging his well-attested appetite for the petite young women of Paris. And while the hedonistic Russian aristocrat concluded his letter to his mistress in the St Petersburg ballet by joking that 'We must annex Russia to this capital city, or else for preference this city to Russia', Rachkovsky treated the proposition more seriously.

In the three years since his arrival, Rachkovsky had transformed a Paris bureau whose operations had lagged far behind the 'excellent and conscientious' work being carried out in Berlin and Vienna. Brushing aside rivals with a mixture of cunning and sheer dedication, Rachkovsky had made Paris the main bastion of 'the systematic and covert surveillance of the Russian emigration abroad' which Plehve, then overall chief of the police department and now deputy interior minister, had declared to be his top priority.

Nevertheless, the changes came at a price. As well as the basic running costs of the outfit, which included payments to freelance agents and to traitors in the revolutionary ranks for information rendered, there were the *portiers* and postmen to bribe for turning a blind eye to the perlustration of letters (copied and returned within the day) and fees to pay to prostitutes, whose reports of pillow talk afforded Rachkovsky access to the intimate thoughts of the émigré community. And whilst he had managed to negotiate an increase in the bureau's budget, first to 132,000 francs and then by a further 50 per cent, there were fresh mutterings in St Petersburg about the lack of any conspicuous return on its investment, with Kropotkin's release and Tikhomirov's continued propaganda activities causing particular unease. Hampered by the bureaucracy of the Sûreté that impeded any cooperation, Rachkovsky had been playing a clever game, designed to ensure steady rather than spectacular results. It was now becoming clear, though, that to secure his position he needed a sensational success. The opportunity finally presented itself at the end of 1886.

'On Saturday night printing press in Geneva successfully destroyed by me, fifth volume of the *Herald* and all revolutionary publications. Details by post,' Rachkovsky telegraphed to St Petersburg on 11 November, signing himself off as Monsieur Léonard, his wife's maiden name. And he was more than happy to oblige when the reply came through from Interior Minister Dmitri Tolstoy breathlessly requesting 'the technical details of the operation, how you infiltrated, at what time, how long was needed for the destruction, what measures were taken not to be noticed'. The enterprise, Rachkovsky informed his superiors, had been initiated following the receipt of high-quality information about the location of the press from a disgruntled ex-associate of the People's Will. Based on this, Rachkovsky had drawn up a plan of the building, subsequently refined by enquiries carried out by his agent Wadyslaw Milewski in Geneva, whose powers of persuasion had convinced the caretaker that he was the rightful owner of the presses and secured access to the premises.

Milewski, Henri Bint and another man, quite possibily the agent Cyprien Jagolkovsky, had embarked on their methodical destruction of the works at nine in the evening and had continued through the night. The personal risk to them was great, since under Swiss law anyone who killed an intruder on their property was immune from prosecution, and as they moved from shelf to shelf the agents allowed themselves only the light of matches to work by, to avoid detection from the street. Gallons of acid, brought from Paris for the purpose, were poured on to the type, melting several hundred kilograms of metal beyond use or repair; a similar quantity of type would be scattered in the streets as the intruders left. Hundreds of copies of the *Herald* too were destroyed, past and present editions, along with editions of Herzen's and Tikhomirov's works due for clandestine delivery into Russia; Rachkvosky's agents tore them up, page by page, until knee-deep in shredded paper and barely able to move.

It was half-past four in the morning when they finally left, breaking the lock to indicate forced entry and protect the caretaker from retribution, and planting false evidence to suggest that the crime was the direct responsibility of a rival political group rather than simple vandalism. As they travelled back to Paris that morning on separate trains, their blistered hands testified to a gruelling and nerve-racked night, but the rewards were considerable, both for them as individuals and for Rachkovsky's organisation. Amidst much rejoicing in St Petersburg, Rachkovsky received 5,000 francs and the Order of St Anna, Third Class; his agents got 1,500 apiece, while any questions that had remained over the effectiveness of the Paris *agentura* were, for the moment, answered.

Such an audacious cross-border incursion may well have been without precedent in the history of policing, and owed its success to the operational shortcomings of the Sûreté. Its ex-director, Gustave Mace, was one of those frustrated by the Sûreté's inefficiency, explicitly citing its overly laborious process when pursuing fugitive criminals to the frontier. He described how a report filed in the early morning had to pass through the municipal police, the first bureau of the first division to the local *commissaire* where 'after a respectable sojourn in various offices, [it would be] examined by a clerk, who draws up a memorandum some lines long in which there does not always appear all the information of value in seeking the suspect', before finally returning to the Sûreté for action late in the evening. Had French policing been more efficient, things could have been different: *Le Journal de Genève* might have been printing news of the Russians' arrest, rather than lapping up stories planted by Rachkovsky to feed the internecine squabbles of the revolutionary exiles.

There was relief in St Petersburg that the Geneva venture had passed off without an international incident. Eager to avoid anything that could prompt further questions about the raid, Count Tolstoy declined Rachkovsky's request to be allowed to press his advantage by planting further forged documents apportioning blame for the press' destruction that would undermine both Plekhanov and Tikhomirov. Rachkovsky was not easily deterred. Having proved to himself how a maverick approach to the niceties of policing and diplomacy could reap results, he set about harrying the revolutionaries in both Switzerland and France with even greater vigour, and scant regard to propriety.

In Russia, surveillance units strove to be inconspicuous, assisted by the extensive wardrobe of disguises held by the police department in Moscow. Among the émigrés abroad, however, the aim was to intimidate rather than simply to gather intelligence, and Rachkovsky's agents made their presence known in the most sinister of ways, generating the illusion of ubiquity. So effective were they in this that many émigrés succumbed to paranoia that a vast network of *mouchards* was on their tail, rather than the few dozen that Rachkovsky actually employed. Once again Rachkovsky's policy was vindicated when, in 1887, contrary to all previous policy, the Russian government formally requested that France actually desist from expelling any further nihilists, realising that whilst under the keen eyes of the Paris *agentura* they would pose far less of a threat than if they were sent to England or Switzerland.

Intoxicated by his successes, Rachkovsky began to seek even greater prizes. Strolling out of the embassy building in the rue de Grenelle in 1886 and 1887, he would have heard newspaper vendors tickling the interest of passers-by with news of an anarchist bomb thrown into the Paris Bourse, or the dramatic theft by 'The Panthers of Batignolles' of money and jewels from a socialite painter's apartment 'in the name of Liberty'. Meanwhile, wherever he looked, the freshly rebuilt architecture of the area around the embassy would have provided a visual reminder of the fatal last days of the Commune, when cannon fire from the rampaging Versaillais had devastated the nearby Croix-Rouge crossroads. The latent anxieties of the French were transparent to Rachkovsky, as they were to the futurological artist Robida, and would provide a broad canvas for his psychological games. A dab of terrorism here, a flick of anti-Jewish incitement there, all mixed in with a spot of warmongering, and the spymaster might just be able to bring Russian autocracy and French republicanism into the improbable alignment that had proved elusive for so long. For the moment, though, his usual duties had to come first.

*

To judge by the circulation of anarchist newspapers in France in the mid-1880s, the movement could claim at most a few tens of thousands of followers, including casual sympathisers. Yet circumstances could hardly have been more propitious for the growth of an ideology that was internationalist and egalitarian. In the vexed area of labour relations, the troubles around Lyons in which Kropotkin had been caught up had migrated to Anzin, on the Belgian border in the north-east, then flared up too at Decazeville in the Aveyron, hundreds of miles to the south-west, where the government was obliged to station troops in the spring of 1886 to deal with the violence. Meanwhile, following France's occupation of Tunisia in 1881, its overseas activities once again became a source of shame and anger to the socialists. Since 1883 Jules Ferry's government had pursued a policy of colonial expansion in South East Asia, to offset the effects of economic recession at home and help assuage the loss of Alsace and Lorraine to Germany. War with China was the result: a piece of adventurism that enjoyed only fragile support at home. When faulty intelligence reported that the Battle of Bang Bo was a defeat for the French expeditionary force in Tonkin, the belief in Paris that the force was in an irredeemable position precipitated the fall of Ferry's administration.

The leading figures of the radical left were quick to trace the common thread between the diverse iniquities of the age. 'We didn't want to send troops to Tonkin and Tunisia,' Louise Michel raged to audiences who were easily roused. 'High finance becomes high crime.' Rochefort spoke out tirelessly for the oppressed of Tunisia, arguing for the release of those who had resisted French rule, and when a subscription in *L'Intransigeant* raised funds to help strikers arrested in confrontations at the Anzin colliery, he delivered the money in person. France's industrial workers and her young soldiers were victims alike, he proclaimed, sent to die for the profit of their masters, whether killed in the fighting for Tonkin or mangled in machinery, as many hundreds were every year.

There were others, though, Rochefort told his readers, who were prepared to go far further in their opposition to colonialism, revealing that Olivier Pain, his companion in the escape from New Caledonia and his secretary since, had been executed by Lord Kitchener in the Sudan as a spy for the Mahdi, the mystical Arab leader who besieged the British in Khartoum and shook Britain with the killing of General Gordon. And once again, Verne seemed to echo the experiences of those associated with his occasional co-author, Paschal Grousset, when in 1886 he presented the eponymous *Robur the Conqueror* to the world. A pioneer adventurer of the skies, the hero's fearsome vessel the *Albatross,* a heavier-than-air equivalent of Nemo's *Nautilus,* serves the cause of liberation by turning its firepower on the exploiters of Africa. Rochefort himself, ever the egotist, would have been more likely to see in Robur's adventures a metaphor for his own contrarian campaigns.

Having been elected to Parliament as a Blanquist in 1885, and having then resigned in high dudgeon to publicise the crimes of colonialism,

Rochefort was now eager for a new tub to thump. Edouard Drumont, whose father had hired Rochefort thirty years earlier for his first job at the department of architecture, was championing one promising cause with his newly founded *La France Juive*: a periodical that was sworn to expose the undermining of French society by cosmopolitan Jews. The subject, already close to Rochefort's heart, had additional appeal at a time when the uncle of Joseph Reinarch – the object of Rochefort's personal loathing over the exposure of his special pleading to the tribunal that had tried the Communards – was among three Jewish 'promoters' mounting a public-relations whitewash on behalf of the Panama Canal Company. For bubbling under the surface of the company's reassuring message were rumours about delays and mismanagement in the construction of the canal and fears of economic scandal and collapse.

The first issue of shares in the Panama project in 1881 had been quickly taken up, with those who had missed out on the 300 per cent profit made by the early investors in Ferdinand de Lesseps' Suez project determined not to do so again. Eight years was what they had been told it would take for de Lesseps, the universally acknowledged genius of the age and France's national treasure, to reshape the world by cutting a forty-five-mile canal through mountain ranges 800 feet high to link the Atlantic and Pacific oceans. Five years on, however, the proceeds of that first feverish sale of stock had been all but spent on barely one sixth of the construction, necessitating further investment, with a lottery loan the proposed means of raising it. De Lesseps was brazenly dismissing concerns and again promising completion by 1889, in time for the centenary of the Revolution, but the newspapers were unearthing buried reports about delayed progress and the story refused to die. Anti-Semitism and the merry-go-round of political folly and incompetence alone, however, were not sufficient to boost either Rochefort's profile or the languishing circulation of *L'Intransigeant*. In desperate need of a cause to promote, fortune now brought him General Boulanger.

It had been Georges Clemenceau's idea to appoint the glamorous Boulanger as minister for war in de Freycinet's reformist government of 1886, with a brief to deliver an army reformed on truly republican lines. The choice was an odd one for an old radical to make, given that Boulanger was an ex-Versaillais officer. Louise Michel remembered only too well Boulanger's part in the savage defeat of the Communard soldiers who had set out for Versailles on Gustave Flourens' *grande sortie* in a spirit of fraternity. The memory of most on the left, though, appeared to be shorter, and the wounds that had prevented Boulanger from participating personally in the Bloody Week continued to provide him with dispensation from any lingering blame. Eventual victory in the colonial war for control of Tonkin, achieved while he was director of the war office, had burnished the general's prestige, but it was his attitude towards those two bugbears of the left – colonial occupation and the treatment of strikers – that helped extend his appeal beyond the usual constituency for a military hero. His expressions of unease over the French strategy in North Africa had cost him his command of the garrison there, while as the minister responsible for troops sent to pacify strike-racked mines in the Aveyron, he had announced to the Chamber of Deputies in April 1886 that 'at this very moment, every soldier is perhaps sharing his rations with a miner'.

Soft soap it may have been, but the sentiment endeared Boulanger to those for whom an army commander with the common touch, alive to the suffering of the hungry masses and to their deeper emotional need for a sense of national purpose, was a most appealing prospect. Moreover, he was handsome and dashing, with an elegantly styled beard, handlebar moustache and an impressive black steed, on which he regularly rode out in public; and what France truly craved in late 1886, with the most wanton part of her soul, was the immediate glory of the cavalry charge: the chance for revenge on Germany. At the Bastille Day celebrations at Longchamp in July 1886, President Grévy was left waiting in vain to receive the salutes of the column of soldiers who, rather than looking right, towards him, as they passed, instead turned left to Boulanger.

Rochefort had always had something of a soft spot for a man in uniform, especially one who could combine the smack of firm leadership with liberal tendencies: during the dying days of the Commune in 1871 he had, after all, pressed the young General Rossel to assert himself as a military dictator. In Boulanger the ideal was made incarnate: a tribune of the people who had not flinched when it fell to him to inform his old mentor, the duc d'Aumale, that as an Orléanist claimant to the throne he was to be discharged from the army, yet who would equally readily speak hard truths to the tired old professional politicians in the council of ministers. And during the winter of 1886, mounting military tension with Germany allowed Boulanger to establish a reputation as 'General Revenge', a national saviour who strengthened frontier fortifications and sought to even ban performances of Wagner's operatic paean to Teutonic chivalry, Lohengrin.

With conflict in the air, the anarchists saw an opportunity for revolution. Elisée Reclus came under suspicion from the French police of planning 'a seditious movement whose aim is to thwart the efforts of the

French armies'; so too did Kropotkin, who proposed that each French city should declare itself a revolutionary commune as a focus for resistance. Friedrich Engels, meanwhile, demonstrated his usual perspicacity in military matters by warning the German high command that, were hostilities to break out, the conflict would rapidly turn into a continent-wide conflagration, as deadly as the Thirty Years War and bringing in its wake 'the collapse of countless European states and the disappearance of dozens of monarchies'.

Seventy thousand troops were mobilised across the border, in response to Boulanger's bellicose statements, with the result that nearly every other continental power stepped up its military preparations. Rochefort weighed in to fuel war fever, revealing in *L'Intransigeant* that Bismarck had warned the Red Cross to prepare field hospitals, and had offered Provence, Nice and Savoy to Italy if it would join the attack: a Boulanger dictatorship, the newspaper proposed, was France's only hope. That he was providing Bismarck with the pretext to rouse nationalistic support in the weeks before the German elections did nothing to dent the general's rising popularity. Yet wiser heads, fearing what might happen if actions were allowed to match the rhetoric, held France back from mobilisation, and once the elections in Germany had passed, the situation began to cool. Clemenceau now realised, however, that in underestimating 'Boulboul' he had loosed on to the political stage a man of dangerous charisma.

For Rachkovsky, a brinksman and provocateur by instinct, the situation must have held a fascination that was far from disinterested. Although Boulanger's belligerence made him an unnerving figure for the Russian government, which knew itself to be in a parlous state of military unreadiness, the Okhrana chief deployed his propagandists in the French press to publish spuriously alarmist assessments of German intentions. For whilst not in Russia's national interest, by encouraging heightened tension in the Franco-German relationship Rachkovsky could promote his own importance as a conduit for key intelligence, and he doubtless drew on the contacts he had made among Boulanger's associates to monitor and influence the general.

Keeping track of Boulanger's alliances was a complex business, though, since the 'man on the horse' acted as a magnet for malcontents from across the political spectrum. The Blanquists, still in thrall to the myth of their own revolutionary chief who had died in 1881, eagerly gravitated to the general's camp in the hope of causing the kind of social crisis from which they might profit. Ambitious men like Louis Andrieux, the ex-prefect of police and bitter antagonist of Rochefort, were lured by the hope that working with Boulanger would propel them into power. And crucially, the funding for Boulanger's political insurgency came from the likes of the fabulously wealthy Duchess d'Uzès, inheritor of the Cliquot family's champagne fortune. An arch-monarchist, who under the pseudonym 'Manuela' pursued an artistic sideline sculpting statues of saints for the Sacré-Coeur, it seemed scarcely credible that d'Uzès should bankroll the atheist populist that Boulanger appeared to be. Everyone had their reasons, though, and agendas of their own to advance.

While Juliette Adam handed over the editorship of *La Nouvelle Revue* to Elie de Cyon, in order that he might better coordinate with Katkov's *Moskovskie vedomosti* over their campaign for a Franco-Russian alliance, others in her circle took a more purely esoteric approach to international affairs. The occultists' first foray into geopolitics had been to court the maharajah Dalip Singh to stage an insurrection against British rule, offering the inducement of a Franco-Russian alliance that they were in no position to deliver. Their fanciful aim then may have been to facilitate access to the technologically and spiritually advanced Holy Land of Agartha, buried deep under the mountains of Asia, from whose Grand Pandit their own guru d'Alveydre claimed to have learned the secrets of synarchy. In 1887, however, they turned their attention to matters closer to home.

Gérard Encausse, the scientific hypnotist at the Salpêtrière who was now beginning to establish himself as a mystical visionary under the name 'Papus' had, together with Paul Adam, a bon viveur, Boulangist and literary acolyte of Fénéon's decadent movement, been engaged for some time in the investigation of consciousness, and the possible interpenetration of times past, present and future. History as it was experienced, they had come to understand, was merely an echo of strife and turmoil in the spiritual realm, and France's defeat at the Battle of Sedan was the clear consequence of the superior invocatory powers of Prussia's scryers. At a personal level, Encausse fought duels over accusations that he had attacked his enemies with volatised poison, but was alert too to conflict on a larger scale. If Boulanger was going to wage war, they must have concluded, then it was the patriotic duty of France's psychic brigade to be in peak condition and free of earthly distractions.

It was Encausse who remarked at around this time on the feline cunning that Rachkovsky concealed beneath his jovial exterior, but as 'Papus' he too knew how to bear a grudge, and whilst his revenge would be slow in coming and far from ethereal, the Okhrana chief ignored him at his peril. In the present circumstances, though, Rochefort must have seemed to offer Rachkovsky a more reliable means to influence the international situation. After all, he had predicted with suspicious clairvoyance the next flashpoint in the stand-off with Germany: a border incident involving espionage, such as was triggered by the arrest in German Alsace of the French police superintendent, Schnaebele. Moreover, with the secret documents in question concerning Bismarck's intrigues in the Balkans, the situation had a Russian angle that de Cyon and Katkov were quick to exploit. Russia and Germany squared up in a war of words, with the Russian government rejecting Bismarck's offer of a free hand in the East in return for being allowed to act with impunity in the West, asserting that if Europe was to be the theatre of war, then it was ready.

After the new French foreign minister, the late Gustave's younger brother, Emile Flourens, finally secured the release of the spy a week later, Boulanger recklessly taunted Bismarck with having run scared of the Russian press, while from the sidelines Rochefort lambasted the Jewish financiers of Germany for their supposed role in orchestrating the crisis. With forgery, intrigue, nihilists, anti-Semitism and geopolitical manipulation all involved in the debacle, if Rachkovsky did not have a hand in it, then he would surely have had sleepless nights calculating how he might claim this territory as his own.

Concerned by the rising tide of popular acclaim for Boulanger, the general's colleagues in the cabinet finally realised that they must act to curb his power, but when ousted from his post, Boulanger immediately received 100,000 write-in votes at the next by-election, and had to be hurriedly 'promoted' to command the army division based in Clermont-Ferrand, deep in the Auvergne. Unfortunately, sending an idol into the wilderness wasn't so easy. Tens of thousands of grief-stricken Boulangists turned out to block the path of his train in July, before at last letting it roll with plangent cries of 'You'll be back! You'll be back!' And return he did, sooner than the crowds might have expected. A corruption scandal involving the sale of state honours by Daniel Wilson, the son-in-law of President Grévy, led to the fall of Grévy's government and a power vacuum just waiting for the general to fill. From November 1887, throughout the following year, France was a frenzy of Boulangism.

Such was the extremity of emotion around Boulanger that it had even begun to attract the attention of researchers at the Salpêtrière and elsewhere, for whom the psychology of the crowd rather than the individual posed interesting new challenges. Their studies diagnosed Boulanger's fanatical supporters as suffering from hysteria, a symptom of which, as

Encausse knew very well, was the susceptibility to hypnosis. As Jules Liégeois, of the rival Nancy school of psychologists, would write, 'Nihilists, anarchists, socialists, revolutionaries – all kinds of political and religious fanatics – don't they become . . . criminals by the force of suggestion? On days of popular agitation, the crowd – composed of many good individuals – turns fierce and bloodthirsty . . . the beast is unleashed.'

From her magnificent town house on the Champs-Elysées, plumply louche in black gown and diamonds, the Duchess d'Uzès pumped out money to the general's campaign in the vain hope of seeing the republic brought down, while the general himself seemed ready to horse-trade his principles for monarchist support. It was a vision of anarchy, in its most pejorative sense: of myriad factions each hell-bent on destruction and chaos in the search for power; and a Boulangist campaign without even the self-respecting consistency to decline contributions from rich Jews, despite its overt anti-Semitism. And within this broad church, there was even a place for the anarchists themselves, whose affections were bought with some part of the campaign's three million francs of champagne money.

Louise Michel herself, who had previously disdained the general, discovered enough cynicism to see how Boulanger might serve her political purposes, and finally agreed to accept donations from Duchess d'Uzès on behalf of her various charitable interests. 'She confirmed that the extreme left will ally itself with the right,' wrote one police informant, seemingly well placed to know her mind. 'She believes that the demonstrations being organised by Rochefort will be extremely effective, and will help spread anarchist ideas.' Michel even allowed herself to be drawn into involvement with the Ligue des Femmes, established by d'Uzès, who had charmed her by requesting a copy of Kropotkin's *Paroles d'un révolté*.

Then, at the end of the year, the Panama Canal Company went bankrupt. The tens of thousands of bourgeois who had staked their savings on an engineering project so strongly tied to national pride, were devastated. Little in French national life, it seemed, could any longer be believed in; everything was a fraud, an illusion, a sleight of hand. 'One can no longer mistake that what is taking place today, what the coming year has in store, is the decisive crisis of the republic, coinciding, by a singular irony, with the ostentatious celebration of the French Revolution,' wrote one veteran political commentator at the turn of the year. It seemed that the general's time had truly come.

A fortnight later, Boulanger won a crushing victory in a Paris by-election. 'A l'Elysée, à l'Elysée,' tens of thousands of his supporters cried as they massed outside the Café Durand where their idol was dining, sensing that the *coup d'état* they had so often called for was now inevitable. Fatally, though, Boulanger hesitated. He would, he told the gathering of his political intimates, rather win power legitimately at the next election; then he promptly disappeared into the night, to celebrate his success in the arms of his beloved mistress. Had Rochefort been right all along in lauding his fundamental modesty and honesty, or did the general merely suffer a loss of nerve?

The acerbic wit of the professional politicians who had stayed up late to gauge the threat to their careers left no doubt as to their disdain: 'Five-past twelve, gentlemen,' remarked one, consulting his watch, 'five minutes ago Boulangism started to fall on the market.' 'He's set us a good example,' said the president, Sadi Carnot, 'let's all go to bed, too.' But behind the relief and the jokes, those in government must have still felt disquiet: they had come to grips with Boulanger and Boulangism, but what of the deep currents of popular disenchantment on which his rise had depended? Remove the lightning rod, and who might then be struck down?

*

Louise Michel was made for suffering and martyrdom, wrote the publisher Monsieur Roy in his preface to her memoirs. 'Born 1,900 years earlier, she would have faced the wild animals of the amphitheatre; born during the Inquisition, she would have died in the flames.' Others in thrall to Louise Michel's magnetism reached for similar images. In his ballad Verlaine depicted her as Joan of Arc, perhaps thinking of the 'exalted' state Michel entered in moments of political passion: the anarchist equivalent of the religious ecstasies that the Church believed were being blasphemed in Charcot's public experiments involving his hysterics. Alternatively, Verlaine may simply have been hinting at the fate she courted, at a time when the nationalistic right was erecting a rash of statues to the Maid of Orleans, while the left countered with effigies of its own freethinking martyr, Etienne Dolet. And indeed, only two months after the hanging of the Haymarket martyrs, little noticed for the moment in a Paris caught up in its own drama, Louise Michel did come close to a kind of martyrdom of her own.

She was addressing a meeting in the Channel port of Le Havre, challenging her bourgeois audience to see the light before the revolution overwhelmed them. The mood was hostile to her, but not more so than in most of the provincial towns she visited. Then, without warning, a young man approached the stage. He proudly declared himself a Breton before raising a pistol and firing twice. One bullet lodged in Michel's hat, the other deep in her left temple.

'I'm fine, really fine' she wrote to a solicitous Rochefort the next day, but she was putting on a brave face. Despite the game attempts of a local doctor to extract the bullet from her cranium with his pen, it had lodged too deep to be easily retrieved. Journalists were issued with accounts dismissing the wound's severity, but the police in Paris soon learned the truth from their agents: 'she is fainting frequently and the problem with her sight gets worse every day,' wrote one. Yet somehow she survived. The wound would not kill Michel, an expert confirmed, but the long-term effects as the bullet wandered through her brain were unpredictable.

Forgiving to a fault, Michel swiftly turned her attention to her would-be assassin, whose acquittal she was determined to secure. He was a 'subject of hallucination', she informed the readers of L'Intransigeant, 'a being from another age' made brutal by living in a tumultuous era of transition, and like the patients in the Salpêtrière, not to be held responsible for his actions. A week after the attack, she even wrote to Charcot himself, pleading for science to come to the defence of her assailant. In the era of the freelance assassin that was now dawning, of the terrorist armed with his bomb and revolver and a mania to make his voice heard, the sanity or otherwise of those convicted would assume a new political significance. For was anarchism itself a form of madness, or was it the rest of the world that was insane?

15

The Revolution is Postponed

London, 1887–1890

So sweeping had been Peter Kropotkin's dismissal of England as a 'land impermeable to new ideas' after the anarchists' London Congress of 1881 that the transformation in its radical life in the six years that had passed took him aback. Addressing the Socialist League's anniversary commemoration of the Paris Commune in March 1886, he left his audience at the South Place Institute in no doubt of his conviction that they were meeting 'on the eve of one of those great uprisings which periodically visit Europe'. George Bernard Shaw, who was probably present that evening, would later remark of Kropotkin that 'his only weakness was a habit of prophesying war within the next fortnight', with revolution to follow in its wake. Few could have denied, though, that the period between Kropotkin's imprisonment in 1883 and his release from Clairvaux prison in January 1886 had seen tensions rise across the Continent and beyond, with Britain no exception.

'How to promote the greater happiness of the masses of the people, how to increase their enjoyment of life, that is the problem of the future,' Joseph Chamberlain, the reforming Liberal mayor of Birmingham had recently diagnosed. By extending the franchise to all working men, his party had already fulfilled the key demand of the Chartist movement twenty years earlier but times and expectations had moved on. The Liberals' failure to adopt his proposals to guarantee the property of the rich in return for welfare protection for the poor, led the working masses to question whether the cosy duopoly of political parties, whose alternating rule Morris would liken to a politely fixed football match, could ever deliver effective representation for their views.

For such opinions to be proclaimed in public, however, was profoundly unnerving for those in authority, and the police were called upon to intervene. Dod Street in the East End had seen the first concerted action against the Socialist League, when socialist street preachers had been driven from their pitches while trying to address a crowd of 10,000 demonstrators against the curtailment of free speech. Then, when the packed public gallery of the courtroom shouted its fury at the sentences passed on eight men arrested, who included Frank Kitz, the police waded in with sticks and fists. Attempting to shield Marx's daughter Eleanor from the fray, William Morris was among those beaten and taken into custody. But in the spectacle of violence deployed to protect the interests of a complacent middle class, Morris saw similarities with pre-revolutionary France and declared that by dragging this hypocrisy into the open the socialists had 'gained a complete victory over the police'.

If Morris' optimism about a British revolution had seemed fanciful in the autumn of 1885, within a few weeks of Kropotkin's release from prison early in the New Year, events in London appeared a harbinger of class war. The occasion, at which Morris was not personally present, was a march from Trafalgar Square to Hyde Park by those who had lost their jobs in the difficult economic circumstances. An initial blow would be delivered the following February when, in Morris' absence, another meeting of the unemployed marched the same route. Ten thousand strong, as the crowd passed the Tory Carlton Club and the Liberal Reform Club, insults and missiles were hurled, with one army veteran memorably raging that 'we were not the scum of the country when we were fighting for bond-holders in Egypt, you dogs!' Peering from their windows, outraged members jeered back that the mob needed the smack of firm discipline, although the sound of breaking windows in Piccadilly, where the indigent of Whitechapel, Shoreditch and Limehouse were looting the shops, may have made them tremble that they might rather be on the receiving end of physical chastisement.

In the aftermath of the riot, even *Blackwells Magazine* had written of 'Black Monday' as the germ of a British revolution, while for days London had quaked at rumours that an army from the East End was preparing to attack under cover of the thick fog that had descended. Seeing a middle class 'so terrified of the sight of the misery it has created that at all hazards it must be swept out of sight', Morris looked forward to further repression that would feed the fires of popular discontent. Readiness, though, was essential. 'We have been taken over unprepared by a revolutionary incident,' he wrote in the *Commonweal*, urging his readers to become quickly 'educated in economics, in organisation, and in administration' so as to be ready when such an opportunity presented itself.

Sentiment may have led Kropotkin to esteem France as the cradle of revolution, but improbable as the situation must have seemed to him, in early 1886 Britain held out the riper promise. Although thousands turned out in Paris to hear him speak after his release from prison, hungry for words of guidance and inspiration from anarchism's lost leader, he had no further taste for the rough hospitality of the Third Republic. Weakened by illness and with a wife and young child to support, the idea of a secure refuge clearly appealed; news of the suicide of his brother Alexander in Siberia, unable to face the prospect of release after fourteen years' internal exile, would shortly confirm his own determination to avoid further spells in prison. Moreover, Britain promised him a vehicle for his developing ideas, for during the latter months of Kropotkin's incarceration in Clairvaux he had been approached by Charlotte Wilson, the Cambridge-educated wife of a stockbroker and sister of a Liberal Member of Parliament, with a proposal to establish an anarchist newspaper in London. Crossing the Channel in March, he settled his family as temporary guests in the home of his old friend Kravchinsky.

The intellectual environment of London to which Kravchinsky introduced Kropotkin was highly congenial: one peopled by men who were at least intrigued by his ideas, like William Morris, and often wholly sympathetic to them, and women who were frequently as smitten by the charm of the unlikely revolutionary as by his impressive and enquiring mind. Coming in the immediate aftermath of the Black Monday riot, the annual commemoration of the Paris Commune had special piquancy, and the following months witnessed a slew of works that engaged with the unfulfilled promise of 1871 and its continued relevance to the political life of Kropotkin's new friends. Eleanor Marx led the way, with her translation of Lissagaray's ten-year-old magisterial work of myth-making, *Histoire de la Commune*; William Morris and Belfort Bax revisited the subject, yet with the same romantic desire to cast the victims of the Bloody Week as having chosen 'to bury themselves in the smoking ruins of Paris rather than . . . allow socialism and the revolution to be befouled and degraded'. Then, in 1887, Henry Hyndman drew out the urgent relevance of their historical accounts in his provocatively titled pamphlet *A Commune for London*. 'It is in the power of London', he wrote, 'to lead the way in the great social revolution which will remove the crushing disabilities, physical, moral and intellectual, under which the great mass of our city populations suffer at the present time.'

For all his personal antipathy to Hyndman, his old sparring partner from the Social Democratic Federation, Morris undoubtedly shared his sentiments. 'The East End of London is the hell of poverty,' John Henry

With the railways into Paris closed by the siege of 1870, the platforms of the Gare d'Orléans became production lines supplying balloons to Nadar's aerostatic service.

An anonymous photograph looking down from the Butte Montmartre onto the artillery park that housed many of the National Guard's cannon, whose attempted seizure by the regular army was the catalyst for civil war.

Père-Lachaise cemetery, scene of the last stand of the Communards on 28 May 1871; the survivors were executed against what would become known as the Mur des Fédérés, at the rear of the cemetery, which remains a site of annual pilgrimage.

It would be three decades before the anarchist artist Maximilien Luce exorcised his traumatic childhood memories of the Bloody Week in his vast canvas of 1903/4, *A Paris Street in May 1871*.

For those communards deported to New Caledonia, eight years would pass before an amnesty allowed them to return.

A surge in peaceful political activism by Russia's radical youth in the 1870s prompted severe Tsarist repression; many hundreds were imprisoned for long periods without trial.

Within weeks of the Tsar's death, seemingly spontaneous pogroms against the Jews swept through Russia.

In early 1881, less than two years after The People's Will faction adopted a strategy of terrorist violence, Tsar Alexander II was finally killed by bomb-throwing assassins.

When Rachkovsky arrived in Paris in 1884 fumigators had been installed to protect against the cholera epidemic then sweeping southern Europe.

New conceptions of disease suggested irresistible metaphors for social malaise. Here a cartoon from the anarchist newspaper Père Peinard proposes that Capitalism should be seen as 'The True Cholera'.

The French artist who illustrated the murder of Colonel Sudeikin, Rachkovsky's police mentor, exaggerated the number of assailants but not the brutality of the attack.

Although a historical illustrator by trade, the most extraordinary work of Albert Robida offered visions of airborne commerce and technological warfare that recollect the work of Jules Verne.

Spectators on the Eiffel Tower view the celebrations of the Franco-Russian alliance that Rachkovsky had helped orchestrate from behind the scenes.

The only known photograph of Peter Rachkovsky

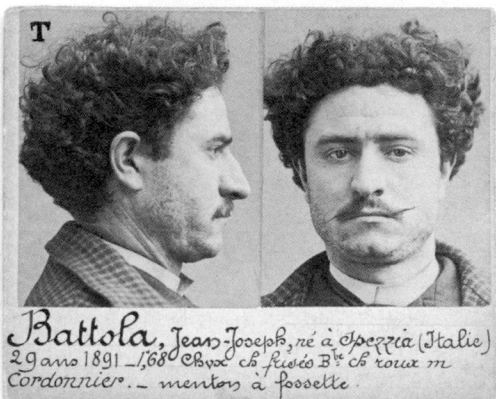

Battola, Jean-Joseph, né à Spezzia (Italie)
29 ans 1891 1,68 Chvx ch fusés Bt ch roux m
Cordonnier. — menton à fossette

By the 1890s, after years of struggling
to have his anthropometric system of
criminal identification accepted,
Alphonse Bertillon was the pride
of the Paris Prefecture of Police.

Among the many anarchist refugees to England who
had their details recorded were Jean Battola who as
'Degnai' was said to be the instigator of the Walsall
bomb plot, and Charles Malato, Rochefort's secretary
and the author of *The Delights of Exile*.

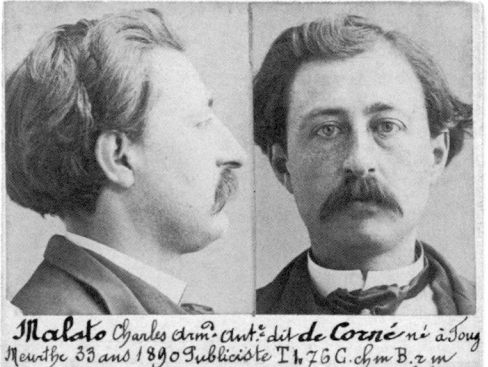

Malato Charles Arm. Ant. dit de Corné né à Joug
Meurthe 33 ans 1890 Publiciste T 1,76 C. ch m B.z m
verrue à 2 ç gl s œil f.

Though photographed by Bertillon
after his arrest, it was a very different
image of the anarchist bomber
Ravachol that his comrades promoted
that of the iconic martyr.

The garrotting of innocent anarchists accused of insurrection in Xerez was a significant incitement to terrorism for their comrades in France and elsewhere.

Two months after Bourdin was killed when the bomb he was carrying exploded near Greenwich Observatory, Pauwels died similarly during a planned attack on the Madeline Church in Paris, his corpse photographed by the police.

The bomb that Emile Henry left in the Café Terminus in February, 1894, was intended to strike directly at the bourgeoisie as they enjoyed their leisure.

By 1893 the anarchist of the popular imagination was a megalomaniac hell-bent on destruction;
the airborne anti-hero of sixteen-year-old E. Douglas Fawcett's *Hartmann the Anarchist* deviates
from type only in his concern for his mother's disapproval.

Paul Signac's *In a Time of Harmony* of 1895 offered an alternative vision of an
anarchist utopia in the wake of the recent terrorist attacks in Western Europe.

Mackay would write. 'Like an enormous black, motionless, giant Kraken, the poverty of London lies there in lurking silence and encircles with its mighty tentacles the life and wealth of the City and of the West End.' Venturing frequently into the maw of the monster for speaking engagements in Shoreditch and Whitechapel, or simply to research and more fully understand its misery, Morris was shocked by what he found. Commenting on the hovel in which the Socialist League stalwart Kitz lived, he confided to a friend: 'It fairly gave me the horrors to see how wretchedly off he was; so it isn't much wonder that he takes the line he does.' Affluent London society was, he believed, 'so terrified of the misery it has created that at all hazards it must be swept out of sight'. And yet, all the while, the finely appointed homes of the wealthy, some furnished from Morris' own interior design shop on Oxford Street – which had itself narrowly escaped the Black Monday window-breaking – offered the dispossessed a tantalising, infuriating glimpse of warmth, satiety, ease and comfort. 'If you want to see the origin and explanation of an East London rookery you must open the door and walk in upon some fashionable dinner party at the West End,' remarked Edward Carpenter, whose absence from the capital gave him an outsider's clear perspective on its iniquities.

Despite criticising Carpenter for his withdrawal from the political fray, Morris clearly found the simple life at Millthorpe in Derbyshire deeply appealing, with its sparse furnishings and meals of home-grown vegetables shared from a single wooden plate. It was during a visit in 1886 that he read the newly published novel by Richard Jefferies, *After London*, a vision of a post-apocalyptic Britain returned to the state of untamed nature that its countryman author so cherished. 'Absurd hopes curled around my heart as I read it,' Morris wrote and the book's premise lodged in his imagination. A country lapsed into barbarism and dominated by feuding warlords was scarcely what Morris aspired to, but the notion of beneficent erasure – of a London reduced to ruination and submerged in swampland, and a society purged of all the corrupt influences that had led mankind astray since the Middle Ages – spoke directly to Morris' deepest political and imaginative instincts.

The affinity between Kropotkin and Morris was apparent to both, even though their political positions remained distinct, and frequently at odds. The Russian found in his new friend a shared aptitude for viewing contemporary issues with a long historical perspective, and this would lead to a fruitful cross-fertilisation of ideas in the years to come. For the moment, however, Morris allowed himself to indulge his taste for fantasy – whether dreaming of revolution tomorrow, or the distant prospect of Utopia – while

Kropotkin's attention was drawn to concrete planning for the day after the existing authorities and institutions had been toppled.

During his years in Clairvaux, experimental gardening had provided Kropotkin with a seemingly harmless occupation. And though the scurvy from which he had suffered suggests he lacked green fingers, tilling the soil had focused his thoughts on the necessity of ensuring tangible benefits to the masses in the immediate aftermath of social upheaval, in order to cement their loyalty and avoid the problems of starvation that he mistakenly saw as having helped defeat the Commune. 'To what should the two million citizens of Paris turn their attention when they would be no longer catering for the luxurious fads and amusements of Russian princes, Romanian grandees and wives of Berlin financiers?' he pondered. His proposals would not be published in book form until some years later, as *The Conquest of Bread*, but it was already clear to him that the equal distribution of food was key. He imagined parklands and aristocratic estates handed over to smallholders as common land, along with the credible promise of 'a more substantial well-being than that enjoyed today by the middle classes'.

'We are living at the close of an era, during which the marvellous advance of science [has] left social feeling behind,' an article asserted in the first edition of Kropotkin's and Charlotte Wilson's newspaper *Freedom* in October 1886, which was printed on the presses of Morris' *Commonweal*. In the narrow lecture hall created out of the old stables at Kelmscott House, Morris' home in Hammersmith, west London, the path to the future was thrashed out in meetings attended by the leading lights of socialism in Britain. Kropotkin was 'amiable to the point of saintliness, and with his full red beard and loveable expression might have been a shepherd from the Delectable Mountains,' Shaw would write, and it may well have been he too who wrote the report of the first, halting speech that a self-conscious Kravchinsky attempted, after months of persuasion, in his broken English.

It was an environment that encouraged cosmopolitan participation. Kropotkin entertained his audience with apocryphal stories of Russian settlers in the United States outwitting the Native Americans and stolid frontiersmen alike. And along with Shaw, William Butler Yeats and Oscar Wilde added an Irish flavour to the proceedings, the latter organising a petition against the execution of the Haymarket martyrs, and working out the ideas that would eventually appear in his overtly anarchist essay 'The Soul of Man Under Socialism'. Ford Madox Ford, then known as Hueffer, and a young H. G. Wells comprised the core of the English literary contingent, though many other writers and artists put in an occasional appearance. But amidst the ferment of amicable debate, the distrust and animosity that had torn apart the Social Democratic Federation and seemed to poison socialist unity at every turn, in England as abroad, could not be laid to rest.

'The anarchists are making rapid progress in the Socialist League,' Engels remarked wearily in the spring of 1886. 'Morris and Bax – one as an emotional socialist and the other as a chaser after philosophical paradoxes – are wholly under their control for the present.' Morris clearly saw the atmosphere of toleration as a source of strength, considered himself to be 'on terms of warm personal friendship with the leading London anarchists', and readily accepted the principle that 'the centralised nation would give place to a federation of communities' with Parliament of use only to facilitate the latter stages of the transition. Even the Fabian Society toyed with anarchist ideas for a while, with Shaw, a leading light, admitting that 'we were just as anarchist as the Socialist League and just as insurrectionary as the federation'. When Morris visited the Glasgow branch of the league, soon after Kropotkin had addressed them, he appeared pleasantly surprised to find his colleagues turned 'a little in the anarchist direction, which gives them an agreeable air of toleration'. It would not be long, though, before Morris discovered that his positioning of the league 'between parliamentaries and anarchists' could only aggravate the hardliners on either side, and Shaw came to see the Fabians as suffering 'a sort of influenza of anarchism': a more deadly and rampant form of the 'children's ailment' on which Engels had poured scorn.

The summer of 1887 was marked by the withdrawal from the league of Bax, Eleanor Marx and her husband, Edward Aveling, angry at what they thought had come to be a 'swindle' that used their support for ends that they could not endorse. Neither this, though, nor the bloodletting in the 'brothers' war' between the German contingent, in the form of Reuss' resignation that May and the Commonweal's subsequent publication of a list of suspected spies and informants, helped settle matters. Accusations continued to fly and recriminations simmered, with the fault lines increasingly drawn in intractable terms of class. The ownership of 'anarchism' itself was also perversely contested, and Kropotkin found himself stranded in the middle of the factions.

David Nicoll, a strange young man who until recently had styled himself an aesthete, frittering away a sizeable inheritance on theatrical speculation and extravagant velvet outfits before his unstable mind led him to extremist politics, recollected how his hard-line 'individualist' associates within the league poured scorn on those who grouped themselves around Kropotkin's *Freedom* newspaper. 'We looked upon them as a collection of middle-class faddists', he wrote, 'who took up with the movement as an amusement, and regretted that Kropotkin and other "serious" people ever had anything to do with them. But they called themselves "Anarchists!" and that had great influence with many of our international comrades.' The ideological differences were minimal, with the key exception of the violent methods advocated by the opponents of the *Freedom* group. 'If the people had only had the knowledge, the whole cursed lot would have been wiped out,' was the punishment for scabs proposed during one strike by Henry Samuels, a militant figure from Leeds with a high opinion of his own abilities, who had married into the émigré French community. 'Fire the slums and get the people into the West End mansions,' fulminated Charles Mowbray, an ex-soldier and tailor from Durham with a widow's peak and drooping moustache, whose controlling presence as an orator had seen him among those charged after the Dod Street riot.

'The noblest conquests of man are written on a bloodstained book,' wrote Joseph Lane in his *Anti-Statist Communist Manifesto*, a clear and well-argued response to the more moderate socialists who had left the league. 'Why evade the fine old name which for years has rung out in the van of the socialist movement throughout the world?' Charlotte Wilson reprimanded him for failing to embrace the term 'anarchist' in favour of a 'clumsy' alternative. Her criticism must have rankled deeply with a man who had devoted his life to a cause, fostered by him from the grass roots up. His circumspection about simplifying his political beliefs with catch-all labels that seemed to cause only contention, and signified an adherence to the worst aspects of the individualist creed, was surely wise.

In Sheffield, for the moment, Carpenter kept such unpleasant bickering at bay, thanks to a modesty and self-effacement that the city's *Weekly Echo* newspaper evoked in awestruck terms. Instead Carpenter threw himself into opening the Commonwealth Café, an enterprise inspired in part by the small-scale Utopia described in Walter Besant's novel of 1882, *All Sorts and Conditions of Men*. In Besant's story, a communal workshop is established by a brewery heiress, Angela Messenger, where the seamstresses were kept entertained by edifying readings, and kept healthy by leisure breaks for tennis and gymnastics. On visiting Carpenter's café, one local journalist was overcome with religious emotion: 'One could not help thinking of another upper room of considerable importance in history, where not many mighty and not many learned were present . . .

there was another Carpenter not a bit more exclusive: one who had nowhere to lay his head; who wore the purple only once and then in mockery.' To those caught up in the political factionalism of the capital, the Christlike Carpenter offered calm conciliation in his 1887 book *England's Ideal*, with the advice to 'Think what a commotion there must have been within the bud when the petals of a rose are forming! Think what arguments, what divisions, what recriminations, even among the atoms!' By then, though, William Morris was already doubting that he could keep up the 'pig-driving' necessary to hold the league together for even a few more months.

External factors too were putting pressure on the movement. The work of philanthropic and religious organisations such as the Salvation Army in the East End increasingly offered practical benefits to the poor of a kind that the anarchists could only promise in some nebulous future. And the year of Queen Victoria's Golden Jubilee would see a monumental expression of their presence rise up in the Mile End Road.

Three storeys high, with a swimming pool, cast-iron galleries, vast hall and rib-vaulted library inspired by the medieval Prior's Kitchen in Durham, the East End's 'People's Palace' was, proclaimed *The Times*, a 'happy experiment in practical socialism' that would 'sow the seeds of a higher and more humane civilisation among dwellers and toilers in [that] unlovely district'. Neither Kropotkin nor Morris could have questioned the nobility of its stated aim of providing all with opportunities previously open only to the aristocracy; Oscar Wilde even applied unsuccessfully to serve as its secretary. The education it promised, though, watched over by the busts of England's greatest poets, was unlikely to be one that would cultivate revolutionary sentiments in the tens of thousands who passed through its doors every week. If they were in any doubt about how it would reinforce the existing social order, the socialists need only have looked at the guest list for the opening of the People's Palace on 21 June 1887. The German kaiser was present, dressed in the silver and white livery of a Teutonic knight, while the honour of opening the Queen's Hall, its centrepiece, went to King Leopold II of Belgium, whose private army was then embarking on its campaign of terror against the natives of the Congo Free State.

Queen Victoria also attended, though she had very nearly been indisposed. Twenty-four hours earlier, a ceremony of thanksgiving for her reign had been held in Westminster Abbey, during which it had been the intention of Fenian militants to blow up both her and her ministers. Only a delay in the ship carrying them from the United States had intervened, according to the press reports of her merciful escape. In fact, the truth was rather different. The plot itself had been initiated and guided over a period of many months by agents of the British police, with the acquiescence of Lord Salisbury's Conservative government; the decision to allow it to progress so far was a risk calculated to heighten popular outrage when the danger was finally exposed. Furthermore, the indirect target of the provocation was Charles Parnell and the other moderate advocates of Home Rule, whose names it sought to blacken. Had any of this been known, it would have provided a sharp warning to Britain's socialists that they might expect similar treatment at the hands of the police.

*

The origin of the provocation lay in the rivalry between two men, Edward Jenkinson and Robert Anderson, both ambitious to make their name in the policing of Fenianism, and with an arrogance that led them to believe that they could play politics too. Three years earlier, Jenkinson had been transferred to London, where Anderson, an Irishman by birth, was already working alongside Adolphus Williamson, the chief of the Metropolitan Police's counter-subversion division, Section D. Expertly manipulating interdepartmental tensions, the newcomer had outflanked the heir apparent to claim Section D as his own fiefdom, with thirty agents at his disposal and a direct line of accountability to the Home Secretary.

'The four essentials for a policeman are truthfulness, sobriety, punctuality and tremendous care as to what you tell your superiors,' 'Dolly' Williamson advised those who worked for him. Jenkinson ignored the first point and embraced the last wholeheartedly. Indeed, such was the secrecy with which he ran his operations that whatever suspicions his colleagues may have harboured about quite how he landed such a remarkable tally of arrests during the Fenian bombing campaign of 1883 to 1885 were almost impossible to prove. Something catastrophic would have to happen for more serious questions to be asked.

'The sands of destiny, they are almost run out, is the crash of all things near at hand?' was the kind of question that Anderson, a strong believer in Christian millenarianism, liked to ponder in his spare time. When a bomb placed beneath the urinals used by the Special Irish Branch demolished part of Scotland Yard, it must have seemed to those in the building that the End of Days had arrived. But for Anderson it heralded a fresh start. The new head of the CID, James Munro, who shared Anderson's Unionist politics and religious leanings, recalled him from the Home

Office backwater to which he had been posted and together the pair set about tracing the underground Fenian networks active in mainland Britain. Time and again their investigations exposed unknown agents run by Jenkinson with a cavalier disregard for both his loyalties to the Metropolitan Police and the basic principles of law enforcement, as he coached them to twist their testimony to suit his own agenda.

Reprimanded, Jenkinson nevertheless persisted in his clandestine activities, trimming his strategy to the prevailing political wind at Westminster, where Salisbury's Conservative government had now come to power. Only after it was revealed that the ringleader of the conspiracy to import dynamite from America for the Jubilee Plot was in fact a veteran British agent operating out of Paris and New York, and now being run by Jenkinson, was action taken to remove him from his position. As much as the risk Jenkinson's actions had posed, however, by toying with catastrophe, it was the lack of coordination that was most hazardous, as he maintained what Munro described to his superiors as 'a school of private detectives working as rivals and enemies of Scotland Yard'. For Anderson too had embarked on a simultaneous intrigue of his own, forging documents that supposedly revealed Parnell's links to terrorism and leaking them to *The Times* for its 'Parnell and Crime' exposé, that had begun early in 1887.

Henceforth the Metropolian Police's counter-subversion activities would be unified under a single Special Branch, supervised by Munro, its brief now widened beyond the Irish threat alone. Heading the Branch was Chief Inspector Littlechild, whose officers included the impressive young tyro William Melville, who had done sterling service as a liaison and surveillance officer in France, and others who brought with them valuable skills acquired under Jenkinson's tutelage.

In the past, Britain had always viewed with disdain the kind of political police that Continental tyrannies relied upon to enforce their will. In Special Branch, however, Britain now had the makings of just such a department, ready to turn its attention to fresh fields of investigation. As the fight to free Ireland took its place alongside that to liberate Britain from the capitalist yoke, and to raze the institutions of state rule across Europe that kept men and women in economic and spiritual bondage, Special Branch would be ready: watching and waiting, Jenkinson's methods never quite forgotten.

*

The scene in Trafalgar Square on Sunday, 13 November 1887 was so dramatic that William Morris 'quite thought the revolution had come'. For the previous few months, unemployment in Britain had been rising rapidly, and Trafalgar Square had again become the venue for those without work to express their discontent, as well as housing a permanent contingent of the dispossessed. Up to 600 men and women slept rough in the square every night, to be joined during the day by thousands more who had walked in from the East End, for whom the People's Palace remained an irrelevance as long as their basic needs were not met. When, two days after the execution of the Haymarket martyrs on 11 November, Hyndman's Social Democratic Federation staged a protest rally against the Irish Coercion Act recently passed by Lord Salisbury's government, the scene was set for confrontation. Thousands of constables from the Metropolitan force lined up four deep to enforce the ban on public meetings in the square which had been pronounced the previous week; large reserve units of infantry and cavalry from the army regiments stationed in the capital were present as backup. It was precisely the kind of situation that Salisbury's two-year-old government knew it might precipitate, by passing the draconian Coercion Act, which suspended civil rights without time limit: an ideal opportunity for the government to present itself as the guardian of law and order.

The circumstances were unnervingly reminiscent of those in Chicago's Haymarket two years earlier when the fateful bomb had been thrown, but it took only the first police advance for Morris' bold assessments of the left's readiness for revolution to be exposed as naïvety. The retreat soon became a rout, with those at the front and stragglers left behind beaten ferociously by the police, with fists and batons. 'I don't know how fast the sturdy Briton is expected to fly,' Edward Carpenter told a reporter from the *Pall Mall Gazette* immediately afterwards, 'but in our case I suppose it was not fast enough, for in a moment my companion (a peaceful mathematician, by the way, of high university standing) was collared and shaken in the most violent – I may say brutal – manner. I remonstrated, and was struck in the face by the clenched fist of "law and order".' 'Running hardly expressed our collective action,' according to Shaw, cornered in nearby High Holborn: 'we *skedaddled*, and never drew breath until we were safe on Hampstead Heath or thereabouts.'

Bloody Sunday was, the *Pall Mall Gazette* declared, 'a Tory *coup d'état*', though such was the lack of organisation and mettle among those would-be insurrectionists attending the demonstration that the infantry had been unused and the cavalry never ordered to draw their sabres. As a consequence of this restraint, only three protesters had died, though 200 attended hospital while many more were afraid to present themselves for treatment. That the list of casualties was not much longer was a clear indication of the complete absence of the spirit of revolution that Morris, Hyndman and so many others had convinced themselves was abroad. 'I was astounded at the rapidity of the thing and the ease with which military organisation got its victory,' Morris admitted, having calmed his nerves, though not yet ready to face the crushing reality of the socialists' failure. A more honest account of the disappointment of the day, though, was offered by Shaw: 'On the whole I think it was the most abjectly disgraceful defeat ever suffered by a band of heroes outnumbering their foes a thousand to one.'

Yet the forces of law and order would not become complacent. One of Melville's colleagues in the new Special Branch was a man named Sweeney, an ardent reactionary who had joined the Metropolitan Police a few years earlier having been too short in stature for the Royal Irish Constabulary. Sweeney, it seems, was clear about where the new challenge for Special Branch lay. It was around the time of the Jubilee, he would later recollect, that the anarchists 'began to grow restless. They held frequent meetings; there was quite a small boom in the circulation of revolutionary periodicals. Then, as now, England was a dumping ground for bad characters, and London thus received several rascals who had been expelled from the Continent as being prominent propagandists.' Such sentiments were echoed in a Home Office internal communication, which described the émigrés as 'a violent set and utterly unscrupulous'.

In other countries, too, eyes were turned towards London as a seedbed for violent activity. From early 1887, reports had been sent to the Paris prefecture suggesting that instructions to what remained of the terrorist underground in Russia were no longer coming from France but London and even New York, with Hartmann and Kropotkin strongly implicated, and anarchists across the Channel said to be seeking gelignite for the assassination of the tsar. The claims, though confused and far-fetched, were summarised for the French cabinet, and may have found their way on to Rachkovsky's desk. However, it was on the advice of his agent Jagolkovsky, who had assisted in the raid on the People's Will press in Geneva, that the Okhrana chief now turned his attention to London and the anti-tsarist groups coalescing there.

*

A keen empire-builder, Rachkovsky straight away set about establishing an Okhrana presence in Britain following a possible personal visit in

June 1888. The man he hired for the job was an old freelancer with the Russian police department, Wladyslaw Milewski, who had served as the case officer in Paris for those non-Russian agents and informants previously run by the Barlet Brigade. And as when the Okhrana had originally established itself in France, it is likely to have been from ex-officers of the native police that Milewski recruited his agents in England, while the air of secrecy around the pseudonymous 'John' suggests that he may even have been a moonlighting Met officer. If the Okhrana had indeed decided to retain the services of an insider, no one would have been a better investment than the rising star of Special Branch, William Melville; his long service in France, liaising with the Sûreté and handling informants and provocateurs with an interest in Fenian affairs, may well have brought him into contact with the Paris Okhrana. Years later, Rachkovsky would hint at some pecuniary relationship, but Melville would always make a point of officially distancing himself from the Russian.

The priorities that Rachkovsky detailed for Milewski in London, too, can only be guessed at, though it is safe to surmise that they entailed at the very least the demonisation of Russian émigrés, who had so scrupulously distanced themselves from violence. Would a strategy of intimidating surveillance prove as effective in subjugating the old nihilists here as in France, or might the strategy used by Jenkinson against the Fenians, and Anderson against Parnell, work better? Anti-Semitism and the fear of anarchism were two promising routes in France, if linked to nihilism in the popular imagination, but would England be so responsive?

Rachkovsky's visit to London in the summer of 1888 would have coincided with the matchgirls' strike at the Bryant and May factory in the East End. Three weeks of protest led by Annie Besant, with whom Kravchinsky had lodged on first arriving in the country five years earlier, extracted an undertaking from the management of wholesale improvements in the terrible working conditions. For the Labour movement it provided important evidence of what might be achieved through concerted action, even when carried out by those with no prior organisation. Such moderate methods offered lean pickings for the Okhrana if they wished to demonstrate to the British public the threat from Russian Jews and extremists among the East End immigrants. Before the summer was out, however, the Whitechapel slums would throw up an exemplary case of how quickly general unease could turn to terror when popular attention was focused through the prism of violent crime, and the monstrous 'Kraken' given shadowy, human form.

Violence was an everyday hazard in the notorious area, and the desperate poverty that drove its female inhabitants to prostitution made them more vulnerable than most. What distinguished the murder of Mary Ann Nichols, whose body was discovered in a backstreet during the afternoon of 31 August 1888, was the brutal nature of the attack and the mutilation of the corpse: the neck severed through to the spinal cord and the torso half eviscerated. A week later, when Annie Chapman was found similarly butchered barely half a mile away, the crimes became national news. A further fortnight after that they became an international story, when the taunting predictions of further deaths in a letter received by the Central News Agency from 'Jack the Ripper' were realised: two more mutilated women were discovered on the night of Sunday, 30 September.

As journalists competed with the police in speculating as to the Ripper's identity, the circumstances of the two most recent murders allowed those with a political agenda to suggest that the killer might come from the underworld of revolutionary immigrants. The body of Elizabeth Stride, the first of the two to die, was found close to the rear entrance to the International Working Men's Club on Berner Street, one of seven revolutionary clubs set up by Joseph Lane in the east of the city, where lectures and classes were held on Sunday evenings with such prominent figures as Kropotkin frequently in attendance. Then, on a door jamb close to where the second body, of Catherine Eddowes, was found, a message had been freshly scrawled in white chalk: 'The Juwes are (not) the men that will (not) be blamed for nothing'. Witnesses disputed the position of the '(not)' after a policeman had hastily rubbed out the words, fearing that they might incite a pogrom.

There were suggestions that the strangely spelled 'Juwes' might imply Freemasonic connotations, while contemporary commentators variously construed the double negative as indicating that a Frenchman or Cockney was the Ripper – if indeed the message had been chalked by the murderer. Fascinating and unfathomable, the hideous deeds of the serial killer generated, then as now, a myriad of possible perpetrators to haunt the imagination. Special Branch ledgers of the period have been construed to suggest both that the killings were carried out by the Branch itself, to cover up Jenkinson's employment of Catherine Eddowes and her husband John Kelly as agents, and that Anderson and his officers suspected it to be a Fenian plot conceived to humiliate the Metropolitan Police.

That Anderson, a religious zealot, might have been keen to promote the notion of Irish involvement is quite credible. Soon after his appointment as assistant commissioner that summer, he had been sent away to Switzerland for an extended rest cure, where he must have hoped to remain for the duration of the Parnell Commission's inquiry into the letters he had secretly helped forge to incriminate the Irish leader. Having viewed the Whitechapel murders, from a distance, as a useful warning to immoral women to stay off the streets, and one that the authorities should not go out of their way to prevent, he was certainly indignant at being recalled to deal with the continuing killings.

For a period after 30 September, however, most observers expected that the murderer would be found among the local population of immigrant Jews and political extremists. As far away as Vienna, the British ambassador Augustus Paget was persuaded by an informant that the killer was Johann Stammer, a member of the anarchist International operating under the alias of Kelly, and when Scotland Yard refused to pay for the informant to travel to London to present his evidence, Paget personally provided £165. The Paris Embassy's refusal to meet the informant's demands for another £100, en route, brought an end to that avenue of enquiry: but at the beginning of November, Madame Novikoff, eager to find an angle on the Ripper story for propaganda purposes, contacted the Okhrana in Paris to request additional information on another political extremist, this time Russian. Where the rumours about Nicholas Vasiliev started is uncertain, but as stories of his involvement bounced between newspapers in France, Britain, Russia and America, the biography of this elusive – and quite possibly non-existent – character received an interesting spin: he was 'a fanatical anarchist,' both the *Daily Telegraph* and the *Pall Mall Gazette* reported, who had emigrated to Paris in 1870, shortly before the Commune.

With even the *Illustrated Police News* depicting Jack the Ripper as a vicious caricature of the eastern European Jew, thick-nosed and with large crude ears, Rachkovsky, now back in Paris, could surely not have been more satisfied had he planned the whole gruesome sequence of murders himself. Coming at almost the same time as the publication by his erstwhile agent Madame Blavatsky of *The Hebrew Talisman*, which claimed the existence of a Jewish conspiracy for worldwide subversion, such prejudiced reporting of the Whitechapel murders was more grist to the mill.

Before long the press was peddling fresh rumours and proposing new criminal types – the butcher with the bloodied apron or the aristocratic dandy – for their readers to chew over and, by early 1889, with no new murders to report, interest in the Ripper began to wane. Nevertheless, the brutal myths that the killings had generated seeped into the fabric of the East End, adding their hellish stench to what was, as three contemporary observers commented, 'a kind of human dustbin overflowing with the dregs of society', or a 'vast charnel house' whose denizens lived 'in such artificial conditions as practically to be cut off from the natural surface of the earth' and from which, it was predicted, a plague would soon spread across the city.

Charles Booth's investigators were just beginning their survey of London, pounding the streets to collect data for the Poverty Maps that would first appear in 1889, coloured to represent the life experience of the capital's inhabitants according to a seven-point scheme: a firelight glow of oranges and reds for ease and affluence, chilly blue for those slums whose inhabitants suffered the greatest deprivation. The areas from Whitechapel out to the docks of Limehouse and Wapping were coloured like a great, sprawling bruise.

For Malatesta, though, back from four years in South America, the workers of the East End, immigrants and indigenous alike, possessed an energy to force change that impressed him.

*

Since his sojourn in England after the 1881 London Congress, Malatesta had seen a lot of the world. In Egypt he had fought the British in the cause of independence; returning to his homeland of Italy he had evaded a police hunt for the perpetrators of a bomb attack by hiding in a container of sewing machines; then in Patagonia he had laboured for three months in sub-zero temperatures prospecting for gold to fund anarchist propaganda, only to have the few nuggets he had found confiscated by the Argentine state. In Buenos Aires, though, he had discovered something more precious still: with 60,000 peasants from Mediterranean Europe arriving in the city each year, at a rate higher even than those of eastern Europe pouring in to London and New York, he found a receptive audience for his ideas.

Working in a range of industries to win his colleagues' trust, Malatesta had galvanised their belief in anarchism. In January 1888, the Bakers Union in Buenos Aires, whose members had previously satisfied their anti-authoritarian urges by turning out dough-based products with names such as 'nun's farts' and 'little canons', staged its first strike, and later in the year the Shoemakers Union followed suit. Learning from those he taught, and under the guidance of the older Irish anarchist Dr John Creaghe, Malatesta realised how militant trade unionism might advance his ideas of social revolution, and in four manifestos published in the space of two years he refined his ideological position. Whether or not his return to London in 1889 was due to pressure from the vexed Argentine authorities, there was no doubt that in the time he had been away both Britain and Europe had become more receptive to his ideas.

Industrial action continued intermittently in the French mining regions, and in Italy there were the first signs of the *fasci* groups of radical syndicalists challenging landowners over their mismanagement of agriculture. Meanwhile, the frequency of anarchist meetings and weight of anarchist publications in Belgium surpassed that of any other socialist group, and recent years had seen strikes and protests tend towards insurrectionary violence that the Catholic government had struggled to quell. In Spain too, where Malatesta had travelled on a mission for Bakunin more than a decade before, anarchism had taken deep root, unifying the peasantry of Andalucia and the industrial workers of Catalonia with uncommon success, setting the stage for a long-lasting struggle against the clerical and political authorities. From a base in London, Malatesta could reach out to this diffuse body of support, through frequent forays to the Continent and the regular publication of a new paper, *L'Associazione*. But as Kropotkin had found before him, the British capital could now afford inspiration of its own, even to a veteran anarchist.

Trade with the empire was the lifeblood of Britain, and London's docks its fast-beating heart. Only a few weeks after London's gas workers had won themselves an eight-hour day by striking, a walkout by 500 men from one dock in the summer of 1889 caused it to miss a beat. Then, almost immediately, 3,000 stevedores, nearly the entire workforce, followed suit. Within a fortnight, they were joined by 130,000 more Londoners from all trades and industries, omnibuses abandoned in the streets as their drivers and conductors flocked to protest. 'The great machine by which five million people are fed and clothed will come to a dead stop, and what is to be the end of it all?' wondered the *Evening News and Post*. 'The proverbial small spark has kindled a great fire which threatens to envelop the whole metropolis.' And it seemed it would rage on. Just when a lack of funds threatened to force the dockers back to work, a huge donation arrived from their colleagues in Australia to save the strike. Solidarity seemed to stretch around the globe.

It was a moment of the kind that the leading anarchists of the last decade had long awaited, brimming with the potential for revolutionary change. Yet the most outspoken foot soldiers of the Socialist League remained on the fringes of the strike, preferring to exploit the holiday atmosphere that engulfed the East End to propagandise rather than engage with the more reformist agenda of those trade unionists who had devoted so much time and effort to preparing the ground among the dock workers. 'Members of the league do not in any way compromise their principles by taking part in strikes,' pronounced the *Commonweal*, whose editorial policy William Morris could no longer effectively steer. When the strike ended with the dockers settling for their initial pay demands being met, Malatesta, Kropotkin and others, though unsurprised, could not hide their disappointment. The scale of the popular protest had changed the political game in Britain, radically altering any calculation of how best the transformation of society might be effected. But the strike had also underlined just how cripplingly close the internal divisions within the anarchist movement – between 'associationists' such as Malatesta and the firebrand 'individualists' – came to being an outright schism.

Among each nationality to be found in London, the differences were writ large, with the 'individualists' eschewing the hard work and onerous compromises of practical politics and collective endeavour in favour of the untrammelled egotism of the criminal. So absolute was their position, indeed, that it seemed less as though anarchists were sloughing off the repressive dictates of society by illegal action, than that those disposed to criminality were adopting anarchism as a political figleaf.

Prominent among the Italian émigrés, Parmeggiani and Pini were so outraged by the suggestion of a socialist newspaper in Italy that their political espousal of expropriation was merely a cover for robbery, and that their pernicious influence suggested them as police agents, that they had travelled across Europe to attempt the assassination of its editor, Farina, by stabbing. After Pini's arrest in Paris during their return journey to London, Malatesta would frequently meet with Parmeggiani, but it was an uneasy relationship. Jean Grave, since Kropotkin's imprisonment, the effective editor of *Le Révolté*, renamed *La Révolte* since its move to Paris, came out in favour of the individualists' position among the French, arguing that each man must act according to the dictates of his conscience, though the suggestion that this might extend as far as pimping his wife or turning police informant suggests a certain irony. When Grave in turn was imprisoned, however, the newspaper's line would further harden under the caretaker editorship of Elisée Reclus' nephew, Paul. Meanwhile, 1888 had seen hardliners and outspoken firebrands take over the Socialist League, among them Henry Samuels, Charles Mowbray, David Nicoll and even Frank Kitz, all of whom drifted ever more towards the individualist extreme.

William Morris strived to maintain the organisation as a broad church, but the strain was growing. 'He disliked the violence that was creeping into his meetings,' Ford Madox Ford would recollect, wryly adding that 'He had founded them solely with the idea of promoting human kindness and peopling the earth with large-bosomed women dressed in Walter Crane gowns, and bearing great sheaves of full-eared corn.' But there was a growing swell of resentment towards Morris among the more headstrong anarchists who, on one occasion, terminated a meeting in Hammersmith by throwing red pepper on the stove: an event observed and noted by a Special Branch informant. 'Morris, who used to walk up and down the aisles like a rather melancholy sea captain on the quarter-deck in his nautical pea jacket was forced to flee uttering passionate sneezes that jerked his white hairs backwards and forwards like the waves of the sea,' Ford would remember.

'Agitate! Educate! Organise!' Morris had written only a few months earlier. 'Agitate, that the workers may be stirred and awakened to a sense of their position. Educate, that they may know the reasons of the evils they suffer. Organise, that we and they may overthrow the system that bears down and makes us what we are.' But for Morris socialism had always been about the imagination: the capacity to inhabit, in prospect, a better world of spiritual and artistic fulfilment. When he started writing *News from Nowhere* in late 1889, it was not simply out of the need to reconcile his practical and ideal politics, nor to answer the ugly, mechanised and corporatist version of socialism predicted in the American Edward Bellamy's 1888 book *Looking Backward*. It was to present a cogent vision of the world as he wished it to be, as a means to inspire hope and courage.

'There were six persons present, and consequently six sections of the party were represented, four of which had strong but divergent anarchist opinions,' the narrator tells us in the preface, preoccupied with the factionalism of the league. A night of tossing and turning, however, propels him into a twenty-first century in which the nuisances of the 1880s have vanished, replaced by the communism of which Morris dreamed, realised down to the last detail: a federalised society, living in simple harmony, its craftsmanship underpinned by technology that supported the relative leisure enjoyed by its citizens rather than alienating them from the creative pleasures of work. It was a neo-medieval Utopia, informed perhaps by Kropotkin's research into guilds as a model for post-revolutionary organisation, but also Morris' belief that medieval man had accepted limits on his freedom willingly because they were 'the product of his own conscience'.

Whilst Morris moulded his ideal society of the distant future from the best of the past, the proximate cause of the revolution out of which it was born was drawn from his own experience: a massacre of demonstrators in Trafalgar Square by troops serving the military dictatorship of 'a brisk young general'. Conflating Boulanger and Bloody Sunday, along with strong echoes of the Paris Commune, Morris demonstrated how in minds permeated by socialist education such brutality from the authorities would provoke revulsion and a successful general strike. Aided by 'the rapidly approaching breakdown of the whole system founded on the world-market and its supply; which now becomes so clear to all people', and a food supply guaranteed by the revolutionaries, the logistics of which Kropotkin was also researching and would present in his *The Conquest of Bread*, power would shift from the privileged to the workers with relatively little bloodshed.

Dynamite would be held in reserve as a last resort: the passive resistance of unarmed protesters would win the day. Sailing up the Thames at the end of the book, and back into the reality of 1890, the narrator expresses the hope that 'if others can see it as I have seen it, then may it be called a vision rather than a dream'. There were darker visions at work, though, beside which Morris' promised Utopia would struggle to take root.

16

Deep Cover

Paris, 1887–1890

From the centre of his web of operations in the Russian Embassy, Peter Rachkovsky's operations against the émigrés continued, his methods becoming ever more subtle and various. The psychological game he played during 1887 with Lev Tikhomirov, the effective leader of the rump of the People's Will in exile and among his highest priority targets, called for particular patience and self-restraint. By forgoing the simple gratification of eliminating the man who had ordered Sudeikin's murder, he hoped to achieve an altogether more profound reward.

It had been on Clemenceau's suggestion that Tikhomirov had disappeared to the echoing seclusion of a rented house in Le Raincy to the east of Paris, during the commotion caused by Kropotkin's release from prison and as the Russian government pressed for all revolutionaries harboured by France to be expelled. At first, the solitude came as a relief, after years of unrelenting anxiety and unpleasantness. It had been a torment for a refined and fastidious man of considerable intellectual accomplishment such as he to live cheek by jowl with cruder companions among the émigrés of Paris, eating his meals direct from the paper in which the food came wrapped. Worse by far, though, had been the surveillance agents whose perpetual presence tightened the screw on his insecurity. 'In the street he is constantly turning round. He is in a half-trembling state,' wrote a journalist who interviewed him at the time, while so grave had been his disturbed mental state that at one point a friendly visitor had felt obliged to call the doctor. At Le Raincy, Rachkovsky's agents were still in attendance, loitering at the end of the overgrown garden, but the nature of the siege was at least clear.

The tense, still atmosphere in the house had another explanation. For weeks on end, after his son fell ill with spinal meningitis, Tikhomirov had tended the boy as others despaired, forcing open his mouth to spoon in the medicine that no one else believed could save him. And while the outside world of the belle époque looked to General Boulanger to fill its hollowed-out soul with military glamour and nationalism, it was the old mystical religion that poured into the spiritual void felt by Tikhomirov. A positivist atheist, he had found himself praying, albeit in 'an unconventional way', offering whatever bargains he could to the Almighty in exchange for his son's life. Miraculously, the boy survived.

An intellectual and a writer, Tikhomirov had never been suited to the life of an active revolutionary and his nerves had long been frayed. Imprisoned during the round-ups of the Chaikovskyists a decade earlier, he had witnessed at first hand the vicious beating administered to Bogoliubov by General Trepov: an object lesson in the powerlessness of the outsider. After his release, Tikhomirov's more robust companions in the People's Will had tried to insulate him from situations requiring physical courage, but his vulnerability had been confirmed when the police were tipped off about his subversive activities. Attempts to lie low after the tsar's assassination only brought further fears of exposure: he was haunted by the memory of watching those convicted of the killing drawn on carts beneath his apartment window, while he nearly fainted with fear lest the maid recognise them as his friends. Then, exiled in Geneva, he had made the catastrophic decision over how to deal with Degaev's confession of treachery that resulted in Vera Figner's arrest. Even the murder of Colonel Sudeikin, which he had instructed Degaev to carry out, had backfired by focusing the Okhrana's attention even more ruthlessly on the émigrés abroad. He now found himself unable to avoid the more fundamental question of whether his entire revolutionary career had been a terrible mistake.

Rachkovsky's agents tracked every shift in Tikhomirov's mood, and noted his every movement: the gradually lengthening walks in the garden at Le Raincy with his convalescent child, their picking of berries, conversations with local children, even his patting of dogs. Back in Russia it had been Rachkovsky himself, while operating undercover among the revolutionaries, who had identified Tikhomirov to the police, and knowing of his psychological fragility, Rachkovsky may have always considered him susceptible to turning. After a second raid on the Geneva press in early 1887 turned up fragments of paper bearing Tikhomirov's despairing scribbles, Rachkovsky stepped up the pressure.

Crucial assistance was provided by the journalist Jules Hansen, recently added to the Okhrana payroll on a retainer of 400 francs a month.

A small, bespectacled man with a retiring demeanour, Hansen's lack of physical presence had earned him the nickname 'the shrew' in his native Copenhagen; to those in the know, however, the quality of his contacts at the Danish and tsarist courts and his powers as a propagandist fully warranted the more respectful sobriquet of 'the president'. Under Hansen's guidance, such esteemed journalists as Calmette of *Le Figaro* and Maurras of *Le Petit Parisien* turned their fire on the revolutionary émigrés, with Tikhomirov their prime target. Fodder was provided by an incriminating pamphlet entitled *Confessions of a Nihilist* – published under Tikhomirov's name, but in reality forged at the embassy. Rachkovsky also engineered the publication of an anonymous attack on the 'uncontrollable rule' that Tikhomirov and Lavrov allegedly exercised over the émigrés. Caught in a pincer movement, Tikhomirov had scant emotional resources left to deal with the attacks.

With feline cunning, in the autumn of 1887 Rachkovsky had moved in for the kill, targeting Tikhomirov's innate elitism, which vainly saw the utopian dreams of the Chaikovskyists as having been squandered by the actions of the ignorant. The approach Rachkovsky made was surprisingly solicitous, proposing that the Okhrana sponsor Tikhomirov to the tune of 300 francs to pen an account of the intellectual journey that led him to renounce revolution and terrorism: an opportunity to settle his account with the merciful God who had saved his son. The result was a triumph for Rachkovsky. On its publication, *Why Did I Stop Being a Revolutionary?* created a sensation. Uninhibited not only in its denunciation of terrorism, but its refutation of the entire rationale of the author's past life, it was the product of a nervous breakdown, yet deftly projected its psychological origins on to the subjects of its critique. 'Our ideals, liberal, radical and socialist, are the most enormous madness,' he wrote, 'a terrible lie, and furthermore, a stupid lie.' Tikhomirov's unconditional regret that his 'misguided former colleagues' had failed to recognise autocracy as the most fitting form of government for Russia led Rachkovsky to suggest that he seek the path of atonement, and petition the tsar – God's holy representative on earth – for forgiveness.

Tikhomirov's appeal to the tsar in late 1888 was timely. The first attempt on Alexander III's life little more than a year earlier had served as a reminder of the continuing terrorist threat, while the execution of those responsible had stoked the outrage and resentment of a new generation of revolutionaries. In quick succession new radical circles were formed by Blagoev, Tochissky and Brusnev, only to be as speedily

suppressed by the Okhrana, which was operating with a new professionalism from its base on the Fontanka Quay in St Petersburg. The death of
one of the People's Will's assassins who was hanged, however, lit a fire
that would burn quietly for many years before flaring up to consume the
country. When Alexander Ulyanov, a brilliant law student, went to the
scaffold, the childhood desire of his equally able younger brother, Vladimir
Ilyich, to be in everything 'like Sasha' was now translated into the revolutionary field. Thanks in part to Rachkovsky's suppression of the People's
Will, the young man looked for leadership to Plekhanov, who had scorned
Tikhomirov's book.

Among the Russian elite, however, Tikhomirov was greeted as the
returning prodigal: there were even private dinners with Pobedonostsev,
who arranged for him to do penance in a monastery and placed his writings on the school curriculum. Once back in Paris, Tikhomirov was
welcomed into the most fashionable salons, the firm friend of Juliette
Adam and Madame Olga Novikoff, who now divided her time between
London, Paris and the Riviera. His response to personal attacks in the
left-wing press testified to the influence of the company he was keeping,
but perhaps also to the elusive nature of the double standards by which
they lived: 'The Jews! The scum!' Tikhomirov cursed, unaware of the
strange hypocrisies that allowed the arch anti-Semite Novikoff to carry
on an affair with the Jewish author of *The Conventional Lies of our
Civilisation*, Max Nordau. ('We can only snatch an occasional moment,'
she panted, in one letter to him of December 1888. 'I can't believe I am
trusting what a woman says, but you are not a woman in spirit' he replied,
somewhat ungallantly.)

Rachkovsky's long manipulation of Tikhomirov had finally defeated
the man responsible for the murder of Rachkovsky's mentor, Colonel
Sudeikin, and who had described the members of the Holy Brotherhood
as 'political savages and adventurers, parasitically sucking the people's
lifeblood'. Unlike the funding for most of the 'perception management'
that Rachkovsky was engineering in the French press, the money for
discrediting Tikhomirov had come not from the Okhrana coffers, but his
own pocket. But if Rachkovsky, bitter that Degaev had slipped through
his hands, craved his enemy's complete destruction, the rehabilitation of
a chastened, pious Tikhomirov was a great propaganda coup in the eyes
of those who mattered, and the pragmatic Rachkovsky must have known
that it served his purposes well.

Now married to a Frenchwoman, Rachkovsky had recently moved to
a grand villa in the western suburb of Saint-Cloud: a property to which

his salary from the Okhrana is unlikely to have stretched, even with bonuses for his continued success. In the Paris of the late 1880s, anyone well connected and with an iota of cunning could create a fortune; kickbacks were so easy to come by. The Russian ambassador, de Mohrenheim, certainly took advantage of the opportunities, accepting vast secret donations from the Panama Canal Company for his connivance in its deception, and was also said to be in receipt of a regular slice of the interest paid by the Russian government on the huge French loans arranged by his friend, the Franco-Danish financier Emile Hoskier, so that Russia need no longer be in such deep debt to Germany. During the winter of 1888, 640 million rubles of debt were transferred from Berlin to Paris, and collecting the crumbs from the table made de Mohrenheim a rich man. It seems likely that Rachkovsky feathered his own nest too, safe in the knowledge that, at a time when Russia's goodwill was so valued, for the French press to investigate the financial interests of its embassy staff would have been nothing short of unpatriotic. And yet to those with a vested interest in the transactions, the corruption appeared brazen. For his attempts to mediate a rival loan deal, Elie de Cyon received a cool million francs, but at the cost of what remained of his tattered reputation, being labelled as one of the greatest 'rascals of our age' by the French, and 'a mendacious and venal Jew with revolutionary tendencies' by the Germans.

Rachkovsky's diplomatic and propagandist sidelines were proving ever more absorbing to him. Besides lobbying for the French foreign ministry to decline to take Bulgaria's side in a disagreement with Russia, there would soon be the delicate matter of the rifles manufactured by the French company Lebel on which to keep an eye. While the initial order, after a sample had impressed Grand Duke Vladimir, commander of the Russian Imperial Guard, might only be for 5,000, if every member of the Russian army received the weapon, as their French counterparts had, it would facilitate military coordination between the countries. But Rachkovsky was stretching himself thin. If he was to be effective in pursuing his other interests, it was essential that he maintain the indispensable nature of his counter-subversive work as the Okhrana's spymaster.

With the centenary of the French Revolution in 1889 fast approaching, when Paris was to host a Universal Exposition, there would be abundant opportunities for him to work his wiles. That Russia would not officially attend – having used Kropotkin's release as a pretext to announce its withdrawal from a celebration of democracy that the tsar would, in any circumstances, have found distinctly uncomfortable – need not impede his intrigues.

*

One thing was certain, as the great Exposition prepared to open in May 1889: it wasn't going to be Boulanger who brought about a Franco-Russian coalition. Ironically, it was an eccentric Russian religious adventurer by the name of Ashinov who helped precipitate the final collapse of the Boulangist project, when his missionaries mistakenly occupied the fort in the small port of Obock, a French colonial possession in the Gulf of Aden. The new French minister of the interior, Ernest Constans, indicated that he was inclined to treat the incursion as a declaration of war. Perhaps, too, he saw the political potential of the situation, for when the journal of the Boulangist League of Patriots accused the government of betraying the national interest by its hostility to Russia, Constans promptly announced that its editor would be charged with treason, with Boulanger and Rochefort implicated by association. Boulanger promptly took fright and, rather than lead the crowds who were once again baying for a march on the Elysée Palace, allowed the crafty chief of police, Louis Lepine, to bundle him and his mistress on to a train to Belgium, and into exile.

'Not a man, but a wet rag,' Duchess d'Uzès said of her ex-protégé. To all practical purposes, Boulangism was finished, the general's sudden departure seen by most as an admission of guilt. Rochefort's faltering influence over French public opinion could no longer ensure his safety from arrest, and he soon followed his hero into exile. To Louise Michel, the threatened trial and Boulanger's departure were 'just another burlesque, signifying a society in its slow death throes', but the opportunists in government could, for the moment, breathe a sigh of relief. For the few months of the Expo, it was hoped the simmering discontent of the past few years might be contained, or else subsumed in the ferment of artistic creativity that was its correlative. And what better symbol of their optimism than the edifice that had won the competition to be the centrepiece of the Exposition: Eiffel's extraordinary iron pylon, which for the past two years had been gradually rising skyward over Paris, its four great feet held steady by the use of pneumatic props as it grew.

The Panama project may have collapsed, deeply compromising Gustave Eiffel, who had designed the locks needed to lift the boats over the mountains of the isthmus through which dynamite could not blast a path, but his tower now stood as alternative proof that French ingenuity could raise a monument of an unprecedented scale. Conservatives railed against it on aesthetic grounds, filling the letter columns of the press with attacks on how its brute presence overshadowed the elegance of Haussmann's boulevards. To the bourgeoisie, however, Eiffel's great feat of engineering, together with the vast Gallery of Machines, offered conspicuous reassurance that the process of industrialisation that had driven their rising affluence was again gathering pace after years of recession. The tower even held something for all those women who had been such strong adherents of the cult of Boulanger: one admirer of its sheer, phallic assertiveness wrote to Eiffel that 'it makes me quiver in all my emotions', and anecdote suggests that in this she was far from alone.

Among the Expo's thirty-two million visitors that summer, though, seditious elements lurked. Workers descended on Paris in their thousands from the industrial heartlands of Europe, including a sizeable contingent, conspicuous only to the surveillance agents detailed to spy upon them, who had come for the socialist congresses convened to commemorate the revolution of 1789. For residents and visitors alike, the recent launch of Emile Pouget's scabrous newspaper *Père Peinard*, modelled on the revolutionary *Père Duchesne* that had thrived from 1790 and through the Terror, offered a crude call to arms against contemporary injustice, written in the argot of working-class Paris, which its critics claimed to be symptomatic of moral decay. It was with very different eyes that its readers viewed the tower, and the celebrations that surrounded it.

Many of the anarchists from Belgium carried in their minds images glimpsed in the studios of the radical artists' group Les XX, that tore up the rulebook of artistic propriety. James Ensor's depiction of *Christ's Entry into Brussels*, above all – which usurped the Church's monopoly on the most potent icon of spiritual renewal by taking the figure of the Messiah and submerging him in a carnivalesque crowd of self-satisfied bourgeoisie, fringed by vignettes of scatological satire – was an image so shocking that even his colleagues in the group suppressed its public exhibition. The crazed mood that Ensor captured, however, must have seemed close to quotidian in the Paris of the Exposition: a city whose facelift extended far beyond the public monuments to include even the '*maisons closes*', all redecorated in anticipation of the surge in business.

For Elisée Reclus, meanwhile, whose vast and widely acclaimed *Universal Geography* was nearing its nineteenth volume, Eiffel's tower represented a missed opportunity. For in its place might have stood a symbol that would have gladdened the hearts of all believers in social revolution:

the Great Globe, of which Reclus had dreamed since his days in London almost forty years earlier. A statement of universal brotherhood and promise of enlightenment, the design on which he would shortly begin work would pay homage to the ideals of the Revolution, referencing the vast domed 'Temple to Nature and Reason' that the visionary Etienne-Louis Boullée had planned in the 1780s, barely escaping the Terror after being named one of the parasitical 'madmen of architecture'. Even Reclus, however, might have acknowledged that a tower rather than a globe offered a better symbol of the myriad congresses under way in 1889: a tower of Babel.

Two years earlier Louise Michel had embraced the putative new lingua franca of Esperanto, certain that linguistic innovations could facilitate the unity of mankind. 'Everything leads to the common ocean, solicited by the needs of renewal,' she wrote, adopting Elisée Reclus' favourite aquatic metaphor. 'The human species which since the beginning of ages had ascended from the family to the tribe, to the horde, to the nation, ascends again and forever, and the family becomes an entire race.' Yet in the absence of any gathering of Esperanto evangelists, the rival followers of Volapük set new standards of confusion by insisting that delegates to their congress communicate only in the notoriously complex invented language.

Elsewhere in the city, the ideological incompatibility and barely suppressed factionalism of the socialists produced a similar effect, with the sects refusing even to accept temporary coexistence under the same roof. The International Socialist Workers, with their collectivist tendency, convened on 14 July in a tiny music hall, the Fantaisies Parisiennes in the rue Rochecouart, while another congress nearby for the 'Possibilists' was attended by the likes of Henry Hyndman of the Social Democratic Federation, who were committed to operating within the existing framework of politics. Much time and effort at each was devoted to the question of whether to fuse.

Edward Carpenter, whose friendship with William Morris had led him to the congress of International Socialist Workers in its crowded, smoky music hall, reported back to his friends in Sheffield on the chaos of the debate: 'The noise and excitement at times was terrific, the president ringing his bell half the time, climbing on his chair, on the table, anything to keep order.' But with figures of the stature of Vera Zasulich, Plekhanov, Kropotkin and Kravchinsky from the Russian contingent, Liebknecht from Germany, Malatesta's friend Merlino from Italy, and Louise Michel and Elisée Reclus from France, the cacophony was strangely rewarding to those who had previously only read their heroes' words. 'All this', enthused

Carpenter, 'was to feel the pulse of a new movement extending throughout Europe, and emanating from every branch and department of labour with throbs of power and growing vitality.'

The eventual vote accepted a compromise resolution, expressing a desire for union with the members of the other congress but coyly postponing action until it had expressed a preference. Fusion of a kind was swiftly achieved, however, by the arrival of a wave of defectors from the 'Possibilists'. For many of those who had travelled as representatives of their own small clubs – among the British, Frank Kitz from the Socialist League, Eleanor Marx's husband Edward Aveling from East Finsbury, Joseph Deakin and Fred Charles from Walsall and North London, and even Auguste Coulon from Dublin – it was a chance to meet their foreign counterparts, and form international relationships that held the promise of future grass-roots cooperation in building the new world. The small army of translators struggled to keep pace, in the hall itself and as the debates overflowed into the more convivial surroundings of the Taverne du Bagne.

At the heart of the factional differences, though rarely explicit in discussions, was the contested interpretation of the Revolution that was being celebrated. For many, even the year chosen for the centenary was wrong. The Marxists viewed 1789 as the date of significant rupture, when the destruction of the feudal system laid the ground for the next stage on the long journey to a socialist Utopia. It was one that would be brought about by the inherent contradictions of the new, capitalist economic system which, under pressure from a growing class conscious-ness among the industrial proletariat, would tear itself apart in a second revolution. To those of the anarchist persuasion, by contrast, Marx's Hegelian vision of historic forces slowly shifting like tectonic plates to reshape the landscape of society denied the power of individual will to effect change. For them 1789 was merely a moment of half-hearted compromise, and it was from the subsequent, genuinely populist achieve-ments of the revolutionaries that contemporary socialists should draw their inspiration.

Above all, the anarchists should look to the brief moment before the Terror turned cannibalistic, when the sans-culottes, hungry for justice, gloriously demonstrated the potential of the workers to strike out against the tide of history. The blood shed so copiously by the guillotine should not be allowed to obscure that simple truth. By this logic, some even considered Robespierre a martyr to the anarchist cause, having advocated the continuation of the Revolution to its just conclusion, before his excessive zeal had provided the inadvertent catalyst of reaction. The anarchist's highest esteem, however, was reserved for Gracchus Babeuf, the inspiration behind Sylvain Maréchal's *Manifesto of Equals*, the first coherent expression of the anarchist creed, who had lost his life conspiring in bloodthirsty fashion against the Thermidorian Reaction of the mid-1790s.

To accept the version of 1789 promoted by the Third Republic was misleading, Elisée Reclus warned, and it was especially 'important to see how the Revolution helped establish the modern nation-state that has progressively annihilated an invaluable legacy of decentralised, communal institutions.' Yet it was perfectly palatable to the followers of Marx who, as Félix Fénéon observed, preferred 'the complexity of a clock to that of a living body', and longed for 'a society in which every citizen carries a number'. The struggle to realise anarchism's dream of society in an organic state of harmony nevertheless raised profound ethical challenges along the way. Reclus's position, in particular, midway between the anarchist-communists and the pure Bakuninists, left him struggling to square a number of circles, foremost among which was the issue of 'conscientious' criminality, which believed in its right to flaunt the rules of a corrupt society, despite causing injury to others.

'Equality is the ensemble of social facts which permit each man to look another man in the eye and to extend his hand to him without a second thought,' Reclus had written to Louise Michel in 1887, and it was with the same saintly attitude that, in 1889, he revealed the secret of his equanimity: 'to love everyone always, including even those whom one must fight against with unflagging energy because they live as parasites on the social body.' But could violence and mutuality coexist? Was it possible to draw a moral distinction between theft from the rich, and the exploitation of others that had made them so? Where should the limits of acceptability be drawn for acts of 'propaganda by the deed'?

Events only a fortnight before the opening of the congress had brought these issues into sharp focus, when an anarchist group calling itself the Intransigents, though with no connection to Rochefort's paper, was revealed to have emulated the spree of burglaries committed by the Panthers of Batignolles. The Italian Pini, already a wanted man for his murderous escapades in Italy with Parmeggiani, and two Belgian brothers called Schouppe had been arrested after a police raid had found them in possession of a sizeable hoard of goods from homes in France and *La Révolte* defended the crime, insisting that the robberies were carried out solely for propaganda purposes. Reclus too came down decisively in favour of those driven to seek restitution from a bourgeois society whose own wealth had been iniquitously acquired. For interwoven with his deep benevolence was the same steely pragmatism that, ten years earlier, had insisted that the young would have to be prepared to lay down their lives to achieve the social revolution, and who in 1885 was said to be advising his acolytes on how to ensure the success of any repeat of the Commune uprising by seizing the Bank of France and the major rail companies.

*

The moral issues at stake were less complex for the man who had become chief of the Service for Judicial Identity at the prefecture of police, Alphonse Bertillon. It had been a rapid rise. Having had his 'anthropometric method' dismissed by Andrieux eight years earlier, and only tolerated by Mace, Bertillon was now able to introduce it across the French police force. When Pini and the Schouppes were taken into custody, their heads, faces and limbs would have been measured at eleven points to ensure they could be identified again (no expert in calculating probability, Bertillon omitted the twelfth measurement which would have made his system to all intents infallible). But outside the police force the belief in a physiological difference between the law-abiding citizen and the criminal was more hotly debated. Indeed, at a congress of criminal anthropologists, which also took place during the Exposition, leading experts from France and Italy were at loggerheads.

To the French, drawing on the imagery of Louis Pasteur's discoveries in the field of microbiology, the most scientifically plausible explanation for criminal degeneracy lay in cultural influences: the social and economic context in which extremists – the equivalent of microbes – lived was the *bouillon* or 'soup' from which their wrongdoing emerged. The Italians, devout followers of Darwin, with Lombroso their high priest, instead argued for a divergence in the evolutionary paths of the pure and the atavistically sinful: a notion dismissed by their rivals as mere pseudoscience. A comparison of the skulls of criminals and non-criminals would reveal the validity of their claims, they asserted, but the French disdained the suggestion, and the congress ended in acrimony. At least the Italians could have consoled themselves before they left Paris, with an excursion to the quai de Branly, in the shadow of the Eiffel Tower, where the first in a series of tableaux representing the progress of man featured Neanderthals made up with just the heavy brows, misshapen ears and thick lips that they assigned to the atavistic criminal.

In all likelihood, absolute unanimity reigned at only one congress: that of the Freemasons. Outrage was what brought them together, in the face of seemingly well-attested accusations that their secret rites entailed the raising of the devil and human sacrifice. The document that formed the basis for these accusations was published – on the very day that Pini and his accomplices were arrested – by a certain Leo Taxil, who claimed to have received it from a mysterious and elusive woman called Diana Vaughan, purportedly the child of the goddess Astarte by her mystical union with the seventeenth-century alchemist Thomas Vaughan. Smuggled from America to Europe by Vaughan, who was resolved to expose the diabolical heart of Freemasonry, it laid bare a Masonic cult called Palladism, based in the American city of Charleston where the Grand Master of the order spoke to the rulers of hell by means of telephonic apparatus. Taxil himself was an ex-Freemason who had turned against the brotherhood in a spectacular way. During his days as an initiate he had been fiercely anti-clerical, writing pornographic satires against the Pope that his fellow Masons had considered so far beyond the pale that they had pressured him to resign. Since then he had switched his allegiances dramatically, being granted an audience with the Pope he had previously maligned.

That the Catholic hierarchy proved so receptive to his claims of Masonic devil worship was due to the embattled position in which the Church felt itself to be. Displaced from its traditional role shaping young minds by the French educational reforms of the 1870s and 1880s, pinned back into the Vatican by the encroachments of state power in Italy and stripped of its control over clerical appointments in Germany by Bismarck's *Kulturkampf*, across Europe the Church was having to cede power to the state. To explain its difficulties, however, the Catholic Church needed an enemy in its own form: one against which it could pit itself in a Manichaean struggle for which the rhetoric was ready-made. To this end, Leo XIII had dug out an old foe and dressed it up in frightening new clothing: his encyclical *Humanum genus*, of April 1884, painted Freemasonry as a black sect, the progenitor of the evils of the modern world, with socialism, anarchism and communism its evil cohorts, against which his clergy were instructed to fight back with all the weapons of the Congregation of the Inquisition.

Taxil's revelations furnished this ravening monster with witches to hunt, at the very moment when the opinion-makers of a decadent society were themselves demonstrating a growing interest in the occult. Little wonder then that Archbishop Meurin of Paris, one of Taxil's many correspondents in the Church hierarchy, fell for his tales of the satanic Pope in Charleston. All it would have taken for the story to crumble was for Meurin or someone else to unearth Taxil's true name – Gabriel Jogand-Pages – and to look back beyond his Freemasonic days to earlier deceptions: the shoal of killer sharks that harried the coast near his home town of Marseilles, in the nervous weeks after the fall of the Commune, or the submerged Roman city sighted beneath the waters of Lake Geneva. But nobody thought to do so. As a result, with no support but invented witnesses, and no one with the nerve or desire to expose his fraud, Taxil pursued his fiction to ever more vertiginous extremes. 'Compared with the tugboat I had dispatched to hunt for sharks in the coves near Marseilles,' he would later marvel, 'the boat of Palladism was a true battleship . . . the battleship turned into a squadron . . . the squadron grew into a whole navy.' When that time came he would reveal the genuine nature of his enterprise, but for the moment he continued to play the part of Freemasonry's scourge with glee, furnishing his fearful, foolish society with a diabolic scapegoat on to which it could project its many anxieties. Indeed, it is hard not to see the goat-headed devil that is illustrated presiding over the rites in Taxil's pamphlets as yet one more of his in-jokes.

*

Even setting aside the contribution made to the ongoing struggle between progressives and conservatives by Taxil's great fraud, Peter Rachkovsky would surely have followed the career of such a kindred spirit keenly. The manipulation of the credulous contemporary masses was increasingly the spymaster's stock in trade, after all, and the Russian pogroms of 1881 had revealed to him how susceptible the late nineteenth century remained to the superstitious manias of the Middle Ages. Doubtless to his chagrin, he had not yet managed to pull off a coup on anything like the scale of Taxil's, despite having planned a spectacular of his own during the centenary celebrations.

In plotting an outrage to take place against the backdrop of the Expo, Rachkovsky may have remembered that his forebear as de Mohrenheim's pet intelligencer, Wilhelm Stieber, had achieved his most significant success at the 1867 Paris Expo when the near death of Tsar Alexander II at the hands of would-be assassin Berezowski had poisoned Franco-Russian relations. Rachkovsky, though, desired the opposite effect: the yoking of France and Russia together against the common enemy of revolutionary terrorism.

For the past four years the turncoat revolutionary Hekkelman, still operating under the name Landesen and Rachkovsky's most prized undercover agent, had been living in Switzerland. There he had wormed his way into the core group of People's Will policymakers by claiming a sympathetic 'uncle' prepared to pass on profits from the family firm to finance any special projects the nihilists had in mind, most particularly bomb-making. But then, in February 1889, a bomb being tested on the slopes of Mount Uetilberg by two philosophy students, both leading members of the new generation of the People's Will, exploded prematurely: Dembo was mortally wounded, his Polish companion Dembski seriously so. As a result, a number of prominent Russian activists were expelled by Switzerland and Germany, but, like the exploding bomb itself, the reaction was a little too early and not quite damaging enough to serve Rachkovsky's purposes.

The chance that the Expo presented for a publicity coup may have been missed, but it also afforded new opportunities, for it was in the bustling bars of Paris that Landesen, generous to a fault in buying drinks for those who hung on his words of provocation, first encountered an impressionable Russian medical student by the name of Reinstein. He quickly inveigled his way into the young man's life and trust.

'The revolution is not advancing; the energies are asleep; the consciences are dead,' Landesen complained to Reinstein and his friends, repeatedly urging them during the coming months to join him in a bomb-making operation on French soil. Or rather, to undertake the actual production themselves, since Landesen, a dapper, scented and well-suited young man with floppy blond hair, preferred not to remove his gloves. Reinstein at first resisted the provocation, cleaving to Kibalchich's notion that the movement would be dishonoured if it did not make all the materièl it needed within the motherland; but by March 1890, Landesen had persuaded him of the legitimacy of testing explosives outside Russia, with news of a proposed visit to France by the tsar later in the year perhaps providing a practical incentive. The next two months were spent in preparation, bringing into the conspiracy several other violent opponents of the Russian regime, including a number of women with dramatic, first-hand experience of tsarist persecution.

Still only twenty-two years old, Sofia Fedorova had first been arrested five years earlier, when caught taking food and clothing to her imprisoned parents in St Petersburg. Escaping detention, she then set up an underground printing press which was raided and her female colleague seized, but again Fedorova escaped the police, leaping from a window, only to be recaptured and sentenced to eight years of hard labour. For her final escape she slipped over the gunwales of a convict barge in western Siberia, and crossed the 3,000 miles back to St Petersburg, alone and hunted, before making her way to Paris where she heard that the current cause célèbre in the émigré community – the suicide of five women in the prison camp at Kara after one of them had been viciously beaten – involved her old colleague from the printing press. Others in Reinstein's group – some proposed by Landesen, some by Rachkovsky – had reasons of their own for joining the conspiracy, and particular talents to contribute: Lavrenius the inventor; Nakashidze the technician, summoned from London to assist; the brilliant Suzanne 'Tauba' Bromberg, a poor Jewish girl and gold medallist medical student; Dembski, who had survived the accidental blast in Switzerland; and Stepanov, a relative veteran of the revolutionary underworld. Not even Stepanov, though, quite had Fedorova's fiery motivation.

The grenades Landesen advocated were in the shape of tubes and spheres, and featured a novel design: highly explosive panclastite, with a fragile serpentine tube of glass placed at the heart of each bomb to trigger the reaction when it cracked on impact. After gathering to test the devices in woods at Bondy, each member of the group was sent away by Landesen with samples wrapped in newspaper to store until required, along with written details of the part they were to play in the conspiracy. Not all were so naïve as to accept the dangerous gift at face value. Stepanov had nurtured suspicions about Landesen since before the demonstration in the woods: he would later reveal that he considered Rachkovsky's provo-cateur to be 'a real boulevardier' who knew 'the whole of Establishment Paris'. Vladimir Burtsev, absent on an expedition to smuggle revolutionary literature into Russia, wrote from Romania to warn his friends in Paris: he was being tailed by the local Okhrana agents and had finally realised that it must have been Landesen who, having waved him off from the station in Paris, had given Rachkovsky details of his itinerary.

Burtsev's warning arrived too late, though; the die had been cast. Even the handful of plotters who reluctantly approached the French police with their concerns found themselves cold-shouldered for several crucial days. Landesen went to ground, and Rachkovsky's factotum, the journalist Jules Hansen, delivered a complete dramatis personae for the plot to a grateful minister of the interior, Constans, who immediately ordered their arrest. Before dawn on 29 May, French police battered down the doors of the conspirators and the word 'arrested' was written in quick succession next to all but one of the twenty-seven names on their hit list. The four days that the warrant for Landesen's arrest was held up in the system gave him enough time to disappear.

'At last!' cried the tsar, when informed of the interdiction of a revolutionary plot on which he had been continually briefed, 'So France has a government at last!' The contribution made by the arrests to the establishment of friendly relations between Russia and France was, Hansen believed, 'immense', and de Mohrenheim was effusive in his letter to Goron, the prefect of police: 'Your Excellency, Monsieur le Préfet and, permit me to add, my dearest, truest and great friend! . . . I hope to shake your hand in the near future with the greatest, most sincere and unchanging affection and friendly devotion.' The indignation expressed by the French security services when some of the less tractable and more influential powers suggested that they had merely been carrying out orders from St Petersburg soon evaporated in the warm light of such appreciation, and Rachkovsky was more than happy to concede that he had known little of the explosives until informed by Monsieur Loze of the Sûreté. Any lingering awkwardness or unease over the disappearance of Landesen, the leading conspirator, was washed away in a rush of rewards for French functionaries, from police officers to the president. 'They have reached the point of making the republic the *mouchard* of the world,' one old deputy was overheard remarking. 'Ferry bends his knee to Bismarck, but Constans kneels before the tsar.' The world at large, however, accepted the story of the plotters at face value.

Nothing the accused could say in court carried any credibility. 'How many of the bombs did you make?' asked the defence counsel; 'None,' replied Reinstein, 'I received them all from Landesen.' 'Always Landesen,' the lawyer shrugged, dubiously, suggesting that it was too easy to lay all the blame on the one conspirator who got away. And when it was put to Reinstein that neither he nor his companions in the dock required any provocation, he merely replied with resignation, 'Oh! How that would suit the Russian ambassador!' With half the French press in Rachkovsky's pocket, nobody was listening, its readership distracted by reports of Lavrenius' improbable claim that the 'bomb' in Stepanov's possession was in fact an experimental version of a propulsion engine for manned balloons: one that not even the testimony of his old professor and the production of a patent application could persuade the court to accept. Only the sentencing of Landesen to five years *in absentia* roused a degree of unease.

It was left to Rochefort's *L'Intransigeant* to voice its founder's bitter disillusionment, from his exile across the Channel: 'Really, the only punishable fault of the nihilists, so viciously sentenced last Saturday, is to have believed that the France of today is the old France, a refuge for the proscribed and friend of the persecuted.' In fact, the manner in which the bomb plot was presented to the public cleverly struck a number of populist chords, and in other circumstances might easily have persuaded the fickle Rochefort to swing behind the government position. The conspiracy had been Israelite in origin, and backed by Jewish money, announced polemics published in the Russian newspapers *Novosti* and *Grazhdanin,* which emphasised the ethnicity of a number of the plotters and demanded reprisals against Jews throughout the empire. Such an interpretation was promoted in France too, where Edouard Drumont, editor of *La France Juive,* had just founded the Anti-Semitic League of France as 'an instrument of national resurrection' that would 'fight the pernicious influence of the grasping Jewish financiers, whose clandestine and merciless conspiracy jeopardises the welfare, honour and security of France'. And only days before the arrest of the bombers, threats against Baron Adolphe de Rothschild himself had raised fears of an anti-Semitic terror campaign.

'Are they affiliated to our anarchists?' asked *Le Petit Parisien* during the trial of the Russian conspirators. 'It is hardly likely, since their views are not the same and their methods of action are quite different.' The prefecture was furious, and expeditiously presented a summary of its reasons for disagreeing with the line taken by the newspaper to Constans at the ministry of the interior. The police rooted their thesis in the congress of the Anarchist International in Switzerland of 1881, when the Russian delegates had taken it upon themselves to serve their foreign friends at dinner, in expression of brotherhood; 'All true Russian nihilists are anarchists,' one had ingratiatingly told the company, proposing that they should 'act hand in hand in their strikes'; the Lyons bomb attack of that year was said also to have been a joint effort with nihilist technicians; Kropotkin's straddling of the two movements was adduced as evidence, with Elisée Reclus fingered as the fulcrum of their cooperation. Since then, it was erroneously implied, the movements had grown closer together. Memos flew within the government, and a strategy to make anarchism and terrorism synonymous started to take shape.

Rachkovsky should have basked in the success of his enterprise. Within weeks of the tsar's conversion to a new respect for the French government, secret negotiations for a Franco-Russian alliance had been initiated. As a practical gesture, the Russians, after toying with the idea of equipping their army with the British Enfield rifle, upped their order to the Lebel factory at Châtellerault. With Sarah Bernhardt rousing French patriotism to new heights with her portrayal of Jeanne d'Arc at the Théâtre de la Porte Saint-Martin, and Admiral Colomb predicting in his speculative book *The Great War of 189—* that hostilities could break out at any moment, and might be precipitated by an event such as the assassination of a crowned head in the Balkans, both sides were adjusting to the need for amity. A squadron of the French fleet was even invited to visit the port of Kronstadt the following summer, at the time of the annual Russian manoeuvres – a gesture of friendship that would be overshadowed only by the tsar peremptorily declaring 'Enough, enough!' after a single verse of the revolutionary hymn the 'Marseillaise' – and audiences at the opera stood for de Mohrenheim, cheering *'Vive la Russie!'*

Yet still Rachkovsky could not rest. It had been Landesen's own choice to go into hiding and then flee to England, rather than stay and prove to the revolutionaries that he was truly one of them, as Rachkovsky had planned. Now, holed up in the Grand Hotel in the English seaside resort of Brighton, the eight years that Hekkelman had spent under deep cover as Landesen had left him close to a state of mental breakdown. If Rachkovsky was going to ensure that his agent remained safely in the fold, he needed to act decisively, and did so in a letter that was a masterpiece of manipulation. 'Regard an informant as you would a beautiful woman with whom you are having an affair,' the senior St Petersburg policeman, Zubatov, had been in the habit of telling his junior officers. 'Dote upon her. One false move can lead to her disgrace.' Rachkovsky's letter, preserved in a barely legible draft in the Okhrana archives, veers between tenderness and a tone of bullying with an astonishing nimbleness.

'I was so sorry to learn from your last letter how much you are suffering,' he writes to Landesen:

What is it that *drags* you back to that *suffocating* place, from which you so long to escape? Why, instead of allowing your *wounded soul* to heal in peace, do you *let it fester*?

. . . Of course, had you been arrested together with some others (which is what I recommended), then after a few *interesting* days in gaol, you would have been a free man once again . . . But you were tired of this old game. To regret anything now is not only too late but also will not do you any good.

. . . There is no hard legal evidence against you, but suspicions could grow, which, aided by a set of indisputable facts, might lead to a reasonable conclusion. This, as you well know, is more than sufficient, under the revolutionary code, to *sentence you without appeal* . . . Your attackers will no doubt be totally demoralised [when you fight back against] those repulsive, maddened Jew-cries of 'crucify him!' If someone should attack you, try to write something along the lines of the following:

'It is with indignation that I perceive the continuing slanderous attacks on my person at the hands of my *dear* comrades. Like a mob of the possessed, you have lost your common sense and do nothing but howl fiercely to the pleasure of certain . . . Pharisees in our midst . . . Forget my personality and my past and forget how you led me out of Paris after the arrests. Continue to publish articles about me claiming that I had a horde of lovers and a weakness for roulette. Now, having sold out that "nihilists' plot", I can open my own harem and spend my days promenading the boulevards of Monaco like some golden cloud?! Oh, you are not revolutionaries, you are nothing but filthy human waste!'

. . . In my opinion, you have terminated relations with the revolutionaries once and for all, and having anything to do with them, even on a purely personal level, would mean betraying your convictions and do terrible injustice to yourself: you invested all your energy . . . your whole self into the last job. Enough! Try to view your past as nothing more than an unpleasant dream, bring your nerves in order, and try to focus your mind on the future, rather than looking back and torturing yourself over this memory or that. You certainly deserve to live an honest life and do a dignified job – not only as far as [your service to] the government, but also as far as your own conscience is concerned. So enjoy yourself, have some fun and rest until the autumn as the Lord guides you, fully unshackled from your own past and from all obligations. In the meantime I shall be in Petersburg, but on my return we will raise our glasses *to the new tracks along which your life will run.*

This was the head of the Paris Okhrana acting as psychotherapist, priest, life coach and consoling barman rolled into one, and it was a compelling performance. Rachkovsky gently reprimands, then straight away soothes. Indulging Hekkelman's delusion, he appears genuinely to accept that Landesen is innocent in the whole affair, stepping into the dangerous territory where fact and fiction blur. A dose of anti-Semitism is injected to rouse the self-hating Jew in Hekkelman, but swiftly followed by a riposte intended to sting the shy, louche agent into indignation.

More than ever, as Hekkelman, or Landesen – or Arkady Harting, as he would soon become – listened to the sea wash the Sussex beach, he would have known himself to be Rachkovsky's creature. When he later wrote from London to request that noblest of prizes – conversion to the Orthodox faith – Rachkovsky would see to it that his protégé's christening was conducted with aristocrats and diplomats as guarantors: the stigma of being a Jewish boy from Pinsk would be forever erased. A pension of

1,000 francs a month was also agreed. And though there is no record of what services, if any, 'Arkady Harting' performed for his master during his sojourn in England, it was there that a new front was about to be opened in the Okhrana's battle with the revolutionaries, whose propagandist activities were now better organised and more vexatious to Rachkovsky than they had ever been in Switzerland.

Even as the Okhrana chief congratulated himself on his ever growing power, however, one man aboard a ship passing through the Straits of Gibraltar threatened to become Rachkovsky's nemesis. Cursed never to have his warnings about Hekkelman's treachery believed, Vladimir Burtsev's failure to prevent the framing of his comrades in Paris had been followed by the arrest of his travelling companion, again on a tip-off from Landesen, as he attempted to cross into Russia. Under surveillance in Romania, Burtsev had fled to Bulgaria where, again harassed, he had embarked on an English merchantman at the port of Galatz, bound for London. Then, while the ship was anchored in Constantinople, a flotilla of Turkish police vessels had attempted a blockade, telling the captain he must hand Burtsev over to the authorities and the Russian officials who accompanied them. 'I will not,' the captain of the SS *Ashlands* replied, 'this is English territory! And I am a gentleman!'

It was a story the British newspapers would relish repeating on the ship's arrival in London, along with accounts of how a burly Turkish hireling had insistently remained on board, awaiting an opportunity to grapple Burtsev into the sea, to be picked up by the Russian vessel that had followed them out of Constantinople harbour. The myth of English liberalism remained alive, but soon enough even the British press would fall prey to Rachkovsky's wiles.

17

The Russian Memorandum

Great Britain, America and Russia, 1890–1893

The news of General Seliverstov's assassination reached the Russian ambassador, de Mohrenheim, while he was attending the premiere of the new comedy *Dernier Amour* at Paris' Théâtre du Gymnase: a whispered word in his ear that must have caused him to blanch. The ex-head of the St Petersburg police had been found dead in a room at the Hôtel de Bade on boulevard des Italiens, executed by a single shot to the head. It was December 1890, twelve years since Seliverstov's predecessor in the job had been stabbed to death by Kravchinsky. Was the same assassin again at work? A news blackout on Seliverstov's death was imposed, but the garrulousness of de Mohrenheim's entourage soon had the press scrambling to uncover the whole sordid story. The French police agent 'Pépin' reported having heard from an old Communard that, ten years earlier, a revolutionary tribunal in Switzerland had indeed assigned Kravchinsky the task of carrying out the sentence of death that it had passed on Seliverstov. It soon became clear, however, that the alleged perpetrator, now calling himself 'Stepniak', had a watertight alibi, and one rather alarming to the Okhrana: he was, it was said, in America.

Rachkovsky must have been furious that Kravchinsky, who since the conversion of Tikhomirov had become his greatest headache, had slipped through the net. The revolutionary's popularity among the bohemian intelligentsia of England was irksome, but it was the widening scope of his propaganda activities that was most troubling, and which urgently required suppression. Having fled Russia a decade earlier, Kravchinsky had pledged 'to win over the world for the Russian revolution, to throw on the scale the huge force of the public opinion in the most advanced countries'. Recent years had seen the pace of his propagandist effort accelerate and his audience grow ever more receptive.

The acclaimed publication in 1883 of his account of the struggle against the tsar, *Underground Russia*, had opened the way for three further works examining the parlous condition of his homeland. Then, in 1889, his first novel *The Career of a Nihilist* had been published, at a time when his name was being mentioned as a possible compromise leader of the English socialist movement. It was a runaway success. Kravchinsky's talents 'would have made his . . . fortune if turned into the profitable channel of sensation novel writing,' raved *Science* magazine of the book's dramatic narrative, and others concurred. As much as any literary merit the book may have had, though, it was the shocking reports from Russia then appearing in the headlines that ensured its popularity with the circulating libraries that dominated English reading culture. And the impact of those reports was felt on both sides of the Atlantic.

On a tour of Russia in the mid-1880s with the Western Union Telegraph expedition, the American explorer George Kennan had been impressed by his official hosts' apparent cooperation. The result was a book, *Tent Life in Siberia*, which described the exemplary penal colonies he had been shown. Kravchinsky and Kropotkin had both chided him for his credulity. As a consequence, when Kennan secured a commission from *Century* magazine to revisit the tsarist prison camps at Siberia in 1887, he was more thorough in his investigations. His shocking accounts of the abuses endured by the political prisoners overshadowed even the efforts of such esteemed apologists for the tsarist regime as the English editor of the *Pall Mall Gazette*, W. T. Stead.

Despite having shown his guest considerable hospitality, Constantine Pobedonostsev was dubbed by Kennan 'the Russian Torquemada' with reference to the notorious leader of the Spanish Inquisition. Graphic illustrations punctuated articles in a wide range of magazines, bringing home to readers the abject misery endured by Russia's internal exiles. In blistering rain and snow, with guards on either side, columns of the dispossessed were described marching out of St Petersburg, their lanterns swinging forlornly as family members reached out in vain with last letters; then the journey across thousands of miles of wilderness, hard and dangerous, by barge, road and sledge; the overnight stops, shoulders jammed against the barred windows of their compounds as they strained to hand over precious pennies to an old woman in exchange for the scant rations in her basket; and, at last, the godforsaken clapboard towns where they were expected to make a life, labouring under guard, amidst the relentless ice of the tundra.

Since Kennan's return, matters in Russia had deteriorated still further. A crackdown on discipline among the convicts had caused protests, leading to further repression. The mass suicide of women prisoners at Kara, in protest at one of their number dying two days after being given a hundred lashes, was followed in April 1889 by what became known outside Russia as the Yakutsk massacre. An angry demonstration by thirty-four exiles against their ill-treatment had led to reprisals that left four dead, two fatally wounded, and three others condemned to death.

For some time, Kravchinsky had been lobbying influential figures in the English political Establishment in an attempt to coax them away from their liberal complacency and adherence to peaceful protest. 'It is very easy for Alexander III to allow himself to be persuaded that he is doing his sacred duty in maintaining a political regime which is causing such awful misery and sufferings,' he wrote to Mrs Spence Watson, the wife of one of the leading Liberals outside Parliament, insisting that 'in Russia, as everywhere else, freedom will be won by fighting and not otherwise'. Soon afterwards, her husband Robert proposed a society that would raise public awareness of Russia's despotism through a regular series of pamphlets.

Kravchinsky insisted that neither he nor Kropotkin should be named as instigators of the scheme, which he thought would be best publicised as a fundamentally English affair. But questions of presentation were not allowed to delay the launch of the Society of Friends of Russian Freedom on 30 April 1890. Two days later, May Day saw the best attendance yet in a series of Free Russia rallies in Hyde Park, at which speakers included George Bernard Shaw, Marx's sons-in-law Aveling and Lafargue, and the Member of Parliament Robert Cunninghame Graham; as William Morris had advised, the English were not patronising the Russians, but standing as their friends and equals in the struggle. And by the summer the first edition of *Free Russia*, featuring a full exposé of the Yakutsk massacre, was in the hands of readers.

When the Russian ambassador to London, Yegor de Staal, informed St Petersburg that 'the agitation raised against Russia on the grounds of the exaggerated rumours of merciless treatment of prisoners in Siberia has still not subsided', Rachkovsky could offer no immediate answer and several months later was still writing of Britain as 'alien and not at all conducive to the agency's work'. Even Olga Novikoff, with her bulging book of contacts in London high society, was impotent to shift public opinion, grousing to the turncoat Tikhomirov about how 'That accursed Stepniak is inciting each and all in England against all that is dear to Russia. It's a terrible, terrible disaster.' Events in Russia, though, would soon compound their problems, and further boost the circulation of the society's newspaper. When news filtered through of the country's widespread famine, British public opinion was outraged by the Russian government's shameful response.

Fear and pride had conspired to create a climate of denial around the tsar. 'There are no famine victims. There are merely regions suffering from a poor harvest,' he declared when a group of officers proposed cancelling their regimental dinner and donating the cost to the starving, while a subscription by the French people in aid of the famine victims was also rejected. 'Russia does not need charity,' Ambassador de Mohrenheim insisted to the French press while on vacation in Aix-les-Bains, but the fraudulence of the official line was exposed when aid sent secretly by the émigrés, via Leo Tolstoy, was received with pitiful gratitude. And to ensure that the message of tsarist incompetence reached those suffering from it most directly, a lithographic copying centre was set up in St Petersburg to reproduce *Free Russia* for domestic distribution.

Meanwhile, Kravchinsky, previously nervous about his poor spoken English, was finally prevailed upon by Kennan to visit the United States on a lecture tour and, unlike his co-editor Felix Volkhovsky who habitually spoke to audiences wearing chains on his ankles and wrists, he would rely on his verbal powers to make an impact.

Establishing a base in Boston, just as Bakunin had thirty years earlier, Kravchinsky used literary discussion of the novels of Tolstoy and Turgenev as a Trojan Horse to gain him entry into the society of America's literary opinion-makers. 'One of the most important things I ever heard . . . large, bold and massive to an extraordinary degree,' enthused the critical luminary William Dean Howells of Kravchinsky's lecture on novels that were known more by repute than in translation, and took the revolutionary under his wing. After dining with the Russian at home and in his club, and even taking him on a visit to a local fire station where Kravchinsky slid down a brass pole, the American critic's initial impression was confirmed: 'One of those wonderful clear heads that seem to belong to other races than ours.'

But whilst Kravchinsky's message that the pogroms against the Jews in Russia had been propagated by the government struck home, concerns persisted about the violence that underpinned the revolutionaries' own strategy to force constitutional change, with Howells reluctant to lend his name to support for such methods. Others, though, had no such qualms and were happy to sign up, including the author Mark Twain.

'If such a government cannot be overthrown otherwise than by dynamite, then thank God for dynamite!' Twain had proclaimed the previous year, leaping to his feet in the audience at one of Kennan's lectures on the Kara outrage. As an angry sentimentalist, with an outspoken antipathy to that most 'grotesque of all the swindles invented by man – monarchy', Twain was perfectly receptive to Kravchinsky's message, believing that America, having received the support of France in its struggle to overthrow despotism during its own revolution a century before, was beholden to remember its origins and lend its support to those now engaged in the fight for political justice.

The endorsement of such prominent moral arbiters gave Kravchinsky good reason to hope that the idea of Russian freedom would fall on fertile ground, and plans were made to establish an American branch of the Society of Friends of Russian Freedom. Before Kravchinsky could see the project realised, however, a message arrived from Volkhovsky summoning him back to London to assist in resolving tensions with colleagues in Europe that had unexpectedly become inflamed. Under intense pressure to stem the tide of anti-tsarist propaganda, Rachkovsky may have been finding it hard to land a clean blow, but he had been far from idle.

*

In Paris, the rumours about Kravchinsky's involvement with the murder of General Seliverstov had refused to go away merely because it had been shown that he could not have carried out the attack in person. Agent 'Pépin', who had originally pointed the finger at Kravchinsky, quickly came up with a variant account, based on information supposedly received from an anonymous source. The true culprit, he asserted, was a young, London-based Pole called Stanislaw Padlewski, whom Kravchinsky had instructed to kill the general.

There were sightings of Padlewski in Spain and Italy, but no one stopped to enquire further about the real reason for the assassin's frequent trips, in the past, to Paris and Italy, or his unexplained connection with Rachkovsky's old agent, Yuliana Glinka. Nor did anyone give much credence to the lonely voices daring to claim that Padlewski was himself mixed up with the Okhrana, and that the killing was a false-flag operation. It would be more than a decade before one of Rachkovsky's agents, Cyprien Jagolkovsky, revealed his role in Seliverstov's murder, and another ten years before the notion was publicly aired that the Okhrana chief himself had organised the hit to rid himself of a possible threat to his position.

In the meantime, Rachkovsky had doggedly pursued his agenda of demonising the Russian émigrés in the eyes of the British public, in the hope of facilitating political action against them. January 1891 had seen him meet the Russian interior minister, Durnovo, in Nice, to discuss his proposed strategy and his request to be posted to London, since his efforts to date had effectively driven the key émigrés across the Channel. Durnovo's immediate reaction was to report to St Petersburg what Rachkovsky had told him of the ease and affluence that the London émigrés enjoyed thanks to their 'ghastly agitation of the English'. The eventual outcome, however, was the drafting of what would become known as the 'Russian Memorandum' that laid out the argument for why the British government should take action against those enemies of the tsar to whom it had granted asylum. Sent by the Russian foreign ministry to Ambassador de Staal in London, it was then passed on to Her Majesty's Government. Neither Lord Salisbury's tacit support, however, for surveillance of Russians entering through English ports, nor the redoubled lobbying efforts of Madame Novikoff produced the desired effect. 'This is not a very reassuring result,' would be Tsar Alexander's terse reaction to the lack of progress.

There were, however, other weapons in Rachkovsky's arsenal, not the least of which was his seasoned tactic of sowing dissent. Kravchinsky's great talent, well attested by those around him, was his skill as a conciliator, working to bring into alignment the disparate groups of Russian revolutionaries spread across Europe. That ability was put to the test. Even before the first edition of *Free Russia* hit the news-stands, co-editor Felix Volkhovsky had been attacked by Plekhanov's group in Switzerland for his high-handedness in ignoring all those who did not share the newspaper's relatively liberal agenda, and by Peter Lavrov for emphasising the search for political over economic freedom. Thanks in part to Kravchinsky's past kindnesses to Plekhanov, whom he had subsidised to take a rest cure when he was suffering from tuberculosis, the flurry of accusations temporarily abated. But then, during Kravchinsky's absence in America, a series of black operations orchestrated by Rachkovsky, and implemented by the expert forgers at rue de Grenelle, stoked the fires of mistrust and resentment.

First to appear was a pamphlet entitled *A Confession by an Old Revolutionary Veteran*, which accused Kravchinsky and the other London émigrés of having sold themselves to the British police; then, an open letter purportedly written by Plekhanov further denounced the London group. After Lavrov's 'Group of Veterans' had re-established contact between the old People's Will organisations in Russia's major cities, his name too was put to a forged document which lamented that there was no prospect of a social revolution in Russia, announced that its author was to retreat to a monastery, and signed off with an implausible 'Amen'. Those impugned were quick to scorn the ruse, roundly denying any involvement, while *Free Russia* left its readers in no doubt about the documents' true source: 'The spies are dancing a jig,' it confirmed in a note to its readers. Yet for all the inconvenience caused to Kravchinsky, and despite Rachkovsky's boast of the previous autumn that by infiltrating agents into the London émigré community he had brought it 'under our full control', in early 1892, the Anglo-Saxon world remained largely impervious to the Okhrana's wiles.

'S—, I have been given to understand, had been concerned in some very dreadful affairs indeed. Perhaps he would blow me up. Perhaps he would convert me,' wrote one journalist, approaching an interview with the notorious revolutionary with trepidation, only for his fears to be assuaged by an evening spent at Kravchinsky's St John's Wood house. Though the furnishings were somewhat exotic – 'couches and settees had the places that in mere bourgeois homes would have been occupied by stiff-backed chairs' – the man himself was thoroughly congenial: 'capable of enjoying a good dinner', and irresistibly charming as he sat sipping spiced tea and languidly smoking a cigarette. Conversation flowed easily around the sceptical Kravchinsky's adventure of the previous evening, ghost-hunting in Westminster Abbey, and the intriguing prospects raised by psychic research. Always, though, it returned to his perennial theme: the brutality of tsarist Russia, the degradations experienced by its people, and the just cause of revolution in the quest for democracy. So powerful was Kravchinsky's evocation of Russian misery that even his dire prediction that 'when the peasants do wake up, their revolution will put the French one into the shade' was recorded by his rapt interviewer without demur.

Nor was it only the press that Kravchinsky and Volkhovsky courted with their Slavic charm, as they insinuated themselves ever deeper into the supportive sympathy of their British hosts. The Garnett sisters, Olive and Constance, epitomised the susceptibility of literary and artistic bohemia to the Russian émigrés' radical chic, and the strong erotic appeal that they exercised. Constance's decision to live in Fitzroy Square, in the heart of the French anarchist colony, had already singled her out as a woman with a taste for adventure beyond that offered by her timid, bookish and sexually inhibited husband, Edward. Her head was turned first by Volkhovsky and his compelling history of twelve years spent in Siberian exile following the Trial of the 193 and his subsequent escape down the River Amur to Japan, who set about teaching Russian to the sisters.

By turns intellectually austere and vainly sensuous, his very unpredictability seemed to draw in Englishwomen. 'One day he was a pathetic broken down old man, the next he would look twenty years younger, put a rose in his buttonhole, and lay himself out very successfully to please and entertain,' Constance's sister commented, and would marvel that, when he left, 'It is so curious to awake from Siberia to a Surrey Lane.' But if Volkhovsky had been intriguing to the sisters, Kravchinsky was much more so. On being introduced to him when visiting his new home in the model Arts and Crafts suburb of Bedford Park, Constance found him barely resistible. With doting friends like the socially well-connected Garnett sisters, Kravchinsky's respectability was firmly underwritten.

Rachkovsky was not to be deterred. The agents who followed Kravchinsky home on his nightly walks out to the suburbs of West London may have been easily paid off by their mark with the price of a beer, glad to avoid the antagonism from the locals that the presence of shady foreigners evinced, whatever side of the political divide. No similar solution was available, though, when it came to the professional cracksmen paid to burgle the homes of known associates of the émigré revolutionaries, or the thugs hired to beat up young women who worked on the society's stall in Hyde Park, and a general air of intimidation prevailed. Most damagingly of all for the Society of Friends of Russian Freedom, Okhrana agents were also targeting the movement from within.

Alexander Evalenko had first offered his services to the police in St Petersburg in early 1891, when he and his wife had decided to emigrate from Russia to the United States; Rachkovsky's decision to recruit him on a generous salary, under the cover name of Vladimir Sergeyev, was quickly vindicated. Money supplied from the Okhrana purse bought 'Sergeyev' ready access to the Society of Friends of Russian Freedom, on both sides of the Atlantic, and his dedication earned him both a trusted position as the movement's librarian in New York, and the friendship of the ambitious Yegor Lazarev, then the leading figure of the American movement. It took Evalenko's talent for cool dissimulation to allay suspicion of his extravagant donations, but as contributions from genuine well-wishers slowed to a trickle, his funding became ever more crucial, whilst tempting the society into a dangerous dependency upon him.

It was a slow-burn strategy, but one that would ultimately prove hugely effective. Curtailing positive propaganda for the revolutionary cause, however, was only half of the task. Even if weaned away from their sympathy for the anti-tsarist movement, the British and American governments still had to be made to understand the need to take firm action themselves against the 'terrorists' in their midst. America's own industrial unrest, however, would spawn violence of a kind that, whilst directed at plutocrats rather than princes, would powerfully illustrate the nature of the threat.

*

Years later a friend would recollect that Kravchinsky had never appeared happier than during the time he spent teaching impoverished black children whilst on a visit to America. Having come to ask for support from a nation founded upon freedom, he had been taken aback by the levels of inequality he saw, claiming never before to have witnessed such a disparity of wealth in a society. Nor was he alone in viewing the United States as a country much in need of a new revolution of its own. 'When the Americans start, it will be with energy and violence. In comparison we will be children,' Engels himself had recently remarked, and Kravchinsky, on friendly terms with the German, may well have tailored his tone of address with such perceptions in mind. For whereas in England he had always been at pains to offer assurances to the Friends' supporters that 'the only help we shall ever ask . . . is that of bringing the public opinion of free countries to bear on Russian affairs', in his written appeal entitled 'What Americans Can do for Russia' he revealed a far greater and more militant dream: 'to see one day . . . an army spring into existence – not a host, but a well-selected army like that of Gideon – composed of the best men of all free nations, with unlimited means at their command, fighting side by side . . . [for] the supremacy of the triumphant democracy.' The summer of 1892 revealed the germ of what might become such an army among the downtrodden steelworkers of Pennsylvania.

In June 1892, Henry Clay Frick was appointed chairman of the vast Carnegie Steel Company, which amalgamated Frick's own business interests with those of Andrew Carnegie. Having made an extraordinary fortune, Carnegie was now getting on for sixty years old and was content to take a back seat, burnishing his image as a philanthropist and rediscovering his Scottish roots, while Frick brought to bear the same ruthlessness he had shown while building his own fortune as the 'King of Coke'. But the steel workers of the Homestead plant, the centrepiece of Carnegie's empire, presented a challenge. They must, it had been made clear, accept an 18 per cent pay cut and the loss of union rights, or face the sack. But after almost twenty years of deep recession, during which America's leading industrialists had continued to accumulate almost inconceivable wealth, workers labouring long hours for already pitiful wages were in no mood to compromise. Nor did the libraries and meeting halls that Carnegie was busy erecting across the country persuade them otherwise. Evidence of plutocratic vanity as much as genuine philanthropy – whatever the moral message propounded by Carnegie in his 1889 apologia for the 'robber barons', *The Gospel of Wealth* – they were funded by a small portion of company profits that, every year, exceeded the entire wage bill for his workforce. They certainly did not appease the Homestead workers, who came out on strike.

'We think absolute secrecy essential in the movement of these men,' wrote Frick to the Pinkerton Agency, 'so that no demonstration can be made while they are en route.' The paramilitary organization he was referring to comprised 300 freelance security contractors: a tiny proportion of the 30,000 that the Pinkertons could mobilise, which amounted to a force greater than the whole standing army of the United States. While some of the mercenaries sent to Homestead were veterans of past confrontations, most were thuggish greenhorns, hired off the streets of New York, Chicago, Kansas City or Philadelphia, and loaded on to one of the two huge roofed-in barges that had been readied to transport them down the eight miles of the River Monongahela from Pittsburgh with no foreknowledge of their task or destination. It was hoped that what they lacked in experience would, however, be compensated for by the daunting defences that they would garrison: a three-mile palisade around the industrial site, twelve feet in height, topped with barbed wire, with holes drilled at regular intervals to allow concealed rifle fire, water cannon and even a system of piping to spray boiling water at assailants: 'Fort Frick', as it had become known to the thousands of locked-out steelworkers who watched its erection.

The tugs pulled the barges crammed with Pinkertons upstream under the cover of thick fog, but as the men crowded into the boats' dark bellies held their breath, they could hear the voices of striking pickets along the banks on either side. It was two days after the anniversary of the Declaration of Independence, and having celebrated it as patriots, the steelworkers were resolved to defend the town and works that they had built up over the past decade: Carnegie might be the owner, but they were stakeholders whose moral rights were manifest.

It took a single shot, from an unknown source, for violence to erupt. The crates of Winchester rifles stowed on the barges were broken out and distributed to the Pinkerton employees, and a great fusillade followed. The crowd of strikers, dragging their dead and wounded with them, retreated only so far as a series of makeshift barricades on higher ground; the Pinkertons hastily sawed loopholes into the wooden flanks of the barges, through which to level the muzzles of their rifles.

For two days the Homestead workers laid siege to the floating redoubts. Dynamite charges were thrown, exploding on the roof of the barges and causing consternation within; a flaming rail hopper was rolled down the incline towards the river, but stuck in the muddy strand before it could reach its target. All the while, telegrams arrived from around the country pledging support for the workers; their Texas colleagues even promised the loan of cannons. Yet when the Pinkertons finally surrendered and were forced to run the gauntlet of beatings, the strikers' leaders intervened in the name of justice to prevent summary executions. Eager to dissociate themselves from violence, they laid the blame for the uglier behaviour at the door of the plant's Hungarian workers but, above all, on anarchist outsiders who had come to advance their own ideological struggle against capital. Three anarchists were even attacked by the strikers, who recognised that association with the sect that was blamed for the Haymarket Affair would lose them much of the goodwill they had accrued. They were right, but powerless to protect themselves from the inevitable propangandist attacks.

Hardly had the smoke cleared on the Battle of Homestead than the anarchist Alexander Berkman set off from New York for Pittsburgh, armed for action. A Russian Jew from Odessa, Berkman had arrived in America in 1888. Aged eighteen, he was part of the great wave of refugees from the tsar's anti-Semitic policies, fleeing the fear of pogroms to pour through the port of Hamburg and across the Atlantic. Like many of his more radical compatriots, he had quickly gravitated towards the anarchist politics of Johann Most, who subsequently hired him to work as a compositor on the newspaper *Freiheit*, in its grime-encrusted offices down by the Brooklyn Bridge. The relationship between the two men was complicated, however, by their shared passion for a young Russian divorcee, Emma Goldman; she, for her part, was happy to reciprocate the affection of both men. 'Something gripped my heart,' Goldman later wrote of her first meeting with Most, 'I wanted to take his hand, to tell him that I would be his friend. But I dared not speak out. What could I give this man – I, a factory girl, uneducated; and he, the famous Johann Most, the leader of the masses, the man of magic tongue and powerful pen.'

Goldman provided Most with a rare exception to his gruff rule that, other than Louise Michel and Vera Zasulich, all women were 'stupids', and he encouraged her to study and develop her natural talent as a political speaker. Meanwhile, Berkman suffered agonies of jealousy in silence, laboriously setting type, while the woman he loved mounted the stairs to Most's office, not to descend again until dawn. The young compositor's commitment to the doctrine of free love that Goldman advocated was sorely tested, and when Most gave his beloved protégée a bouquet of violets in the middle of winter, Berkman could not help but protest at the indulgent expense, when so many around them were short of food. Most, for his part, simply dismissed his rival as a figure of no consequence. But it was with Berkman that Goldman chose to make a home, and after Most was dragged off to the penitentiary on Blackwell's Island in the spring of 1891, for the second time in three years, the pair set up an ice-cream parlour together in Worcester, Massachusetts, to support their continued work in the anarchist cause.

When Berkman checked into the Merchants Hotel near the train depot in Pittsburgh on 13 July, in the guise of Mr Rakhmetov, an employment agent, it is not known whether he was motivated by pure idealism, or the desire to prove to Goldman that unlike the loquacious Most he was a man of action. The stated purpose of the attack on Frick that Berkman had in mind was propaganda: to demonstrate where the true guilt for the Homestead debacle lay, and to show that, however forcefully the strikers might reject the anarchists' involvement in their affairs, 'the proletariat had its avengers'. Berkman had come armed with a bomb, constructed according to the instructions in Most's booklet *The Science of Revolutionary Warfare*, but Vera Zasulich's famed shooting of General Trepov in St Petersburg seventeen years earlier would ultimately prove the closer model. Having twice been turned away by Frick's receptionist at the Carnegie Steel Company when he requested a meeting, eventually Berkman marched straight past her and into the chairman's office. Dazzled for a moment by sunlight falling through the window, Frick turned from his desk to squint at Berkman who, levelling his pistol, fired three times. Frick hauled himself to his feet, blood pouring from two wounds to his neck, in an attempt to grapple with his assailant, only to be stabbed twice in the side with a stiletto before the belated appearance of his security staff.

Berkman was sentenced to twenty-two years; his accomplices, Bauer and Nold, received five, on evidence that included the distribution of anarchist literature at Homestead. A soldier by the name of Iams, serving with the federal troops deployed to keep the peace around the steelworks, spontaneously shouted 'Three cheers for the man who shot Frick!' His reward was to be hung by his thumbs until unconscious, and drummed out of camp. A legal case brought by Iams' barrister cousin against the army officers responsible caused a minor stir. This time, though, no one dared delineate anarchism's long heritage, right back to Jesus, the great 'Redeemer of Mankind', as Bauer's defence lawyer had done, to the horror of the presiding judge.

The greatest impact of Berkman's attack, though, was on the status and credibility of the leading voices of European anarchism. Only a few weeks earlier, Johann Most had been released from his most recent spell of incarceration on Blackwell's Island. It had been a traumatic experience. On his arrival at the penitentiary, his hair had been cropped close to the skull and beard shaved off, revealing the hideous scar that disfigured his cheek to the mockery of the wardens. The twelve months he had then spent subject to 'the Spanish Inquisition to the United States' had further broken him: endless hours in a cell so small that he had to stoop, under strict orders to do nothing and make no sound, even when members of the public visited to peer in at the inmates. Now at liberty, Most promptly seized the opportunity to demonstrate to the authorities that he was a reformed man by openly criticising Berkman to a reporter from the *New York World*; envy of his romantic rival may have also played a part in the decision to break ranks.

It was a betrayal too far by Most. In Goldman's eyes, nothing could excuse his cowardice and hypocrisy, and the blustering German was finally exposed as the empty vessel that many had long suspected him to be. Goldman, by contast, emerged as a model of candid loyalty and would be named 'Queen of the Anarchists' by the press: a sudden elevation that was nevertheless borne out by popular support within the movement, which only increased when she publicly took a horsewhip to Most. It had been Italian anarchists from the 'Carlo Cafiero Group' who had first inspired the Russian radicals in New York, and Most to whom they had rallied as the 'Pioneers of Liberty', but in Emma Goldman they now found a brave and vocal figurehead of their own race, who would soon attract the attention of Peter Kropotkin and Louise Michel, and international recognition.

Any hope that the Haymarket martyr August Spies had taken with him to the gallows – that the anarchist creed would fire the imagination of the American worker at large – was dead and buried, however. Not even the posthumous pardoning of three of the Haymarket martyrs by Governor Altgeld of Illinois, in 1893, could reverse the surging victory of capitalism, industry and commerce. For even as he took the brave step, the city of Chicago, where radicalism had been rampant only seven years earlier, was busy welcoming up to 700,000 rapt visitors, including many Europeans, to the Columbia World's Fair, and its celebration of the dawning age of 'conspicuous consumption'.

At the time, the novelist Vladimir Korolenko was visiting America in Kravchinsky's footsteps under cover of a journalistic commission, in order to discuss with Yegor Lazarev and other leading figures of the Friends how best to import *Free Russia* into Russia itself. Whilst there, Pinkerton agents in the pay of the Okhrana were constantly on his tail, but their presence was not what most dispirited him about New York and Chicago. His horrified impressions were expressed through the narrator of his novel *Sofron Ivanovich*, who felt himself 'besieged by simple, repetitive advertising which wears its way hypnotically into the brain: Stephens Inks, Stephens Inks, Stephens Inks . . . Pears Soap, Pears Soap, Pears Soap'. During the Fair, not even the heavens above the city were spared, with advertisements projected on to clouds in grim realisation of Alfred Robida's fanciful predictions. Off site, the Marshall Field's department store offered a cornucopia of goods, while on display at the Fair itself were prototypes of products to tempt even the wariest shopper of the future: the high-frequency phosphorescent lighting with which the visionary Nichola Tesla was experimenting, the electrotachyscope and even the first electrical kitchen, complete with washing machine. The latter would actually attract Kropotkin's approval, as an example of technology that would create leisure for the working man and woman.

'Business fever here throbs at will,' wrote a French visitor to Chicago, 'it rushes along these streets, as though before the devouring flame of a fire.' The pursuit of money seemed unstoppable, immune even to economic crisis: the collapse of the New York stock market, the unprecedented bankruptcy of the United States treasury, and the run on banks that would see 500 of them go to the wall before the end of the year, with even greater hardship in store for the country's poor.

Korolenko was not a man who lacked perspective, or one given to easy hyperbole. An ex-internal exile to Siberia in 1879, he had been the only one of his party of convicts to survive the first winter in the freezing wasteland, thanks to the kindness of the women of the local tribe who had taken pity on him. Hardship and suffering were second nature to him, and his writer's eye was drawn to scenes of humanity at its rawest, as in his account of a night-time visit to the slaughterhouses and meat-packing factories of Chicago. But it was the injustices of American society more than any nightmarish scenes of cattle being sledgehammered that horrified him during his month-long stay. By the time he sailed out of New York, the torch borne by the new Statue of Liberty that had shone with such hope on his arrival, seemed to 'illuminate the entrance to an enormous grave'. He said he would rather be back in the Yakutsk penal colony than stay a day longer in the benighted Land of the Free.

The recent arrests of Johann Most and Emma Goldman, in separate instances but both on trumped-up charges, may have influenced his distaste for America, along with the signs of spiritual corruption that he saw in its economic life, but there were more immediate and personal reasons for his stance. Support for the Society of Friends of Russian Freedom had begun to haemorrhage as popular sentiment turned further against politically troublesome immigrants of all hues. And in February 1893, after two previous 'no' votes in recent years, the Senate had finally acquiesced to the tsar's demands that the United States strip his opponents of their privileged 'political' status, ratifying the treaty that would allow them to be extradited as common criminals.

Aghast at the result, Mark Twain challenged the very 'Americanism of the Senate' with its 'bootlicking adulation' of 'tsarist tyranny', while in London Spence Watson thought it 'the saddest news which any lover of liberty can receive'. There too, though, concern was mounting over how long Britain's resilience could last in the face of similar pressures.

*

Europe had not experienced anything quite like the armed confrontation seen at Homestead, but earlier bloodshed during strikes and May Day demonstrations in France and Spain, in 1891, had helped prompt anarchist revenge attacks that generated far more general alarm than Berkman's attempt to assassinate Frick. Britain itself had not been immune from terrorist scares, with anarchists rather than Fenians now bearing the responsibility, and when troops opened fire on rioting strikers at the Featherstone colliery in September 1893, acts of vengeance seemed possible. Furthermore, as in America, immigrants rather than indigenous socialists were seen as the likely source of any trouble; those in the French and Italian colonies primarily, but the Russians too, supposedly by association.

'Known to the outside world as the Terror . . . [the Brotherhood of Freedom] is an international secret society underlying and directing the operations of various bodies known as nihilists, anarchists, socialists – in fact, all those organisations which have for their object the reform or destruction, by peaceful or violent means, of society as it is presently constituted.' The words come not from an Okhrana report, nor the imagination of a Sûreté informant, but from *The Angel of the Revolution*, published in 1893 by the first-time novelist George Griffith, one of an emerging generation of sensationalist writers who would fuse the genres of Vernian science fiction with future war prophecy to create something thrilling but fundamentally reactionary. Verne's *Robur the Conqueror* had become, in Griffith's hands, 'Natas the Jew', his airship no longer a lone sentinel of liberty, but the flagship of a fleet being readied over the horizon to seize the revolutionary moment when the opposing sides in a continent-wide war had fought themselves to exhaustion.

For Kravchinsky and his colleagues, struggling to maintain support for the Society of Friends of Russian Freedom in England and to unify opposition to the tsar's rule among the disparate émigré groups across Europe, the conflation of their endeavours with the apparent anarchist threat to democratic society, as it filtered through into fiction, posed a severe challenge. Their friends remained supportive, expressing intense frustration towards the troublemakers. 'As for anarchism we utterly and entirely condemn it, all of us, Stepniak as much as anyone,' Olive Garnett confided to her diary. 'The blind folly of it makes one lose patience with & account blameable even such a man as Krapotkine.' There were further violent shocks in store, however, in the midst of which, just days short of the end of 1893, a pair of articles by 'Z' and 'Ivanov' would appear in the *New Review* entitled 'Anarchists: Their Methods and Organisation', which drew heavily on the content of the Russian Memorandum, mixing in with their many and varied calumnies the unambiguous assertion that 'Stepniak' and Kravchinsky, the assassin of General Mezentsev, were one and the same.

The allegations that Mezentsev's killer had hesitated several times, for 'psychological reasons', and then 'plunged the knife into the wound again and again' were inaccurate yet graphic and unpleasant. Almost as distressing to Constance Garnett, though, may have been the pointed reference to Kravchinsky's 'shallow theories of free love' and the imputation that his friends in literary circles were being duped. 'Selfishly I feared that I might lose my Stepniak – the artist – in the Stepniak I do not know, the nihilist, the terrorist and —' she would remember, unable to write the word 'assassin'. It was doubtless one effect which the true authors of the 'Ivanov' article, Rachkovsky and Madame Novikoff, had hoped to achieve, though their aim in associating past and present acts of terror, in Russia and France, and potentially in Britain too, was far wider.

When the Russian Memorandum had first been presented to the British government nearly two years earlier, it had emphasised the danger posed by the anti-tsarist émigrés in relation to 'military conspiracies . . . bombs and dynamite'. It was certainly convenient for Rachkovsky that events since had brought home to the western democracies the nature of the threat, on their own territory, reinforcing the message sent out by the 1890 bomb plot that he had contrived with his agent Landesen. But his growing skill in 'perception management' saw to it that appearances were accepted and inconvenient questions suppressed. During the trial of those entrapped in that sting operation, the defence lawyer had tried to expose the Okhrana's role but with scant success, and the possible involvement of the organisation in subsequent acts of 'anarchist' terrorism was scarcely hinted at in print.

Yet while Rachkovsky was forthright in denouncing the conspiracies of his enemies, the scope of his own conspiratorial skulduggery during those years had been far more ambitious. How he had succeeded in keeping his activities concealed for so long is a story in itself.

18

Dynamite in the City of Light

London and Paris, 1890–1892

Almost two decades after their passage to New Caledonia aboard the *Virginie*, Henri Rochefort and Louise Michel again found themselves exiled together on an island, though on this occasion the journey had merely required them to buy a ticket for the boat train across the Channel. Rochefort had arrived first in Britain, in the summer of 1889, fleeing the sentence of transportation to a fortified enclosure that hung over him for his involvement in Boulanger's plot to seize power. Unlike Michel, whose circumstances would be very different when she arrived in July 1890, he lived in considerable comfort. Having sold his Paris home for a reported million francs, and dabbling in the antiquities trade to supplement an income from the newspaper *L'Intransigeant*, still run out of Paris but left in the safe editorial hands of his appointee Edward Vaughan, he soon established himself in a grand town house in Clarence Terrace, overlooking Regent's Park.

He had not, however, left behind in Paris his appetite for either politics or status, and was busily ingratiating himself with his British hosts. To oil his admission to the salons of London he donated a Landseer painting to the National Gallery, but was helped too by introductions from Madame Olga Novikoff, the 'MP' for Russia, as one English wag termed her. A propagandist and diplomatic coquette, Novikoff's relationship with both Rochefort and the English Establishment raised intriguing questions about Russian foreign policy.

Through her friendship with Gladstone and other leading figures in the Liberal Party, Novikoff had long teased Britain with the possibility of rapprochement with Russia and continued to do so; now Salisbury's Conservative Party was showing interest. Yet Britain was increasingly fretful over maintaining its naval pre-eminence and the possibly re-entry of the Russian fleet into the Mediterranean. One naval reform followed another in quick succession; fiction such as *The Taking of Dover* predicted an inevitable war with a Franco-Russian alliance as soon as 1894. As Elisée Reclus had astutely remarked in his *Universal Geography*, whilst seemingly at the height of its power, a lack of geographical cohesion left the British Empire vulnerable to attack. As to Russia and her relationship with France's Boulangists, the press had caught Ambassador de Mohrenheim out paying a visit to the general during Boulanger's spell in the wilderness in Clermont-Ferrand, three years earlier, but since then discretion had ruled. The Third Republic and Alexander III's Russia were, after all, prospective allies, and Boulanger now an enemy of the state.

And yet whilst Boulanger himself was a liability, bellicose and unpredictable, what he represented continued to appeal to Russia as much as it did to Rochefort: a strong nationalism and latent anti-Semitism. Boulanger was no longer a useful cipher, distracted by his love for his mistress, who was now dying: Rochefort had remarked the change, observing that the general's 'thoughts, ears and eyes were elsewhere' when he visited London and the Covent Garden Opera in 1890. Even before Boulanger shot himself dead on his lover's grave the following September, Russia may have been looking for an alternative instrument through whom to shape and shake up republican France.

Were Rochefort a candidate for the role, his supporters could comfort themselves that he had put his radical past behind him: an old Communard had recently leaned into Rochefort's carriage on Regent Street and slapped him with a glove, challenging him to a duel for his betrayal of the cause. Anarchists and Boulangists, though, had joined together against the republic, and distasteful as it was, Novikoff may have hoped that the two extremes of French politics might once again be harnessed in the future. If Rochefort found himself in need of help to build bridges with his old friends on the left, the presence of Louise Michel in London would have been useful. She lived scarcely ten minutes' walk away from his grand house in Clarence Terrace. But that short distance spanned the extremes of London society.

A stone's throw further on from Charlotte Street, where Michel was staying, lay the sheer destitution of the slums of Seven Dials and the St Giles rookery, home to the 'stink industries' whose squalid labour underpinned the glamour of the nearby West End; in these slums 'you burned the stair rails and banisters, the door jambs, the window frames for fuel', and bobbies on the beat were few, being loath to venture in. The enclave north of Soho was one notch better, 400 French households crowding the terraced houses, the pavements walked by what the Baedeker guide charmingly described as 'a motley crowd of labourers, to which dusky visages and foreign costumes impart a curious and picturesque air'.

It had been the May Day demonstrations of 1890, designated at the Paris Congress of 1889 as a date for mass protests demanding an eight-hour day, that had condemned Michel to a spell living in the streets where so many Communards had settled long before. While she was campaigning in the provinces, predicting her own martyrdom in incendiary speeches, the police had swooped to take her out of circulation for the day itself. When told she would be freed, the shameful anticlimax drove her to smash anything to hand in her cell. The doctor who ordered 'her immediate removal to a special asylum for treatment', recorded a diagnosis of 'auditory hallucinations that provoke her to violence'. Michel had long claimed to hear the 'voices from below', but that had been a mere figure of speech. Perhaps the bullet still rattling around her skull had triggered something; more likely, the failure of the demonstrations, in a Paris heavily garrisoned for the occasion, was too much for a woman perpetually tormented by the bitter memory of past defeats to bear.

Michel fitted in easily in London, bringing with her Charlotte Vauvelle, her long-time companion from New Caledonia. A living legend to many, Michel would gossip in the grocery shop of the old Communard Victor Richard, an unofficial clearing house for newly arrived *compagnons*, or drink and curse the republic in the notorious Autonomie Club, which had recently moved to Windmill Street from its previous location only a few doors down from Michel's own home. And when it came to the younger generation of immigrants – for whom the Commune was no longer a source of personal trauma but rather a mythic horror, known only from the sad eyes and gaunt features of those who refused to speak about the past – they adored her. Michel's threat of 'little engines' to be used against the police in the speeches that had prompted her most recent arrest would have been a passport into their hearts.

Commanding the respect and affection of her countrymen was one thing; earning enough to supply even her modest needs, and fund her generosity to the anarchist community, quite another. Michel could, if necessary, rely on the kindness of wealthy friends, with Duchess d'Uzès an obliging patroness, but it was not enough. In her search for financial independence she found herself coming into the orbit of a very different set of Russians from those with whom Rochefort socialised, and indirectly into contact with a Russian government agent of a very different kind to Madame Novikoff.

Michel had met Kravchinsky in Paris during the congress of 1889, and kept his calling card, in the corner of which she had made a tiny sketch in ink; whether of a fizzing bomb or a blossoming tree it is hard to tell. Kropotkin, though, she had known far longer, since the London Congress of 1881, their contentious release from prison on the same date in 1886 forming a further bond. It was to him that she now turned, requesting an introduction to the agency that arranged his lectures, under the impression that Kropotkin was considered almost a god by those around him, and his influence irresistible.

In reality, Kropotkin's affiliation with his old Russian comrades was already becoming attenuated. 'Is it even possible to write the history of our objectives, convulsions and errors, of the egotism of our comrades and their shortcomings?' would be his acerbic reply when asked to contribute to a series of memoirs of leading figures in the nihilist movement. He despaired of Russia being ready for the onerous honour of leading the revolution, as Marx had predicted it would, in his dying years. And when the editors of the newly revived journal of the People's Will approached him to participate in 1891, he would excuse himself on the grounds that he was committing all his strength and attention to the international anarchist cause, in the firm belief that 'every step forward towards the coming revolution in western Europe also hastens the revolution in Russia'. Before long, though, in private he would be laying the same charge of egotism against the anarchists of the West.

Eventually, Kropotkin would secure Michel representation for her lectures, but only by undertaking to be present as her translator; for the moment her English was too accented to be readily intelligible. In the next scheme for which Michel solicited his help, however, his prestige and that of the other prominent names in English socialism that he brought on board could provide an immediate benefit.

The suggestion that Michel found a school to be run on anarchist principles came initially from Auguste Coulon, a half-French, half-Irish member of the Socialist League. It appealed to her immediately as a project that would allow her to reconcile the political engagement and nurturing sentimentality that formed the two poles of her identity; a year after the first progressive private school in England had been founded at Abbotsholme, the moment seemed propitious for the creation of a truly libertarian institution. It would serve those who wanted 'to keep their children out of the hands of those professors of the modern school divinely inspired and licensed by the state, who teach, consciously or unconsciously, the doctrine of popular sacrifice to the power of the state and to the profit of the privileged class'. And who better to partner her than Coulon himself, who boasted scholarly credentials as the co-author of *Hossfeld's New and Successful Method for Learning the German Language*?

A prospectus was printed, and premises were taken at the heart of the French enclave, in Fitzroy Square, whose grand houses, which had been prime addresses for the aristocracy a century earlier, were now subdivided into a maze of cramped rental rooms and workshops or else occupied by affluent British bohemians. Walter Crane provided the woodcut for the school's letterhead, and a quotation from Bakunin was prominently displayed: 'The whole education of children and their instruction must be founded on the scientific development of reason, not on that of faith; on the development of personal dignity and independence ... and above all on respect for humanity.' Morris served on the five-man steering committee along with Malatesta, Kropotkin's involvement assuaging any unease Morris felt at the involvement of Coulon, who was becoming known as one of the more inflammatory contributors to the *Commonweal* for his 'International Notes'.

Michel would teach the piano, Coulon classes in French and German, while among other members of staff was listed a young Margaret McMillan, who in years to come would become the great pioneer of progressive schooling in England. There appeared to be good cause for optimism. Yet on the very day that Michel wrote out the order for the new school's stationery – '6 boxes of pens; 4 bottles of ordinary ink; 6 dozen pen cases' – the British steamer SS *Utopia* sank off Gibraltar with catastrophic loss of life, after hitting submerged rocks. She should perhaps have taken the ship's fate as an omen, and looked for the unseen hazards in her own project, for Coulon had been on the British Special Branch payroll for three months under the code name 'Pyatt', a curious approximation of the name of Rochefort's great journalistic rival of twenty years earlier, Félix Pyat, who had died in 1889. As to his possible relationship with foreign forces, there would later be much speculation. One thing is certain: during Coulon's breaks from teaching, when he stepped out into Fitzroy Square to chat with the neighbours such as the Battolas or perhaps greet Constance Garnett, his actions were rarely disinterested.

*

The Special Branch of the Metropolitan Police had been founded specifically as a corrective to the kind of provocative intrigues and manipulation in which Edward Jenkinson had engaged as head of Section D during the mid-1880s, with near-catastrophic consequences. Since then it had become a victim of its own success, the threat from Fenianism greatly diminished by its efforts in that area, with home-grown socialism hardly a compelling enough replacement to justify the cost of the Branch's work to protect against subversion.

Already, in the previous four years, Special Branch had lost a fifth of its staff, its numbers falling from thirty-one to twenty-five at a time when Britain's foreign spy networks were also being scaled back. Investment in the apparatus of state security was falling across Europe, with the 'secret funds' assigned by the French police cut by half in 1890, and only a belated sleight of hand by the Belgian interior minister preventing a three-quarters reduction in the budget of its Sûreté. Further cuts in Special Branch funding were imminent, unless a pressing danger could be identified. In the Britain of the early 1890s, the greatest risk of sedition appeared to lie in the gathering tide of strikes, but unless labour activism could be shown to entail some element of violent conspiracy, a force such as Special Branch had little legitimate role in its supervision.

The Continent provided clear examples of how the need for their involvement might be made apparent. In 1887, just as a series of general strikes in Belgium was about to force concessions from a strongly Catholic and deeply corrupt government, the high moral ground occupied by the socialist leader Alfred Defuisseaux crumbled beneath him when an associate called Léonard Pourbaix persuaded him to write an ultimatum to the government. The document was manipulated for publication so as to appear to threaten civil war and, following a series of bomb attacks, the socialist party was utterly discredited. Pourbaix himself, it would transpire, had supplied the dynamite, after a secret midnight consultation with the chief of the cabinet. Similarly in France, an escalation of violence around strikes and demonstrations on May Day 1891, provoked by police heavy-handedness, helped create a general sense of emergency, while Landesen's contrivance of the bomb plot in 1890 had stiffened the case for French police action against foreign émigrés.

That the British government should be inhibited about such an approach was unsurprising, in light of its past experience with Jenkinson and the Fenians, but concern for public opinion and its patriotic belief in the virtues of liberalism in matters of policing was a more decisive factor. Lord Salisbury's administration felt obliged to proceed cautiously, while the prime minister himself appeared sceptical about the true extent of the danger laid out in the Russian Memorandum and the reliability of information of conspiracies forwarded from the Okhrana. There were those in Special Branch, however, who felt a visceral antipathy towards anyone or anything that challenged the status quo in Britain, or even the authority of despotic foreign states, and found their own government's timidity deeply frustrating. The most capable and determined among them was William Melville, the rising star of the Branch, whose knowledge of the French language and postings to Paris and the Channel ports over the previous few years would have made him amply aware of the machinations of Rachkovsky and others.

Calculating, perhaps, that his actions if successful, would receive the tacit approval of his superiors, in April 1891 Melville took matters into his own hands. Eschewing the usual diplomatic channels, and apparently keeping both Chief Inspector Littlechild and Assistant Commissioner Anderson in the dark, he wrote to warn the Italian police that Malatesta had left with a companion for Rome, to involve himself in the disturbances planned there for May Day. Then, only a few weeks later, he went much further in conniving with a foreign force. 'I have made the acquaintance of Inspector Melville of the political police,' wrote the Okhrana go-between, an expatriate French journalist named Jolivard to his contact 'Richter'. 'He has offered me his services complaining that his superiors at Scotland Yard act too feebly with regard to the nihilists. *Do not pass up on this chance*, my friend, it will not come your way again.' It was, indeed, a proposition that 'Richter', in reality none other than Rachkovsky himself, could not afford to decline.

In Auguste Coulon, Special Branch had an informant whose activities over the previous few years might have been conceived with the very purpose of effective provocation. His involvement with the Socialist League had begun with the Dublin Branch in the mid-1880s, and he had cemented his position among the hard-line 'individualist' members during the Paris Congress of 1889, when anarchism's moment of glory had seemed near at hand. It was then, presumably, that he had met Louise Michel, but it was the impressionable young anarchists from provincial England that were most beguiled by his outspoken beliefs: men such as Joseph Deakin of Walsall, and Frederick Charles Slaughter, a native of Norwich.

The latter, known by 1891 simply as Fred Charles, having dropped his surname as too sanguinary, offered an object lesson in the career of a new breed of British anarchist. Won over to anarchism by one of Mowbray's speeches, which Charles had heard when serving as a special constable policing the crowd in his home town, he had begun his transformation by joining the local branch of the Socialist League. The political education it offered broadened his horizons and the trip to Paris opened his eyes to a wider world of international brotherhood and possibility. The next step on his journey of self-discovery was to Sheffield, under the saintly tutelage of Edward Carpenter, whom he had met at the congress. Whilst there, though, most notably during Carpenter's lengthy absences on winter vacation to warmer climes, his ideological drift towards 'individualist' extremism had accelerated, thanks in part to the paternal influence of Malatesta's friend from Buenos Aires, Dr John Creaghe.

Having seen too many Europeans arrive in Argentina full of hope, only to be ruthlessly exploited, Creaghe arrived back in England declaring that 'at last the emigration fad is thoroughly played out', and promptly established the *Sheffield Anarchist* newspaper. Its first edition called for a general strike the following January. The policy was consistent with his past work in South America, but the rhetoric soon began to shade into something rather different. 'They'll all be making final arrangements for the revolution! Which Brown [another of the group] says is to come off some time in January next,' wrote Carpenter's lover, George Hukin. There was little Carpenter could do, however, as he cruised through the Suez Canal, admiring the local talent: 'These darkies are very taking – some of them, very good-looking and lively – though you have to be careful as some are regular devils.' And his visit to India and Ceylon was essential, he had written, 'to renovate my faith, and unfold the frozen buds which civilisation & fog have nipped!'

Whilst Carpenter's weekly visits to the guru Gnani Ramaswamy were doubtless enlightening, the susceptible Fred Charles was left to the tender mercies of the hardliners. Sacked from his job for unpunctuality, the spring saw Charles move on to Walsall, in the industrial heart of the West Midlands, where Coulon, no less, had helped find him work as a clerk and translator at Gameson's iron foundry. He was back visiting Sheffield in May and was perhaps still there a few weeks later when Creaghe and his acolytes tricked their way into a public meeting addressed by the African explorer and colonialist Henry Morton Stanley, heckling him and selling satirical pamphlets to the jingoistic crowd. But it was the darkening tone of Creaghe's pronouncements, and of those who visited him in Sheffield, rather than brief moments of frivolity, that characterised the following months.

'If you can find 15 or 20 to join me,' Creaghe wrote in an article for *Commonweal*, 'I promise you we will make an impression on the enemy and do more to make recruits to our cause than all the rest who only preach and write verses'; in the same edition, Charles Mowbray referred to the 'determined men' needed, and clarified that they must be 'acquainted with the power which nineteenth-century civilisation has placed within their reach'. It was a clear call for dynamite, which made nonsense of Creaghe's pretence of taking offence at William Morris' belief that anarchists were all advocates of conspiracy. The only questions were when exactly the conspiracy would come to a head, and who would direct it.

During the latter months of 1891, Mowbray, the equally incendiary Henry Samuels and Coulon himself were all frequent visitors to Sheffield; in all likelihood, only Carpenter's return prevented the city turning into a centre of violent action. Coulon, though, had been quietly building his influence in Walsall too, with Deakin and Charles already in place. Soon after Melville had made his clandestine offer to collaborate with Rachkovsky, Coulon would find the final piece to complete the puzzle and his provocation would be ready to be set in motion.

It was events in France on May Day 1891 that delivered Victor Cailes into his hands. At Clichy, a western suburb of Paris, attempts to disperse a demonstration drove the mob into the town's bars where the seditious toasts raised to the spirit of revolution provoked the police to initiate a shoot-out; the three ringleaders arrested were promptly sentenced to a total of eight years in prison. Meanwhile at Fourmies, a mining town close to the Belgian border, twitchy troops opened fire during a stand-off with marching strikers, killing at least nine, four of whom were women – including the first to die, while pleading with the troops – and only three aged more than twenty-four. Finding himself a wanted man after delivering an incendiary speech in Nantes on the same day, Cailes, a stoker by trade, fled to London.

Ascertaining his new friend's vengeful state of mind, and perhaps supplying Cailes with the copy of the bomb-making manual *L'Indicateur Anarchiste* that was later produced as evidence against him, a solicitous Coulon promptly arranged work for him as a brush-maker at Westley's Factory in Walsall. A foreigner a long way from home, Cailes could not have been more grateful, all the more so for the introduction to Charles and Deakin, and over the summer the three new anarchist friends went about their usual business until, in October, the time came for them to repay Coulon's kindnesses.

The letter came from a mysterious source calling himself 'Degnai' and was addressed to Cailes, but the enclosed design for an egg-shaped bomb was to be realised at the foundry where Charles worked. Deakin was clearly concerned about the new turn of events, and somewhat suspicious, but a letter from Coulon in London soothed and reassured him. The bomb, as Coulon appeared already to have made clear to Charles and Cailes, was for use in Russia, against whose despotic rulers such methods were surely warranted.

None of the three Walsall anarchists, it must be presumed, had heard of Landesen's epic provocation of 1890, although as the time approached for the bomb's completion they did show some wariness. When Jean Battola, Coulon's and Michel's neighbour in Fitzroy Square assigned the role of 'Degnai', had arrived in Walsall to collect the 'infernal machine' earlier in December, the Special Branch surveillance team had to watch him return empty-handed. Their frustration must have been compounded by the announcement at the end of the month of a reduction in the unit's budget that would entail the loss of four constables' jobs. Assistant Commissioner Anderson expressed the view that further cuts would be rash, but he needed evidence. Then on 6 January, Deakin caught the train to London to probe whether the conspirators were being observed. Melville's men pounced as he left the station for the Autonomie Club, a brown paper parcel containing chloroform that he was carrying sufficient to warrant his arrest under the Explosives Act of 1882. His Walsall associates were promptly apprehended too, along with the foundry worker charged with fabricating the device, while Battola was taken into custody a week later. Coulon was left untouched.

A week earlier, on the last day of 1891, a young anarchist poet and friend of Oscar Wilde called John Bartlas had fired a pistol at the Houses of Parliament. It was a futile gesture of the kind that seemed set to characterise anarchism in Britain: a movement full of men who had often been known to take off their jackets but never to fight, as David Nicoll would later remark of one of his colleagues at *Commonweal*. That perception was changed at a stroke by the Walsall bomb plot. Anarchist terror had come to Britain, and if anyone was in any doubt about the scale and reach of its ambitions, they need only have listened to the reading material that came to light at the trial as having been in the possession of the accused.

The Feast of the Opera offered a description of how to plant a bomb that would bring down the house, and then there were the blood-drenched ravings of Parmeggiani's short-lived *L'International*, or the rough imperatives of *Fight or Starve*. There was even the document entitled *The Means of Emancipation* that Cailes himself had written, or at least transcribed: 'to arrive at a complete emancipation of humanity, brutal force is indispensable . . . it is absolutely necessary to burn the churches, palaces, convents, barracks, police stations, lawyers' offices, fortresses, prisons, and to destroy entirely all that has lived till now by business work without contributing to it.' No one seemed to care that at least two of the publications were widely said to be incitements funded by the French police; all were taken as proof that Walsall was part of what *The Times* termed 'a great system' of terroristic activity, stamped with 'the lust of bloodshed'.

It was clear who gained from Coulon's subterfuge. Special Branch's funding was restored and Melville's ascendancy assured; excused by the judge from answering questions relating to his relationship with Coulon, his high-stakes gamble had paid off. Rachkovsky, meanwhile, prepared to publish a pamphlet lambasting the English for allying themselves with the nihilists. 'Bearing in mind . . . the general indignation about the "dynamite-heroes", into which category the nihilists fall,' he commented gleefully to Durnovo, the interior minister and his ultimate superior in St Petersburg, 'our pamphlet will cause a great stir; and it will be the first step of my agitation.' Coulon himself received an immediate bonus from Special Branch of £4 with his weekly pay raised to £2, and was able to continue his double life, suspected by some among the anarchists but not wholly ostracised, yet giving anonymous interviews to the press from his office in Balham in which he claimed to be in the service of the 'international police'.

There were losers too, with the greatest damage surely suffered by the British sense of justice and fair play, in which the public took considerable if often misplaced pride. In a stark example of the abuses that the hysteria surrounding the Walsall trial made possible, a completely innocent inventor from Birmingham spent several weeks in a police cell on account of an innovative device he had designed for blowing up rabbit warrens. Corrosive precedents were being set. Inevitably, though, it was the leading anarchists who experienced the antagonism most fiercely.

Louise Michel had been contentedly teaching her classes, 'sitting in the midst of a group of very intelligent-looking but dirty children,' as shocked visitors remarked, with the single word 'L'Anarchie' written across the blackboard for a history lesson and drawn below it graphic representations of the hanging of the Chicago martyrs and the massacres of the Bloody Week. According to Michel, and to her obvious distress, their enlightened education, free of capitalist indoctrination, came to an abrupt end when bombs were discovered in the basement. 'There is nothing so terrible as to feel oneself surrounded by enemies, without being able to guess either their identity or purpose,' she confided to a friend.

But not even her closest friends could be trusted: the Special Branch ledgers recorded a tip-off from someone intimate with her that 'there is dynamite in London', while a French agent confidently reported that Michel's companion, Charlotte Vauvelle, was an Orléanist spy. And although Coulon was probably responsible for the planting of the bombs at the school, Special Branch knew of a Russian informant among the teachers. Curiously, not long after Rachkovsky informed St Petersburg that the next stage of his agitation was to involve incriminating the nihilists in London as counterfeiters of money, a package of counterfeiting equipment was deposited with

Michel, which she and Vauvelle wisely threw on to a rubbish tip. In the unlikely event that the Okhrana was indeed targeting Michel directly, the explanation may have lain in vindictiveness on Rachkovsky's part towards a woman who sneered at France's developing relationship with Russia, insiting that 'you can't have an alliance between free people and slaves'.

Insofar as Rachkovsky hoped to use terrorism to inflate popular opprobrium of the Russian nihilists, however, in Paris the anarchists appeared intent on doing his job for him.

*

Ever since May Day 1891, an appetite for vengeance had taken a firm hold among the most militant French anarchists, inspired by the example of their colleagues in Spain, who had exploded two bombs in the port city of Cadiz. Alongside the fifteen black flags of anarchist mourning paraded in the funeral procession for those killed at Fourmies had been thirty-two coloured red for revolution, while deeper grievances too were resurfacing. A month later, the inauguration of Sacré-Coeur reopened old wounds, as the French Federation of Free Thought indicated by condemning the ceremony as 'an odious Jesuitical comedy played out on Montmartre in honour of the 35,000 victims of May 1871'. Only the intervention of baton-wielding police prevented a carnivalesque protest featuring a great red crown carried by horsemen from reaching its climax: the draping of a vast red flag over the half-finished basilica. It would not be long before a loosely affiliated band of young anarchist discontents would translate the symbolism of the blood-red banners into violent retribution.

François Koenigstein, better known as Ravachol, had carried out his first known criminal act only a fortnight after the fateful May Day, and it had been a macabre affair. A spurious gesture against authority, the only rational explanation for the twenty-three-year-old's exhumation of Countess de la Rochetaille's rotting corpse was the hope of retrieving jewels buried with her. It was a chilling act that seeped into the public consciousness of a morbid and moribund society. The Café du Néant, opened in Montmartre a few months later, would allow its clientele to sample mortality, sipping absinthe while seated at a coffin lid in the Room of Intoxication, or watching a live human turned to dust in the Room of Disintegration by means of a Pepper's ghost trick. By then, though, the real terror generated by Ravachol would be too immediate for easy sublimation.

Neither the desecration of the countess' grave, nor his subsequent murder of Jacques Brunel, a ninety-five-year-old hermit in the tiny Loire town of

Chambles, had sated Ravachol's appetite for spectacular revenge on a society that had, he believed, deeply wronged him. The spur to fulfilling his destiny seems to have been provided when an insurrection in the wine-producing Spanish city of Jerez on 8 January 1892 had seen around fifty peasants descend on the prison there to liberate friends who had been hideously tortured during interrogation over the bomb attacks of the previous year. The response ordered by Prime Minister Canovas was brutal and wide-spread, culminating on 10 February with the garrotting of four supposed ringleaders: strapped to seats, facing a crowd of soldiers and spectators, a rod was inserted into a cord looped around their neck and slowly rotated to strangulate them. Slower than hanging, far less clinical than the guillo-tine, it was a punishment that spoke of a governing elite who viewed the anarchists as little better than vermin, fit for extermination.

Outrage greeted the news in radical Paris, with one anarchist conclave agreeing that between two and five million deaths and ten to twenty years of warfare were necessary to bring about a revolution. With thoughts of the Clichy confrontation fresh in his mind too, Ravachol could wait only four days, until the feast of the early Christian martyr St Valentine, on 14 February. Then, together with his eighteen-year-old acolyte Charles Simon, known as 'Biscuit', along with the humpbacked anarchist Théodule Meunier and two or three others, Ravachol led an expedition to raid an arsenal at Soisy-sous-Etiolles to the south of Paris, from where the band succeeded in carrying off a sizeable haul of high explosives.

The motive had now found the means, and on a scale that made possible a campaign of terror to rock the French state and its neighbours and shock even the least alarmist prognosticators in the press. Far out into the suburbs, police raids scoured known anarchist hideouts, but without success. Ravachol, having gone to ground just outside the city, bided his time while fabricating the raw materials into timed or fused devices. Two weeks later, a half-cocked explosion, set by one of the Soisy band, blackened the front of Princess de Sagan's town house: either her association by birth with Spain, or by marriage with the glittering world of French high society, had placed her in the firing line. For the start of the real campaign of terror, however, Paris had to wait another fortnight, while Ravachol and 'Biscuit' carried out planning and reconnaissance of targets deemed culpable in some manner for the fate of France's May Day martyrs.

Ravachol's first bomb exploded outside the apartment of Monsieur Benoît, the judge who had presided over the case brought against the Clichy demonstrators; the ground momentarily shook on boulevard Saint-Germain and a few windows shattered, but without causing injury. Then,

four days later on 15 March, a second device, planted by Meunier, struck
the Lobau barracks near the Hôtel de Ville, home to the troops who had
suppressed the Clichy demonstration. It was also the base from which
Thiers' troops had marched out to Versailles, almost exactly twenty-one
years earlier, precipitating the creation of the Commune.

It would be another ten years before the painter Maximilien Luce
could dredge up and place on canvas the image of Bloody Week that
had haunted him since he had witnessed its horrors at first hand as an
eight-year-old: the corpses piled in uncannily desolate streets. Already,
though, his anarchist friends were retracing the old battle lines in stark
new terms, justifying the persistent fear in Paris that, just beneath the
surface of everyday life, the old insurrectionist spirit was threatening to
rise again. Where a generation before the Communards had faced death
together on the barricades, chemistry had now made the means of
waging war against authority readily available, and martyrdom had
become a matter of individual choice.

As if to allow time for the Parisians to confront their own darkest
imaginings, Ravachol paused for nearly another two weeks before committing his next outrage. This time the target was the home of the public
prosecutor in the Clichy case, the explosives were hidden in a suitcase,
and the injuries and devastation caused by the larger bomb far more
extensive. For a brief moment, as the evening newspapers appeared on
the stands, Parisians must have felt that terror had become endemic: the
new condition of their lives. Already, though, Ravachol's campaign had
been doomed by his own pride and boastfulness. Taking lunch in the
Café Véry on boulevard Magenta, he had been overheard by a waiter
bragging about his recent exploits; when the waiter next caught sight of
him in the street, he tipped off the authorities. In the ensuing chase
Ravachol injured one of his police pursuers with a shot from a revolver,
before eventually being wrestled to the ground.

Yet even with Ravachol in custody, the fear did not abate. With some
reports claiming that up to 1,000 pounds of dynamite were still unac-
counted for, it was now the turn of the Parisian bourgeoisie to feel besieged
in their own city, as the defenders of the Commune once had. 'They
dared not go to the theatre, to restaurants, to the fashionable shops in
the rue de la Paix, to ride in the Bois where there were anarchists behind
every tree. The most terrible rumours ran round every morning: the
anarchists had undermined the churches and . . . were robbing and
murdering rich American ladies in the Champs-Elysées,' recalled one
English visitor, while Goncourt commented that, so empty was the city,

it might 'have been devastated by a plague'. Communards and anarchists, powerless and marginalised for so long, could not help but feel a secret pleasure at the effect Ravachol had created. As a personality cult began to develop around him, even Elisée Reclus would write admiringly of Ravachol's 'courage, his goodness, his greatness of soul, and the generosity with which he pardons his enemies, and indeed those who informed on him'.

The same could not be said for those of Ravachol's friends still at liberty, whose silence since his capture had maintained the air of menace. Then, the day before the trial of Ravachol and 'Biscuit' began, Meunier unleashed the most deadly attack yet. His target was the Café Véry, crowded with diners; his purpose to punish the friends of the waiter, Lhérot, who had betrayed Ravachol to the police. Sauntering in for a drink at the bar, the fuse of a bomb already smouldering in a bag that he discreetly deposited, Meunier had only just paid and left when a huge explosion tore the establishment apart, killing both the patron and a customer, and seriously injuring many others. A self-generating cycle of official repression and anarchist retribution was now in motion.

The views of the veteran anarchists became markedly more muted. In conversation with Coulon about the merits or otherwise of nitroglyc-erine for 'social therapy', Louise Michel was persuaded to admit that 'in principle, yes, it is possible to use force for good purposes. That's how the revolution will come about.' Judged by her usual standards, however, it amounted to disapproval. Kropotkin too was increasingly critical, insisting that 'a structure built on centuries of history cannot be destroyed with a few kilos of explosives'. Previously he had deferred to the conscience of the perpetrators of terror, often victims of a corrupt society. Yet faced with an angry young Frenchman called Auguste Vaillant – who in order to escape from servitude in South America as an indentured *peon* had braved the muddy shallows and violent eddies of the River Salado on a raft of his own construction, chancing his luck against the paramilitaries posted along the banks to capture any fugitives – the mild old Russian was said to have spoken 'with great emphasis against physical force and even against revolution brought about by violence'.

Ravachol himself, however, had grasped better than others that in the service of anarchist propaganda nothing carried a greater currency than his own image. A handsome, manly but slick-haired dandy, he was conscious of the effect upon his looks wrought by the inevitable rough treatment dealt out in the police cells to any would-be cop-killer. When Alphonse Bertillon appeared with a camera to snap a '*portrait parlé*' for his anthropometric collection, Ravachol resisted fiercely. 'Why?' asked Bertillon, with a disingenuous professionalism that made his later tractability to corruption all too plausible, 'I have to do this. It is part of my duty.' 'Well, my face is not such a pretty sight, is it?' replied Ravachol, and Bertillon relented, realising perhaps that the prisoner's bruised features would not reflect well on the police who were holding him.

When the official photograph was eventually produced, its subject did indeed appear more presentable: dangerously so, to those looking for an anarchist icon. Artistic impressions published in the anarchist press and elsewhere, alongside extraordinary encomiums from the literary world and transcriptions of the prisoner's own eloquent invective, fixed his public image as the self-sacrificing hero of a society that had lost its way. 'Judge me, members of the jury,' Ravachol told the court, 'but if you have understood me, in judging me, judge all the unfortunates that destitution, allied with natural pride, has made criminals and whom wealth, even just ease, would have made honest people.'

His sentence was surprisingly lenient: hard labour for himself and an absent 'Biscuit' and acquittal for the other three defendants. The novelist Octave Mirbeau, already an eager contributor to the anarchist press, wondered whether the jurors had been afraid 'to kill a man whose mysterious vengeance will not wholly die with him'. The assizes court of provincial Montbrison, however, promptly rectified the error, providing the French anarchists with the martyr denied them by the Paris judiciary. That Ravachol ultimately went to the guillotine for the murder of an ancient hermit did nothing to hinder his lionisation, and the anarchism that he preached until the very moment the blade fell was immediately taken up by myriad other voices. 'After three quarters of a century of dreams, should the last word be left to Deibler [the executioner]?' demanded Charles Malato, the son of a New Caledonian exile who was well acquainted with Ravachol's co-conspirators.

Reclus derived hope from Ravachol's death. 'I am one of those who see in Ravachol a hero with a rare grandeur of spirit,' he wrote to Félix Nadar, the photographer and balloonist, telling his old friend that 'We live from day to day, happy and confident, listening to the great blast of the revolution which is advancing.' A striking feature of many opinions expressed about Ravachol, though, was the appropriation of religious language and symbolism, echoing that applied to the terrorists in Russia a decade earlier, but coming carelessly close to blasphemy. 'In this time of cynicism and irony, a saint has been born to us,' wrote Paul Adam,

the Symbolist novelist and amateur mystic, expressing a common sentiment, while others eulogised Ravachol as a 'violent Christ'.

The defining image of the moment was provided by an iconic ink
sketch by Félix Vallotton for the *Revue Blanche*, which depicted Ravachol
in a muscular refusal to submit to his tormenters, his hair wild and eyes
staring, white shirt stripped from his shoulders as the prison guards force
his straining neck down towards the board of the guillotine: the anarchists' answer to a meek Jesus stumbling under the weight of his cross,
on the way to Calvary.

★

'The old world is collapsing under the weight of its own crimes, and
is itself lighting the fuse on the bomb that will destroy everything,'
Mirbeau wrote in the anarchist literary and artistic newspaper *L'Endehors*
on the day of Ravachol's execution, warning that 'There are certain
corpses that walk again.' The phrase was an exact echo, whether unconscious or not, of that written by Henri Rochefort about Boulanger the
previous September, after the putative dictator had shot himself dead
on the grave of his recently deceased mistress. But while the terrible
'bomb' to which Mirbeau referred would 'contain neither gunpowder
nor dynamite . . . [but] comprised compassion and an idea; two forces
that nothing can withstand', Rochefort longed to see a more cataclysmic
fate befall a French Establishment that he held responsible for his persecution and exile.

'He dreams of the death of Constans,' his hireling editor on
L'Intransigeant had written in 1891, 'and all his letters say that he wants
to kill the minister [of the interior], no matter how, or by what means.'
Stewing in paranoia, with an infinite capacity for delusional self-
righteousness, Rochefort was convinced that his enemy Constans would
arrange his murder if ever he set foot again in his homeland, and considered his own murderousness a just and reasonable response. But the
shame and humiliation produced by a journalistic exposé was Rochefort's
favoured means of attack, and his hand can surely be detected in the
revelations about the scandalous sale by Constans, for personal profit, of
Indo-Chinese antiquities that had been purloined during France's recent
colonial adventures in the Far East.

As the French political Establishment struggled to suppress the far
greater scandal of the widespread corruption surrounding the collapse
of the Panama Canal Company, which had already seen official investigations begun into Gustave Eiffel and the ninety-six-year-old national hero

Lesseps, it was little wonder that agents of the French police watched Rochefort so closely on his surreptitious trips to Belgium. The marquis' ostensible purpose there was to gamble in the casinos at Ostende or else to fight duels, banned in England and France but possible in the nearby sand dunes, against those whom he had defamed or who had slandered him. And whilst spies noted the packet of documents slipped to him at Boulanger's funeral in Brussels, Rochefort himself would later boast that he regularly shook off those who tailed him to make secret forays to Paris, no doubt in search of damning evidence to use against his enemies.

With three Jewish promoters in the frame for organising the gargantuan bribes paid out by the Panama Canal Company to cover up its losses, one of whom was Baron Jacques de Reinarch, uncle of Rochefort's bête noire, the scent of an anti-Semitic scoop had him salivating. But more than that, as the Third Republic teetered on the brink, nothing could have delighted him more than to harness his countrymen's disaffection in order finally to drive it to destruction. It was an ambition shared, of course, by the anarchists, to whom he now reached out.

Money supplied by Rochefort to Louise Michel, which trickled down to those in the colony she deemed most worthy, accompanied perhaps with an acknowledgement of her affluent friend's largesse, may have helped restore his reputation with anyone willing to take a pragmatic view of his past unreliability and egregious Boulangism. Michel, though, while still voluble in her denunciation of injustice and calls for revolution, had increasingly retreated from the intractable human mess of the here and now, for which she could offer only the same old angry nostrums, into a world of animals and the imagination. Her home provided a sanctuary for a menagerie of unfortunates, including a parrot that was reputed to squawk out a parody of her choicest invective; meanwhile she conjured Verne-like visions of the world to come: a global federated society, inhabiting 'underwater cities, contained in submarine ships as large as whole provinces; cities suspended in mid-air, perhaps orbiting with the seasons'. Rochefort indulged her but she was of little use to him. Instead, by hiring Charles Malato as his secretary, Rochefort bought himself direct access to the core of the 'individualist' faction of anarchists. His memoirs are uncharacteristically reticent on the subject, the extent of his dealings with the extremists only glimpsed from police reports, and the reason for them even then obscure. Rather, it is a work of fiction published fifteen years later but looking back to the early 1890s that most vividly evokes Rochefort's clandestine activities at the time.

The clear identification of Rochefort with the sinister 'Comrade X' in Joseph Conrad's short story 'The Informer' surely came close to breaching Britain's libel laws. 'A revolutionary writer whose savage irony has laid bare the rottenness of the most respectable institutions', the character is a cynical, nihilistic coward, described as having 'scalped every venerated head, and . . . mangled at the stake of his wit every received opinion and every recognised principle of conduct and policy'. Comrade X is described as having been born into the nobility and 'could have called himself Vicomte X de la Z if he chose', collects exquisite antiques and works of art, eats bombe glacée and sips champagne in the finest restaurants. Conrad might as well have mentioned the marquis de Rochefort-Luçay's recent endorsement of a proprietary brand of bath salts.

Steeped in the underworld of the London anarchist émigrés, Conrad had published his early poems on the presses of the *Torch* newspaper, while his friend Ford Madox Ford was close to Kropotkin, Kravchinsky and Morris. The impressive factual detail that Conrad included in his stories of this milieu makes his insistence that he drew purely on his imagination, understandable in a novelist, demonstrably disingenuous. When his narrator claims to know about Comrade X 'as a certainty what the guardians of social order in Europe had at most only suspected. Or simply guessed at', his insight need not be dismissed as simple authorial invention. The great secret? That 'this extreme writer has been also . . . the mysterious unknown Number One of desperate conspiracies, suspected and unsuspected, matured or baffled'.

What, though, was the nature of the conspiracies in which Rochefort may have played such a role? Events would soon enough reveal their terrible outcome, but beyond the marquis himself and the anarchists to whom Malato introduced him, it was his trips to the Belgian coast that may provide the best clue as to the third man. For it was there, with the full knowledge and cooperation of the Belgian Sûreté, whose officers Rochefort was said to tip off in advance of any duel that might threaten his health, that Rachkovsky's star agent Landesen had set about establishing himself under a new identity: Arkady Harting.

After many more twists and turns in his extraordinary career, years later Harting would take over the ownership of one of the casinos where, in the early 1890s, Rochefort played the roulette wheels and laid his bets at baccarat. Now, though, Harting was running a game with far higher stakes, in which he could doubtless have found a seat for the polemical French aristocrat with the anarchist friends.

19

Wicked Laws

London and Paris 1892–1894

Rochefort's trips from London to Belgium in 1892 ran against the tide. Until recently the boat train from France had often carried artists and activists on *'un go back'*, or day return to London, the police crackdown in Paris following Ravachol's bombings had now made single fares the rule. Meunier, a wanted man for the Lobau barracks and Café Véry bombings, and Jean-Pierre François, who had been named as his accomplice, on flimsy grounds had already gone to ground in the British capital. Now anyone who feared being swept up in the prefecture's broadening search for co-conspirators and the missing dynamite, or who had got wind of the French government's decision to adopt the old plan drawn up by Boulanger to intern 100,000 suspected anarchists in the event of war, planned their escape to England.

Prominent figures like Zo d'Axa, the founding editor of the avant-garde cultural and political magazine *L'EnDehors*, departed as early as April 1892, hastily handing over the running of the magazine to an inexperienced office junior called Emile Henry. With Charles Malato tempting others with the idea that they could 'jump on the train illegally at Bougainville – buy a Dieppe–Newhaven ticket', the only anarchists left in Paris by the late summer were those who did not have so much as a guilty conscience to hide. And even some of them may have been persuaded to think again by the arrest and imprisonment of Parmeggiani, caught on a clandestine foray to Paris that August, although his crimes of expropriation, attempted murder and incitement to terroristic slaughter were all too tangible.

'Enough of organisation . . . let's busy ourselves with chemistry and manufacture: bombs, dynamite and other explosives are far more capable than rifles and "barricades" of destroying the present state of things, and above all to save our own precious blood.' Such was the cowardly and vicious doctrine preached by *L'International*, established in London by Parmeggiani with Bordes, the ex-manager of *Père Peinard* who would shortly be revealed as a provocateur in the pay of the French police. Yet despite the newspaper's pillorying of Kropotkin and his ilk as 'papacy', 'flatfoots' and 'orators of the philosophical class', Louise Michel, Malatesta and others rallied to Parmeggiani's cause, protesting against his extradition to Italy and fund-raising to pay for a visit by his wife, with Rochefort a generous contributor.

'Oh great metropolis of Albion,' wrote Charles Malato in *The Delights of Exile*, a bittersweet evocation of the anarchists' life in London, 'your atmosphere is sometimes foggier than reason allows, your ale insipid and your cooking in general quite execrable, but you show respect for individuality and are welcoming to the émigrés.' With anarchist visitors like Parmeggiani to contend with, though, it was doubtful how long Britain could remain so tolerant. 'Be proud of these two qualities and keep them,' Malato urged Albion, but the warm welcome and the respect would soon run thin and cold.

The dispatch of the Sûreté's finest, Inspector Prosper-Isidore Houllier, to assist Scotland Yard in the hunt for Ravachol's accomplices had, for a while, provided the anarchists with some levity. Seemingly pursuing a personal mission to seek out the best of Britain's much-derided gastronomy, Houllier's fancy was particularly taken with the whitebait served at the Criterion, though he was partial as well to lunch in the gilded surroundings of the Café Royal. At least he could claim that they were both close to Piccadilly Circus, where he had tried to lure 'Biscuit', now going under the name of 'Quesnay', by posing as a *Figaro* reporter looking for an interview. Needless to say, his target failed to show: that Quesnay was the name of the French procurator general should have warned Houllier that he was being led a dance. But the French inspector appeared oblivious to how farce followed him around.

Turning their attention to Théodule Meunier, Houllier and Melville descended on Victor Richard's grocery store in Charlotte Street with the deputy director of the Sûreté, Fedée, in tow, chasing up a tip-off. Their informant, it seemed, was in on the joke. When the crack police team emerged empty-handed, a mob was waiting, and it took uniformed reinforcements to extract them, in scenes played out to the accompaniment of Zo d'Axa's barrel organ. Subsequently, Houllier and his Special Branch colleagues would chase around London after the vans belonging to a removals company mistakenly linked with the fugitives, while Melville donned the disguise of a hygiene inspector for some unsavoury undercover work, though dressing up seems always to have appealed to him. That the French took to calling Special Branch's favoured son 'Le Vil Melville' points to a more intimidating and nefarious side to his methods, however, confirmed by the decision of Richard, the grocer, and Brocher, who had convened the congress of 1881, to put the inspector himself under surveillance by the anarchists.

Melville's harassment of the anarchist émigrés in London did not stop after Meunier's flight to Canada and Houllier's departure, or with François's return to France, where he was soon arrested. Special Branch agents, often themselves 'in a state of beastly intoxication', according to anarchist accounts, resorted to bully-boy tactics, bribing gangs of 'corner boys' to attack speakers at public meetings before themselves weighing in with 'kicking and thumping'. Even the banana wine that the old Communard exiles to New Caledonia brewed as ersatz champagne, and then drank to their undying comradeship and to drown their sorrows, was prone to being impounded as a potentially explosive concoction.

Nor were the English anarchists excused Melville's rougher methods. After rejecting his offer of £500 to reveal the whereabouts of Meunier ('and that's just for starters'), Charles Mowbray's wife received a sinisterly worded warning from Melville that 'It'll be no joke when your children are howling from hunger.' He was true to his word a few weeks later when, hours after her death, he arrested Mowbray, leaving the infants alone in the house with their mother's corpse. The grounds for Mowbray's arrest were provided by an article published in *Commonweal* concerning the miscarriage of justice in the Walsall case, which asserted that 'Jesuit Home Secretary Matthews, Inspector Melville, and Coulon are the principal actors and two of them must die'. Melville's primary target, though, was the newspaper's co-editor David Nicoll, whom Sergeant Sweeney of Special Branch would testify to having heard deliver the threat verbally during a public meeting in Hyde Park.

Not only had Nicoll dared to challenge the official account of Special Branch's activities in Walsall but he also took every opportunity to publicise his suspicions of provocation and entrapment. In a likely attempt by Special Branch to intimidate him into stopping the dissemination of uncomfortable truths, he had already been arrested shortly after the Walsall debacle for defaming the queen: a charge so ludicrous that a local councillor had felt compelled to stand bail for him. But in court this time neither Sweeney's admission that he had noted down Nicoll's speech from memory only, half an hour after the event, nor Nicoll's insistence to the jury that 'anarchists in the country [are] quiet, peaceable people.

Anarchism [does] not necessarily spell dynamite' cut any ice. The eighteen-month sentence he received must have come as a relief to Melville, who may have had more personal reasons for his vindictiveness towards Nicoll.

Since William Morris' withdrawal from the editorial board of the *Commonweal* in 1890, the tight-knit group of 'individualists' whose wearisome advocacy of violent means forced Morris' depature, had grad-ually turned on one another. Accusations of treachery flew, with Samuels, Mowbray and Coulon all the object of Nicoll's suspicions. What plots were 'Lady' Mowbray and Melville concocting when they were seen drinking together? And what was Henry Samuels thinking of, using his impressionable young brother-in-law, Martial Bourdin, to circulate pamphlets filled with slanderous attacks on Nicoll that Coulon had printed? Inevitably, those Nicoll accused turned the tables on him with counter-accusations, and Frank Kitz's uncharacteristic decision to embezzle the newspaper's funds and flee town left Nicoll isolated and vulnerable.

Already psychologically fragile, the pressures plunged Nicoll into a state of mental turmoil, engendering a paranoia that provided his double-dealing colleagues with a convenient cover. Nicoll's suspicions about Coulon were, of course, well founded, but Mowbray too, Special Branch ledgers reveal, was 'organising secret shadowers of anarchists', while a French agent reported rumours that Mowbray had been involved in the Walsall provocation, working for Russia. Quite when Mowbray was recruited is unclear, but it appears to have been after his arrest by Melville, and may have been a condition of his early release. What, though, of Nicoll himself? Lacking in self-awareness to a painful degree, his own writings seem to hint at some buried connection with the Branch: the nervous crossing out of sensitive passages concerning Melville, or the reference to the inspector's advice that he should recognise in Coulon and Samuels his truest friends, in letters to those he thought he could trust. For all his denunciation of others, had he too, then, at some point been turned, as was suggested, and was he then victimised for betraying Melville's trust?

The notion that the entire *Commonweal* editorial team should, unbe-knownst to one another, have been informants may seem far-fetched, but it was standard practice for the Okhrana, at least, to secure two sources or more in every key group it was monitoring, in order to guarantee the reliability of their reports by means of comparison. As to Henry Samuels, future events would prove the pernicious nature of his influence. What, though, did it say about the effectiveness of Special Branch and Inspector

Melville, if a large proportion of the most incendiary figures in the anarchist movement were indeed in their employ? Handled with skill and integrity, the level of information such informants could provide would certainly vindicate official claims, offered in part as reassurance to foreign forces, that any action the anarchists planned would almost immediately become known to them. It could be counted a success too if they could seed uncertainty and dissent in the movement. Beyond that, though, there were obvious risks.

Even Chief Inspector Littlechild would soon have to admit that 'the "nark" is very apt to drift into an agent provocateur in his anxiety to secure a conviction'. Melville, by secretly offering his services to Rachkovsky, head of the foreign intelligence of Britain's foremost recent enemy on the international stage, had surely come close to treasonable behaviour. So far he had been lucky. The worst result that Walsall had produced was the conviction of hotheads on charges that, unprovoked, their behaviour is unlikely to have warranted: a gross abuse of the justice system but no more. However, were a repeat of the provocation that had brought about the arrest of the Walsall men to result instead in death or injury, the full moral obscenity of the strategy would surely be revealed. Certainly it was one with which neither the people nor the political leaders of the country Melville was meant to serve would have had any truck.

*

'We who, in our houses, seclude ourselves from the cry and sight of human sufferings, we are no judges of those who live in the midst of all this suffering . . . who are driven to despair,' had long been Kropotkin's default position with regard to those anarchists who lashed out at society, as Ravachol, Meunier and the others had done. Personally, though, he was quite explicit that he hated the explosions, concerned that as well as damaging the movement's reputation, they risked attracting criminal elements with no higher purpose, or else young men who craved the easy adrenaline rush of terrorism but lacked the stamina and dedication for the arduous task of building a broad and popular movement. Worse still, he feared that the effects of such violent acts might contaminate the revolution, when it happened, and propel it not towards a Utopia of freedom but instead into the hands of an oppressive dictatorship.

Both he and Malatesta were wary of the Autonomie Club anarchists, men and women of all nationalities who drank and talked amidst a fug of smoke, reclining on the comfortable chairs and sofas beneath portraits of such heroes as Ravachol and the Fenian, O'Donnell, and a poster proclaiming 'Death to Carnot', the French president. 'It is no longer a love for the human race that guides them, but the feeling of vendetta joined to a cult of an abstract idea, of a theoretical phantasm,' Malatesta wrote of Ravachol's disciples in his 1892 essay 'Nécessité et bases d'une entente', in what was an attempt to guide the young, headstrong anarchists away from the doctrine of dynamite. But the new generation of French anarchists, many of whom had flocked to London, were not so easily persuaded.

That summer, before handing over the onerous editorial duties on *L'EnDehors* to Félix Fénéon, the twenty-year-old Emile Henry used the pages of the newspaper to challenge Malatesta's argument. Taking issue with the Italian's assertion that 'hate does not produce love, and by hate one cannot remake the world', he replied that 'To those who say that hate does not give birth to love, I reply that it is love, human love, that often engenders hate.' From an early age Henry had seen how painful a thwarted love for mankind could be, watching his father, an elected member of the Commune, live out his final years as an exile in Catalonia. Emile himself, a brilliant and diligent student at school despite all the disadvantages of his upbringing, had just missed out on the place at one of Paris' *grandes écoles* that might have allowed him to participate in building the bright future to which he aspired. As it was, rejection had set in motion a train of events that over several years would crystallise his sense that 'only cynics and sycophants get a seat at the feast'.

After fleeing his call-up papers, as a criminal deserter every step that Henry took seemed to lead deeper into the political underworld. Seeing Emile in search of a political purpose, his brother Fortune had introduced him to the moderate anarchist teachings of Kropotkin, but when Emile's new interest was discovered, it cost him his job. Then, despite Emile's own rejection of Ravachol's methods as inhumane and counterproductive, Fortune's outspoken support for the bombings led his brother to be arrested in his own apartment and briefly taken into custody. It was a rapid process of radicalisation, accelerated by the sense that he was being persecuted and marginalised. Hard-line veterans of anarchism, the likes of Malato, d'Axa, Fénéon and Constant Martin were now the only friends on whom he could rely, and thrilling discussions about how destruction was the purest form of artistic expression surrounded him.

The bomb that Emile Henry left outside the door of the offices of the Carmaux Mining Company on avenue de l'Opéra on 8 November 1892 was intended to cause the maximum loss of life. An inversion device made according to a design of his own, it was aimed primarily at the bosses of a business that had, in the course of the previous few months, brutalised the striking workers at its mines in the Aveyron. But Henry's definition of economic guilt had become wide enough for him to feel no disquiet that the bourgeois residents of the nearby apartments might die too. Having used a meeting across town as cover for his murderous expedition, Henry returned to his workplace confident that the ghost of Ravachol would soon once again be stalking the streets of Paris. By then, however, the bomb had already exploded, with a rather different effect from that intended.

Alerted by the mining company, police officers had taken the infernal machine to the station on rue des Bons-Enfants for inspection; three of them had lifted it carefully upstairs. Shortly afterwards, Henry's ingenious detonator had triggered. Four officers and the office boy died in terror and agony, their flesh and scraps of uniform spattered over the walls and dangling from the fixtures. It was an act of terrorism quite different in scale and effectiveness from any of the copycat squibs that had followed in the wake of Ravachol. Two days later Henry packed his bags and departed Paris for the safety of London, and the welcoming bosom of his anarchist family. He left behind a France racked by anxieties.

*

It was the nationalistic newspaper *La Libre parole*, published by the notorious anti-Semite Edouard Drumont – with its motto 'France for the French' – which had broken the story of the Panama scandal in September 1892, filling the pages across which it had previously splashed reports of Ravachol's arrest and trial. Its revelations were surely the outcome of the neo-Boulangist and anti-Semitic campaign against the French authorities that Rochefort had been reported as formulating that summer. The outrage over Panama felt by the French public made Rochefort a serious political player once again, visited in London by the ex-prefect of police, Louis Andrieux. He was courted too by those with something to hide, including Cornelius Herz – one of the three Jewish 'promoters' who had arranged the Panama scandal bribes – who offered him 300,000 francs to moderate the follow-up attacks in *L'Intransigeant*, without success. News that Baron de Reinarch, one of Herz's two colleagues, had been found dead the day after his nephew had tipped him off that he was to be prosecuted, and with many doubting the official account of suicide, must have doubly delighted

Rochefort, coming as it did within days of the rue des Bons-Enfants explosion.

'Gradually the land is passing from the native to the foreigner. Jews are becoming the proprietors of the finest farms mortgaged to their advantage,' complained a character in Jules Verne's novel *The Carpathian Castle*, published in 1892, fifteen years after the chief rabbi in Paris had felt compelled to write to Verne's publisher to complain against racial stereotyping. Such anti-Semitism was pervasive in French society in the period, however, and rarely remarked upon. Now, though, a dangerous confluence of circumstances, further excited by some propagandist contrivance, raised the level of anti-Semitic rhetoric to an almost hysterical pitch. An impression of conspiracy was being woven around the Panama scandal with little regard to the collateral damage: the burial of Reinarch's body without an autopsy raised suspicions of foul play, while almost the entire political Establishment, including even Clemenceau, were seemingly implicated in a five-year-long deception of the French people.

The conspiracy had an international angle too with 'X', described as 'the ambassador of a very great power friendly to France – a dashing gentleman, actually, whose financial embarrassments [have long been] a matter of common knowledge in Paris', said to be a beneficiary of bribes on a vast scale. Nor were comments on the recent ostentatious affluence of Baron de Mohrenheim limited to the French press: in a letter to Pobedonostsev, de Cyon calculated the sum total of the kickbacks de Mohrenheim had received at half a million francs, while the same sum had been paid to the late Katkov's Russian newspaper. Most unnerving, though, for the French was surely the queasy sense that not only had the Jewish financiers got their hooks into the ambassador, on whom they pinned their hopes for a geopolitically crucial alliance, but that they were simultaneously in league with those who sought the destruction of their society. Such at least was the drift of an article in Drumont's *La Libre parole* headed 'Rothschild and the Anarchists . . . An International Conspiracy'. The malign influence of the Jews was, it seemed, truly ubiquitous, corroding western civilisation from above and below.

Following the demise of Boulanger and the disgrace of the aged Lesseps, sentenced to prison for five years in 1893, the subject of the most popular souvenir photographs in France would be Louis Pasteur. And it was all too easy for those with half a grasp of his bacteriological ideas, or those of his German rival and colleague Robert Koch, to extrapolate from their findings metaphors for the spread of alien stock by emigration, especially that of eastern European Jewry. Known vectors of disease, with cholera a particular problem that caused a devastating outbreak in the transit port of Hamburg in 1893, the Jewish refugees from the pogroms began to be perceived as a disease themselves, whose virulence must be addressed. In 'The Invasion of Destitute Aliens' of 1892, the earl of Dunraven had written of 'the superiority of the lower order over the higher order of organism – the comparative indestructibility of lower forms of animal life', with veiled reference to the influx of immigrants to the East End. The same year, quarantine officials in New York came under pressure to weed out 'the diseased, defective, delinquent and dependent'.

Even without the learned contribution of such criminal anthropologists as Lombroso, the same principle could be readily extended to foreign subversives entering Britain or America, many of whom were Jewish. Indeed, Sir Basil Thomson, later head of the CID, would look back on the early 1890s with the lamentation that 'if the pharaoh Memptah had been given an efficient intelligent service, there would have been no exodus'. There were, though, other perspectives on the teeming immigrant world of London's East End, which saw not only the difficulties but also the promise and potential of the tens of thousands of new arrivals who were pouring through London docks at an unprecedented rate, and prized the social example that they set.

It was a process that the Fabian Beatrice Webb charted with brio. 'Let us imagine ourselves on board a Hamburg boat steaming slowly up the Thames in the early hours of the morning,' she began her lengthy account of the journey of one exemplar of the 45,000 émigrés from Lithuania, Russia and Poland to disembark in 1891, to the point where 'In short, he has become a law-abiding and self-respecting citizen of our great metropolis and feels himself the equal of a Montefiore or a Rothschild.' The social reformer Olive Schreiner might not have appreciated the capitalistic aspirations imputed to the Jewish families with whom she worked and wrote, but she too felt a passionate admiration for how the tight bonds of the family provided the necessary support and security in a largely hostile environment for members to undertake, with a high frequency of success, a relatively rapid rise through the established society.

For Kropotkin, a regular speaker at the Jewish anarchist clubs of the East End, the social solidarity of the eastern European immigrants represented the idea of 'Mutual Aid' in action: evidence to support his alternative theories for the factors shaping evolution. Infuriated by the publication in 1888 of Thomas Huxley's essay 'The Struggle for Existence', he had immediately set about giving systematic expression to his belief that 'fitness for survival' was best determined not by competition but by cooperation. By working together, rather than striving for dominance, a particular group or species might win an advantage in the search for resources and, thereby, in the perpetuation of their genes. The culmination of a lifetime of study and observation, the series of long essays in the *Nineteenth Century* magazine in which he articulated these ideas during the first half of the 1890s predicted much that the science of genetics would prove about the mechanism of evolution a century later. Nor were the political implications of his research lost on him.

Despite taking on a heavy workload of reviewing and lecturing to meet his family's bills, concurrent with his work on 'Mutual Aid', Kropotkin was developing a practical blueprint for the creation of a society similar to that which Morris had evoked in *News from Nowhere*. Except that whereas Morris the craftsman had shown aesthetic discretion by keeping the electrical cables out of sight, Kropotkin's *Fields, Factories and Workshops* explained how technology could provide for the basic needs of human existence, freeing men and women to lead a just and fulfilled life.

Any such anarchistic paradise was premised on an optimistic view of human nature that appeared increasingly fanciful in the face of the brute, competitive realities of a capitalistic, industrialised world. And yet Kropotkin could now adduce scientific support for a notion that the political realities of the world appeared to belie. For according to the theory of 'Mutual Aid', evolution offered clear, natural validation for the principle of social solidarity both as the means to achieve the ideal communistic future, and as the proof of mankind's inherent perfectibility.

The cause of the East End immigrants was unsurprisingly, then, close to his heart. Whilst on holiday on the Isle of Wight in the summer of 1891 he had written a long letter of reproach to the usually sympathetic French sociologist and author Auguste Hamon, for the indifference Hamon and others on the political left showed to the growing anti-Semitism around them. Putting himself in the position of the hundreds of Jews who supported the Berners Street anarchist club with their subscriptions, he imagined how they must hate those who 'cannot admit that the exploited Jew is a revolutionary just as often (more often, I'd say) than the Russian, the Frenchman, etc., and that the Jewish exploiter is no more nor less than the German exploiter'.

Kropotkin himself, however, would suffer from more than his fair share of prejudice as anarchism became ever more demonised in the popular imagination, the subtleties of his thinking lost on the mass of his contemporaries who failed to differentiate between the political ideals he espoused and the simpler impulse to destruction which so many younger colleagues in the movement were eager to indulge. 'There must be no destruction,' he confided to Ford Madox Ford, in the softest of voices, as they sat in an alcove off the grand Grill Room of the Holborn Restaurant, the dishes clattering around them. 'We must build, we must build in the hearts of men. We must establish a kingdom of God.'

This was the Kropotkin whose soul Oscar Wilde described as being that of a 'beautiful white Christ'. Even the budget fifteen-shilling dinners that the Holborn Restaurant offered to feed a father, mother, governess and four children were so far beyond the vast majority of anarchism's adherents, though, as to evince prejudices of another kind against him too. Seen from outside the movement as being tarred with the brush of violent anarchism, from within it Kropotkin's voice increasingly appeared anachronistic in its moderation. His attitude towards Britain might be premised on a clear understanding that it shared the fundamental author-itarian shortcomings of all nation states, but he could enthuse to Jean Grave that 'Parliament has voted (on the 2nd reading) the 8 hour law for the miners. The Old Gladstone was superb . . . the young want it: I am with them!' It is unlikely that Parmeggiani, for example, would have felt the same.

That Kropotkin's anarchism was sincere and resolute was never in doubt, but increasingly the radical left was tempted into a closer rela-tionship with the political mainstream. In 1893, the tide of strikes that had been building for several years across Europe would reach its high-water mark, and the general election in France saw a huge swing in favour of the socialists with their vote rising to 600,000, twelve times its level a decade earlier. At the same time, a socialist congress in Brussels voted to work within a constitutional framework to achieve representa-tion for labour. With socialism's leaders once again acquiescing to the status quo, just when the prospect of worker-led revolution seemed in sight, anarchism, as embodied by a new generation – many of whom were little more than adolescents – reacted by becoming increasingly egotistical and shrill. The People's Will of the 1870s had been similarly preoccupied by violence, but at least it had possessed a genuine, prac-tical sense of its political goals.

*

Emile Henry had first visited the Autonomie Club soon after his arrival in London in late 1892, high on his recent murderous exploits. No one outside his immediate circle took seriously his boasts of responsibility

for the rue des Bons-Enfants bomb. Nevertheless, the devil-may-care attitude that Henry cultivated led one French informant to speculate that
he was destined for the guillotine, and appears to have made him a focal
point around which the most restive and impetuous of the international
émigrés now coalesced, in their unscrupulous quest for profit and excitement. There was talk that he might set sail for a new life in North
America, as Meunier had now done, but after tasting the fruits of straightforward criminality with an ambitious extortion scam in January 1893,
Henry set aside such plans. From idealist to extortionist was a giant step
for Henry to take, but the five lives he had claimed, albeit inadvertently,
had hardened his attitude, and London provided a convenient base from
which to launch lucrative forays across the Channel.

Among the most seasoned expropriators in the émigré underworld
from whom Henry could learn the trade were many anarchists he would
have known from Paris: the old Communard Constant Martin, Henry's
original mentor in the ways of anarchism; Louis Matha, a hairdresser
and vehement militant, who first helped Henry find his bearings in
London; Placide and Rémi Schouppe, who had been on the longlist of
suspects for the Bons-Enfants attack; the Mexican burglar and propagandist Philippe Leon Ortiz, known to his colleagues as 'Trognon' (his wife
was 'Trognette'); and Alexandre Marocco, a thick-set fifty-one-year-old
Egyptian and veteran of Pini's and Parmeggiani's gang, who as
'Mademoiselle Olga' acted as a fence for stolen goods, while running an
umbrella shop in an unlikely gesture to British respectability. Henry, with
his baby-faced charm, new-found confidence, and a knack for disguise,
soon defined a role for himself within the gang, acting as a trustworthy
lure for its bourgeois French marks, or distracting them while their goods
were liberated. For the best part of a year, the gang plundered the
Continent from the Channel coast to Montpellier in the south, from
Paris to Brussels and over the border into Germany. Or so, at least, seems
likely. For such was the skill of the robbers that even the weight of police
resources committed to placing the anarchist demi-monde under surveillance could not confidently keep track of them or their crimes, as they
crossed and recrossed the Channel, and followed smugglers' rat runs
across borders.

The job of gathering evidence against them was far from easy. Whether
experience had taught them discipline and patience, or their claims to be
motivated by ideology rather than greed were genuine, few of the stolen
goods came on to the open market to be traced. Whilst the occasional
bag of gemstones might be offered quietly to the jewellers of Hatton

Garden, or an *objet d'art* discreetly sold, perhaps to Rochefort or through the antiquities shop opposite the British Museum in which Parmeggiani had invested his own ill-gotten gains after returning from his prison term in France, not enough of the loot turned up to give the police the clues they needed, allowing Henry and his companions to lead them a dance across France.

In England, though, the anarchists now faced a Special Branch under the direction of William Melville himself, with only Anderson as his superior to keep him in check. There is pathos to the formality of his predecessor's last entry in the accounts ledger: 'Ch. Insp. Littlechild left office on 18 March 1893 on three weeks' leave, having his resignation in so as to expire with his leave viz 9 April.' In all his previous entries to the ledger, Littlechild had referred simply to 'self'. Poor health was the explanation given for the forty-five-year-old's departure, though he was well enough to establish himself promptly in a private detective practice. Perhaps he had simply seen which way the wind was blowing. Although debate continued to rumble on concerning the treatment of the Walsall men, with Irish Members of Parliament tabling further questions in the House of Commons, the choice of Melville as Littlechild's successor suggests that those appointing to the post approved of his methods, even if they could not openly condone them.

Seated at his new desk, his broad moustache bristling, Chief Inspector Melville must have felt himself master of his world. Like the telephone apparatus that the mysterious anti-Masonic campaigner Leo Taxil, actually the hoaxer Jogand-Pages, had described Satan using to communicate with his minions from beneath the Rock of Gibraltar, speaking tubes sprouted from the walls of Melville's office, connecting him to every point of the compass. The latest warning of threats could be received and orders issued, insights communicated and intrigues planned. Since 1891 a cable laid beneath the Channel had provided a direct line to Paris, and unlike awkward written records, telephone conversations left no incriminating paper trail. There were other conduits too that he could use to pass information to his foreign colleagues: among the most reliable and productive of the French police informers was 'Jarvis' and it is clear that he and Melville frequently met to exchange information; Lev Beitner, embedded in the Society of Friends of Russian Freedom, may have performed a similar role for Rachkovsky. And should the need arise, on Duck Island in the lake of St James's Park, only a stone's throw from the royal palaces, stood the bombproof bunker of the Home Office's explosives expert, Colonel John Majendie, on whose services Melville might call.

With everything in a state of readiness, a week before he officially took up his new role Melville celebrated by donning a mask and outfit to attend a fund-raising programme of revels staged at Grafton Hall in Fitzroy Square by Emile Henry's dangerous friend, Louis Matha. After the mockery that had accompanied Inspector Houllier's visit to London, the event would have allowed Melville an inward chuckle in revenge. First the foreigners' unpunctuality delayed the curtain rising on 'Marriage by Dynamite', a crude vaudeville scripted by Malato. Then their demonstrations of the cancan left the native English shocked, their mood already soured perhaps by having to sit through Louise Michel's lecture on contemporary art, with its unfavourable compar-isons of Hampstead to Montmartre. At the time, Degas' *The Absinthe Drinkers* was on show in the city, depicting a disreputable couple huddled over a cloudy glass of the intoxicating liquor: the press reaction, reviling it as 'a dirty French picture', articulated the growing unease felt in London towards such foreigners. Whether Melville was a follower of the fine arts is not known, but squeezed in among such characters in the fug of the Grafton revels he would undoubtedly have concurred with the critics.

The population of the anarchist enclaves had further swelled in the course of the year, to such an extent that the sudden and unexpected arrival of thirty Spaniards from Buenos Aires was reported to have merely 'caused a stir among anarchists here'. Having docked at Liverpool and then travelled by train to Euston station, they marched down the Tottenham Court Road to the Autonomie Club, where billets were arranged for them in hostels or on the floors of already overcrowded homes. A further half-dozen from Italy – whose anarchists comprised the most noxious 'pests to society' and scroungers, according to Special Branch officer Sweeney – were lodged in the offices of the *Torch* newspaper, where the children of William Michael Rossetti, Her Majesty's secretary to the Inland Revenue, were thrilled to host them.

'Poor children,' Olive Garnett had remarked not long before, 'they want so much to know some desperate characters and no one will intro-duce them': tea with Kropotkin in the refreshment room of the British Museum had been as close as they got. Now she was appalled at the hypocritical blitheness with which the eldest sibling, Helen, was prepared to print articles calling on readers of the *Torch* to commit bombings of the kind that she would never contemplate undertaking herself. The unsurprising result of their folly, according to Madox Ford, another family friend, was that their home was subsequently 'so beset with English detectives, French police spies and Russian agents provocateurs that to go along the sidewalk of that respectable terrace was to feel that one ran the gauntlet of innumerable gimlets'.

After the fogs and harassment that ground the anarchist émigrés down in London, those who dared visit Paris in July 1893 must have relished the colourful uproar around the Bal des Quat'z Arts. Setting out from the Moulin Rouge, a fancy-dress cavalcade dreamed up by students from the Ecole des Beaux-Arts and featuring debauched emperors, Cleopatras and courtesans had brought the subculture of the avant-garde to the streets as it progressed towards the Latin Quarter, where it arrived at dawn. Concerns about dancers in 'immodest attire' and charges of licentiousness prompted a heavy-handed police response, however, leading the students to barricade themselves into the old streets of the Left Bank where they stayed for several days. With a vote of confidence tabled in the Chamber of Deputies over the mishandling of the affair, it seemed artistic anarchy had come close to toppling the French government. But the time was surely coming for anarchism to express itself again in more serious ways.

'If one could know the microbe behind each illness . . . its favourite places, habits, its methods of advance,' Dr Trélat wrote, 'it would be possible, with a *bonne police médicale*, to catch it at just the right moment, stop its progress and prevent its homicidal attack.' While the application of the language of disease and its spread to human migration may have been scurrilous, the disciples of Pasteur were respectful in drawing an explicit comparison between their research and the inquiries conducted by the police and the judiciary. Nowhere was the analogy more apt, though, than in relation to the cryptographic work of Eugène Bazeries, known variously as the 'Lynx of the Quai d'Orsay', the 'Napoleon of Ciphers' and simply the 'Magician', whose success in breaking an alpha-numerical code used by the émigré anarchists may well have helped bring the spate of international robberies to an end.

Gradually, during the latter months of 1893, members of the gang containing Emile Henry, who had himself once been nicknamed 'Microbe', began to be picked off by the police. In September, Ortiz was arrested in Paris and charged with burglaries and associated acts of violence in Mannheim and Crespin earlier in the year, while November saw an extensive and carefully coordinated operation by the French and Belgian police to corner and capture Rémi Schouppe while in the act of exchanging stolen goods in a suburb of Brussels. Anyone even faintly familiar with bacteriology would have known, though, that until the last microbe was eradicated, the risk of disease remained.

Retreating to London, Henry may have remembered the final words of Clément Duval, a member of the Panthers of Batignolles and a hero of anarchist expropriators, as he was led out of court seven years earlier to face a life sentence on Devil's Island: 'Ah, if ever I am freed, I will blow you all up!'

The autumn of 1893 brought a resumption of anarchist attacks on the Continent. First came a revenge attack in Spain for the execution of Ravachol, when two bombs thrown by Paulino Pallas at the captain general of Catalonia left him with barely a scratch but killed a handful of bystanders. Then, on 7 November, a terrible massacre took place in the Liceo opera house in Barcelona during a performance of *William Tell*, that old favourite of the People's Will terrorists: nine women were among the twenty-nine killed by bombs dropped into the orchestra stalls in revenge for the suppression of the Jerez revolt. The consequences would be disastrous: a further ratcheting of the repression, with the Spanish anarchists left no other means to express their discontent than further acts of terrorism.

In France, an attack of a different nature took place on 12 November at the Bouillon Duval, a canteen set up by a butcher from the nearby market of Les Halles to serve good cheap food to the masses, but which had been quickly taken over by a bourgeoisie who enjoyed the frisson of slumming it. 'The French working man, though he could eat at the Bouillon Duval as cheaply and much better than in his usual greasy spoon, was too proud to thrust himself upon the society of people better dressed than himself,' the obituary of its founder would observe. With money no object, however, the young unemployed cobbler Léon Leauthier did not stint on his last meal as a free man, feasting on a menu that now stretched beyond the basic bouillon to offer fresh game, roast meats and fine wines. Then, before the bill arrived, he abruptly crossed the room and plunged his knife into the chest of another diner, apparently at random, with the single thought that 'I shall not be striking an innocent if I strike the first bourgeois that I meet.'

That his victim turned out to be Serge Georgevitch, the Serb ambassador to France who, like de Mohrenheim, had been implicated in the Panama bribery scandal, prompted some talk of conspiracy. It was generally accepted as perfectly plausible, though, that simple despair and envy of the ostentatious profiteering of bankers and the bour-geoisie had impelled Leauthier's action.

The reaction of the London colony to events abroad was predictably excitable. It was the opera attack in Barcelona that stirred them most, for the dramatic scale of the devastation. An outspoken Samuels took the lead in articulating the mood: 'I claim the man who threw the bomb as a comrade,' he told an audience at the South Place Meeting House. 'We will fight the bloodsuckers by any means . . . We expect no mercy from these men and we must show them none.' His rhetoric was consistent with that of the *Commonweal*, now under his editorship, whose series of meetings on the subject of 'Dynamitism' drew eager audiences; the produc-tion of the Incendiary Cigar, Lorraine Fire, Fenian Fire and Pholophore recommended by Most and the *Indicateur anarchiste* may well have been on the agenda. The newspaper *Liberty*, though, was clear in asserting that the more bloodthirsty pamphlets then circulating were 'inspired by Melville with the object . . . of preparing public opinion for the expulsion of foreign émigrés'.

★

It had been a satisfactory year for Peter Rachkovsky, quite apart from developments involving the anarchists and the benefits for his own campaign against Russia's émigré dissidents. On 12 October, the Russian fleet had anchored off the French naval port of Toulon, the Third Republic reciprocating its own ships' visit to Kronstadt in 1891, which the public at large saw as initiating the new relationship. Rachkovsky knew differently, having worked and deployed his agents for several years to help bring about a secret alliance.

That autumn, Rachkovsky could sit down to a celebratory Okhrana dinner, served *à la russe* with one course following another in the manner now fashionable in Paris. Outside the city had gone wild for the sailors' visit, the cries of '*Vive la Russie!*' reverberating as the carriages carrying dignitaries made their way up the rue de Lyon. 'There are two million French people who wait to attest with their acclaim the indissoluble friendship and union between our two nations: Russia and France,' wrote Charles Dupuy, the president of the council. Perhaps the only shadow was cast by the implication of Rachkovsky's mentor de Mohrenheim in the mess of the Panama bribes, but Dupuy had at least promised to see to it that the press would be prevented from publishing any further embarrassing revelations about the Russian ambassador.

On 9 December, a fortnight after Dupuy's bill to curb press freedoms

had been defeated in a vote by France's deputies, Auguste Vaillant, radicalised by his cruel experiences in Argentina, entered the Palais Bourbon
where the parliament met. Ignoring Kropotkin's personal warnings against
the use of violence, he proceeded to hurl a bomb, rather clumsily, into
the Chamber of Deputies. The shrapnel of nails did as much harm to
his nose as to the one politician injured, though several female visitors
were said to have fainted after being scratched by the projectiles.
'Gentlemen, the session will continue,' Dupuy coolly announced.

Pope Leo XII would commend Dupuy for his sangfroid, but others
were dubious. 'Oh! The bravery of Dupuy!' scoffed one anarchist, within
earshot of the French commissioner of police, 'It didn't cost him much!
He knew better than anyone that the bomb was not dangerous!' The
explosive power of the bomb had indeed been minimal: a fact due, some
said, to it having been manufactured and supplied by the Municipal
Laboratory. Vaillant, however, would insist that he had patiently gathered
the chemicals necessary before making the glass fuse for the device, which
had been intended only as a protest rather than to cause death.

Most leading anarchists interviewed were prepared to laud Vaillant's
act. 'You must balance it out. On the one side, a few voluntarily sacrificed lives of our own plus a few others' lives; on the other side, the
happiness of all humanity, and the end of war and want which together
claim many more victims than do a few explosions,' explained Louise
Michel to a reporter from Le Matin who visited her new suburban home
in East Dulwich. The acerbic cultural critic Laurent Tailhade considered
it a 'healthy warning', but went on to offer a chilling reformulation of
aesthetic theory for a dawning era of terrorism: 'What do a few human
lives matter if the gesture is beautiful?' Others, though, looked again to
provocation and conspiracy, asking why the police had made so little
effort to apprehend the mysterious accomplice who Vaillant told them
had bankrolled the bombing. And intriguingly, Edouard Drumont's La
Libre parole pointed the finger at Germany and England which, it claimed,
were using the émigré anarchists 'to kill every ideal in French souls, to
destroy that faith in Christ which has rendered the French invincible'.

The government's response was swift: so swift, in fact, that Vaillant's
attack seemed almost to offer a pretext for legislation to be implemented
that had been under consideration for some time. A slew of draconian
measures, the 'Lois Scélérates', or 'Wicked Laws' as they became generally known, were rushed through the chamber, starting with a bill to
outlaw anarchism, voted in only three days after the chamber had been
bombed: the bill decreed that henceforth it would be a criminal offence

to promote, publicise, encourage or exonerate the anarchist idea, punishable by up to two years in prison, while to be involved in any violent action, regardless of outcome, was liable to capital punishment. The resistrictions on the press did not yet amount to all that Ambassador de Mohrenheim had been promised by Dupuy, but the additional 80,000 francs of funding allocated to the police would surely have delighted Rachkovsky who, a few weeks later, would contact the French foreign ministry, behind his own government's back, in an attempt to promote the idea of an anti-anarchist convention.

On Boxing Day, the novelist Huysmans, immersed in a spiritual crisis of his own, expressed the prevailing mood among those sickened by the revelations of the Panama scandal. 'The infamous and fateful year 1893 is coming to an end' he wrote to a colleague and friend, 'In France, at least, it has been nothing but a heap of filth, so much so that it has made one sympathise with the anarchists throwing bombs in parliament, which is the rotting image of a country in the process of decomposition . . . in an old world that is cracking apart at the seams; Europe seems drastically undermined, as she heads into the sinister unknown.'

In London, Vaillant's attack had seen the tempo of anarchist 'chatter' about terrorist plots continue to increase, with *La Cocarde* informing Paris early in the New Year that the émigrés had decided that their main targets should be stock exchanges, religious buildings and political institutions. A report to the French cabinet from the 'special commissioner' warned that nearly all émigré anarchists believed in the assassination of heads of state as the most effective means of propaganda. By then, Emile Henry had almost certainly returned to Paris having weighed the reality of Vaillant's failure: the gesture might have been beautiful and bold, but the execution and consequences were dismal. A further demonstration of the anarchism's potency was now required, Henry decided, to set the record straight, and to avenge the death sentences that awaited Vaillant and the Barcelona bombers.

Henry's original objective in early Ferbuary 1894 was to assassinate the French president, Sadi Carnot, but tight security around the Elysée Palace thwarted him. Wandering the streets in search of an alternative target, the example of the Liceo opera house in Barcelona must have passed through his mind as he glanced into the cafés and restaurants of Paris, estimating the likely number of bourgeois fatalities he could cause; repeatedly he walked on when it seemed too low a price at which to rate his own life, faced with almost certain arrest and execution. For it was now to be a whole social class who would feel the force of his attack: a class so reckless and irresponsible that, lost in their lives of leisure, they gave no thought to easing the poverty that surrounded them.

'Are those children who die slowly of anaemia in the slums, for want of bread in their home, not innocent victims too; those women ground down by exhaustion in your workshops for forty centimes a day, whose only happiness is that they have not yet been driven into prostitution; those old men turned into machines so you can work them their whole lives and then cast them out on to the street as empty husks?' As Henry settled into his seat at the Café Terminus and sipped his drink, he would have had plenty of time to ponder how he might justify the action he was about to take before a court of law.

The café, situated in the facade of the grand Hôtel Terminus at the entrance to Saint-Lazare station, was already filling up with after-work drinkers on that February evening, but Henry waited until he was satisfied that he could cause the greatest mortality. At that instant, he lifted his large bomb from its hiding place and launched it towards the diners nearest the orchestra. The noise and devastation were terrible, the blast destroying the immediate area and shattering the windows, while shrapnel ripped through flesh and furnishings and embedded itself in the ceiling and walls, leaving two dead and others dying. Henry, clutching a pistol beneath his jacket, made a bid to escape, but a crowd gave chase, persisting even when he turned and fired, emptying the chambers of his revolver. Two of his pursuers, one of them a policeman, were wounded by bullets before Henry was finally brought to bay.

The trial would be a tense affair. Bulot, the prosecuting lawyer, had been the intended victim of one of Ravachol's bomb attacks, and was determined not only to secure justice but to humiliate Henry in the process, while all Henry's wasted education welled up into angry wit and bilious eloquence that would prove endlessly quotable. 'Your hands are stained with blood,' the judge told him. 'Like the robes you wear, Your Honour,' Henry quipped back. His display delighted the likes of the aesthetic Félix Fénéon, who claimed that Henry's acts had 'Done far more for propaganda than twenty years of brochures by Reclus and Kropotkin'. It was the rousing conclusion to Henry's final speech, though, that would truly resonate with the friends he was leaving behind:

You have hanged us in Chicago, beheaded us in Germany, garrotted us in Jerez, shot us in Barcelona, guillotined us in Montbrison and Paris, but anarchy itself you cannot destroy. Its roots are deep: it grows from the heart of a corrupt society that is falling apart, it is a violent reaction to the established order, it represents the aspiration to freedom and equality that struggles against all current authority. It is everywhere, which means it cannot be beaten, and ultimately it will defeat you and kill you.

20

The Mysteries of Bourdin and the Baron

London and Liège, 1894

At around one o'clock on 15 February 1894, three days after Emile Henry's bombing of the Café Terminus, Special Branch was on a high state of alert. Henry Samuels was meeting his younger brother-in-law Martial Bourdin for lunch in the International Restaurant near Fitzroy Square. The same day, a French informant penned the only report that the prefecture ever received that focused exclusively on the two men. Neither the source nor the nature of the intelligence that prompted such attentiveness by the police on either side of the Channel is known. However, the sighting of a 'Bourdin brother' in Paris a week earlier, in conversation with Henry, may well have raised the alarm.

Leaving the restaurant Samuels and Bourdin travelled together to Westminster where they parted, Bourdin crossing Westminster Bridge to the south side of the Thames. It was at that moment too, by curious coincidence, that the Special Branch undercover agent also lost the scent. 'I never spent hours of greater anxiety than . . . when [the] information reached me,' Sir Robert Anderson, Melville's superior, would remember. 'To track him was impracticable. All that could be done was to send out officers in every direction to watch persons and places that he might be likely to attack.' Where and when Bourdin had collected the small, home-made grenade that Special Branch clearly knew to be in his pocket by this stage, together with £13 worth of gold, would remain a mystery.

Boarding a tram in the direction of East Greenwich, Bourdin took a seat at the rear, but gradually moved forward towards the driver, eager perhaps to peer through the windscreen at what lay ahead, or else from a fearful man's simple instinct for company. It was half-past four when he reached his stop near the edge of Greenwich Park and the afternoon light was already dying away in the west. He began to climb the zigzag-ging path up the hill. Behind him lay the Thames, on either side of which London stretched away beneath a hanging blanket of smoke from its fires and factories; ahead, the powerful symbol of the Greenwich Observatory, named a decade earlier as the site of the Prime Meridian, in the face of competition from Jerusalem and Paris, a decision to which the latter still refused to acquiesce. Was revenge for Henry's arrest on his mind, and was the Observatory truly his target: the guardian of the point in space from which the worldwide tyranny of time, oppressor of the working man, was calibrated? Or was it merely that the park was the agreed venue for him to hand over the bomb to whoever had commis-sioned its production?

At eight minutes to five, a flash suddenly lit up the fog-laden air: jolted by the sound of a 'sharp and clear detonation', two assistants in the Observatory's Computing Room noted the time. Whether pausing to prime the bomb, or tripping on the path, Bourdin had accidentally trig-gered the device. Two children were the first to reach the dying man, on their way home from school. The scene that greeted them was appalling: flesh and fragments of bone had been flung through the air to hang in trees, while the force of the impact had wrapped a section of sinew around the iron railings of a nearby fence. 'Take me home' was all Bourdin could gasp, his left hand and forearm blown off, his entrails spilling out, but instead he was carried to the nearby Seamen's Hospital, where shortly afterwards he expired.

Late the following evening, police raided the Autonomie Club, to which Melville gained entry by means of the secret password of knocks. While the chief inspector disdainfully puffed on a cigar, all those present were detained and interrogated, and the premises was subsequently closed until further notice. There were no angry crowds to block his exit this time, though, as there had been when he had visited Richard's shop with Houllier eighteen months before; as the dramatic news sank in, popular feeling turned against the anarchists as never before, and the next time the police were called out in force to the Charlotte Street area it would be to protect its radical citizens against an angry English mob.

Many émigrés reacted with consternation to the news from Greenwich: 'Anarchists were not so blind to their own interests and well-being as to forgo by their conduct the right to asylum that England so generously offered to political refugees,' one told the *Morning Leader*. But whilst an attack that killed or injured innocent victims, like those perpetrated by Ravachol or Henry, would surely have caused the British press to close ranks in outrage, the mysterious circumstances of Bourdin's death in Greenwich simply invited further investigation.

Among the anarchists themselves, rumours of provocation were rife in the days following the debacle, with the greatest suspicion focused on Henry Samuels, whose influence on the younger man David Nicoll would express in his recollection of a scene from the Autonomie Club a few weeks earlier, of 'little Bourdin sitting at the feet of Samuels, and looking up into his eyes with loving trust'. Nicoll's own misgivings about Samuels had long been a matter of record but already that January the first edition of the newspaper *Liberty* – founded by James Tocchati, a veteran of Morris' Socialist League, in order to provide a moderate counterbalance to *Commonweal* – had explicitly accused him of working for Melville.

Determined to exculpate himself, Samuels briefed the press about Bourdin's 'erratic behaviour' at their lunch on the fateful day, but professed himself certain that when they had parted – insisting that this was outside the restaurant at 2.50 p.m. – his brother-in-law had no intention of bombing the Observatory: his plan, he thought, must have been 'either to buy the explosive or to experiment'. Samuels' purpose was clearly to put time and space between himself and the incriminating material but his version of events rapidly began to unravel when a witness came forward to testify that he had seen them together in Westminster. Forced to concede that he had lied, Samuels now volunteered that on their journey across the city they had been 'pursued by' detectives. His new contortions, though, raised as many questions as they answered. If Samuels had known that he and Bourdin were under surveillance, why had he tried to pretend that they had parted earlier, unless he could rely on the police to keep his secret? Was it not more likely that Samuels himself was both the source of the bomb and the money that Bourdin collected along the way, and in league with the police?

While Samuels' amateurish attempts at deception were easily exposed, his old friend and colleague Auguste Coulon, still on the Special Branch payroll, played the journalist from the *Morning Leader* with an altogether more deft professionalism. Speaking anonymously, and unidentifiable to his old colleagues, Coulon was interviewed in the jeweller's shop in South London in which he now maintained an office lined with books on the theme of anarchism, the better to understand the subjects of his infiltration. As an array of clocks and watches ticked away the time, as if in portentous countdown, and his Swiss assistant tinkered at a workbench, Coulon divulged that he had been aware of plots brewing and had recently been on Bourdin's trail, but had relaxed his attention on the fateful day in the mistaken belief that the plot would not come to a head until the following Saturday. Having established his authority on the subject, he then persuasively asserted that the authorities would have to take 'steps to cleanse from their midst the criminals that now infest London. Too long has London been an asylum for European murderers, forgers, and thieves.'

The argument that Coulon advanced for the benefit of the newspaper's readers would have been welcomed by Melville, as by his associates abroad, but all were likely to have been disconcerted by his accompanying boast that 'I am in the service of the International Secret Police, which is subsidised by the Russian, German and French governments.' That Coulon may have been taking money from all three in a freelance capacity was perfectly possible, but the idea that cooperation between the national police forces amounted to anything like the official organisation he evoked was as fanciful as the much-touted notion of a vast concerted anarchist conspiracy. Yet Coulon's self-regarding admission perhaps hinted at something almost as extraordinary, whose existence none of those involved would wish revealed: a clandestine arrangement that had grown out of Melville's back-channel offer to Rachkovsky of his personal assistance, two years earlier. It may moreover have been upon such a foundation that the Okhrana chief hoped to build when he had approached the French foreign ministry, only weeks before Bourdin's death, to call for an anti-anarchist convention, in the move that had so angered his superiors in St Petersburg.

David Nicoll, at least, was in no doubt that Bourdin had died as the result of an elaborate intrigue involving police agents, and was unafraid to point the finger in print. Even before the explosion at Greenwich, he had charged Coulon with having received £70 to help reignite Melville's 'delectable game [of] dynamite outrages'; now Henry Samuels, whom he had previously considered 'too much of a fool to be a spy, but . . . the sort of man whom a spy could make good use of', was elevated to the status of a full-blown agent provocateur. And then there was Dr Fauset MacDonald, a well-heeled medical practitioner who had thrown in his lot with the *Commonweal* group the previous year: he too was now labelled a police agent, from whose surgery the chemicals could be supplied to produce explosives. As for a motive, Nicoll believed that 'A few dynamite explosions in England would suit the Russian police splendidly, and might even result in terrifying the English bourgeoisie into handing over the refugees to the vengeance of the Russian tsar.'

Nicoll's apprehension of the conspiracy that had been woven around

Bourdin was corroborated by an improbable source more than a decade later, when Joseph Conrad wrote *The Secret Agent*. Despite Conrad's assurance to his publisher that the plot was 'based on inside knowledge of a certain event', which was clearly the Greenwich bombing, in certain respects the novel presented a rather schematic cross-section of the anarchist world of the period. Comrade Ossipon may be taken as a slightly facetious version of Kropotkin; Yundt of the firebrand Johann Most. But when Verloc, the equivalent of Henry Samuels in Conrad's account, who habitually works as a nark for Chief Inspector Heat, recruits the Bourdin character, Stevie, into bombing the Observatory, he is in fact acting on the behest of Mr Vladimir, assigned the position of first secretary at the Russian Embassy but an obvious avatar of Rachkovsky.

Conrad would later protest, perhaps too much, that the work was drawn primarily from imagination. In reflecting on a realm where fact and fiction were constantly and intentionally being blurred, however, his well-informed storytelling may come closer to illuminating the truth than documentary sources that are so often partial and distorting. As to the true quality of the 'inside knowledge' about which Conrad boasted, the proof lies in the figure of the novel's purveyor of explosives, 'The Professor', whose elusive factual counterpart, bearing the very same sobriquet, is today known only from French police files that remained locked away in the Paris prefecture until long after the novelist's death. In one intriguing report, the real 'Professor' is said to have supplied Emile Henry's mentor, Constant Martin, with dynamite; in another, more significantly, the French informant states that 'Russian anarchists have confirmed that the school for the manufacture of bombs is in London and that the Professor is a Russian refugee'.

Unfortunately for the anarchist movement as a whole, in the London underworld of early 1894, it was all too easy for those accused by Nicoll to dismiss his suspicions as far-fetched: a further symptom of his paranoia, whose disruptive effects were beginning to weary even those who had some sympathy for the poor man's plight. For whilst rumours that Bourdin's intended destination had been Epping Forest, where he intended to test the bomb, may have carried echoes of the Landesen plot of 1890, they hardly constituted proof of Russian involvement. Furthermore, claims by anarchists to have received unsolicited deliveries of explosive materials, of which they had then wisely disposed, shortly before Special Branch ransacked their homes in search of incriminating evidence, could be easily explained away as anti-police propaganda. And when a pair of anarchists, Ricken and Brall, who had previously been suspected by neighbours of manufacturing bombs, suddenly disappeared, two days after Bourdin's death, the move suggested the remaining members of a terrorist cell hastily going to ground, more than it did innocents fleeing persecution.

It was perhaps fortunate for the sake of Nicoll's sanity that he did not know what the agents of the Paris prefecture had reported about the comings and goings of the London anarchists in Paris in the weeks before the Henry and Bourdin bombings. Had he done so, his paranoia would surely have reached a dangerous pitch. He would have been disturbed enough to learn that Dumont, an ex-colleague of Ravachol who was now part of the clique around Coulon that Nicoll had named as provocateurs, had been troublemaking in the city: indeed, early in January, Charles Malato had been so infuriated by Dumont's incendiary rhetoric in Paris that he had threated to go there 'to sort him out'.

What, though, would Nicoll have made of the reported meeting between Emile Henry and a 'Bourdin Brother' only days before the attack on the Café Terminus? If it were Martial Bourdin who had crossed the Channel to meet his fellow bomber, that would surely point simply to some coordination of their attacks. But what if it was Henry Samuels who had made the trip to meet Henry, using his wife's name as he sometimes did, not least when applying for the British Museum Library card that was used to gain entry to specialist works on the manufacture of explosives? Both recent bombs could then have been linked to one suspected agent provocateur, with others in the background. And what questions might then have been asked about the true provenance of the earlier attacks in which Henry had been involved, or that committed by Vaillant, or even those carried out by the anarchist Christ, Ravachol, Dumont's late friend?

No such doubts about who truly benefited from the self-sustaining cycle of anarchist terrorism seem to have troubled Emile Henry's associate Louis Matha, whom Agent Z6 had reported leaving London on the day of the Greenwich bombing to rejoin Henry's brother Fortune in Paris, where they meant to stage another dynamite outrage. Exactly a month later, however, while Henry read *Don Quixote* to pass the time as he awaited trial, it was another of his old accomplices by the name of Pauwels who set out for La Madeleine, in what was to have been the latest of a series of attacks on ecclesiastical targets in Paris. Yet in a near repeat of the accident that had befallen Bourdin, the device he was carrying exploded prematurely as he entered the church.

If the two events suggested a consistent flaw in design or manufacture of bombs supplied to the anarchists, however, whether accidental or preconceived, it did not deter the part-time art impresario Félix Fénéon – who had earlier stored bomb components in his desk at the war ministry on Henry's behalf – from venturing what seemed like a small-scale attack on his own initiative. The bomb he concealed in a flowerpot on the windowsill of the Café Foyot, just across the road from the Senate chamber in the Palais de Luxembourg and a favourite watering hole of its members, exploded as intended, but injured only his old friend Tailhade who happened to be drinking nearby. That it took out his eye seemed oddly like poetic justice for the man who had so coldly acclaimed Henry's destructive artistry, and yet the bomb's effect was to sustain the widespread sense of terror.

Paris once again lived in fear, as it had after the attacks by Ravachol and his gang: the bourgeoisie stayed at home and policemen handed in transfer requests, while the sound of scenery collapsing backstage at the Gaîté theatre was enough to send the audience rushing for the exits. The Third Republic and its new left-leaning government, patently incapable of defending the institutions of politics or religion against the anarchist bombers, and with the general public now in the firing line, had been further destabilised. For Henri Rochefort, dining with anarchist friends in London on the very day that Pauwels had blown himself up, the situation must have seemed quite satisfactory.

The previous year had seen Rochefort substantially repair his relationship with the anarchists themselves, telling Le Gaulois that they were more sinned against than sinning: 'the true anarchist is not dangerous for he tolerates without complaint the promiscuous presence of agents provocateurs'. Furthermore, Louise Michel had recently extracted a large donation from him on their behalf, while police agents reported that anarchists and nihilists regularly visited his home to solicit his largesse. Did this generosity, that might be considered material assistance to those involved in the violence, buy him the kind of malign influence enjoyed by Conrad's fictional Comrade X? If so, it might have made for a rather uncomfortable evening on 15 March, when his fellow diners included Constant Martin, a linchpin of the campaign of robberies that had involved Emile Henry, and Emile Pouget who had been sent to prison with Louise Michel for the bread riots a decade earlier. For on their way to the dinner from the Charlotte Street enclave, some would have passed the window of the undertaker's shop in Tottenham Court Road, where the image of Martial Bourdin's face, photographed as he lay in his coffin and showing all the puncture marks of the shrapnel from his bomb, offered a grim reminder of what waging war against the state could cost.

By April, it was once again Meunier's dossier that topped the pile on Chief Inspector Melville's desk. With the bomber of the Café Véry said to have returned from Canada, the hunt was resumed. The associates of known militants found themselves under pressure to provide information, presumably in return for indemnity from prosecution. Bourdin's close friend Charpentier was arrested for burglary, while Rousseau, the watchmaker who had given Henry work, was also detained. In due course, he and Coulon were considered the most likely candidates to have betrayed details of Meunier's movements.

Melville's coup in Walsall had briefly won him celebrity status and now the chance finally arrived for him to cement his reputation for decisive action. Having forewarned journalists, on 12 April the chief inspector and his troops staked out the boat train preparing to depart from Charing Cross station. Then, just as Meunier was about to board, Melville himself appeared from his hiding place and wrestled the outlaw to the ground. Lively representations of the scene were rushed out in the illustrated magazines: real-life detective heroism for a public whose appetite for such things had soared since the *Strand* began publishing the Sherlock Holmes stories by Conan Doyle in episodic form two years earlier. But where the phenomenal popularity of the fictional sleuth was based on regular monthly instalments of his adventures, Melville would have been confident, as he escorted Meunier out of Charing Cross station, that he could provide his public with a dramatic sequel far sooner than that.

In fact, it was only two days after Meunier's arrest that Inspector Sweeney took a seat at the front of a bus bound for Clerkenwell, next to a twitchy Italian teenager. For the previous fortnight Special Branch agents had been watching the eighteen-year-old Francis Polti, knowing that some weeks earlier a middle-aged anarchist drifter calling himself Emile Carnot had approached Polti to take part in a bomb plot. Since then, the police had shadowed him up to the hospital in Highgate, where his wife lay dangerously ill after the recent birth of their twins, and around pharmacists' shops closer to his home in Saffron Hill, observing as he assembled the necessary components.

It was 'a weary and thankless task' for the surveillance agents, Sweeney would complain, 'telegraphing for relief to come to one place when you've already had to leave to go halfway across London in pursuit'. Finally, however, they had tailed him to Mr Cohen's iron foundry in

Clerkenwell, from where he and Carnot – whose real name was Giuseppe Farnara – had commissioned the bomb's casing. Realising that once Polti was back in the slums of the Italian quarter he might 'easily give his pursuers the slip in the maze of alleys and courts', and fearing that the device might prematurely explode as Bourdin's had done, Sweeney moved to make the arrest as soon as he saw Polti's hand enter the bag.

The motive for his planned attack, Polti declared, was to avenge himself on the British tourists who deluged the cities of his native Italy in droves each year: those Cookites who were 'destroying the natural beauties of the place and making scorching, sunbaked boulevards where were formerly olive-shaded lanes'. The outraged eloquence, though, was that of a journalist writing in a *Pall Mall Gazette* article two years earlier; Polti's explanation appeared quite bathetic in light of the bombs that had recently shaken the ministries in Rome in revenge for the government's brutal suppression of the anarchist uprising. An unsent letter from Polti to his parents left no doubt that he had indeed planned a suicide attack for the following day, but his words lacked the brazen clarity of Farnara's 'I am guilty; I wanted to kill capitalists.' Perhaps, to the impoverished teenager, the glory of martyrdom in the anarchist cause simply offered an escape from the burden of fatherhood. What seems certain is that he was a dupe, his reference to the 'Royal Exchange' rather than the 'Stock Exchange' as the intended target, an obvious example of poor rote learning. The crucial question was on whose behalf, if any, Farnara had put him up to it.

The newspaper *Justice* was as forthright as it dared be: 'Somehow it does seem to us that the great Melville has possibly engineered the whole thing. We don't say that he has, of course. Nevertheless, we cannot but remember that a serious anarchist plot in England would be very convenient just now, especially an Italian or French anarchist plot.' A plot by Russian nihilists would have been even better, of course, but they had learned to be more cautious than their impetuous and gullible anarchist peers. If the Polti and Farnara conspiracy was useful in some respects for the chief inspector, however, in others it represented a considerable personal risk, and its early interdiction was a necessary act of caution. For shortly after the Greenwich bomb explosion, the Home Secretary, Sir William Harcourt, had been overheard in the lobby of the House of Commons reprimanding the assistant commissioner, Sir Robert Anderson, whose responsibility it was to supervise Special Branch. 'All that's very well,' he had said, 'but your idea of secrecy over there seems to consist of keeping the Home Secretary in the dark.'

Ten years before, during his previous tenure at the Home Office,

Harcourt had adamantly opposed the use of agents provocateurs, arguing that 'the police ought not to set traps for people'. It must have been clear to Chief Inspector Melville that were some terrible error in Special Branch's management of a bomb plot to expose his illicit plans to undermine the principles of liberal Britain, he could expect no quarter from its political masters. And yet with each successive coup against the anarchists, Melville's reputation rose, and with each outrage abroad, so too did the perceived need for robust policing of the émigrés. It must have been with some delight, then, that just a week after Polti's arrest, when the air was still thick with awkward rumours of provocation, Melville received news of a series of explosions that had rocked the city of Liège in Belgium. His delight, however, would have been premature. Any hopes he had of presenting the Belgium bombings as final proof of an international terrorist network would soon evaporate.

Liège, nestling in the deep folds of hills close to Belgium's industrial heartland, was no stranger to terrorism. Nor was it unfamiliar with the effects of agents provocateurs, with the Catholic and government conspiracy that had framed the socialist leader Pourbaix, seven years earlier, still fresh in many memories. More recently, in 1892, the city had been the first to be struck by the international wave of terrorism that had since reached from Barcelona to Rome, and Paris to London. Though largely unremarked upon outside Belgium, the attacks had been in response to the mayor's decision to ban May Day demonstrations, and had targeted the more affluent areas of the city, causing considerable damage and alarm but no injuries. Moineaux, a leading Belgian anarchist, had been convicted of the bombings, together with fifteen other *compagnons*, but to the surprise of many in the city, a local cabaret owner called Schlebach, widely blamed for initiating the violence, had been acquitted on the judge's instruction.

As May Day approached in 1894, mounting tensions and resentments appeared to augur a new round of trouble. A month earlier, a huge clerical march had roused the indignation of the local socialists, since when it had been reported that an anti-socialist organisation over 500 strong was planning to demand tougher restrictions on the labour movement's activities. Against a backdrop of recent pit collapses at nearby coal mines which had cost many lives, and press reports of an army of tens of thousands of America's unemployed converging on Washington, DC to demonstrate, the socialists of Liège, a powerful force, were not inclined to submit without a fight. Where normally the result might have been strikes and demonstrations, however, the start of Emile Henry's trial at the Court of Assizes appeared to inspire the anarchist faction to emulate his bloodier example.

The first bomb exploded on the evening of 1 May itself, the Saturday of the week in which Henry's advocate had opened the case for his defence. Wedged into an angle of the right transept of the medieval pilgrimage church of Saint-Jacques, the sixty cartridges of dynamite, weighing more than six kilograms, produced a devastating blast. Windows were shattered, a large hole was blown in the floor and many of the great stones supporting the vaulted roof cracked; had the charge been positioned only slightly differently, the ancient nave would have been brought down. Within minutes, the sound of the explosion had drawn a crowd of several hundred. Troops from the Belgian army had to be drafted in to keep order, but the young man seen sprinting away from the blast escaped unrecognised.

Awaiting news of the attack at his lodgings in Schlebach's cabaret club was the well-dressed Baron Ernest Ungern-Sternberg. A pale and rather corpulent figure with blond hair and a moustache tinted with red, his somewhat anomalous presence appears to have aroused no prior suspicion. Having arrived in Liège some months earlier, he had established himself as a charismatic presence in the anarchist community, equipped in advance with a descriptive list of its most significant members, to guide him in winning their trust. It was he who had commissioned one local activist called Muller to steal a sizeable quantity of dynamite from a store in nearby Chevron earlier in the year. And as witnesses would attest, 'The joy of the Russian was fierce' upon hearing of the damage caused by the Saint-Jacques bomb.

Ungern-Sternberg held his nerve as the police began their investigation with the round-up of predictable suspects, remaining in Liège for the moment to ensure that the series of attacks he had initiated and helped plan was seen through. Having already accompanied the anarchist Muller in collecting the casings and fuses from an elegant town house in the rue des Dominicains, it appears probable that on 3 May he joined him in placing the next device outside what was taken to be the home of Monsieur Renson, the president of the Court of Assizes. The explosion this time, in a residential area, was of a similar force to that in St Jacques and caused even more alarm and distress: the facades of buildings all around were ravaged and one old woman reported having been thrown from her bed on to the floor. As for the intended victim, the Monsieur Renson who was badly burned and blinded turned out to be not the scourge of anarchists, but his namesake, a popular local doctor.

'It is to be doubted that it will bring anarchism many new adepts,' the social democratic newspaper *Le Peuple* remarked of the attack, with considerable understatement. Before dawn broke the baron had fled, leaving the anarchists of Liège to face the music, the additional bombs still in their possession, should they choose to use them.

Claims that events in Liège provided final proof that the anarchists were involved in a truly international conspiracy appeared to be corroborated when one of the documents left behind by the baron conveniently listed eight Germans, two Dutch and five locals among his accomplices; reports in the German press claimed quite mistakenly that Kropotkin had been arrested in Russia. Meanwhile, under interrogation the Liège anarchists began to divulge more information about the baron himself. He had, the police were told, urged one of the anarchists he knew best to 'come with me, you can be part of a big spectacular' before setting off alone for Paris, two days before the Café Foyot bombing. Others testified to how he had planned a similar attack on the Café Canterbury in Liège that had only failed due to last-minute nerves on the part of the assigned bombers; how he had spoken too of his involvement with plots in London, his boasts seemingly borne out by information contained in his private papers. Following a further explosion outside the home of the city's mayor, bombs were discovered in the Théâtre-Royal foyer and close to a prominent banker's house, while warnings that the baron had been scouting a local gasworks raised further alarm. Despite the inevitable concern with the safety of Liège's citizens, however, there remained many awkward questions to be answered.

At the prefecture in Paris, the police tried to join the dots. Information supplied by their London-based agent, Léon, that Henry's dangerous friend Marocco and others had recently visited Brussels gave substance to the notion of cross-border coordination among the anarchists. Léon even provided the class and number of the carriage in which they had travelled, in support of his theory that so short were the distances to be travelled in Belgium that London-based anarchists might themselves have carried out the attack in Liège and still caught the return train. Marocco himself was said to be quite openly advising visitors that the Liège bombings and that in the Café Foyot in Paris were linked. Meanwhile, there were reports from Geneva that the Russian colony there had known of the Liège attacks in advance. In this case, though, the agent noted that the nihilist suspected of funding them 'always has a well-filled wallet': a shorthand signal, in this context, that he was an Okhrana agent.

In the past Rachkovsky had always been able to keep any hard evidence of provocation at arm's length, relying on friendly figures in the local police, where such operations were undertaken, to intervene and prevent the exposure of his agents. The Paris prefecture had done so with admirable efficiency in 1890, turning a blind eye to the false passport sent to Landesen from the Russian Embassy and ensuring that he was given enough time to make good his escape before their officers swooped; for his part Chief Inspector Mace of the Sûreté had been generously decorated by the tsar. Melville too had done a good job of silencing David Nicoll's inconvenient revelations about Walsall, at least for a while: it was only unfortunate that awkward scruples high up the chain of command in England meant that his rewards would have to wait. Rachkovsky must have thought his operations in Belgium were at least as secure, guaranteed by the position of respect that his foremost agent held there.

Rachkovsky had made every effort to provide the new life and identity for which Hekkelman had pleaded while holed up in the Grand Hotel in Brighton, after the sting operation of 1890. The stigma of his Jewish birth had been erased in grand fashion, with Count Muraviev and the wife of Imperial Senator Mansurov drafted in as godparents for his baptism in the chapel of the Russian Embassy in Berlin. But his christening as 'Arkady Harting' was only the beginning of the makeover. Rapid elevation to the position of state councillor was followed by an attachment, in 1892, to the Russian legation in Brussels, where the Belgian Sûreté, in full knowledge of his true identity, expressed their admiration for his undercover work. It was the next event in Harting's life, however, that would have most reassured Rachkovsky that Liège was safe for the Okhrana's operations: his protégé's marriage to the local high-society beauty, Marie-Hortense-Elizabeth-Madeleine Pirlot, nine years Harting's junior and the niece of a key figure in the city's judiciary. The dowry was 100,000 francs, with twice that sum gifted by her parents to help the newlyweds establish a home on the rue des Dominicains, while the presence of the Belgian attaché to the French ministry of the interior as one of four witnesses conferred on the union the appearance of an official sanction.

Yet all those efforts had been in vain, it now seemed, thwarted by the foolish incorruptibility of the Russian consul in Amsterdam, and the excessive zeal of the Liège police. For while the attention of the press and the police had initially focused on Schlebach and the 'Academy of Anarchy' that was said to operate out of his club, papers and letters found in the baron's rented room there had shifted the emphasis of the official inquiry. And when news had arrived from the police in Amsterdam that the man

known best to his old associates as 'Le Russe' had been turned over to
them by the Russian consul, on whose mercy he had thrown himself, the
Liège authorities had broadened their investigation.

Rachkovsky can have had little warning of the approaching storm when,
sitting at his desk on 5 May, only four days after the Saint-Jacques bomb
and within hours of the baron being handed over to the Dutch police,
he was passed a message that a visitor had asked to see 'Monsieur Léonard'.
Just as great, though, was the surprise of the Belgian official sent to track
down the man whom letters found in the baron's room revealed as the
financier of the Liège bomb conspiracy. He would have double-checked
the address in his dossier before entering the grand courtyard of the
Russian Embassy on rue de Grenelle, and surely paused again before
mounting the steps beneath the canopied entrance. However, the momentary but unmistakable flicker of recognition in the face of the doorman
at the mention of 'Léonard' suggested he was on the right track, while
the long interval between his request being passed through and his polite
but firm ejection from the building surely confirmed it.

In the Okhrana's offices in the east wing, Rachkovsky himself may
have felt tempted simply to close his eyes tight and hold his breath, in
the hope that the awkward reality of the situation would melt away. For
'Léonard' was his wife's maiden name which he, in common with Henry
Samuels, regularly borrowed for his double-dealing. Seeing the imminent ruin of his reputation and the collapse not only of the great
conspiracy he had woven but the wide network of agents he had
constructed, he instead moved swiftly into firefighting mode. With the
Ungern-Sternberg family, well-known Baltic aristocracy, telegraphing
Amsterdam that their relation, whose passport had recently been stolen
in Gibraltar, bore no resemblance to the man described, Rachkovsky's
options were limited. Determined to save his agent Cyprien Jagolkovsky
from exposure, he applied pressure on the Dutch police who were holding
the 'baron' to free him, which they did: tellingly, Jagolkovsky's route
back to Russia involved a period spent in hiding in London with Dumont,
about whom Nicoll and Malato had harboured such strong suspicions.
At least with the 'baron' removed as a source of potential embarrassment, the Okhrana chief could turn his attention to perception management, though with so many secrets out in the open the process would
be long and laborious.

By the time of the trial of the Liège conspirators, nine months later,
Rachkovsky had comprehensively secured his position, due in part

perhaps to strings pulled by Harting in Liège. In the course of the cross-examination, 'Le Russe' was endlessly referred to, and yet 'Ungern-Sternberg' was not to be blamed: Monsieur Seny, the *juge d'instruction*, informed the court that he had travelled to St Petersburg in person to question the accused, and declared him wholly innocent. The name of Jagolkovsky was never mentioned. *Le Peuple* reported how the Russian consul in Amsterdam, when 'interviewed afresh, refused to reply, hiding behind professional secrecy', while evidence that the bombs had been collected from Harting's house on the rue des Dominicains was also suppressed. Even Muller changed his story, insisting that he had been mistaken in thinking that the baron had helped him carry out the attack on Renson. And as for Monsieur Léonard, who had channelled the funds for the bombings to Schlebach via an anonymous female sympathiser, the judge ruled that a case could not be brought against a man who did not exist.

The truth about the scope of the Okhrana provocation conspiracy in 1894 that encompassed Liège, London and Paris, and the covert involvement of foreign police services, remains elusive today. The file on Cyprien Jagolkovsky held by the Belgian Sûreté was immediately transferred to the cabinet office, where it soon disappeared into the ether, as did the court transcripts; those of Emile Henry's private papers that were not spirited away by friends in the hours after his arrest were impounded by the French interior ministry. Later they would be joined in oblivion by the documents relating to the Okhrana's activities in London at the time, as well as Special Branch ledgers that were said for decades to have been destroyed; since their inconvenient reappearance shortly prior to 2002, their retention has been defended, and heavy redaction undertaken. And yet beneath the whitewash, the fragmentary outline of the relationships that Rachkovsky and his co-conspirators were so eager to conceal can still be discerned.

What is known of events in Liège that spring reveals the modus operandi of Rachkovsky's agents: a model that conforms closely to that of the 1890 sting operation in Paris, was echoed at Walsall, and surely replicated elsewhere. A charismatic figure like the baron or Landesen or Coulon, burning with idealism and determination, presents themselves as an inspiration to impressionable youths who talk a good fight but lack the means. The material is provided, or else commissioned with detailed instructions for its acquisition or manufacture. Funds are supplied from a distant and affluent benefactor, ideally through an intermediary, of a generosity that dazzles any doubters. Secondary agents provocateurs, recruited locally,

affirm the credulous recruits in their sense of purpose. And if the execution of attacks is part of the plan, the bombers' own preferences may be
solicited but are then refined, to ensure maximum impact on public
opinion.

So to what had the counterfeit 'baron' been referring when he told
a group of cowardly Liègeois anarchists that 'You should see how we
do things in Paris', or when he alluded to his part in plots in London?
His involvement in Fénéon's attack on the Café Véry seems highly likely;
the coincidence of the unfortunate Pauwels' bombing of churches and
the baron's choice of Saint-Jacques as the first target in Liège, intriguing.
And then there was Dumont, Jagolkovsky's associate in London, who
had raised such suspicion in Paris the month before Henry's bombing
of the Café Terminus, and who had been part of Ravachol's group when
their raid on the dynamite store, reminiscent of that at Chevron near
Liège, had supplied the large haul of explosives used in any number of
the attacks that followed. As for Samuels and Coulon, they were bit-
part players at least in the whole mad cycle of violent retribution that
Rachkovsky's wiles had kept spinning. Rochefort, if he had a role,
unquestionably had his own agenda too.

A year after the Greenwich bombing, a disgruntled ex-sergeant in
Special Branch called MacIntyre would be the first to go public on the
use of agents provocateurs against the anarchists. 'Their intrigues produce
conspiracies,' he wrote in *Reynolds News*, his confirmation of long-
standing suspicions about the Walsall Affair eliciting a letter from Coulon
confessing to his role. For all Melville's attempts to discredit him,
MacIntyre was surely right to say that when such a provocateur 'finds
the prevailing danger is diminishing in quality . . . He manufactures more
"danger".' In 1898, Sir Robert Anderson, the assistant commissioner,
would admit as much, acknowledging 'emphatically that in recent years
the police have succeeded only by straining the law, or, in plain English,
by doing utterly unlawful things, at intervals, to check this conspiracy'.
It would be another two decades before a veteran of the French police
would admit the force's involvement in luring Vaillant into bombing the
Chamber of Deputies.

David Nicoll evoked the human cost of such tactics with great pathos.
'Romance and novelty there are,' he wrote of the anarchist's life, 'though
sometimes the delightful vision comes to an abrupt termination, changing
suddenly like a lovely face into an opium vision of something horrible
and devilish. This was the fate of some friends of ours, who dreamed of
regenerating the world, and found themselves, thanks to the machinations

of a police spy, doomed to a long term of penal servitude.' The fate of others was more abrupt.

The twenty-first of May 1894 was a day of executions. In Paris, Emile Henry was guillotined, while in Barcelona, the six men convicted of the Liceo opera house bombing faced a firing squad. As widely expected, their deaths heralded the next wave of revenge attacks. Three weeks later, an anarchist assassin tried and failed to shoot dead the Italian prime minister, Crispi, whom he held accountable for the imprisonment of over 1,000 socialists after the risings in the south of the country. Eight days after that, in Lyons, another Italian, Sante Geronimo Caserio, would meet with greater success: dashing from the crowd as the French president Sadi Carnot's carriage passed, he hauled himself up on to the running board and plunged a dagger into his victim's chest. Few were convinced by the assassin's insistence that he had acted on his own initiative, having simply caught a train from his home near the Mediterranean and then walked the rest of the distance to carry out the act, nor by the anarchists' disavowal of all knowledge of him.

Around the world, increasingly draconian measures were taken to counter the terrorist threat. In America, mere adherence to the anarchist cause had already become a crime, and any who espoused it were barred from entering the country. In July, France added a Press Law to the anti-anarchist armoury that the 'Wicked Laws' already constituted. The same month, Italy caught up by enacting three exceptional laws to ensure public security, known collectively as the 'Crispi Dictatorship', that imposed harsh restrictions on freedom of speech and association. Sentiment in Britain too was swinging against the anarchists.

'Society is asking how long the British metropolis will be content to afford a safe asylum for gangs of assassins, who there plot and perfect atrocious schemes for universal murder on the Continent,' opined the leader article in the *Globe*. Alarmist accounts of the terrorist threat, previously the preserve of the sensationalist novels, now became the subject of supposedly factual reportage in the popular magazines. The *Strand* published an article entitled 'Dynamite and Dynamiters' which disingenuously denied any intention to 'give rise to alarm or be an incentive to disturbed or restless nights', while offering the most blood-chilling accounts and illustrations of the destructive power of anarchist bombs. *Tit Bits* upped the ante, scooping an interview with a 'gentleman holding a high position in the detective force' who confided his concern that the anarchists were now turning their attention from conventional to biological terrorism, using the spores of typhus and yellow fever to spread viral contamination. Following the model of Rachkovsky's anti-Semitic propaganda, the immigrant masses were to be transformed in the popular imagination from inadvertent vectors of disease into intentional agents of infection.

21

A Time of Harmony

Paris, London and New York, 1894–1896

The Utopia for which veterans like Reclus and Kropoktin had strived for so long was finally plain to see. Paul Signac had begun work on his vast canvas *In the Time of Anarchy* in 1894, while the campaign of bombings and assassinations was at its most intense, but the scene he envisioned was a world apart from the chaos and ruination to which most now thought anarchism aspired. In Signac's modern-day Eden, fruit hung from trees within easy reach, babies explored freely, women danced in elegant but loose dresses and men read or played *petanques*, stripped to the waist, while couples gazed out over the sea. A distant steam tractor implied the benefits of technology but did not intrude on the balmy peace of the Mediterranean landscape.

Signac had ignored Kropotkin's famous call of a decade earlier for artists to 'depict for us in your vivid style or in your fervent paintings the titanic struggle of the people against the oppressors' or 'show the people the ugliness of contemporary life and make us touch with a finger the cause of this ugliness'. Instead, his restorative paradise evoked the kind of world in which Reclus had advised workers to spend their leisure, the better to counteract the bestiality of their labour, and for which Kropotkin had more recently supplied the logistical foundation in *Fields, Factories and Workshops*. Reclus himself would have been in his element there. 'I see him yet,' a friend of the geographer would later recollect, 'close to the waterside, making islands, capes and archipelagos in the sand with his stick, to amuse some child, and saying, "This is the ideal place to teach geography."'

The influence of the two venerable anarchists on Signac went far deeper, though, than his choice of subject matter. The pointillist method of constructing images through the application of minute paint dabs, that characterised the neo-Impressionist style of Signac and his late friend

Seurat, had first been inspired by Reclus' descriptions of running water, and only later developed by reference to recent innovations in optical theory. Reclus, a true poet of nature as Kropotkin said of him, saw how closely mankind and its environment were informed by one another: that aesthetic harmony encouraged social well-being, promoting the intellectual, moral and spiritual growth of its members and, conversely, that 'the planet's characteristics will not have their complete harmony if men are not first united in a concert of justice and peace'. Signac had visualised that reciprocity at its most benign, and for him the very perceptual process by which adjacent spots of colour blended into a shimmering whole in the eye of the beholder, as musical notes did in a complex composition, was itself a potent metaphor of the political harmony that the coming social revolution would herald. To many of his artistic peers, however, Signac's gesture of solidarity with the older generation of anarchists must have seemed curiously anachronistic, at the very least.

The propaganda value of all the articles written by Reclus and Kropotkin were as nothing, Félix Fénéon had pronounced, beside the bomb attacks by Vaillant and Henry, with the latter's attack on the Café Terminus especially noteworthy, 'being directed toward the voting public, more guilty in the long run, perhaps, than the representatives they elected'. In 1890, Signac had painted a full-length portrait of Fénéon in profile, in which the swirling psychedelic background, 'Rhythmic with Beats and Angles, Tones and Tints', suggested the lily-carrying impresario of the post-Impressionist and Symbolist movements conjuring an unknown aesthetic cosmos into existence. 'Everything new to be accepted requires that old fools must die. We are longing for this to happen as soon as possible' Fénéon had since written, in this case out of impatience for Camille Pissarro's work to receive due recognition. Increasingly, though, his belief in violent rupture as the necessary mechanism of progress had spilled over from his artistic concerns into political activism. In common with the large numbers of Signac's cultural peers who had spent months or years in a self-imposed London exile among the most extreme of the 'individualist' anarchists, the aura that surrounded Fénéon by 1894 was that of the dynamite blast.

That spring, when police raids were netting more than 400 anarchists suspected of conspiracy, Elisée Reclus was in Belgium, where he had finally gone with the intention of taking up a fellowship at the Free University in Brussels, which he had delayed until the nineteenth and final volume of the *Universal Geography* was complete. Wisely, the French authorities declined to pursue him, recognising that quite apart from the international furore his arrest might cause, the prosecution of a man of such high intellectual standing would muddy the convenient image of anarchism as the preserve of thugs and degenerates. Signac too was left unmolested, despite his name appearing, together with those of many other cultural figures, on a document seized by the police that listed the circulation of *La Révolte*. Yet when thirty anarchists accused of promulgating terror were arraigned in France that August, Fénéon found himself in the dock, together with the artist Maximilien Luce. Alongside them were Grave and Sébastien Faure, both of whom were reluctant speakers, together with a selection of other journalists and a handful of inarticulate career criminals from among Parmeggiani's gang of expropriators, many of them recent members of the London colony. With Emile Pouget and Constant Martin both in hiding, Fénéon was free to command the stage.

The charge against him was of conspiring with anarchists and keeping explosive materials concealed in his desk at the war ministry, in relation to the bombing of the Café Foyot. The incidental accusation of having spied for Germany was clearly absurd, but in other respects the case against him had a firmer foundation than certain outraged sections of the press claimed. By making the case as much about crimes of thought as of action, however, the authorities provided Fénéon with a field of battle tailored to his talents.

'You were seen conversing with an anarchist behind a gas lamp,' challenged Bulot, who was once again prosecuting for the state, his occasional fumbling of the cross-examination perhaps explained by the emotion of having himself narrowly escaped one of Ravachol's bombs. 'Could you explain to me,' Fénéon asked, turning insouciantly to the president of the court, 'which side of a gas lamp is its behind?' And when the president reminded the court how the mercury that Fénéon had admitted keeping for Henry might easily be made into an explosive fulminate, Fénéon had a smart riposte: just as it could be made into thermometers and barometers. Emile Henry had shown a quick tongue too, of course, until silenced by the guillotine, but the glowing tributes paid to Fénéon by such respectable character witnesses as the poet Mallarmé lent the acerbic logic of his responses something like a moral weight when set beside the sophistry of the prosecution.

The French authorities had intended the Trial of the Thirty, as it became known, to be a slick spectacle that would demonstrate the necessity and efficacy of the 'Wicked Laws' in defending the state and its citizens.

Having started its hearings less than a month after President Carnot's assassination, only one outcome to the trial seemed likely. The police, though, had overreached themselves in attempting to construct a case that conflated the theorists of anarchism with those who merely used the ideology as political cover for their habitual violent criminality. The result was that by the end of the trial in late October 1894, in all but three instances of serious but non-political violence, either the charges were dropped or acquittal ensued. 'Not since Pontius Pilate has anyone washed their hands with such solemnity,' Fénéon had quipped after Bulot opened a package from a 'well-wisher' that proved to be full of human excrement. However, although his facetious wit had afforded the 'individualist' anarchists outside the courtroom a crumb of comfort, the events of the previous year had left the movement high and dry, its press almost silenced and its lost momentum almost impossible to regain.

In retrospect, the Trial of the Thirty can be seen as marking a watershed in the history of French anarchism, between a period of terroristic violence and one of more considered attrition against the existing structures of society. The moderation of the jury's verdict reflected the unease that was widely felt in French society when people compared the harsh treatment meted out to those conspiring in the cause of a more just society, feared and despised as they widely were, with the leniency shown towards many of those involved in the Panama scandal, which had defrauded the French people of untold millions of francs. But while the trial may have helped release the dangerous pressure that had built up on both sides, the attitude of the authorities towards the anarchists in its immediate aftermath was scarcely conciliatory.

The mood among the London émigrés was variously depressed, chastened and pathetically vituperative. 'Most of them have lost their exaltation; others regret having ever become part of the anarchist movement and want to return to France,' concluded the prefecture's regular summary of its intelligence in October. The 'Wicked Laws' still threatened harsh penalties, though, and even the most remorseful were to remain trapped for the foreseeable future in an exile that became ever less congenial. Colleagues in Paris were warned by both Rochefort and Grave that coming to London had become a risky business and was inadvisable, but they would only have needed to read the articles in French magazines about the constant preparedness of the Home Office's resident bomb expert, Colonel Majendie, to understand how vigilant the British police remained. A spate of bomb attacks on London post offices in August may have proved to be the work of an indigenous anarchist from Deptford, but the French and Italian émigrés continued to feel the hot breath of Melville's agents on their necks.

With no other outlet for their violent urges, the expropriators turned on one another. Parmeggiani, frustrated as his gang went their separate ways, waved a revolver when Marocco accused him of stealing his share of the ill-gotten gains. For others, a long visit by Emma Goldman provided a welcome distraction, although her friendship with the informant Mowbray, who had recently accompanied her on a lecture tour of America, said little for her judgement. Her presence at least inspired thoughts of greener pastures, despite the harsh restrictions that the United States had imposed on anarchists entering the country. One French anarchist, Mollet, who had come into a sizeable inheritance, even set up a travel agency in Liverpool to facilitate passage for all those wishing to cross the Atlantic. Louise Michel herself appeared intent on doing so, though she wavered over which side of the equator should be graced with her presence.

The end of the year brought further bad news, this time from the penal colony of Devil's Island off the coast of Guyana, where many of those responsible for the most notorious crimes of recent years were serving sentences of hard labour. A number of anarchists had risen in revolt, stabbing four of their warders in vengeance for a convict beaten to death by a guard. Forewarned by informers, however, the authorities quickly reasserted control, hunting the miscreants down in bestial fashion. Hiding in a tree, Ravachol's accomplice Charles Simon ('Biscuit') was used for target practice. His body and that of Leauthier, who had stabbed the Serbian ambassador in the Bouillon Duval restaurant, were among eleven to be thrown to the sharks.

At any other time in the previous three years, such brutality would have aroused hot talk of vengeance among the London émigrés, but what meagre conspiracies the French police agents now reported had instead an air of desperate futility. Only the new young Tsar Nicholas in Moscow, who had recently inherited the crown on the death of Alexander III, was deemed a fitting target. With Rochefort turning off the tap of funding to the émigré communities, however, and in the absence of further nefarious investment from Rachkovsky and the Okhrana, any such murderous expeditions seemed certain to remain a pipe dream. Such, at least, must have been the hope of the more senior anarchists in London, who had for some time been edging towards a more outspoken denunciation of dynamite.

The previous March, soon after the bombs at the Café Terminus and in Greenwich, Louise Michel had gone on record as saying that terrorism was irrelevant to the general struggle. It was a view that Malatesta would echo in his critical essay on the subject, 'Heroes and Martyrs', observing that 'with any number of bombs and any number of blows of the knife, bourgeois society cannot be overthrown, being built as it is on an enormous mass of private interests and prejudices and sustained, more than it is by force of arms, by the inertia of the masses and their habits of submission'. However, a reputation, once acquired, is hard to live down.

For many years, Malatesta's commitment to the cause of social revolution had led him to plot and plan its advent wherever the prospect seemed most promising; it was no accident that his travels around Europe, since his return from South America, had frequently coincided with strikes and demonstrations. The confrontations that ensued often led to violence, initiated by one side or the other. An almost inevitable outcome was the recourse to terrorism by anarchists for purposes of revenge. The repeated linkage of Malatesta's conspiratorial presence and the use of dynamite led many, in the police forces of Europe and even among his colleagues, to suppose a causal relationship where it did not necessarily exist. Even his denunciations of individualistic violence, including his tart exchange of views with Emile Henry in 1893, were consequently seen as a ruse to misdirect attention away from his supposed role in such plots.

The wave of 'anarchist' terror that had swept the Continent was a millstone for Malatesta. He had been a suspect in the case of the rue des Bons-Enfants bomb in 1892, which Henry had in fact planned himself, and was thought by many to be the guiding hand behind others in Spain and Italy. During the weeks before the Café Terminus bombing it was his presence rather than that of either Henry or 'Bourdin' which attracted the heaviest surveillance, while his movements and contacts in London were consistently reported with an assiduousness that applied to few other émigrés. Accused in one report of having been 'involved with' President Carnot's assassin, Caserio, and in another of being 'satisfied' with the result of the attack, in the face of all evidence to the contrary, the image of him presented by French police agents was like that in the Englishman W. C. Harte's memoir *Confessions of an Anarchist*: 'the most dangerous plotter of modern times – who however . . . when the death of kings and presidents is in the air – appears in the background'. When Malatesta reviled dynamite, the authorities swiftly claimed it was because he 'prefers daggers that are sure to strike their predetermined target', and would long continue to insist that 'he wraps himself in mystery'.

Malatesta's predicament exemplified that of the movement as a whole. The demonisation of the movements in the 1890s had provided the press with a compelling shorthand for the anarchist as a malign figure in the shadows, a bomb beneath his coat and hell-bent on destruction, and it was a cliché that enemies on all sides found highly advantageous to exploit. Even Signac's innocent painting found itself tarred with the same brush. Up on the slopes of Montmartre, Henri Zisly's anarchist group Les Naturiens pursued a libertarian existence that echoed Signac's bucolic idyll, perplexing the police with their defiant choice of a life of near savagery in such close proximity to the metropolis. But while they won converts with their neo-Gaulish festivals and vegetarian banquets in honour of Rousseau, it was an attempted dynamite attack on the Sacré-Coeur in July 1895, rising ever higher on the skyline, and fantastical sketches of the destruction such a blast might cause published by the anarchist lithographer Théophile Steinlen, that caught the public imagination. These seemed to the general public to be a more credible representation of what life would be like *In the Time of Anarchy* than Signac's flower-strewn paradise.

In recognition of the adverse circumstances, Signac altered the title of his painting to *In the Time of Harmony* but not even this compromise could secure its place in Victor Horta's revolutionary art nouveau House of the People in Brussels, for which it had originally been destined. In fact, the previous year the Belgian authorities had revealed their nervousness towards anarchism, even in its most peaceable form, with the Free University's last-minute decision to cancel Elisée Reclus' fellowship. The decision had proved counterproductive. Rather than leave Brussels, Reclus had found an alternative venue for his lectures in the Freemasonic Loge des Amis Philanthropes, where his willingness to debate ideas with his audience had so energised the pedagogic process that, such was the demand to attend, arrangements were made for a breakaway New University to open its doors the following September.

Reclus had demonstrated how anarchists could turn marginalisation to their advantage, using their exclusion from the mainstream to shape new opportunities and a new identity that might in time deliver the objective of social revolution. While resident in Belgium, the geographer even took up the composition of songs to carry anarchist propaganda to the francophone peasantry. The project that was dearest to him, though, was the revival of his plans for a Great Globe, for he believed that 'in the solemn contemplation of reliefs you participate so to speak with eternity . . . Globes must be temples which will make people grave and respectful.' Conceived now on a scale of 1:100,000, at over a quarter of a mile in diameter, a third as high again as the Eiffel Tower and nearly twice the height of the Sacré-Coeur, Reclus hoped that it would be commissioned for the 1900 Paris Expo, where it would reassert the values of the Enlightenment which commerce and religion threatened to obscure.

It is amusing to imagine what Special Branch and French police agents in London must have made of the diagrams that Reclus sent to his nephew Paul, one of those charged *in absentia* in the Trial of the Thirty and who had remained in partial exile for some time after the amnesty of 1895. Complete with its proposed superstructure housing the external observation platforms, in profile the pointed egg-shape of the globe bore a strong resemblance to that of the most advanced terrorist grenades, whose eye-opening function it was meant to supersede. The allusion was surely unintentional, though, and the path to acceptance would not be easy for either Reclus' proposals or the anarchism they projected.

In 1891, Oscar Wilde had proposed a geographical metaphor of his own for the development of socialism. 'A map of the world that does not include Utopia is not even worth glancing at,' he wrote in his essay, 'The Soul of Man Under Socialism', 'for it leaves out the one country at which Humanity is always landing.' Since then, anarchists had ventured into treacherous territory in search of their ideal. Even now, though, as veterans of the recent rough seas charted a course to new and diverse destinations, the shores that awaited them held unforeseen hazards of their own.

'There is a growing sense of harmony and reconciliation,' Louise Michel had written, 'the reactionaries are less harsh than they used to be, and the bombs are past history.' But while the bombs may have fallen silent, her statement was otherwise wishful thinking, as would be shown in the onslaught of criticism to which the anarchist elements at the congress of the Second International would be subjected when it convened in London in July 1896. A determination that anarchism should remain recognised as a legitimate socialist creed, socialism in its ultimate and purest form indeed, had led Malatesta to help organise the event, but any hopes he may have had of shaping the agenda from the inside were soon revealed as futile.

'The only resemblance between the individual anarchists and us is that of a name,' Reclus had recently protested, but not even the campaign of denigration waged by Parmeggiani's L'Anonymat group against Kropotkin, Malato and Pouget could persuade the Marxists and social democrats to acknowledge the reality, when there was so much for them to gain by not doing so. 'What we advocate is free association and union, the absence of authority, minds free from fetters, independence and well-being of all. Before all others it is we who preach *tolerance* for all – whether we think their opinions right or wrong – we do not wish to crush them by force or otherwise,' Gustav Landauer reminded the delegates, but failed to shame Liebknecht, Lafargue and the other Marxists into matching those ideals. Minds were made up, even before his assertion that 'What we fight is *state socialism*, levelling from above, bureaucracy', setting the stage for a coup even more decisive than that staged by Marx and Engels against Bakunin a quarter-century earlier.

Having delayed her planned move to America to be present at the congress, Louise Michel attended for its second day and the showdown. The dice were heavily loaded against the anarchists, who were poorly represented: offers by Special Branch to subsidise the cost of a one-way Channel crossing at the time of the amnesty the previous year had left the once thriving London colonies sadly depleted. The followers of Marx, by contrast, had succeeded in packing the congress with delegates shipped in from Germany and Belgium as well as many local supporters. Malatesta's oratory failed to break down their disciplined obstructionism, despite the attempts of the British trade unionist Tom Mann and others to win him a hearing. 'Were I not an anarchist already, that congress would have made me one,' wrote Michel, after witnessing the expulsion of her colleagues; an excommunication, in effect, by a new 'state religion' of Marx with its own 'infallible hierarchy'.

Even this decisive schism in the socialist movement was not without its benefits, however, with many of the heretics from the congress impelled towards a consensus on the vexed question of how the future society to which anarchism aspired should be organised. For too long, the rival claims of communism and collectivism – ownership in common, or on a cooperative basis, with some degree of private property – had clouded anarchism's clarity of purpose. Now, the young Fernand Pelloutier joined with Emile Pouget to clarify the issue. Inspired by the dynamic example set by the British unions, and his own recent work in France in bringing together the representation of different industries with the city-specific work of the *bourses du travail*, Pelloutier advocated 'a hybrid of anarchist and trade unionism known as anarcho-syndicalism or revolutionary socialism'. The project breathed new life into the vision of autonomous but associated units of economic activity that Proudhon, Bakunin and Kropotkin had all held up as a viable basis for social transformation, but also provided a robust base from which eventually to launch a general strike, as the mechanism for effecting peaceful revolutionary change.

The London Congress of 1896 was notable too, however, for those who were absent: Kropotkin, Kravchinsky and Morris. Kropotkin, weary of the predictable and unproductive debate that characterised past meetings, and perhaps reading the runes, had decided in advance not to attend. It was not only the final marginalisation of the anarchists, though, that caused the congress to mark the end of an era. The recent death of Kravchinsky and failing health of Morris would have left Kropotkin, had he attended, without two of those contemporaries closest to him.

The valedictory tone of *News from Nowhere* in 1890 had marked William Morris' turn away from socialism and back to his artistic activities, in particular the exquisite printing of the Kelmscott Press, but since 1893 he had once again begun to appear at public meetings of the Social Democratic Federation. Its brand of bureaucratic socialism was scarcely more to his taste, though, than the anarchism that had driven him from his own Socialist League, and he had wearily bemoaned to a leading Fabian that 'The world is going your way, Webb, but it is not the right way in the end.' The last lecture he delivered before his death that autumn was to the newly formed Society for Checking the Abuses of Public Advertising, denouncing the plague of billboard advertising that had begun to disfigure the landscapes he so loved and from which he had drawn such inspiration. As a sideways attack on the capitalist culture of consumption, it chimed perfectly with the oblique approach to revolution increasingly being adopted by his lasting friends in the anarchist movement.

It had been almost a year earlier, however, standing on the steps of Waterloo station on 28 December 1895, that Morris had delivered his final outdoor address to the mourners at Kravchinsky's funeral, 200 of whom then boarded the train run by the London Necropolis Company to accompany his coffin on the twenty-mile journey to Brookwood Cemetery. 'It was a significant and striking spectacle, this assemblage of socialists, nihilists, anarchists, and outlaws of every European country, gathered together in the heart of London to pay respect to the memory of their dead leader,' *The Times* told its readers. The sadness of those present was all the greater that his death was so premature and unnecessary, while its cause seemed scarcely credible, in the case of a man who had always lived by his wits.

Recent years had undoubtedly imposed great strains on Kravchinsky, as he risked the safety of even those closest to him in the cause of Russian freedom, only to find himself repeatedly thwarted in his task by the ruthless efficiency of his enemies, and the unscrupulous tactics that they were prepared to employ. When, on the eve of 1894, he had sent Constance Garnett into the depths of icy Russia on a risky mission to distribute money and collect information, she had returned deeply unnerved by the police surveillance to which she had been subjected, and which had caused her to burn all her entire precious cargo of letters and documents back to

London before she reached the border. Almost as bad, it had been while she was away, leaving her six-month-old baby in the care of her husband, that Rachkovsky had placed the article in the British press that exposed her beloved Kravchinsky as Mezentsev's murderer and made pointed reference to his 'shallow theories of free love'. The personal awkwardness was as nothing to Kravchinsky, however, compared to the damage being done by the Okhrana to the Society of Friends of Russian Freedom.

With a new efficiency, the Russian police department had distilled the product of its intensive surveillance of suspected subversives, in Russia and abroad, into a diagrammatic representation of the whole vast web of revolutionary activity. Taken in isolation, the colour-coded lines that fanned out from the central individual on each chart allowed seemingly tenuous relationships to be traced deep into the revolutionary under-world, revealing complicity where least expected; cross-referenced, with up to 300 suspects mentioned on each sheet, they mapped the far-reaching curiosity of a formidable police state. This system alone might have explained why a large portion of the printed material smuggled into Russia by the Friends failed to reach its destination, but the true, uniden-tified cause actually lay closer to home.

Some of the packages whose shipment the Okhrana agent Evalenko, posing as the Friends' American librarian 'Vladimir Sergeyev', had volun-teered to oversee were destroyed by him as soon as they arrived from the presses; others he forwarded to Russia having supplied details that allowed their interception by the border police. Meanwhile, in London, the Okhrana agent Lev Beitner had so thoroughly infiltrated himself into the organ-isation and the society surrounding it that when he applied for a reader's ticket for the British Museum Library, it was Garnett's own brother, Richard, an employee, who provided a reference. Drawing on the intelli-gence he had gathered, Rachkovsky reported to St Petersburg that Kravchinsky and his associates were involved with other previously antag-onistic émigré groups around Europe in the creation of 'a central organ-isation that would unite them all and help to join efforts and resources, forge and sustain contacts with revolutionaries back home'.

A unified distribution network might bring together the disparate émigré groups in a common front; without it, they would surely only atomise further. Rachkovsky was determined to see it sabotaged, and his agent Evalenko had already begun the dirty work, helping to seed the discord between Lazarev and Kravchinsky that, ironically in light of Kravchinsky's past actions and reputation, had its origin in his resistance to Lazarev's demands for the Russian revolutionary movement to adopt more militant tactics. Then, having effectively destroyed the American wing of the Society of Friends of Russian Freedom from within, in late 1895 Evalenko was recalled to London to continue his mischief-making there.

Early that summer, Constance Garnett's sister Olive had written of how Kravchinsky had confided in her that he 'wanted a new life, to elope with someone, not to be set down to work'. There was perhaps an element of flirtation in the words of a man who had once taught the art of coquettishness to Vera Zasulich and knew that both Garnett sisters doted on him and despised his wife. However, after fifteen years of onerous exile, with little progress to see for his efforts, Kravchinsky's anguish was probably all too real. As the year drew to an end, and the rest of London prepared for Christmas, Kravchinsky remained hard at work thrashing out the details of a new journal that he was to edit, which would create a united front of Russian socialists and liberals against autocracy. On the subject of elopement, he appeared to have reconciled himself to quietly cuckolding Constance's husband Edward, and had 'promised to get a bear's ham from Russia' for his visit to the Garnett family's new country cottage when it was completed in the New Year. First, though, on 23 December, he was scheduled to attend a crucial meeting to discuss editorial policy.

From Kravchinsky's home in Bedford Park in West London, whose calm streets Camille Pissarro had recently painted, it was only a short walk to where Volkhovsky and Lazarev awaited him. Both were old friends, veterans of the Trial of the 193 twenty years before, but in Lazarev he would face a man reconverted to terrorism, quite possibly under Evalenko's influence, and determined to sway Kravchinsky, a founder member of the Independent Labour Party, from his commitment to the principle that social justice should be achieved through peaceful change. Distracted or distraught, Kravchinsky's state of mind can only be guessed at when, swinging his legs across the stile at the end of his road, he wandered on to the tracks of the North London Railway. Rounding the distant bend, the attentive driver pulled on the power vacuum brakes of his engine, but when the train came to a stop Kravchinsky's body lay mangled beneath the second carriage.

Foul play was ruled out, suicide not mentioned. Friends considerately explained the accident by reference to Kravchinsky's early experiences in the Bosnian gaols, an episode never before mentioned, where he had supposedly acquired the ability to will himself deaf in order to stay sane amid the cacophony. 'How else could I endure English dinner parties?' they remembered him joking. Olive Garnett cropped her hair in grief. Rachkovsky's reaction to the news was doubtless rather different.

22

Conspiracy Theories

Europe and America, 1896–1901

Taking stock in early 1896, Rachkovsky could have reflected on two turbulent but largely efffective years for himself and the foreign Okhrana. In the weeks before the bombs of Henry and Bourdin had exploded, he had appeared more vulnerable than at any time since his arrival in Paris. Neither the fact that he had recently exercised 'more influence on the course of our rapprochement with France than did our ambassadors', in the words of the Russian finance minister, Sergei Witte, nor his success in 'exerting pressure on the local press . . . in the battle against the émigrés' in London, had been enough to make his position secure. Ambassador de Mohrenheim, his supporter for many years, looked ripe for ignominious retirement, tarnished by his involvement in the Panama scandal and deemed increasingly unreliable after a debilitating bout of influenza, while Rachkovsky had been criticised for his indiscreet dealings with the French government.

The visit that January of Ivan Manasevich-Manuilov from the ministry of the interior, whom Rachkovsky suspected of collecting 'information about my personal life, my financial position abroad, about the staff of the *agentura*, and about my relations with the prefecture and the embassy in Paris', must have appeared the prelude to his removal from post. Yet Rachkovsky had quickly turned the situation around, swatting away 'the nimble Jew' who was 'ready to do anything for a goodly sum', and earning fitting recognition for his efforts. The bonus of 10,000 rubles that he received in April, nominally for his work in swaying the press, must also have been in tacit acknowledgement of his feats of provocation: fortunately for him, it was paid before the embarrassment of Liège. Yet, despite Liège, few of his superiors could have doubted that Rachkovsky's deft exploitation of the anarchist bombings was largely to thank when, late in the year, the Russian department of police's magazine *Obzor* reported 'a marked cooling of the English towards the supposedly innocent but persecuted Russian dissidents'.

The way ahead, though, was less clear. A flurry of warnings from British and French police about mooted attacks on Russian targets after the death of Alexander III, and the involvement of a group of Berlin anarchists in a planned assassination of the new tsar in Moscow, maintained a sense of imminent danger. So too did the discussions between Lazarev and Burtsev, among others, about a renewal of revolutionary violence in Russia to offset the drift towards reformism in the movement led by the charismatic Georgi Plekhanov and his Social Democrats, the official standard-bearers for the ideas of Marx. Times were changing, though, and Rachkovsky had to reposition himself accordingly: both with regard to the declining threat of terrorism in the West, and more crucially the change of ruler in Russia.

Rachkovsky appears never to have been a favourite of the late tsar, who had once scrawled the single word 'villain' next to Rachkovsky's name in an official report. And yet for fourteen years, Alexander III's towering physical presence and authority had maintained stability and held Russia on a tight course of religious and political conservatism. In stark contrast, his son Nicholas, on hearing of his succession, is said to have wept not for his lost father but at his own unreadiness to inherit the throne: a sound self-assessment that would leave him dependent on the influence of his advisers. According to one popular joke, so fickle was the young tsar that whoever had last spoken to him could be considered the most powerful man in Russia, with the serious consequence that the court was riven by factionalism. It was a situation whose risks were illustrated in tragic fashion on the very day of Nicholas II's coronation in the gilded splendour of the Kremlin's Uspensky Cathedral, when his entourage had insulated the new tsar from news of the stampede by peasants on the nearby Khodynka Field that had left almost 1,400 dead. The decision that he would proceed as planned to a ball at the French Embassy left a lasting impression of callous aloofness on the peasant population, which compounded their irritation at Nicholas's recent dismissal of proposals for constitutional change as 'senseless dreams'.

For Rachkovsky, there was no option but to choose sides and his preference was clear: the progressive Witte, determined to drag peasant Russia into the modern world. Witte was still an enthusiast for railway expansion, as he had been when he claimed to have seeded the idea of the Holy Brotherhood, and an advocate of an active credit system, migration to cities and the division of labour. Implicit in Rachkovsky's choice

of patron, however, was the acquisition of powerful enemies: the politically conservative Plehve, who as director of police had never quite trusted
Rachkovsky, and Pobedonostsev, procurator of the Orthodox synod, a
deeply thoughtful man who nevertheless hated all originality and innovation, and was committed to the resettlement of migrant peasants in
villages subject to the traditional social binding of church and family.
Rachkovsky's audience with Pope Leo XIII in the Vatican, where he
allegedly attempted to broker a rapprochement between the Catholic and
Eastern Orthodox Churches, might almost have been designed to pique
Pobedonostsev. Witte must have hoped that ease and wealth had not
blunted Rachkovsky's capacity for subtler intrigues and that he could rely
on him to serve his interests. The coming years would be fertile in opportunity.

*

One crisp October morning in 1896, dignitaries gathered on the Left
Bank of the Seine near the Esplanades des Invalides for the ceremony
to lay the cornerstone of the bridge that would be France's tribute to
Alexander III. Standing slightly apart, Rachkovsky looked on hawkishly.
The safety of Tsar Nicholas II, there to honour his late father, was
always the Okhrana chief's top priority and should have commanded
his full attention. Yet despite his duties, Rachkovsky may have allowed
himself to exchange a knowing glance with one or two familiar figures.
Boisdeffre was present, the general with whom he had dealt over the
French alliance, as was Henri Rochefort who had travelled a long way
politically since 1881, when the nihilists had entrusted him alone with
the inside story of a previous tsar's assassination. That the reactionary
soldier and the radical marquis had recently found common ground
was strange enough, with Rochefort considering his new friend for the
Boulanger role in the dictatorship of which he still dreamed. Stranger
still, though, was the possibility that both shared a secret with the Russian
spymaster that was far more explosive: one that within weeks would
seep out into the public domain.

The Dreyfus Affair, when it broke that November, would redraw the
political fault lines that divided French society, with dramatic effect. Nearly
two years had passed since Maurice Barrès had described the ritual humiliation of the Jewish army captain from the ministry of war convicted of
spying for Germany, in terms reminiscent of those more usually applied
to the criminal degenerate. 'As he came towards us with his cap thrust
down over his forehead, his pince-nez on his ethnic nose, his eyes dry

and furious, his foreign physiognomy, his impassive stillness,' Barrès wrote, 'the very atmosphere he exuded revolted even the most self-controlled of spectators.' In a brutal spectacle, the braid and buttons were ripped from Dreyfus' uniform by a towering blond Breton, who then proceeded to break the disgraced officer's sword over his knee; a prelude to Dreyfus' transportation to Devil's Island, where only weeks before the rebel anarchists had been massacred. A scintillating literary talent whose anarchism had brought him full circle to that dangerous place where the extremes of right and left overlap and where an extreme form of nationalistic socialism would later be born, Barrès relished the scene, and few public figures questioned the sentence unless, like Clemenceau, to criticise its leniency. Now all that was about to change.

The first challenge to the soundness of the verdict came from another anarchist, the journalist Bernard Lazare, who had been an outspoken presence at the recent London Congress. For while Barrès, Drumont and Rochefort had spent their time feeding fresh meat to the beast of anti-Semitism, hungry again after gorging itself on the Panama scandal, Lazare had taken a considered interest as further evidence came to light. The proof of Dreyfus' guilt – an incriminating document purportedly in his handwriting – had been thrown into doubt by the discovery in a war-ministry wastebasket of a suspicious letter bearing an identical hand: that of a Major Esterhazy. Battle was joined in the press, with neither side conceding an inch. The socialists were slow to engage, and two months later Jules Guesde would still be insisting that the passion evinced by the affair was merely a 'bourgeois civil war'. Many anarchists, though, recognised behind the anti-Semitism a more far-reaching reactionary agenda that had forged a fearsome cohesion in the radical, nationalistic right. Louise Michel, torn between her gratitude to Rochefort on the one hand and, on the other, friendship for the passionate Dreyfusard, Sébastien Faure, was rare in remaining neutral: a position that left her utterly isolated.

As Rochefort wove a complex conspiracy claiming that a Jewish syndicate was conspiring against France, did he know that his amplified prejudice was merely providing a smokescreen to conceal a real conspiracy that was scarcely less alarming? If so, he had aligned himself not only with General Boisdeffre but with key figures from the earlier struggle against terrorism. When the graphology expert Monsieur Gobert refused to bow to pressure from the military to verify the letter, Alphonse Bertillon, the criminal anthropologist, was happy to step in with elaborate justifications of Dreyfus' guilt. Most intriguing of all, however, were the rumours that circulated of a Russian angle to the skullduggery. Forged intelligence overstating France's military strength had, it was suggested, been supplied to reassure the late tsar as he wavered before signing the alliance; Dreyfus' imprisonment in solitary confinement was to prevent him from divulging what he knew. If true, it would have put both Boisdeffre and Rachkovsky in the frame.

The French government, however, issued a statement absolving all foreign embassies of involvement in the affair, but the full truth will never be known, for as the novelist Emile Zola would mention in his famous open letter to President Faure of January 1898, 'papers were disappearing, then as they continue to do to this day'. And yet, in a revealing paradox, other papers were simultaneously appearing in the most mysterious ways, with Esterhazy claiming that the document used to exonerate him, fraudulently as it proved, had been handed over by a 'veiled lady' outside, of all places, the Sacré-Coeur.

Frauds and forgeries were, of course, a practised part of Rachkovsky's repertoire of intrigue, and it is tempting to imagine him taking a connoisseur's interest in other successful practitioners. Might he, then, have been in the queue of top-hatted gentlemen waiting to check in their sticks and umbrellas at the cloakroom of the Paris Geographical Society on Easter Monday 1897, a strict requirement for admission to the auditorium on this most intriguing of nights? Against a backdrop of heightening political tensions, the foyer was abuzz with the promise of an appearance by a certain Diane Vaughan. Descended from the seventeenth-century English mystic Thomas Vaughan, it was said, she was the author of *The Restoration of Palladism, a Transition Decreed by the Sanctum Regnum to Prepare the Public Cult of Lucifer.* She was also the alleged source of the extraordinary revelations about satanic Freemasonry made by the ex-Freemason Leo Taxil.

Rachkovsky would certainly have admired Taxil's ambition, or rather that of Gabriel Jogand-Pages, the true identity of the charlatan. Building on a decade of fantastical fear-mongering, in the autumn of 1896 Taxil had been the prime mover behind the Anti-Masonic Congress, marching through the streets of Trent at the head of a torch-bearing procession 18,000 strong. A petition from Spain asserting that Freemasonry was indeed a 'dark and diabolical sect, the enemy of God' contained more than 100,000 signatures, while there was little ambiguity about the anti-Semitism later in the declaration by delegates, including dozens of Catholic bishops, that Freemasonry was the 'Synagogue of Satan'. After much pleasurable alarmism had been indulged in, though, doubts had finally been raised about the reliability of Taxil's sources. The Geographical Society event was the outcome: Jogand-Pages' punchline to his grotesquely overextended joke.

To begin with Taxil regaled the audience with an account of his earlier hoaxes: the scam of the sharks troubling the fishermen of the Riviera, the year after the Commune, and of the mysterious city under the waters of Lake Geneva that so many travelled to see while anarchism was being defined nearby. And yet, he teased, 'compared with the tugboat I had dispatched hunting for sharks in the coves off Marseilles in my early years, the boat of Palladism was a true battleship . . . the battleship turned into a squadron. And when Miss Diana Vaughan became my auxiliary, the squadron grew into a full navy.' Taxil had fooled even the Pope, despite having previously satirised His Holiness' sexual habits: invited to the Vatican, he received a papal endorsement of his campaign against the Masons. And yet every word that Taxil wrote or spoke had been a fraud. Those terribly plausible stories of devils with telephones, of orgiastic rituals and Satan's global conspiracy were revealed, to widespread astonishment, as so much nonsense. Among the audience at the Geographical Society whose anger and astonishment Jogand-Pages now fled, only the winner of the prize draw for a typewriter left with anything other than shattered illusions. And even he was the unwitting victim of yet another joke: the 'Diana Vaughan' whose name Jogand-Pages had borrowed, was a saleswoman for Remington.

'They accepted my tales as gospel truth,' Taxil observed of those he had duped for so long, 'and the more I lied for the purpose of showing that I lied, the more convinced they became that I was a paragon of veracity.' To anyone of good conscience these words would have invited them to question the appeal of conspiracy stories that flattered their most atavistic tribalism; to someone like Rachkovsky they merely inspired greater deviousness.

The opportunity for Rachkovsky to implement the lesson of Taxil's audacity may have arisen not long afterwards. Sergei Witte, his powerful political ally, had responded to attacks made on him by de Cyon in the *Nouvelle Revue*, with their dangerous claims that he was conspiring to seize power, by trying and failing to force their author's return to Russia. Stripped of his Russian nationality, and with French hospitality exhausted, de Cyon had taken up residence in Switzerland as a stateless person, and it was to his villa in Territet that Rachkovsky's agents pursued him, in a raid reminiscent of that on the People's Will's presses a decade before. Their objective may have been the seizure of material incriminating de Cyon himself. It would later be claimed, however, that they had discovered a very different kind of document: one that would shock and astound readers with a vivid blueprint for the long-gestated Jewish takeover of the world.

How *The Protocols of the Elders of Zion* came into existence is even more obscure than the hidden details of the Drefyus Affair. And yet, for all the many theories about the provenance of the forged document, with its cunning representation of anarchists, socialists, Masons and liberals as the dupes of a diabolic Jewish plot, its roots clearly lie in the world over which Rachkovsky presided. It is not only the contemporary allusions that point to such a conclusion: the construction of the Paris Métro, for example, or the document's own claim to be the secret agenda of the first Zionist Congress, organised in Basel in the summer of 1896 by Theodor Herzl and Max Nordau, whose secret lover was the Okhrana agent Madame Novikoff. Nor is it the employment in the Okhrana's Paris offices at the time of the skilled forger Matvei Golovinsky, who like Rachkovsky and his loyal French agent Bint was an old member of the Holy Brotherhood.

The most telling facts of all concern, rather, the literary work on which the forgery was based, *The Dialogues between Machiavelli and Montesquieu in Hell*, a satire of Napoleon III's despotic manipulation of public opinion, and the context of its composition in 1867 by Albert Joly, while he was an exile in Brussels. Thirty years on, few would still have remembered Joly's work, long since out of print. But when Joly had been in Brussels, so too had Rochefort, who may well have consulted him about routes by which to smuggle *La Lanterne* into France. Albert Joly, moreover, was the brother of the lawyer Maurice Joly, who had defended Henri Rochefort before the military tribunal in 1872 at Gambetta's request, and would subsequently be hounded to suicide for it by his client. If anyone had proposed the old booklet to Rachkovsky as the basis for a trick to demonise the Jews, Rochefort appears the likeliest candidate.

When Herzl witnessed the humiliation of Captain Dreyfus in 1895, it was the visceral anti-Semitic hatred he saw and felt in the crowd that convinced him that only in a Jewish homeland could the safety of his race be guaranteed. At the time he cannot have guessed the sordid intrigues that had led to the scene, but still less can he have imagined the conspiracy that would be forged to demonise the Zionist movement he founded. Rochefort and Rachkovsky had both demonstrated, in their different ways, that they had few scruples when it came to settling scores and making their political points.

*

Compared to the knotty intrigues that Rachkovsky was ravelling and unravelling in France, the problem posed by the enquiring mind of the revolutionary movement's counter-intelligence agent Vladimir Burtsev in London should have been relatively straightforward to resolve. Yet despite Rachkovsky's best efforts, Burtsev continued to be an irritant. 'The conflict of the Russian government with revolutionaries has long ago lost its primitive character and has now become a regular science,' Burtsev wrote, and responded accordingly. Having himself been the victim of betrayal on more than one occasion, he set about compiling an archive of notes and dossiers on police agents for the purposes of rooting out informers and provocateurs. For anyone to turn his own techniques against him was intolerable for Rachkovsky, but his antipathy towards Burtsev may have had a personal edge too.

For several years Rachkovsky had run a honey-pot operation against Burtsev. The woman involved was Charlotte Bullier, a rich young widow and possible cousin of Rachkovsky's agent Henri Bint. Bullier first met Burtsev in Paris in 1892, winning his trust with an offer of assistance in evading the French police. Over the next two years they conducted a tempestuous affair, in the flesh and by letter, as Bullier repeatedly sought and failed to lure her lover abroad for romantic trysts, in order to deliver him to her Okhrana paymaster. If Burtsev sometimes felt dazed by the experience, it may have been due as much to the sleeping drugs with which she dosed him, in order to read and report on his letters, as mere sexual obsession. Either way, he nearly fell prey to her wiles. Eventually answering her invitations to travel to Marseilles to be with her, he found himself locked into his cabin. Bullier's attempt to get her captive to Russia was only foiled by the lack of transport, although the head of the police department in St Petersburg was tempted to dispatch a warship from the Black Sea fleet for the purpose.

The gifts and intimate notes exchanged between Bullier and Rachkovsky hint that he too was in thrall to her charms, perhaps exacerbating his antipathy to Burtsev. When in 1897 the revolutionary finally overstepped the line, publishing a newspaper called *Narodovolets* that advocated a resumption of the old terror tactics of the People's Will, Rachkovsky was certainly ready to pounce. The first signs were not encouraging. A demand from Russia's chargé d'affaires in London that Lord Salisbury's government take urgent action against Burtsev was diplomatically dismissed. 'I could not answer for it that upon that jury some person might not be found, whose prejudices might prevent him from recognising the heinousness of the offences with which the prisoner has been charged,' the prime minister explained. His authorisation of a secret payment for Hilda Czarina, a 'speciality dancer' from Brighton, to change her name, at the request of the Russian Embassy, scarcely made amends. Rachkovsky, though, knew someone who shared his disdain for the 'pedantic concern' that the English displayed towards ancient legal tradition, and could help him negotiate the obstacles.

For the benefit of his superiors, Chief Inspector Melville grumbled at having 'to play the part of host to the Russian secret service' during the tsar's visits to Queen Victoria at Balmoral, but the time he spent there with Harting and Rachkovsky appears to have been perfectly convivial, and in private correspondence with the latter he sang to a very different tune. Burtsev and his associates were 'common murderers', Melville informed Rachkovsky, whom he would like to 'chase from one end of London to the other' and whose prosecution, he thought, would help 'alert the public and the government to the menace posed by the anarchists'. Doubtless the gifts of gold jewellery from the tsar went down well with Melville's wife, but even setting aside his underhand offer to assist Rachkovsky in 1892, the chief inspector's disdainful attitude to the democratic rule of law was shocking, if nothing new.

Consistently regarding the police as 'correct' in their stance towards the international émigrés, and the electors as wrong-headed, Melville had written to his French counterpart Fedée as long ago as 1893 of his intention 'to open the eyes of the English public to what the anarchists are really like'. At the time one senior civil servant had recently advised his minister that the public would only accept further police powers for the control of immigrants under 'the immediate pressure of alarm and indignation at the perpetration of bombings here'. And yet despite Rachkovsky's best efforts to create such circumstances the following year, Lord Salisbury's Aliens Bill had failed to pass through Parliament. Now, though, late in 1897, having advised his friend Rachkovsky how best to apply political pressure for Burtsev's prosecution, Melville could look forward to a small consolation.

Burtsev was arrested on 16 December in the foyer of the British Museum Library. Melville had the added pleasure of seeing his officer invade London's great temple of learning, whose stacks had nourished the subversive passions of so many native and émigré troublemakers down the years. Burtsev's lodgings were swiftly raided and his archive impounded; a question had to be asked in Parliament before assurances were forthcoming from Special Branch that the material would not be passed on to the Okhrana. When Burtsev's case finally came to court, the public gallery was packed with British policemen in plain clothes, to prevent genuine spectators gaining admission, and Kropotkin, Chaikovsky and

Volkhovsky were among only a handful of Burtsev's friends able to find a place. Rachkovsky himself declined to attend, lest his presence incite anti-Russian feeling.

Burtsev attempted an appeal to the British sense of fair play. 'We ourselves would naturally prefer to write books than make bombs,' he told the court, asking that it give the same answer to Russian despotism as the captain of the SS *Ashlands* had, years before, when the Okhrana demanded he hand Burtsev over in Constantinople harbour: 'I will not; I am a gentleman.' Ten years of hard labour for incitement to murder Tsar Nicholas II was what the prosecution demanded, but Burtsev was sentenced to only eighteen months, which he served first in Pentonville, then in Wormwood Scrubs. Rachkovsky's subsequent letter to Melville was full of sarcastic praise for an English jury system that both men knew had half thwarted their plan. The prime minister too must secretly have been disappointed. While Burtsev had been awaiting trial, Salisbury had proposed an entente to Russia and was asking for help in the 'delicate' matter of stemming the tide of Jewish immigrants. An exemplary punishment for Burtsev would have suited him well.

*

If Burtsev's imprisonment was only a moderate victory for Rachkovsky, he would be able to console himself with greater successes as more assassinations turned the tide of political opinion ever further in his favour. Indeed, an event in Trafalgar Square the previous May had already inspired the murder of the Spanish prime minister, Cánovas. Ten thousand people had gathered there to listen to a group of innocent escapees from the infamous Montjuich prison in Barcelona, who exposed the terrible wounds inflicted on them in an attempt to extract confessions of their part in the bomb attack on the previous year's Corpus Christi procession in the city. Inflamed by what he had seen and heard, a southern Italian by the name of Michele Angiolillo acquired a pistol and left for Paris, where he paused only to attend a lecture by Henri Rochefort, before heading for Spain in search of vengeance. Deterred by a friend from attacking the royal family, he instead tracked Cánovas to a spa town where the prime minister was taking a cure, and there shot him dead.

Then, in September 1898, in circumstances of similar tranquillity, on the shores of Lake Geneva with Mont Blanc rising sublime in the background, the sixty-one-year-old queen of Hungary and empress of Austria fell victim to yet another Italian anarchist, Luigi Lucheni. Sissi, as the empress was affectionately known, was walking down to the lakeside when the man stepped into her path from behind a tree. The blow to the chest was sudden and unexpected and then her assailant fled. 'What could that man have wanted? Perhaps to steal my watch,' she muttered as she hurried on, so as not to miss her ferry. It was not until it had steamed away from the jetty that she felt any pain. The stiletto blade had barely left a mark as it entered her heart, but within half an hour she was dead.

Lucheni was caught and brought to the late Empress's hotel, smiling, quietly cynical, where the manager's son-in-law struck him in the face; an Austrian baron had to be restrained from doing worse. For those enjoying their privileged leisure in the pure autumnal air, the attack represented an incomprehensible eruption of violence from a distant world. 'I have avenged my life,' the pitiful lone assassin would tell the court, 'long live anarchy and death to society!' Often misinterpreted, 'propaganda by deed' had finally come to mean no more than envious arbitrary retribution; the last resort of the hopeless, the damaged and the dispossessed.

One week after the empress' death, a plan for an international police league was jointly proposed by the Swiss and Austrian government; by the end of September Italy had seized the initiative by issuing invitations to the leading nations to attend a conference on the subject, to be held in Rome that November. It was, in effect, the revival of the scheme that Rachkovsky had tried in vain to initiate nearly five years earlier, but one that Russia now welcomed after the recent foiling of a planned attack in Moscow. Once again western anarchists had provided technical assistance in planting explosives in a renovated church where the tsar was to worship. Wires emerging from freshly applied plaster had aroused suspicion, in the nick of time.

Agreement among the twenty-one countries that attended the Rome Anti-Anarchist Conference in late 1898 was inevitably elusive, but by the end of a month of discussions a consensus had been thrashed out. 'Anarchism' would be defined as any activity 'having as its aim the destruction, through violent means, of all social organisation': broad enough, at a push, to encompass Russia's revolutionaries, yet explicitly refusing to dignify such violence with any plausible political motive that might be used to mitigate criminal charges. Information would be shared and new legislation enacted internationally, to facilitate the suppression of 'anarchism'; the possession of explosives would be outlawed, and a mandatory death penalty prescribed for the assassination of heads of state.

Only Britain declined to sign, despite the presence among the international police delegates of the Home Office's dynamite expert, Colonel Majendie, who believed that the only way to eradicate terrorism was to ensure that its perpetrators and advocates were 'debarred from either shelter or sympathy in any part of the civilised world'. However, as Anderson briefed the Home Office soon after the conference closed, the British government's position had been determined not by its liberal idealism but by the cynical calculation that any tightening of its laws might 'reveal to anarchists the limits which the police were supposed to keep within'.

'The congress opened and shut its doors with no more noise than a congress of spectres,' wrote Louise Michel. 'The sound of a single human voice (that of the English delegate) refusing to sign measures contrary to liberty, made the phantoms vanish like a nightmare fleeing before dawn.' She must have already filed the article before she learned that it would appear in what was to be the last ever edition of the *Adult*, the journal of the Legitimation League, which campaigned for equal rights for those born out of wedlock, along with a raft of other libertarian causes. The prosecution of its editor George Bedborough for attempting to 'debauch and corrupt the morals of the liege subjects of our Lady the Queen' indicated a new desire in Special Branch to stamp out anarchism in whatever form it found it.

When, three years earlier, Melville's forerunner as chief inspector, Littlechild, by then working as a private investigator hired by Lord Queensbury, had produced the evidence that secured the conviction of Oscar Wilde for gross indecency, Wilde's advocacy of anarchism had been entirely incidental to the question of sexual morality. Sweeney's infiltration of the league and entrapment of Bedborough, from whom he bought a copy of Havelock Ellis' *Sexual Inversion*, and his gloating at having stopped a 'Frankenstein's monster' in its tracks, indicated a rather sinister shift in Special Branch's agenda. It was all the more disturbing in light of the end-time beliefs of its overseer, that spare-time millenarian Robert Anderson, whose exegesis of the Book of Daniel, published in 1895, identified the Zionist call for a Jewish homeland as a sign of the approaching apocalypse which he so earnestly craved. 'Democracy in its full development is one of the surest roads to despotism,' he wrote, 'the voice of prophecy is clear, that the HOUR is coming, and the MAN.'

As convener of the Anti-Anarchist Conference, Italy's fear of an international threat would prove well founded, with more assassinations by its citizens and on its soil not long in coming. But whilst familiar names would be linked to the killings, their involvement was once again rather different than it appeared, though that would not prevent further calumnies being heaped upon them.

Having disappeared from London in 1897, Malatesta had reappeared soon after in Ancona at a time of peasant riots, only to be arrested in 1898 and transported for a term of five years to the island of Lampedusa, where several thousand socialists had been sent in recent years on grounds laid down in the Crispi Laws. With the connivance of the governor of the penal colony, yet another dramatic escape ensued, by fishing boat to Malta, and by the following August, Malatesta had made his way to the United States. A month later he was addressing the émigré silk workers in Paterson, New Jersey, and it was there that he became himself a victim of the violent emotions that were washing through the movement, when an argument with hard-line individualists ended with a shot wounding him in the leg. Before a second shot could be fired, his assailant was disarmed by, it was said, a compatriot whose experience of the Italian legal system echoed Malatesta's own: Gaetano Bresci.

Bresci, though, was himself no moderate, and was even then practising his own marksmanship, shooting the tops off bottles in his yard. Outraged by the treatment of protesters in Italy the previous year, when an army cannon had opened fire on a crowd, a group in Paterson would nominate him as its agent of revenge. It was a task he accepted as an honour since his own sister had been among the ninety killed, and having returned to Italy, on 29 July 1900 he shot dead King Umberto, whose reign had begun twenty-two years earlier with the release from prison of Malatesta and Kravchinsky.

In rural Ohio, Leon Czolgosz, the son of Polish immigrant farmers and rabbit trappers, followed the news reports of Bresci's trial devotedly. His parents noted how he took the paper to bed with him, but did not recognise the extent to which he idolised Bresci. Soon he started attending anarchist meetings in Chicago, sometimes three a week, and in May 1901 was in the audience in Cleveland for a lecture delivered by Emma Goldman, towards the end of her three-month speaking tour with Kropotkin, in which she 'deprecated the idea that all anarchists were in favour of violence and bomb-throwing'. Whether he had met the two luminaries of the movement before, at the Hull House educational settlement in Chicago, as some would suggest, he now approached Goldman for advice on what he should read to advance his understanding of the cause, which she was happy to supply.

Once back in Chicago, however, Czolgosz's behaviour became stranger and more obsessive, and his views more incendiary and outspoken. 'Say, have you any secret societies?' he asked his new comrades, 'I hear that anarchists are plotting something like Bresci; the man was selected by the comrades to do the deed that was done.' By late August, his colleagues had begun to suspect him as a police provocateur and, when he failed to appear at their meetings for a while, published a description of him in *Free Society*, together with a warning that they had 'confirmed themselves of his identity and were on the point of exposing him'.

A few days later, President McKinley was dead, gunned down with a revolver that Czolgosz had hidden in his bandaged hand, at the Pan-American Exposition in Buffalo. 'I done my duty,' was all he had to say as he was apprehended in the Temple of Music, while outside the film crew from the Edison Company, who had been following McKinley's visit, had to satisfy themselves with the reaction of the awaiting crowd. Unlike many anarchist assassins or bombers of the recent past, Czolgosz could offer no eloquent justification for his action, referring merely to his dislike of McKinley's talk of prosperity when so many were poor. And despite Goldman's recommendations, he had read little anarchist literature, the members of the Chicago group told police.

Called upon to explain the assassin's state of mind and his motivation, medical experts seized the opportunity to ride their hobby horses. One stated baldly that Czolgosz had been 'drifting towards dementia precox of the hebephrenic form', another declared himself certain that 'he was not a degenerate because his skull was symmetrical and his ears did not protrude, nor were they of abnormal size'. Based solely on his reading of the newspaper reports, Cesare Lombroso was willing to venture a bold diagnosis from the far side of the Atlantic, declaring that Czolgosz was, like all anarchists, 'under the spell of a kind of monomania, or the absolute obsession by a single idea which produces hypersensitiveness and makes them excessively sensitive to the influence of others'.

The crux of the assassin's trial, however, was precisely the issue that the Rome Conference had worked so hard to render inadmissible: whether there could be any mitigation for anarchist violence, on the grounds of insanity or political belief. A witness for the defence, Mr Channing was in little doubt of the defendant's madness, even if that madness had proved evanescent: given temporary release by the murderous act itself, he suggested, the delusions had for the moment dissipated, to the extent that Czolgosz had little sense of what he had done. To this, the sophistry of an opposing expert provided a convenient answer: since whatever delusion Czolgosz had suffered from was consistent with a set of political beliefs, he could be considered perfectly sane. Which was to say, in effect, that all anarchists suffered from a special kind of madness, that was reprehensible rather than exculpatory. It was so neat a formulation that even when the superintendent of police in Cleveland testified that he had found no clear link between the accused and any anarchist organisation, his opinion was easily set aside.

Only a few years earlier, Kropotkin had thrilled to news of technological advances from the Chicago World's Fair, but he would have been less pleased to hear how certain innovations were applied in 1901. The electric chair was still a relatively novel form of capital punishment, barely ten years old, when Czolgosz was strapped in and subjected to three high-voltage surges; forbidden to film, Edison's company nevertheless made it a public execution by means of a reconstruction.

Across America, anarchists faced a harsher purge than anything since Haymarket. Emma Goldman was arrested and interrogated, those in Chicago who had published their concerns likewise; Johann Most, who had the almost comic misfortune to have rerun an old article on tyrannicide to fill a space in *Freiheit* a week before the assassination, was sent to prison for another year; Alexander Berkman, less than halfway through his twenty-two year sentence for the attempt on Frick's life, was returned to solitary confinement; John Turner, the English anarchist who had converted the young David Nicoll years before, was detained entering the country for a speaking tour and placed in a cage, too low for him to stand, until deported.

It was left to Benjamin Tucker, the editor of *Liberty*, to make the case that not all anarchists were alike: that many of their number in America were lawyers, teachers, librarians, college professors, inventors and even millionaires. To the extent that anyone paid attention, his words can only have raised fears of the hidden enemy in their midst. America, it seemed, had already decided to espouse the simple 'truth' that McKinley's successor President Theodore Roosevelt would succinctly express in 1908: 'when compared with the suppression of anarchy, every other question sinks into insignificance'.

Agents Unmasked

Russia, London and Paris, 1901–1909

For an anarchist to avert an attempt on Rachkovsky's life, after all that had transpired, would have required enormous moral self-discipline. Yet such was surely Kropotkin's intent when, in 1900, he condemned a plan by the young revolutionary Nicholas Pauli to assassinate the Okhrana chief. Whether Pauli was a true threat to Rachkovsky was questionable. Rachkovsky certainly led his superiors in St Petersburg to believe so, but by boasting of the danger the spymaster may simply have meant to burnish his reputation as sedition's greatest foe. However, Pauli's plot would have had disturbing echoes for Rachkovsky. Usually scrupulous in vetting his informants, Rachkovsky had allowed Pauli to insinuate himself into his trust, just as twenty years earlier his mentor General Sudeikin had fatally misjudged Degaev. That no political murders had been committed in Russia since that time can have afforded Rachkovsky only small comfort, since he surely foresaw that the fashion for assassination in western Europe would soon spread east with a vengeance.

Even before President McKinley was killed in 1900, the officials of the tsar's government lived in mortal fear. Then, in February 1901, the education minister Bogelpov was shot dead, and a month later, potshots were fired into Pobedonostsev's apartment. Both attacks were perpetrated by recent graduates of St Petersburg's universities, where tension had been rising after the police had publicly beaten student demonstrators in contravention of the unwritten rules of engagement. They were seen, though, to presage a far larger confrontation between revolutionaries and the dominant forces of reaction – one that the authorities were prepared to meet head-on. 'We shall provoke you to acts of terror and then we shall crush you,' one captured revolutionary was told by the St Petersburg chief of police, Zubatov.

Zubatov's strategy was taken straight from Rachkovsky's playbook, but when it came to the informer Evno Azef, Zubatov and Rachkovsky disagreed. It was Zubatov who had first recruited Azef as an informant in 1893, sending him to Germany; more recently he had recalled him to Moscow, ignoring Rachkovsky's past expressions of disquiet about his reliability. Azef had quickly appeared to repay Zubatov's trust, his reports providing an inside view of the Russian émigrés' efforts towards unification. What was more, he rose quickly through the ranks of the Socialist Revolutionary Party, officially founded in Russia only in 1902, and became a key member of its combat unit, whose members playfully referred to themselves as 'anarchists' in homage to the bombers and assassins in France, Spain and elsewhere. Provocation may or may not have been the original reason for Azef's infiltration, but was almost inevitable if informants became involved in the planning and execution of terrorism in order to retain credibility with their colleagues. In the case of an agent with Azef's amoral attitude, the risk of treachery was considerable. For the moment, though, he successfully countered any doubts that his police handlers expressed about his reliability with accusations of his own concerning their blundering response to his warnings.

Somewhat surprisingly, it was another element of Zubatov's highly interventionist policing strategy that ultimately cost him his job. Calculating that the economic circumstances of Russian workers were of greater interest to them than abstract ideas of political and constitutional change, in May 1901 Zubatov had gained the support of General Trepov, the head of the police department, for the creation of police-funded unions to manage popular discontent. The tactic had seemed to work. Less than a year later, 50,000 union members came out to celebrate the fortieth anniversary of Tsar Alexander II's emancipation of the serfs, and Zubatov was promoted to director of a special section of the police department, with a brief to extend the initiative across the provinces. But his tenure was to be short-lived. In the summer of 1903, when strike action by the police-funded unions rapidly spread across southern Russia, the hardliners gained traction with their argument that there should be no concessions lest the masses be encouraged to ask for more.

For Zubatov, it spelled the end of his career. Plehve had recently inherited the ministry of the interior, following the assassination of the previous incumbent Sipyagin by the combat unit in which Azef was prominent. Now Plehve seized the opportunity to mount a proxy attack on his rival, the finance minister Sergei Witte, of whom Zubatov and Rachkovsky were favourites. Zubatov was stripped of his position, scurrilous rumours were circulated that he was a secret revolutionary sympathiser, and funding of the unions abruptly cut. Even as the revolutionaries gained strength, bitter splits in the government were hindering the work of the police.

'New times – new problems; the sooner we reorganise the better,' Rachkovsky had written to his superiors, but Trepov's replacement, Alexei Lopukhin, had started asking awkward questions about the legitimacy of the Okhrana man's activities in Paris. There was, of course, ample evidence for Rachkovsky's abuses of power. In addition to the bombings in Liège and the role of his agent Jagolkovsky in the assassination of General Seliverstov, there was his exploitation of contacts in the French police to settle personal scores, and his profiteering. Fees for brokering commercial deals between France and Russia had bolstered his salary of 12,000 rubles to make him a rich man, but there was the suspicion too that he had used some part of the foreign agency's considerable budget to play the stock market. Such dubious practices might, though, have been allowed to pass unnoticed were it not for the petty factionalism at the tsar's court.

Rachkovsky's Achilles heel proved to be his fraught relationship with the mystical demi-monde of Paris. The fact that those inclined to intrigue were perennially attracted to the esoteric had made the murky waters of mysticism an irresistible fishing ground for Rachkovsky, and had doubtless yielded a good catch, some years before, as he orchestrated the Franco-Russian alliance. However, in the process he had made dangerous enemies, and it was one of these, Gérard Encausse, who returned to haunt him. The occult credentials of Encausse, once an assistant hypnotist at the Salpêtrière hospital but now better known as the seer 'Papus' and a Gnostic bishop, had brought him to the attention of the Russian imperial family. In 1901, writing as 'Niet' in the right-wing *Echo de Paris*, he had censured Rachkovsky and Witte for their alleged conspiratorial dealings with a Jewish financial syndicate, and was now intent on using his influence to destroy them.

'I want you to take serious measures to terminate all relations between Rachkovsky and the French police once and for all,' the tsar wrote to Durnovo, now the senior figure in the government; 'I am sure that you will carry out my order quickly and precisely.' The consequences for Rachkovsky were devastating. Nothing could save him, not even the replacement of Durnovo as chairman of the committee of ministers by his patron, Witte. Stripped of both his position and influence in France, he had no option but to accept an old friend's offer to manage a factory in Warsaw. It was a long fall from grace for the man who had been the most feared security agent in western Europe, but more twists and turns of fate lay ahead for him before the current struggle for power in Russia was resolved.

Among the criticisms levelled at Rachkovsky was that he had 'created in the public opinion abroad the belief that Russia stands on the brink of revolution and that its political order is in danger'. In reality, it was merely a question of Rachkovsky revealing the reality of what most within the Russian government feared. 'Twenty years ago when I was director of the department of police,' Plehve told Nicholas II on his appointment, 'if someone had told me that revolution was possible in Russia I would have smiled, but now we are on the eve of that revolution.' It was partly a ministerial pitch for resources and latitude, of course, just as the alarmist reports he forwarded to Witte were intended to force his rival on to the back foot. There is no doubt, though, that Plehve sincerely believed in the urgent imperative of neutralising the revolutionaries' appeal to Russia's peasants and industrial workers. And if that meant manipulating those peasants' most atavistic instincts, then he was more than happy to countenance such a policy.

The provocations contrived by Rachkovsky and Zubatov had been as nothing compared to those employed in the Bessarabian city of Kishinev in the spring of 1903. The police and interior ministry were scrupulous in ensuring that the origins of the pogroms could not be traced back to them but, unlike in 1881, this time their hand was clearly behind everything, from the incendiary manifestos that began to circulate that Easter to the document proclaiming that the tsar exonerated in advance all those who attacked the city's Jews. When more than twenty groups of armed youths spread out through the city, late in the afternoon of 6 April, the police stood aside. Nor did they make any attempt to intervene as the gangs rampaged through the Jewish quarter, murdering, mutilating and raping the occupants of any house not marked with a white cross. Nearly fifty were dead and hundreds seriously injured before Plehve instructed that the killing should be stopped. Smaller-scale pogroms would occur across Russia in the following months, deflecting popular discontent with the government on to an easy target, as anti-Semitic propaganda became widespread.

The idea of the global Jewish conspiracy had a long pedigree in Russia, with the publication of the *Book of Kahal* preceding the Odessa pogrom of 1871, while the appearance of Osman Bey's *World Conquest by the Jews* a decade later coincided with revenge attacks for the tsar's assassination. Following the massacre in Kishinev, in August 1903 the notion was propagated anew by the publication of *The Protocols of the Elders of Zion* in

Znamya (the *Banner*), the organ of the nascent extreme nationalist movement the Black Hundreds, a recrudescence of the worse aspects of the
Holy Brotherhood of the early 1880s. But whilst the Holy Brotherhood
had supposedly been the brainchild of a young Witte, and had numbered
Rachkovsky among its members, it was now Plehve who was playing the
anti-Semitic card most aggressively, while Witte sought to calm the situation, under pressure from the western European bankers on whose
financing his project of modernisation relied. Had the 'discovery', or
rather forging, of the *Protocols* really been the brainchild of Rachkovsky,
following the raid on de Cyon's villa, the document's extraordinary propagandist power would already seem to have escaped his control.

The delegates attending the congress of the Russian Social Democratic
Party in Brussels that July saw clearly how the Kishinev pogrom and its
imitations would, according to the resolution proposed by the Marxist
Georgi Plekhanov, 'serve in the hands of the police as a means by which
the latter seek to hold back the growth of class-consciousness among the
proletariat', and were urged to expose the reactionary origins of anti-
Semitism. By demonstrating how easily the masses could be led by their
baser instincts, the pogrom also illustrated his assertion that the peasantry would prove readily tractable to government bribes should revolution
ever truly threaten. To counter this, argued Vladimir Ulyanov, soon to
be known as 'Lenin', a conspiratorial party of dedicated revolutionaries
should be formed to lead the masses on the straight path to victory. It
was a proposal quite at odds with the populist principles of the movement, but Lenin and his recent ally Plekhanov had contrived a coup,
ensuring that, during the congress, their supporters would be in the
majority. Outvoted, the veterans of the movement, including Vera
Zasulich, were ousted from their posts on its journal *Iskra*, and by a clever
propagandist sleight of hand, permanently labelled as a minority, or
'Mensheviks'. Lenin and his cohorts asserted their brief claim to be the
majority: the 'Bolsheviks'.

It was a tragedy for Zasulich, who had been the agent of reconciliation between Plekhanov and Lenin after their past disagreements, and
was now the butt of their humour, the former joking to his new friend
that 'she takes me for Trepov', presumably in reference to the chief of
police whom she had tried to shoot dead a quarter-century before. Plehve,
by contrast, was more than satisfied by the schism, but also that the ascendancy of the little-known theoretician, Lenin, simplified the task of the
police, whose tactics were already adapted to combating the kind of militancy he proposed. The interior minister's strategy had certainly made

considerable advances against the Social Revolutionaries: by late 1903 its combat unit had been reduced to a mere rump under the direction of the police agent Evno Azef, following the arrest of the team's charismatic leader, Gershuni. Even the protracted campaign for concerted international action against subversives had gained new momentum, as a result of President McKinley's assassination, and the ten countries who convened in St Petersburg in March 1904 finally agreed on a 'Secret Protocol for the International War on Anarchism', supporting information-sharing and deportation. Britain, France and the United States stayed away, but even they were prepared to cooperate. Any resentment Rachkovsky felt at the lack of credit he received for a scheme that Plehve had opposed when Rachkovsky had originally presented it years before would soon receive a bloody salve.

Security around Plehve was tight. Rarely did he set foot outside the headquarters of the police department on the Fontanka Quay, where he kept an apartment; when travelling by rail, a special carriage was at his disposal, permanently guarded by police, whose doors would be locked and blinds lowered whenever it slowed into a station. Arrangements at his summer residence on Aptekarsk Island were no less rigorous, as the members of the combat unit sent to assassinate him with bombs and guns in July 1904 discovered. The attack failed, thanks to information supplied by Azef, who had himself bullied the reluctant conspirators to proceed. Only two weeks later, though, a bomb thrown into Plehve's carriage by a member of the same unit as he drove for his daily meeting with the tsar blew the interior minister to pieces.

As director of the police department, Lopukhin was convinced that Azef's double-dealing was responsible for Plehve's death. The evidence was ambiguous. His tip-offs had led to the arrest of members of a rival group that had also been preparing an attack on Plehve, but perhaps only to prevent them from stealing his glory, and although Azef insisted that his warnings about the combat unit's own plans had been sufficient for any competent police force to have prevented the attack, the truth was that they had in many respects been misleading. As for Azef's personal motive: he was himself a Jew and had been seen shaking with fury after the Kishinev pogrom and cursing Plehve. On the wider context of the assassination, Lopukhin would later conclude that it had been Witte's long-nurtured plan to use the revolutionaries to get rid not only of his rival, but subsequently of the tsar himself, who Witte saw as inadequate to the task of modernising reform that circumstances so urgently required of him, and whom he wished to replace with his brother Grand Duke Michael.

The assassination of Plehve was certainly convenient for Witte who shifted the blame for the government's least popular policies on to his dead rival. Among the most catastrophic of these was the ongoing war with Japan. Russia had provoked hostilities partly with the aim of raising nationalistic support for the tsar, but it had backfired from the very beginning, when the Japanese had inflicted serious damage on the Russian navy with a surprise attack. Since then, things had gone from bad to worse with further defeats in the Far East. Moreover, a British declaration of war had only narrowly been avoided when Russian ships sailing through the North Sea on their way to the Far East had opened fire on the boats of the British fishing fleet on the Dogger Bank, in the mistaken belief that they were Japanese raiders. The error was due to faulty intelligence supplied by Arkady Harting – the one-time Hekkelman and Landesen – on board the ship *Esmeralda* to winkle out subversive officers in the fleet.

'Plehve's end was received with semi-public rejoicing,' reported one English journalist. 'I met nobody who regretted his assassination or condemned the author. This attitude towards crime, although by no means new, struck me as one of the most sinister features of the situation.' Azef's decisions now seemingly vindicated by the court of public opinion, he was confirmed in his delusion that he was an absolute moral arbiter, judge, jury and executioner. And such was the thrall in which he held Rachkovsky's ineffectual replacement Rataev that, having returned to Paris, there appeared to be no brake on Azef's ambitions. The reports that he filed from revolutionary conferences could not be faulted, but his setting up of bomb factories boded ill, while his fascination with flying machines was still more ominous. In 1904, the last novel by the ageing Jules Verne, written under the influence of his reactionary son, once again caught the tenor of the times: a sequel to *Robur the Conqueror* entitled *The Master of the World*, its 'hero of the air', who had freed African slaves in the first book twenty years before, has become merely another amoral nihilist: a megalomaniac hell-bent on shaping the world to his demented will. Azef fitted the type exactly.

*

A lifetime spent among the anarchist community of France and the London colony had taught Louise Michel a certain detachment when it came to the endemic problem of agents provocateurs. 'We love to have them in the party, because they always propose the most revolutionary motions,' she joked in a letter to Henri Rochefort when he tried to warn her against one suspicious character. It was just another example of the wistful humour that now characterised correspondence between the veterans of the movement: 'Year One is so long in coming!' Kropotkin had commented regarding a discussion about the approaching 'Age of Liberty'.

Tireless to the end, Michel continued to tour France giving lectures, her clothes bundled up in a white cloth, her face ever more wrinkled, her shoulders more stooped. The crowds had shrunk too, down from the thousands she had once routinely attracted to mere hundreds. 'People here are fools,' she said of the French. 'It seems history is going to pass them by. But look at Russia . . . There'll be spectacular events in the land of Gorky and Kropotkin. I can feel it growing, swelling, I can feel the revolution that will sweep them all away, tsars, grand dukes, the whole Slavic bureaucracy, that entire, enormous house of death . . .' In the course of several years of intermittent illness, Michel had experienced trance-like moments of mystical insight, but her prescience had never before been so acute.

Aged only sixty-eight, Michel was still touring when she died in January 1905. Her frail body, that had endured so much, was carried back from the provincial town in which she had been lecturing; for its arrival at the Gare de Lyon, several hundred troops were summoned to maintain public order. As the cortège passed through Paris, from the centre out to the eastern suburbs, past Père Lachaise where the Communards had made their last stand to her final resting place in Levallois-Perret, the crowd swelled to tens of thousands: nothing like it had been seen, it was said, since the funeral of Victor Hugo. 'Long live the Russian Revolution! Long live anarchy!' they shouted, though the first news of events in St Petersburg can only just have been coming through.

On the morning of 22 January, six columns of workers from the industrial suburbs had converged in the Russian capital and set off for the Winter Palace, where they would present a petition to the tsar or his representatives asking for labour reform and an end to the futile war against Japan. It was a Sunday, and the icons and imperial symbols they carried aloft, like the songs they sang in honour of the tsar, signalled patriotism and piety: a message of peaceful intent that had been communicated in advance to the authorities. The authorities, though, appeared not to have heeded it. Blocking the procession's approach to the palace were 12,000 troops, their guns loaded with live rounds which, when fired into the approaching marchers, mowed down up to 200 and injured hundreds more.

Elisée Reclus saw Russia's 'Bloody Sunday' as heralding the glorious dawn of revolution. His enthusiasm was only dampened when, hurrying to Paris to deliver a speech, he succumbed to debilitating fatigue and had to ask a friend to deliver it for him. 'Alas! I should speak to them in words of fire, and I only have an asthmatic puff to give them,' he bemoaned to Kropotkin, whose own expectations of what would ensue were as high as his own. Yet Reclus' hopes that events in Russia would herald 'the conciliation of races in a federation of equity' showed little sign of being fulfilled. Whilst anger at the events of Bloody Sunday had indeed compounded widespread and growing dissatisfaction with the tsarist autocracy, while the many strikes and minor insurrections that followed were a clear demonstration of latent threat, they were far from sufficient to wash away the regime. Nor did the architecture of repression show any sign of crumbling.

Even the origins of the January revolution were muddied by the police's use of conspiratorial tactics. At the head of the procession of workers to the Winter Palace had been Father Gapon, a man whose passionate commitment to the workers' cause, throughout the years that he had led and organised the Union of Russian Factory and Mill Workers, had won him their high esteem. Walking beside him was Pinhas Rutenberg, a prominent member of the Socialist Revolutionary Party, who had flung Gapon to the ground when the bullets started to fly. In saving his life, however, he cannot have known that Gapon had been close to the police for several years, his organisation one of those bankrolled by Zubatov. The massacre of the protesters in St Petersburg was primarily the result of confusion, poor communication and official overreaction, but the shock it generated served the purpose of those arguing that it was necessary for the authorities to tighten their grip.

In a period marked by significant losses for the anarchist movement, Elisée Reclus chose a good moment to die, buoyed up on news read to him by his daughter of the mutiny of the crew on the Russian battleship *Potemkin* in June 1905. He was not one of those old hands of 1871 who blamed the demise of the Commune on its lack of military ruthlessness, but the thought of a battleship in the hands of its workers, free to roam the oceans, surely resonated deeply with both the geographer and the anarchist in him as he approached the end. For a few minutes in the midst of the Black Sea, when the sailors of the Russian fleet refused to fire on the renegades and allowed the *Potemkin* to sail away between a line of ironclads, it seemed that the long-gestated naval insurrection might indeed take hold. Barely ten days later, however, after pleas by the *Potemkin's* crew for a sympathetic country to refuel and provision the ship had fallen on deaf ears, the ship was abandoned in a neutral port, and would subsequently be renamed *Panteleimon* in an attempt to erase awkward memories of the episode. If the revolution was to progress to the stage of armed insurrection, the weapons would have to be supplied from outside Russia, even if that meant soliciting the support of hostile governments.

Since the latter years of the previous century, growing international tensions had increased the likelihood of war between two or more of the Great Powers, and it seemed quite possible that a general conflagration of the kind that many had long predicted would be the outcome. France and Russia were allied in the case of war being declared on one or other, but the consequences if either initiated an attack was less certain. Equally, the question of what role Germany and Britain would play, whether as allies or enemies, had taxed the imagination of military planners and speculative novelists alike, with all permutations rehearsed. To revolutionaries like Kropotkin, however, such questions were less relevant than his expectation that the outbreak of hostilities would prompt an international general strike as a prelude to revolution, the prospect of which had helped focus minds at recent socialist congresses.

Conflict with the underestimated Japan may have seemed an unlikely midwife of revolution, and yet it was anger at defeats inflicted by the Japanese navy, as well as with their own ill-treatment by officers, that had provoked the mutineers on the *Potemkin*. Moreover, it was Japanese intelligence, in the person of Colonel Akashi the military attaché in Stockholm, that agreed to furnish the putative revolutionaries in Russia with the material needed for the struggle.

The Okhrana had become aware of details of the plan to transport Japanese-funded weapons via Finland thanks to its interception of correspondence between Nicholas Chaikovsky and the captain of the SS *John Grafton*. The operation to track its cargo would be led by Arkady Harting, newly installed as head of the Berlin bureau: the 1,000 reports it sent to St Petersburg in less than two years spoke of his determination to make his mark. Other agents had been deployed to seven ports on the English, Dutch and Belgian coasts to signal the ship's departure; Lev Beitner and his wife, also now an agent, were reporting from the heart of the émigré community in Brussels. Azef, meanwhile, had persuaded his colleagues to designate him as the man to collect their share of the vast consignment of 5,000 pistols, more than 10,000 Swiss rifles, and millions of rounds of ammunition at the far end.

Intelligence from Harting that the *John Grafton* was due to dock near Jakobstad on the Gulf of Bothnia reached St Petersburg soon enough for the battleship *Asia* to intercept and force her aground on sandbanks. Explosions were set off to suggest that the arms had been destroyed in the ship's hold, but what really happened was typically opaque, with the captain of the *Asia* seemingly bribed to allow at least some of the weapons to be salvaged.

Kropotkin, grieving over Reclus' death, neverthess shared the Frenchman's optimism that Russia would be the scene of the long-awaited revolution and was determined to take an active part. 'The real anarchist party, in the true sense of the word, is in the process of final formation in Russia,' he would claim that autumn, having begun training with a rifle for his role on the barricades on his planned return to the land of his birth, after a thirty-year absence. He was briefly encouraged by the emergence in St Petersburg on 13 October of the first soviet, or workers' council, whose inspiration was broadly anarchistic, though Leon Trotsky would later appropriate much of the credit. The publication four days later of the tsar's constitutional October Manifesto, in which he renounced autocratic rule, and his ministers' strategic decision to allow time for the political mood of the country to settle before further repression, gave the soviet a temporary reprieve. But then, on 3 December, an insurrection in Moscow provided the pretext for the full wrath of the police department to be unleashed.

'You would only be one among many, and you above all ought not to be exposed to any accident in this year in which we have already lost Louise Michel and Elisée Reclus,' the future historian of anarchism, Max Nettlau, wrote to Kropotkin, arguing against his return to Russia. It was good advice. The fighters who took to the streets in Moscow might have looked down at their rifles – vintage 1871 Vetterlins salvaged from the *John Grafton* – and imagined themselves the heirs and avengers of the Communards, but they too faced defeat. The retribution they suffered may not have been anywhere near so sanguinary as that of Bloody Week, but the police action supervised by Colonel Gerasimov was ruthless enough. And behind Gerasimov stood a superior who saw the crushing of revolution as a ticket to job security and the St Petersburg high life: Peter Rachkovsky.

Witte's loyalty to Rachkovsky had seen him recalled to the police service at the beginning of the year, a fortnight after the uprising in January 1905 and within twenty-four hours of the SR combat unit's assassination of Grand Duke Sergei, a profoundly conservative influence on his nephew, the young Tsar Nicholas. After the series of pale imitations who had tried to fill his shoes, the original intriguer found his stock at a premium, regardless of the antipathy of the imperial family. It was Gerasimov's footwork that led to the foiling of a bomb attack intended to kill four senior tsarist figures during a commemoration service for Alexander II, and the subsequent seizure of twenty bomb-makers in a raid on the Hotel Bristol in St Petersburg. Nevertheless, Rachkovsky basked in the reflected glory, and his contribution was rewarded in July with the creation for him of the new post of chief of police for the Russian Empire.

After three years languishing in Poland, the old Paris chief was again in his element. The presses he installed in the basement of the police department churned out propaganda to deviously incite resistance to the compromises offered by the tsar in the October Manifesto, with the aim of raising the political temperature. His encouragement of the nationalist movement, the Black Hundreds, and of militant cells in the associated new Union of the Russian People further fanned the flames of civil strife. Yet Rachkovsky could not escape the ghosts of his past. By early 1906, Sergei Witte's influence in government was waning, and yet still the extraordinary power vested in Agent Azef continued to wreak havoc with the Okhrana's attempts to control the revolutionaries.

The fate of Father Gapon, the ambiguous figure who had led the 1905 demonstration, revealed the extent to which things had got out of hand. Within days of Bloody Sunday, his beard shaved off, Gapon had fled Russia for France. From Marseilles he had travelled to Rome, then to Paris and on to London where he stayed in the family home of Ford Madox Ford, and met with the émigré revolutionaries, throwing in his lot, it was said, with the arms smugglers. Such business, though, seemed almost incidental to the delight he took in his celebrity. The defrocked ex-priest slipped easily into the role of playboy, putting behind him the not so distant memories of comforting dissident convicts on their way to penal exile. Fame and luxury fed his sense that he had become untouchable, however, and bred incaution. Returning to Russia in November 1905, possibly in a deal to ensure him safe passage, Gapon renewed his relationship with the Okhrana, undertaking to play the part of peacemaker. As part of the arrangement, in February 1906, he also agreed to recruit the Socialist Revolutionary Rutenberg, the man who had saved him on Bloody Sunday. For Gapon to reveal his secret dealings with the Okhrana to Rutenberg, however, was a fatal miscalculation, for the loyal socialist informed the party leadership and steps were taken to terminate both the traitor Gapon and the man who was pulling his strings, Rachkovsky.

Rachkovsky must have approached his meeting with Azef a few weeks later with some trepidation, given the complexity of the agent's allegiances and cover stories. He had, after all, recently avoided several proposed rendezvous with Gapon and Rutenberg, correctly suspecting them to be a trap, since when Gapon had fallen silent. Even steeled to hear the worst, however, Rachkovsky can scarcely have predicted how Azef's mockery would force him to gaze into the abyss of doubt and insecurity into which his own nefarious activities had in the past plunged so many others. 'Do you know where Gapon is now?' Azef taunted; 'He is hanging in a lonely country house . . . and you could easily have shared his fate.' It was a shameless assertion of the power Azef now wielded over his controller.

Within days of his confrontation with Azef, Rachkovsky was once again dismissed from his post for misconduct, and reduced to serving as a shadowy intermediary between officialdom and the reactionary militias. There was a generous golden handshake and his Order of St Stanislas, the highest of the honours he had so far accrued, was upgraded to First Class, though the tsar doubtless agreed to both with bad grace. Rachkovsky's methods, however, lived on in police policy. Indeed, Witte's successor as chairman of the committee of ministers, Peter Stolypin, who became Russia's prime minister in July 1906, would go so far as to declare that, 'it is the duty of all to acquire provocateurs and increase investigations in every direction'.

The rapidly burgeoning number of Okhrana agents was nevertheless far outpaced by the recruitment of informants, to the extent that one observer remarked on how before long there would be no one left in Russia who was not either a spy or spied upon. As the quality of evidence required for the conviction of revolutionaries fell, the apprehension of suspects by the official police was supplemented by citizen's arrests by the Black Hundreds, and during the latter months of 1906, a system of mobile courts martial was established to process cases promptly and *in situ*. By October 1906, 70,000 of the regime's supposed enemies had been detained, and over the next three years, 26,000 were sentenced to death or hard labour, and roughly 3,000 executed. So vast were the numbers that death and punishment became hideously close to abstractions. Whereas a decade earlier a single anarchist bomb explosion, or punitive execution by the state, roused half the world to protest, now such occurrences could pass almost unnoticed amidst the generalised violence.

Yet despite the rapid process of depersonalisation, individuals and their relationships still played a crucial role. After the demotion of Rachkovsky,

Azef showed a new dedication to the Okhrana and Gerasimov, who since taking over as his contact had demonstrated a refreshing concern and professionalism towards his powerful agent. It was as though mutual respect was all Azef needed to remain loyal. Azef's days, though, were numbered.

Since Vladimir Burtsev's release from Wormwood Scrubs prison in 1899, he had returned to his anti-tsarist work, first in England and then Switzerland. If anything, persecution had sharpened his desire to root out informants and provocateurs, lending his freelance counter-intelligence activities a new ruthlessness as he slowly closed in on Azef. A letter purportedly delivered to him in 1905 by a 'veiled lady', that useful fiction familiar from Esterhazy and the Dreyfus Affair, had raised suspicions about one member of the party's combat unit, Tatarov, who had been hunted down to his family home in Warsaw and stabbed to death. The tip-off, though, referred to Azef as a second traitor.

Throughout his years as a police agent, Azef had become adept at deflecting any suspicions of his treachery. On this occasion, he easily persuaded colleagues, with whom he had conspired on numerous assassinations, of the malicious absurdity of the charge. Bitter experience, though, had taught Burtsev to take nothing at face value and he was not so easily mollified. The foreknowledge of the group's activities that the police showed did not appear to have stopped with Tatarov's elimination. And the more Burtsev investigated Azef, the closer his profile seemed to that of an Okhrana agent: he would plot attacks but always absent himself from their execution, and had repeatedly been in locations across Europe when betrayals had taken place. When Burtsev spotted him – one of Russia's most wanted men, driving through St Petersburg, untouched and carefree at a time of mass arrests – the unthinkable became for him a certainty. Others, though, would require more persuasion.

So began a lengthy period of research for Burtsev. He went first to Paris in search of evidence and, eventually, in 1908, back to London. As much as things had changed there since his arrest, more had stayed the same. Chief Inspector Melville may no longer have been with the Special Branch, having stepped down from his post somewhat abruptly, shortly after Rachkovsky had been eased out of his job at the Paris *agentura*. The subsequent unease in the Metropolitan Police over informants and provocation may suggest a cause. And yet, freed from the straitjacket of political accountability to pursue a semi-official freelance career, his fortunes had only risen, as he engaged in 'spectacular duties which entailed extensive travel on the Continent' and finally accepted the rewards and honours from foreign governments that his previous position had required him to decline. Nor could the employment of former officers of Special Branch by the Okhrana, at generous rates, leave any doubt about the close relationship between the organisations. The intimations of past complicity in Joseph Conrad's novel *The Secret Agent*, published in 1907, had passed largely unnoticed, due to its small original readership. Burtsev, however, would have had no difficulty equating the fictional Mr Vladimir with Rachkovsky, or believing that the novel's dark elements of intrigue, provocation and betrayal were thinly fictionalised reportage.

The breakthrough came for Burtsev with the decision of Russia's disgraced ex-director of police, Lopukhin, to divulge enough of what he knew about Azef to prove his guilt. Whatever Lopukhin's motivation, whether a desire to have the last word in his long-running rivalry with Rachkovsky, or to avenge the murder of his patron Plehve that Azef was suspected of orchestrating, his admission saved Burtsev from humiliation and probably worse. For the revolutionary movement was deeply wounded by Burtsev's claims, and he himself had been summoned to trial in Paris, in the apartment of Azef's Socialist Revolutionary colleague, Boris Savinkov, on the rue La Fontaine.

Past the looping filigree of the art nouveau Castel Béranger next door Burtsev walked, day after day in the autumn of 1908; past the police tails assigned to Kropotkin, Figner and Lopatin; and up the stairs to the spartan room in which the Jury of Honour sat in judgement. And day after day he met their cold stares of accusation that cast him as the villain, with no ally except Kropotkin who had more experience in such matters, and replied to their questions with further evidence. Finally, though, Burtsev was compelled to play his trump card, in breach of his word to Lopukhin, after which Azef's guilt could no longer be disputed.

Even after the jury had announced its verdict, however, distrust gnawed deep, the uncertainty created by Azef's conviction almost as damaging as the original treachery. Despite the jury's sensational decision, still not everyone would accept Azef's guilt, and he was allowed to escape the court's sentence of capital punishment and slip away, hiding at first in a Balkan monastery. Once the excitement of the trial had died down, Kropotkin found himself unable to shake off concerns about the tangle of duplicities, past and present. 'Among other things,' he wrote to Burtsev, 'the question that troubles me is this: did Chernov and Natanson know that Azef was in the service of the police, and did they consider him to be their great Kletochnikov or not?' Chernov was a founder member of the Socialist Revolutinary Party, the others names from long ago: Natanson, whose embryonic circle Chaikovsky had inherited in the early 1870s; Kletochnikov, the People's Will mole in the police, the first and perhaps the only man whom Rachkovsky had trusted too much.

Just before Christmas 1908, Kropotkin went to Switzerland on the instructions of his doctor, who had advised clear mountain air after the damp of England. It was his first visit since he had been expelled in 1881. Though sixty-six and in weak health, Kropotkin could not be held back from spending his time there revising the text of *The Great French Revolution*, a grass-roots re-examination of the seminal event, first conceived on his release from Clairvaux prison in 1886. There must have been free moments for memories too, though: of his work with Reclus, tracing the outlines of anarchism, all those years ago; of the congresses and the endless, tiresome arguments; of the nights he had sat, his political vision as yet unformed, listening to tales of the brief, wondrous life of the Commune. And yet recent experiences had surely shaded such optimistic memories with pathos. 'Unhappy Europe! Thou shalt perish by the moral insanity of thy children!' said the fictional Russian ambassador at the end of Conrad's *The Secret Agent*. Kropotkin may have felt similarly, when informed of the exposure of yet another turncoat. 'But what is this?' he complained, 'Now the revolution has become a sport: "If they arrest me, I will go over to their side!"'

Okhrana infiltration agent turned chief of the Berlin station Arkady Harting was, for once, in no mood for devious games. On New Year's Day, 1909, he bluntly demanded of his superiors in the police department that Lopukhin be punished for the information he had divulged to Burtsev, with the result that Lopukhin was promptly dispatched to a posting in Siberia. Harting may well have guessed that after Azef's exposure, he would be the next target of Burtsev's investigative zeal, and that Lopukhin might divulge his true identity too. For Burtsev was caught up in his own private psychodrama. Years before, he had twice been tricked by his old friend Hekkelman into defending him against accusations of treachery: an error on Burtsev's part that had since cost many comrades their lives or freedom. Would Burtsev now conclude that tearing down Hekkelman's carefully constructed new identity as 'Harting' was his best chance of catharsis?

After years of patient research, Burtsev's revelations about Harting were perfectly timed. Harting had only recently been posted back to Paris as head of Rachkovsky's old *agentura*, to all appearances an elegant European aristocrat and famous socialite who had added the *grand cordon* of the Légion d'honneur to a drawer full of similar decorations. But then, on the morning of 15 June 1909, the story broke. 'The Scandal of the Russian Police' screamed the headline in *La République*, in what was a common theme. The fêted baron was revealed to be none other than Michel Landesen, the fugitive bomber of the Raincy Affair, sentenced by a French court to five years *in absentia* in 1890.

'Do you really think he is Landesen?' one newspaper interviewer asked Burtsev, who appeared astonished by the question; 'Believe me, I know Landesen deeply – we started our careers together,' he replied. For years Burtsev had avoided the subject of his misguided friendship with Hekkelman, when they were both young men. That he now spoke of it openly was a sure sign that he felt released from guilt's spell. 'Two years ago it came to our attention that Harting was not Harting, that he was a mysterious being, on whose past it was preferable not to lift the veil,' he told *L'Humanité* in an interview published as 'The Reign of the Provocateurs – Azef No. 2'. In publication after publication, the details of the 1890 bomb plot were once again laid before the public, except now with the last, shocking piece of the jigsaw inserted.

Quizzed by the press, Inspector Loze's memory failed him. The journalists were quick to point out to their readers that as well as having headed the French investigation of the bomb plot, the inspector had also served on the committee that had awarded Harting the Légion d'honneur. Goron, the chief of the Sûreté in 1890, confirmed that there had been an official cover-up: the prefecture and the Okhrana, he recalled, had acted hand in glove. It was an acute embarrassment for the French government, and all the more so when Clemenceau, as president of the council, was forced to admit that a file discovered in the ministry of the interior proved that it had indeed known the truth all along. Before long *Le Soir de Bruxelles* joined the fray, dragging up the strange case of Monsieur Léonard and the Liège bombings of 1894, which had received so little coverage at the time. Harting was shown as being at the heart of that plot too. The government might have counted itself lucky that the unravelling of the Okhrana's conspiracies to provoke terrorism and create fear and hatred went no further.

Having lifted Harting from Paris at the first inkling of trouble, the Okhrana was determined that he should enjoy its protection, arresting one man merely for recognising him in a St Petersburg restaurant. In Belgium too the local Sûreté stood ready to guard him on his return to his wife's house against the revolutionaries sent to carry out the death sentence that had been passed in secret by the central committee of the Socialist Revolutionaries. It was soon clear, though, that he could not carry on his life as before, simply by moving on whenever word arrived that his executioners had caught his scent. There were rumours of a pension for him to retire to London under a new identity, or else to South America, but suddenly the Okhrana records fall silent. In 1910, Harting vanished into thin air. In the same year, Rachkovsky also left the scene, dying in circumstances that are somewhat obscure.

Speaking in the French Chamber of Deputies, the socialist Jean Jaurès expressed the outrage of the nation: 'I personally know French citizens who, on French soil, have been subjected to investigation and frisking by Russian police agents,' he protested. It would be brought to an end, Clemenceau promised, as would the surveillance of foreign émigrés to France. Twenty years on, Rachkovsky's intriguing, which had seemed so astute at the time, had compromised the very cause it had set out to serve. Few lessons had been learned, though. Already, in the Okhrana's encouragement of Lenin's Bolsheviks, seen as a group with no future that might nevertheless help fragment the revolutionary movement, the law of unforeseen consequences was once again at work.

24

War and Revolution

Europe, 1914–1932

In the years preceding the Franco-Prussian War of 1870, members of the International League of Peace and Liberty, Elisée Reclus among them, had cherished high hopes that their project for a federated Europe might ensure a lasting peace. Even after the war's outbreak, the solidarity with the besieged workers of Paris shown by socialists in the Reichstag and striking workers in Chemnitz and elsewhere had kept that flame alight. In the decades since, though, the flame had faltered: renewed conflict had been avoided more by the mutual fear of the Great Powers than by the force of fraternal idealism. And yet, as the moment of greatest danger approached in 1914, Jean Jaurès appealed once more to the workers of France and Germany to halt the slide towards a continent-wide conflagration by means of coordinated general strikes.

Those hopes were finally dashed on 31 July 1914, only hours before France began the fateful mobilisation of her armies, when Jaurès himself was shot dead. The assassin was a member of Action Française, an ultranationalist organisation born out of Boulangism, nurtured by Henri Rochefort and his anti-Semitic associates, and given distinct form during the Dreyfus Affair. Since then it had spawned a violent subculture of its own, breaking the revolutionary left's monopoly on terroristic violence with an attack on Alfred Dreyfus during the ceremony to install the ashes of Emile Zola in the Panthéon in 1908; Dreyfus' recent, belated exoneration of any lingering guilt had roused its members' ire, but he had escaped with only a light wound. Now, a year after Rochefort's death in Aix-les-Bains, the assassin's bullet had ensured that the marquis' forty-year campaign for vengeance against Germany would not again be thwarted.

It was, of course, another assassin, Gavrilo Princip who, a month earlier on 28 June, had precipitated the impending catastrophe by his shooting dead of Archduke Franz Ferdinand of Austro-Hungary and his wife in their car as they drove through Sarajevo. The bloodied cobblestones of the Balkan city were a long way, in every sense, from the Sussex countryside around Brighton, where Kropotkin now lived, or the middle-class English Utopia of Hampstead Garden Suburb, to which he sent his letters to Kravchinsky's widow, Fanny; and yet they were linked: on the bookshelves of the assassin Princip and his co-conspirators in the Serbian underground movement, two works took pride of place – *Memoirs of a Revolutionary* and *Underground Russia*. From them, and from the practical example of the old People's Will, the Serbian nationalist movement to which Princip belonged had drawn inspiration and courage for their bid to end Austro-Hungarian rule in the Balkans and promote a pan-Slavic agenda.

As co-signatories to the anti-anarchist pact agreed in St Petersburg in 1904, Austro-Hungary expected Serbia to mount a comprehensive investigation of the conspiracy. Equally, it required the cooperation of Russia to pressure its fellow Slavs into compliance. The Serbs' continued reluctance to concede fully to Vienna's demands, even as the situation gusted towards a crisis, perhaps betrayed an uneasy conscience over covert official involvement with the conspirators, if not in the plot against the archduke itself. The Serbian police, after all, had enjoyed a good relationship with the Okhrana, learning from its methods. Nevertheless, the tension might have been defused, and the archduke's murder have resulted in nothing more than an expulsion of diplomatic hot air, or at worst a minor regional confrontation, had not Austro-Hungary prepared to enforce its will by punitive military action, and the military alliance between France and Russia set in motion the engine of wider war. For as a member of the triple alliance with Germany and Italy, the mobilisation of Austro-Hungarian forces against Serbia triggered the terms of the binding agreement that required a response in kind by the governments in Paris and St Petersburg.

As the man whose intrigues had helped secure the Franco-Prussian alliance and the St Petersburg Pact, Peter Rachkovsky must therefore bear his own small part of the blame for the outbreak of the First World War. Though dead, his influence lingered on as the Great Powers heaved their armies into readiness in the summer of 1914, and would continue to do so for many years to come.

*

The point at which conflict on a continent-wide scale became inevitable eludes easy identification, so various were the contingent factors. But when

German and Austro-Hungarian military preparations were reported in mid-June, the tsarist regime's fears for its own survival certainly served to make it more likely. Russia's participation was a gamble. To back away from the fight would show weakness in the face of the nationalistic swell in public opinion, and risk revolution, but so too would defeat in a war for which Russia was ill prepared despite an annual military budget larger than Germany's. Mobilisation was ordered, and the tsar's apparent decisiveness was rewarded with the support of the country's socialists, while pacifist dissenters had no choice but to scatter into exile. The unity of the Russian people when faced by a national challenge would, it was hoped, effect a spiritual renewal and restore respect for the tsar. The immediate effect of the mobilisation, however, was merely to provoke Germany to respond in kind.

For the anarchist movement, all war amounted to what Kropotkin had declared it to be in his essay of 1881, 'La Guerre': the ultimate betrayal of the individual by the state and by capitalism, in search of profit. It had long campaigned against militarism and conscription, and still clung to the hope that the international solidarity of the oppressed masses might stymie the warmongering folly of nation states. And yet, from the moment hostilities broke out in August 1914, Kropotkin expressed himself a passionate supporter of the Allied war effort.

It was not naïvety about the scale of the tragedy about to unfold that turned Kropotkin's position inside out: on that matter he and Reclus had been many years in advance of most observers. Rather, it was the very Manichaean dimensions of the struggle that he judged as necessitating the temporary suppression of all other principles. German aggression was, Kropotkin had come to believe, an apocalyptic threat to Enlightenment civilisation, which sought 'to impose on Europe a century of militarism' along with the horrors of 'state socialism in cooperation with Bismarckian policies'. It was a danger of which he had been warning for many years, and developments in the revolutionary movement internationally had only confirmed his position. Marx and Bismarck had been, he asserted, two sides of the same coin, and it was in the defeat of Germany on the battlefield that the malign influence of both might be stamped out, and the coming revolution saved from the centralising tyranny of Marx's disciples. Those who failed to recognise what was at stake were sleepwalking into a totalitarian nightmare.

'In what world of illusions do you live that you can speak of peace?' Kropotkin wrote to Jean Grave, as the French army and the British Expeditionary Force attempted to regain their footing in the face of the

German onslaught. His letter urged Grave to summon his countrymen and women to raise a people's army that would take to the hills south of Paris to defend the capital in a superhuman effort of resistance, and inspire the continent with their ideals of liberty, communism and fraternity. Persuaded by the argument, if not the strategy, Grave was among a small faction of sympathisers that, with Kropotkin, issued the *Manifesto of the Sixteen* that autumn to explain their position. 'If the anti-militarists remain mere onlookers of the war,' he wrote, 'they support by their inaction the invaders; they help them to become still stronger, and thus to be a still stronger obstacle to the social revolution in the future.' Even Kropotkin's closest friends, however, were for the most part hurt and mystified by his ostensible volte face which was, Max Nettlau averred, merely the result of an old man's obtuse sentimentalism. 'He spoke of France as the land of the Revolution, and I said France had lived on its revolutionary reputation for many years, and had exhausted the claim to be considered so now.'

On any clear-sighted assessment, the idealistic nation whose rebirth Kropotkin had described in his *The Great French Revolution* of 1909 had indeed long since been worn away by wave upon wave of political pragmatism. In the absence of an alternative, however, France continued to represent for Kropotkin an almost mystical model of anarchistic aspirations, its society a honeycomb of resilient autonomous cells, their iconic form replicated from microcosm to macrocosm. It was the France symbolised by the 'Hexagon', officially adopted as its symbol during the Terror of 1793, that was capable of generating by its example a great transnational hive of federated endeavour; France the aggregate of its communes, each a scaled version of the 'great beehive' which Kropotkin had used in his book *Fields, Factories and Workshops* as an image of the artisanal workshops of Paris.

Opponents might have pointed to how the advent of war had sealed the fate of the one surviving anarchist project in France that had striven to put Kropotkin's ideals into practice. Founded by Sébastien Faure near Rambouillet in 1904, the colony named La Ruche, or the Beehive, had offered a libertarian education with the aim of raising the healthy, rational citizens to lead the march to social revolution. To illustrate his point, however, Kropotkin might in turn have offered a simple reminder of the disputes that had long dogged the interpretation of apian collaboration. Since for every account of the benign 'spirit of the hive' nurturing each individual contribution to what the playwright and Gnostic-sympathiser Maurice Maeterlinck referred to as 'the science of the chemist, the geometrician, the architect and the engineer', there was another claiming that it demonstrated the virtue of internalising rules or laws promulgated by a centralised state, and of a militaristic social structure.

Kropotkin's stance on the war ran deeper than any of the tactical and ideological disagreements of the past, setting him irreconcilably at logger-heads even with Malatesta, a respected colleague for the best part of forty years. Unlike Kropotkin, the Italian had never allowed himself to develop any affection for the state, or assign especial virtue to a particular national character. For long periods since the turn of the century Malatesta had been largely inactive except as a journalist, while he struggled to earn a living in England as an electrician, sherbet-vendor and even salesman of chicken incubators; intermittent forays back into activism had only hard-ened his truculence and resolve. Instinctively critical of terroristic violence, he had nevertheless held back from publishing his article on the subject, convinced that ventures such as La Ruche were symptomatic of a tendency among anarchists to 'let themselves fall into the opposite fault to the violent excesses'. His occasional positive contributions, though, had been influential and his attendance at the 1907 Anarchist Congress in Amsterdam had helped reinvigorate a movement that had drifted too far under the influence of syndicalism, and instill it once again with something of the old insurrectionary zeal. Indeed, it was his disagreement with Kropotkin over his wishful belief in spontaneous revolution that had originally opened up a gulf between them. In psychological terms, though, the two men's very different experiences of life as exiles in England may also have shaped their attitudes to the war.

Since settling in England in 1887, Kropotkin's existence had been far from that of the propertied Russian aristocracy into which he was born. The long hours of piecework reviewing, crammed in between his own studies, writing and lecturing in order to pay the bills on the various small rented properties in which his family lived, had taken their toll on his weakened constitution, and periods of intense application were punctu-ated by frequent bouts of ill health. But whilst he was familiar with the horrendous life of the urban underclass from his propaganda work in the East End and around the country, and had witnessed and campaigned against the persecution of the Walsall martyrs, Burtsev and others, Kropotkin personally had been untroubled by such hardships. Held in high esteem by the scientific Establishment, and even by the more radical sections of the political Establishment, he had enjoyed a status from which he could allow himself to recognise in a functioning liberal parliamen-tary democracy – even one that was yet to be elected by universal franchise

– the germ of an acceptable polity. He was even known to muse, or perhaps half joke, that a constitutional monarchy such as Britain's might be a guarantor of something resembling an anarchistic society.

Malatesta, by contrast, was the perpetual outsider, and had seen nothing at the margins of British life to suggest that he should modify his heart-felt enmity towards the state, or its representatives. Since before the London Congress of 1881, he had been widely suspected by the British police as a terrorist mastermind, and had been subject to Special Branch surveillance for much of the 1890s. Never, though, had he come so close to being implicated in violent crime as in December 1910, when a blow-torch that he had lent to a Latvian émigré was found at the scene of a burglary whose perpetrators, holed up in Sidney Street in East London after shooting dead three policemen, were subsequently involved in a dramatic shoot-out with the British army, in what became famous as the 'Battle of Stepney'. On that occasion, Malatesta escaped prosecution but then, in 1912, an Italian spy whom he had denounced exploited British libel laws to have him imprisoned for three months. He only avoided expulsion thanks to a demonstration in Trafalgar Square, led by the unions and attended by Vera Figner, and a forthright letter to the press from Kropotkin.

Though Malatesta insisted that the British people were his friend, he was clear that their government was not. Lloyd George, the Chancellor of the Exchequer, was according to Malatesta 'the most perfect kind of philanthropic and religious hypocrite'; his reforms to introduce welfare a mere sop. He presumably felt a far greater distaste for Winston Churchill. Despite Malatesta's own denunciation of the Sidney Street revolution-aries, the fact that Churchill had grabbed headlines when, as Home Secretary, he visited Sidney Street during the 1910 siege, would have sick-ened Malatesta. Unable to place the slightest faith in the call to war against German aggression made by such Establishment politicians, in the autumn of 1914 Malatesta's open letter, 'Anarchists have forgotten their principles', predicted that after what would be a long and crippling conflict 'there will be more militarism than before. One side wanting revenge, the other wanting to remain prepared against their revenge.' Much as he regretted it, the breach with Kropotkin was never to be repaired. 'It was', he would later recollect, 'one of the saddest and most tragic moments of my life (as doubtless for him too), when after hard discussion, we parted as adversaries, almost as enemies.'

The weight of disappointment must have lain heavy on him, consid-ering his failure yet again to foment a revolt against the Italian government in the early summer of 1914. Malatesta had established a sizeable following among the dock workers of Ancona where he based himself during previous visits in 1907 and 1913, and circumstances seemed so propitious, with Italy unsettled after a recent foretaste of war against Turkey in North Africa. His contacts throughout the socialist movement in his homeland were strong, and in the preceding year he had successfully cultivated the young editor of the party's leading newspaper, *Avanti!*, Benito Mussolini. The son of an anarchist, Mussolini had translated Kropotkin's *The Great French Revolution*, which he thought 'overflowing with a great love of oppressed humanity and infinite kindness'; he had even praised in print the revolutionaries involved in the Sidney Street siege, whom Malatesta had disowned. But for all the high hopes of the Red Week which followed the killing of two demonstrators by police in Ancona, the putative insurrection fizzled out when the unions called off their strike. And by the time Malatesta returned to London in August, his meetings and correspondence with Mussolini may have caused him some foreboding that Italian socialism might assume a dangerously nationalistic and even authoritarian aspect under the pressures of involvement in a continent-wide war: a war which Italy would join in 1915, breaching its previous promises to the Allies that it would confront Austro-Hungary, in the first instance, and subsequently Germany too. 'Let the way be opened for the elemental forces of the individual, for no other human reality exists except the individual,' Malatesta would have read in one letter from Mussolini, though he can little have suspected his bellicosity of being sponsored by the British secret service.

*

The obduracy of Belgian resistance, especially around the heavily fortified city of Liège, delayed the initial German advance into France for several days during August 1914, and the sacrifice at the same time of 200,000 Russian soldiers, dead or captured in the terrible Battle of Tannenberg on the Eastern Front, bought time for the forces of the Entente to steady their nerve and stabilise their front line. But as the French soon learned, the result would merely be a stalemate, as the opposing armies settled into a war of grinding attrition, waged across a barely shifting line of barbed wire and bomb craters. As the first Christmas of the war passed, and then the second, the quagmire of the Western Front drew in ever more millions of troops to fight and die in the most futile of battles.

Having staked so much of his faith on liberal Britain, Kropotkin at last received some vindication for his position on the home front. In the government's desperation to retain the loyalty of its citizens, who were being asked to sacrifice far more than ever before in the national cause, whole swathes of the socialist programme of reform for which Hyndman and others had argued for thirty years, consistently reviled by the Establishment for their efforts, were passed into law. The contribution to the war effort made by women in men's jobs would even lead to their being granted the vote, as anarchists had demanded ever since Louise Michel had chaired the meetings of the Women's Vigilance Committee during the Siege of Paris. By early 1917, however, Kropotkin's attention had turned to events in the land of his birth. His stalwart defence of the Allies' participation in the war had been intended to protect the revolutionary tradition of France but now, as his late friend Elisée Reclus had predicted in 1905, Russia appeared about to claim her destiny and fulfil the 'rights of man' that the French Revolution of the eighteenth century had betrayed.

The war had inflicted catastrophic casualties on Russia, its operations constantly compromised by poor communication technology and ill-educated soldiers. Whilst German military intelligence had built on the achievements of Wilhelm Stieber in the war of 1870, the emphasis placed by Russia on its efforts to suppress revolution now left it floundering on the battlefield, unable even to fall back on the ingenuity shown forty years earlier by the besieged defenders of Paris. For whereas the desperate French had then improvised their aeronautical postal service and experimented with the most improbable methods of communication, conscripted Russian peasants now chopped down telegraph poles for use as fuel. A single, disastrous offensive in 1915 saw over a million Russian troops taken prisoner, and even the breakthrough achieved the following year by dint of General Brusilov's strategic brilliance failed to quell growing disquiet in the ranks, after the tsar, who had appointed himself commander-in-chief, neglected to capitalise on the advantage.

Away from the front, the atmosphere grew febrile during the winter of 1916 as bread shortages stoked fears of looming social disorder, and exposed the tsarist court – over which Tsarina Alexandra and her latest mystical adviser Rasputin presided in the absence of her husband – to ever more scurrilous rumour and the hatred of broad swathes of public opinion. Not even the murder of Rasputin that December, however, could stem the tide of discontent and by late February 1917 attempts at the violent suppression of spontaneous mass protests in St Petersburg at the shortages of bread had propelled the city into a state of open revolt. Even the most prominent fulminators of revolution were caught unawares. As power in the city devolved to the twin institutions of the Provisional government and the Soviet of Workers' Deputies, following the garrison's refusal of orders and then its desertion, and central authority began to collapse across the empire with even villages declaring themselves 'autonomous republics', the tide of change became irresistible. It took the intervention of his generals to convince Tsar Nicholas that his abdication was unavoidable, but for all his air of denial he must already have known the game was up. A fortnight earlier, Gérard Encausse, Rasputin's forebear as the imperial family's favourite mystic, had died in Paris: as long as he lived, he had promised, the tsar would retain his crown.

On being appointed minister of justice in the Provisional government, Alexander Kerensky, who alone also served on the executive committee of the Soviet, cemented his position as the great hope of the new Russian politics by ordering the immediate release of all political prisoners. Forty years after he had last seen his homeland, Kropotkin received the news with exultation: 'what they reproached us with as a fantastic Utopia has been accomplished without a single casualty,' he wrote, not quite accurately and wholly prematurely. Yet even amidst the excitement he may have felt a twinge of envy. In accordance with Kerensky's instruction that the returning martyrs of the revolution should be greeted with public acclamation, Vera Figner and German Lopatin, along with other 'heroes and heroines of terrorism', were given the imperial box of the Mariinsky theatre at a celebratory concert: 'old gentlemen and several old ladies, with grave, worn, curiously expressive and unforgettable faces'.

'I shivered to think of all that the little party stood for in the way of physical suffering and moral torment, borne in silence and buried in oblivion,' recorded the French ambassador, Maurice Paléologue, as the orchestra struck up the 'Marseillaise'. When reviewing a French naval squadron in 1893, Alexander III had cut short its rendition after a single verse, but now it was Russia's new national anthem, its conclusion met with cries of 'Long live the Revolution!' and 'Long live France!' Mounting the conductor's podium, elegant and 'utterly unaffected', in calm, level tones Figner intoned a litany listing all those who had died under tsarist persecution, reducing nearly all those present to tears. 'What an epilogue to Kropotkin's *Memoirs*, or Dostoevsky's *Memories of the House of the Dead*!' Paléologue averred, but Kropotkin himself was not there to bear witness.

The effects of Kropotkin's past imprisonment and a life spent sublimating disappointments had undoubtedly accelerated the ravages of time on a man who, half a century earlier, had been able to endure a journey post-haste from Siberia to St Petersburg, much of it by sled. By 1912, he was writing to Edward Carpenter to express his regrets that they would be unlikely to meet again as he only ventured up to London from his south coast retreat during the summer months. Nevertheless, the prospect of a victorious homecoming rejuvenated Kropotkin to the extent that within a few weeks of the Mariinsky concert he embarked at Aberdeen for the North Sea crossing, his decision to transport fifty crates of books to Russia, with only his wife to assist him, a true bibliophile's statement of intent.

In St Petersburg, now renamed Petrograd as a patriotic gesture, the popular reception that greeted Kropotkin recalled that which Paris had always shown his old friend Louise Michel on her homecomings from exile. Despite his train not arriving until two o'clock in the morning, a crowd 60,000 strong was waiting at the station to cheer him on his way to a formal audience with Kerensky, with only the absence of those who opposed his position on the war to mar the celebration. Kropotkin's advice was widely solicited during the summer of 1917, and willingly offered in private meetings with Kerensky and Prince Lvov, a long-time reformer and the original head of the Provisional government. And yet the turmoil of political uncertainty and almost untrammelled possibility into which he had plunged seems to have left Kropotkin somewhat bewildered. When offered the education portfolio in a Provisional government that already included Boris Savinkov as assistant minister for war, Kropotkin declined, true to his long-held principle that all centralised government was corrupting to popular autonomy. And yet the efforts of Jacobin elements to seize power left him close to despair and he won a rapturous response from across the political spectrum at the State Conference of all parties, held in Moscow at the end of August, by appealing for Russia to become a federal republic, similar to that of the United States.

The political atmosphere had long been filled with factionalism, but as the year progressed and the authority of the Provisional government seeped away, the worst features of the French Revolution and the Commune looked set to repeat themselves, with new forms of Jacobinism taking root. Only a few days before the old revolutionaries had taken their bow at the Mariinsky theatre, the most dynamic and ruthless figure of the new generation had made his return from Switzerland. It was nearly thirty years since Lenin had been drawn into the revolutionary underworld by the execution of his brother. Talent and determination had seen him navigate the hazardous waters of socialist politicking with alarming deftness, but his own rise and that of his Bolshevik Party had been helped too by timely assistance from its natural enemies. As far back as 1905, when Lenin had been lecturing at an East End socialist club during a visit to London, Special Branch officers had intervened to save him from the fury of a mob that believed him to be a police spy, and subsequently the Bolsheviks had received lenient treatment by an Okhrana hoping to drive a wedge through the revolutionary left. More recently, Lenin's return to Russia had itself required the cooperation of the German intelligence services, who clearly thought that his disruptive presence there, funded in part from their coffers, might hasten Russia's military collapse.

Both strategies in turn now proved almost too effective, as Lenin bypassed the bourgeois stage of revolution that Marxist dogma demanded, and progressed immediately to that of the workers and peasantry. Tentatively allied with the anarchists to form a proletarian vanguard, in July Lenin's Bolsheviks had come within a hair's breadth of toppling the Provisional government and seizing power in a *coup d'état*. Accused of high treason and impugned as a German agent, Lenin had gone to ground, secretly winning over the expanding network of soviets from their crucial support for Kerensky's regime, while reflecting further on the military and political lessons to be learned from the failure of the Commune: a subject he had studied and written about over many years. Unlike Kropotkin and the Russian anarchists, who agreed that federalism and devolved autonomy must be encouraged, Lenin concluded that, having bided its time, a revolutionary elite must seize power and implement a centralised revolutionary programme. Peace, Lenin insisted, should be made with Germany at almost any cost, in contradiction of the Provisional government's policy.

After months of mounting economic crisis, military setbacks and increasingly violent expressions of discontent, the October Revolution saw Lenin's plan come one step closer to realisation. With most members of the Provisional government apprehended in the captured Winter Palace and summarily imprisoned, power passed into the hands of the All-Russian Congress of Soviets of Workers' and Soldiers' Deputies, laying the ground for their subordination to a dictatorship of the proletariat, for which Lenin had called in his recent work, *The State and Revolution*. Failing to read the runes, significant numbers of anarchists continued to lend Lenin their support, viewing recent events as a vindication of their belief in revolution by mass action. But whilst Lenin's insurrectionary leadership prompted a number of contemporary observers to liken him to Bakunin, Lenin would not have appreciated the comparison. As the Bolsheviks tightened their grip on power they soon turned mercilessly on those whom it had briefly served their purposes to tolerate.

During the autumn of 1917, Kropotkin had kept a low profile, while privately complaining of Bolshevik rule that 'this buries the revolution', and when the envoy of President Wilson of America visited him the following spring, he confided his hatred of the Bolsheviks as 'aliens, enemies of Russia, robbers and gangsters, set upon looting and destruction'. He had always thought Lenin dangerous and now considered him despicable too, his request for an armistice in the war with Germany adduced as evidence that he had sold out his country and the revolution, despite Lenin's professed belief that the cause of Marxist revolution would be best served by the victory of a socially advanced Germany. 'Revolutionaries have had ideals,' Wilson's envoy would recollect him saying, 'Lenin has none. He is a madman, an immolator, wishful of burning, and slaughter, and sacrificing. Things called good and things called evil are equally meaningless to him. He is willing to betray Russia as an experiment.' For the moment, though, Kropotkin kept his powder dry, restricting his public utterances to theoretical matters and hoping that in 'two or three hard years', the worst of the horrors of Bolshevik revolution may have passed.

The political ideas with which Kropotkin engaged nevertheless posed a dangerous challenge to the structures of Soviet rule, drawing inspiration from an England which the Germanophile Lenin despised, and whose attempt to interfere in Russian politics, clandestinely and later by military means, infuriated him. When Kropotkin lectured the Federalist League on the historical lesson that 'federation led to unity and how the opposite path of centralisation has led to discord and disintegration', it was the example of the British Empire which he cited, while in his capacity as president of the Society of Relationships with England, he sought to create links with his adopted home of many years as a source of humanitarian assistance.

And yet, for all their differences, Lenin appears to have looked upon the old anarchist philosopher with a certain grudging respect, which Kropotkin would attempt to exploit. Invited to a meeting with Lenin in Moscow in April 1919, the discussion was wide-ranging as they debated how the revolution should develop and Kropotkin lobbied on behalf of the beleaguered cooperative movement, in which he placed great hope. With Bolshevik violence already beginning to sweep the country, eradicating enemies of the new regime through imprisonment and large-scale summary executions, every word of the futile discussion must have stuck in Kropotkin's throat. In future, he would not be so diplomatic.

The demolition of Boris Korolenko's cubist statue of Bakunin, less than a year after it had been commissioned, vividly illustrated how quickly opportunistic inclusiveness had slipped into intolerance. All around, Kropotkin watched his friends and allies suffer persecution, and by early summer he himself had been driven out of his Moscow apartment by Bolshevik wiles, and sought refuge on a smallholding in the town of Dmitriev, forty miles from Moscow. The timing of his move into rural seclusion was well advised, coming as anarchists, together with the Mensheviks and the 'left' faction of the Socialist Revolutionaries, launched insurrections against Bolshevik rule in Petrograd and in cities across Russia, and embarked upon a series of assassination attempts, aimed in part at undermining the armistice and renewing hostilities. Both were causes with which Kropotkin had much sympathy, and his outspoken views on the necessity of war against Germany risked identifying him with a strategy in which Boris Savinkov would later claim to have been sponsored by the French government.

Infuriated by the arrest of his daughter, Sophie, while she was attempting to return to England to raise humanitarian funds, Kropotkin finally gave vent to his moral disgust. His anger spilled into a letter addressed to Lenin, which the Bolshevik leader received as he convalesced from the serious wounds inflicted by a Socialist Revolutionary assassin. 'To throw the country into a red terror, even more so to arrest hostages, in order to protect the lives of its leaders is not worthy of a party calling itself socialist and disgraceful for its leaders.' It was a bold act on Kropotkin's part, just when the Bolsheviks' suppression of what the anarchists and the Left Socialist Revolutionary Party claimed as a 'Third Revolution' was about to reach its bloodiest pitch, and seemed almost to be inviting a response that would bind his fate to that of his more militant colleagues. His only punishment, though, was continued obscurity and an equal share of the hardships that were visited on the Russian people as the cold winter closed in, the burgeoning civil war reducing still further their meagre supplies of food or fuel.

*

'Many too many are born and they hang on their branches far too long. I wish a storm would come and shake all this rottenness and worm-eatenness from the tree!' Friedrich Nietzsche had written in the mid-1880s, in his work of esoteric philosophy *Thus Spoke Zarathustra*. The intervening years had seen diverse attempts to answer his subsequent call for 'a declaration of war on the masses'. Cesare Lombroso and his followers had set out to identify the symptoms of atavism, but laid the intellectual groundwork for those who argued that deficient stock should be eliminated from the gene pool. Others, such as Enrico Ferri, had proposed a role for capital punishment in expediting natural selection, since 'It would therefore be in agreement with natural laws that human society should make an artificial selection, by the elimination of antisocial and incongruous individuals.' For such a policy to work, though, required the commission of crimes of a kind at which even the vast majority of anarchists baulked. Other theorists argued straight out for the sterilisation of undesirables.

In the two summers immediately preceding the war, Kropotkin had dragged his tired old limbs, weakened by his own past experiences of incarceration as a criminal, to the congresses first of the eugenicists and then of the British Medical Association to protest their position. His compassionate involvement with the immigrant slum-dwellers of London's East End had confirmed to him that poverty rather than inherited debility lay at the root of most crime and most physical underdevelopment; to suggest that sterilisation could solve such problems was simply to express a violent hatred of the poor. And yet the cost of the struggle against Prussian militarism that he had passionately advocated had been an indiscriminate cull of the world's youth, with eight million killed in the course of the Great War. The appetite for eugenicist solutions would for a while be muted, but Europe's leaders now had to ensure a future free of war and in which death on an industrial scale had no place.

When the victorious Allies convened their Peace Conference in 1919 to assign prizes and penalties in search of a lasting settlement, the threat of anarchist terrorism still haunted the politicians of the West. Neither the common cause that the anarchists in Russia were making with western interests in their struggle against Bolshevism, nor the unheeded campaign for peace by the majority of the movement, had erased the stigma of anarchism's long association with terrorism. In selecting a city to host the conference, the organiser's first choice, Geneva in neutral Switzerland, had to be abandoned on the advice of the international police that it remained a hotbed of anarchist assassins. It was therefore in Paris that the victors and their petitioners convened on what Clemenceau, the French president, arranged to be the anniversary of France's humiliation on 18 January 1871, when Wilhelm I had been crowned kaiser of the newly united Germany in the Hall of Mirrors at Versailles. The switch in location did not prevent Clemenceau himself from being seriously wounded by a shot fired by an anarchist into his car, while he was travelling to a meeting to discuss, once again, the vexed question of whether Russia's revolutionary government should be allowed to participate in the conference.

That Lloyd George, by now prime minister, could suspect the anarchist responsible for injuring Clemenceau to have been working for the Bolsheviks illustrated how poorly informed the western leaders were about developments in Russia, where the anarchists were involved in a fight for survival against the Bolsheviks. Restricted communications, fostered by a western blockade of the country, prevented greater understanding. Nevertheless, there were some in Allied circles who harboured a degree of sympathy for how the relatively obscure Bolsheviks had been impelled to seize power by the cruelty of the tsarist autocracy and the predations of capitalism, and to look forward to a time when the ferocity of the revolution would soon give way to peaceful, social democratic rule. Such hopes, though, were at odds with the presence of over 180,000 Allied troops on Russian soil, and their support for the White Army's campaigns, which were then approaching their high-water mark. For even while political arguments for engagement with the Bolshevik government were advanced, the overriding desire in the West was that the revolution be contained lest it prove infectious.

Nowhere was the fear of contagion more apparent than among the Italian delegation, trapped in fraught negotiations over their territorial claims to the Adriatic port of Fiume, while under intense domestic pressure from the extremes of both left and right. 'What will happen in our country?' asked the Italian foreign minister, Sonnino, of the other Allied representatives who were resisting his argument for Italy to be granted a more generous allocation of land from the old Austro-Hungarian Empire, immediately supplying the answer that 'We shall have not Russian Bolshevism, but anarchy.' If Lloyd George and others thought such upheaval a price worth paying for a lasting settlement in the Balkans, the 'madness' they predicted on the streets of Italy was not long in coming, with clashes between squads of militant socialists and the nationalist Fasci di Combattimento increasingly frequent and violent. It was an 'anarchy' fomented by extremist parties of all hues, but one in which the Italian anarchists themselves played a prominent part. And, just as it had five years earlier, the task of catalysing a movement prone to factionalism and defections into a dynamic force fell to Errico Malatesta.

The dramatic reversal of fortune that Malatesta's return to Italy in late 1919 represented could not quite match that of the old heroes of the revolution in Russia, lifted out of interminable exile in Siberian labour camps and thrown before the adulation of the Mariinsky audience. Yet for the small, bearded figure greeted by a cacophony of claxons and the clamour of stevedores lining the docks as his ship entered the port of Genoa, the contrast with the anonymous existence he had endured for much of the last twenty years in London must have been overwhelming. The following day, Christmas Day, the city's workers turned out in their tens of thousands to greet him, and when he arrived in Turin four days later, the crowd was estimated to be more than 100,000 strong, its cries of 'Long live Malatesta! Long live Lenin!' brimming with the hope of international revolution. The linkage of his name with the Bolshevik leader, and the implied equivalence of their positions, cannot have sat easily with Malatesta, who would write that 'To achieve communism before anarchism, that is before having conquered complete political and economic liberty, would mean stabilising the most hateful tyranny.' Insofar as the Bolsheviks had come to power through alliances of convenience and a conspiratorial insurgency, however, he appeared briefly ready to embrace their example.

The recent parliamentary election in Italy had left the socialists with the largest block of representatives and, buoyed with success, they proposed a great march on Rome to force the government to cede power. Malatesta's anarchists, and the nationalists of the right, headed by the poet and politician Gabriele d'Annunzio, who in the absence of agreement from the Peace Conference had shortly before occupied the disputed port of Fiume in a paramilitary raid, would make common cause. Their alliance was an amusing idea – two passionate but diminutive orators, with diametrically opposed political ideas, one zealous to demolish centralised power, the other to seize it – but their nationalism and socialism certainly promised a potent and hazardous mix. Unsurprisingly, though, the coalition quickly fractured: the triumphal entry into Rome would have to wait for a leader in whom the two ideologies had fused into a more perfect and monstrous hybrid. The possibility of revolution flared brightly, only to be quickly extinguished. A general strike called in the autumn of 1920 saw soviets set up across the industrial north of Italy, but the mainstream socialist movement stepped back and Malatesta was arrested, with more than eighty other leading anarchists. The following summer, when the strategy was tried again, in a last-ditch attempt to check the brutal rise of Mussolini's new fascist party, Malatesta was still in prison, petitioning for an early trial and staging a hunger strike, and his ultimate acquittal came too late for him to regain the initiative.

In 1922, half a century had passed since Malatesta had attended the

Saint-Imier Congress of the anti-authoritarian International as the protégé of the ageing Bakunin. He returned that year to celebrate the anniversary with yet another bout of the ideological bickering without which, it seemed, no meeting of anarchists would be complete. Malatesta, though, was himself now aged sixty-eight, and long past being riled by such disagreements, however insolent his detractors must have seemed. Rather, the experience occasioned from him a statement of mature pragmatism concerning the current status of the cause to which he had devoted his life, and the duty of anarchists in the event of revolution: 'the problem' was, he wrote in a newspaper article, 'of greatest interest in the present time, so full of opportunities, when we could suddenly face situations that require for us to either act immediately and unhesitatingly, or disappear from the battleground after making the victory of others easier'. An anarchist revolution, he urged his readers to recognise, would only be possible once the majority of the population were anarchist in outlook, and yet only the educationalists in the movement believed that the overthrow of the current political regimes should be deferred until such a time. It therefore fell to anarchists to work with the reality of whatever revolutions should occur, resisting authoritarianism, whilst accepting that 'For us violence is only of use and can only be of use in driving back violence. Otherwise, when it is used to accomplish positive goals, either it fails completely, or it succeeds in establishing the oppression and the exploitation of some over others.'

The article was a model of restraint and modest self-sacrifice, appearing as it did in *Umanità Nova*, the newspaper that Malatesta had founded in 1919 and whose offices and presses had recently been broken up in a raid by blackshirts. By the time the article was published, in October 1922, the fascists would have been cheering Mussolini's March on Rome, and his usurpation of the position of prime minister. Malatesta alone remained to deliver the valedictory wisdom of the whole generation of anarchists of which he had been a part to a world that had disdained their ideas and demonised those who had propounded them. Even amidst the turmoil and horror of recent years, it seemed, the vision of equality, justice and harmony to which they aspired had less appeal than the experiments in violent authoritarianism that public apathy and tribal atavism had allowed to take root. 'The establishment and the progressive improvement of a society of free men can only be the result of a free evolution; our task as anarchists is precisely to defend and secure the freedom of that evolution,' Malatesta's article concluded. In his mind, perhaps, was the memory of Reclus and Kropotkin, who had lent their scientific genius to that cause.

Kropotkin had died more than a year earlier, on 8 February 1921, his last great work – an *Ethics* that was, he insisted, not specifically anarchistic, but simply 'human' and 'realistic' – unfinished. The previous year he had enjoyed visits from Emma Goldman and Alexander Berkman, deported back to Russia by America for conspiring against the military draft, and had echoed the horror his guests had expressed at the direction taken by the revolution, writing to chastise Lenin in the sternest terms. Likening his policies to those of the 'darkest Middle Ages', he questioned the sincerity of his purported ideals, and asked plaintively 'What future lies in store for communism?' He needed some hope to cling on to, but would have to supply his own. While his wife Sasha eked out meals from the produce of their frozen vegetable patch during that last winter, Kropotkin's scant reserves of energy had been spent on recording his reflections on the terrible whirlwind of revolution all around him, which had slipped human control and become something worse than he could ever have imagined. With no end in sight to civil war and massacres and terror, the two years he had predicted that it would take for the elemental fury to burn itself out had stretched to five, but after that, he still insisted, would 'begin the constructive work of building the new world'. Though built, however, it was not to be the world of which he dreamed.

Kropotkin's burial in the cemetery of the Novodevichy monastery in Moscow was to be the last time that the anarchists would gather in numbers in Soviet Russia. Having at first shown the kind of insensitivity to political principle that only the most brutish regime could muster, by announcing a *state* funeral for a man who had always fought against the power of the state, the security organs of the Bolshevik government did all in their power to hinder the attendance of those imprisoned anarchists who had been promised parole for the purpose by Lenin himself. As Kropotkin's body lay in the ballroom where, as a young prince dressed in Persian fancy dress, a lifetime earlier and in a very different world, he had first caught the attention of the tsar, thousands visited to pay their last respects, the atmosphere tense with rumours of duplicity by the Cheka, Dzerzhinsky's secret police who had inherited the mantle of the Okhrana, along with its methods and many of its staff. Spontaneous outbursts of speechifying fury against Lenin and his cohorts marked the funeral itself. Days later, the final, ruthless suppression of Russian anarchism began.

Malatesta's last years, spent in fascist Italy, resembled the isolation that Kropotkin had suffered under Bolshevik rule, though in Malatesta's case the house arrest was official and stringently enforced. That he was left to reflect alone on the miserable fate of his anarchist colleagues in Italy's

worst prisons was the cruel privilege accorded to his venerable reputation, and a rare example, perhaps, of Mussolini's sentimental attachment
to a man he had once esteemed. Not even anarchist bids to assassinate
Mussolini, on at least two occasions, could jeopardise Malatesta's strangely
protected position, thanks perhaps to his words cautioning against violent
resistance to the regime. Following the suppression of his newspapers,
he was left untouched to grow old in voiceless frustration, finally dying
in 1932.

Coda

For half a century following the Paris Commune, socialist revolution had been an abiding fear for democracies and autocracies alike, with 'anarchism' all too often the label fixed upon for the festering resentment that threatened violence to the status quo. It had been Elisée Reclus who had argued in 1876 that by embracing the notorious title of 'anarchist' with which others had tarred them, those who dreamed of a social revolution that would truly free mankind of all inherited institutions and authority would at least win recognition for their ideas. Instead, they had merely singled themselves out for opprobrium. Practicable as its ideals may have been, or not, anarchism had believed in the inherent perfectibility of humanity, far more than humanity had been willing to trust its own good nature. When alienation and a thirst for vengeance had driven a few misguided youths to perpetrate violence in anarchism's name, the state's response had often been so disproportionate as to force the fulfilment of its own prophecy, even when that response was sincerely conceived for the protection of society. Moreover deception on the part of the organs of state security, rather than sincerity, was generally the rule.

Inevitably, then, when the revolutions finally arrived, in one form or another, it was not the anarchists – battered, demonised and wary, on principle, of accepting or imposing discipline – who assumed power. 'The majority of anarchists think and write about the future without understanding the present,' Lenin had written in 1918. 'That is what divides us communists from them.' Mussolini, having conquered that future through an appeal to crude nationalism, similarly condescended to the movement whose humane ideals he had outgrown, asserting that 'Every anarchist is a baffled dictator.' But if naïvety was anarchism's fatal flaw, it was one that clever, moral men such as Reclus and Kropotkin must have consciously struggled to maintain: the siren song of authoritarianism in the supposed cause of the greater good would have been only too easy to heed. That way, though, as history would prove, lay only shipwreck and servitude.

'The internal rivalries aren't important,' Louise Michel had written at a time of intense factionalism; 'I think that each of the "tendencies" will provide one of the stages through which society must pass: socialism, communism, anarchism. Socialism will bring about justice and humanise it; communism will refine the new state and anarchism will be its culmination. In anarchism, each will achieve his own fullest development . . . Man, because he will no longer be hungry or cold, will be good.' That her words now read more like a route map to spiritual enlightenment rather than to political power is revealing. For whilst Kropotkin and others fiercely rejected Marx's and Engels' slighting of anarchism as a utopian doctrine, throwing the charge straight back in their faces, it was nevertheless the transcendent idea of heaven on earth, albeit underpinned by scientific theories as to its achievability, that carried the movement through endless years in the wilderness.

It was no accident that anarchism, more than any other element of socialism, should develop its own martyrology, casting itself in the tradition of the persecuted Gnostics and Anabaptists, and its enemies as a latter-day Inquisition. Inheriting the attributes of radical religion, its adherents could see themselves as the oppressed heroes in a Manichaean struggle for progress, and as such found eager recruits in the field of artistic expression, where bloodless revolution was a generational event and spiritual fulfilment through creativity the ultimate prize. Too few recognised, however, that the most important battle that the revolutionary movement needed to fight was in the field of counter-intelligence.

*

Although never an outright partisan of anarchism, Vladimir Burtsev showed exemplary tenacity in answering the intrigues of the Okhrana with investigations of his own. He would continue his crusade to uncover their spies, informants and provocateurs but could not match his success in exposing Azef and Harting, and by 1914 a number of ill-founded accusations had lost him the trust of those who, not long before, had looked to him for their protection. Briefly he flirted with Bolshevism, before turning implacably against Lenin.

The lives of many Russians who were prepared to reassess their loyalties were transformed, one way or the other, by the October Revolution of 1917: ex-Okhrana agents turned leaders of a soviet, like Rachkovsky's forger Golovinsky, or revolutionary populists like Chaikovsky, who would lead the anti-Bolshevik government of the Northern Region during the civil war, around Archangel. For Burtsev it merely brought more of the same. Arrested on Trotsky's first orders he would once again be sentenced to the Trubetskoi bastion of the Peter and Paul fortress, just as he had been twice before under the tsar. After his release and flight abroad, the 'Sherlock Holmes of the Revolution' would accept a job with the British secret services that allowed him to continue his fight against tyranny from the margins; the challenges for an émigré dissident were much as they had always been, only with Lenin rather than a tsar now in the Kremlin.

The trajectory of Burtsev's career had left him with few illusions about where the current of political poison ran, from its source in Rachkovsky's Okhrana, through into the murky waters of the interwar years. The inquiry into the provenance of *The Protocols of the Elders of Zion* began in earnest in 1920, when, in an article titled 'The Jewish Peril: A disturbing pamphlet', *The Times* had asked 'What are these "protocols"? Are they authentic? If so, what malevolent assembly concocted these plans, and gloated over their exposition: prophecy in part fulfilled, in parts far gone in the way of fulfilment?' In addition to the newspaper's revelations concerning the work's plagiarism of Joly's *Dialogues*, the Russian Princess Catherine Radziwill revealed that Golovinsky himself had given her a copy in 1904, along with an explanation that Rachkovsky had indeed commissioned the forgery. However, neither of these new pieces of evidence could weaken the purchase that the *Protocols* had established as a propaganda weapon against Bolshevism, whose leaders were largely of Jewish extraction. Within a couple of years, two books elaborated on how the predictions in the *Protocols* had already been realised. *Secret World Government*, by an old Okhrana bureau chief called Spiridovich, and *World Revolution*, by the English proto-fascist Nesta Webster, fingered the diabolical banking family of the Rothschilds for everything from inciting the American Civil War and financing the Paris Commune, to the assassinations of Lincoln and Alexander II.

Societies turned upside down by war and revolution craved simple explanations for their misfortunes, and if blame could be laid squarely at the door of a conspiracy by an easily identified and little-loved ethnic group, so much the better. A touch of mysticism made the notion more intoxicating still: an account, for example, by the young Alfred Rosenberg of how, on opening a copy of the *Protocols* while a student in Moscow during the summer before the October Revolution, he had sensed 'the masterful irony of higher powers in this strange happening'. A leading member of the German National Socialist Party since 1919, who would go on to be Nazism's leading racial theorist, Rosenberg's publication of a German translation of the *Protocols* in Munich in 1923 provided inspirational reading for his close colleague Adolf Hitler while in prison following the failed Beer Hall Putsch of that year.

The seed fell on fertile ground, prepared years earlier when the teenaged Hitler had attended meetings held in Vienna by sympathisers with the Union of the Russian People, which Rachkovsky had helped found. Now, with the leisure that prison afforded him, the arguments he had heard there for the extermination of the Jews, hardened by the fictional fears of world conspiracy propagated by the *Protocols*, were burnished with the same abuse of science that had been used to strip the immigrant centres of anarchist militancy of their humanity, decades before. 'The struggle in which we are now engaged', he wrote in *Mein Kampf*, 'is similar to that waged by Pasteur and Kock in the last century. How many diseases must owe their origins to the Jewish virus! Only when we have eliminated the Jews will we regain our health.'

Not long after Malatesta had died, it was the enduring toxicity of the *Protocols* that brought Burtsev to Berne in Switzerland in 1935, where the local Jewish communities had lodged a legal challenge against the book's Nazi propagators. For too long the mystery of its provenance had fed public curiosity, and allowed the unscrupulous to insist that it was genuine. Laying to rest any residual uncertainty had become a moral imperative, which even the lack of hard, documentary evidence could not be allowed to impede. Alexandre du Chayla, who had corroborated Princess Radziwill's wholly unreliable tale of Rachkovsky's involvement with an account of his own meeting with the *Protocols'* first Russian editor, Sergei Nilus, agreed to testify; the secret 4,000-franc fee he commanded was yet another symptom of the ugly opportunism that had all along surrounded the book. Boris Nikolaevsky, the historian who, five years earlier, had had the chance to inspect a suitcase containing Rachkovsky's private papers, agreed to conceal from the court his own conviction that the claims of Radziwill and du Chayla were groundless.

Burtsev was faced with a dilemma of his own, for whilst he had a good story to tell of how the *Protocols* had arrived in the world, one that was clear and coherent, it lacked any sure foundation. For when he had approached Rachkovsky to buy his collection of key Okhrana documents and a fragmentary memoir, his offer had been rebuffed, and, following the revolution of 1917, the vast and precious archive of the Paris Okhrana vanished into thin air, or into smoke and ash, as would later be claimed. There was little doubt, though, about which way Burtsev would jump.

And just as he had learned from the Okhrana's methodology of surveillance and record-keeping in the 1890s, modelling his counter-intelligence activities on theirs, he now played his part with aplomb in weaving a myth of Okhrana conspiracy around the document's origins as strange and compelling as that contained in the *Protocols* themselves: one that drew together high finance, espionage, diplomacy, court intrigue and personal rivalry. It is a testament to the subtle complexity of Rachkovsky's devious mind that Burtsev's story remains to this day only too plausible.

Rachkovsky's dark genius would be demonstrated too by the abiding influence that the Okhrana's methods exercised over the clandestine war waged between the heirs of communist revolution and capitalistic democracy for decades to come. The sixteen crates containing the lost archives of the Paris Okhrana finally came to light in 1957, proudly revealed to the press by the Hoover Institute in California, into whose safekeeping they had been entrusted by the last tsarist ambassador to France after he had smuggled them out of Paris in the 1920s. Since its inception in 1947, the Central Intelligence Agency had, it would later be revealed, analysed the archive closely in the process of developing its own tradecraft. The same thing was happening on the other side of the Iron Curtain. When it lifted, Oleg Kalugin, the highest-ranking Soviet intelligence officer ever to cast light on the inner workings of the KGB, confirmed that Okhrana methods had also been taught to the organisation's agents throughout the Cold War. There is a striking irony in the fact that, while the Okhrana files and piled boxes of crumbling agent reports in the Paris Prefecture of Police provide a treasure trove of insights into late nineteenth-century policing of terrorism, only in Britain – so proud in the nineteenth century of its liberal traditions of policing – is access to the scant surviving documentary evidence of Special Branch's early anti-anarchist activities still tenaciously guarded. Democracy and the existence of a political police force are, it seems, perhaps only compatible as long as certain more uncomfortable truths about the price of political stability are kept secret.

The greatest experiment in communism and the greatest abuser of its ideals, the Soviet Union was not, of course without its own more grotesque hypocrisies. But however undeserving its leaders' claims to be the custodians of the nineteenth-century dream of freedom and equality, it is likely that, without them, the early dreamers might never have been memorialised. There might have been no Kropotkin Street and Metro station in Moscow, no crater named after Kibalchich on the dark side of the moon; and who would have thought to place a ribbon cut from a

Communard flag in the rocket named *Voskhod*, or *Dawn*, which launched into space in 1964?

From space, humankind could finally gaze upon the delicate blue globe that was its home, as Elisée Reclus had once planned to make possible through the artifice of his epic construction. Such a vision would, he was certain, prise open even the stoniest heart to the apprehension of a fraternity that ignored national borders, and divisions of class or religion. The world as it might one day be.

List of Illustrations

The anonymous photograph of the artillery park, *Parc d'artillerie de la Butte Montmartre (18 mars 1871)* is from of the Musée Carnavalet in Paris; Maximilien Luce's *A Paris Street in May 1871, or The Commune* on page 2 is courtesy of the Musée d'Orsay, Paris, © Photo RMN - Hervé Lewandowski. On page 3, the arrest of a suspected Nihilist in St Petersburg and the assault on a Jew in the presence of the military at Kiev are from the *Illustrated London News* of 6 March 1880 and 4 June 1881 respectively, the assassination of the Tsar from *L'Univers illustré*, March 1881. The assassination of Sudeikin in St Petersburg on page 4 is from *Le Monde Illustré*, 1884, as is the image of measures taken against the epidemic: the disinfection hall at the Gare de Lyon, 1884. 'Capitalist: The Real Cholera' is taken from the German edition of Dubois's *Le Peril Anarchiste* (Die Anarchistische Gefahr, Amsterdam, 1894), along with the reproduction of the woodcut of Ravachol before the guillotine on page 6. On page 5, the celebrations of the Franco-Russian alliance on the Eiffel Tower are from *Le Petit Journal*, 11 November 1893; the reproduction of Robida's drawing in *le Vingtieme Siecle* is from Beraldi's *Un caricaturiste prophète*, Paris, 1916. On pages 6 and 7, the image of Bertillon's judicial anthropometry comes from *Le Journal Illustré*, 16 November 1890, the garroting of thc Xerez anarchists from *Le Petit Journal*, 27 February 1892, and the Café Terminus explosion from *Le Monde Illustré*, No. 1925, 1894. The photographs of Malato, Battola and the dead Pauwels are courtesy of the Paris Préfecture de Police, all rights reserved. On page 8, *Shelling the Houses of Parliament* comes from *Hartmann the Anarchist, or, The Doom of the Great City* by E. Douglas Fawcett, London, 1893; Signac's *Au Temps d'harmonie*, photographed by Jean-Luc Tabuteau, is courtesy of the Mairie de Montreuil. The archive of Louis Bonnier containing the designs for Reclus's *Globe Terrestre* is held by the Centre d'archives d'architecture du XXe siècle, Cité de l'architecture et du patrimoine, and the image is published courtesy of the Lordonnois family. All other illustrations are from the author's private collection.

Notes on Sources

Concern for the portability of a book that is a work of wide-ranging synthesis has led to discursive bibliographical notes being provided for each chapter, rather than specific footnotes. The intention is to assign credit to all those whose research has been most useful, provide an overview of the original research undertaken in particular areas, and to signal those rare instances where a greater degree of licence has been employed in reconstructing scenes. Detailed citations and additional material, including many digressions that had to be excluded from the published text, can be found online at www.theworldthatneverwas.com or via www.alexbutterworth.co.uk. It is hoped that, over time, the site will provide a growing resource for those interested in the individuals and themes that figure in the book or are tangential to it.

Prologue

My account of Kropotkin's involvement in the 1908 Jury of Honour draws on descriptions of visits he had made to France in recent years. When Kropotkin had disembarked at Dieppe in 1896, the French police had been forewarned by Special Branch and put him straight back on the next boat to England: only in 1905 had his return been officially sanctioned. Confino offers a vivid account of his illicit visit in 1901, based on letters and police reports: the trips to a Turkish hammam, visits to Clemenceau and tea with girls in Tyrolean straw hats all under surveillance by the 'international police'. On that occasion he gave agent 'Sambain' the slip and would have recognised him again in 1908. In fact the jury first convened in the home of Roubinovitch, only moving to Savinkov's apartment shortly afterwards, while for security Kropotkin stayed with the artist Bréal, as G. Marx observes. Some licence is therefore taken in re-creating the street scene, and Kropotkin's reflections on a changed Paris and his journey through its streets, though less than by Gaucher in his description of the three old revolutionaries descending from a carriage; in other respects, however, his account of the trial is informative. Figner's memoirs tell of life in Schlüsselburg, and the eighteen years Lopatin spent in solitary confinement; Fischer mentions her suggestion to Burtsev of suicide. Miller discusses Kropotkin's concern with agents provocateurs and fears regarding penetration of the anarchist movement; he also elucidates how dispirited Kropotkin was by the experience of the trial. Accounts of the investigation and trial appeared in Burtsev's journal of history, *Byloe*, though a degree of ambiguity surrounds Lopukhin's testimony and the ex-police chief's motivation for cooperating, as Ruud and Stepanov consider. Zuckerman, Rubinstein and Geifman all survey the career and trial of Azef; the latter favours an interpretation that he was never more than incidentally disloyal to his police employers, lending too little credence to the testimony of revolutionaries. My sense of the iconoclastic optimism represented by art nouveau comes from Sutcliffe. The various recollections of the Commune are noted in Kropotkin's autobiographical writings, while the papers that Savinkov had to clear each day were work in progress on his novel *Pale Horse*.

1 *A Distant Horizon*

The description of Reclus' early life is drawn largely from his own correspondence and from Fleming; Heath informs my evocation of his time in London, Nord his involvement in the Peace League, Rykwert the background of French socialist thought in Saint-Simon, Fourier and Proudhon. Dunbar's article introduced me to Reclus' fascination with Wyld's Globe, while Sennett and Welter illuminated the influence of Etienne-Louis Boullée. The letters from Reclus to Nadar during the period of the siege suggest a significant involvement by Reclus in the aerostatic experiments to which both Ishill and Kropotkin allude in their obituaries of the geographer, rather than the more cautious interpretation in Dunbar. The scene of Reclus' balloon flight is nevertheless imagined, the aeronaut's experience drawing on Fisher, whose research into the imaginative struggle to maintain communication links from Paris was informative, as was his evocation of the ballooning events at the Expo. The extraordinary snails, however, are found in Horne's incomparable history of the war and Commune, while the revolutionary resonance of ballooning, and the Montgolfier tradition, is from Schama. Costello makes the connections between Verne and Nadar, the anagrammatic hero Ardan in *From the Earth to the Moon*, and explores the cultural importance of the submarine. In light of the uncertain reliability of Stieber's memoirs, corroboration of his claims from secondary sources has been sought, both in the writings of his near contemporaries such as Tissot, in the *Byloe* article 'Count Bismarck', and in more recent scholarly works by Höhne, Wilms and Schoeps. Stieber's perspective on the meteorological tests is also an invented vignette; Deacon informs my sense of Stieber's early foray to London, while Wheen gives Marx's side of the story. Marx's antipathy to Proudhon and Bakunin and his attempt to counter their influence is apparent in his letters; Engels' notion of Reclus as contaminated by their influence is reported in W. O. Henderson as is Engels' role in reporting the Franco-Prussian War and the fact that he filed reports for the *Pall Mall Gazette* from London, out of fear of how

Stieber might treat him were he in Versailles; from Henderson is also the glee that he and Marx felt at the fate of France. Avineri explores Marx's original attempts to avert the Paris insurrection. Williams contextualises and often subverts Rochefort's own account of the autobiographical *Adventures of My Life*, whose extraordinary appeal to France in what Flaubert called its 'abnormal mental state' is explored by Christiansen. Molnár is referred to for the socialist reaction to the birth of the republic; Bury for the overheated Vatican Council on infallibility on the very eve of the outbreak of war, where cardinals were accused by the Pope of revolutionary tendencies; Jellinek for the social effects of the war and the fumigation after the victory parade.

2 Communards

Despite the somewhat adulatory tone of her biography of Louise Michel, Thomas provides the core source for her career, embroidered by Michel's own autobiographical writings and correspondence, while Guillemin's interpretation of the code of Hugo's *Carnets Intimes* offers insights into their relationship. Sources for Michel's involvement in resisting the seizure of the Montmartre guns include Jellinek; Edwards, who surveys the grass-roots enthusiasm for the Commune and its educational imperatives; Christiansen, whose discussion of the Joan of Arc phenomenon in France during the war casts the Red Virgin in an interesting light; and Williams for his account of the murder of the generals. The *Official Journal* and *Le Mot d'Ordre* offer a powerful sense of the internal life of the Commune while Horne and Tombs afford a more considered overall appraisal, the latter evoking the excitement of the Commune and its social reforms, but questioning the reality of the final armed resistance by women. Gildea quotes Edmond Goncourt thanking God for civil war, in words identical to those Horne assigns to Thiers: it has been assumed that their response was indeed shared. Boime conveys Courbet's unreasonable optimism and explores the iconography of the destruction of the Vendôme column; Pernicone presents Costa's bewildered reaction to the sense of unreality surrounding the Commune's impending demise; Costello quotes Verne's impression of Daumier's cartoon. Although the paradox of Marx's minimal and largely unsupportive role in the Commune and the excessive credit he would later be accorded is only touched upon, W. O. Henderson and Avineri suggest a murky cynicism, due in part to letters perhaps forged by Stieber, while Verdes offers an account based on French police reports from London; Dmitrieff's role is discussed by McClellan. The letters of Elie Reclus recount details of the tragic sortie, while Elisée's own describe the circumstances of his capture; Rochefort's autobiography considers Thiers' role in the original construction of the forts. The English response to events in Paris is largely drawn from Martinez, while my sense of the utopian and dystopian fiction of 1871 is from T. Clark and Beaumont; Beaumont and Tombs both allude to the vicious attitude adopted towards the Communards by the Church: from the Pope down to the priest at Versailles.

3 From Prince to Anarchist

Along with Kropotkin's own *Memoirs of a Revolutionist*, two biographies have been of particular assistance in describing Kropotkin's early life: those by Woodcock and Avakumovic, and Miller, to which I have returned for specific investigations. Information on the Fell railways comes from Pemble, Byrnes' biography of Pobedonostsev explores the residue of French intellectual life left behind by the Grand Armée, while the letters between Kropotkin and his brother Alexander chart their political development. Complemented by Meijer, Figner's memoirs provide a moving account of the everyday life in the community of émigré Russian students in Switzerland, as do Engel and Faure, who context-ualise their studies, in intellectual and political terms. Gaucher examines the appeal to Russia's youth of Peter Lavrov, who must regrettably remain a background figure in this story, and the compelling charisma of Nechaev, though it is Hingley who quotes Nechaev's calls to arms: 'Now, friends, let us start the drama.' Avrich and Morris have both examined the relationship between Bakunin and Nechaev, while Leier has recently provided an effective survey of Bakunin's wider career. Wheen, with a biographer's sympathy for Marx, is unsparing in his attack on Bakunin's anti-Semitism, which held the Jews to be 'a single exploiting sect' and insisted that 'every popular revolution is accompanied by a massacre of Jews: a natural consequence . . .'; Jensen lays bare Bakunin's equally reprehensible belief that all progress must be 'baptised in blood'. The account of life among the members of the Jurassian federation, 'the last Mohicans of the International' according to Bakunin, derives in part from material in Guillaume and from Enckell, with the culture of watchmaking taken from Jaquet and Chapuis. Titov was useful on the origins of the Chaikovsky Circle, as were others concerning the mission 'to the People', and Venturi on the naïvety of the idealistic youths in their mission and on Kropotkin's Manifesto. Tikhomirov's memoirs of his attempts at propaganda at the time are found in his *Conspirateurs et policiers*. Fleming was once again an important reference point for Reclus' biography, prompting further research regarding agents' reports in the AN, *Papiers Elisée Reclus*, and the APP, folders BA a/1502 and 1237.

4 Around the World in 280 Days

Rochefort's own *Adventures* provides the main source for my description of his circumnavigation of the globe, tempered by Williams' eagle eye for his subject's manifold hypocrisies, as for example in the rumours that his escape from Paris had been betrayed by Grousset. Jellinek, however, is the major source for the activities of the tribunal operated by the council of war. Similarly, Thomas' biog-raphy of Louise Michel, and Michel's own writings provide the mainstay for Michel's journey to New Caledonia, supplemented by additional sources for the digressions along the way. The correspondence of Engels and of Reclus illuminate perceptions of the Spanish uprising, while Anderson in *Under Three Flags* affords a useful summary of the situation in that country, as part of a far wider history of Hispanic anarchism at the time. The imaginary sharks between Prato and the Catamans are inevitably the work of Jogand-Pages, or Taxil, and form part of his own account of his hoaxes, delivered to the Paris Geographical Society in 1897, but appear too in his APP files. Costello considers contemporary myths of the sea and its monsters, as transformed by Verne's imagination; Day examines the suggestions that Michel was the original author of *20,000 Leagues*, dismissing her candidacy in favour of George Sand; the world tours are Pemble's subject. As for the anarchist ideas discussed on board *La Virginie*, Rykwert is helpful; the key document regarding anarchism from the time of the French Revolution is the Babouvist *Manifeste des Egaux*. Pain's memoir of Rochefort, along with the accounts of other escapees, gives a colourful picture of New Caledonia, as does Gauthier, but the indispensable work is Bullard's exceptional study of the deportee's life. The account of the escape is largely taken from Rochefort's own *From Nouméa to Newcastle*, though corroborated by others: his companions recorded his souvenir-hunting en route to America. I would have liked to quote Whitman's *Oh Star of France* at length, but it can be found in Boime, who expertly distils the impact of the Commune in America, as well as its aftermath in an amnesiac France, through the transformation of the Parc Monceau. An old doctoral thesis by Martinez remains the definitive source for the Communard emigration to London, evoking the Charlotte Street colony and its inhabitants' antipathy to Rochefort's hauteur, with further information from Kellet. Madox Ford sheds light on growing up with Communard domestic staff, Bertall on the contemporary belief that 'the actors have but retired behind the scenes'. Porter examines British policing at the time, for which documents in Home Office files 9335 29553 and 45 9303 11335 at TNA are essential reading.

5 To the People

The activities of the Chaikovsky Circle are well represented in Venturi and Footman, with Kravchinsky's *Revolutionary Russia* providing a propagandist account that reveals much about how the radical youth of Russia understood their mission, including the assertion that 'in 1870 the whole of advanced Russia was anarchist', and his *Career of a Nihilist* gives a fictional interpretation of similar experiences; Taratuta draws on a mass of Russian material for her narrative of his life. Billington examines the positive beliefs that impelled the radical movement, whose sense of intellectual suppression fuelled its drift towards violent tactics, and the role of the journal *Znanie*, as does Coplestone, with his interest in Pisarev. Suvin and Fetzer explore the Russian science fiction of the period and its utopian content, Fetzer as editor of a useful anthology. Doskoevsky's visions of a utopian society on another planet corrupted by a lie, in *The Dream of a Ridiculous Man*, and of the proto-blogging habits of a future society are particularly intriguing. In light of the many deaths of radicals while held in prison without charge, Florovsky's discussion of the belief held by the Comtean, Nicholas Fedorov, that 'the new age of science would make possible even the resurrection of the dead', is plangent. The descriptions of Cyon's confrontation with the St Petersburg students in Kennan and Fox are complementary; my sense of the reactionary backlash to such ideas derives from Byrnes and Berglund; Figner, Hingley, and Daly are, with ascending degrees of critical distance, informative regarding the police crackdown on the activists. Dr Veimar's insistence on retaining some independence and that 'I cannot join any circle', whilst facilitating prison breaks and assassinations – an interesting position – comes from Miller who, once again together with Woodcock and Avakumovic, supplies the core of Kropotkin's story.

6 Forward!

The Manual of Guerrilla Warfare that Kravchinsky was said to have written remains a tantalising notion on which his impressive biographer Taratuta, uncharacteristically, sheds little light: it is mentioned by Guillaume, who published Kravchinsky's letter from Santa Maria Capua Venere prison, and the manual is said by Nettlau to have circulated in manuscript form until at least the mid-1890s, but is not preserved in GARF or TsGALI. My account of Kravchinsky's Bosnian adventures, improbable as certain incidents may seem, are drawn from Taratuta's thorough research, as are details of the letter sent by Klements to Chaikovsky. The writings of Pick and Gould on Lombroso and criminal anthropology form the basis of my discussion of this theme, the former also alluding to the contemporary perception of southern Italy as being almost African in temperament. Bakunin's insistence that 'we must make unceasing revolutionary attempts', which I imagine being repeated by Malatesta, was written to Debagory-Mokrievich in 1874. The narrative of the Matese expedition, from the availability of the Puglia cache of arms to its ultimate failure, is constructed from the research of Masini and Ravindranathan: the latter noted the mysterious aristocrat for whom marriage to Kropotkin was the price of her financial support, as though she were akin to Bakunin's patroness Princess Zoe Obolensky, without supplying the accurate but more mundane explanation. Pernicone too contributes to my evocation of the Matese expedition, while Bakunin's powerful first impressions of Malatesta after his Alpine crossing are taken from his work, which is also interesting on the marriage of Cafiero to the Russian radical Olympia Kutuzov before the Italian consul in St Petersburg in 1874. It is Vakhrushev, however, who reveals that the same consul, in the pay of the Third Section, betrayed her presence in Russia to the police in 1877; he also exposes the patron of Lavrov's propaganda work in London, Balashevich-Pototsky, as another Third Section agent. Kimball cites a letter from Lavrov's chief assistant, Smirnov, that recounts how pressure from such agents in London had driven the émigré Sibiryakov to madness and expresses the fear that the same fate might befall Kropotkin. The edition of *Forward!* In which Frey's letter appeared was published in August 1874. The tension between the Godmen and radicals forced to share overnight accommodation comes from Frolenko; the main narrative of Chaikovsky in America from Hecht and Yarmolinsky, the latter of whom quotes Faresov on Malikov's disenchantment with Cedar Vale. Hoig captures the wild atmosphere of Wichita, while Miner sets out the painful history of the Wichita tribe and the 'Happy Valley'. The idea that 'the anarchists are simply unterrified Jeffersonian Democrats' is first articulated by Benjamin Tucker; Foner is the source for the scandalous circumstances of Hayes' election as president and the terrible treatment of railroad workers, also in Stowell; d'Eramo for the military operations that saw soldiers deployed from 'redskins' to 'reds'. Adamic and Schveirov throw light on the violent world of labour relations, Mackay on the Pinkerton Agency's involvement in it.

7 *Propaganda by Deed*

Concerning both Jogand-Pages (aka Taxil) and Elisée Reclus the APP files for this period are revealing. In the case of the hoaxer, his scurrilous journalism, frauds and sale of aphrodisiac pills are all noted, along with the anti-Catholic sentiments he shared with Garibaldi in an extraordinary exchange of letters that refer to the priesthood as 'black crocodiles'. In the case of Reclus, whose book *La Terre* had laid out his theory of the existence of a single landmass in the Jurassic period, the informer who progresses from describing him as a 'dreamer' to 'most active' appears to be Oscar Testut. However, it is hard to imagine how a man described by Christiansen as writing a book that claimed the Commune was a form of red Freemasonry with tentacles across the Continent could have gained Reclus' trust. Again, Miller and Kropotkin's own writings provide much of the detail of his life, but Cahm is the source for his claims to scientific socialism, and the anti-intellectualism that temporarily divided him and Reclus. Cahm's work has also informed my understanding of the theoretical debates at the congresses of the period, though others too deserve much credit here: Jensen for his exploration of the idea and practice of 'propaganda by deed', Fleming for her insights into Guillaume's resistance to the 'distressing ambiguities' of the term 'anarchist', and Taratuta on the attendance at Ghent of Costa as representative of the imprisoned Matese group. Kropotkin's brief presence at the congress under the name 'Levashev' is traced from the AGR files, which also shed light on the true status of his 'marriage' to Sarah Rabinaria. Haekel's eugenicist interests are discussed by Pick, his anti-Semitic nationalism by Weindling; the obsequies for Bakunin are from Ravindranathan. Liubatovich, quoted by Eyel, testifies to Kravchinsky's tutorship in coquetry in a letter to Anna Epstein; regrettably, Siljak's biography of Zasulich, *Angel of*

Vengeance, was not published in time to be consulted, nor was Matthias' *Im Geruch eines Bombenwerfers* concerning Johann Most. Trautmann is my main source for the life of Most, along with his own *Memoiren*, his book *Die Bastille am Plotzensee*, and articles in *Freiheit*, while his comments concerning Reclus are taken from Ramus, in Ishill. My sense of the pressure brought to bear on Switzerland by her neighbours derives from Vuilleumier; of anarchist influence on the Egyptian nationalist movement from Vatikiotis and Un Vecchio; and of the curious origins of the financing of the Suez Canal from Rykwert. Lee offers an excellent critique of *The Begum's Millions*, though I give more weight to Grousset's role in the novel's composition, while the social references examined by Chesneaux too are of interest.

8 *Spies and Tsaricides*

The early life of Rachkovsky is detailed in Brachev, drawing extensively on the archives of the Okhrana's foreign agency, though Aronson in his article for *Kniga* 'The Jewish Press in Russia', quoted by Poliakov, implies a rather later date than April 1879 for his appointment as managing editor of the newspaper *Russian Jew*. His feline demeanour is alluded to by Encausse, quoted in Cohn, while the physical description comes from his police file, compiled by Kletochnikov himself; Vakhrushev supplies further details of their friendship in the Third Section's offices and of Rachkovsky's exposure of Tikhomirov. The ruthless instincts Rachkovsky shared with Stieber and his dislike of the Prussian are assessed by Höhne, who also reveals the tip-off by Stieber regarding the Winter Palace bombing, based on Swiss sources, and the sensitivities surrounding the tsar's mistress. The main source for the chapter's history of Russian terrorism, however, is Footman, whose hugely impressive biography of Zhelyabov is a model of elegant economy, supplemented by Hingley regarding the train attacks and the conspirators' ultimate execution. Clutterbuck's thesis defines the signature technique of the Russian bombers as the use of an electrical charge to detonate homemade explosive, using a spotter and often tunnelling, but his argument that the Fenians rather than the nihilists were the true pioneers of dynamite terrorism is inconsequential. Gaucher describes Plekhanov's resignation at the Voronezh Congress; Gaucher and Laporte were also the sources for the later story of Zhelyabov's betrayal by Okladsky. Liubatovich's disagreement with Tikhomirov, together with information about the death of Kravchinsky's premature baby, is found in Engel; details of Figner's role in the plots, including as mistress of the cheese shop and seducer of the stationmaster, are drawn from her memoirs; Confino quotes Engels musing to Marx on whether Nechaev was a provocateur or merely behaved like one. The reversals suffered by Russia in the Balkans are chronicled by Kennan; the rise of anti-Semitism in Russia by Byrnes and Poliakov, who considers the misrepresentation of the tsar's Slavic assassin, Grinevitsky. Daly, Monas, Wright and

Zuckerman cast light on Loris-Melikov's 'Dictatorship of the heart' and the suspension of the Third Section.

9 Inconvenient Guests

The memoirs of Andrieux are a fount of entertaining gossip and reveal the self-regarding and capricious figure of whom his secretary Louis Lepine, later Paris' most effective police prefect of the period, would comment 'What was he not? The only thing he lacked, and that only just, was to be a dictator.' Andrieux's insights cover everything from the police 'reptile fund', to his funding of the anarchist newspaper, Michel's praise of the nihilists and the seizure of anticlerical publications by Taxil. As Rhodes points out, Bertillon was one blind spot for Andrieux, who was unimpressed by the string-pulling of Bertillon's illustrious father, president of the Society of Anthropology, and refused to back his experiments. For the furore around Hartmann's arrest, the petitions for his release and the sleight of hand that resolved the situation, the APP and AN provided a rich resource: there is an echo of Reclus' advocacy of the name 'anarchism' as a name in Hartmann's declaration, noted by Senese, that '"Nihilist" is a word that interests the West and hence it is desirable to use it.' Joll and Kennan furnish the detail of France's military preparations and the geopolitical background to the chapter; the hugely successful tombola for the New Caledonian exiles, which saw money subscribed from both sides of the Atlantic, is mentioned by Martinez. Williams is the source for Rochefort's coinage of the term 'Opportunist' and cowardly reputation as a duellist, Jellinek for the background to his insults against Gambetta and Reinarch, while Rochefort's own *Adventures* and newspaper *L'Intransigeant* of March 1881 celebrate his scoop concerning the Geneva nihilists. Agent reports from his APP file for that month cover his banqueting there and advance warning of the London Congress. The Joly file in the same archive reveals the fact, intriguing for historians of the *Protocols*, that Rochefort's lawyer and the author of the *Dialogues* were brothers, the former committing suicide at this time, in 1878, the latter a few years later. Sutcliffe examines the technology that transformed Paris; Barrows and Martinez the loss to France of skilled Communards; Casselle paints a vivid picture of the Expo, coordinated by Adolphe Alphand, and explains how the council of ministers pinned the blame on Andrieux for the 1881 confrontations at Père Lachaise.

10 Voices in the Fog

The description of Michel's return is taken from her memoirs and from Thomas, as are other details of her life at this time. Regarding relations between the Belgian and British police, Dilnot revealed the corruption scandal, Keunings deals with the Sûreté's reforms, and Sherry the outing in disguise on which

Vandervelde accompanies Vincent. Vincent's reforms are examined by Porter, who also paints a memorable portrait of Williamson, but whose works are drawn on most extensively concerning the trial and arrest of Most. Carlson provides Most's incriminating quote, 'May the day not be far off when a similar occurrence will free us from tyranny', Trautmann gives details of his principled defence lawyer. Like Porter, Quail is a major source for the chapter, as for so much regarding British anarchism: details taken from his work including Neve's smuggling operation using mattresses and the punishment of the informant, and the informed speculation that Charles Hall who attended the London Congress was a police spy. Oliver recounts the eventual exposure of Serreaux five years later, Miller the disputes surrounding his involvement in the congress, the prospectus for which, signed partially anagrammatically by Brocher as 'Rehorb', lies in the IISH [Int 240/4]. Among those attending, Malatesta's recent background prior to the congress appears in Nettlau, but Dipaola's unpublished thesis, drawing on material in the Italian archives, provides captivating detail on his life in London at the time: the chinks in the wooden partitions of his lodgings through which Vincent spies, the whitewashed windows of the workshop he shares with Hartmann, behind which the device they are inventing is merely a pea-shelling machine for a competition, and his visits with Chaikovsky to the British Museum Library: Emsley refers to Special Branch's request in 1883 for access to readers' records. For the background to the discussion of 'propaganda by deed' and Cafiero's call in *Le Révolté* to spread the anarchist gospel 'by spoken and written words, by the dagger, the gun, dynamite', Jensen and Cahm are both informative. The former notes the paradox of anarchists praising the use of dynamite by the People's Will, whose hierarchical organisation they should have found abhorrent; he also notes the anarchist activity in Lyons; it is Vizetelly who explodes the myth of the Black Hand. Kropotkin's offhand dismissal of England in favour of France, despite the presence in the West End of a theatrical adaption of the Verne novel *Michael Strogoff* that he is said to have inspired, is quoted by Oliver. Shipley evokes the Rose Street club's Christmas party; Fleming, Cafiero's incipient madness; Williams, the Union Générale *krach*; Poliakov, the anti-Semitic backlash. I was delighted to discover in the APP file for Jogand-Pages that Taxil's satirical response had been to sell notes printed for the 'Banque Sainte-Farce', for which he was arrested on the boulevard des Italiens. Madox Ford reports Kropotkin's belief in the 'perdurability of the rabbit', Kimball the flocks of spies who attended him; details of his arrest are taken from the AN files and of his trial from Fleming and Gallet.

11 *The Holy Brotherhood*

'From above a hidden hand pushes the masses of people to a great crime' wrote Simon Dubrow, the historian of the Jewish people, to the government-appointed Pahlen Committee in 1883. The question of whose the hand was behind the pogroms – and it existed – is a vexed one. Most have blamed reactionary elements, though Alexander III himself thought them 'the work of anarchists' (*Russkii Evrei*, 12 May 1881) and there was indeed anti-Semitism within the People's Will, and even more a desire to exploit the chaos to revolutionary ends; Poliakov traces, in nascent form, the correlation between anti-Semitism and those who rejected modern life, as vegetarians, anti-vivisectionists and back-to-nature cultists. Klier presents the most persuasive argument, for genuinely spontaneous violence, which Plehve sent urgent telegrams in an attempt to quell; nevertheless, Berk's suggestion that many stationmasters on the railway were members of the Holy Brotherhood identifies a possible mechanism for the persistent spread of the pogroms. Peregudova presents her findings from the GARF archive, F. 1766.OP.1.D.1–5za (1881–1883) concerning the Brotherhood and offers a useful introduction to it, though it is quite thoroughly examined by Talerov and by Lukashevich who maps the Brotherhood's structure, alludes to Tchaikovsky's involvement and considers Sudeikin's criticisms of it. 'Sviashchennaia druzhina (Pis'mo v redaktsiiu)' was Kropotkin's insurance, to be disclosed by *The Times* should any ill fate befall him. An entry in the APP file on Loris-Melikov, BA 1162, for June 1881 makes clear the scorn in which the Brotherhood was held throughout western Europe. Marx and Engels, in the preface to the 1882 Russian edition of *The Communist Manifesto*, refer to the new tsar as 'a prisoner of war of the revolution', while in Russia he was known simply as the 'Gatchina prisoner'; 'K biografii Aleksandra III' in *Byloe*, however, reveals his letters of 1885 demanding that the military follow his orders to slacken restrictive security around him. Footman is among the sources for Kibalchich's pleas for scientific validation for his rocket design. Pipes is the source for much of Degaev's double-dealing, Tidmarsh for Sudeikin's intended power grab, Brachev for his engagement with the Holy Brotherhood and recruitment of Rachkovsky, and 'Degaevshchina' in *Byloe*, April 1906, for the post-mortem after his murder. Lemke examines Sudeikin's operational innovations, which contributed to the capture of Figner, and considers Semiakin's report that compared the Paris office unfavourably with the activities of the consuls in Vienna and Berlin; the career of Korvin-Krukovsky is largely reconstructed from his APP file, BA 881. The scene of Rachkovsky's arrival in Paris is imagined, referencing fumigators described in Pemble; Kantor reveals Duclerc's opening of police files on the émigrés to Zhukov, presumably including APP BA 196, which identifies the flat of the author L'Isle Adam as a focal point for those planning attacks in Russia. Zvoliansky's support of Rachkovsky and the recruitment of Hekkelman draws on Agafonov and Fischer, who pinpoints the student friendship between Hekkelman and Burtsev that the latter in *Chasing Agents Provocateurs* appears eager to obscure. Daly reveals the Holy Brotherhood's previous employment of Bint, from the Barlat Brigade, while Kennan suggests that Juliette Adam's St Petersburg visit in January 1882 included private dinners with Paul Demidov, a prime funder of the Brotherhood. Rachkovsky's polite dismissal of de Mohrenheim's interference is taken from Svatikov, his letter to Fragnon quoted by Johnson. Yarmolinsky and Biriukov are the source for Frey in Russia, Frey's letter of 2 July 1886 for his lobbying of Kropotkin and Kravchinsky in London on the 'religion of Humanity'.

12 *A Great News Tide*

Martinez is the source for Hyndman's visit to the Commune, together with a young Conservative barrister who found 'much in it to deserve . . . the admiration of an intelligent and practical statesman', Hulse for his decision to found the Democratic Federation to 'undertake the propaganda that Marx and Engels were neglecting in England'. It was Hulse's prismatic account of the lives of five diverse socialists in England – Kropotkin, Morris and Kravchinsky among them – that helped crystallise the structure of this book, as well as furnishing much pertinent detail concerning the relationships between them. It is primarily Tsuzuki's account of Carpenter's life that informed his appearances, in combination with research in SCL, and Rowbotham's earlier writings: sadly, her magisterial biography of Carpenter was published too late to figure in my research. Noteworthy in the appendix of Carpenter's *My Days and Dreams*, the foremost of his own works to be used, is his explanation that his opposition strength of conviction stemmed from being born at what he regarded as the zenith of commercialism. Reclus' warning against withdrawal to the life of the small community is found in 'An Anarchist on Anarchy'; Rykwert discusses the irony that although Ruskin's books had a wide readership, they failed to rouse the British middle class to social action; while Kinna discusses how Morris' purpose in 1883 was 'to reconcile Marx with Ruskin'. Her work together with that of Thompson and, above all, McCarthy's masterful biography of Morris have informed my sense of the origins and development of his socialism, with Morris' own *How I Became a Socialist* and *Collected Letters* the obvious autobiographical point of reference. For a grass-roots perspective on the tensions in the movement, the 'bloodthirsty resolutions' that had earlier concerned Scheu and the part played by Lane in the schism, Quail is once again invaluable, as is Shipley for Kitz's sense of the socialist tradition and his relationship with Morris. In many respects, Kravchinsky remained something of a mystery even to his close friends, Kropotkin reflecting in the commemorative pamphlet *Vospominaniia o Kravchinskom* of 1907, 'We know about the external occurrences in his life, we possess his works, but we know too little about his interior life: it slips away from us.' BA 1133 and 196 in the APP reveal the extent of confusion at this time in France over his true identity, something which Olga Novikoff attempted to resolve in Britain by the insinuations about the murderer of General Mezentsev in her *Pall Mall Gazette* article of July 1886. Whyte considers her role in British life and the propagandist value of her brother's death; Szamuely, British attitudes to Russia more generally. Hollingworth, Hulse and Senese all contributed to my sense of Kravchinsky's propaganda strategies and

his place in the British socialist movement; the Russian's use of the words 'toy revolutionaries' comes from Shaw, whom Kravchinsky alone could argue into silence,
quoted by Senese, Maudsley and intellectual degeneracy are discussed in Pick, while
Beaumont's survey of British utopian writing has been of great assistance.

13 The Making of the Martyrs

The far-flung network of imperial German police agents informed Berlin,
according to Hohne, that Most 'promises to kill people of property and position and that's why he is popular'. From the arrival of the 'king-killer', through
his tour speaking to audiences that included, by *Freiheit*'s reckoning, 5,000 in
the Cooper's Union Great Hall, to his evasive manoeuvres after Haymarket,
Most's American career is closely tracked by Trautmann. Lingg's association
with Reinsdorf and others that upstaged Most, is revealed by the *Chicagoer
Arbeiter-Zeitung* of 30 April 1885. Three historians have provided the bulk of the
information deployed in the chapter after the economic and social conditions
of Chicago, of which Green's well-contextualised account of the bombing and
martyrdom of the convicted men is the most recent. Nelson and d'Eramo both
discuss the parties for the Commune and the Dawn of Liberty: the former
explores the organisation of the socialists and the basement paramilitaries; the
latter is illuminating on the addresses at Pittsburgh in 1883, the subject of the
Red Squads, the industrialists' purchase of a Gatling gun and, latterly, the planting
of bombs at Chicago's anarchist headquarters in the wake of the Haymarket
debacle. Victor Dave's torn letter of resignation from the Socialist League was
found in file 1205/1 at the IISH, a tangible artefact of the 'Bruderkrieg' explored
by Carlson, who considers the intrigues of the elusive figure of Reuss, and Neve's
smuggling operations, and Quail, who additionally discusses Lane's organisational success, Morris' excitement at the idea of imminent revolution, and Engels'
concern about the anarchists of the Socialist League. Abraham Cahan wrote of
Eleanor Marx's 'brilliant words' to a gathering of 3,000 in New York in protest
against the persecution of the Haymarket Martyrs, Oliver of the previous South
Place meeting she addressed, alongside Kravchinsky and Kropotkin.

14 Decadence and Degeneration

The sentiment unleashed at Hugo's funeral is described by Robb, who also examines the myth surrounding the republican author, of whom Zola wrote that he
had 'become a religion in French letters, by which I mean a sort of police force
for maintaining order'; Shattuck quotes Barrès on the erotic sublimation of grief,
and his work informs my sense of much about Paris during the period. Bullard
discusses the memories and myths of the savagery at Satory that haunted the
Communards. Freud's letters convey his impression of the uncanny city; Pick

surveys the state of French psychiatry, considering Charcot's ideas of visual derangement as a symptom of mental degeneracy, from which he thought the 'roaring colourists' of post-Impressionism, as Nordau refers to them, might be suffering. Anderson, B. describes the second exhibition of the Salon des Indépendants, at which Seurat and Signac burst upon the scene, while Roslak's sensitive study of Signac traces a thread through artistic and anarchistic theory and Reclus' understanding of the world as a geographer; Hutton puts their work in a social and cultural context. I am gratified to find my own interpretation of *La Grande Jatte* roughly coincides with that of Robert Hughes. While promoting the pair of artists, Félix Fénéon found time to edit the mess of Rimbaud's extraordinary poems into the exquisite shape of *Illuminations*, as I discovered in Halperin's biography. The ballad to Louise Michel by the young poet's lover, Verlaine, which appeared in *Le Décadent* in December 1886, compares her to Joan of Arc and says she is 'far' from Leo Taxil. Expelled from the Freemasons five years earlier for publishing the salacious *Secret Love Life of Pope Pius IX*, Taxil aka Jogand-Pages had recently rediscovered Catholicism; the claim in the APP report of 25 July 1885 that 'nobody, absolutely nobody believes in the sincerity of this conversion' was misguided, as the coming decade would amply prove. On the demi-monde of nightclubs and cults, Shattuck, Sonn, Casselle and Varias all offer fascinating detail, the last quoting Crueul's 'a thing to be mocked'; Costello describes the Robida projection shows and Jouan explores his images; Debans cites the Russian's desire to annex Paris; Brachev, in *Foreign Secret Service*, quotes Encausse on Rachkovsky's liking for Parisian girls. André unpacks the tangled world of mysticism and details Encausse's other life as Charcot's hypnotist; Osterrieder makes the links between d'Alveydre, Danish royalty, the Pandit and the conspiracy with the maharajah. The story of the Boulanger phenomenon is derived from many sources, but best diagnosed by Gildea as what happened when the 'republican concentration' broke down. The general's interest in the Decazeville miners comes from Barrows, that of Rochefort in those at Anzin and in the soldiers sent to Tonkin from Williams, who also recounts the marquis' suspicious ability to predict the steps to a coming conflict with Bismarck, and his demands for a dictatorship; the gossip about Pain and the Mahdi is from Rochefort's *Adventures*. Boulanger's friend, Captain Hippolyte Barthélemy, published *Avant La Bataille* at the time of the Schnaebele Incident, insisting that any rapprochement with Germany be through force of arms. Reclus, in his letters to Groess, expected war, while one agent's report in APP BA 75 claims he was preparing 'a seditious movement . . . to thwart the efforts of the French armies'; at the same time, Engels was warning Germany that any war would draw in the continent, cause destruction equal to the Thirty Years War and 'be followed by the collapse of countless European states and the disappearance of dozens of monarchies'. Rochefort in his *Adventures* blamed the whole incident on 'German financial Jewry' yet, as Williams remarks, took Jewish money for the Boulangist campaign. Kennan reveals General Bogdanovich's attempt to orchestrate a Franco-Russian alliance as early as January 1887. Mace expresses his frustration with the organisation of the police in his memoirs, while Stead describes its factionalism and inefficiency, and Longoni the waiting room. Agafonov, Vakhrushev and Zuckerman are among the sources for Rachkovsky's Okhrana operation in Paris, Gaucher for the Moscow disguise wardrobe, and *Byloe* of July 1917 for the details of the printing-press raid. The APP file on de Mohrenheim records France's anxieties about his movements, *Le Temps* for 2 December 1887 the packed meeting at Salle Favie addressed by Michel, and the dynamite threats made there. Barrows quotes the conservative Mazade on the 'decisive crisis'; she also considers how psychologists of crowd activity such as Taine and Le Bon analysed the Boulanger phenomenon and socialist protests. The letters written by Michel after her shooting are published in the collection *Je vous écris de ma nuit*.

15 *The Revolution is Postponed*

'We can only rest quietly at Clairvaux and do our best to avoid dying of anaemia and dysentery,' Miller quotes Kropotkin writing from prison, though Hulse remarks on his lack of green fingers as an experimental gardener. Kennan is the source for Russia's regret that he survived to be freed and the diplomatic repercussions, police reports in TNA F7 12519–20 for July 1887 for British concern over his influence as an exile in London. My sense of the Dod Street riot and the ensuring trial derives primarily from McCarthy and Quail, and of Black Monday and Bloody Sunday from both Porter and Tsuzuki. The debate around the extent to which, for all his denials, Morris was an anarchist is a fascinating one, though there is space here only to note the contributions of Bantman, Cole, Thompson and Kinna, who also discusses his call to educate, his views on class conflict and society's complacency, and the political trap of the Coercion Bill; Holroyd is the source for Shaw's memories of 'skedaddling', Oliver for his remarks about the anarchism of the early Fabians. She also traces the early biographies of Nicoll and Samuels, to which Quail contributes, along with insights into tension between Charlotte Wilson and Lane concerning the title of his publication. Rowbotham, and Carpenter's *My Days and Dreams*, are the source for the Commonwealth Café, whose location in an old debtors prison offered, she suggests, a reminder of the iniquities of capitalism. Beaumont contextualises Carpenter's observation regarding the West End dinner party, the implied voyeurism of which, taken with his comments elsewhere regarding the 'huge human creature' that will one day 'shrug its back and shake us into the dirt', brings to mind the Kraken of Mackay. The effectiveness of the Salvation Army and the ban on fortune-telling are discussed in Fishman's wonderful book on the East End. Regarding the People's Palace, Garnett is interesting on how its social significance was perceived at the time, Beaumont on its philanthropic origins and literary context, while reference to Mrs Wilson's curious prescience regarding the threat to Victoria is found in Oliver. The background to the rivalry of Jenkinson and Anderson is

from Porter and Campbell, while my attention was drawn to the approving presence on documents of Salisbury's 'S' by Robert's review of the latter; Clutterbuck
discusses the Fenian intrigues, Cook the role of Melville as port watcher: a task
explored by Johnson. Porter, again, is the source for Ambassador Paget fingering
Stammer as the Ripper, Deacon for Le Queux's claim in *Things I Know* that
Rasputin had indicated the guilt of an Okhrana agent named Nideroest, and
http://www.casebook.org/suspects/ for Vassily as a candidate. Clutterbuck
alludes mysteriously to Special Branch suspicions of Fenian involvement in the
Ripper murders, while Lowdes, whose website suggests that she has been prosecuted for publishing photographs of the un-redacted Special Branch ledgers to
which she too had access, alleges the Branch's own culpability. Fischer is the
source for the hiring of 'Murphy' and 'John' by Rachkovsky's agent Milewski.
'Malatesta's personal life remains to be written,' writes Levy, lamenting the 'scant
outlines available in largely hagiographical works . . . scattered letters and . . .
police spies' on whose testimony, pending his own mooted biography of the
Italian, I have to some extent relied; in addition to Nettlau and Dipaola, both
Ruvira works consider his activities in Argentina, Jensen the troublesome Pini
and Parmeggiani. Cahm and Hulse explore Kropotkin's views on expropriation
and his work towards 'The Conquest of Bread'; Byrnes casts surprising light on
Pobedonostsev's passion for Morris and Novikoff's role in indulging it; Pick illuminates Le Bon's idealisation of medieval communes, whose role in the social
vision of both Morris and Kropotkin warrants closer consideration than was
here possible.

16 *Deep Cover*

The atmosphere of the Raincy house rented by Tikhomirov at the time of his
son's illness is described by him in *Vospominaniya;* a contemporary description of
the Russian's state of mind and history of nervous afflictions is found in Rosny's
'Nihilists in Paris' in *Harper's,* August 1891, and reflections on his apostasy in
Gleason. Vakhrushev is the source for the role played by Rachkovsky in applying
pressure, Fischer for Hansen's part in publishing Tikhomirov's confessions to
compromise him; Agafonov, as well as discussing the second raid on the printing
works, quotes the Okhrana chief on the 'relationship of obligation to myself' in
which he placed Hansen for intelligence purposes, while Kennan considers
Hansen's background and reputation, and also examines Grand Duke Vladimir's
early expressions of interest in the Lebel repeating rifle. Tidmarsh probes the
ideological reasons for Tikhomirov's move, quoting his belief that the Russian
'people has degenerated terribly', and Maevsky who sees him turning equally on
his old colleagues, 'misfits . . . puerile and limited personalities'. The greatest
defence of the revolutionaries against the slurs of *Why I Ceased . . .* came from
Plekhanov, in *A New Champion of Autocracy.* Webb and André have illuminated
the murky world of Parisian mysticism; the dates of de Mohrenheim's visit to

Clermont-Ferrand were, according to various press reports, 26 July and 10 August 1887. Casselle quotes d'Uzès' opinion that Boulanger was a 'wet rag', and offers a panoramic overview of the 1889 Expo, from the Eiffel Tower, and those who criticised and thrilled to it, to the Palais des Machines, a 'Hell of work where so many diabolical machines furiously gesticulate'; Sutcliffe too contributes to my sense of the event. Thomas is the source for Michel's interest in argot and Esperanto, Varias for 'the great hatching' and the Volapük Congress; disagreements at the criminal anthropology congresses are covered by Harris. The account of the two socialist congresses is drawn from Tsuzuki, McCarthy, Bernstein, the files of the IISH on the Congrès International Ouvrier Socialiste de Paris, letters home from Carpenter in the Sheffield archives, and Joll's *Second International*; his *Europe 1870*, the first book I ever read on the period, still informs my sense of the prevailing economic conditions. Reclus' letter that advocates 'love everyone' is quoted by Clark and Martin, while my knowledge of Tarrida's lecture on 'anarchism without adjectives' comes from B. Anderson. Poliakov credits the Franco-Russia rapprochement, in part, to Rachkovsky 'showing that Catholic France and Orthodox Russia had to fight against a common Jewish enemy', while Clarke explores fictional expectations of the next war. Goron's memoirs conceal the duplicity of the French police in relation to the 1890 bomb plot but are interesting on its external circumstances; *Byloe* for 1908 sheds more light, as do the AN and APP files, and a number of studies drawn from them; R. Henderson refers to attempts by the conspirators' defence lawyer, Millerand, to expose Rachkovsky and Hekkelman, though neither the court nor the press rose to the bait. Zuckerman quotes Zubatov's advice on the informant as a 'beautiful woman': the scrawled draft of Rachkovsky's letter to Hekkelman, held in the Okhrana archive at F10003 K162 P12a11a, required painstaking decipherment and is presented here, I believe, for the first time. Two views of Burtsev's flight from Constantinople aboard the *Ashlands* are found in *The Times* of 19 and 20 January 1891, and Burtsev's own *Chasing Agents Provocateurs*; whether or not the burly man who boarded the ship was Bint being a key point of variance.

17 *The Russian Memorandum*

The surface detail of Seliverstov's assassination along with speculation about the perpetrator's identity and motive are taken from British press reports in the *Daily Graphic*, *Justice* and *Commonweal* from late November 1890, and from APP file BA 878, which implicates both Padlweski, the pseudonym of Otto Hauser Dyzek, and Rochefort's *L'Intransigeant* for abetting his escape. The suggestion that his death was ordered by Rachkovsky, with Jagolkovsky's involvement, comes from *Byloe* for February 1918, while Brachev intimates Plehve's suspicions on the same subject. It is agent Pépin who finds the old Communard to testify to the revolutionary death sentence passed on Seliverstov in Montreux a decade earlier; *Le Figaro* of 11 March 1890 that reports Kravchinsky in Washington, supposedly 'exhibited' by Kennan at the city's zoological garden alongside Hartmann and Degaev. The APP file on 'Krawtchinsky' summarises his 'Herculean strength' despite his medium height, and suggests that he 'represents very well what the English call a "gentleman"': an impression consonant with Edward Garnett's fanciful idea, quoted by R. Garnett that 'A goddess fell in love with a bear – and so was born Stepniak', who also refers to Olive's comments about the 'confidential' tone in which the Russian delivered his speeches. The journalist who spends the night with 'Stepniak' is Earl Hodgson, out of which he spins a booklet. Senese, an important source for Kravchinsky's career, quotes Hubert Bland as proposing in June 1888 that 'Stepniak' should lead the English socialists, while Saunders refers to his letter to Mrs Spence Watson. Hollingsworth examines the prehistory of the Society of Friends, with its first unproductive meeting in 1886, and he, Senese and Taratuta inform my understanding of its effective foundation in 1889. W. O. Henderson mentions Kennan meeting Volkhovsky and Lazarev on his visits to Siberia, while Byrnes is the source for his encounter with Pobedonostsev, who supposedly tried to read some Emerson every day. In addition to those mentioned above, Budd and Billington examine Kravchinsky's reception by America's literary society, Moser the composition of Career of a Nihilist, while the world of William Dean Howells is beautifully evoked by Cohen, whose book was a structural inspiration for this one, though notable for its elegance and concision. De Mohrenheim's refusal to countenance offers of assistance during Russia's famine is covered extensively in reports and clippings in his APP file, the Gaulois interview being dated 5 September 1892. The report of a Geneva brochure detailing Kravchinsky's supposed sell-out to England was by Agent 'Auguste' on 16 April 1892 and is in the Russian's APP file, while the Okhrana archives and Shirokova reveal the extent of the similar frauds and forgeries it carried out at this time. R. Henderson has unearthed important evidence in GARF regarding the date of the Russian Memorandum in the form of Durnovo's draft; Senese notes Obzor's glee at progress in shifting British public opinion. Engels' prediction concerning the 'energy and violence' of an American revolution is from a letter of March 1892 to Hermann Schluter; the Okhrana's interest in the United States and use of surveillance there are from Taratuta, who had access to files in GARF concerning the New York and London branches of the foreign agency whose contents have since disappeared. Burgoyne, writing journalistically in the immediate aftermath of Homestead, and Krause are my main sources for the battle with the Pinkertons, with sidelights from Trautmann, who treats Most's various periods of imprisonment on Blackwell's Island, his horsewhipping by Goldman for disparaging Berkman after the latter's arrest, and accusations concerning his supposed plans to terrorise Chicago with dynamite during the World's Fair. Concerning the Columbus centenary event itself, I have drawn on Larson and Gilbert; the cloud projections are from Costello, the economic and consumerist life of the city in Fogarty; I regretted the lack of space to consider W. T. Stead's When Christ Comes to Chicago. Kimball deals with the 'saddest news' of the extradition law and the process that led to this conclusion.

18 *Dynamite in the City of Light*

For Rochefort's experiences in London, including the confrontation in the carriage, his art donations and Boulanger's visit, his *Adventures* and Roubaud are the source, but Williams and the police reports in his APP file, BA 1250, strip away much of the glamour of his exile, and regarding the general, Baylen adds detail. The suicide of Rochefort's eldest son only four days before his departure from France is sidelined in his memoirs, just as the suicide a few years previously of a Swiss maid who was said to be the lover of both father and son: it added to a toll of those associated with him that had begun with the daughter of his alleged mistress, in 1872, already included both Joly brothers, and to which Boulanger and Jacques de Reinarch would soon be added. The Belgian casino visits and duels, the mysterious package at Boulanger's funeral, his white hair and Hertz's visit are all recorded by police agents, Norrit and Agent Z in particular, whose sources include Vaughan, the stand-in editor of Rochefort's *L'Intransigeant*, who reveals details of paranoia concerning a vendetta against Constans, while 'Dumont' reports on his clandestine visits to France, allegedly with the assistance of Clemenceau. It was Sherry who many years ago first awoke my interest in the intrigue around the anarchist terror campaign, in light of Conrad's fiction, and his study of 'The Informer' is even more revealing when set beside archival sources; Michel's expression of dislike for 'your' Rochefort to d'Uzès is reported by the duc de Bruissac. Thomas and Michel's own writings are the source for her life at this time, including suggestions of Vauvelle as an Orleanist spy, while the redacted Special Branch ledgers appear to suggest that Vauvelle was an informant for the British police too; Clutterbuck's unrestricted access to this material reveals most fully Coulon's employment under the cover name 'Pyatt'. Porter presents a characteristically balanced view of Special Branch, but argues that those trained in unscrupulous Irish countersubversion themselves subverted the liberal values of the period, creating a disjuncture with the 'myth' of limitless English hospitality that Bantman examines in light of its propaganda value to the French émigrés. It is Porter too who suggests a vested interest in the Walsall case for a Special Branch threatened with budget cuts; the comparison with Continental forces in this and their use of provocateurs comes from Stead, in the case of the Paris prefecture, and Carpenter, Moser and Keunings regarding the Belgian. In sketching a life of Melville, Cook hints at his more sinister side, but it is R. Henderson's meticulous examination of the letter from Jolivard to Richter from the Okhrana archive (f 102, d 3, op 89 [1891] delo 4 'Svedeniia po Londonu' ll. 80:1, 17 May 1891, 24 May 1891, cited by Henderson) that finally confirms Melville's nefarious connivance with Rachkovsky: the latter's pencil annotation of Richter as 'mon pseudonym' establishes the link. Many at the time thought Nicoll deranged to suggest that 'It is only lately that English police agents have followed the example of their foreign associates in manufacturing plots', although in *Commonweal* for

February 1891 'our comrade Mendelsohn' had warned of imminent 'sham dynamite plots' by the Russian police. Melville's maverick tip-off to the Italian Embassy about Malatesta's movements was discovered by Dipaola, though Coulon handed over at least one note about his presence among the marble-workers of Carrara: the claim at the time by the highly respectable Bruce Glasier that Coulon was 'a spy in the pay of the French government' surely underestimates his usefulness to the nebulous 'International Police'. Following a path charted by Tsuzuki and Rowbotham, the Sheffield archives illuminated Carpenter's unfortunate absences at the time when Charles and others there fell under the influence of Creaghe: his career is examined in O'Toole, who also explores Vaillant's experience as a *peon* in Argentina. File MD 259 proved especially revealing about Carpenter's championing of Charles, whose involvement with the bomb he excuses in *My Days and Dreams* as the action of one of those men who 'having the love of humanity in their hearts . . . are able to believe in the speedy realisation of an era of universal goodwill'. According to *Hansard*, the questions were raised in the House between February and April 1892, the Liberal MP Cunninghame Graham especially vocal in challenging the possible involvement of agents provocateurs. Fleming and Herbert cast new light on the martyrology that the well-covered story of Ravachol's terror spree and execution prompted; Rhodes describes Bertillon's professionalism towards him as a photographic subject. Malatesta's reactions, some from the APP, are examined by Levy; those of Reclus by B. Anderson ('rare grandeur'), his *Correspondance* ('the bombings will not prevent us') and Clarke ('end of an epoch'); Jensen, Cahm and Miller consider those of Kropotkin, who appears as a 'white Christ' in Wilde's 'De Profundis' and about whose 'saintliness' Hulse quotes Shaw. Rouvaloff in *Lord Arthur Savile's Crime* and the conflation of Zasulich and Perovskaya in the eponymous heroine of *Vera* reveal Wilde's wider interest in the Russian revolutionaries, as does his *The Soul of Man Under Socialism*; like Wilde, Shaw consulted Kravchinsky over his *Arms and the Man*. Madox Ford describes the post-bomb hysteria in Paris, the Holborn restaurant and the Rossetti children, about whose desire for danger Olive Garnett writes, and whose hospitality towards expelled Italian anarchists interested the Home Office. Henry's nickname of 'microbe' comes from Merriman's excellent new biography, published only in time for cursory reference to be made, while the bouillon is in Harris, and the virologist-as-detective in Latour. The historical lineage of anarchism from the Gnostics through the Mazdaks to the Anabaptists was traced at the time by Garin; the openness of their organisation remarked upon by Dubois.

19 *Wicked Laws*

This chapter and those on either side warrant a book in themselves to tease out the intricacies of the relationships, motivations, intrigues that gave rise to a period of little more than two years that were rich in incident, and their social, political and cultural impact. Merriman's recent volume achieves this admirably for France by focusing on Emile Henry, though it is an account that gives scant attention to the influence of Russia and to the unseen but guiding hand of the Okhrana, in relation to which the bombs and hysteria appear to me to be at most surface turbulence. The somewhat synoptic and reductive account given in this book covers territory familiar from many sources, from Joll to Kedward, Anderson to Vizetelly. It finds little space for the tensions and distrust in the émigré colonies of London, the nuanced ideological differences that the bombings generated or the sense of eavesdropping and claustrophobia that is evoked by running reports of French police agents and informants, and the multiple perspectives they offer. Among the more unusual details of the chapter, Rollin is the source for Dupuy's promise to de Mohrenheim, the payment to Vaillant to rent a room for his bomb-making, and Jacot's mockery of Dupuy's foreknowledge. Rollin's extraordinary work of investigation into the deep historical origins of the *Protocols* was published in 1939 but ruthlessly suppressed during the Nazi occupation of Paris, never to receive the attention it deserved, and in the course of my research I have repeatedly found myself treading in his footsteps. Porch writes about Boulanger's plan to intern anarchists and Bazaries, while the APP émigrés anarchist files contain both examples of the code and reports of concerns about it; Lavenir writes about the course of the idea of 'terrorism' and the 'terrorist' from the revolutionary State Terror of Robespierre and the guillotine. Shattuck briefly explores the invocation by the anarchist martyrs of their scientific and artistic heroes, Darwin, Spencer, Ibsen and Mirbeau, though how violence became aestheticised, in parallel to criminals adopting anarchist ideas, is a subject that warrants further study. B. Anderson is moving on the subject of the future care of the daughters of condemned anarchists: Santiago, convicted of the Liceo bombing, pitifully remarked of his own that 'If they are pretty the bourgeois will take care of them'; Vaillant's only child was fought over by his comrades and Duchess d'Uzès, but eventually became the ward of Sébastien Faure and, before long, his underage lover. Clutterbuck first revealed Littlechild's parting entry in the Special Branch accounts ledger, Porter his comment on 'narks', Dilnot the assumption of disguises by Melville, Bantman the French perspective on the British watchers at French ports and the surveillance of Melville mounted by the anarchists; my research in the Special Branch ledgers indicated Mowbray's role helping organise the surveillance of the anarchists. The image of Melville telephonically connected is from the *Westminster Budget* of 23 February 1894. As well as dealing with Conrad's treatment of the Greenwich bombing, Sherry examines the literary references to 'The Professor', a mysterious figure in the context of Le Raincy, mentioned by Ruud and Stepanov quite vaguely: my own research has noted his appearances in APP, which suggests his identification with the 'Professor Mezenoff' who lectures on dynamite in Paterson and is reported occasionally elsewhere in America as carrying a bomb in his pocket for demonstration purposes. Rachkovsky's reprimand for promoting an anti-anarchist congress is found in 34, VA, 2 of the Okhrana archive, as is the menu for the agency's celebration of the Franco-Russian alliance.

Beaumont summarises *The Year of Miracle*, with its purging plague, while Weindling considers the cultural impact of epidemics and how it overlaps with justifications for later genocide; the Verne novel criticised by the rabbi was *The Carpathian Castle*; Huysmans' farewell to the year 1893 is from a letter to Arij Prins.

20 *The Mysteries of Bourdin and the Baron*

The propaganda successes of which Rachkovsky boasted to Durnovo in January 1894, and for which he was rewarded that April, effectively entailed, as the *Daily Chronicle* acknowledged on 28 February, the publication of an abridged version of the Russian Memorandum. The seizure of Henry's private papers by the French ministry of the interior were disclosed by *La Patrie* on 22 May; B. Anderson, quotes Clemenceau on society's equally savage revenge for the bomber's own savagery. The reports of Malato's concerns about Dumont and about the 'Bourdin brother' present in Paris that January come from the APP, as does information about Rochefort's dinner with anarchists in March; R. Henderson considers the identity of 'Bourdin' in the context of British Museum Library membership in his *Library History* article. The core examination of the press reaction to Greenwich and the contribution of Samuels and Coulon is provided by Sherry and Quail, while the background to the tension between Samuels and Nicoll and the latter's suspicion of Coulon, along with his cover as 'Diamond Setter and Jeweller' is derived from IISH files (2011 and 2018 respectively), as is Nicoll's claim, at the time of his second arrest, that 'Under the rule of Lord Salisbury and his political police, Russian methods are coming into fashion' (2016). It is interesting to note that the sell-out first printing of Nicoll's 'Walsall Anarchists' pamphlet appeared on the very day of the Greenwich explosion. His correspondence with Nettlau, in the IISH, indicates his belief that Bourdin's accidental death was due to the inadvisability of carrying 'sulphuric acid and chlorate of potash . . . in close combination', remarked on by the Home Office's Colonel Majendie. Dipaola's Italian sources suggest that the spy Lauria led to Farnara's arrest, while Clutterbuck quotes the redacted Special Branch ledgers as listing for 30 June, 'Blanqui (Lauris for Farnaro) – £10', a very sizeable payment: Quail suggests the involvement of a mysterious third man, Pemble a context for Polti's supposed anti-tourist motive. The change in British attitudes following the bombings is traced by Shpayer-Makov, the response in the sensationalist fiction and journalism of the time by Porter, Eisenzweig and Melchiori. For the recent history of anarchist militancy and police intrigue in Belgium, Linotte, Keunings and Moulaert are excellent sources, though the documents mentioned by the former as held by the Liège archives now appear to have been lost, compounding the problem caused by the removal of the file for Jagolkovsky/Ungern-Sternberg from the Sûreté archives at AGR, by the cabinet office. To reconstruct events in Liège required painstaking cross-reference of diverse archival sources: Vervaeck is an invaluable guide to those in Brussels, from which so much of the 'lost' life of Hekkelman aka Landesen aka Harting can be reconstructed; APP BA 1510 provides a French perspective on activities in Belgium, including useful press reports; the Okhrana archive, suspiciously muted regarding Liège, does include a document in French from 5 May about the unknown visitor to the rue de Grenelle embassy urgently demanding to see M. Léonard. Coming at the moment when the Belgian police were searching for the Léonard mentioned in the letters abandoned by Ungern-Sternberg as living at that address, the scene in the embassy has been imagined: *Plaisirs de Paris* mentions its restricted opening hours. It is curious but surely only coincidental that Encausse attended an esoteric congress in Liège only days before the first bomb exploded. In the absence of available official records of the trial, I tracked down a running daily transcript in the local Belgian socialist paper, *La Peuple*, which illuminates the 'fix' to conceal the Okhrana's role; reports by agents Z1 and Jarvis in June 1894 in the APP files go some way to tying up the London end of the network of provocation. MacIntyre's confessions about Special Branch provocation and its corrupt practitioners were in *Reynold's News* starting 14 April 1895, and are discussed in Porter. Agafonov reports Rachkovsky's meeting with Pope Leo XIII and discussion of ecumenicalism; Fischer the proposed exchange of diplomats between Russia and the Vatican.

21 *A Time of Harmony*

Clark and Martin consider Reclus' progressive educational ideas, Jacqmot and Fleming the crisis around his university appointment in Brussels and the creative reaction to it: the Flemish he had learned from a fellow prisoner in the barges after his capture in 1871 stood him in good stead. This instance of disowning association with individualist anarchism is found in Reclus' letter to Renard of 27 December 1895; his revival of ideas for a Great Globe, thoroughly explored by Dunbar and Welter, first found expression in Reclus' pamphlet, 'Project de construction d'un Globe terrestre a l'échelle du cent-millième'. The punctured 'exaltation' of the London colony is the subject of many agent reports in the APP; Rochefort's *Adventures* cast an alarmist eye on the well-documented Trial of the Thirty as the prelude to an 18 Fructidor, date of the *coup d'état* of 1797 by the Directory. Lee's work once again parallels my own curious concatenation of interests in Verne and Pompeii, in his examination of the metaphors of a Paris haunted by the Commune, the 'political volcano' in Zola's *Paris*, and the Vesuvius that Montmartre might become were anarchist plans for the bombing of the Sacré-Coeur to come to fruition. The intended title of Signac's painting was taken from the popular ballad 'Quand nous serons au Temps de l'Anarchie', such songs being a pronounced feature of the anarchist cultural landscape; Malato's line on the future Golden Age is from an 1893 article of his in *La Revue Anarchiste*; Signac's adoption of it and response to Kropotkin's demands is quoted by Herbert, his acknowledgement of his debt to Grave, by Varias. Roslak's superb study of Signac's art deftly draws together science, politics and aesthetics, to my sense of which Hutton, Shattuck and Sweetman also contribute; Joll in *Anarchists* quotes Fénéon that 'Old fools must die'; Clark, writing about Seurat, astutely observes that 'rather than being anarchism's painter he was the painter anarchism made possible', which applies in slightly different terms to Signac too; tangentially, Boime draws attention to how long it took the painter Luce to reconcile himself to the traumatic memories of the Bloody Week of 1871 in his work. Gaucher is my source for the organisation and schematic representation of the Okhrana's surveillance of revolutionaries within Russia and R. Garnett for the expedition on which Kravchinsky sent Constance Garnett: an adventure that seems particularly appealing in the context of Kropotkin's comment in his memoirs that Alexander III felt intimidated by 'educated women . . . wearing spectacles and a garibaldi hat'. The Garnett family variously remembered Kravchinsky's promise of a ham and loss of hearing in the Turkish prisons, and his desire to elope: David and Olive, in her diaries, respectively. The account of his death is from Taratuta, with a nod to Senese; of his funeral from *The Times* of 30 December; and of his posthumous popularity at seances from the Hon. John Harris, *Inferences from Haunted Houses and Haunted Men*. McCarthy is the source for Morris' last year, his words to Webb and his death. Kropotkin's recurrent overwork and *grippe* is tracked by Slatter, Marshall mentions Landauer's appeal to the 1896 congress, whose schism is analysed by Joll, Michel spoke optimistically of 'harmony and reconciliation' to *Le Paris*, while Thomas recounts how the Dreyfus Affair caused her to become isolated.

22 *Conspiracy Theories*

The role played by Rachkovsky in the Franco-Russian alliance, referred to as 'mystical' by Adam in *Le Matin*, and how his diplomatic and financial interests courted trouble, are alluded to by Ruud and Stepanov: considered alongside the large number of historians of the Okhrana archive who have already been mentioned, their work is an important source for its activities at home and abroad. Laporte mentions Alexander III's scribbling of 'crapule' next to Rachkovsky's name, Figes recounts the joke about the fickle Tsar Nicholas, and Byrnes considers the influence of Pobedonostsev's conception of the 'good society'. The Dreyfus Affair has generated a mountain of studies: for its antiSemitism I have looked to Poliakov and Stanislawsky, the former quoting Herzl's reaction to Dreyfus' formal humiliation and Zionism, Doise on the suggestion of a Russian angle, which Giscard d'Estaing dismisses, I am not sure reliably. Williams discusses the disdain with which anarchists and nihilists regarded Rochefort, regarding him useful only as a 'demolition hammer'. De Cyon's predicament and the raid on his villa are covered by Fox and Kennan, with Cohn's exploration of the .origins of the *Protocols* admirable if no longer definitive, and with Lepekhine offering new candidates for their authorship and Hagemeister a more circumspect view; it is Svatikov who places Golovinsky in Paris, working for Rachkovsky. Katz touches on Taxil, but details of the 'historical and philosophical conference, with light projections' convened by Jogand-Pages at the Paris Geographical Society are taken from the APP file. My understanding of the moral policing undertaken in late 1890s London, including Bedborough and the Legitimation League, comes from Bunyan, Calder-Marshall and Porter: in the aftermath of the Wilde trial, even the homosexual Carpenter found his work sidelined and was cast out by his publisher Fisher Unwin. Sweeney's memoirs, though, make no bones about his prejudices and conviction that 'We should at one blow kill a growing evil in the shape of a vigorous campaign of free love and Anarchism': a far cry from the belief of Home Secretary Harcourt, in the case of the free-thinking Foote's crime of blasphemy in 1882, that 'more harm than advantage is produced to public morals by government prosecutions of this kind'. R. Henderson's thesis, which must now be considered the authoritative source on the prosecution of Burtsev, drew my attention to Bullier's honeytrap operation against him, with its echoes of the Holy Brotherhood's plan to use femmes fatales to seduce and kill fleeing terrorists; it also quotes Salisbury's 'delicate' negotiation with Russia over Jewish immigration. His thesis builds on foundations laid by Hollingsworth, Kimball, Senese and Porter, to whose work I also refer. The Foreign Office's views of 1892 on public hostility to an Aliens Act are in TNA FO 27/3102, its changed position regarding Burtsev in FO 65/1544; the case of Hilda Czarina is discussed in HO 45/9751. Burtsev published his opinion on the 'regular science' of Russian policing in *Narodovolets* 3, 1897; Quail quotes Nicoll's impression that Fitzrovia was teeming 'with vermin in the shape of spies'. Kingston recounts Melville's complaints about hosting Okhrana agents, Cook offers more on his relationship with Rachkovsky: his report to the police department apparently names Melville McNaughten as the source of comments on 'common murders', though Chief Inspector William Melville seems a more likely candidate as his 'longtime associate' in light of his letter to the latter praising the jury system, in 35/Vc/folder 3. The Corpus Christi meeting in Trafalgar Square is described by Rudolf Rocker, quoted by B. Anderson who traces Angiolillo's subsequent movements; details of the assassination of Empress Elizabeth are from Jaquet. Majendie's views on the Anti-Anarchism Conference are in TNA HO45/10254/X36450, those of Michel in the *Adult* of February 1899 while Quail quotes those of Kropotkin, who considered the murder of Sissi to be an act of insanity. In an intriguing aside, Jensen refers to the bomb attack in Lisbon of February 1896 on a doctor who had certified an anarchist to be insane: an issue considered by Dr Channing soon after McKinley's murder, which is covered in detail by Rauchway: Trautmann discusses the determination in America to uncover an anarchist conspiracy; Theodore Roosevelt's bold assertion is found in the Congressional Record.

23 *Agents Unmasked*

The notion that Rachkovsky's life was saved by Kropotkin in 1900 emerges from Confino's study of his letters, while the causes of his dismissal from his Paris post, including his antagonism to the tsarina's favourite 'Master' Phillipe Vachot and his maverick press campaign for the 'League for the Salvation of the Russian Fatherland', are detailed in *Byloe*'s account of his career, in 1918. Yet the meticulous care with which Rachkovsky had once vetted his agents, dismissing many recommendations from his superiors, is drawn out in Fischer; my sense of the police department at this time is informed by Ruud and Stepanov, Peregudova and Zuckerman, and of its involvement with the extreme right in particular from Lauchlan. Azef's biography is drawn largely from Rubinstein and Geifman, who disagree substantially on the extent to which he betrayed his police paymasters, with the latter arguing that where possible he remained loyal; on this, bearing in mind the testimony of figures close to Azef, including Savinkov, who Geifman deems less reliable than police sources, I tend to favour Rubinstein. That the anarchists in the West increasingly looked to Russia for encouragement is apparent long before the revolution of 1905, with Most urging the readers of *Freiheit* in 1903 to 'Let your models be comrades in Russia. Their example glows like an ember in the anthracite of anarchist achievement': at the time of his death the newspaper that Marx and Engels had predicted would survive only six months was approaching its third decade. For Most, Trautman is the source, for Michel's last years, Thomas. It is in letters of 1902 to Guillaume that Kropotkin dismisses Marx as 'A German pamphleteer'; Miller and Woodcock both discuss his eagerness to return to Russia, and Reclus' regrets about his 'asthmatic puffs' are expressed in a letter to his old friend found in his own collected correspondence. I regret that narrative logic prevented a closer consideration of the ironies that clustered around Reclus' declining years. Among these are the characterisation of him as Kaw-djer in Verne's *The Survivors of the Jonathan*, which creatively conflates the wreck of the Commune, Reclus as an early guru of South American colonies, and his perceived status as a benign seer: the 'arch-Druid' as his friend the educationalist and pioneering urban planner Patrick Geddes described him, while secretly negotiating for none other than Andrew Carnegie, with whom Kropotkin refused all contact, to fund Reclus' globe. The latter information comes largely from Dunbar, the former from Fleming. Gapon's activities abroad are illuminated by his APP file, with a sidelight from Madox Ford; Rachkovsky's near escape when Gapon was entrapped and hanged and Azef's taunting of his handler come from Gaucher, with information about his renewed career in Russia from Brachev, as well as sources mentioned above. It is Porter who reveals that Special Branch saved Lenin from a lynching as a spy in the East End during one of his five visits to London, Walter who suggests that Kropotkin intervened to secure his release from custody in 1907. The irony that Lenin used the same cover name as Rachkovsky, 'Richter', is picked up by R. Henderson while Deacon discusses the revolutionary counter-espionage outfit in the East End, similar perhaps to the 'Revolutionary Police Department' set up by Bakai in Paris, who attempted to track down and execute Harting after his exposure. Rubinstein explores the connection between the Okhrana and Lenin's Bolsheviks, through its agent Malinkovsky, Brackman the recruitment of Stalin, then known as Koba, as an informant by Harting. The sources for the Jury of Honour are substantially covered in the notes for the Prologue. Regarding Harting's later career, Fischer was useful on surveillance of ports, and Futrell on Harting's interdiction of arms smuggling, Chaikovsky's fund-raising for which is found in Budd. The most fascinating detail, however, emerges from AGR, in particular folders SA 126, 32762 and 302: the protection he was accorded by the Belgian Sûreté, and his role in Manchuria during the war against Japan, on the way to which, on board the *Esmeralda*, he targeted the British fishing fleet. The best source for the drama of his exposure, however, on the very day the Versaillais butcher General Gallifet died, are the AN files. Harris sheds light on the phenomenon of the Apache gangs, Porch quotes Jaures on the affront of Russian agents active in Paris. It is in *Misalliance* that one of Shaw's characters observes that 'anarchism is a game'.

24 *War and Revolution*

For Malatesta's detestation of Lloyd George, as for the campaign against his deportation in 1912 and much else that followed, Levy is my main source. Nettlau offers a somewhat partisan account of his various forays back to Italy and his contact with Mussolini, whose praise for the Houndsditch shoot-out and translation of Kropotkin's memoirs are discussed by Joll in *Anarchists*, which also contains a fascinating survey of the diverse backgrounds of those who joined the colony of Aiglemont, established by Emile Henry's brother, Fortune. Malatesta's rebuke for Kropotkin's support of the war appeared in the Russian's old newspaper *Freedom* in November 1914. Tsuzuki quotes the letter from Kropotkin to Carpenter; it is a bitterly ironic companion piece to that from W. T. Stead only a week before he sailed on the *Titanic*, held by SCL. Far from vanishing forever, Harting contributed to the Belgian war effort, as AGR 32762 reveals. Miller is the source for the fears Kropotkin expressed over the effect of German victory on Russia and his return in 1917, Fischer for Burtsev's past employment by Lenin, MacMillan for the Peace Conference, including the concern over anarchists in Geneva and the attempted assassination of Clemenceau. Walter remarks that Kropotkin refused even to stand for the royal toast at the Royal Geographical Society dinners in London, but his approval of the British constitutional arrangement is echoed in the old anarchist encountered by Arthur Ransome on his visit to the anarchist headquarters in St Petersburg in March 1918 who averred that 'England before the war was an almost perfect expression of an anarchist state'. The cursory account of the October Revolution and the Terror are drawn from Pipes and Figes; the latter refers to Goldenburg's misplaced belief that the Bolshevik leader was Bakunin's heir, Chaikovsky's role in the civil war, the arrest of Kropotkin's daughter and his angry letter to Lenin. Wilson alludes to the importance of the bread supply in revolution as the one area on which Kropotkin and Lenin could agree, while Merriman quotes the former's rebuke of the latter's attack on 'every honest feeling'. Otherwise, the story of Kropotkin's sad final days, hoping that the storm will soon pass while working on his *Ethics*, draws on Miller and more on Woodcock; Wexler describes the visit of Goldman and Berkman, which like that of President Wilson's envoys is scarcely covered.

25 *Coda*

It was in January 1881 that Michel expressed her transcendent view of anarchism to *Le Gaulois*. Files in AGR reveal that the Belgian casino owned in later life by Harting was in Blankenberge, where Rochefort had gambled in the early 1890s: the co-owner, perhaps coincidentally, had the same name as the Dutch police official who had been involved in the Ungern-Sternberg case after the Liège bombings, but had kept silent at the trial. Even in 1927, the director of the police judiciate in Belgium was writing the barefaced lie to the *procureur* of the French Republic that his organisation held no file on Harting. Carey alludes to Hitler's admiration for Kock; Hagemeister questions the widely propounded account of Rachkovsky's role in authoring the *Protocols*, but does not dismiss it.

Select Bibliography

PRIMARY

Archives

AN	Archives Nationales, Paris
AGR	Archives Générales du Royaume, Brussels
APP	Archives of the Prefecture of Police, Paris
GARF	State Archive of the Russian Federation, Moscow
HI	Hoover Institute, Stanford University
IISH	International Institute of Social History, Amsterdam
SCL	Sheffield City Library
TNA	The National Archives, Kew, London
TsGALI	Central State Archive of Literature and Art, St Petersburg

Books and Articles

Anderson, R. *A Defence of the Book of Daniel against the 'Higher Criticism': Being the preface to the fifth edition of 'The Coming Prince'* (London, 1895); *The Lighter Side of My Official Life* (London, 1910)

Andrieux, L. *Souvenirs d'un préfet de police* (Paris, 1885)

Bax, D. and Morris, W. *A Short Account of the Commune of Paris* (London, 1886)

Bernstein, E. *My Years of Exile: Reminiscences of a Socialist*, trs. Miall, B. (London, 1921)

Bertall (pseud.) *The Communists of Paris 1871. Types-physiognomies-characters* (Paris, 1874)

Brissac, duc de *La Duchesse d'Uzès, 1847–1933* (Paris, 1950)

Brust, H. *I Guarded Kings: The Memoirs of a Political Police Officer* (London, 1931)

Burgoyne, A. G. *The Homestead Strike of 1892* (Pittsburgh, 1979)

Burtsev, V. *Protocols of the Elders of Zion: A Proved Fraud* (Paris, 1938); *Chasing Agents Provocateurs* (Moscow, 1991)

Carpenter, E. *Towards Democracy* (London, 1895); et al. *Forecasts of the Coming Century* (Manchester, 1897); *My Days and Dreams: Being Autobiographical Notes* (London, 1916)

Channing, W. 'The Mental State of Czolgosz: The Assassin of President McKinley', *American Journal of Insanity* (Utica, 1902)

Cherep-Spiridovich, A. I. *The Secret World Government; Or, 'The Hidden Hand'* . . . *100 Historical Mysteries Explained* (New York, 1926)

Conrad, J. *The Secret Agent. A simple tale* (London, 1907); *Under Western Eyes* (London, 1911)

Cyon, E. de *Nihilisme et anarchie* (Paris, 1892)

Debans, C. *Les Plaisirs de Paris. Guide pratique et illustré* (Paris, 1867)

Dubois, F. *Le Péril anarchiste* (Paris, 1894)

Fawcett, E. D. *Hartmann the Anarchist* (London, 1893)

Figner, V. *Memoirs of a Revolutionist*, trs. Daniels, C. and Davidson, G. (New York, 1927); *Polnoe sobranie sochinenii*, 6 vols. (Moscow, 1929); *Posle Shlissel'burga* (Leningrad, 1925)

Ford, F. M. *Return to Yesterday: Reminiscences, 1894–1914* (London, 1931); *Ancient Lights and Certain New Reflections: Being the Memories of a Young Man* (London, 1911)

Garin, J. *L'Anarchie et les anarchistes* (Paris, 1885)

Garnett, D. *The Golden Echo* (London, 1954)

Garnett, O. both ed. Johnson, B. C. *Tea and Anarchy! The Bloomsbury Diary of Olive Garnett, 1890–1893* (London, 1989); *Olive and Stepniak: The Bloomsbury Diary of Olive Garnett, 1893–1895* (Birmingham, 1993)

Garnett, R. *Constance Garnett: A Heroic Life* (London, 1991)

Goldman, E. *My Disillusionment in Russia* (New York, 1923)

Goncourt, J. and E. *Paris Under Siege, 1870–1871: From the Goncourt Journal*, ed. Becker, G. J. (London, 1969)

Goron, M. F. *Les Mémoires de M. Goron, ancien chef de la Sûreté*, 4 vols. (Paris 1896, 1897)

Griffith, G. *The Angel of the Revolution: A Tale of the Coming Terror* (London, 1893)

Grousset, P. *L'Affaire Dreyfus et ses ressorts secrets* (Paris, 1899)

Guillaume, J. *L'Internationale. Documents et souvenirs, 1864–1878* (Paris, 1905)

Hamon, A. *La Psychologie de l'anarchiste-socialiste* (Paris, 1895)

Hansen, J. *L'Alliance Franco-Russe* (Paris, 1897); *Ambassade à Paris du Baron de Mohrenheim* (Paris, 1907)

Hart, W. C. *Confessions of an Anarchist* (London, 1906)

Hodgson, W. E. *A Night with a Nihilist* (Fife, 1886)

Hugo, V. *Carnets intimes, 1870–1871* (Paris, 1953)

Hyndman, H. *A Commune for London* (London, 1887)

Jefferies, R. *After London, or Wild England* (Oxford, 1980)

Kennan, G. *Siberia and the Exile System* (New York, 1891)

Korolenko, V. *Bez yazyka – Matvei Lozinskii* (Moscow, 1895)

Kropotkin, A. *Petr i Aleksandr Kropotkiny. Perepiska*, ed. Lebedev, N. (Leningrad, 1932)

Kropotkin, P. *La Conquête du pain*, preface by Reclus, E., third edition (Paris, 1892); *Fields, Factories and Workshops* (London, 1899); *Mutual Aid: A Factor of Evolution* (London, 1902); *The Great French Revolution* (London, 1909); *Ethics,* ed. Lebedev, N. (Moscow, 1922); *Correspondence* (Moscow, 1932); *Kropotkin's Revolutionary Pamphlets*, ed. Baldwin, R. (New York, 1970); *Selected Writings of P. A. Kropotkin*, ed. Martin, M. A. (Cambridge, Mass., 1970); *Memoirs of a Revolutionist* (New York, 1971); *The Essential Kropotkin*, ed. Capouya, E. and Tompkins, K. (New York, 1975)

Lane, J. *An Anti-statist Communist Manifesto* (Cambridge, 1985)

Le Bon, G. *The Crowd: A study of the popular mind* (Marietta, 1982)

Lenin, V. 'Lessons of the Commune', *Zagranichnaya Gazeta (Foreign Gazette)*, 2, 23 March 1908; 'Street Fighting (The Advice of a General of the Commune)', *Forward!*, 11, 23 March 1905

Littlechild, J. G. *The Reminiscences of Chief Inspector Littlechild* (London, 1894)

Lissagaray, P. O. *History of the Commune of 1871* (London, 1886)

Lombroso, C. *Les Anarchistes* (Paris, 1897)

Mace, G. P. *La Police parisienne, aventuriers de génie* (Paris, 1884)

Machtet, G. A. *Preriia i pionery* (Moscow, 1986)

Mackay, J. H. *The Anarchists* (Boston, 1891)

Malatesta, E. 'Pietro Kropotkin – ricordi e critiche di un vecchio amico', *Studi Sociali*, April 1931; 'Kropotkin, Malatesta e il congresso internazionale socialista rivoluzionario di Londra di 1881', ibid., April 1934

Malato, C. *Les Joyeusetés de l'exil* (Paris, 1897)

Marx, K. and Engels, F. *Collected Works*, 47 vols. (Moscow and London, since 1975); *Selected Letters: The Personal Correspondence, 1844–1877* (Boston, 1981)

McMillan, M. *The Life of Rachel McMillan* (London, 1927)

Meredith, I. *A Girl Among the Anarchists* (London, 1903)

Michel, L. *Les Microbes humains* (Paris, 1886); *Le Monde nouveau* (Paris, 1888); *Mémoires de Louise Michel, écrits par elle-meme* (Paris, 1886); 'Je vous écris de ma nuit': *Correspondance générale de Louise Michel*, ed. Gauthier, X. (Paris, 1999); *Souvenirs et aventures de ma vie* (Paris, 1983); *La Commune* (Paris, 1898)

Mirbeau, O. and Grave, J. *Correspondance* (Paris, 1994)

Morris, W. *Chants for Socialists* (London, 1885); *News from Nowhere* (London, 1891); *Letters of William Morris to his Family and Friends*, ed. Henderson, P. (London, 1950); *The Collected Letters of William Morris*, ed. Kelvin, N., 4 vols. (New York, 1984–1996); *Journalism: Contribution to Commonweal, 1885–1890* (Bristol, 1996); *The Collected Works of William Morris*, 24 vols. (London, 1910–1915, reprinted 1966)

Most, J. *The Science of Revolutionary Warfare* (New York, 1885); *The God Pestilence* (New York, 1883)

Nettlau, M. *A Short History of Anarchism*, trs. Pilat, I. (London, 1996); *Errico Malatesta: The Biography of an Anarchist* (New York, 1924)

Nicoll, D. V. *Life in the English Prisons: The Walsall Anarchists* (London, 1894); *The Greenwich Mystery* (Sheffield, 1897)

Nordau, M. *The Conventional Lies of Our Civilization* (London, 1895); *Degeneration* (London, 1895)

Pain, O. *Henri Rochefort* (Paris, 1879)

Paleologue, M. *An Ambassador's Memoirs* (Paris, 1923)

Reclus, E. *Evolution et révolution* (Geneva, 1880); 'An Anarchist on Anarchy', *Contemporary Review*, May 1884; *Correspondance*, ed. Dumesnil, L. 3 vols. (Paris, 1911–1925)

Richards, V. (cd.) *Malatesta, Life and Ideas* (London, 1965)

Robida, A. *Le Vingtième siècle, la vie électrique* (Paris, 1892)

Rochefort, H. *De Nouméa à Newcastle (Australie): récit de son évasion* (Paris, 1874); *The Adventures of My Life* (London, 1896)

Schaak, M. J. *Anarchy and Anarchists: A History of the Red Terror and the Social Revolution in America and Europe* (Chicago, 1888)

Stead, W. T. *The MP for Russia: Reminiscences and Correspondence of Madam Olga Novikova* (London, 1909)

Stepniak, S. *Underground Russia: Revolutionary Profiles and Sketches from Life* (London, 1883); *Russia Under the Tsars* (London, 1885); 'What Americans Can Do for Russia', *North American Review*, 153, November 1891, pp. 596–609; *Nihilism As It Is* (London, 1894)

Stieber, W. J. C. E. *The Chancellor's Spy: The Revelations of Bismarck's Chief of Secret Service* (New York, 1980)

Sweeney, J. *At Scotland Yard* (London, 1914)

Thomson, B. *The Story of Scotland Yard* (London, 1935)

Webster, N. *World Revolution: The Plot Against Civilisation* (London, 1921)

Wilde, O. *The Soul of a Man Under Socialism* (London, 1891)

Yarros, V. *Anarchism: Its Aims and Methods* (Boston, 1887)

Zola, E. *L'Assommoir* (Paris, 1877); *Paris*, trs.Vizetelly, E. A. (London, 1898)

Periodicals

Byloe (Paris, 1909; St Petersburg, 1917); *Chicagoer Arbeiter-Zeitung*; *Commonweal*; *Le Cri du peuple*; *Daily Graphic*; *Le Décadent*; *L'Echo de Paris*; *L'Eclair*; *Freiheit*; *Freedom*; *Le Figaro*; *Le Gaulois*; *Golos minuvshago*; *Hansard*; *Harper's New Monthly Magazine*; *L'Intransigeant*; *Le Journal Officiel de la Commune*; *Justice*; *Katorga i ssylka*; *La Libre Parole*; *Mercure de France*; *Morning Advertiser*; *Morning Leader*; *Na chuzhoi storone*; *New Review*; *Obzor*; *Osvobozhdenie*; *Pall Mall Gazette*; *Paterson Labor Standard*; *Le Pays*; *Le Peuple* (Liège); *Probuzhdenie*; *Le Révolté* (Geneva, 1879–1885; Paris, 1885–1887); *La Révolte* (Paris, 1887–1894); *Reynold's News*; *Science*; *Le Soir*; *Le Temps*; *Les Temps Nouveaux*; *New York Times*; *The Times*; *Westminster Budget*

SECONDARY

Unpublished Dissertations

Bantman, C. 'Anarchismes et anarchistes en France et en Grande-Bretagne, 1880–1914: Echanges, représentations, transferts', PhD thesis, Université de Paris 13, 2007

Clutterbuck, L. 'The Progenitors of Terror: Russian Revolutionaries or Extreme Irish Terrorists?', PhD thesis, University of Portsmouth, 2002

Dipaola, P. 'Italian Anarchists in London (1870–1914)', PhD thesis, University of London, 2004

Henderson, R. 'Vladimir Burtsev and the Russian revolutionary emigration: surveillance of foreign political refugees in London, 1891–1905', PhD thesis, University of London, 2008

Manfredonia, G. 'L'individualisme anarchiste en France, 1880–1914', PhD thesis, IEP de Paris, 1984

Martinez, P. K. 'Paris Communard refugees in Britain, 1871–1880', DPhil thesis, University of Sussex, 1981

Books and Articles

Adamic, L. *Dynamite: Class Violence in America* (New York, 1934)

Agafonov, V. K. *Parisian Secrets of the Tsarist Okhrana* (Moscow, 2004)

Anderson, B. *Under Three Flags* (London, 2005)

André, M. S. and Beaufils, C. *Papus, la belle époque d'occultisme* (Paris, 1995)

Auerbach, L. (ed.) *Miscellanies of Secret State Councillor Dr Stieber* (Berlin 1884)

Avakumovic, I. and Woodcock, G. *The Anarchist Prince: A Biographical Study of Peter Kropotkin* (London, 1950)

Avineri, S. *The Social and Political Thought of Karl Marx* (Cambridge, 1968)

Avrich, P. *Bakunin and Nechaev* (London, 1987)

Barrows, S. *Distorting Mirrors: Visions of the Crowd in Late Nineteenth-Century France* (Yale, 1981)

Baylen, J. O. 'Madam Olga Novikoff, Propagandist', *American Slavic and East European Review*, 10, 1951, pp. 133–57

Beaumont, M. *Utopia Ltd: Ideologies of Social Dreaming in England 1870–1900* (Leiden, 2009)

Becker, H. 'Johann Most in Europe', *Raven Anarchist Quarterly*, 1, 4, March 1988, pp. 291–331

Berglund, K. (ed.) *Imperial and National Identities in Pre-Revolutionary, Soviet and Post-Soviet Russia* (Helsinki, 2002)

Berk, S. M. *Year of Crisis, Year of Hope: Russian Jewry and the Pogroms of 1881–1882* (London, 1985)

Bevir, M. 'The Rise of Ethical Anarchism in Britain, 1885–1900', *Historical Research*, 69, June 1996, pp. 143–65

Billington, J. H. 'The Intelligentsia and the Religion of Humanity', *American Historical Review*, 65, 4, July 1960, pp. 807–21

Biriukov, P. I. 'Leo Tolstoi and William Frey', *Minuvshie gody* (St Petersburg), 1908, pp. 69–91

Bishop, P. 'Protocols of Zion Forger Named', www.telegraph.co.uk, 19 November 1999

Boime, A. *Art and the French Commune* (Princeton, 1997)

Brachev, V. S. *Foreign Secret Service of the Police Department (1883–1917)* (St Petersburg, 2001); *Masterminds of Political Investigation in Pre-Revolutionary Russia* (St Petersburg, 1998)

Brackman, R. *The Secret File of Joseph Stalin: A Hidden Life* (London, 2001)

Budd, L. J. 'Twain, Howells and the Boston Nihilists', *New England Quarterly*, 39, 3, September 1959, pp. 351–71

Bullard, A. *Exile to Paradise: Savagery and Civilization in Paris and the South Pacific, 1790–1900* (Stanford, 2000)

Bunyan, T. *The History and Practice of the Political Police in Britain* (London, 1976)

Bury, J. B. *History of the Papacy in the Nineteenth Century (1864–1878)* (Cambridge, 1930)

Byrnes, R. F. *Anti-Semitism in Modern France* (New Brunswick, 1950); 'Pobedonostsev's Conception of the Good Society: An Analysis of his Thought After 1880', *Review of Politics*, 13, 2, April 1951, pp. 169–90

Cahm, J. C. *Kropotkin and the Rise of Revolutionary Anarchism, 1872–1886* (Cambridge, 1989)

Calder-Marshall, A. *Lewd, Blasphemous and Obscene: Being the Trials and Tribulations of Sundry Founding Fathers of Today's Alternative Societies* (London, 1972)

Campbell, C. *Fenian Fire* (London, 2002)

Carey, J. *The Intellectual and the Masses* (London, 1992)

Carlson, A. R. *Anarchism in Germany, Vol 1: The Early Movement* (New Jersey, 1972); 'Anarchism and Individual Terror in the German Empire, 1870–1890' in Hurschfeld, J. and Mommsen, W. J. (eds.) *Social Protest, Violence and Terror in Nineteenth and Twentieth-Century Europe* (London, 1982), pp. 175–200

Carpentier, C. and Moser, F. *La Sûreté de l'état: histoire d'une déstabilisation* (Gerpines, 1993)

Casselle, P. *Paris républicain, 1871–1914: nouvelle histoire de Paris* (Paris, 2003)

Chapelier, E. and Gassy, M. *Anarchists & The International Language Esperanto* (London, 1908)

Chesneaux, J. *The Political and Social Ideas of Jules Verne*, trs. Wikeley, T. (London, 1972)

Christiansen, R. *Paris Babylon: The Story of the Paris Commune* (London, 1996)

Clark, J. P. and Martin, C. (eds.) *Anarchy, Geography, Modernity: The Radical Social Thought of Elisée Reclus* (Oxford, 2004)

Clark, T. J. *Farewell to an Idea* (Yale, 1999)

Clarke, I. F. *The Tale of the Next Great War: 1871–1914* (Liverpool, 1995)

Cohen, R. *A Chance Meeting: Intertwined Lives of American Writers and Artists, 1854–1967* (London, 2004)

Cohn, N. *Warrant for Genocide: Myth of the Jewish World Conspiracy and the Protocols of the Elders of Zion* (London, 1967)

Cole, G. D. H. *William Morris as a Socialist* (Norwood, 1977)

Confino, M. 'Pierre Kropotkine et les agents de l'Okhrana: étude suivie de treize lettres inédites de P. Kropotkine à un groupe d'anarchistes russes', *Cahiers du monde russe et soviétique*, 24, 1–2, 1983, pp. 83–149

Cook, A. *M: MI5's First Spymaster* (Stroud, 2004)

Coplestone, F. C. *Philosophy in Russia: From Herzen to Lenin and Berdyaev* (Indiana, 1986)

Costello, P. *Jules Verne: Inventor of Science Fiction* (London, 1978)

Daly, J. *Autocracy Under Siege: Security Police and Opposition in Russia, 1866–1905* (DeKalb, 1998)

Day, H. *Louise Michel, Jules Verne: de qui est Vingt mille lieues sous les mers?* (Brussels, 1959)

Deacon, R. *A History of the Russian Secret Service* (London, 1972); *A History of the British Secret Service* (London, 1969)

d'Eramo, M. *The Pig and the Skyscraper: Chicago, A History of Our Future*, trs. Thomson, G. (London, 2003)

Dilnot, G. *Great Detectives and their Methods* (Boston & New York, 1928)

Distel, S. *Au temps d'harmonie* (Paris, 2001)

Doise, J. *Un Secret bien gardé* (Paris, 1994)

Drachtovich, M. M. (ed.) *The Revolutionary Internationals, 1864–1943* (Oxford, 1966)

Dunbar, G. S. *Elisée Reclus, Historian of Nature* (Hamden, 1978); 'Elisée Reclus and the Great Globe', *Scottish Geographical Magazine*, 90, 1, 1974, pp. 57–66

Edwards, S. (ed.) *The Communards of Paris, 1871* (Cornell, 1973)

Eisenzweig, U. *Fictions de l'anarchisme* (Paris, 2001)

Ellmann, R. *Oscar Wilde* (London, 1987)

Emsley, C. *The English Police* (London, 1991)

Enckell, M. *La Fédération Jurassienne: les origines de l'anarchisme en Suisse* (Lausanne, 1991)

Engel, B. A. *Five Sisters: Women Against the Tsar* (London, 1880)

Fauré, C. (ed.) *Quatre femmes terroristes contre le tsar: Véra Zassoulitch, Olga Loubatovich, Elisabeth Kovalskaia, Véra Figner*, trs. Chatelain, H. (Paris, 1978)

Ferraris, L. V. 'L'assassinio di Umberto I e gli anarchici di Paterson', *Rassegna Storica del Risorgimento*, LV, 1, January–March 1968, pp. 47–64

Fetzer, L. (ed.) *Pre-Revolutionary Russian Science Fiction: An Anthology* (Ann Arbor, 1982)

Figes, O. *A People's Tragedy: The Russian Revolution 1891–1924* (London, 1996)

Fischer, B. B. *Okhrana: The Paris Operations of the Russian Imperial Police* (Virginia, 1997)

Fisher, J. *Airlift 1870: The Balloons and Pigeons in the Siege of Paris* (London, 1965)

Fishman, W. J. *East End 1888* (Philadelphia, 1988)

Fleming, M. 'Propaganda by the deed: terrorism and anarchist theory in late nineteenth-century Europe', *Terrorism*, 4, 1–4, 1980, pp. 1–23; *The Anarchist Way to Socialism* (London, 1979)

Florovsky, G. *Puti Russkago Bogosloviia* (Paris, 1937)

Fogarty, R. S. *All Things New: American Communes and Utopian Movements, 1860–1901* (Lanham, 2003)

Foner, P. S. *The Great Labor Uprising of 1877* (New York, 1977)

Footman, D. *Red Prelude: A Life of A. I. Zhelyabov* (Yale, 1945)

Fox, F. 'The Protocols of the Elders of Zion and the Shadowy World of Elie de Cyon', *East European Jewish Affairs*, 27, 1, 1997, pp. 3–22

Freymond, J. and Molnár, M. 'The Rise and Fall of the First International' in *The Revolutionary Internationals* (Stanford, 1996)

Frolenko, M. 'Iz dalekogo proshlogo', *Minuvshie gody* (St Petersburg), July 1908

Futrell, M. *The Northern Underground* (London 1963)

Gallet, L. 'La presse lyonnaise et les anarchistes: le "procès des 66" de 1883', *Mémoire de maîtrise d'histoire*, dir. Lequin, Y., Université Lumière-Lyon, 2 (2000)

Gaucher, R. *Les Terroristes (de la Russie tsariste à l'OAS)* (Paris, 1965)

Gauthier, X. *La Vierge Rouge: Biographie de Louise Michel* (Paris, 1999)

Geifman, A. *Entangled in Terror: The Azef Affair and the Russian Revolution* (Wilmington, 1999); 'The Security Police in Late Imperial Russia' in Geifman, A. (ed.) *Russia Under the Last Tsar: Opposition and Subversion, 1894–1917* (London, 1999)

Gilbert, J. B. *Perfect Cities: Chicago's Utopias of 1893* (Chicago, 1991)

Gildea, R. *Barricades & Borders: Europe 1800–1914* (Cambridge, 1987); *Children of the Revolution* (London, 2008)

Gilman, D. *Decadence: The Strange Life of an Epithet* (London, 1979)

Giscard d'Estaing, H. *D'Esterhazy à Dreyfus* (Paris, 1960)

Gleason, A. 'The Emigration and Apostasy of Lev Tikhomirov', *Slavic Review*, 26, 3, 1967

Good, J. E. 'America and the Russian Revolutionary Movement, 1888–1905', *Russian Review*, 41, 3, 1982, pp. 273–87

Gott, T. 'The Spirit of Revolt: Anarchism, Drugs, Social Unrest' in Bascou, M. *Paris in the Late Nineteenth Century* (Canberra, 1996)

Grob-Fitzgibbon, B. 'From the Dagger to the Bomb: Karl Heinzen and the Evolution of Political Terror', *Terrorism and Political Violence*, 16, 1, September 2004, pp. 97– 115

Gould, S. J. *The Mismeasure of Man* (New York, 1981)

Green, J. *Death in the Haymarket: A Story of Chicago, the First Labor Movement and the Bombing that Divided Gilded Age America* (New York, 2006)

Grigorieva, E. V. *Revolyutsionno-narodnicheskaya emigratsiia kontsa 19 veka (Revolutionary and Populist Emigration at the End of the 19th Century)* (Moscow, 1970)

Guillemin, H. *Victor Hugo par lui-même* (Paris, 1962)

Hagemeister, M. 'The Protocols of the Elders of Zion: Between History and Fiction', *New German Critique*, 103, 2008, pp. 83–95

Halkin, L. E. 'Liège, la première Internationale et la Commune', *Revue Belge de Philologie et d'Histoire*, 44, 4, 1966, pp. 1160–73

Halperin, J. U. *Félix Fénéon, Aesthete and Anarchist in Fin de Siècle Paris* (Yale, 1988)

Harris, R. 'Understanding the Terrorist: Anarchism, Medicine and Politics in *Fin de Siècle* France' in Clark, M. and Crawford, C. *Legal Medicine in History* (Cambridge, 1994)

Hasty, O. P. and Fusso, S. *America Through Russian Eyes, 1874–1926* (Yale, 1988)

Heath, R. 'Elisée Reclus', *Humane Review*, October 1905

Hecht, D. *Russian Radicals Look to America, 1825–1894* (New York, 1968); 'Lavrov, Chaikovsky and the United States', *American Slavic and East European Review*, 5, May 1946, pp. 138–61

Henderson, R. 'Russian Political Emigrés and the British Museum Library', *Library History*, 9, 1–2, 1991, pp. 59–68

Henderson, W. O. *Life of Friedrich Engels* (London, 1976)

Herbert, E. W. *The Artist and Social Reform in France and Belgium, 1885–1891* (New Haven, 1961)

Hingley, R. *Nihilists: Russian Radicals and Revolutionaries in the Reign of Alexander II (1855– 81)* (London, 1967); *The Russian Secret Police: Muscovite, Imperial, Russian and Soviet Security Operations* (New York, 1970)

Höhne, H. *Der Krieg im Dunkeln: Macht und Einfluß des deutschen und russischen Geheimdienstes (War in the Dark: Power and Influence in the German and the Russian Secret Service)* (Munich, 1985)

Hoig, S. *Cowtown Wichita and the Wild, Wicked West* (Albuquerque, 2007)

Hollingsworth, B. 'The Society of Friends of Russian Freedom: English Liberals and Russian Socialists, 1890–1917', *Oxford Slavonic Papers*, 3, 1970

Holroyd, M. *Bernard Shaw, Vol. 1: The Search for Love* (London, 1998)

Horne, A. *The Fall of Paris: The Siege and the Commune, 1870–1871* (London, 1965)

Hulse, J. *Revolutionists in London: A Study of Five Unorthodox Socialists* (Oxford, 1970)

Hutton, J. G. *Neo-Impressionism and the Search for Solid Ground: Art, Science and Anarchism in Fin de Siècle France* (London, 1994)

Hyde, R. *Printed Maps of Victorian London* (Folkestone, 1975)

Ishill, J. *Peter Kropotkin: Memorial Volume* (New Jersey, 1923); *Elisée and Elie Reclus: In Memoriam* (New Jersey, 1927)

Israel, A. *Les Vérités cachées de l'affaire Dreyfus* (Paris, 1999)

Jacqmot, R. 'L'affaire Elisée Reclus, ou l'effet d'une bombe', *Bulletin Mensuel de l'Union des anciens étudiants de l'Université Libre de Bruxelles*, April 1958, pp. 5–13, and May 1958, pp. 11–16

Jaquet, C. *La Secrète à 100 ans: histoire de la police de sûreté Genevoise* (Geneva, 1993)

Jaquet, E. and Chapuis, A. *Technique and History of the Swiss Watch From its Beginnings to the Present Day* (Boston, 1953)

Jellinek, F. *The Paris Commune of 1871* (London, 1939)

Jensen, R. B. 'Criminal Anthropology and Anarchist Terrorism in Spain and Italy', *Mediterranean Historical Review*, 16, 2, 2001, pp. 31–44; 'The International Anti-Anarchist Conference of 1898 and the Origins of Interpol', *Journal of Contemporary History*, 16, 1981, pp. 323–47; 'Daggers, Rifles and Dynamite: Anarchist Terrorism in Nineteenth-Century Europe', *Terrorism and Political Violence*, 16, 1, 2004

Johnson, R. J. 'Zagranichnaia Agentura: The Tsarist Political Police in Europe', *Journal of Contemporary History*, 7, 1–2, January-April 1972, pp. 221–42

Joll, J. J. *The Second International 1888–1914* (London, 1955); *The Anarchists* (London, 1964)

Jouan, R. *Voyages très extraordinaires dans le Paris d'Albert Robida* (Paris, 2005)

Kantor, R. M. 'Frantsuzskaia okhranka o russkikh emigrantakh' ('The French secret police on the Russian émigrés'), *Katorga i ssylka*, 2, 31, 1924

Katz, J. *The Occult Tradition: From the Renaissance to the Present Day* (London, 2005)

Kedward, R. *The Anarchists: The Men Who Shocked an Era* (London, 1971)

Kellet, J. 'The Commune in London', *History Today*, May 1983, pp. 5–9

Kennan, G. *The Decline of Bismarck's European Order* (Princeton, 1979); *The Fateful Alliance: France, Russia and the Coming of the First World War* (New York, 1984)

Keunings, L. 'Les grandes étapes de l'evolution de la police secrète en Belgique au XIXe siècle', *Bulletin trimestriel du Crédit communal de Belgique*, 43e année, 3, 1989, pp. 3 30

Kimball, A. 'The Harassment of Russian Revolutionaries Abroad: The London Trial of Vladimir Burtsev in 1898', *Oxford Slavonic Papers*, VI, 1973, pp. 48–65

Kingston, C. *A Gallery of Rogues* (London, 1924)

Kinna, R. *William Morris: The Art of Socialism* (Cardiff, 2000)

Klier, J. 'The Russian Press and the Anti-Jewish Pogroms of 1881', *Canadian-American Slavic Studies*, XVII, 1, 1983, pp. 199–221; 'Unravelling the Conspiracy Theory: A New Look at the Pogroms', *East European Jewish Affairs*, XXIII, 2, 1993, pp. 79–89

Krause, P. *The Battle for Homestead, 1880–1892: Politics, Culture, and Steel* (Pittsburgh,1992)

Laporte, M. *Histoire de l'Okhrana, la police secrète des tsars, 1880–1917* (Paris, 1935)

Larson, E. *The Devil in the White City: Murder, Magic, and Madness at the Fair That Changed America* (New York, 2003)

Latour, B. *The Pasteurization of France* (Cambridge, Mass., 1988)

Lauchlan, I. 'The accidental terrorist: Okhrana connections to the extreme right and the attempt to assassinate Sergei Witte in 1907', *Revolutionary Russia*, 14, 2, 2001, pp. 1–32; 'Separate Realm? The Okhrana Myth and Imperial Russian "Otherness"' in Chulos, C. (ed.) *Imperial and National Identities in Pre-Revolutionary and Soviet Russia* (Helsinki, 2002)

Lavenir, C. B. 'Bombs, Printers and Pistols: a Mediological History of Terrorism', *History and Technology*, 19, 1, 2003, pp. 54–62

Ledger, S. and Luckhurst, R. (eds.) *The Fin de Siècle: A Reader in Cultural History, c.1880–1900* (Oxford, 2000)

Lee, D. P. 'The Catastrophic Imaginary of the Paris Commune in Jules Verne's *Les 500 Millions de la Bégum*', *Neophilologus*, 90, 2006, pp. 535–53

Leier, M. *Bakunin: A Biography* (New York, 2006)

Lemke, M. 'Our foreign investigation 1881–1883', *Krasnaia letopis*, 5, 1923

Lepekhine, M. 'The findings of Russian historian Mikhail Lepekhine', *L'Express*, 18 November 1999

Levy, C. 'Charisma and Social Movments: Errico Malatesta and Italian Anarchism', *Modern Italy*, 3, 2, 1998, pp. 205–17

Linotte, L. 'Les manifestations et les grèves dans la province de Liège de 1831–1914' in *Archives de la Sûreté Publique* (Liège, 1964)

Livesay, H. C. and Handlin, O. (eds.) *Carnegie and the Rise of Big Business* (London, 1999)

Longoni, J. C. *Four Patients of Dr Deibler* (London, 1970)

Lukashevich, S. 'The Holy Brotherhood, 1881–83', *American Slavic and East European Review*, 18, 4, December 1959, pp. 491–509

Mackay, J. A. P. *The Eye Who Never Slept* (Edinburgh, 1996)

MacMillan, M. *Peacemakers: Six Months That Changed the World: The Paris Conference of 1919 and its Attempt to End War* (London, 2001)

Maitron, J. *Le Mouvement anarchiste en France* (Paris, 1951)

Marsh, J. *Back to the Land: The Pastoral Impulse in Victorian England from 1880 to 1914* (London, 1982)

Marshall, P. H. *Demanding the Impossible: A History of Anarchism* (London, 1992)

Martin, A. *The Mask of the Prophet: The Extraordinary Fictions of Jules Verne* (Oxford, 1990)

Marx, G. T. 'Thoughts on a neglected category of social movement participant: The agent provocateur and the informant', *American Journal of Sociology*, 80, 2, September 1974, pp. 402–42

Masini, P. C. *Gli Internazionalisti: La Banda del Matese* (Rome, 1958)

McCarthy, F. *William Morris: A Life For Our Time* (London, 1994)

McClellan, W. *Revolutionary Exiles: The Russians in the First International and the Paris Commune* (London, 1979)

Meijer, J. M. *Knowledge and Revolution: The Russian Colony of Zurich (1870–1873)* (Assen, 1955)

Melchiori, B. *Terrorism in the Late Victorian Novel* (London, 1985)

Menshikov, L. *Okhrana i revoliutsiia. K istorii tainykh politicheskikh organizatsii v Rossii*, 3 (Moscow, 1925); *Russkii politicheskii sysk za granitsei* (*The Russian political investigation abroad*) (Paris, 1914)

Merriman, J. *The Dynamite Club: The Bombing of the Café Terminus and the Birth of Modern Terrorism in Fin de Siècle Paris* (New York, 2009)

Miller, M. A. 'The Intellectual Origins of Modern Terrorism in Europe' in *Terrorism in Context*, Crenshaw, M. (ed.) (Pennsylvania, 1995); *Kropotkin* (Chicago, 1976); 'Ideological Conflicts in Russian Popularism: The Revolutionary Manifesto of the Chaikovskyists', *Slavic Review*, 29, 1970, pp. 1–21

Miner, H. C. *Wichita: The Early Years 1865–80* (Nebraska, 1982)

Monas, S. *The Third Section: Police and Society in Russia under the Tsars* (Cambridge, 1961)

Morris, B. *Bakunin: The Philosophy of Freedom* (Montreal, 1993)

Moser, C. *Anti-Nihilism in the Russian Novel of the 1860s* (The Hague, 1964)

Moulaert, J. *Le Mouvement anarchiste en Belgique, 1870–1914* (Belgium, 1995)

Naimark, N. *Terrorists and Social Democrats: The Russian Revolutionary Movement under Alexander III* (Cambridge, 1983)

Nelson, B. C. *Beyond the Martyrs* (New Brunswick, 1998)

Noll von der Nahmer, R. *Bismarcks Reptilienfonds* (Mainz, 1968)

Nord, P. 'Republicanism and Utopian Vision: French Freemasonry in the 1860s and 1870s', *Journal of Modern History*, 63, June 1991, pp. 213–29

Nordhoff, C. *Communistic Societies in the United States* (New York, 1875)

Oliver, H. *The International Anarchist Movement in Late Victorian London* (London, 1983)

Osterrieder, M. 'From Synarchy to Shambala: The Role of Political Occultism and Social Messianism in the Activities of Nicholas Roerich', paper presented at the conference on 'The Occult in Twentieth-Century Russia' (Berlin, March 2007)

O'Toole, A. *With the Poor People of the Earth: A Biography of Dr John Creaghe of Sheffield and Buenos Aires* (London, 2005)

Patsouras, L. *Jean Grave and the Anarchist Tradition in France* (Middletown, 1995)

Pemble, J. *The Mediterranean Passion: Victorians and Edwardians in the South* (Oxford, 1987)

Peregudova, Z. I. *Politicheskii sysk Rossii (Russia's Political Investigation)* (Moscow, 2000)

Pernicone, N. *Italian Anarchism, 1864–1892* (Princeton, 1993)

Phillips, W. M. *Nightmares of Anarchy and Dreams of Revolution in English and American Literature, 1870–1910* (Bucknell, 2003)

Pick, D. *Faces of Degeneration: A European Disorder* (Cambridge, 1993)

Pierrot, J. *The Decadent Imagination 1880–1900*, trs. Coltman, D. (Chicago, 1981)

Pipes, R. *The Degaev Affair: Terror and Treason in Tsarist Russia* (Yale, 2003)

Poliakov, L. *The History of Anti-Semitism*, trs. Howard, R. (London, 1966)

Porch, D. *The French Secret Services: From the Dreyfus Affair to the Gulf War* (New York, 1995)

Porter, B. 'The Freiheit Prosecutions, 1881–1882', *Historical Journal*, 23, 4, 1980; *The Origins of the Vigilant State: The London Metropolitan Police Special Branch Before the First World War* (London, 1987); *The Refugee Question in Mid-Victorian Politics* (Cambridge, 1979)

Quail, J. *The Slow-Burning Fuse: The Lost History of the British Anarchists* (London, 1978)

Rauchway, E. *Murdering McKinley: The Making of Theodore Roosevelt's America* (New York, 2003)

Ravindranathan, T. R. *Bakunin and the Italians* (Montreal, 1998)

Rhodes, H. T. F. *Alphonse Bertillon: Father of Scientific Detection* (New York, 1956)

Robb, G. *Victor Hugo* (London, 1997)

Robbins, R. G. *Famine in Russia: 1891–1892* (New York, 1975)

Roberts, A. 'When the Prime Minister Plotted to Kill the Queen', review, *Daily Telegraph*, 9 May 2002

Rollin, H. L. V. *L'Apocalypse de notre temps. Les dessous de la propagande allemande – d'après des documents inédits* (Paris, 1939)

Roslak, R. S. 'The Politics of Aesthetic Harmony: Neo-Impressionism, Science and Anarchism', *Art Bulletin*, 73, 3, September 1991, pp. 381–90

Roubaud, N. *Henri Rochefort intime* (Paris, 1954)

Rowbotham, S. 'Anarchism in Sheffield in the 1890s' in Pollard, S. and Holmes, C. (eds.) *Essays in the Economic and Social History of South Yorkshire* (Sheffield, 1976)

Rowbotham, S. and Weeks, J. *Socialism and the New Life: The Personal Politics of Edward Carpenter and Havelock Ellis* (London, 1977)

Rubinstein, R. E. *Comrade Valentine: The True Story of Azef the Spy* (New York, 1994)

Ruud, C. A. and Stepanov, S. *Fontanka 16: The Tsar's Secret Police* (Montreal, 1999)

Ruvira, G. Z. 'Errico Malatesta y el anarquismo argentino', *Historiografía y bibliografía americanista*, XVI, 3, 1972; 'Anarchisme et mouvement ouvrier en Argentine à la fin du XIXe siècle', *Le Mouvement social*, 103, April–June 1978, pp. 14–17

Rykwert, J. *The Seduction of Place: The History and Future of the City* (New York, 2000)

Salé, M. P. and Papet, E. *L'Art Russe dans le second moitié du XIXe siècle: en quête d'identité* (Paris, 2006)

Saunders, D. 'Vladimir Burtsev and the Russian Revolutionary Emigration (1888–1905)', *European History Quarterly*, 13, 1983, pp. 39–62; 'Stepniak and the London Emigration: Letters to Robert Spence Watson (1887–1890)', *Oxford Slavonic Papers*, 13, 1980, pp. 80–93

Schama, S. *Citizens: A Chronicle of the French Revolution* (London, 1977)

Schleifmann, N. 'The Okhrana and Burtsev: Provocateurs and Revolutionaries', *Survey*, 27, 1983, pp. 22–40

Schoeps, J. H. 'Agenten, Spitzel, Flüchtlinge: Wilhelm Stieber und die demokratische Emigration in London' in Schallenberger, H. and Schrey, H. (eds.) *Im Gegenstrom* (Wuppertal, 1977)

Schveirov, R. 'Chicago's great upheaval of 1877', *Chicago History*, 9, 1, spring 1980, pp. 2–17

Senese, D. *S. M. Stepniak-Kravchinksy: The London Years* (Newtonville, 1987); 'Le Vil Melville: Evidence from the Okhrana File on the trail of Vladimir Burtsev', *Oxford Slavonic Papers*, 14, 1981, pp. 147–53

Sennett, R. *Flesh and Stone: The Body and the City in Western Civilization* (New York, 1996)

Shattuck, R. *The Banquet Years: The Origins of the Avant Garde in France, 1885–World War I* (London, 1968)

Sherry, N. *Conrad's Western World* (Cambridge, 1980)

Shipley, S. *Club Life and Socialism in Mid-Victorian London* (London, 1971)

Shirokova, V. V. 'From the history of connections between Russian revolutionaries and émigrés', *Osvoboditelnoe dvizhenie v Rossii*, 8, 1978, pp. 41–52

Shor, F. R. *Utopianism and Radicalism in a Reforming America, 1888–1918* (Westport, 1997)

Shpayer-Makov, H. 'Anarchism in British Public Opinion, 1880–1914', *Victorian Studies*, 1988

Siemann, W. *Deutschlands Ruhe, Sicherheit und Ordnung* (Tubingen, 1985)

Skirda, A. *Facing the Enemy: A History of Anarchist Organization from Proudhon to May 1969*, trs. Sharkey, P. (Edinburgh, 2002)

Slatter J. 'The Correspondence of P. A. Kropotkin as Historical Source Material', *Slavonic and East European Review*, 72, 2, 1994, pp. 277–88

Smith, E. E. *The Okhrana* (California, 1967)

Snell, R. review of Thomson, R. *The Troubled Republic: Visual Culture and Social Debate in France, 1889–1900*, *Times Literary Supplement*, 5350, 2005

Sonn, R. D. *Anarchism and Cultural Politics in Fin de Siècle France* (Nebraska, 1989)

Squire, P. S. *The Third Department: The Political Police in the Russia of Nicholas I* (Cambridge, 1968)

Stanislawski, M. *Zionism and the Fin de Siècle: Cosmopolitanism and Nationalism from Nordau to Jabotinsky* (California, 2001)

Stead, P. J. *The Police of Paris* (London, 1957)

Stedman-Jones, G. *Outcast London: A Study in the Relationship Between Classes in Victorian Society* (New York, 1984)

Stowell, D. O. *Streets, Railroads, and the Great Strike of 1877* (Chicago, 1999)

Sutcliffe, A. *Paris: An Architectural History* (Yale, 1996)

Suvin, D. *Metamorphoses of Science Fiction* (Yale, 1979)

Svatikov, S. G. *Russkii politicheskii sysk zagranitsei (Russian political investigations abroad)* (Rostov-on-Don, 1918); 'Iz istorii politicheskoi politsii zagranitsei' ('On the history of the political police abroad'), *Na chuzhoi storone*, 8, 1925

Sweetman, D. *Explosive Acts: Toulouse Lautrec, Oscar Wilde, Félix Fénéon and the Art and Anarchy of the Fin de Siècle* (London, 1999)

Szamuely, H. *British Attitudes to Russia, 1880–1918* (Oxford, 1982)

Talerov, P. I. 'P. A. Kropotkin Targeted by the "Holy Brotherhood"', trs. Slatter, J. *Revolutionary Russia*, 14, 2, 2001, pp. 123–30

Taratuta, E. A. 'Fridrikh Engels i Sergey Mikhailovich Stepniak-Kravchinsky', *Nauka i zhizn*, 7–9, 1965; *S. M. Stepniak-Kravchinsky: Revolutionary and Writer* (Moscow, 1973)

Thomas, P. *Karl Marx and the Anarchists* (London, 1980)

Thompson, E. P. *William Morris: Romantic to Revolutionary* (Stanford, 1988)

Thomson, R. *The Troubled Republic: Visual Culture and Social Debate in France, 1889–1900* (Yale, 2005)

Thurschwell, P. *Literature, Technology and Magic Thinking, 1880–1920* (Cambridge, 2001)

Tidmarsh, K. L. 'Lev Tikhomirov and a Crisis in Russian Radicalism', *Russian Review*, 20, 1961

Tissot, V. *La Police secrète prussienne* (Paris, 1884)

Titov, A. A. (ed.) *Nikolai Vasil'evich Chaikovskii. Religioznye i obshchestvennye iskaniia* (Paris, 1929)

Tombs, R. *The Paris Commune 1871* (London, 1999)

Trautmann, F. *The Voice of Terror: A Biography of Johann Most* (Westport, 1980)

Tsuzuki, C. *Edward Carpenter 1844–1929* (Cambridge, 1980)

Turner, F. M. *Between Science and Religion: The Reaction to Scientific Naturalism in Late Victorian England* (New Haven, 1971)

Un Vecchio (pseud.) 'L'anarchismo in Egipto', *La Protesta Umana*, 40, San Francisco, 9 January 1904

Vakhrushev, I. S. 'Russian revolutionaries and foreign secret service of the tsarist regime in 1870s and 1880s', *Osvoboditelnoe dvizhenie v Rossii*, 8, 1978, pp. 53– 70

Varias, A. *Paris and the Anarchists* (New York, 1996)

Vassilyev, A. T. *The Okhrana: The Russian Secret Police* (Philadelphia, 1930)

Vatikiotis, P. J. *The History of Modern Egypt: From Muhammad Ali to Mubarak* (London, 1991)

Vâtre E. *Henri Rochefort, ou la comédie politique au XIXe siècle* (Paris, 1984)

Venturi, F. *Roots of Revolution: A History of the Populist and Socialist Movements in Nineteenth-Century Russia* (Chicago, 1983)

Verdes, J. 'Marx vu par la police française 1871–1883', *Cahiers de l'ISEA*, S, 10, August 1966, pp. 83–120

Vervaeck, S. *Inventaire des archives du ministère de la justice, administration de la Sûreté publique, police des étrangers, dossiers généraux* (Brussels, 1968)

Vizetelly, E. A. *The Anarchists: Their Faith and Record* (London, 1911)

Vuilleumier, M. 'Elisée Reclus et Genève', *Musées de Genève*, 12, 114, 1971, pp. 9–13; 'Les Proscrits de la Commune en Suisse, 1871', *Revue Suisse d'Histoire*, 12, 1962, pp. 498–537

Walter, N. *The Anarchist Past and Other Essays* (Nottingham, 2007)

Webb, J. *The Flight From Reason: The Age of the Irrational* (London, 1971)

Weindling, P. J. *Epidemics and Genocide in Eastern Europe, 1890–1945* (Oxford, 2000)

Weiss, S. 'Wilhelm Stieber, August Schluga von Rastenfeld und Otto von Bismarck', *Francia*, 31, 3, 2004, pp. 87–112

Welter, V. M. *Biopolis: Patrick Geddes and the Life of the City* (Cambridge, Mass., 2002)

Wexler, A. *Emma Goldman in Exile* (Boston, 1992)

Wheen, F. *Karl Marx* (London, 1999)

Whyte, F. *The Life of W. T. Stead* (London, 1925)

Williams, R. L. *Henri Rochefort, Prince of the Gutter Press* (New York, 1966)

Wilms, R. *Politische Polizei und Sozialdemokraten im Deutschen Kaiserreich (Political Police and Social Democrats in the German Empire)* (Frankfurt, 1992)

Wilson, E. *To The Finland Station* (New York, 1940)

Wolfgang, M. E. 'Cesare Lombroso' in Mannheim, H. (ed.) *Pioneers in Criminology* (London, 1960)

Wright, P. 'Loris-Melikov: Russia, 1880–1881', *History Today*, 24, June 1974, pp. 413–19

Yarmolinsky, A. *Road to Revolution: A Century of Russian Radicalism* (London, 1957); *A Russian American's Dream* (Kansas, 1965)

Zhukhrai, V. M. *Tainy tsarskoi okhranki. Avantiuristy i provokatory* (*Secrets of the Tsarist Okhrana. Careerists and agents provocateurs*) (Moscow, 1991)

Zuckerman, F. S. *The Tsarist Secret Police Abroad: Policing Europe in a Modernising World* (New York, 2003); *The Tsarist Secret Police and Russian Society, 1880–1917* (New York, 1996)

Acknowledgements

The anarchist Utopia of selfless cooperation may not have come much closer in the last hundred years, but throughout the years of this book's preparation I have been fortunate enough to experience something like it in microcosm: any shortfall in the area of Mutual Aid is my own.

In France, the archivists at the Prefecture of Police under M. Gicquel, including Oliver Accarie-Pierson, Jean-Daniel Girard, Bernard Goupy and Mélik Benmiloud were invariably helpful on my repeated visits, as were Catherine Mérot and her colleagues at the Archives Nationales; Rossana Vaccaro at the Bibliothèque Jean Maitron, Université de Paris 1 deserves particular gratitude for visits to the stacks during closed hours, when the rest of Paris was on strike. In Amsterdam, I enjoyed the attentive care of Ella Molenaar at the International Institute of Social History, while Pierre-Alain Tailler at the Archives Générales du Royaume in Brussels was kind enough to direct me towards his exceptional assistant Felip Strubbe, whose committed burrowing generated some remarkable late revelations. The magisterial guidance of Zinaida Peregudova at the State Archive of the Russian Federation in Moscow was greatly appreciated, even on those occasions when eagerly awaited files proved empty.

In America, Ronald M. Bulatoff at the Hoover Institute at Stanford University elucidated the complexities of the Okhrana Archive, while the library staff at the universities of Kansas and Rutgers expedited my microfilm investigations. In Great Britain, Janet Allen at Senate House Library of the University of London and Katya Rogatchevskaia at the British Library have been of particular help, while a Carlyle bursary from the London Library has enabled me to continue to use its remarkable resources; the staff of all three institutions, and those of the Bodleian Library, the National Archives in Kew, the University of Birmingham library and the Sheffield City Archives have all been patient with my enquiries. I have appreciated too the courtesy shown by Nigel Shankster in the archives of the Metropolitan Police, despite our differences of opinion.

In this regard, the Freedom of Information case that I initiated to gain access to the Special Branch ledgers from the 1890s has, over its prolonged course, evinced much generous legal advice: from Julia Apostle and Martin Soames at DLA Piper, John Ashton of the FOI Ltd Consultancy and Vanessa Milton at Random House. At the Information Commission, overwhelmed with applications, I have found Jo Pedder, Adam Sowerbutt, Antonia Swann and Caroline Howes to be consistently professional, prompt and scrupulous in their work on the case: the contrast with my experience of the Information Tribunal has been striking.

Among the many individuals who have shared with me their specialist knowledge and advice are Regula Boschler, Dr Lindsey Clutterbuck, Michel Cordillot of Université de Paris 8, Frank Engehausen of the Historisches Seminar at Heidelberg University, Aleksandr Ivanovich Kokurin, Dr Julia Mannheim and Adhaf Soueif; the doctoral theses of Dr Bob Henderson and Dr Pietro Dipaolo revealed some fascinating insights. Many friends too have helped in their various ways: Sarah Adams, Roland Chambers, Scott Goodfellow, Saira Shah and Pedro Ferreira with introductions, Jerry Brotton with references, Benjamin Carter with copying, Rachel Holmes with tussles over Tussy, Chris Morgan Jones with cocktails, Melissa Morandi with the geography of a fighting retreat, Tom Reiss with an untraceable book, Vijay Sharma with a prod in the right direction and John Wyver with a pointer to the right *mairie*. Colleagues among the governors at the Margaret McMillan Children's Centre have provided a living example of the journey to Utopia. The sustained interest of Simon Ardizzone, Andy Beckett, Gail Eisenstadt, David Gale, Sara Holloway, Spencer Hyman, Deborah Levy and Stanislav Sermedjev has been a comfort, as has that of Ed Davey, whose database-building skills have been invaluable. Dominique Shafer's late secretarial contribution was a godsend.

Sylvie Audoly, Brian Heller, Lisa Gallagher, Susanne Lea, Antoine Audouard, Anne-Marie Stott, Thomas Guillot and Galina Vinogradova have all provided the warmest of hospitality on my travels, while Constantin Tublin and Natasha Smirnova may well have saved me from frostbite in the depth of a Russian winter. I could not have had more delightful surroundings in which to write than Grove House, courtesy of Polly McLean and Rose McAfee, or to complete the book than Casa dei Fichi, for which my thanks to Jamie and Katherina Bielenberg-Bulloch and Christopher Bielenberg. The loan of *Otherwise* by Martin and Naomi Jennings has kept me afloat, Lesley Cusse's password, connected. For their unconditional patronage, however, my deepest gratitude is to Stewart and Tamsin Wilkinson: Ivy Cottage is the refuge that every writer needs.

I have been supremely fortunate too in my research assistants, Luba Vinogradova, and Nika Frank whose youthful brilliance as a translator of Russian and German, scholar and critic I scarcely deserved. Dr Constance Bantman, Stephen Hancock and Professor Bernard Porter have all given greatly of their time to offer thorough, engaged and astute critiques that have saved me from many errors; they are, of course, exonerated of all responsibility for any that remain. Financial assistance received from the Authors Foundation, administered by the Society of Authors, in the form of a K. Blundell Trust award, offered a lifeline when completion of the archival research was in jeopardy, and was much appreciated.

Jörg Hensgen, Rowena Skelton-Wallace, Kay Peddle and Liam Relph at Bodley Head have offered timely support, David Milner an acute and sympathetic eye and ear; particular thanks are due to Will Sulkin for his unstinting commitment to the book in difficult circumstances and despite the author's seemingly cavalier attitude to deadlines. Far more than an agent, Patrick Walsh has negotiated many obstacles on the book's behalf: his team at Conville and Walsh, in particular Alex Christofi and Jake Smith-Bosanquet, deserve plaudits too. In New York, Christie Fletcher and Melissa Chinchilla found it the best of homes at Pantheon, where I am truly grateful for the support, enthusiasm and patience of Dan Frank, Jeff Alexander and Danny Yanez.

My greatest gratitude is due to my family, whose love, support and tolerance have been endlessly tested. My parents, Ros and Bas Butterworth, to whom I owe so much, and my in-laws, Penny and Sebastian Carter, have given of their time without complaint. Half the lives of my delightful children, Matilda and Thomas, have been spent in the book's shadow, yet they have thrived regardless. For that and so much besides I owe a debt of inexpressible gratitude to my wife, Rebecca Carter, whose extraordinary human qualities are matched by her supreme talent and tenacity as an editor: a vocation which she has long deserved to practise without domestic distractions.

Index

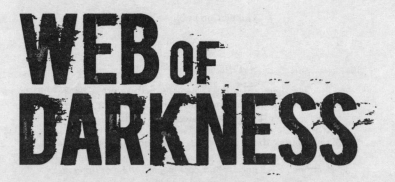

WEB OF DARKNESS

BALI RAI

CORGI

WEB OF DARKNESS
A CORGI BOOK 978 0 552 56212 6

First published in Great Britain by Corgi Books,
an imprint of Random House Children's Books,
A Random House Group Company

This edition published 2014

1 3 5 7 9 10 8 6 4 2

The Random House Group Limited supports the Forest Stewardship
Council® (FSC®), the leading international forest-certification organisation.
Our books carrying the FSC label are printed on FSC®-certified paper. FSC is
the only forest-certification scheme supported by the leading environmental
organisations, including Greenpeace. Our paper procurement policy can be
found at www.randomhouse.co.uk/environment.

MIX
Paper from
responsible sources
FSC® C016897

Set in 12/16 pt Requiem by Falcon Oast Graphic Art Ltd.

Corgi Books are published by Random House Children's Publishers UK,
61–63 Uxbridge Road, London W5 5SA

www.randomhouse.co.uk
www.randomhousechildrens.co.uk
www.totallyrandombooks.co.uk

Addresses for companies within The Random House Group Limited
can be found at: www.randomhouse.co.uk/offices.htm

THE RANDOM HOUSE GROUP Limited Reg. No. 954009

A CIP catalogue record for this book is available from the British Library.

Printed and bound in Great Britain by
CPI Group (UK) Ltd, Croydon, CR0 4YY

To all the pupils, teachers and librarians who
have been so wonderful over the past decade,
in schools and colleges across the UK and
beyond. A massive, massive thank you.

Lily

I used to be all the things that a teenage girl should be – normal, happy, outgoing. I had friends, and I had dreams. I did well at school, and I was popular. Everyone liked me, or at least most people did. My life was easy and I had my entire future to think about . . .

I had this friend – more a sister, if I'm honest. She sparkled with energy and light and I would have done anything for her. Sometimes she annoyed the hell out of me. Other times she made me laugh so hard, I'd nearly wet myself. Every time, she showed me what true friendship was about. I loved her. I still love her . . .

Only, I don't see her any more.

A predator walked into our lives. The sort of

monster you never think you'll meet. The sort that preys only on others. You see faces on the television news, and staring at you from under lurid, printed headlines – but you never think they'll come for *you* . . .

This man, this *thing*, did come. He brought shades of pain and evil into my life that I could not comprehend. He caught my life in his web and wrapped me up so tight that I will never be able to escape. It was nothing to him – just a game that he enjoyed . . .

I didn't understand true evil until he arrived in my life. I always thought such things had a reason for existing. He showed me how wrong I was. Sometimes there is no reason. Sometimes there just is . . .

PART ONE

Did you like the page?

The Spider sits in his darkened room, his face the only thing illuminated by the stark glow of his computer's monitor. He waits for his partner in crime – the OTHER – to respond.

It was pretty special, comes the reply. *You're a twisted genius.*

It was nothing, the Spider replies. *Remember the first girl – Emma Wallace?*

How could I forget her? She brought us together.

The German boy too – what was his name?

Lukas Adler, recalls the OTHER. *He lasted about two weeks.*

Pitiful creatures, both of them, the Spider replies. *This time will be different. Are you sure you wish to proceed?*

His accomplice takes time to reply. While he waits, the Spider logs onto another computer – a laptop.

If we plan correctly, the OTHER eventually writes, *we will be fine.*

The planning is my domain, the Spider tells him. *Do not forget that.*

I won't. You have your skills. I have mine. Talking of which – I have buyers for those photographs. They were very interested in the videos too.

Then I will supply them. The price will be higher this time.

Don't worry, the OTHER replies. *They will pay.*

So, the Spider asks again. *Are you sure you are ready for this? The risks will be high.*

I know.

The Spider chuckles to himself. *High risks*, he writes, *bring high rewards.*

I can't wait, types the OTHER.

We should meet. Discuss our strategy.

Is that wise?

Have I ever let you down?

No.

Later, the Spider watches from the shadows, as Girl #1 sits at her desk, oblivious to his presence. Her webcam is on, but goes unnoticed. Her keystrokes are logged. He has access to her entire online world.

Her life is caught in his web. Soon, he will devour her . . .

1

'Did you say summat?'

I was sitting in the café of a local supermarket when the voice rang out.

I looked over. Manisha Patel was doing her usual. She glared at Amy who was walking past their table. Both were almost sixteen; in my year at school. One used to be a friend, the other was definitely not.

I watched Amy lower her head and walk on towards the exit. She slouched, like she was carrying rocks on her shoulders. My heart hurt for her.

Manisha hadn't finished, though. 'I'm talking to you, lard ass!' she yelled.

I saw Amy shrink further down into her coat and felt a wave of anger. Next to me, I could tell that my best friend, Tilly, was like a tightly coiled spring.

'Stop it, you nasty cow!' she snapped. And before I knew it, Tilly had shot out of her seat and stormed across the café to Manisha and her friends.

'Oh, look.' A perfectly manicured finger pointed towards Tilly. 'Hey, Amy. Here comes your super-hero.'

Manisha was one of the rich girls. You know the type, always immaculately dressed – a different outfit for every day, complete with expensive bags, shoes and accessories. She was spoiled and self-obsessed. On the outside, she seemed to have everything – apart from intelligence, manners and a heart, that is. Her threatening eyes were narrow and set into a thin, bony face with a square chin. Her friends were almost as bad – like mini-me versions of Manisha. They sat now and watched Tilly with the same twisted, mean expressions their leader wore.

'You leave Amy alone!' my best friend screamed.

Amy looked at Tilly for a moment, before lowering her gaze again, embarrassed. I was so frustrated. Why didn't she ever stand up for herself?

It was January and dead cold so the warm café was packed. And we were making a scene. The adults around us mostly glared and shook their heads and I felt a surge of embarrassment. As Tilly and Manisha stared each other out an old lady got up to complain.

Manisha didn't look bothered. She grinned. 'What you gonna do, Tilly?'

Tilly had a thing about bullies – and I knew she wanted to protect Amy. It was just her nature, sticking up for the underdog. Her porcelain cheeks started to colour. Her icy-blue eyes were like melted Arctic water, and they drilled into Manisha's face. I could see she was about to go crazy. Tilly was tall and skinny, with long legs and a tiny waist, but if it came to a scuffle, she could more than match Manisha, I knew. All the sport she did had made her strong.

'You lot have gone too far,' Tilly warned. 'It's time everyone left Amy alone. I'm telling you first.' She jabbed a finger right into Manisha's arm. The silver *Sisters Forever* charm that I'd bought her for her tenth birthday clinked against her Pandora bracelet. My matching charm hung from my left wrist.

'If she lost some weight,' began one of Manisha's gang, 'maybe she'd—'

The girl who'd spoken, Ria Smith, didn't get to finish. I watched in disbelief as Tilly grabbed her plate full of chips and beans, and dumped it on her head. It was something I might imagine doing but never would. I'd be too scared of the consequences. Tilly didn't care, though.

It happened in a flash. Every pupil in the café started to laugh or cheer – not necessarily because they disliked Manisha and her mates. They were just enjoying the drama.

I saw the security guard approaching fast, and pulled Tilly away. 'Come on!' I said. 'We'd better go.'

Ria, Manisha and the rest started yelling and complaining. I thought of baby vultures, fighting with each other.

As we made our way to the door, I looked for Amy, to see if she was OK. But she'd already gone . . .

There are so many targets for a predator as skilled as the Spider. The virtual world is filled with easy prey.

He finds the things that make them scream inside – the horrors that they fear most. The insecurities that they hide from the rest of the world. The overweight, the depressed, the pathetic and the mentally unstable . . . He exposes those secrets for all to see. He takes victims who are almost broken and pushes them over the edge. A degree of skill is required for this. An ability to pull apart the defences people erect to protect their inner selves.

Girl #1 is a classic example. Too stupid to care about, too ugly to miss. She knows what she is; knows that her life will always be plain and humdrum. He has watched her fall apart – from the jibes on Facebook, to her search for like-minded people. Those looking for a way out.

Most of his past victims have been random strangers – picked out in chat rooms and social-media sites around the globe. Technology has made the world so much easier to get around. The Spider has woven his threads in the USA, in Europe and in Asia, careful to maintain a geographical distance. Yet he has never received credit for his work – and he has not asked for it. He has been content to linger in the shadows – anonymous, silent, patient . . .

But things have changed. The thrill needs to be reawakened. This time it will be different. This time will be like the first. He is crawling out of the darkness again. Moving out from the virtual and back into the real world. It will be a bigger test of his skills.

2

The 'Diary of a Fat Bitch' page had started a few weeks earlier. Someone had posted it on Facebook, and though we thought it was probably Manisha because she was the worst of the bullies, she was denying it. It was beyond mean, too far, as Tilly had said, and I just felt so bad for Amy – the subject of the 'diary'. I couldn't begin to imagine how it made her feel.

Amy wasn't exactly a close friend, but I'd known her for most of my life. Like Tilly and me, we'd met at junior school, and then later our mums had become friends.

She'd always been a bit chubby as a little girl but back then she didn't seem to care. The trouble really started when we got to secondary school. The boys were the first. A group of them, led by Jamie Walker, made up stupid rhymes about her size. Then Manisha and her bitchy gang joined in.

And Amy reacted by shutting herself off. We grew further and further apart. Every time I tried to talk to her, she would just clam up and walk away. All her old friends, including Tilly, got the same reaction. As we made other friends it was like Amy had just given up, or something. And as she became more and more isolated she seemed to get bigger and bigger; now she spent most of her time alone.

The Facebook page was the worst thing, though. It was public so that anyone could see it and comment, and full of really heartless jokes. Someone had even photoshopped a picture of a whale in a bikini, posted it and tagged Amy. It was so cruel.

When Amy didn't report the abuse, Tilly and I decided to instead. We found the violations procedure online and went directly to Facebook. It had finally been taken down two days before Tilly went mad in the café. Too late to help Amy. Her already shitty school life had been torn apart all over again.

That's what I considered as I knocked on her door, later that evening. She lived only three streets along from my mum and me so I'd decided to stop by there on my way home. I couldn't get her face in the café out of my head and I wanted to check she was OK – even if she had pushed me away every other time I tried to speak to her recently.

'Hey!' I tried to sound cheerful as she opened the door and saw me standing on the step.

Amy didn't look happy. Her brown eyes narrowed. 'Why are you here?' she almost whispered.

She'd grown her light brown hair – long enough to cover her pale brown eyes. Her clothes were loose and baggy so you couldn't really tell what size she was any more, but actually she was really pretty. Only now you had to look past the misery and her hair to see it.

'Are you OK?' I asked. 'You know – after earlier?'

Amy shook her head. 'Don't care,' she told me. But her shoulders seemed to curve inwards, telling me otherwise. 'I don't need your help. Or Tilly's. I'm fine.'

I shook my head. 'But you can't let Manisha keep speaking to you like that,' I replied. 'Or anyone else.'

'Too late for that,' she told me flatly.

'What do you mean?' I asked.

She looked down at her feet. 'Oh, nothing . . . Well, I better go back in – homework to do and stuff.'

She was pushing me away again. 'Can't I come in?' I suggested brightly. 'Maybe we could have a proper catch-up? Or do you want to nip to Costa or something?'

Amy shook her head. 'No thanks. I'm OK,' she replied. 'I've got other friends now. People I've met online. People like me . . .'

I shrugged. I wanted to know what she meant; which people like her? I let it go, though. She really didn't seem to want me around. Well, I'd tried my best. But when she looked at me, the sadness in her eyes made me want to cry and I couldn't leave.

'Amy . . . I'm sorry.'

'Why are *you* sorry?' she replied. 'You're one of the few people who *isn't* mean to me.'

'Because you have to deal with this,' I told her. 'You think you're alone, but you don't have to be. I know we haven't been that close for a bit, but you can hang with Tilly and me. Like we used to.'

Amy shook her head again. 'Listen, I'm fine,' she said with more conviction. 'Honestly, Lily – it might not look like it but I'm dealing with things . . .'

'But . . .'

Amy just repeated herself and then shut the door in my face.

'*Aargh!* I get so angry,' Tilly said.

She lounged on her purple Ikea duvet as I told her more about my earlier visit to Amy's.

'I just want to slam Manisha's head into a table whenever I see her,' she added.

Tilly only lived in the street behind mine, so after remembering that Mum was going to be late, I'd gone over to hers. We were like sisters. Mum called us the Lily and Tilly Show. I loved my best friend more than anyone, but she could be seriously fiery. If you messed with her, or people she liked, she would snap and do silly things. Like dumping a plate of food on your head. She could be kind too, but she defended her friends like a lioness with new-born cubs.

'How does hurting Manisha help anything? You'll just get yourself into trouble.'

We were in her bedroom, messing about online. Her Facebook page was open. In a second window, so was mine.

Our friend, Danny, was fending off comments about his sexuality. Danny was openly gay, and most of the lads at school didn't even pretend to be OK with it. The Asian lads were the worst. Vicious. I think it was because Danny's from the same background as them. It was like they couldn't handle the idea of a British Asian gay boy.

Even though he didn't seem to need it, Tilly was always ready to step in and defend Danny. He was my favourite person online – funny, savage, rude. He was like a caricature of a bitchy gay man, with bells on. Seriously, that boy had a put-down for every occasion. We were quite close, having met at junior school, and behind the bravado, I was one of the few people who Danny really spoke to. For most people, he wore a mask, sometimes even with Tilly – who often got irritated by him. He guarded his real emotions like they were jewels, but I knew that secretly all the horrible comments were wearing him down.

The lads saying stuff online were wannabe bad boys with homophobic issues. They didn't quite dare do it at school, but saying it online – not right to his face – was easier for them, the cowards. They called him all kinds of names. Tonight, Danny had just effortlessly confirmed how stupid they were.

Yeah, he'd written. I've seen you eye my ass when your boys ain't with you. Pop over and pop it out, babe. Lemme see what you got. #pencildick.

I saw it and burst into giggles.

'What?' Tilly asked, looking up from the text she was sending.

I pointed at the screen. 'Look at how Danny's just dissed this idiot!'

When she saw Danny's reply, she sniggered too, and for a moment we forgot about Amy. But only for a moment.

'I'm going to write something nice about Amy,' Tilly said.

'Huh?'

'After earlier,' she replied. 'What do you reckon?'

I smiled at her – the lioness defending her cubs again – and I wanted to hug her. But Ria Smith had got there first, and she wasn't defending Amy. She was slagging Tilly off, and had compared Amy to a baby elephant.

Dunno where the Fat Bitch page went but someone should bring it back. That was the best laugh ever. Like, seriously! PMSL every time!

Tilly almost growled at the screen.

'Forget about it,' I said. 'Ria isn't worth your anger.'

I maximized my page. A load of posts clogged up my news feed, mostly from people at school. Some of them had posted pictures or videos of themselves – with new haircuts or showing off their latest gadgets. A lad called Daniel wanted me to like some band page. Molly Cooper, another of the self-obsessed tribe but nicer than Manisha and her lot, had posted a 'rate my looks for a rate back' selfie. She was all tiny tight red shorts and a white boob top, and had about fifty likes – most from lads. Just the usual crap.

In the top left corner, I had some friend requests. I clicked on the little icon, and looked down the list.

'You got any good books?' Tilly looked up from her phone again and asked out of nowhere.

'Books?'

'Yeah — you know those things with covers and words in them. We *like* them?'

'I've got a few,' I replied, smiling at her random question. 'But you didn't give the last one back.'

Tilly pointed to a mess of clothes and shoes in the corner of her room. 'It's under there,' she told me. 'I think.'

'I'm not searching under all your dirty knickers!' I told her.

'Come on! I'm in the mood for something girly and real. Though,' she added, 'I don't want anything about undead lovers, nerdy magicians or anything like that.'

I started to think through what I'd read recently that Tilly might enjoy when one of the friend requests particularly caught my eye.

It was from a boy I didn't recognize. I did recognize that he was hot, though. And I *mean* seriously, seriously attractive.

'*Hello!*'

'Hmmm?' said Tilly.

'Look!' I tapped on the picture.

Tilly's eyes nearly popped out of her head. 'OMG!' she squealed. 'Who's he?'

On my screen was a lad with dark chestnut hair, pale blue eyes, and the most amazing ripped abs and chest I'd ever seen. He looked like a Hollister model. His tag said 'Benedict Pablo, NYC, USA'. I hit confirm so fast I thought the button on the keyboard would break.

'I dunno,' I replied. My tummy was turning, and not in a horrible way. He was gorgeous.

'But . . . she said, as my new friend messaged me immediately.

Hey Lily – Thanks for the friend confirmation. Good to be talking to ya! You're very pretty. Holla back, if you wanna chat, yeah?

'Wow,' I replied. I couldn't think of anything else to say.

The Spider places his feet on his desk and smiles. The mouse and mat sit in his lap, as he takes control of another computer. Weaves another section of his latest web.

Boy #1 hasn't noticed that his browser address is faked, or that his webcam has turned itself on. The boy is too busy searching the Web for nude pictures of celebrities. A cursory glance at his search history reveals his preference for one particular actress. The woman in question is stunning but her acting leaves much to be desired.

This is the knowledge the Spider used to send his virus across – a Remote Access Trojan that gave him control of the infected PC, so that it became his slave. The boy was so eager to download 'new and exclusive nudes' that he clicked on every prompt given. Like stealing candy from a baby, if clichés are your thing . . .

Then Boy #1 met the woman of his dreams. Older, experienced and looking for a fling – she found him in a chat room, and they exchanged details. Boy #1 was eager to connect with his new friend. So eager that he didn't stop to think. He is communicating with her now – a chat-room session in which he cannot see her. However, thanks to the virus, she can see him . . .

The webcam begins to record the boy's actions – something the Spider has no desire to watch. Such things excite the OTHER. The recordings are for him and his kind. For the Spider the video is simply a lever; something he will use later on . . .

The Spider gets up and walks across the room to yet another laptop. Girl #2 is also oblivious to the webcam light above her screen. She is too busy crying at comments on Facebook. In public, she is sassy and confident. In private, she bubbles with insecurity. A pathetic creature.

When, finally, she stops blubbing, the Spider makes himself comfortable. As several more laptops around the room watch their prey silently, Girl #2 begins to undress for bed, and the Spider watches and records every single move she makes . . .

3

'I can't believe how fit he is,' said Tilly the following morning.

We were in the English Hub – a new part of school – waiting for our lesson to start. Tilly had been talking about Benedict all morning, and I was hoping she'd stop. I didn't want everyone else knowing my business – it was embarrassing. Tilly didn't mind what people thought of her – she didn't care. But I was the opposite. The thought of anyone knowing my innermost feelings filled me with dread.

Molly Cooper gave a loud giggle and I looked over. She was by the stairs, chatting to one of our best friends, Max. She was made-up – looking more ready for a night out than a day at school – and I could smell her perfume from where I stood. Molly was really pretty, but the makeup gave her a hard look.

Max saw us and waved, and Tilly rolled her eyes at him. He winked back.

'I dunno whether I dislike her or feel sorry for her,' I told Tilly.

'Who?'

'Molly,' I said. 'Do you think she's really insecure?' She knew lads were eyeing her up whatever she did. It was like she wanted their constant attention.

'Stuff Molly,' she replied, eager to change the subject. 'We're talking about American Boy.'

'He's probably got the wrong girl,' I told her. 'He'll see more of my pics and realize.' I wasn't exactly photogenic, and in most of my Facebook ones I looked terrible. I'd been checking them overnight, and I was convinced that once he'd been through them, Benedict would un-friend me.

'You should totally upload a selfie,' said Tilly. 'Do what Molly would do.'

'No way!'

'Nothing nasty,' she continued. 'Just flash a bit of cleavage – you've got enough. I'll take some photos of you if you like.'

Just thinking about it made me feel a bit ill. No way was I letting Tilly do that. He'd take one look at my huge bum and wobbly thighs and run a mile. It was easy for Tilly to be confident about her figure – she was a goddess. I was the dumpy girl who looked on as the boys all chatted up my best mate. At least, that's how I felt sometimes . . .

'Tilly!' I protested. 'He's made a mistake – the last thing he wants to see is *more* of me.'

Tilly gave me a funny look. She was wearing slim-fit jeans with a yellow polo shirt and purple Converse. Her hair was piled up on her head, like a white-blond pineapple.

'Mistake?' she asked. '*How* – he requested you, remember?'

'Yeah, I know,' I told her. 'I just can't believe it.'

'Tell me about it,' she replied, grinning. 'Those abs . . .'

'I thought I was gonna faint,' I said. 'Wonder why he contacted me, though. It's a bit random.'

Tilly looked at me like I had two heads or something. 'Er . . . who *cares?*' she said. 'He's *fit!*'

Max came over and asked what we were talking about.

'Girl-stuff,' said Tilly, before pretending to be sad. 'But never mind about us – you go back to Molly. We know you love her more than us.'

Max shook his head and smiled. 'Molly's OK,' he said. 'You know that, really.'

'Fair enough,' Tilly replied. 'But she can be a bit

much at times. She's *so* pretty but she hides it under all that makeup. I feel like scrubbing it off and telling her to love her real face.'

Max grinned. A couple of younger girls walked past, looked at him and giggled. I didn't blame them; he was tall, athletic and had a jawline that most actors would die for. He was wearing a white shirt, open at the collar, with straight brown chinos and beige desert boots. His sleeves were rolled up and a silver chain that he always wore hung round his neck. It had a ring on it, which I guessed was of sentimental value. He was never without it.

Miss Theobald turned up and unlocked the door to her room. She was in her late twenties but dressed like an old woman in plaid skirts, thick brown tights and matching sensible shoes. Her blouse was ruffled along the button-line.

'In you go,' she ordered.

'Miss,' I replied.

She acknowledged me with a smile, which I returned. English was my favourite subject, although I was in top set for everything except science.

Tilly asked if I fancied Benedict. It felt like the world's silliest question, ever.

'Who wouldn't?' I replied. 'He's a model.'

'What – is he even fitter than Kane?' She winked at me.

I felt myself blush. Kane was another of our close friends, and I'd fancied him for ages. We'd known each other for a long time, though, and you know that thing where lads become your friends and nothing else happens? That was what Kane and me had. Besides, he wasn't interested in me. Boys like him never were. I'd tried flirting with him but I was useless at it. The lines I said in my head, all sophisticated and rom-com, weren't the words that came out of my mouth. I was too shy, too beige, if that makes sense. I was easy to ignore and didn't stand out. Not like Tilly, who made people turn their heads when she walked into a room. She was like a dazzling sunset compared to me. Which is why I thought Benedict had made a mistake.

'Did you talk to American Boy after you left mine?'

'Message,' I corrected. 'You don't *talk* to people with a keyboard.'

'Whatever, *nerd*,' said Tilly.

'Like *that's* an insult,' I replied. 'I'm proud to be a nerd!'

'You're changing the subject, babe.'

I shook my head. 'I haven't replied yet — I'm playing it cool.'

Tilly rolled her eyes. 'Bad move!' she advised. 'You play hard to get and he'll start chatting up some other girl. You need to reel his sexy ass in!'

'I don't even know him,' I said. 'And besides, he's from New York. He's not about to ask me out.'

Tilly looked thoughtful as we sat down. The rest of our class started filing in too.

Danny joined us. 'Hello, darlings,' he said, grabbing Tilly in a hug. 'Any juicy gossip for me?'

'We were discussing Lily's FB conquest,' Tilly explained, pushing him away. 'Model looks, abs of steel, and American too.'

Danny grinned, flashing impossibly straight, pearly teeth. 'Tasty,' he said. 'But those Americans only look good until their mid-thirties. After that the grease-soaked burgers and colossal sandwiches turn them into elephantine right-wing bastards who want to bomb anyone with a burqa on. Trust me . . . '

'Not all of them,' I said. 'My cousin is American and he's not—'

'How would you *know*?' Danny grinned. 'You're Asian, girl. You've probably got enough cousins to populate a small planet. I bet you don't even know all of their names.'

I smiled. My dad had come from a huge Punjabi family. Not that I knew them well. After he'd died, they stopped calling my mum. I saw them now and then but we weren't close. And Danny was right – there were a lot of them.

'You've got a point there,' I conceded.

'*We* were talking,' Tilly said to Danny, nodding in my direction. 'I didn't hear an invitation for you to take over. Now if you wouldn't mind . . .'

'Ooh – jealousy,' Danny replied. 'I won't steal your girlfriend, babe, I promise.'

'Sit down and shut up, there's a good little boy,' Tilly told him.

'Touchy this morning, aren't we?'

'I'll bloody touch you in a minute,' warned Tilly.

I grinned at both of them. Their love/hate banter always made me smile, because underneath it they were the same – fiery, loud-mouthed and sometimes a bit rude. The number of times I blushed and grinned simultaneously at something either had said was untrue.

They didn't get to finish their spat, though, because Miss Theobald started her lesson. And you didn't cross her. I swear, some days I thought she would stab us all, the looks she gave. She was continually disgusted with everything.

Tilly grinned. 'Bet she's a bit frustrated,' she whispered.

'What – sexually?' added Danny.

'*Danny!*' I replied. 'You can't say that – it's just wrong . . .'

'Yep,' he replied. 'Wrong, probably sexist and politically incorrect too. But who cares?'

After school, we went into town. Tilly wanted to look at shoes, I wanted a coffee, and Danny just moaned about having to go home. Tilly dragged us through five shops before we left her to it. We told her we'd wait in Costa Coffee. It was Danny's turn to pay, and as I sat and waited I checked my iPhone.

I had a few messages, including one from Kane. I felt weirdly excited as I read it. He was in town and wanted to meet up. He'd even signed off with a kiss, although just the one. If he really liked me, I thought, he'd have added two kisses, at least.

'Who was that?' asked Danny, setting my coffee down.

'Kane,' I replied.

'Ooh – your favourite boy,' he said, looking sympathetic and making me feel even sillier. 'Sorry,' he said immediately. 'That was a bit insensitive of me, wasn't it?'

I shook my head. 'It's OK,' I replied. 'A girl can dream. How about you – how are things?' I asked.

He shrugged. He was about five eight, like me, with short dark hair, bright russet eyes and a smile

32

that made you want to snog him. His nose was sharp, his cheekbones high, and a wispy beard covered his square jaw. 'I'm as well as any persecuted minority can be,' he sighed.

I knew Danny's moods and the sigh was a cue – a signal that something had happened.

'What?' I asked, putting my phone down and getting a bit worried.

'My dad,' he replied. 'He's been chatting to some moron at the *gurdwara*. Reckons he can *fix* me.'

'*Fix* you?' I asked, before realizing what he meant. 'Oh . . .'

'Some bogus holy man who sorts out gay boys. Probably points our willies in the right direction . . .'

'I thought your old man was getting used to—'

'So did I,' interrupted Danny. 'Big fucking lie, that was.'

'Danny, I don't know what to say . . .' I couldn't imagine what his family life was like. My mum was great and we talked about most things. I realized how lucky I was, to have that sort of relationship.

'Don't matter,' he said, putting on a fake smile. 'I'll just buy another phone, or get some new shoes. Retail therapy will make it all better – just like the adverts tell us.'

I didn't pry any further, deciding to wait until we

had more privacy, and when Kane arrived Danny started discussing coursework with him. I picked up my phone to message Tilly and tell her to hurry up, but the Facebook app caught my eye.

I opened it and saw that I had a message from Benedict:

Was kind of waiting for you to holla back, babe. What – you don't like?

I must have blushed because Danny raised his left eyebrow and smirked. 'Are you looking at rude stuff?' he asked, stirring a huge amount of sugar into his drink.

'No,' I replied. 'Just some lad on Facebook.'

Kane looked up. His hair was in tight braids, and his mocha skin seemed to glow. I caught his eye and felt sort of embarrassed and guilty at once. 'What lad?' he asked quickly.

I shook my head. 'Doesn't matter,' I told him, feeling even guiltier, even though there was nothing going on between us.

'But you're blushing,' Danny pointed out. 'It *does* matter, obviously.'

I shook my head again, and wished that Danny would shut up. 'Just some boy,' I protested. 'In New York. He's sent me a message.'

'Show!' demanded Danny, grabbing at my phone and nearly toppling the table.

'Oi!' I shouted.

Kane was looking straight at me and I felt a twinge of panic. Weird or what? A couple seated nearby turned round, looking disgusted. I managed to keep hold of my phone but my face felt hot with embarrassment. The other customers must have thought we were morons.

'Show me, then,' Danny continued. 'Or is he that ugly?'

I blushed again. 'That's just it,' I said. 'He's fit. Like, really, *really* gorgeous.' I gave Kane another fleeting look.

'Sister,' said Danny, 'if he's *that* lovely, you'd show us . . .'

I sighed and gave Danny my phone. 'He's called Benedict,' I said.

Danny studied the screen, and then zoomed in. 'Wow!'

'See, told you.'

'Lily – he's absolutely *stunning*. Are you *sure* he's not gay?'

I smiled and shook my head. Kane mumbled something under his breath.

'What?' I asked him.

'Nothing,' he replied, looking away.

'Forget him – tell me about American Boy!' Danny insisted. 'Is this what you and Tilly were jabbering about this morning?'

35

'I don't know anything about him,' I replied.

'What?' asked Kane. 'Some random bloke just contacted you?'

'Yeah,' I replied. 'He just wants to be friends.' I took back my phone and put it away. 'Like I said, I don't know anything about him.'

He finds Girl #1 in her regular chat room. She is asking questions but no one replies. How unfortunate can one person be? the Spider wonders. Ignored in the real world, ignored virtually too. Still, not for long . . .

How are you? he types.

    Hey! I hoped you'd be in here, she replies.

    Are you ready?

    Yeah.

    And . . . ?

    Does it hurt?

    No – not really. Besides, when it's over, what does a touch of pain matter?

    Don't like pain, she tells him.

No one does, he replies.

Do you think they'll care?

Of course, he says. *You'll be remembered.*

Like that girl you told me about?

Yes – just like her.

For ever?

Yes – for ever.

I think I'm ready, she tells him.

You must be sure. You must do it right.

I know.

He tells her how to set up. To make sure that she posts the video blog first.

I can help, of course, he adds.

Would you?

I said that I would.

Seriously – will it hurt?

Forget about that, he replies. *Right now, they don't see you. They think you're a nobody. They ignore you. After this, though, they'll never forget who you are. This is a new world – you'll live for ever on the Web . . .*

I'll be a somebody?

A celebrity. A face on T-shirts and Internet blogs. A sensation . . .

When can we meet?

I'll be on again, same time tomorrow. We'll arrange it then.

Promise?

I won't let you down, he replies. *I am not like the others.*

Later, the Spider reminisces . . . It is a cold, wet November afternoon, in Balham, South London, years ago. He has skipped uni and decided to go home. The house he shares with five others sits on a side street, off Bedford Hill. The others are at lectures. Or so he thinks . . .

He enters through the rear kitchen door. The sink is overflowing with used dishes and the cooker covered in a thick layer of grime. He ignores the mess and walks into the living room, the stench of cigarettes and weed assaulting his senses. He takes the stairs and is halted by a muffled sound. It is a girl's scream. It comes from upstairs . . .

Excitement rises in his chest. He goes to investigate.

One of his housemates, his hair long, his chest bare, stands in front of a bedroom door. 'What are *you* doing here?' He is surprised.

The Spider, a few years older, can smell the boy's fear, and see it in his youthful face. 'Who's in your room,' he asks.

'No one!' the boy lies. 'Just some girl I met.'

More sounds come from his bedroom. Thuds, followed by a loud crash.

39

The Spider smiles. 'I think she's trying to escape,' he says.

'I don't know what you're talking about,' replies the boy, yet his face betrays him again.

When the girl screams once more, he drops his pretence. He crashes through the door and the Spider follows. Inside, a young girl, perhaps fourteen, wriggles in his grip. She is blonde, waif-like and half-naked. Her dirty clothes, lying across the room, suggest she lives on the streets.

'Please!' the boy pleads. 'It's not what it looks like. She told me she was eighteen!'

The Spider notices the camcorder lying on the floor. He grins.

The girl's expression changes. No longer does she think she'll be rescued.

'Keep her quiet,' he tells the younger man, as he closes the door behind him.

As the boy's eyes widen and his mouth falls open, the Spider picks up the camera. 'Would you like me to film?' the Spider asks. 'You seem to have your hands full already.'

The girl screams again. Her name is Emma Wallace.

4

When I checked Facebook a day later, I had three
more private messages from Benedict. I read each of
them, and smiled:

Holla back then, babe?
Great pic of you in that blue dress!
You got some seriously pretty eyes, girl!

I was sitting in Mum's car at Sainsbury's. She'd
gone back to collect the debit card she'd forgotten at
the till, which was unusually scatty for her. But she'd
had a long day so I didn't wind her up about it. A
green BMW pulled in next to Mum's red VW Golf.
It seemed a bit close and I gave the driver a glare
before realizing it was the IT technician from

school. I half smiled but he ignored me, locking his car and walking off, phone in hand. Most of our teachers lived around the school, so we saw them all the time.

I looked at my iPhone again, wondering how to respond to Benedict. I wanted to seem interested but not *too* keen. I didn't want to get all Molly Cooper on him. In the end, I decided to play cool. I doubted he'd be around anyway, and I didn't know the exact time difference between Leicester and New York.

I looked at his picture and smiled again. He was *so* gorgeous. Part of me began to wonder if he was even real. Like, was someone winding me up maybe?

Hey Benedict! Thanks for the friend request. I'm a bit confused though. How come you picked me?

I closed the app, thinking any reply might take a while, but my FB alert went off almost immediately.

Hey – she lives!!!?

I shook my head. The boy was *eager*.

Wow – that was quick – LOL!

Again, it took only seconds for him to get back to me.

Bored, you know? Just chillin' – surfing the Net. You've cheered me up! You OK?

Cool – just shopping with my mum.

Mum as pretty as you?

Prettier – she's hot!

This was true. I looked like her – only she was skinnier than me, and prettier. She had long dark hair, big chocolate eyes and a smile that always made you feel better. When we went shopping together, I often caught men eyeing her up. She was a babe.

Doubt that – you're gorgeous! And we've got loads in common.

How'd you know that?

I saw your 'likes' lists. Read most of your favourite books and I love Bob Marley too!

We exchanged more little messages until my mum turned up. I told Benedict to contact me later. But when I got in, he'd already sent three more messages.

'You're always on that phone,' said Mum as we unpacked.

I looked at her. The worry lines around her eyes were growing deeper, and she looked tired. She taught at a different school to mine, and her work got her down.

'If my PC wasn't so rubbish, maybe I wouldn't be on the phone,' I told her.

'That's not what I meant,' she replied. 'Try the real world for a change.'

'Mum!'

I'd wanted a laptop for ages – something that

worked and didn't crowd my desk like an ancient monument. My PC was so old that Tilly laughed whenever she came over. She called it the 'abacus'.

'I'll get you a laptop when I decide to,' said Mum. 'Now put the chilled stuff in the fridge.'

Ten minutes later, I was at my desk. I kept my PC on constantly, and never signed out of Facebook or anything else, otherwise getting back in took for ever. It did mean that Tilly often hijacked my Facebook page when she came over – but only to leave messages about how much she loved me, and other, more random stuff.

On Facebook, one of Benedict's messages in particular made me grin.

Got three things I love. Baseball, burgers and beautiful ladies. If you came at me with a quarter-pounder and Red Sox tickets, I'd just die.

I didn't know who the Red Sox were so I searched the name before replying.

How come a New York boy loves a Boston baseball team?

My mom is Boston all the way. She never gave me no choice.

What about your dad?

He died when I was a kid. Never really knew him.

I felt bad instantly.

44

You still there?

Yeah – sorry about your dad. Mine died when I was young too. I feel horrible.

Don't. You weren't to know – how could you?

But I just assumed.

What happened to your dad?

I wondered what to say. I missed my dad all the time, but as each year passed, I started to forget stuff about him. That made me feel really guilty and I'd only ever talked to Mum and Tilly about it. But something about Benedict's interest made me feel warm inside. I liked that he cared enough to ask.

It's hard to think about. Dad just never came back from work one day. He was driving home and there was accident and he died.

That's cruel, Lily. Life can be awful sometimes. Mine died from a heart attack, so my mum says – sudden too. I never really knew him much.

Do you miss him?

Every day.

His reply rattled me a bit – but not in a bad way. I had always believed I was odd for not letting my dad's memory go, but Benedict was just like me – and that felt lovely.

It's weird. Some days I think about him a lot, others he's hardly there. Makes me feel guilty.

He wouldn't want that, Lily. I don't think any father would. You shouldn't feel bad about that. It's natural, I guess. Besides, there's always something positive that comes from a negative.

I wondered what he meant.

How so?

We've got losing our fathers in common. Like, we understand how that feels. Instant connection sorta thing.

Later, when he'd signed off, I thought about our messages. I'd had two boyfriends, ever. Both of those were stupid little girl crushes – and neither lasted more than a few days. The first had been Will Baker, who bought me a white chocolate muffin and wanted to hold my hand in school as a reward. After him, Tilly paired me up with Faisal Mulla. That lasted for about a week until I went off him. He had bad breath and was really immature. He got upset when I dumped him, and I felt awful for ages.

What I'd *never* had was that spark you were supposed to get with a proper boyfriend. The chemistry I'd read about in books, or in the movies Tilly and I liked watching together. Often I'd see couples on the street, so caught up in each other that they ignored the world around them. Couples who seemed to be attracted to each other like magnets. I'd never had that connection with anyone.

There was Kane, who had been my dream boy for ages now but who would never want someone as plain as me. He didn't even know I liked him. The atmosphere didn't exactly crackle with desire when we spoke, either. But chatting online with Benedict seemed easy. It seemed so natural. And he understood about my dad too, and cared enough to ask. That felt like it *meant* something.

Then Tilly's voice popped into my head.

I thought you couldn't chat to people online, you pedantic cow? it said.

Eyeing Benedict's photo again, I felt all warm and fuzzy inside.

Downstairs, Mum was marking coursework and having a glass of red wine. She smiled, and asked if I was OK.

'Yeah,' I told her, as I remembered that I'd seen her ex-boyfriend today at school. He was an ex-teacher who'd gone on to become a governor there. 'By the way – I saw Dave earlier.'

Mum raised an eyebrow at the mention of him. 'Oh?' she replied. 'How was he?'

'We didn't really chat,' I told her. 'I just waved at him.'

'And you're telling me this because . . . ?'

'I dunno,' I replied, smiling. 'Playing Cupid?'

My mum's relationship with Dave had lasted

three years. He'd even moved in with us. After a dodgy start, I grew to really like him – he was cool and funny and listened to great music. When he left two years ago, I'd cried. And my mum had been unhappy ever since – at least that's how I saw it. She had never explained why they'd split up, even though I'd asked, but I guess it was her business. Which is what she thought too.

'Mind your own, miss,' she said. 'I *do* need to speak to him, though.'

'You *know* you still love him,' I told her.

'*Lily* . . .'

Her tone was a warning. A sign that I'd overstepped the line. I told her I was going to read a book.

'Hallelujah,' she replied. 'Time away from that *stupid* phone.'

The Spider's virtual life is a busy one. Each thread he weaves links to every other. A lesser man might get confused and make a mistake, but not the Spider.

He crosses to a different laptop, signs into the account of yet another false persona – a thirty-year-old female executive called Charlotte – and sends a message to Boy #1.

Can't stop thinking about you. We need to meet.

The boy is waiting, as though he's anticipated the message – longed for it to arrive.

I wanna meet you too. When?

Soon, baby, soon. I have to be careful – stupid laws.

I know – I'm nearly 16 – this country is ridiculous. Anyone suspicious?

No, Charlotte – I haven't told anyone. Just you and me.

Be careful babe. I can't get caught.

You won't. So when do we get together?

I've got a few things to sort out, but after that. A week – maybe two?

Really?

Yes, really.

Excited now . . .

Look – I've got to go. I'll message you later – on your phone.

OK.

Maybe you can show me more? I like when you do that.

I like it too, but I want to SEE you. Is your webcam still broken?

Yes and I've been too busy with work to get it fixed. I'll sort it out soon, I promise. And you'll like what you see.

I can't wait.

Nor can I.

The Spider sits back, as his mobile phone lights up. It's the OTHER – his fellow traveller on the Dark Side of the Web. Do I have some plans for you, the Spider thinks. He smiles and answers the phone . . .

5

That weekend, I went into town with Tilly. I wanted to talk about Benedict and the messages we'd been sending each other, but didn't know where to begin. I'd meant to speak to Tilly earlier but hadn't found the right moment yet. Part of me wanted to keep him all to myself, just for a while, and then there was my fatal flaw too – embarrassment.

I wasn't getting much chance anyway because Tilly was on about the summer holidays, still five months away. We had our GCSEs to deal with first.

'We're not going away,' said Tilly. 'Mum can't afford it.'

'So we'll spend summer *together*,' I said. 'Just you and me. Celebrating our great results and planning the future.'

'In bikinis, sipping cocktails in the garden?'

'Er . . . no,' I said, almost shuddering at the thought of people seeing me in a bikini. 'Besides – it'll probably rain the whole time.'

'Bloody hate this country sometimes,' said Tilly.

We got off the bus, to a couple of harsh glares. Tilly was often loud in public, so I was used to the dirty looks. I didn't like it exactly, but I loved Tilly too much to say anything. Town was packed with shoppers, and a street market was on. Food, jewellery and exotic ingredients. As we walked past a hog-roast stall, my stomach started to grumble. I saw the stallholder pass across two rolls crammed with pork and onions. I wanted to grab them and run.

'Do you think I'm fat?' I asked my best friend, still thinking about bikinis. 'Like, all joking aside?'

I was wearing leggings with black boots and a navy floral print dress over the top. It was one of the five combinations I usually wore for school so that the bitchy girls wouldn't call me a tramp. Being a girl at our 'no uniform required' upper school was hard work. So many expectations to live up to. And no matter how much I pretended not to care, I couldn't help it. No one wanted to stand out. No one wanted to be like Amy.

'No,' said Tilly. 'Why even ask that again? You know I think you're gorgeous.'

I shrugged. Tilly annoyed me sometimes by being so loud, but I must have annoyed her too with my weight paranoia. I guess we were evens.

'Just wondered,' I replied. 'I was thinking about Amy and all the crap people give her.'

Tilly stopped to look at some rings. 'Amy?' she asked, as she picked through the stock.

'Yeah,' I said. 'I just don't think she's that fat,' I added. 'Like, do those people who bully her think I'm fat too?'

Tilly gave me a puzzled look. 'Why would they think that?'

'Because I'm not that much smaller than Amy,' I pointed out. It was true. I was a size twelve at least – what were people saying about my thighs and arse?

Tilly smiled. 'And why should you be?' she asked. 'I mean – look at me. My ass is so bony my knickers don't stay up!'

'Yeah, well mine is so big I can't find any knickers to wear!' I replied.

'No it isn't,' she replied. 'You are a babe – a voluptuous, pretty, lovely babe. Any boy would be lucky to have you.'

'My bum is *huge!*' I protested.

'Don't be such a drama queen,' said Tilly. 'Besides,

53

all that perfect body stuff is crap anyway. When I'm rich and famous, it'll be for my brains, not plastic tits and anorexia.'

Later, as we ate Wagamama's for lunch, Tilly asked why my body shape bothered me so much.

'You shouldn't care,' she added. 'Your body isn't the only thing that makes you a person.'

I shook my head. 'I know I *shouldn't* be bothered,' I said, pushing some udon noodles around with chopsticks. 'I just can't help it.'

'This have anything to do with Benedict?' she asked, a sly grin breaking on her face.

'No!'

Tilly giggled. 'That means yes!' she squealed. 'Has he been in touch again?'

I nodded. 'Every day,' I revealed. 'He's really nice.'

Tilly ate some of her chilli-beef ramen. 'Nice?' she asked after swallowing her mouthful. 'What the hell does nice even mean?'

'As in he's *not* a dickhead?'

'Yeah,' she said, 'but *nice*? Cardigans are nice. *Grandmas* are nice.' She grinned again. 'What did Benedict say?'

I found a prawn, and put it in my mouth. It was delicious – hot and fiery. I only replied when I'd eaten it all. 'Just that he likes me,' I said. 'Calls me pretty and stuff.'

Benedict seemed to have a much higher opinion of my looks than I did.

'OOH LA LA!!!' said Tilly. 'You lucky cow!'

I shook my head. 'He's in New York, remember?' I reminded her.

'So?'

'So,' I continued, 'even if he does like me, we can't go and watch a film or something.'

Even as I spoke, in my head I saw us strolling through town, hand in hand, laughing and joking. It was a fairy tale, though – a scene from Hollywood – it was never going to happen.

'What if he came to England one day?' asked Tilly.

'Yeah – and what if WAGs had brains . . .' I rolled my eyes.

'You never know,' said Tilly.

I looked up and recognized our form tutor, Mr Warren, waiting to be seated. He was our favourite teacher. He was young and cool, and he treated us like adults. He wore brown desert boots, dark blue jeans and a yellow tartan-checked shirt, and his light brown hair was cut short. He had deep brown eyes too, which Tilly loved.

'Oh my God!' I whispered.

'What?'

'Mr Warren – on his own!'

Tilly turned her head so fast I thought her neck might snap. 'Where?' she asked, before spotting him – *just* as he saw us. As her face did a beetroot impression, I waved.

Mr Warren walked over, smiling. 'Hello, girls,' he said. 'Enjoying your weekend?'

'Hi, sir!' I replied. 'Are you on your own?'

He made a point of looking around to check. 'Looks that way, Lily,' he said.

'You can sit with us,' I told him. 'If you want to.'

Tilly shot me a dirty look, as Mr Warren shook his head. 'Oh, thanks, girls, but I'm meeting a mate,' he told us. 'He's late.'

'Oh,' said Tilly, pretending not to care. 'We were nearly finished anyway.'

'Yes,' said our form tutor. 'I can see that. Have fun.' He turned and walked back to the till area.

I smiled at my best friend. 'How red did you go?' I joked.

'Shut up!'

'I forgot – you *likey* Mr Warren.'

'No!' she protested. 'He's just nice, that's all.'

'What?' I asked. '*Nice* nice, or nice like *Benedict* nice?'

* * *

56

We window-shopped for the rest of the afternoon, before heading to mine to watch DVDs. Mum was away – at a teachers' union conference that sounded about as interesting as beige knickers look.

Tilly was hungry again, and I wondered where she put it all. Her speedy metabolism made me envious. We ordered pizza and cookie-dough, and I felt guilty even before it arrived. Not that I'd eat much anyway – I never did. My relationship with food was like that – look, want, feel guilt, avoid. It did my head in.

'You've got a message,' Tilly said, nodding at my phone.

It was Benedict again – but I ignored it. I *wanted* to respond, but a girl *can* seem too eager.

'I'll reply tomorrow,' I told her. 'Tonight is sister time . . .'

'Don't be getting all lesbo on me,' she joked.

'As if . . .'

My phone vibrated again – a text this time. I read it quickly.

'Danny,' I said. 'Wants to come over and talk.'

Tilly nodded. 'Up to you,' she said. 'Your house.'

'But what about girlie time?' I asked.

She grinned. Her big blue eyes sparkled above almost perfect teeth. Her hair was tied up, and her ears were small and sort of pointed at the top. She looked like an ice-blonde pixie. My best friend was seriously hot.

'Who's a bigger girl than Gay Singh?' she asked. 'PJs, pizza and penis-talk – perfect!'

I replied to Danny – telling him to bring booze, which he often 'borrowed' from his dad's stash. It was usually cider.

Tilly asked for my phone when I was done.

'Why?'

'I want to check out Benedict some more,' she said. 'You know – make sure he isn't playing you or anything . . .'

'Check out his muscles, more like,' I joked.

Despite the humour, I felt a pang of jealousy – something I'd never felt before where Tilly was concerned. I felt guilty.

'You OK?' she asked.

'Yeah,' I told her. 'Why?'

Tilly shook her head. 'You looked a bit distant for a moment, that's all.'

'I'm fine,' I told her.

She nodded and took my phone. 'OMG!' She zoomed in on Benedict's abs.

6

Benedict kept up the regular contact, starting the next day. Videos, messages – my Facebook wall had never been so busy.

Molly Cooper liked most of them, and I wondered whether she had sent Benedict a friend request after seeing how good-looking he was. Knowing her, she'd probably sent him a selfie too, just to *introduce* herself. Molly was pretty and nice enough – but she was self-obsessed. She wanted to be famous – like the celebrities she followed fanatically on Twitter. But as far as I knew, she didn't act or sing, or do anything that might bring her fame. She just fantasized about being talent-spotted and becoming an overnight sensation. Like fame was all that mattered.

Several of Benedict's messages were flirtatious, and the last one asked when I could chat again.

I replied eagerly.

Sorry I missed you. Had a girl-only night with my best friend, Tilly – our names rhyme! Tired today. You around?

I hit *send* and switched to Twitter, where Danny was posting positive quotes about being homosexual, and re-tweeting some of the vile insults he was receiving as a result. When I switched back to Facebook a few minutes later, I saw that Benedict had responded.

Hey – no worries about last night. You good?

Yeah – what about you?

Benedict took a while.

Sorry babe – had to help my mum with something. I've got a shoot next week – excited.

My brain went into dim-mode because I was so tired.

What shoot?

A modelling shoot, babe. Got a contract with GAP here in NYC. Big job.

I grinned to myself. This lad, who was an *actual*, like, no bullshit *model*, wanted to be my friend. Not only that – he thought I was pretty and flirted with me online. Yet again, I couldn't believe my luck. All I needed was for him to suddenly appear in Leicester and I was set.

Was wondering about that too, Benedict. So, you're really a model then?

Yeah and call me Benny – my mum and my friends do. Did you think I was lying?

I felt bad and cursed myself for making him feel that way.

Not lying – just thought you might be boasting or something. Boys I know do that stuff.

Baby – you just met a different kinda boy.

How different?

Like all the way different, Lily. I ain't one to play a girl. Don't need to. I'm happy about who I am. You should be too!

Who says I'm not?

No one, Lily – I was just guessing. When I call you pretty or beautiful, you seem embarrassed by it.

That's because I'm not beautiful. I'm not ugly, I know – but beautiful . . . ?

See – you're asking for my opinion. You shouldn't care what I think, babe. If I don't like you, that's my problem. Same goes for anyone else who you know.

Don't get you.

I couldn't *stop* wondering what people thought of me. It was something that bothered me all the time. I knew it was silly but I couldn't help it.

Never ask for someone's opinion of your looks. You are what you are. People accept that or they can fuck off!

Benedict's advice struck at something inside me. It seemed clear and real, even more than Tilly's had seemed. How could some *lad*, online, make more sense than my best friend?

He continued.

Like you know those girls that ask to be rated according to looks?

I know some of those.

I see it all, Lily. They want strangers to rate their asses or their boobs or whatever. They got no self-respect.

Yep – know some of them too.

One of your friends – Molly Cooper – she sent me a pic. Hold on – I'll forward it to you.

She's not my friend. Not exactly.

Benny took his time, so I messaged Tilly, to ask about a project we needed to hand in.

You got email, Lily? Facebook won't let me attach a photo for some reason.

I sent him my address and waited. My PC tower's fan began to croak and splutter, and I thought it might catch fire. The screen went black and then came back on. It had been doing that for a while. I just knew it was ready to die.

Check your inbox, Lily.

When the photo finally downloaded, it showed Molly lying on her bed, wearing just a very tight yellow skirt and black bra. Another of her famous selfies. I went back to Facebook, feeling annoyed. I didn't hate Molly, but sometimes she was difficult to like. What possessed her to do things like that? And then I started to feel bad about judging her. Maybe I was just jealous of her looks and figure, I thought. Which made my judgements unfair. I tried to calm down before replying, and when I did, I said only a little of what I was actually thinking.

That's typical of her.

It's girls like her I was talking about. She's too blatant. I like my girls to have more class.

My phone vibrated – Tilly telling me she was on her way round.

Molly's OK – just a bit insecure, I reckon. And what do you mean your girls??? How many you got? LOL.

You're funny, babe. You know what I meant. I like girls like you.

But you hardly know me???

Getting there. Hopefully we can be real good friends???

Hope so too.

And I really did. I liked our chats and I liked Benedict. It was like having a boyfriend, or at least *sort* of. Someone to tell what I was thinking and feeling who wasn't Tilly or my mum. They were great, but having a boy to talk to was exciting.

Gotta go in a minute, Benedict. Stuff to do.

Shame but I'll holla at you later. Maybe we can hook up via webcam??

Ah – no webcam. My PC was made before the invention of the Internet I reckon!

You should get one. I've got a spare if you'd like???

Doh! You're in New York – what you gonna do – fly it over to me?

You ain't heard of the post? They don't got that where you live?

Let me see if I can get one here.

Up to you, Lily, but I got one just lying here – unused. Why waste your money?

Don't worry, I'll get one.

Up to you, like I said, but this is just going to waste. Don't say I didn't ask!

I won't – better go. Lovely to talk to you.

You sure I can't post that webcam to you?

I'll let you know. Speak to you later, yeah?

Yeah.

Things are moving quickly with Boy #1. He pays no attention to online security. He doesn't disguise his IP address or use any sort of proxy server. He doesn't even clear his search history or empty his cache. Everything the Spider needs is sitting there, waiting to be taken – photos, files, deleted items. The Spider can change his desktop wallpaper or hijack his social-media accounts – even send emails in his name. And considering just how much pornography the boy consumes, it makes no sense that he does not attempt to cover his tracks. Oh well, it's his funeral . . .

The Spider likes to play games. He enjoys pulling the strings and making his victims dance. He's an expert too – been doing it for a long, long time. The Web is full of fools with low self-esteem – people just begging for acceptance. For some meaning to be given to their sorry little lives. The Spider weaves his threads around such people.

He has been watching this group for a while – biding his time. He started with the fat girl – she was the first and the easiest. He used her friend list on Facebook to find more victims. The OTHER's special interest in young ones made the choosing so much easier. His accomplice's tastes mean nothing to the Spider, however. His interest isn't sexual. The Spider does this because he wants to – because he *can*.

Now the Spider is ready to act. Thing is, they'll never see him coming. They'll never see him because . . .

Well, because this time he's already there . . .

7

That evening Mum realized we didn't have any milk. She was busy marking school projects, so she sent me out into the cold. The general store was only five minutes' walk away, but I complained anyway. I wrapped myself up in a thick navy jacket, and wrapped a light blue scarf around my neck. The sky was cloudless and the temperature had fallen. I walked quickly, my hands in my pockets.

As I approached the shop, I passed a busy Indian restaurant. I cut across the packed car park, watching families walk out, all happy and smiling, and I thought about my dad. Then I saw her – Amy. She was sitting on the low wall that circled the pub, on her own. She had a thin grey hoodie on, and her skin was scarlet in the cold. She didn't hear me, and jumped when I called out her name.

'You scared me,' she complained.

'Why are you sitting out here?' I asked. It was freezing – the sort of night when you only went out properly wrapped up, if at all. Yet here was Amy, shivering and sniffing back snot, and occasionally wiping her nose with a sleeve.

'Just thinking,' she told me.

Her long hair was packed under a black cap, and she rubbed her hands together to keep them warm. I felt myself growing concerned and didn't really understand why.

'Thinking about what, Amy?'

She shrugged, flashed me a quick glance and then looked away. 'Just stuff,' she said. 'You remember when we were eight?'

Her question was so random that I didn't know what to say. This situation was odd. It felt like something was happening but I didn't know what.

'I came to your birthday party – me and Tilly together?' she added.

'Oh yeah,' I said, taking a seat beside her. 'What about it?'

'Oh, nothing,' Amy replied. 'I was just remembering – that's all. You were always really nice to me. You and Tilly both.'

I nudged her with my shoulder – trying to cheer

her up. But my attempt felt inappropriate and it didn't work anyway. Amy still looked so glum.

'We were friends,' I said. 'Why wouldn't we be nice to you?'

'Guess you were, once,' she replied. 'Dunno about recently . . .'

'What about the other day – when I came to see you?' I asked, feeling a bit miffed. I knew we weren't close but I'd never ignored Amy or been unkind to her. Tilly had dumped food on someone's *head* to stop them bullying Amy. 'I was trying to help then, but you just shut the door in my face.'

'I know,' she said, as two lads rode past on mountain bikes. 'I'm sorry about that – it was mean.'

I shook my head. Amy might have been acting a bit weird but she wasn't nasty. If I'd been through her ordeal, I think I'd be feeling the same way. 'You were angry and upset,' I replied, hoping she'd realize that I wanted to understand. 'You're not mean, Amy. It's just not you.'

'Still wasn't right,' she said. She was hunched forward, her shoulders raised, and her clothes had a musty odour.

'So what *are* you doing here?' I asked again. I had a sense that something was wrong, but unless Amy told me what that was, I couldn't help. And I really felt as though she needed help.

'Just ... nothing,' she said. 'I was bored and I wanted some fresh air.'

I looked at my phone. It was nearly eight p.m. and the shop was about to close. 'Wait here,' I told her. 'I have to grab some milk. You want anything?'

Amy shook her head. But in the shop, I remembered that she loved Mars bars. I bought us one each, and went back to where she was sitting. Behind me, the shopkeeper locked his doors.

Amy hadn't moved. If anything, she had curled up even more – and she looked very, very cold now.

'Why don't you come over to mine?' I asked her. 'Mum'd love to see you.'

'Can't,' she said. 'I have to go.'

'Well, have this then,' I replied, handing her the chocolate bar. 'You like these, yeah?'

She took the Mars and smiled. 'Love them,' she said, her eyes showing just a hint of sparkle.

She had plump pink lips, shaped like a Cupid's bow, and really smooth, olive skin. I wondered why people couldn't see how lovely she was. Why was her weight the first thing they noticed? Amy was a babe underneath it all.

'Didn't you puke on my presents at my eighth birthday party?' I asked her.

Amy nodded. 'Yeah – I had too much lemonade!' she replied. 'But you didn't even get angry.'

I smiled. 'I know – weird, huh?'

'You went and got kitchen towels,' Amy continued, 'and tried to clean me up. That was so cool.'

'All I did was spread the puke over your face,' I said, grinning at the memory. 'Mum had to do it properly.'

'Yeah – she was always lovely.'

'She still is,' I told her. 'Come on – come round and say hello.'

'Things change,' said Amy. 'You've moved on, and I'm not the same any more.'

'That's because you're unhappy,' I told her.

Amy put the Mars in the pocket of her hooded top and shook her head. The wind began to pick up around us, and I shivered.

'I'm not unhappy any more,' she replied. 'Yeah – I hate the bullying and that, but I don't care any more – not really. I've found something else.'

'What . . . or who?'

But Amy just shook her head slowly and stared off into the distance. I watched a grey BMW drive past, and recognized the driver. It was Dave. I wondered if he was going to see Mum, and I felt excited – like I was a child again. Dave had never replaced my dad but he'd come close. He'd been there for me – always interested in my life and my friends, pushing me to improve at school. The thought of him and Mum getting back together made me happy. But then I stopped being so stupid. Talk about jumping to conclusions. Dave lived near us – he could have been going anywhere. I had no reason but hope to think that he might be getting back with my mum.

Amy stood up. 'I'd better go,' she said.

'Who have you found?' I asked. 'You said something similar the other day too.'

Amy shrugged again. 'Just some friends online,' she told me. 'People who understand what I'm going through.'

'Like a support group or something?' I asked, hoping it was what she meant. I'd spoken to my mum about Amy's problems in the past and recalled her suggesting something similar. It was exactly what Amy needed – to be around people who made her feel good and didn't judge her over something so stupid as weight.

Amy nodded. 'Yeah – something like that,' she said. 'Take care, Lily.'

'Come and have lunch with me and Tilly tomorrow,' I told her. 'Just once?'

Amy half smiled. 'Let's see what tomorrow brings,' she said, walking off.

I watched her for a while before heading in the

opposite direction. When I got in, Dave wasn't there, and my heart sank a little – silly, but true. He and my mum were perfect for each other. If only they could see that too. Disappointed, I went up to my room. I was supposed to be studying – GCSEs were looming like a thunderstorm on the horizon. I had dreams about becoming a lawyer or maybe doing something for a publisher. I loved the idea of getting paid to work on novels. Only it all seemed so far away, the road blocked by a huge mountain called exams. Exams that I had to revise for, if I stood any chance at all.

But Benedict was online, as were Danny and Tilly, so instead of working towards the brighter future I dreamed of, I sat up and messaged them instead, only stopping when my eyes grew sore.

The Spider watches the recording again. He smiles all the way through. Girl #1 is good. Better than he ever imagined. Meeting her had been exciting. Being his real self, out in the actual world, had been exciting. The shock on her face was worth everything. But nothing was more exhilarating than watching the story end . . .

Girl #1 is on screen. She's in some woods. Her eyes are wide, her mousy hair oily. Eyes rimmed with red, clothes dishevelled, black cap skewed, she looks much older than her fifteen years. She is talking to the camera – reading something the Spider helped her to write. The Spider is filming every word.

'. . . *understand how it feels,*' she continues. '*To be ignored and treated like nothing.*'

She holds up a picture. A pretty brunette teenager stares out. Her cheeks are sunken, her eyes tired. The headline above tells of tragedy and innocence lost.

'*Well, this,*' she tells her audience. '*This is Maya Brown. She was nobody until she went. Now she lives for ever. Don't believe me? Google her name . . .*'

She shows more photographs, printed from the Net. Ginny Peters, Bradley Coombs, Tyler Jenkins . . .

'*They were all nobodies, but not any more. This life is so average. There's nothing to do, nowhere to go. Just the same old thing, all the time. Just school and home and town and Facebook. It's all so regular. One day you'll wake up, all of you, and it will be over. You won't ever be famous. You won't ever be rich. You'll never have the dream job you wanted. You'll be middle-aged, with your dreams buried and your energy gone. Not me, though. I'm going to live for ever. You laughed at me, called me names. Now I'm going to look down on you, as you cry at my grave. And I'm gonna have the last laugh . . .*'

The Spider feels a surge of adrenalin – *of control.* He is exhilarated, energized and ecstatic. And he realizes something else too. He is *addicted* – fixated. He wants more of this feeling – more of this power. He wants to bathe in his dominance – his supremacy over others.

Does God exist – and if so, is *this* how He feels?

8

Two days later, as Tilly and I entered student reception at school, Molly Cooper ran past, crying her eyes out.

'What's *she* done?' asked Tilly. 'Posted a clothed selfie by mistake?' Tilly was joking but her timing was off, and she knew it. As soon as the words left her mouth, I saw guilt in her eyes. 'Me and my big mouth,' she said.

I wondered why Molly was crying and was about to go and ask her when Danny and Kane appeared. The skin around Danny's eyes was red and puffy because he'd been crying, and he looked stunned.

'What's going on?' I asked them. I felt a touch of panic – something was wrong.

'Amy,' Kane said softly. 'Ain't you heard?'

Kane's usually handsome face was strained. He was tall and muscular, with braided hair and a beautiful friendly smile. Only there was no sign of his smile that morning. Seeing his expression, and hearing him mention Amy made me even more uneasy.

'Shit is bad,' he added.

My stomach caved in on itself. Molly and Danny crying about Amy? Kane acting like the world was about to end?

'What *about* Amy?' Tilly asked him. She looked confused too.

'She died,' Kane revealed. 'Last night – she killed herself. Left a video blog. It's been on telly this morning . . .'

I felt Tilly take hold of my arm. I wanted to puke. My hands grew cold. I fought back tears. I'd only seen her the other night. I hadn't even told Tilly about it yet. How could she be dead?

'Oh God!' Tilly whispered. 'Amy . . .'

I saw the principal, Dr Woods, walk in, her expression grave. With her were two police officers and a couple of governors, one of whom was Dave – I spotted his tall, broad ex-rugby-player frame.

He saw us and came over. 'Are you OK?' he asked, his eyes wandering from me to my friends and back again. 'All of you?'

The air around me felt heavy, as though it was trying to crush me. I could hear my blood pumping. 'We've just heard,' I told him, wiping my eyes.

'It's a terrible business,' he said, his icy-blue eyes serious and sad. 'If you need anything at all – just ask. That goes for all of you.'

'Thanks, Mr Thomas,' said Tilly.

'Mum said she'd call you,' I told him. Somehow, even in my shock, the little girl that wanted Dave back in her life spoke up. And I'd called Tilly's timing bad?

Dave nodded but his eyes looked cheerless. 'I'd really like that,' he said. 'I'd better go now, though.' And he walked off with the other governors and the police.

'Get to your forms, people!' Dr Woods called when we didn't move on. 'Please!'

The four of us trudged to Mr Warren's room, past other equally dazed pupils. There was a hush around the corridors that I'd never experienced before – stunned silence everywhere. Our form tutor was by his door, talking to Mr Dhindsa, one of the deputy principals. Kane walked on to his own class.

'No idea,' I heard Mr Dhindsa say.

'Surely it has to matter, Kal?' replied Mr Warren. 'She'd been bullied . . .'

They saw us approach, and stepped to one side,

eager to keep their conversation private. In the room, we found people crying, and others whispering to each other. Manisha was sobbing into her cashmere scarf. I looked at Tilly, whose face had turned scarlet.

'You stupid little bitch!' she screamed at Manisha.

I understood Tilly's rage. Manisha and her gang had tormented Amy. If it wasn't Amy's weight, it was the labels she didn't wear, or the trips she couldn't afford to go on. If Amy *had* killed herself because of bullying, Manisha and her friends were partly to blame. And there she was, crying like her own sister had died.

But now wasn't the right time for a fight.

'Tilly – leave it,' I said, holding her back.

Manisha stood and swore at Tilly.

'You *dirty* little hypocrite,' yelled Tilly. 'How *dare* you cry after giving her all that shit!'

'You don't know nothing!' Manisha yelled back.

'You little slag!' Tilly leaped at Manisha and grabbed her wavy hair.

Manisha screamed.

'TILLY ANDERSON!!!' It was Mr Dhindsa, and he did not look pleased. His bearded face was set in anger. 'GET TO MY OFFICE – NOW!'

Tilly let go and pushed Manisha away.

'You get told, bitch!' Manisha crowed. 'Run along . . .'

Tilly tried to grab her again, but Mr Warren intervened. He whispered something in Tilly's ear, and she calmed down almost instantly, though her face was still flushed, and she glared at Manisha. 'Stupid cow!' she spat.

'Come on now, Tilly,' said Mr Warren, his tone soothing and assured. 'This isn't how to deal with what you're feeling.'

Then he led her away towards Mr Dhindsa's office and Manisha turned to me.

'You got anything to say?' she asked, throwing down a challenge.

Before I could react, Danny stepped in. 'I wouldn't wanna be *you* later,' he told Manisha. 'Tilly's gonna *murder* you. Not before time, either. Your hair looks like a melted plastic wig – Tilly would be doing you a favour.'

'Who cares what you think?' spat Manisha. 'Batty bwoi!'

'Shut up!' I yelled, surprising myself and everyone else – I usually avoided confrontation. Only I was angry and upset, and at that moment I didn't care at all. And you know what? It felt good too, like a release.

Mr Dhindsa heard everything. 'Manisha Patel,' he said. 'My office too.'

'But, sir!' she protested. 'That cow attacked me!'

Mr Dhindsa shook his head. 'Homophobic comments won't be tolerated,' he told her. 'I don't care why you were fighting, or with whom. Two days' exclusion.'

'*What?*' Manisha moaned. 'How is that even *fair?*'

He led her out too, and the rest of us sat down.

A couple of lads glared at Danny. When I warned him, he just shrugged it off.

'Not to worry,' he said. 'They're probably wanting a snog.'

I wanted to smile, but there was nothing there but sadness and anger. And the memory of my last conversation with Amy. I could smell her musty clothes and feel the warmth from her body as we sat on that wall. The look of childlike pleasure in her eyes when I gave her the Mars bar. After that, I couldn't stop the tears, and I wanted to go home and be with my mum.

We were summoned to the hall in year groups later that morning, Year Sevens first, and then working up towards our year. No one spoke as we filed in – which was really unusual – and apart from a few sobs, there was an eerie quiet. Dr Woods was waiting for us, alongside one of the police officers. She looked as shocked as the rest of us. Our form tutors lined the hall, and I saw Tilly sitting near Mr Warren. I nodded at her, and she half smiled.

I sat with Danny, Max and Kane and whispered to them, 'What's going on?'

Kane shook his head. 'Dunno,' he replied. 'But got to be summat to do with Amy.'

'Yeah,' I said, 'but why are the police still here?'

I looked around the hall, and the young IT tech caught my eye. He was geeky-looking, with long dark hair and round glasses. But it was his T-shirt that I noticed. It was bright red, with a peace symbol, a love heart and a baseball printed on it. Underneath were the words 'Peace, Love, Red Sox'. I immediately thought of Benedict.

Mr Dhindsa spoke first. He thanked us for being mature, then asked that we remain quiet for our principal's talk. A small murmur went round.

'Year Eleven,' began Dr Woods, 'I know that most of you are aware of the tragic news this morning, indeed perhaps from last night. As a school, we are conscious of the situation, and I have decided to speak to you directly. Amy's death has shocked and saddened each of us. As a school, we will face the days and weeks ahead together. We will also show support and sympathy to the family of our dear departed friend, pupil and peer. Alongside all of you, I feel a deep sense of grief and disbelief. I do not think words can convey the dreadful effect Amy's loss will have on her family.'

She cleared her throat, and I shot Tilly another glance, only she didn't notice. Instead, she leaned towards Mr Warren and said something. Our form tutor shook his head but didn't reply.

'However,' Dr Woods continued, 'we must also consider the circumstances in which Amy chose this most terrible of fates. I suspect many of you know what I'm talking about, but let me explain to those who do not. It has been brought to my attention that Amy was severely bullied, both at school and online . . .'

Another murmur went up, followed by excited whispers.

Mr Dhindsa stood up. 'Year Eleven!' he yelled. 'You've behaved impeccably so far. Don't ruin it now . . .'

Dr Woods cleared her throat again. The police officer standing next to her looked stern with his cropped grey hair, narrow lips, and pointed nose. His eyes were serious and his jaw clenched.

'The accusations I've received are very, very grave,' Dr Woods told us. 'I have seen evidence of the abuse Amy suffered online – her parents provided me with it. And, let me tell you, Year Eleven, it made me cry. The vile and nasty victimization that

I saw is *completely* unacceptable. As of *this* morning, any further incidents of a similar nature will result in instant, *permanent* exclusion. I cannot stress strongly enough how *serious* this episode is. As a school, we will not tolerate such behaviour from our pupils . . . real *or* virtual.'

I heard a few gasps around the hall as Dr Woods gathered her thoughts. I thought about Amy and the nasty jibes she'd suffered on Facebook. Some of the people sitting in the hall, looking shocked and saddened, had been the same people who had hounded her. I felt myself getting angry again.

Danny put his hand in mine.

'What?' I whispered.

'Nothing,' he said, his eyes watery. 'Just sad . . .' He used his other hand to wipe away tears as our principal resumed.

'We've had no choice but to call in the police. There *will* be an investigation into this matter, and let me stress this – *anyone* proven to be involved in these disgusting actions will be in serious trouble. The good name of our school will not be tarnished in this way. I hope that I am making myself absolutely clear on this. You are only months away from your final exams – do *not* let your futures be ruined by such behaviour.' Dr Woods turned to the policeman. 'DI Meadows will now speak to you.

Afterwards, you will be split by gender. The boys must go to gym. Ladies, you will stay here. Anyone unable to show our guests the proper respect will be excluded. I am in no mood to forgive today, Year Eleven. I suggest you heed that warning.'

Five minutes later, the lads had gone, and Tilly came to sit next to me.

A policewoman joined Dr Woods – tall and slim with dark brown eyes and short blonde hair. 'Ladies,' she said sternly, as some of the female teachers shut the hall doors, 'we need to have a chat about Internet safety . . .'

9

School finished at lunch time, after Dr Woods
decided to close early. I was having trouble with
some science coursework, so I went to the library to
get a book. To be honest, I just wanted something
to take my mind off Amy's death. Tilly and Max
came with me.

The library was next to reception – a huge room
with glass panels for walls; we called it the goldfish
bowl. Our librarian, Mrs Band, was busy getting rid
of pupils. When she saw me, she shook her head.

'Sorry, Lily,' she said. 'I'm closing – orders from
on high.'

'Just two minutes, miss?' I pleaded.

Mrs Band gave me a warm smile. She had
spiky hair, dyed purple, and big hoop earrings. I

liked her. 'Go on then – but be quick,' she replied.

As I searched the shelves, Max asked what we'd done after the assembly.

'Just stuff about online safety,' Tilly told him. 'Like we need adults to tell us about that.'

'We got the same talk,' said Max. 'Not that I care. Well, I've got anti-virus. But all that stuff about Facebook settings and being careful who you chat to? I've never cared about that stuff.'

I grabbed the chemistry textbook I needed. It was dense and unexciting and it didn't stop me thinking of Amy. The book, Max's words, the library – none of it did. I thought about Benedict. Our virtual friendship felt *real*. I suddenly wanted to chat to him and wondered if he'd sent any more messages. I was sure he'd care about Amy and how I was feeling over her death.

'Didn't you hear what that policewoman said?' I said. 'It's happening all the time, mostly to teenagers – bullying, death threats – all that stuff. It's seriously scary.'

I wondered how people didn't spot that they were being targeted. Like, it would have been obvious, surely? Amy's voice spoke out in my head – telling me that she'd met people like her online. Again, I found myself wondering which people she'd been talking about.

'The Web is full of idiots,' said Max. 'Facebook is just a joke. Look at all the abuse people write on there. Look at what Amy suffered – and how many people in our year thought that was funny. It's sick.'

Tilly rolled her eyes. 'But you could just *block* the morons,' she pointed out. 'Like that man who followed me on Twitter last year?'

I nodded. The man she was talking about, some middle-aged loser, had been a random troll. It had been the usual stuff – jibes about being a slag and all that. It only stopped when she blocked and reported him, and his account was suspended.

'*We* know that,' I said to her. 'But what about, like, girls in Year Seven?'

Max nodded. 'She's got a point, Tilly,' he said. 'Like, if someone was chatting to me – say an adult or something – I'm mature enough to handle it. We're not kids any more. I can talk to anyone I want. But a Year Seven . . . ?'

It was only later, at my house, that Max mentioned Amy. I think the three of us had been avoiding mentioning her by name. Not intentionally – just because it was so horrible. It made sense, I guess, but didn't stop me feeling a bit guilty. We were in the living room, drinking tea with the telly on, even though no one was watching it. Tilly was on an armchair and Max sat next to me on the sofa. I was glad to be at home, rather than sitting in some café or, worse still, at school. I felt safe and warm at home, and I needed that comfort.

'I saw the video on TV,' Max told us. 'The one Amy left before she . . .'

His words hung in the air for a while, like ghostly echoes of something we didn't want to face.

In the end, Tilly grimaced. 'Why would the news show that?' she asked. 'That's just exploitation, isn't it?'

Max shrugged. 'They love stories like this,' he said. 'I read news websites all the time. The media jump on this stuff.'

'It's nasty,' I said. 'Like they even care about Amy.'

Using her name made me tearful and then embarrassed. I turned away, staring at the mantel-piece, where a photo of Mum and me sat in a silver frame.

'I can't believe this is real,' I eventually said. 'It's just . . .'

Tilly got up and came over to me. She put a hand on my shoulder. 'We're bound to feel this way,' she told me. 'I've got this sense of guilt nagging at me.'

'Me too,' said Max.

'Why do you feel guilty?' I asked.

'I keep thinking we should have helped her,' he replied.

I thought about the last conversation I'd had with her, and the way Tilly had defended her from Manisha in the café. 'How could we have helped any more than we did?' I asked.

When Max didn't reply, I repeated myself. 'How?'

'By being her friends, maybe,' he replied. 'We didn't even try.'

'Tilly did – and so did I,' I told him. 'I spoke to her two nights ago. She didn't want my help. She was distant – like she wanted to push everyone away.'

Max gave me an intense, almost unsettling look. 'That happened after the Facebook thing,' he said. 'She was OK before that.'

I shook my head. Max was so wrong. 'No, she wasn't,' I told him. 'She's been bullied since we started at this school. Like, seriously bullied, and normal everyday shit too. I never thought she'd do something like this, though. I feel so sorry for her parents. Imagine having to face *that*?'

Amy had been found in some woods, close to a new-build estate called The Grange. Loads of pupils we knew lived there. She'd hanged herself from a tree, using climber's rope – at least that's what we'd heard. The thought of it sent a shiver running down my back.

'The video was so bad,' Max added. 'Like, she was looking forward to dying.'

'That's ridiculous,' I replied, but something began to bother me. Something about Amy's words that last time I'd seen her. Only I couldn't quite work out what.

'Honestly,' said Max. 'Wait until you see it.'

'I don't want to watch it,' I said. 'That's just *nasty*.'

'They only showed a snippet,' he told me. 'But she'd been planning it. That's what she said in the bit I saw.'

'Planning to kill herself?' asked Tilly, her expression as confused as mine.

Max nodded. 'She reactivated her Facebook page,' he continued. 'Then she posted a link to this chat room. The video was on that. She sent the link to everyone on her friends list.'

I'd been late for school, and had forgotten my phone, so I hadn't seen the link. I went and grabbed it from the kitchen but the thing is, I didn't *want* to see it. I shook my head.

'The chat room was for people who want to commit suicide,' he said softly.

'Huh?' I asked, astounded. 'A *suicide* chat room?'

I thought I knew my way around the Web quite well but I'd never heard of a suicide forum before. I felt a bit stupid for being so ignorant, but then why *would* I have known? I wasn't some ghoul, prowling around, searching for misery.

'*Exactly* that,' replied Max. 'The Internet is fucked up sometimes . . .'

'I bet her parents didn't know,' said Tilly.

'Exactly,' Max agreed. 'Like, she probably hid it. I would, if someone was bullying me like that. My parents don't know shit about what I do online. They don't even care.'

'But why hide *abuse*?' Tilly asked. 'You'd just report it – surely?'

Max shook his head this time. 'Think about it,' he said. 'Facebook, Twitter – all that stuff – it's, like, fifty per cent of our lives, *at least*. Molly Cooper spends her *whole* life on there.'

I nodded because Max was right – about all of us. I tried to remember the last time I'd just turned up at Tilly's house, without having messaged, texted or called her first. I couldn't.

'Being embarrassed online,' he said, 'is the same as in real life. *Worse*, even. Imagine if someone stole a dodgy pic of you and put it on your Facebook page?'

I shuddered at the thought. 'You'd be gutted,' I said, an understatement of epic proportions.

'I chat to people all the time but I'm not naïve like Amy. The people I chat to can't take advantage of me. I'd spot it straight away. Imagine your most private moments online for everyone to see.'

'It would be hellish,' I told him.

'More than that,' Max added. 'It would mean instant public shame. People at our school would pass it on faster than flu. You'd never be able to show your face again.'

My phone buzzed with a text as Tilly offered to make more tea. It was my mum, asking if I was OK. I actually shook my head as I replied.

The answer was no. I was very much *not* OK.

10

Amy's Facebook memorial page was up by the evening. A picture of her – altered to include angels and clouds – dominated it. I'd never seen the photo before but she looked about fourteen – her soft brown eyes shining and a massive, warm smile on her face. Her hair was tied back, and she looked happy and pretty.

The page already had nearly a thousand likes and people had taken photographs of where Amy had been found and posted them. Flowers covered the ground nearby, close to a police cordon. The page was also inundated with messages of sympathy. Some of them were calm, but many were almost hysterical. I ran down the list of posters. Alongside people from school, I saw the names of adults – many probably random strangers – from across the UK. Some of the people who'd bullied her had posted. It made me feel a bit sick.

My phone buzzed – Tilly asking if I'd seen the page. I rang her back.

'Unbelievable,' I told her.

'Manisha Patel is on there,' she replied angrily.

'I know – have you seen what she wrote?'

Manisha's message made my stomach churn. It read:

Rest in Peace beautiful angel. The Gods will watch over U. Forever you're friend. My tears are 4 U, angel. RIP.

I shook my head at her cheek.

'Stupid cow didn't even get her grammar right!' said Tilly.

I didn't comment. Instead I glanced at my message icon. 'Are you going to watch the news?' I asked Tilly, as I checked my messages.

'I don't know,' said Tilly. 'I want to, but I can't – if that makes any sense?'

'Yeah, it does,' I told her. 'Has your mum said anything?'

'Not much,' Tilly replied. 'She's just shocked like everyone else. How about yours?'

'She sent a text earlier, when you and Max were round,' I told her.

I wanted Mum to come home, so that I could talk to her and tell her how I felt. My heart was heavy and I couldn't stop thinking about Amy.

I remembered that Amy had tagged everyone in her video post. I checked into my own Facebook page and saw the link. My hand hovered over the mouse. A tiny part of me wanted to watch, but I just couldn't bring myself to do it. I knew that if I did, her face would haunt me all night. The only people who deserved that were the bullies who'd tormented her.

I rang off. Benedict had sent me several messages – mostly asking where I was or what I'd been doing. I replied, saying I'd been at school. But when he didn't reply immediately, I felt deflated. I really wanted his company right now.

In the end I deleted the video post Amy had left, removing any possible temptation to watch her final words. Then I went back to her memorial page, and regretted it immediately. A woman from London – Diana Burrows – had written the latest comment. I couldn't believe what it said:

Another true British angel taken from us. Yet still they let the immigrants in. Maybe if we had time for our own kids, they might not kill themselves? Bet the liberals are glad – room for another scrounging immigrant kid in our schools. RIP English Amy – you will not be forgotten.

I was astounded and angered at once. What the hell went through some people's minds when they posted stuff online? I wondered who the page administrator was, and why they weren't editing it properly. How deranged did someone have to be, to post something like that? I loved the Internet, but sometimes it made me *so* angry. Danny popped up in the instant message box.

Seen the racist shit?

Yeah – WTF?

Bitch like that – they should fly her to Africa and make her bring up black babies for free.

I knew that Danny was trying to lighten the mood, but it didn't work. I was too upset, and too annoyed at what I'd just read.

I'm stunned, Danny. Someone needs to delete it. Have you seen Manisha's post too?

Seen it? It nearly made me puke!

Danny stopped messaging and after reading some more posts, I returned to my inbox. Benedict had replied.

Hey you!

I tried to smile but failed. I had this aching sensation in my belly. When I replied, it was short and pointed. I didn't mean it to be, but my mood was strange.

Horrible day at school. This girl died.

Yeah, babe, I know. I'm so sorry. Some of your friends posted about it.

I wondered which friends Benedict was talking about.

The one that sent me that pic – Molly? he answered before I even asked the question.

I felt suddenly annoyed at him. Why was he talking about that cow?

She's no friend of mine.

When I failed to write anything else, he worked it out.

She tagged me in a post. Nothing in it, babe.

You must have requested her. How did she tag you otherwise?

Yeah I did. Thought she was your friend?

What gave you that idea?

My mood was sour, and I *wanted* to argue with him. I wanted to let off some steam. Yet, moments earlier, I'd wanted to tell him everything that was going on inside my head.

Downstairs, I heard my mum come in and a sense of relief washed over me. I decided to sign off, hoping that Benedict wouldn't take it the wrong way.

Look – things are weird ATM. Chat later, yeah?

I'm here if you need me, Lily. Anytime, OK?

Thanks. I have to go.

I signed off, glad that Benedict had been so

understanding, and went downstairs. Mum was in the living room, answering emails.

She looked up. 'I was just about to come up,' she said. 'You OK?'

I shook my head. 'I *saw* her, Mum,' I replied. 'Just the other night when I went to get milk.'

'Sunday?'

I nodded. 'She was OK,' I said. 'I *saw* her and she was OK.'

I felt my lower lip tremble. My legs began to feel like warm jelly.

'How can she be dead?' I sobbed. 'She was OK. How can she be *dead* . . . ?'

My mum jumped up and grabbed me. She held me close and started to whisper in my ear. She told me that I was fine and that everything would be OK. I felt like a five-year-old again – scared of the dark and unable to sleep. For a while, I forgot all about the world and cried until my eyes and throat grew sore.

Later, when I should have been sleeping, I went back online with Benedict. I felt guilty about before – I didn't want him to think I was some moody teenager and stop talking to me. I needed to chat. I needn't have worried, though; he was great – constantly reassuring me that there was nothing I could have

99

done to change things for Amy. I ended up telling him things that only Tilly really knew about me.

I just wonder all the time what people think of me – I know that makes me sound self-obsessed.

You're not that, Lily, believe me. I see people in my world who could win Olympic gold for self-obsession. You're just a bit insecure, that's all.

I was still surprised at how easy he was to chat to. I'd never been able to talk like this to any boy, ever. Not that I'd even tried. Most of the boys I knew would probably run a mile if you wanted to talk about feelings or real stuff.

You're not like other boys. You seem to understand how hard it is.

My mother had the same issues, Lily. Lots of women do. It's the crap they get fed by the media.

Yeah – I know. It drives me mad. Like one week they say some actress has a bikini body to die for and the next, they're slagging her off and saying she has cellulite. It does my head in.

I wondered whether he'd get tired of my moaning, but the opposite happened. He actually wanted to discuss what was on my mind. It made me grin like a lunatic.

Forget about it, Lily – seriously. Like, if your thighs are just a bit wider than the accepted norm, who cares? That makes you like most women. These models, even people like me, we're not the norm. We're the freaks.

I panicked slightly – did he think I was having a go at him?

I'm not saying that, Benny. I'm just annoyed that I have these issues when I understand where they come from.

So lose them, babe. Tell yourself every day to love the body you have.

What – my wobbly arse and thunder thighs? Gonna take some loving – LOL!

Don't get mad, babe, but seems to me like you want to feel insecure. Like you don't want to change. You're just so down on yourself. Makes me sad.

I didn't know whether his last response made me angry or not. He seemed to have a point. I spent so much time picking at myself that the idea of change was an almost impossible dream. What if he was *right* – what if I *was* wallowing in my own stupidity. I knew what had made me feel this way, so why wasn't I changing it?

You're kind of like a self-help guru, Benny. I think you've just summed me up. I don't like it but I think you might be right.

Think about it, you're pretty, funny? Who cares if you don't have the perfect ass or whatever? Like, really?

I took a deep breath. I really liked him.

I wish you were here now.

I wasn't joking either. He might have lived thousands of miles away, but he was getting to me. He was the first lad who made me feel wanted and appreciated. It was like he knew the right answer to every question I asked. If only he didn't live so far away.

We flirted some more and then I had to sleep. Benedict had helped, though – he had taken much of the edge off my emotions, and replaced some of the sadness with warmth. As I closed my eyes and smiled, I wondered if I'd ever meet him for real.

The OTHER drops his bag on the floor.

'What is that?' the Spider asks him.

'The things you asked for – for the girl?' replies the OTHER. 'This is what's left.'

'Store them,' says the Spider. 'We will need them soon enough.'

'There is another ready?'

The Spider grins. 'Take a look,' he replies, calling up several recordings. He plays the first.

'Oh dear,' says the OTHER. 'What a silly young man.'

'Your choices were good,' the Spider tells him. 'Perfect.'

'I know them all,' the OTHER replies. 'That's why I chose them for you.'

'I think the boy will need more help than the girl. She was happy to go. This one may take some persuading.'

The OTHER shows his surprise. A glint of excitement shines in his eyes. 'This is so much more satisfying than before,' he says.

'It is the next step,' the Spider replies. 'We were always going to step offline again. It was just a matter of time.'

The OTHER watches another recording begin. 'My friends,' he tells the Spider, 'they would pay handsomely for this footage.'

'I thought as much,' the Spider replies. 'Shall I send these to you?'

The OTHER nods. 'Thank you,' he says. 'So when do we move on to the next one?'

'We must be careful,' the Spider replies. 'We need to wait a little while longer. Soon, though.'

'I'm eager,' the OTHER replies.

'Eagerness leads to mistakes. Patience is the key,' the Spider tells him.

Later, when the OTHER is gone, the Spider goes over his strategy. The key is to control at least eighty per cent of the moves. The rest – unknown variables – can be guessed at and accommodated. Very little is left to chance – a lesson the Spider had to learn the hard way.

11

The following morning Amy's face was everywhere. In the newsagent's, I counted seven papers with the story, including our local – the *Mercury*. They'd all used the same picture too – the one from her Facebook memorial page, but without the angels and stuff. I didn't want to see the news but I had no choice. It was almost impossible to avoid. I paid for my bottle of water and left, just as some Year Nine lads started talking about Amy's death. One of them asked if dying like that would hurt. *Seriously?*

School was weird again. Mr Warren just nodded when I walked into form. He was sitting at his desk, messing with his laptop. He looked tired, sad and stressed out.

'You need help with that, sir?' asked Tilly, who had arrived before me.

'Got it covered,' Mr Warren replied, without looking up.

Tilly scowled. 'What?' she asked when I shook my head.

'Why the face?' I said. 'He's probably just as shocked and upset as we are.'

'Doesn't mean he can be rude,' she replied. 'Especially not to us . . . we're his best pupils.'

'Everyone's on edge,' I told her. 'Including you. Mr Warren doesn't mean it. He's too lovely to be mean on purpose.'

Tilly, normally so well presented, looked terrible. She'd tied her unwashed hair into a ponytail, and not bothered to change her clothes.

'You OK?' I asked.

'Yeah,' she snapped. 'Why?'

Annoyed that she was snapping at me, I looked away. Tilly wasn't the only one having trouble dealing with Amy's death. When I turned back to my best friend, she seemed to be about to say something, but Mr Dhindsa walked in before she had the chance.

'Lily – I need you for a while,' he said. 'Can you come with me?'

'Me?' I asked. 'Why?'

Mr Dhindsa smiled, showing his straight, pearly-white teeth through his thick, dark beard. 'I'll explain on the way,' he said. 'It's nothing serious.'

We went to his office, where I found the police-woman who'd spoken to us the day before.

'This is DC Evans,' said the deputy principal. 'She'd like to talk to you.'

I gulped and felt myself blush. Even though I'd done nothing wrong, I felt a pang of shame. 'Am I in trouble?' I asked.

DC Evans smiled. 'If I had a pound for everyone who says that.' She was wearing jeans and a white shirt, and carried a black shoulder bag. I wondered why she wasn't in uniform. 'I'm helping with family liaison,' she told me. 'I've been attached to Amy's family at this difficult time.'

I gulped down more air and felt a bit queasy. 'I don't understand,' I replied.

DC Evans nodded. 'We're investigating the events running up to Amy's suicide,' she explained. 'She was bullied quite severely, as I'm sure you know. I'm gathering information. I'll be speaking to a few pupils. You're just first on my list.'

I nodded and felt slightly relieved. 'Everyone knew about the bullying,' I told her.

'Exactly – the problem is that no one reported it.'

Again, I wondered why she was talking to me. I

felt a creeping sense of paranoia, followed by severe guilt because I was thinking about myself and not Amy. She was the one that mattered. Besides I *had* reported it, only I didn't get the chance to tell her straight away.

DC Evans shifted in her seat. She held a notebook, and a red pencil stamped with the letters 'HB' in gold. 'Did you know that Amy kept a diary?' she asked.

'No,' I said. 'We used to be close but we sort of grew apart after coming to this school. She was a loner.'

The policewoman nodded slowly. 'Well,' she said, 'she seemed to like *you*.' I must have looked shocked because DC Evans explained, 'Amy mentioned you in a passage. She claimed that you helped her, when she was being picked on.'

I nodded. 'Yeah – a couple of times,' I told her. 'Me and Tilly – that's my best friend. The last time was in the café at the supermarket.'

'Who was involved?' the policewoman asked. 'Who was bullying Amy?'

I stopped myself from replying right away and thought. If I mentioned Manisha and the others, they'd be in trouble. But if I didn't speak out, I'd be betraying Amy – and she deserved better than that. This wasn't a lunch-time argument over something stupid. Amy was *dead*. There was no choice.

'How many names do you want?' I asked the officer.

'All that you know of,' DC Evans replied. She shifted position again and I waited a moment before answering.

'Manisha Patel,' I said. 'Mostly, but there were others too – Ria Smith and the rest of Manisha's gang.'

As she wrote down some notes, DC Evans nodded. 'And what about this Facebook page?' she asked. 'Do you know who created it?'

I shook my head. 'I only looked at it twice,' I replied. 'It was nasty.'

The officer looked at Mr Dhindsa. He glanced at me but said nothing. The expression in his eyes was serious. But not as serious as the look on DC Evans's face. Her brow was creased and her eyes bored into mine.

'So you didn't comment or report it?'

I nodded. 'We both reported it,' I told her, before looking away from the intensity of her stare.

'You and . . . ?'

'Tilly Anderson,' I replied, glancing at Mr Dhindsa. He gave a little nod.

DC Evans made more notes. 'Did you report

it immediately?'

This time I shook my head. I felt terrible – ashamed and guilty and sad all at once. 'No – but I should have,' I said. 'I know I was wrong not to.' I wanted to cry.

Mr Dhindsa gave me a warm look and shook his head. 'At least you *did* report it,' he told me.

'Who were the regular abusers online?' asked DC Evans. 'The ones who bullied Amy the most?'

This time I didn't pause before replying. I gave her a list of the worst offenders – people who seemed to delight in making Amy miserable. The officer noted every name, as I realized that I hadn't mentioned the last time I saw Amy.

'There's something else,' I told them.

'What's that?' asked DC Evans, her expression changing and her eyes lighting up.

'I saw her,' I revealed. 'On Sunday evening – down at the local shops.'

DC Evans put her notebook down. 'You *saw* Amy?'

I nodded.

'Did you speak to her?'

'Yes – she was sitting on the wall outside the pub – The Blues?'

'I know it,' said DC Evans. 'Was she alone?'

'Yeah – just sitting there in the cold. I told her to

come back to mine but she walked off.'

'Did she say anything to indicate that she might be suicidal?'

I shook my head. 'No – she said she wasn't bothered by the bullies any more,' I replied. 'She was on about meeting people like her on some chat room. Said they were helping her.'

DC Evans grabbed her notebook and wrote quickly.

'That's important, isn't it?' I said.

DC Evans nodded. 'It could be,' she replied. 'It's certainly very helpful. Can you try and recall everything she said and maybe let me know?'

'What – right now?'

She shook her head. 'No – I think that's all for the moment,' she said. 'If you remember anything else, or want to expand on what you've said already, just let Mr Dhindsa know. He has my contact details.'

'OK,' I told her.

'Just one more thing,' said the officer.

'Yes?'

'Has anyone else you know been subjected to anything similar?'

I thought about it and then shook my head. 'No,' I replied.

The Spider is back in London, some fifteen years earlier. He is about to be kicked off his course. He sits in a pub close to Clapham Common and fumes. He cannot believe his own stupidity.

He has been hacking into the university computers – all for fun. He doesn't care about altering grades or anything like that. He does it for amusement – enjoys messing with people's lives. Moving around graduation details, deleting entire year group histories, altering databases. The results have been small-scale, comical. Nothing to warrant this.

Some snot-faced whizz kid from India solved the mystery. The Spider did not take care. He left trails because his weaving skills were not ready. The web he'd created was too thin, too flimsy. It failed quickly . . .

Now he faces the end of his university career. His misdemeanour will follow him. No other institution will have him. Which is why he's in the pub. Waiting for an acquaintance of his housemate. A man who not only shares his housemate's appetites but also has the cash to feed them when he chooses. The man has work for him. Nothing major, but it's a start.

Soon, his new career will offer greater opportunities and the Spider will be able to put his mistakes behind him. His skills honed, he will be ready to strike again . . .

12

I spent the evening sorting out my science course-work, before checking in to Facebook. I was hoping Benedict would be waiting for me. He'd made me feel so much better the night before.

Hey babe – you OK?

Hey Benny – yeah fine . . . No, not really. Oh, I don't know, I'm sorry.

Don't apologize. Do you want to talk?

Yes.

Guess Amy dying made you think of your dad?

It was like he could read my mind.

Not exactly but sort of – if that makes sense.

I understand – I know how that feels.

Like, it was more about Amy, you know, but I think my reaction was based on Dad. That's why I'm so mixed-up, maybe.

You're bound to feel weird, Lily. It's only natural.

Sometimes you say just the right things, Benny. It didn't get any better today either.

Hard day?

Tough – I got questioned by the police.

WHY????

The Amy thing – they wanted to know who was bullying her.

Did you say?

Yes.

I thought about what I'd done, and how it might haunt me. If Manisha and the others found out, I'd get serious grief. Thing is, I guessed that DC Evans had asked plenty of other people too. And anyway it had been the right thing to do. Amy deserved it. Manisha and her gang could go to hell.

I gave her a few names. A horrible bitch called Manisha, some other idiots . . .

Well done! If more people reported these things . . . How are you feeling?

Benedict's interest gave me that warm feeling again. He was the first lad I'd known to ask about my emotions. It felt lovely. It was so annoying that he was so far away. I realized that I wanted him close. I was falling for him and that felt odd. New and weird.

I feel good for giving the names to the police. But I feel numb too because Amy is gone and it doesn't feel real. It's not as bad as when my dad died, but she didn't deserve any of this.

I told you, babe – your emotions are natural. You're a good person – it was bound to affect you this way.

I saw her – the night before she died. She was acting weird.

Benedict took his time to reply.

You saw Amy?

Yeah. She was acting odd but it was nothing that made me think she might do what she did. I keep wondering if I missed something. Like, in my head there's this nagging feeling that she said something important, only I don't know what that was.

What did she say?

That's the problem, Benny – I can't really remember anything important. It's just this feeling I have.

What about the police – what did they say?

The policewoman thinks it might be important. She told me to think about it and get back to her.

And have you?

Not yet. Amy was telling me about meeting people just like her online. She said they were helping her.

Did she give any clues – any names that could help the police?

No – she just mentioned it. She was visiting suicide chat rooms so it must be important. It's hard to know. The police officer didn't give anything away.

No names at all?

None – but maybe the police can investigate. They can search computers and stuff, can't they?

Yes. You did good, Lily. Amy would have been proud of you. Your dad too, I reckon.

His words made me well up and gave me goose bumps. I wished for the millionth time Benedict lived up the street so that I could go and be with him.

Thank you for saying that, but nothing I do can help Amy now, can it?

You can help her memory, Lily. Perhaps bring peace to her parents – what do they call it on TV? Closure . . .

I don't believe in closure. I don't think you get used to people you love dying. You just learn to cope with it.

Maybe you're right, but remember that Amy wanted to die. Nothing you could have done can change that.

How do you know that?

Saw the news reports.

What – in New York?

Yeah – it made the papers here.

That's crazy.

Yeah. Did you get a webcam yet? I want to see your pretty face and talk for real. I want to be able to see your emotions, babe. Like, interact properly. Who am I trying to kid? Mostly, I just wanna see your gorgeous smile . . .

I felt myself blush, and even though he couldn't

117

see me I looked away from the screen. If he had been there, right then, I think I might have snogged him. He made me feel great inside. I made a mental note about the webcam.

I haven't had time. Soon, I promise.

Look – I'll just send you mine. No problem. I'll pay for the postage.

It's OK, honestly – I'll get one. Just busy with stuff.

But I want to see you.

I got that warm feeling again. My emotions were on a roller coaster. I had these growing feelings for Benedict, and that made me happy. But Amy was in there too. And my dad. My head felt light and my thoughts were jumping around randomly. I felt a bit dizzy. I looked at the last reply and wanted to smile. Only, I couldn't.

If you want to see me, look at my photo albums. Although they aren't very nice.

Already done that and they were great! Want to see more.

Haven't got any more.

Take some photos of yourself – post them? Please?

I shook my head and this time the smile came. What harm could a simple self-shot do? I told myself. The thought of it made me feel like a rebel. For a moment, I wondered if Molly felt the same way when she posted selfies. Was it something you could get addicted to? And was I a hypocrite for slagging her off, when I was about to do something similar? Then I saw Amy's face and I started to think about how life was short. Plus I really liked Benedict.

OK – I will.

I grabbed my phone and reversed the camera. Only, every time I posed, my face looked podgy and I wasn't happy.

I can't. I look fat.

You're not fat! You're a real girl. A gorgeous girl. You shouldn't be so hard on yourself.

You don't have to look at my bum in a mirror.

People come in all shapes and sizes, Lily, I've said this to you before. It's what they do and how they are as a person that matters. You're warm and lovely and damn pretty too.

I'm blushing.

Come on, babe – just a few pics – please?

As I thought about taking a pic, Benedict sent one of himself. It was of his body – no face. He was wearing red jeans, with the button fly undone so that his white boxers were showing. His stomach was solid and ridged with muscle. A thin line of dark hair ran from his belly button down into his underwear. I felt myself blush.

Benny!

119

You like????

Yeah!

Your turn!

No way! I'm not showing you my underwear.

Nothing nasty, I know you're not that kind of girl. Just a teaser – please??? If you do, I'll tell you my great news.

Tell me first.

No – pic first!

Better be good – this news . . .

You'll love it – promise!

OK – YOLO. Give me a second.

I lay down on bed so I could get a good angle, opened three buttons on the top I'd worn for school and held the camera up. The picture looked OK and I liked it. Not slutty or nasty. Just a peak of my bra – nothing explicit. I snapped.

Uploading it from my phone now, Benny. My PC is shit. Please don't ever show it to anyone else!

Cool – can't wait! And of course I won't share it. It's gonna be all mine, babe!

We chatted some more before Benedict saw my selfie. His reaction made me grin like a fool.

OMG!!! Lily – you're beautiful!

No I'm not!

Even though I was protesting, Benedict's words made me feel great. I felt like a proper woman, not some kid.

Lily! You're amazing. Man, if I lived in England . . .

My grin morphed into a beam so wide my jaws started to ache. I'd never had a reaction like this from anyone.

I bet you meet loads of gorgeous girls. I'm just ordinary.

Models are vain – you're cool! Wow at the underwear too.

Just an ordinary bra.

On anyone else, ordinary, yeah. On you though! Man, I might need to lie down a while . . .

You nutter! Now tell me the news.

You got a company called Next in England, yeah?

Yeah – why?

They might want me to model for them.

No way!

Yeah – said they want me to come see them at their offices – like next month.

I felt like screaming but managed to hold it in.

But their offices are near me! Like, here in Leicester.

I saw that. We're just sorting out the details . . .

OMG!!!!

Is that all the reaction I get?

YAY!!!!!!!!!!!!!!!!!!!!!!!!

Better!

I can't believe it!

Send me your address then – I'll post the webcam

and then, when I get there, I can come pick you up.

This is just mad!!!!

In my head, I wondered if I was having a day-dream. It all felt so unreal – so perfect. It was like someone had taken my deepest desires and made them come true. I felt like a heroine in a romance novel.

We'll be able to meet up – catch a drink or some-thing . . .

I know!

Can't wait to meet you in the flesh, babe – especially after seeing you tonight. Send me those details.

I tried to hold in the second shriek but it was too strong. I jumped on my bed, and buried my face in my pillow to muffle the sound. I screamed my head off – until Amy's face reappeared in my mind. The happiness vanished and the guilt returned, and I wished that I could just shut my eyes and forget everything but Benedict.

PART TWO

Four weeks later . . .

The OTHER sits patiently, waiting, watching. Girl #3
is on her way. He eyes the pay-as-you-go mobile he
picked up in Asda. The Spider clued him to their use.
They made perfect sense – untraceable, disposable,
anonymous . . .

The girl is nervous when she arrives. He smiles at
her. Her features relax immediately. She looks around
the deserted street, then climbs into the car. He smiles
again before speaking.

'You made it,' he says.

'Yeah.'

'Are you OK?'

The girl looks around, turns back to him –

smiles. 'Yeah. Where you taking me today?' she asks.

'I know a great pub – it's in the countryside. Quiet – no one will know us.'

'Sounds great,' she tells him.

'I was worried you might back out – maybe have second thoughts,' he tells her.

The girl shrugs. 'So was I,' she says.

'But you came?'

'Yeah,' she tells him. 'Here I am. Again.'

The Spider's new web is growing bigger. He is ready to strike again. Boy #1 will be next.

For the Spider, sitting in the shadows had become monotonous. The pleasure had diminished. This feels new. It feels like a challenge. It feels like destiny.

But the risks are great. It is easier to hide inside the Web. The real world presents many more challenges. The real police aren't as dim-witted as their cyber cousins. They will investigate and make connections. The Spider knows he cannot slip up like he did when he was younger. One mistake, one loose thread, and his creation will come tumbling down. He must weave, trap, devour and move on. He is not ready, yet, to be caught . . .

13

Kane looked at the menu and shook his head.

'Too much choice,' he said. 'Do I go Cuban, Peruvian or Brazilian?'

We were in Las Iguanas, a restaurant in town, with Danny and Tilly. Since Amy's death we had all had our heads down, working hard. It was nearly March, and our GCSEs were coming up fast. I wanted to do well, but I wasn't great at exams. Constant revision would be the only way to get the grades I wanted.

So, the meal was a treat, and I was glad of the break. My life had been a roller coaster of school, coursework and revision. In between, I'd managed to keep up with my social life, but mostly online. Actually seeing my friends apart from Tilly was getting harder to do. And Amy was always there too – her death still too difficult to comprehend.

Danny told Kane his choice was obvious. 'If there's Brazilian on the menu, then take it,' he told him. 'Nothing else will do . . . I wonder if they'll let us order proper cocktails.'

Tilly shook her head. 'Not in here,' she told him. 'They'll want ID.'

'Silly people,' Danny replied. 'I fancy a drink.'

'What you should be fancying is a makeover,' said Tilly with a smirk.

He was wearing bright green chinos, a strawberry red shirt and white plimsolls, and looked great. Not many lads could handle that look, but Danny could wear anything – the lucky git.

'I was going to bite back,' Danny told her. 'But I'm scared you might taste foul.'

Tilly grinned. 'If you're lucky, I might let kiss my arse,' she replied.

'EWWW – Tilly!!!!' I complained.

Kane stayed out of it, content to study the menu. When he caught me staring at him, he smiled. His hair was unbraided, so it sat tall and wide in an Afro that I loved. It was awesome.

'This place is cool,' he said. 'Who chose it?'

Danny held his right index finger in the air. 'That

would be me,' he said. 'I'm a person of immense good taste.'

The restaurant was almost empty, but the food was nice and we had discount vouchers. As I scanned the dishes on offer, I noticed Tilly kept glancing at her phone. I wondered what she was waiting for.

'Expecting a text?' I asked.

'No, nosy bum, I'm not,' she replied, before grinning. 'Why?' Her hair was piled up, her face free of makeup, gorgeous as always. She had Cupid's bow lips that were naturally deep pink, and her ears stuck out just a tiny bit too much.

'You keep looking at your phone,' I said. 'You got a new man?'

I was only joking; if Tilly had met someone, I'd be the first to know. But Danny reacted like a shark at the taste of blood.

'Someone say new man?' he asked.

Tilly shook her head. 'Nothing to report but Lily's overactive imagination,' she said.

'What about you?' Danny added, turning to me. 'You still having your online romance with model boy?'

I felt myself blush and glanced at Kane. He didn't seem to notice, as he watched people walk past the window. Part of me wished that he would. Kane was the opposite of my online crush. He was an *actual* crush. I mean, I really liked Benedict, but I was beginning to realize that we might never meet. He had talked about modelling for Next but nothing had been decided.

'Earth calling Lily Basra?' said Danny.

'Huh?' I asked.

'American Boy?'

'Oh,' I said. 'Yeah, we still message. Why?'

Danny shrugged. 'Just taking an interest,' he replied.

'You mean you've run out of hot gossip to spread,' said Tilly.

Danny grinned. '*Well*,' he replied, 'all this exam stuff is boring. No one is doing anything with anyone else. It's all so *stale* . . .'

'Like your aftershave,' said Tilly.

Danny flipped her a finger, as I decided what to eat.

'He sends me a lot of messages,' I said after a while.

'How many is a lot?' asked Danny.

'Like, I dunno, twenty a day sometimes,' I replied. 'And he's always online too.'

'That'll be boredom,' said Danny. 'I watched a show on Sky about models and they lead really weird lives. Lots of spare time on their hands . . .'

Kane finally looked at me. 'Do you like him, though?' he asked.

How should I reply? The last time I'd mentioned Benedict, Kane hadn't looked too impressed. See, I still had a thing about Kane. But that wasn't going anywhere.

'Yeah,' I said. 'But he's not like a boyfriend or anything. He's just someone I'm close to.'

'Close?' asked Kane.

'Yeah,' I replied honestly. 'Like, we chat and he asks me stuff about my life.'

'Twenty times a day, though?' Danny chipped in. 'Is that a bit *odd*?'

'No,' I protested. 'He's not odd – just a bit . . . insistent.'

Tilly grinned. 'Insistent to the point of being annoying,' she said.

I looked away, annoyed and embarrassed.

Tilly realized and put her hand on my arm. 'Sorry,' she said.

'It doesn't matter,' I replied.

Only it *did* matter. Tilly knew that I was having doubts about Benedict because we'd spoken about it. Benedict's constant messages were strange, but not in a horrible way. If I'm honest, I was enjoying the attention. No boy had ever done that with me before. It felt good. But, at the same time, it bothered me too. I had been spending so much time chatting to him I hadn't done enough revision. I was feeling confused and I didn't want the whole world to know my business.

After we ordered, Tilly asked if I was mad at her. 'I'm sorry – big-mouth syndrome,' she added.

'It's OK,' I replied. I really didn't want to fight with Tilly about this.

She leaned in close and whispered in my ear, 'Kane seems a bit jealous.'

'*Ssh!*' I whispered, praying that Kane hadn't heard her.

She nodded towards the toilets. 'Girl time,' she announced out loud.

Kane shook his head when both Tilly and I stood. 'Always the same,' he said. 'Can't you go separately? Like, do you help each other or summat?'

'*Eww!*' said Tilly. 'That's gross, Kane!'

'You can't blame him for asking,' said Danny. 'It's such a weird thing.'

'It's not *weird*,' said Tilly. 'It's just *beyond* your level of comprehension. It's a *girl* thing.'

'Have fun, then!' Danny replied. 'In the *toilet*, you skanks!'

Once we were alone, Tilly repeated herself about Kane.

'He's not jealous,' I told her.

'Seemed that way to me,' she replied. 'Ooh – imagine having two boys after you, Lily!'

'Not going to happen,' I replied. 'Besides, why would either of them want someone as mixed-up as me?'

'You're not mixed up,' said Tilly.

'Really?' I asked. 'I have this great thing with Benedict, and I love that he cares about me. But at the *same* time, I don't like that he cares so much, and I still want Kane. How is *that* normal?'

'Who cares about normal?' she replied. 'Hedge your bets and pick the best one. There's nothing wrong with that.'

'Yes there is,' I said. 'It's not fair on Benedict, is it?'

'He's not here,' she pointed out needlessly. 'And what if you never meet? Are you going to carry a torch for some boy you only know via Facebook?'

'I'm *so* confused!' I complained. 'And all I should be thinking about is my exams.'

Tilly shook her head before examining herself in a wide mirror that sat above the washbasins. Then she looked at my reflection, her expression serious.

'You know what you said – out there?' she asked.

'About what?'

'Me having a new man – well, you were right,' she revealed.

'*Really?*' I asked, getting excited, even though truthfully I was a little hurt that she'd only just mentioned it. Thing is, Tilly hadn't had a boyfriend in ages and I was happy for her. And I'd told her all about Benedict – over and over again. It was nice to hear about her feelings for a change.

'Yeah.'

'What's he like?' I asked. 'Is he at our *school?*'

When she didn't reply I nudged her.

'Tilly?'

She shook her head. 'He's older than me,' she revealed. 'Like – not lots older but a bit . . .'

'Huh?'

'I'll tell you everything later,' she replied. 'Our food will be ready and I need a pee.'

'How *much* older?' I asked.

She squeezed my hand. 'Later,' she said. 'I need to pee.'

Afterwards, the lads went off and left Tilly and me by Town Hall Square. It was sunny but cool, and the area around the fountain was busy.

'So, come on, tell me about this older man,' I said.

Tilly shrugged. 'He's a *bit* older,' she said, 'but we aren't *doing* stuff. He said I have to be sixteen before anything like that.'

Stuff meant sex, I guessed, and I blushed. It wasn't something I properly knew much about, beyond what I'd learned in school, and by reading.

Occasionally I'd see something on screen too – either a TV show or on a DVD – but it felt like a distant thing – something that other people did. Tilly had more experience than me. She'd slept with one boy, a Year Twelve, at a party that I'd missed in the summer, but that was it. I wondered how old this new man actually was.

'Age?' I asked.

Tilly shrugged again, and I knew then that she was holding something back. She had clear reactions to things – black and white – and I knew them all Or at least I thought I did.

'What is it?' I asked.

'Nothing,' she said, before reconsidering. 'I mean nothing major. He's just more experienced than me.'

'How much more experienced?' I said. A pang of worry caused me to frown.

'Well, he's not a boy,' she replied, which didn't tell me much.

'Tilly!'

'He's older,' she repeated, 'but it's not like he's some sixty-year-old pervert. Don't worry about it. I'm not—'

'You mean he's a proper adult man?' I asked.

Tilly nodded. 'But he's not a weirdo . . . honestly.'

'Sounds a bit dodge to me,' I said without thinking.

It was a big mistake. Tilly's expression instantly hardened and I felt a surge of anxiety. I didn't want to upset my best friend, but I was worried by what she was telling me. She's the only person I would have questioned like this too. Normally I would have avoided an argument but Tilly was too important. I thought she was doing wrong and I wanted her to know.

'What's that supposed to mean?' she asked, unimpressed.

'Well – what kind of older man dates a schoolgirl?'

'I'm no *girl*!' she snapped, and I saw her fingers begin to clench and unclench. This was one of her tell-tale signs. She was angry.

'Tilly – how old is he?' I was getting properly worried. If he had been eighteen or something, she'd have just told me. Only she was deflecting my questions, which mean that he was really older.

She shook her head, her face flushed with colour. 'You know what?' she said. 'I thought you'd understand – not judge.'

'I'm not judging—' I began.

'Yeah, you are!' she replied. 'Well, you can stick your opinion!' She stormed off, heading back towards town.

'Tilly!'

She didn't look back and she didn't respond.

The Spider cannot believe his eyes. Girl #3 is typing a message to the OTHER. He slams his palm against the desk. Rules . . .

I really enjoyed last night, she writes. *Just a shame it had to end.*

Don't worry, the OTHER tells her. *One day we'll have all the time we need.*

Soon?

Yes. Are you being careful?

Of course. I'm not stupid.

I know that, but we have to tread carefully. I can't get caught.

Don't worry. I know how to keep a secret. When can I see you again?

Tonight?

I can get out between 7 and 9 p.m. – is that OK?
That's great! Usual place?
I can't wait!
Make sure you don't tell anyone.
I won't – stop worrying.
OK – I'll see you later.

The Spider waits until they have signed off. He grabs
one of several mobile phones and calls the OTHER.

'Yes?'

'You have broken the rules,' the Spider tells him.

'Rules?'

'You've made contact with her.'

The OTHER coughs. 'Are you watching me now?'
he asks.

'Not you – *her!*' the Spider yells. 'Have you lost
your mind?'

'It's nothing – there is no connection to you.'

'Everything is connected to me.'

'I thought you understood my interest.'

'I do – but there are rules. They protect us. This is
a big problem.'

'Why?'

The Spider pauses to think. When he is ready, he
speaks. 'We need to meet,' he says.

'When?'

'As soon as possible.'

'Where?'

'I'll message you.'

'I'm sorry if I've done something wrong.'

'We'll talk again.'

The Spider sits and reconsiders his options. A weakened web is a dangerous one. Just one loose thread could bring the entire structure crashing. And the Spider cannot allow that to happen. No matter *what* the cost.

14

I was at the front door, keys in hand, when our next-door neighbour, Mr Samuels, waved to me from his front garden. I dumped my bag on the step and went over to him. His hair was white, and he had really kind, light brown eyes. He wore his usual brown chinos and a short-sleeved beige shirt that showed off the army tattoo on his left arm. He was one of those happy, smiley people who always found the positive in everything.

'Lily,' he said, as I approached, 'I've got something for you.'

'Really?'

He nodded. 'It's a parcel,' he told me. 'I would have dropped it off yesterday but I had to go out.'

'Oh,' I replied, wondering what it could be. I

hadn't ordered anything and it wasn't my birthday.

He went into his house, returning with a small brown cardboard box. 'It's very light, whatever's in here,' he told me.

'I don't know what it is,' I replied.

Mr Samuels grinned. 'A present, maybe,' he suggested. 'From a secret admirer?'

I smiled, took the package and said I'd see him later.

Only the package wasn't the most important thing on my mind. That was Tilly, who wasn't answering my messages. I wondered how angry she was. I wanted to talk to her, but I'd seen her like this before. Until she calmed down, there was no point. I never thought I'd be the one she was so mad with, though. When she was ready, she'd either reply to a text or pick up when I rang. I just had to give her time.

Before getting down to some schoolwork, I checked Facebook to see if Benedict had left any messages – he hadn't. The parcel was sitting on my bed, and I grabbed it excitedly.

'Wonder what you are?' I said.

Whatever was inside had been sealed in bubble wrap and surrounded by polystyrene chips. Little bits of the annoying stuff fell out. Static charge made them stick to my jeans and the duvet cover. I tried to brush them away, without success. When I finally unsealed the wrap, a Microsoft webcam fell out.

'What the hell?' I said, glancing at my ancient PC.

I checked the package but couldn't find any sender details, but I guessed who'd sent it. It had to be Benedict. At first, I smiled but then something dawned on me. I'd never actually given him my address, so how had he sent me a webcam without it? Had he Googled my address somehow? I sat down at my PC and sent him a message.

You around?

His reply took a while, and I scanned my home page as I waited. Molly had posted a link to some model agency, claiming that they were about to offer her a contract. As usual, a load of lads had liked the status, and one of them had requested a personal photograph. I wondered if things like that made Molly feel more self-confident.

Always around for you, Lily. How you doing today?

I'm good. You?

OK – just bored. Waiting for my next job to start. You've been a bit quiet lately – you OK?

Yeah – just busy with revision. Besides we chatted the other night.

Two days is too long, babe. I want to chat to you every day.

Is there something you want to tell me?

About?

A webcam?

Oh it arrived at last! Great!

So you did send it?

Yeah – you asked me to?

I sat staring at the screen. What did he mean I'd asked him? I thought back to our previous conversations but I could only remember turning his offer of the webcam down.

I don't remember that. When did I ask you?

The other week, when I told you about my Next modelling thing? Are you losing your memory, Lily? Are you OK?

I didn't ask for it.

Yeah you did – why would I send it otherwise, babe?

But how did you get my address?

You gave it to me. Are you sure you're OK, Lily? – you don't seem right today.

I'm fine – but I didn't send you my address and I didn't ask for this.

Scroll back through our conversation. It's all there, babe.

So I checked and saw that Benedict was right. There it was in black and white – my address. How weird that I'd blocked it out. I *had* been mixed-up for a couple of weeks after Amy had died; my mind had been all over the place, and I'd had trouble sleeping.

143

I'd forgotten about homework that had been set a couple of times, which wasn't like me, so I supposed it made sense I'd forgotten about this too. I was embarrassed about being so short with Benedict. When it was just me being stupid.

Oh, really sorry – maybe I did.

You sure you're OK, Lily?

Yes. I've been so busy, I must have forgotten.

Hook the camera up, then – I want to see you!

I glanced at the pile of books on my bed. I was really tempted by seeing Benedict face to face, but I had revision to do and my exams were too important. I needed to listen to my sensible head and not my mixed-up heart.

Like a warning sign, Mum poked her head round my bedroom door. 'I don't think Facebook is on the curriculum,' she said sternly.

'I know,' I replied. 'I'm just about to come off and revise for English. Promise.'

Mum smiled at me. 'You'd better,' she warned.

As soon as she'd gone, I went back to Benedict.

Look, I have to go – sorry. I really have to revise.

Come on babe – just five minutes?

Sorry.

Don't be so cruel. Please?????

I can't – I have to work. I'll hook it up when I get some free time – promise.

You're making me beg, Lily!

Please Benedict – I can't fail my exams. I'll hook it up next time, OK?

Five minutes won't hurt.

I felt myself growing annoyed. Why couldn't he just listen to me?

I'm serious. I have to go. Catch you later?

Don't tease, Lily . . .

I watched the screen for a few more moments, then turned away, and opened my copy of *Romeo and Juliet*, but I couldn't concentrate. Instead, I thought back to the night I'd given Benedict my address. I hated forgetting things; I wasn't a disorganized person but my memory was still drawing a complete blank.

I just couldn't recall doing it at all.

The Spider sits on a bench – watches joggers run past. The park is drenched in late-evening sunshine. A gang of youths walk two Staffordshire bull terriers along the outer path. One dog is brindle, the other a patchwork of black and white. Across the way sits Leicester University, and a war memorial cast in stone.

The Spider is thinking, considering. He knows what needs to be done. When the OTHER arrives, moments later, he looks sheepish. The Spider shakes his head. Establishes power . . .

'You're late,' he tells his fellow traveller.

'Traffic, work,' the OTHER replies.

'Tell me why you have put us in danger?' the Spider asks.

The OTHER sits down too. 'I didn't think,' he replies.

'But I made the rules clear,' the Spider reminds him. 'No move that isn't planned. No contact that isn't secure. Where is the difficulty in comprehending that?'

'No difficulty.'

'So – why?'

The OTHER resists an urge to punch the Spider. He isn't afraid. The Spider, for all his delusions, is a weed. Violence is not where his aptitude rests. It's not what makes him so dangerous. The threat is in his other skills and their shared history. The Spider *knows* things . . .

'I made a decision – I was wrong,' the OTHER says.

'You like this girl?'

The OTHER shakes his head. 'No more than any before her,' he explains. 'She is simply an opportunity too good to miss.'

'You realize that she will have to go?'

The OTHER nods. 'I thought as much after our last phone call.'

'She is the only one who can connect us,' the Spider points out. 'I didn't come here to get caught. I came to bring you closer to the action. I will not be found out.'

Again, the OTHER nods his understanding. 'Does she have to go immediately?' he asks.

The Spider shakes his head. 'No,' he explains. 'The

next two are ready and there will be much attention. You can't drop her too suddenly. We have to proceed with care.'

'We've already drawn attention,' the OTHER replies.

'Yes,' the Spider tells him, 'but we have been in control of those . . . *situations.* Your actions have taken control from us.'

'How so?'

'The girl is an unknown variable. We can't trust her completely.'

'I'll deal with that. She'll listen to me.'

'What if she talks to her friends?' the Spider asks. 'Tells the one she is always with?'

'She won't . . .'

The Spider is amused and angered in one. 'I asked you what would happen if she did talk,' he snaps. 'Who would be arrested and taken from the game?'

The OTHER realizes and nods slowly. 'That would be me,' he says.

'And only *you* know about my presence,' the Spider explains. 'What if you get caught and throw my name to the police?'

'I would never do that,' the OTHER insists.

'How can I be sure?' the Spider asks. 'My only guarantee is that, with the girl gone, there is no more risk.'

The OTHER shrugs. 'Shall I take care of it?' he asks.

'No,' the Spider tells him. 'I will decide when and how to proceed. Is that clear?'

The OTHER nods. 'I have found more buyers,' he adds. 'For the recordings.'

'Men like you?' asks the Spider. 'With your predilections?'

'Are we not the same?'

The Spider smiles. 'I am *nothing* like you,' he replies. 'I have no interest in sexual matters. You've always known that, haven't you?'

The OTHER stares out across the park. A family of four walk the far path, and a game of football ends as the light draws in. 'Why do you do this, then?' he asks.

The Spider stands and stretches his legs. 'Because I can,' he replies.

'So you're just a troll?'

The Spider throws him a furious glare. 'You of all people should know that I'm no troll!' he spits in disgust. 'Where would you and your fellow pederasts be without my efforts? What would you watch?'

'I meant no offence,' the OTHER tells him.

'I'm sure that is true,' the Spider replies. 'After all, you've seen what I can achieve. Would you like me to prey on you?'

The OTHER lifts an eyebrow. 'No.'

'Then we know where we stand,' the Spider replies. 'I shall be in touch.'

He saunters off, towards the city centre, his eyes blazing . . .

15

Tilly stayed angry with me. I'd left her to stew for a day before calling, and *then* sent text messages, but she'd ignored them all. And two days later, she *still* wasn't talking to me.

Danny and Kane realized there was a problem when, for the first time ever, Tilly and I didn't eat our lunch together. Benedict was annoying me too. Nothing major – he'd just been pestering me with messages again. My Facebook inbox was full of them. It was as though he wanted an instant response, all the time. And that just wasn't possible.

The dining hall was packed and noisy, and it stank of musty clothes, food and even a little BO. I felt a little lost without Tilly.

'Just stuff,' I lied to the boys. 'We'll be fine.'

Only I wasn't sure that was true. This was something new for Tilly and me – a place we'd never been to, and I couldn't handle it. I wanted my girl back, preferably minus the new boyfriend.

'But you're like sisters,' said Danny. 'Not to mention being my number one bitches . . .'

'Stop worrying,' I replied. 'Seriously – it's nothing.'

But it *was* something. It was *huge*. And I was determined to sort it out.

I saw Tilly in the corridor, towards the end of lunch. She was standing chatting to Mum's ex, Dave, who saw me and waved. Tilly didn't even look at me, though, and I walked away after giving Dave a return wave. In afternoon registration, she sat on her own, close to Mr Warren's desk.

Manisha walked in and saw that Tilly wasn't sitting with me. I waited for her to say something, but for once she kept her big mouth shut.

Tilly was talking to our form tutor, and when I glanced at her, she looked away. I felt horrible and my eyes grew moist.

'She won't even look at you,' Danny whispered in my ear. 'Seriously, babe – like, WTF?'

'She's angry with me,' I whispered back. 'She'll be OK soon.'

Danny raised a plucked eyebrow. He smelled of vanilla and spice – a women's perfume that I loved. 'Angry about what?' he said.

'It's nothing,' I told him. 'Just girl stuff – honest.' *And now I'm lying to you*, I thought. *What a fantastic friend I'm not.*

'But I'm an *honorary* girl,' Danny replied. 'You can tell me anything.'

I shook my head. 'It's personal,' I told him. 'But I'll sort it out, promise.'

'You'd better,' he told me, looking a bit hurt, as Jamie and his pals sauntered in.

'Move, you likkle *anti*-man!' Jamie whispered at Danny.

'Make me, you skidmark,' Danny replied, his voice much louder.

'Something wrong, Danny?' asked Mr Warren.

Danny shrugged. 'Nothing beyond the usual, sir,' he said. 'Jamie was just admiring my eyelashes.'

Jamie scowled and walked away, as Mr Warren cleared his throat.

'Right.' Our form tutor stood up. 'Quite a few notices this afternoon, so listen up.'

As he read out the messages, I smiled again at Tilly but she just rolled her eyes. Then Mr Dhindsa appeared at the door, with the policewoman, DC Evans, in tow. Mr Warren stopped and asked them to come in. A few whispers circled amongst my classmates.

'We'd like to speak to Manisha Patel,' said Mr Dhindsa.

'Huh?' asked Manisha. 'Why?'

I wondered what was going on. After my initial chat with DC Evans all those weeks ago, when I'd given her a list of names, things had calmed down. So why was she back and wanting to talk to Manisha now?

'Just a few questions,' said our deputy principal. 'Won't take long.'

Manisha sighed, grabbed her bag and nudged me as she walked out. I thought it had to be about Amy, but why now, after so long? DC Evans gave me a quick glance and smiled. I managed a half-smile in return before they left.

'What's that about?' whispered Danny.

'Dunno,' I said.

I guessed that the police investigation was a slow process. From what I'd seen on the news, they were still making enquiries – Amy's family hadn't even been able to hold a funeral. I wondered if they were beginning to deal with the nastiest of Amy's tormentors. It was about time.

'Do you think she'll lock the evil munchkin up?' joked Danny. 'Save me from stabbing her with her own false nails?'

Mr Warren shushed us and continued to read out notices. As he finished, we all filed out, except for Tilly, who stayed put. I went back in and confronted her.

'Go away,' she said softly.

I couldn't believe it. 'Tilly!'

'You're supposed to be my best friend,' she replied. 'But all you did was judge me.'

'No, I didn't,' I told her, my voice low so that Mr Warren, who was on his laptop, wouldn't hear. 'I was just worried about you.'

Tilly stood, and Mr Warren looked up. 'Everything OK?' he asked us.

'Yeah, fine,' I told him.

'Perfect,' added Tilly.

He gave us a bemused look. 'Get to lessons, then.'

In the corridor, Tilly walked off and I had to rush to catch her up.

'Oi!'

'Go away!' she demanded.

'No!' I yelled, not bothered who heard us this time. 'Stuff you and stuff your bullshit!'

Tilly's eyes widened and her mouth fell open. I don't know what came over me, but it had been building for days. Once I'd finished school, done all the revision I needed and had time to relax, I was so tired that I couldn't even keep my eyes open. And then, when I did sleep, I saw Tilly's face or Amy sitting on that wall outside the pub, her skin pink with the cold.

'I'm not talking to you!' snapped Tilly.

'Don't you dare act so childish with me,' I told her. 'You want to destroy our friendship over something so *stupid?*'

Tilly looked at her feet, her face taking on colour.

'Well, I won't let you!' I insisted.

When Tilly looked back at me, I saw she was crying. 'I'm sorry,' she whispered. 'But it's your fault. You think I'm a slut.'

I shook my head. What the hell was she on about? There was no way I'd ever call my best friend something so horrible. Tilly was annoying and moody sometimes but she wasn't that.

'When did I call you a *slut?*'

Tilly looked back down the corridor nervously. She was right: Mr Warren could probably hear us. We needed privacy – well, as much as you could find in a school.

Our maths lesson was beginning but it was all revision so I wasn't worried about being late for it. This was more important. 'Come on,' I said, 'let's talk in the gym toilets.'

We went downstairs, past reception and the dining hall. To the left was a corridor that led to the gym, and the quietest toilets in school. As we entered, a couple of Year Seven girls were inside chatting about some pop star and how much they loved him. When they saw us, they looked a bit scared and scuttled out quickly. I checked all four cubicles, making sure we were alone. The walls and floor were slate grey, and the basins stainless steel. The only light was artificial, and harsh.

'Right,' I said, satisfied that no one could hear us. 'Tell me.'

'Tell you what?' said Tilly, drying her eyes with a tissue from her bag.

'Why you've been ignoring me.'

She shrugged. 'Because you don't like my new boyfriend,' she said.

'I've never met him, so how can I not like him?' I asked.

She looked away. 'I thought I could tell you anything,' she whispered.

'You can.'

Her face was paler than usual, and she hadn't ironed her clothes either. I began to worry about her. She didn't look right.

'You said you wouldn't betray me,' she added. 'Remember?'

'What?'

'When we came to this school,' she continued.

'You said you were my best girl for ever. That you'd always support me.'

Of course, I knew the exact moment. It had been in our first form room. We were sitting together, sizing up the strangers who would become our new classmates. We'd been scared and excited at the same time – sisters facing a brand-new world together. Yet here we were now. It was breaking my heart.

'Yeah,' I told her, 'I remember that. And I haven't betrayed you. I've just been honest because I love you.'

Tilly started to reply but couldn't. She burst into tears.

'How old is he?' I asked. She still refused to say. 'Tilly?'

She shook her head and dabbed her face with more tissue. 'Doesn't matter,' she told me. 'You wouldn't care anyway. You ain't bothered that he means something to me. That we love each other . . .'

That threw me. My super-cool, street-smart sister was in love. 'How can you love him, Tilly?' I asked. 'How much do you have in common?'

'You don't understand!' she moaned.

'I'm trying!' I replied. 'But you're fifteen years old . . .'

She shook her head. 'I know what I'm doing,' she

told me. 'And if you don't believe me, then maybe we should forget it . . .'

'Forget what?' I asked, growing anxious.

'This!' she replied. 'This friendship, or whatever! If I can't trust you . . .'

I tried to stay calm, but I couldn't. Something inside me snapped. 'You're going to cut me off over some creep?' I asked. 'Some man who thinks it's OK to start a relationship with a schoolgirl?'

Tilly's eyes turned fiery. 'Don't you *dare* call him that!' she spat. 'You haven't got a clue – not one!'

'Really?' I replied.

'Yeah!' she spat. 'And I'm done with this!'

I was so angry, I didn't stop to think. 'Fine, if that's what you want,' I said, unable to believe what was coming out of my mouth. I felt genuinely queasy too.

'Whatever,' she replied. 'You did this, Lily . . . not me.'

I shook my head. 'Do your parents know?' I asked.

She grabbed my top and shoved me against the basins, her grip tight. I was too shocked to struggle.

'Don't you dare tell anyone!' she warned. 'If you do, I'll fucking kill you!'

I'd started to cry too, and through my tears I saw something in Tilly change. Right up until that point, our fight hadn't seemed real. Like, it was just bickering or whatever. Now, I knew it was serious and that hurt. *Bad*.

'You're doing this over some *man*?' I whispered, the snot bubbling in my nostrils.

'He's not just some man!' she shouted. 'I *love* him!'

The girl is obviously embarrassed and looks away, across open fields. The OTHER taps his finger against the steering wheel – impatient. He hasn't time for this – he needs to get back to work. The car's interior is plush – leather seats and soft-touch plastics, with aluminium inserts along the dashboard. The engine is running, a Beatles CD playing.

'Well?' he asks. 'Have you told anyone?'

The girl shakes her head but cannot look at him. He knows that she is lying.

'I need to know,' he tells her. 'We could get into serious trouble.'

She turns back and nods slightly. 'Sort of,' she replies. 'But no details. She doesn't know your name or anything like that.'

He grips the steering wheel with both hands now, his anger increasing. 'Who?' he asks. 'Who did you tell?'

'Just Lily,' she replies. 'No one else.'

The OTHER thinks for a minute. Curses her in his head. *You stupid, stupid, girl . . .* 'And who will Lily tell?' he asks.

'No one,' the girl tells him. 'She won't betray me.'

'How can you know?'

The girl gazes at him, and despite his anger, he takes a sharp breath. She is flawless. 'I know,' she replies. 'I'm not stupid.'

He nods. 'Why did you tell her?' he asks. 'Why didn't you listen to me?'

'She guessed,' fibs the girl. 'She asked if I had a new man and I told her. Nothing else. No details, no names . . .'

'Did you tell her my age?'

'No! I told you I'm too smart for that.'

'So she doesn't know I'm older than you?' he asks.

'Not how much older,' she tells him, her gaze steady, her eyes unblinking. 'I know how dangerous this is for you. I don't want you to get into trouble.'

'You shouldn't have said *anything*,' he explains. He puts his hand on her knee, so narrow and delicate in his grip.

She lays her head on his shoulder. 'I'm sorry, Dave,'

she tells him. 'It'll be fine, though. Lily would never tell anyone else.'

He strokes her cheek, the skin smooth and warm, like the surface of a pebble in the sun. 'We can't know that,' he whispers. 'What if she does?'

'I'll talk to her,' the girl tells him. 'Make sure.'

The OTHER lets it go, for the moment . . .

Later, after he drops the girl off, he calls the Spider.

'Yes?'

'She told someone,' he admits. 'The best friend.'

'Oh dear,' the Spider replies. 'Now we have two unknown variables. You see how quickly our control slips away?'

'I see,' the OTHER replies. 'And I apologize.'

'I will have to think,' the Spider tells him. 'Make new plans.'

'Are you watching Lily?' asks the OTHER.

'Not yet,' the Spider admits.

'So what shall I do?'

'About Lily knowing your secret? Nothing.'

'So you'll deal with it?'

'Yes. I want you to buy another phone, and deliver your current one to me.'

'Why?'

'Threads,' the Spider explains, yet again. 'Never stick to the same one for too long. They grow weak quickly and are easily compromised. That's how you get caught. Hiding your tracks is essential.'

'I'll do that now – get a new phone.'

'And I will decide where to go next,' the Spider replies. 'What do you know about Lily?'

'Quite a lot,' the OTHER tells him. 'She's clever but shy and I've never seen her with a boyfriend. Her dad died when she was young. She lives with her mum, close to the school – I know both quite well. Why?'

'Leverage,' the Spider replies. 'Just in case she is tempted to report your little mistake. I need more, though – I know those things already.'

'Oh – OK, I'll have a think. What shall I do about my girl?'

'Have your fun while you can,' the Spider tells him. 'She is fast approaching her date of expiry . . .'

16

Tilly went home, and I spent the afternoon in a daze. I couldn't get over her anger towards me. I kept wondering if I was wrong. Was I overreacting? Only, I knew that I wasn't. I couldn't lie to her, or pretend things were fine. Instead of concentrating on maths and science, I couldn't stop thinking about her mystery man – who he was and why he imagined dating a schoolgirl was acceptable. I knew for a fact he wasn't a teenager, otherwise she'd have told me, and it wouldn't have been such a big deal. No, he was older than that, I was sure, and that worried me. Loads of scary thoughts ran through my head. Images of evil paedophiles preying on my best friend. On my sister . . .

After school, I walked home alone. I saw Max by

our local chip shop, chatting to some lads. I hadn't spoken to him for a few days but I didn't stop, I just wasn't in the mood. My bag started to vibrate as I walked and, thinking it was Tilly, I got my phone out. Only it wasn't her — it was Benedict sending me more Facebook messages. I opened the app and went to my inbox. The last three posts were just odd.

Lily? You there, Lily?
Oh come on, Lily!!!
Please . . . ? Lily??? Are you there? Answer just once so I know. I won't be able to sleep otherwise.

As I read, the worry about the webcam was back. I really couldn't remember asking for it, or giving him my address. I know I must have done, but there was something not quite right. And I didn't want to think about it either — I just wanted to sort things out with Tilly.

And when I reached my front door, I got my chance. Tilly was sitting on the front step. When she looked up, I could see she was distraught.

'Didn't think I'd see you again,' I told her.

'Didn't think I'd come here,' she replied. The skin around her eyes was puffy and her face was drawn, her cheeks hollow.

166

'Why *are* you here?' I asked. 'I thought we were done?'

She shrugged. 'Got some of your stuff,' she replied, pulling books and CDs from her bag.

I felt like some boy, getting dumped. I never thought that Tilly could have been so hurtful – not to me. 'You can keep them,' I said.

'I just want you to pay attention to me,' she replied. 'Like, listen and not judge.'

'How am I judging you?' I asked.

'It's not what you think – this thing with . . .'

'*See?*' I replied. 'You won't even tell me his name.'

She shrugged again, and she suddenly seemed so small – like a sparrow, all tiny and hunched up. It wasn't her at all – it wasn't *my* Tilly. A couple of cars passed us, and three doors down some kids laughed and joked with each other, throwing water bombs made of blue, yellow and red balloons. Two young girls, maybe eight years old, walked past wearing matching Superdry tops in different colours – peach and lilac.

'That used to be us,' said Tilly. 'Remember?'

I nodded.

'We used to talk about clothes and boy bands, and when we'd get to wear makeup,' she added.

'And we never did,' I replied.

'Hate makeup,' she said. 'Hate boy bands now too.'

'Why are you *really* here?' I asked.

She stood and brushed off her dark jeans. My stuff was still in her hands. 'To return these,' she said.

'Don't lie,' I replied. 'You could have dropped them off anytime.'

When she looked at me all I saw was sadness, and it made me want to cry.

'I wanted to say sorry,' she finally admitted.

'Sorry?'

She nodded. 'I shouldn't have grabbed you like that,' she said. 'I'm sorry for swearing at you too.'

'OK.'

Only I wasn't sure that it was OK – not really. Her attack had hurt physically *and* emotionally. I understood that she'd been angry, but still . . .

'What about you?' she asked.

'What *about* me?' I asked.

'Your turn to apologize.'

I looked at my things. The spine of a Sophie Mackenzie thriller stood out – one that we both loved. So did a Bob Marley CD – my mum's.

'I'm sorry we argued,' I said.

'And . . . ?'

'And *what*?' I asked.

'That's all you're sorry for?' she asked.

I shook my head. How could I make my feelings clear? How could I get through to her?

'It still just feels wrong.'

Tilly watched the road for a moment. A pink and white ice-cream van appeared at the end of the street, playing an annoying, twinkly tune.

'If I was you,' she admitted, 'I'd think the same thing.'

'Exactly,' I replied.

Tilly shook her head and I sighed. We weren't getting anywhere. 'It's not, though,' she insisted. 'It's just a problem because of other people.'

'And that doesn't bother you?'

'Yeah, it does,' she told me. 'But I'm not worried for me.'

'Huh?' I asked.

'I'm worried for *him*,' she said. I couldn't help being reminded of a documentary I'd seen. It had been about abuse victims who were *so* damaged they defended their abusers to the end.

'*Him?*'

'Yeah,' she said. 'Our society is a *mess*, Lily. Like, he's not some seedy paedophile, but who'll believe that – if we get caught?'

I wondered if she was repeating what he'd told her. This didn't sound like her at all.

'No one will believe it,' I replied.

Tilly smiled. 'See?' she said. 'You do get it.'

'No,' I countered, 'I don't. It's obvious that he's

169

way older than you, Tilly. He's an adult man carrying on with an underage girl. That makes him seedy. Decent guys don't do that.'

'I'm gonna be sixteen soon,' she pointed out. 'Would it be wrong then?'

'Depends,' I said. 'Like, if he's some lad a few years older than us, then no—'

'*But?*'

'If he's older than that . . .' I trailed off.

'His age doesn't matter,' she insisted. 'When I'm sixteen, it won't matter. We just have to be careful until then . . .'

I shook my head. 'You think your mum will see it that way?' I asked.

'She won't know,' said `Tilly. 'You aren't going to tell her. I *know* you. You're my *girl* . . .'

'What if *I* was seeing someone older?' I asked. 'Like, what if I was with some thirty-year-old?'

'He's not thirty,' she replied.

'I wasn't talking about his actual age, Tilly!' I snapped.

'Then what . . . ?'

'Wouldn't you protect me?' I added.

'Yeah,' she said immediately. 'Of course I would.'

'Even if I was besotted?'

'I'd back you all the way,' said Tilly. 'Unless you were getting hurt.'

'So you understand my point, then?'

'I'm not *being* hurt,' she replied. 'We love each other . . .'

I wanted to slap her I was so angry, but I kept my emotions in check. Whoever the man was, he had got inside her head. I wondered if I should tell my mum. I didn't want to – the perfect solution would be for Tilly to realize what a creep he was and dump his ass.

'I can't do this,' I told her.

'What?'

'*This*, Tilly,' I replied. 'I can't just stand here, pretend nothing is wrong.'

'We're having a disagreement,' she told me. 'That's all this is . . .'

'Is that why you've brought my things, Tilly?' I asked. 'Because this is *nothing*?'

Tilly looked at my stuff and shook her head, but she didn't reply. It all felt too weird. She had come round as though everything was final and we were falling out for good. Yet at the same time she was trying, in her own way, to sort things out. The fact that her emotions were so jumbled added to my concern for her.

'Who is he?' I tried one last time.

'When he can't get into trouble,' she replied. 'That's when I'll tell you.'

'And you're sleeping with him?'

She gave me an intense stare. 'None of your business,' she said, which meant that she was. I was stunned. *My* Tilly was too smart to get played. The girl in front me was like someone else. Someone I didn't know at all.

'Tilly!'

'Look, take these things,' she said. 'Take them, calm down a bit, and maybe I'll call you later.'

I nodded. 'I won't change my mind,' I told her. 'I won't accept this crap.'

Tilly smiled. 'I've worked that out,' she replied. 'It's no big deal, babe. Just forget about it and we can move on.'

'So, you think everything will stay the same?' I asked.

She nodded. 'Unless you stop judging me,' she replied. 'Sorry, again, about this afternoon . . .' She handed me my things and walked down the stone path to the pavement.

'Tilly . . .?'

I was going to tell her that I was sorry and that I wouldn't judge her, but I didn't. It would have been a lie. She turned, held up her left arm and showed me her *Sisters Forever* charm.

'I love you, Lily Basra,' she told me. 'Please don't forget that . . .'

The Spider observes and smiles . . .

Boy #1 starts with confusion, and slowly but surely his face echoes rage and fear, embarrassment and shock. Watching him feel each emotion excites the Spider. *This* is why he does it. This is the feeling of power that he craves like a drug . . .

The boy is tapping at his keyboard, frantically clicking with his mouse. He's attempting to delete the post. Easily done. The boy has a major problem, though. The Spider has tagged the link to all the boy's friends. He's also activated the fake blogs. No matter what the boy does now, the footage is out there. It is burrowing its way into the very fabric of the Web.

The boy stares in horror at the screen – and the Spider knows why. What the boy sees, he sees too.

People are beginning to comment. Girl #2 – the one who spends most of her life online – is first to react. Her response will be typical:

You dirty little bastard! You ain't right in the head!

The Spider has plans for Girl #2, but she'll keep. For now, he has another role to play. He logs in as Charlotte and sends a private message. Chaos surrounds the boy, so Charlotte will be his guide . . .

OMG – what happened?

Charlotte – thank God! I don't know what's happening. Someone must have hacked my account and got this video.

I know – I saw it. What the hell?

It's the last webcam session we did. How could someone record it?

I don't know? Are you OK?

Course I'm not fucking OK!

I'm sorry, babe – stupid question. Can I help?

I'm trying to delete everything but it's on loads of sites. If my parents see this too – I'm dead.

Can't you just remove it completely?

No, Charlotte – people have shared it already. I'm dead.

No – you listen to me! I'll protect you.

How? How the fuck do I get out of this? My parents will kick me out!

You don't know that they've seen it yet.

But they will.

The Spider opens a second window. Logs into the boy's email account. He attaches the offending video. Sends it to his mum and dad. To his grandmother too. You're right, he thinks as he returns to the conversation, they WILL see it . . .

You could come to mine? You know – if things get too difficult?

How can things get any worse? I can't go back to school, I can't go out. I'm finished, Charlotte.

So come to mine . . .

When?

Tonight. I've got to work late – until about midnight.

But people will find me.

We'll move, babe. Get another place. Somewhere far away. I'm due some time off soon – we could go to Spain or Italy?

Really? You'd do all that for me?

I said so, didn't I? I'm not some stupid teenage girl – I'm a grown woman. You and me – we're made for each other.

But we've never met. I've never even seen your face . . .

Of course we've met, babe. Just because it's online doesn't mean we're not real. I've just got to be careful. Something like this could ruin my career.

Where do we meet?

There's a Subway shop near my office – London Road, in town?

I know it.

Go down the side street next to the shop. There's an alley, first left. The car park is there.

Why don't I just come to your place?

No – someone might see you. Besides, it'll be quicker if you meet me outside work.

Car?

BMW 320D.

Midnight?

Make it just after. And, Max?

Yeah?

Just come as you are – don't bother to pack any stuff; we can buy new stuff once we get abroad. So try not to worry. I'll make everything right – I promise.

Thank you.

No thanks needed, Max. It's my pleasure. Really . . .

17

When the doorbell rang an hour after Tilly left, I hoped she'd returned. But it was *Kane* on the doorstep.

'Hey!' he said.

'Hey, Kane – come in.' Despite everything, my mood lifted. I couldn't help the smile creeping onto my face.

He followed me back to the kitchen, where my annoying chemistry revision sat untouched on the table.

'Still having trouble with that?' Kane asked.

'Yeah,' I told him. 'I feel like pulling my hair out every time I look at it.'

'I was just passing,' he said. That sounded a bit odd. Kane didn't live anywhere near me, why would he have been passing by? Had he made a special trip to come and see *me*?

'You don't need an excuse,' I told him. 'You're always welcome.'

He was wearing an indigo shirt, open at the collar, with navy jeans and brown Timberlands. His dark skin seemed to glow and I kept glancing at his almost-perfect hands. I'd known him since junior school, and fancied him since I was, like, eleven. Even my actor crush, Will Smith, had been inspired by Kane's smile.

Kane looked around, studying the kitchen. 'This is different,' he said.

'Mum got it redone last year,' I explained. 'Has it been that long since you've been here?'

'Must be.'

I watched his long, slender fingers as he picked at something invisible on the table surface. He obviously had something on his mind – that must be why he'd come round.

'What's up?' I asked.

'Have you heard from Max?' he asked.

'No – why?'

Kane looked straight at me. His honey-coloured eyes were warm and inviting. If they had been a pool, I would have jumped right in. 'He's been acting strange,' he said. 'Like, we arrange to meet and then he lets me down last minute. Or he doesn't reply to messages and calls.'

'I haven't noticed,' I replied, instantly thinking of Tilly and our argument – our friendship group was sort of falling apart. 'He's been distant recently, but he always does that when we have exams. I just thought he was concentrating on revision.'

Kane nodded and picked at something on the table again.

'Maybe he's got a girlfriend?' I suggested.

'Yeah, he has, kind of,' Kane revealed.

'What – and you didn't say?' I must have sounded like Danny.

Kane shook his head. 'It's like with you and your boy online,' he told me. 'None of my business.'

I paused and wondered how to respond. Benedict's constant messages were getting more and more annoying each day. Now, the real boy I would have given my right arm for was sitting opposite me. Having him so close just made that clear.

'He's not my boyfriend or anything,' I said eventually. 'We just chat about stuff. We've never even met.'

'I thought he was Mr Model?' said Kane.

'That's what he does,' I replied. 'But he's in America.'

'Don't you Skype or anything?'

The webcam popped into my head. It was still sitting on my bedroom floor, unused. 'You know how old my computer is, I didn't have a webcam until the other day,' I told him. 'Benedict sent me one.'

That little nagging sensation returned, and it was doing my head in.

'So why haven't you hooked it up?'

'Too busy,' I said. 'GCSEs come first.'

Kane nodded again, and I felt bad for not telling him the whole truth. Yes, I'd been busy, but Benedict and the webcam thing made me feel uneasy.

'So, is he still annoying you?'

'Huh?' I asked, shocked at his question. I hadn't told him I was annoyed with Benedict. Was he reading my mind?

'You said he was insistent – when we were in Las Iguanas?'

Why was Kane so interested in Benedict? It couldn't be because he was jealous. Or could it? I pushed the thought out of my head. I was being silly. Boys like Kane didn't fancy girls like me. They went for the real beauties – the Tillys of this world. Even Molly, when she wasn't wearing her warpaint. I was no match for them. I pictured Kane sitting staring out of the window in Las Iguanas. I could have *sworn* he hadn't been listening.

'He's just been acting odd,' I explained. 'I told him I'm really busy and he doesn't seem to care – he just wants to chat all the time. The other day, I told him I was going and he just carried on messaging me, even though I wasn't replying.'

'Sounds like he's really into you,' said Kane.

I knew Benedict liked me – he'd told me plenty of times – but I didn't want Kane to know that, for some reason. I decided to downplay it, remembering what Tilly had said about hedging my bets. Only not by lying to Kane.

'He likes me,' I admitted. 'But I also think he's just a bit lonely. I'm like a *confidante*, maybe?'

'In that case, he sounds a bit weird.'

I nodded. In my head, I made a choice. It was a *risky* choice, but I decided to go for it anyway. I decided to tell Kane the truth. 'That's what I was thinking,' I said. 'Like, this webcam. I don't even remember giving him my address, but I must have forgotten I had and he posted it here. I thought that was odd.'

Kane raised an eyebrow. 'You must have told him,' he said. 'Otherwise, how could he send it to you?'

'That's the *point*,' I explained. 'Like, I *know* I must have told him, it's there in our Facebook chat history, but I can't remember doing it. It's confusing me – I don't normally forget things like that.'

'*And* . . . ?'

I gave him an enquiring glance.

'Feels like there's something you're not telling me, Lily,' Kane added.

I shrugged and picked up my phone. I found Benedict's increasingly odd messages and, despite feeling a little apprehensive, showed them to Kane. 'Here.'

Lily? You stopped caring about me, Lily?
Lily????????????????
Please tell me if I've done something wrong, babe. I wanna connect with you so bad. Why won't you reply????'
LILY!!!!!!!!!!!!!!!!!!!!

As he read them, Kane shook his head. 'OK,' he said when he'd finished. 'He's definitely *insistent* . . .'

'I'm a bit creeped out by it,' I said. 'Is that awful?'

Kane shrugged. 'I would be,' he replied. 'Man sounds like he's got some issues.'

'We've told each other a lot,' I revealed. 'Like, about feelings and stuff. I think he's just a bit hurt that I haven't been responding so quickly. I feel bad about it, but I just haven't got time . . .'

'You and me both,' said Kane. 'Revision is killing me.' He stood up, as though he was about to leave, and I felt a pang of hurt. How could he leave after I'd just confided in him?

'You going already?'

He shook his head. 'Nah,' he said. 'I'm making tea, seeing as you didn't ask.'

'Sorry!' I was *that* happy Kane was hanging around my reply had emerged like a squeal of delight. As I watched him fill the kettle, I forgot all about Benedict and his webcam.

'I'm stuck on that stuff too,' Kane added, nodding towards my revision notes. 'Maybe we can work on it together. You know – two heads and all that . . .'

I nodded, desperate not to give my emotions away. I felt like *tweenie* watching a new video by her favourite boy band. 'OK, but no distractions,' I warned. 'I'm turning my phone off.'

Kane grinned, as I remembered why he'd come round in the first place. I'd been so caught up in my own crap I hadn't asked him any more about Max.

'OK, Miss Basra,' he said. 'Anything you say.'

'Tell me about Max first, though,' I replied. 'You sounded worried.

Kane shrugged. 'I am,' he said.

Mum came in around eight p.m. with Dave in tow.

183

They were smiling and I could smell wine on Mum's breath. I resisted the urge to smile but inside I was really pleased to see them together.

'Hello, Kane!' said Mum, sounding a bit tipsy. 'Haven't seen you in ages. How's your family?'

Kane's mum and dad were from Jamaica, which is where his older brother, Alfonso, had been born. They'd lived in England for twenty-three years, and Kane and his sister, Carmen, had been born here in Leicester.

'Great, Mrs Basra. Nice to see you.'

Dave looked at the mess on the table and smiled. 'Good to see you're taking your exams seriously,' he said, glancing from me to Kane.

'Hey, Dave,' I replied, giving my mum a sly look. 'You OK?'

He nodded. His face was flushed and I could see little shaving cuts on his neck. He was wearing a grey suit over a light pink shirt and grey tie combination. He looked cool.

'I'd better get going,' Kane said, standing up.

'No, no!' said Mum. 'Don't leave because we're here. Have you had something to eat?'

'Not yet,' I replied, when Kane didn't answer. 'I thought we could have the leftover lasagne?'

Mum went to the oven and turned it on. 'I'll heat it up for you,' she said. 'Dave and I need to talk over some stuff anyway. You two can carry on working.'

Dave looked at his watch. 'I've got to be somewhere around ten, Laila,' he said.

Mum nodded. 'We'll be done by then,' she replied.

'I can reheat the lasagne,' I told her.

Mum smiled. 'OK,' she said. 'Have fun, you two.'

As they walked off to the living room, Kane grinned. 'They're a bit pissed,' he said.

'Hope so!' I replied. 'Means they had a good time. I'd love it if they got back together.'

'Is it OK for me to stay a bit longer?' asked Kane. 'I don't have to.'

I tapped a finger against a chemistry textbook. 'Yes you do,' I told him. 'You're not going anywhere until we crack this rubbish!'

Kane laughed. 'OK then,' he replied. 'I'm all yours . . .'

In my head, my delighted *tweenie* voice squealed.

As the drugged boy sleeps, the Spider watches and smiles. The boy is tied to a bed, fully clothed. His ankles and wrists are bound with wire and duct tape. The OTHER, having delivered this quarry for him, has gone.

The boy had been shocked, in more senses than one. The cattle prod sent electricity coursing through his body. Anger, confusion and fear cascaded over him when he realized his MILF wasn't all she'd promised to be. Both things had knocked him cold.

Just wait until he wakes up, the Spider thinks. *Now THAT will be fun . . .*

He leaves the basement room and heads back to his office. Several laptops sit idling. He wakes one of them. His fingers are a blur as they tap in commands.

Somewhere else, a webcam comes to life. On the Spider's screen, an image appears. A teenage girl's bedroom, dark except for the glow of a small table lamp. In her bed, Girl #2 is soundly asleep. The Spider watches for a moment. Such a waste of precious time, he thinks, before logging off.

She does not know it yet, but soon Girl #2 will be sleeping for ever . . .

18

I found out at school. There was a buzz – not excitement exactly – more amusement and shock. At the gates, a gang of lads laughed and joked. They all had their phones out.

'This is some *sick* shit, bruv,' one of them said.

I ignored the rest of their conversation, walking through the main entrance. Normally I'd see Tilly or Danny hanging out by the library. But they weren't around.

'It is sick!' I heard an Asian Year Eleven say to his mate.

'Imagine being him, though,' the first one added. 'Like, having to come school and that.'

'No way is he showing his face at school today,' said the second.

I checked my phone. I had several text messages waiting. Every single one was from Tilly – we'd fallen out, so what was going on? But it was the fifteen missed calls that made me realize something was wrong. I looked at the list and saw two names – Tilly and Danny.

'Shit!' I whispered, as Kane walked in wearing a serious expression. He didn't smile at me.

'You seen it?' he asked me.

I shook my head, my stomach starting to churn. 'Seen what?' I asked. 'What's going on?'

Kane rubbed his head. His eyes grew narrower. 'What – you seriously ain't seen?'

'No, I fell asleep straight after you left, and then overslept,' I told him. 'What's happening?'

'It's Max,' he revealed.

'What about Max?'

Kane looked around, making sure no adults could hear. 'He posted a video on Facebook – last night when we were at yours. It's nasty.'

I felt my eyes widen. 'Nasty how?'

Kane looked away for a second. 'You know,' he said, like he was uncomfortable. 'Like – him sitting at his computer, in his boxer shorts and that . . .'

I shook my head. '*Kane?*' I asked. 'Tell me what you're on about!'

He looked around again, just to be sure. 'Max

189

filmed himself . . . er . . . *masturbating*. Then he put the video on FB.'

The horror in my expression must have been obvious. It had to be a mistake. Max would never have done that – no way.

'*See?*' said Kane. 'I told you it was nasty.'

'I don't believe it!' I replied.

Kane nodded. 'I don't want to believe it either,' he said. 'But it's true. I've seen it.'

I shook my head. I wasn't having it. 'His page must have been hacked. That's the *only* explanation.'

Kane ushered me into the library. Mrs Band was at her desk, working. She saw us and smiled. We went over to the Teen Fiction shelves – out of her earshot.

'Thing is – I can believe his FB getting hacked,' Kane continued, 'but what about the *other* sites?'

'What other sites?'

'He posted the video on a couple of blogs and linked them to FB,' Kane explained.

'So? That doesn't mean he wasn't hacked,' I pointed out, though I didn't really know what I was talking about.

'Fair enough,' said Kane, 'but he still videoed himself doing *that*. Unless he's saying it's not him in the clip.'

'Did you watch it?' I asked.

Kane looked sick. 'It got taken down quick,' he told me, 'but I watched a few seconds. Just wanted to be sure.'

I saw Tilly walk in with Danny. Both wore strained expressions. Tilly actually tried to smile at me, though. I smiled back before returning to my conversation with Kane, relieved. Despite the situation, maybe things with Tilly were fixable, after all.

'And it *was* definitely him?' I asked.

'Yeah, and it wasn't good,' said Kane.

As Tilly and Danny joined us, I shook my head in disbelief once more.

'I've been trying to call Max all morning,' said Tilly. 'He won't answer.'

Danny lowered his voice to a whisper, as I saw Dr Woods, Mr Dhindsa and Mr Warren gather in the corridor outside. 'Probably hiding in shame,' he replied. 'Have you seen his wall today? It's, like, swamped with nasty comments.'

Tilly nodded. 'I saw it this morning . . . I just don't get it,' she said. 'Why would Max do that?'

Danny looked at Kane, shaking his head. 'Come on, now, Ice Queen,' he said. 'What do you think hetero boys *do* all night?'

Tilly fought back her anger. I could see it in her eyes, and I understood it too – Danny was being flippant at the wrong time.

I think Danny realized it before Tilly snapped at him. 'I *know* what they do,' she replied. 'I just don't know why he'd record himself and post it.'

'He wouldn't,' I said, looking into her eyes and hoping that our argument was over. 'Come on – he's our friend. We know him. I'm gonna call him.'

'No point,' said Kane. 'I've been trying all morning too, like Tilly. He isn't picking up.'

Kane was about to say something else when Dr Woods walked in. She looked tired and irritated. 'Form rooms,' she ordered. 'Now, please!'

As we walked out, Kane finished what he was saying. 'I know why he was recording it,' he said. 'I'll tell you later, though.'

Tilly shook her head. 'No – tell us now!' she demanded.

'Later,' Kane insisted. 'Dr Woods looks pissed off.'

I caught up with Kane by the gates, as school ended. He was watching DC Evans getting out of her car. This time she was in uniform and wearing a hat. She looked tense.

'What's that about?' he asked me.

'Dunno,' I replied, avoiding the officer's gaze as she passed us and entered main reception.

'Have you heard from Max?'

I shook my head. 'And I'm worried.' I'd checked my phone obsessively all day. Nothing.

Kane ran a hand across his head. 'Me too,' he admitted. 'Sent him plenty of texts this afternoon. He ain't replied to one.'

'No surprise,' I said. 'Like, just *imagine* how he's feeling.'

'Don't want to,' he told me.

'So, tell me why Max was recording himself,' I replied. 'And why didn't you tell me all of this last night?'

Kane's expression darkened and he averted his eyes. 'I dunno why,' he said. 'Didn't feel right, I guess. It was Max's secret. She's some woman – like, this older babe he met online.'

'What older babe?' I asked. 'Is this the girlfriend you were on about yesterday?'

'Yeah,' said Kane. 'He didn't give a name, though. Just said he was in some chat room and this woman messaged him. They were webcamming and that . . .'

'*What?*' I thought of Benedict and the webcam he'd sent. He might have annoyed me recently, but at least he wasn't into shit like this.

Kane looked at me and shrugged. 'What can I say, Lily?'

'I want you to tell me the truth,' I replied.

'OK,' he said, 'but it's seedy, you get me?'

'Seedier than wanking online, for the world to see?' asked Tilly from behind me.

'Hey, Tilly – you OK?' I asked.

Tilly ignored me and I felt deflated. After the way she'd been earlier, I thought we were over the worst. Now I realized that I might be wrong. Tilly was my best friend but she could easily walk away and find someone else. She was chatty and fun, and exciting. I wasn't. I'd always felt lucky to have her on my side. Now I was scared that I might never have her on my side again, and it hurt.

'Well?' she asked Kane.

Kane nodded. 'She started sending him pics and that,' he told us. 'Then she wanted videos and he sent them.'

I shook my head. End-of-school chatter echoed all around us. Parents, parked on double-yellows despite the warning signs, waited for their Year Seven angels. The sun peeked through white clouds and a gentle breeze floated across the fields behind school. It could have been any normal afternoon – except it wasn't.

'Max was doing *that*?' I said in surprise.

'Yeah,' said Kane. 'He showed me a pic of the woman – *proper* MILF.'

'Kane!' yelled Tilly. 'I *hate* that term!'

Mother I'd like to—! I hate it too, I thought, only it wasn't important. Max was our only concern, surely?

'You know what I mean,' Kane protested. 'Anyway – he really got into it. He was staying up all night and that . . .'

Once again, I couldn't believe what I was hearing. Max just wasn't like that. How could there be an entire hidden side to him that I hadn't spotted? He wasn't my best friend but I knew him better than most. How did I not see? But, then again, maybe we all kept stuff from each other. I glanced at Tilly and thought about her secret.

'Did this woman know how old Max was?'

'Yeah – *course* she knew his age,' Kane replied. 'That's why she messaged him – younger man and all that.'

'Shit – what's going on?' Tilly asked suddenly.

I followed her gaze to main reception. Mr Warren was standing with Mr Dhindsa. Dr Woods and DC Evans quickly joined them, and then Dave's car – a BMW – pulled into the drive too. Something was up.

'Look at their faces,' Tilly added. 'Something's wrong – I'm telling you.'

Mr Warren looked towards us and I raised my eyebrows. He shook his head just once. We didn't move as DC Evans and Dr Woods approached us.

Both wore grim expressions, and our principal looked worn out. Her usually immaculate skirt was wrinkled and her hair was a mess.

'Have any of you heard from Max Jones?' asked Dr Woods.

'You're his friends, right?' added DC Evans, eyeing us all.

'Yes . . .' Tilly replied.

Dr Woods seemed to look to DC Evans for approval. When the officer nodded, she continued. 'Someone posted a video on Max's wall last night,' she told us. 'I'm sure you're all aware of this.'

'The whole school knows,' admitted Tilly.

'It's much more serious than that,' said DC Evans.

'Serious how?' I asked, getting worried.

'Max is missing,' she replied.

The Spider smiles as he watches the latest photo download. Girl #2 is wearing tiny red shorts and little else. She types a message.

You like?

She doesn't realize that her webcam is on. That she is being recorded. The Spider isn't just looking at her self-shot photographs. He's watching her as she takes them. Soon, he will reveal them to the world.

You look amazing, babe.

Better than the other girls?

They aren't even on the same planet. Never mind the same league.

Promise?

I promise.

So rate me out of ten?

Like, a MILLION, babe.

You're just saying that.

No way! You're model material – like I told you.

My thighs are too fat.

Your thighs are beautiful.

What about my bum?

Just perfect.

When will you offer me the contract?

Soon – just got to show the agency these shots.

So, like, I'll be famous?

Yeah, babe – the whole world is gonna know your name.

Can't wait! I've wanted to be famous since I was five.

The Spider shakes his head. Such self-obsession, in one *so* young. Girl #2 wants fame. Soon she will have her desire.

Time for the next cliché – how's it go? Oh yeah . . .

Be careful what you wish for . . .

19

The police launched an appeal after they spoke to us. But two days later Max still hadn't turned up. I was becoming more and more afraid that something awful had happened. I recalled Max talking about Amy's death. He'd said only naïve people got exploited online. That they left themselves open to public shame. One sentence went round and round in my head.

You'd never be able to show your face again.

Is that what had happened to Max? Was he so scared, so ashamed, that he'd run off to hide? I wished that I could talk to him – to tell him that his friends cared. That we wouldn't judge him over what he'd done. But despite endless calls and texts from us all, he wasn't replying. The last time I'd tried, his phone had been off.

The police were particularly concerned about the woman Max had interacted with online – her name was Charlotte – and I wondered if that was where he was now. Had he run to her? After interviewing us with Dave and Dr Woods present, we were asked to keep quiet about her. Kane was the only one who really knew anything about her – and even then, only what Max had told him. The police wanted time to confirm the facts, said DI Meadows. DC Evans's expression had told me everything – this was serious.

That evening, after I'd had to convince my mum that I was safe online, I caught up with Benedict. I'd been feeling awful for ignoring him, and had decided to apologize. I still felt uneasy, as I'd confided in Kane, but not so much. Thinking about Max had made me realize that friends were important, and Benedict obviously liked me. He wouldn't have been so wound up otherwise. And even though he'd been acting a bit weird, I liked him too. When we connected, he seemed genuinely upset.

Just a quick message would have done, Lily.

Sorry, Benny. I don't know what to say.

I thought we were friends, you and me?

We are. I've just been really busy and now Max has gone and I fell out with Tilly too.

Oh no – what happened with Tilly? I thought you were like sisters?

We are – at least we were. Just girl stuff though. I'm really hoping it'll blow over soon.

You know you can tell me anything, Lily.

Yeah – I know.

I wondered whether I *wanted* to tell him. I was sort of torn too, between him and Kane, and how I felt about both of them. I'd never had any lad interested in me before, and now it felt like I had two. With Kane, it was just that – a *feeling* and nothing more, and I considered whether I was being stupid. Like, was Kane just being friendly, and was I reading too much into it?

With Benedict, I knew he liked me, but I wasn't sure whether that was enough. The odd messages and the webcam bothered me. And, besides, he lived in another country. He seemed real and unreal at once, if that makes any sense?

Kane was completely real, though, and given the choice, I'd pick him every time. The problem was that I didn't have that choice – I just wanted it to happen. And that didn't mean it would.

Are you still there, Lily?

Yeah, I was just thinking.

About your problem with Tilly?

No – that's just over her new man. It's nothing, I'm sure.

What then?

Max – my friend who's missing.

Maybe he's just hiding out – like he's upset and wants some time to himself?

I hope that's all it is.

He'll probably turn up in a day or so – you'll see.

It's just weird.

What?

First Amy dies, then Max goes missing. It's like there's a curse on the school or something.

You and Max were close huh?

We're good friends. Have been since we started at the school.

Close enough, then.

Don't wanna go to school tomorrow.

So don't. Stay home and chat to me.

But what about the time difference?

I'm always online.

I've noticed that. You ever sleep?

Not much. When I do, though, I dream of you!

Charmer!

Got any more pics?

No.

Connect the webcam?

Not today – I still have to revise. It's important to me, Benny. I want to get the best grades I can. You understand, don't you?

Yeah but I just want to see your face – only for a moment. To see your smile . . .

Why?

Because you're lovely, Lily.

Look – as soon as I get a chance, I will, OK?

Guess that will have to do. For now.

I'd told Benedict I had to work and was just getting into my revision when Danny messaged me. The police were holding a press conference about Max, live on Sky. I didn't have a TV in my room, so I ran downstairs to watch. DC Evans sat next to her boss, DI Meadows. His face was bright red and he was sweating. DC Evans's expression was stony.

'We've had several reports but nothing concrete,' said DI Meadows. 'We would urge anyone with information to contact us. The number to call is displayed on the screen.'

Another question was fired at the policeman, but I couldn't hear it.

'Yes – we are treating it as suspicious,' said Meadows. 'There is a natural investigative window for these cases of forty-eight hours – after which unease grows. Right now, we're concerned that Max hasn't attempted to make contact with his family or friends. He hasn't taken any clothes or a bag either. The only things he took are his wallet and phone, and the clothes he was last wearing. The nature of our search is urgent. We need to find him.'

My mum walked in as I watched. Her face was drawn and the skin under eyes was dark. She looked exhausted.

'How long now?' she asked.

'Huh?'

'Since Max went?'

'Three days almost,' I said. 'He went in the middle of the night. Didn't even take any clothes or anything.'

Mum shook her head. 'That's not a good sign,' she told me. 'People who run away take stuff.'

I nodded. 'That's what I was thinking,' I told her. 'You could ask Dave – he's coordinating between the police and school, so he might know more. I saw him earlier but he's more likely to tell you.'

'I might do that,' she told me.

When I didn't respond, Mum put her hand on my shoulder. 'You OK?'

'No,' I said. 'After Amy, and now this – no . . .'

Mum kissed me on the cheek. 'Don't hold your feelings in,' she told me. 'I'm here for you, OK?'

'Thanks, Mum,' I replied.

On the screen, DI Meadows held up some clothing. He told reporters that Max was wearing similar items, and then showed a photo of him.

'*Will the Jones family be making a statement?*' asked another reporter.

DI Meadows shook his head and I could see that he was annoyed at the question. '*Right now,*' he said forcefully, '*I would request that the family be left alone. This is not a circus, it's a missing person's case. If they decide to speak to the press, you'll be the first to know. Until then, please respect their wishes.'*

Meadows answered some more questions—mostly repeating what he'd already said. I turned off and went back upstairs. Fifteen minutes later, I saw that I had a message from Benedict.

Another pic of me – enjoy!

I scrolled up the screen and found it. My mouth fell open and I blushed, even though I was the only person in the room. The tiny hairs on my forearm began to tingle, as though something was crawling across them. I couldn't bring myself to reply.

It was another shot of Benedict's crotch. Only this time he was naked.

Lily?

I logged off.

Ten years earlier, the Spider is sitting at a table in downtown Manhattan. He looks across the Hudson River, towards Jersey City, the skyline busy with cranes and construction work. His day job takes him into the financial district, temping for a multinational bank.

Today, however, he is moonlighting. This is his night shift. A man approaches, his bulk barely contained within his chocolate-brown leather coat. His head is square, his black hair shaved, and his jaw looks as though it is carved from granite. Behind him, two equally huge men loiter by a black Mercedes S-Class. They look like primates in thousand-dollar suits. They couldn't get closer to the stereotype of Russian mafia if they tried.

The boss is called Grigori and he takes the seat opposite the Spider.

'Boss,' the Spider says in greeting.

'What do you have?' Grigori asks, waving away a passing waiter.

The Spider reaches into his nylon backpack and pulls out an envelope. He shows Grigori the contents – a stack of CD-Rs. Each one contains the financial details of a thousand unsuspecting bank customers from across the world.

When the Spider explains this, Grigori smiles. 'How much?' he asks.

'If you give me regular work,' the Spider tells him, 'you can have these for free. I can get as many more as you wish.'

'What work do you do?'

The Spider takes his laptop from his bag. 'Industrial espionage, hacking, viruses, specialist porn. Whatever you need. I have some examples of my work here, but we'll have to look at this stuff in private,' he tells Grigori.

The gangster grins. They stand and walk to his car.

20

Mum didn't complain when I told her I couldn't face school the following day. She just nodded and gave me a hug. I didn't have much on anyway. The lessons were mostly catch-up and revision sessions, and I could revise at home. I tried to sleep but I couldn't stop thinking about Max and Amy, or Benedict's stupid pic, or my argument with Tilly. So I lay in bed, staring at the ceiling, all of it churning around my head.

The nude pic had really bothered me. It made me question Benedict's motives. I kept thinking about how pushy he'd been over the webcam – going on and on about it. At first, I hadn't even noticed he was being so insistent. That only happened when the messages started becoming more frequent. Now, though, I had the sense that I was being played. Was that really all he'd wanted – some slapper to show him her boobs? Was I supposed to look at his naked pic and send one in return? The thought of it made me angry and miserable at the same time.

Around ten a.m., Kane messaged me to see where I was. I looked at my phone for ages before replying. When I did, I told him the truth, and said I'd be around all day.

You want me to come over?

If you want to.

After school then?

Yeah – that would be cool.

OK.

I had a shower and got dressed, before making some toast. In the living room, I couldn't concentrate on my revision so I watched telly on the widescreen that Dave had hung on the wall when he'd lived with us. I flicked channels, hoping to find something good – or at least something that wasn't a repeat. I didn't manage it and had to settle for *Blackadder* Series 2 – something Mum had got me into after I'd gone off *Mr Bean*. As Rowan Atkinson's rubbery face made me smile, my phone buzzed again. Tilly . . .

You avoiding me?

No. Why would I do that?

Because you hate me?

I don't hate you, Tilly. You hate me.

I don't hate you. I was just angry, that's all. I miss you.

I miss you too.

Reading those words made me smile. I wanted nothing more than to have her back, properly. I couldn't lose her because I'd never find another friend like her. She was my girl.

So why are you off school?

Didn't feel right. Can't stop thinking about Max.

Me neither but I'm here.

Bully for you, Tilly Poo! Why don't you drop by later? Kane is coming over after school.

Can't. Got stuff to do.

I immediately thought of her new man, and shook my head. I was still hoping that she'd see sense and get rid of him.

With him?

No – with Mum. See you tomorrow?

Yeah.

The house was a mess, so after *Blackadder*, I tidied and vacuumed. I was tempted to check my PC – see if Benedict had been back in touch, but I didn't. I wasn't sure how I felt. Instead, I tried to revise, but I couldn't think straight. In the end I found a 1980s film called *The Breakfast Club* on Netflix and settled down to watch.

The film was great – lots of music my mum loved and cool characters. I dozed off at the end and only woke up when my phone buzzed for a third time. I thought it might be Tilly again, but it wasn't. It was Danny and he was obviously off school too.

Sky News. NOW.

I switched channel, shuddered at what I saw on screen, and burst into tears.

'Police investigating the disappearance of Leicester teenager Max Jones tell Sky sources that they have discovered a body. No identity confirmed, as yet, but we'll bring you updates as soon as they happen on the UK's fastest news channe . . . Once again, Sky sources can confirm that police investigating the whereabouts of missing Leicester teenager Max Jones have discovered a body. More on this breaking news story when we return . . .'

The Spider sits and reads through a long list of messages, his mind wandering. He has never failed. Each of his victims has been carefully nurtured and none has ever escaped . . .

Yet here he is – unable to understand why this one won't fall for his trap. She is dismissive of his efforts, ignorant even. He's tried several well-worn strategies but she has rebuffed each one. The Spider has been doing this for a long time. He is not about to be beaten by her . . .

As he reads back through their interactions, he begins to smile. With what he knows already, and what she is yet to discover, perhaps it is time to up the ante. To raise his game . . .

21

A cemetery sits opposite Leicester University. An iron railway bridge crosses the ring road next to it; the bridge has a walkway. Max was found on the tracks below. He'd hanged himself – using the same type of rope as Amy had used. It had snapped, which is why he'd fallen. At least that's what the news reports said.

I was out for a walk, five days after Max's body had been discovered. My mind was numb, my thoughts haphazard. I crossed Regent Street, passing Oadby Fish Bar and an Asian food store. There was no pattern to my route. I was just wandering really. A Sikh man, his turban bright orange, pulled up to the kerb alongside me. He got out and entered the Desi Meat Shop. He drove a silver Mercedes and his young kids were in the back, fiddling with their phones. A lorry rushed past, heading south on the A6, towards my house.

At the BP garage, I went left up Stoughton Road. Danny's family lived half a mile away, in a massive detached house with a gated drive and tennis courts. I thought about sending him a text – but couldn't be arsed. I just wanted to be alone – to think. I'd normally confide in Tilly, but our relationship wasn't great. Yeah, we were talking, but our recent conversations were played out with an elephant in the room. Besides, she was in town with her mum.

I thought about Kane, but something stopped me from calling at his house. Since Max had been found, Kane hadn't been over to mine. I still wasn't sure what was going on between us – if anything even was. I had a mountain of revision too, but I didn't care right then. I couldn't get Max out of my head.

The media had been camped outside school all week. They were around Oadby village too – asking about Max. We'd been advised to avoid them again, but it was difficult. They were like ants. The story was even bigger now Max was dead. And the suicide-pact theory was growing more popular. Never mind that Max and Amy barely spoke, or that there was no evidence that they'd planned anything together. Even my mum's regular newspaper – normally quite calm and sober – was hyping things.

Online, Max had his own memorial page to match Amy's. Facebook was packed with discussions about him. Like, why had he posted a sick video of himself? And, why did he commit suicide? That sort of thing. There were trolls too – loads of them – making nasty comments. I couldn't stomach it – couldn't even click on my Web browser icon. So I hadn't spoken to Benedict since he'd sent me that picture.

Not that I wanted to. Occasionally I wondered whether I was being unfair – after all, it was only a picture – and I started to feel bad about it. Maybe I was being a killjoy; maybe it was just a bit of harmless fun. Thing is, it didn't feel that way. It felt wrong, and added to the webcam appearing out of the blue, and the odd messages that I'd shown Kane, I was a bit creeped out by my American friend.

I found a bench, sat down and took out my phone. I went into the Facebook app, but it took ages to update. When it finally loaded, I felt like throwing it away. Benedict had left nearly *thirty* messages. I blinked when I saw the amount. Blinked again and shook my head. I could have ignored him but I decided to stop being so lame and reply. I thought about how lovely he'd been at first, how

I'd started to have feelings for him. So what had changed? Why was he suddenly being so needy and odd? It felt like he was letting me down – throwing away something wonderful – and that made me sad. He'd made me believe in him but now it just felt wrong. And so quickly too – no wonder I was confused.

Hey Benny – that's a lot of messages.

His reply was instant.

WTF???????

You angry?

No – I'm happy that you've ignored me.

Things are bad here – I told you.

I know. We have media too. I read about Max – I'm sorry.

Why? You didn't know him.

Yeah – well I'm sorry anyway.

I didn't like that pic you sent.

I guessed. Why not?

Because I'm not that type of girl.

That's very judgemental. Am I that type of boy?

I don't know.

Thanks for that. I thought we had a connection, Lily?

We don't even know each other. Not really.

That's why I sent the pic. Why I talk to you on here. Thought we were making a connection. Guess I was wrong.

That's not fair.

How could he say that? Making a connection was about trusting each other and becoming better friends. It wasn't about showing each other naked selfies. Well, not in my world, anyway.

What's not fair? That I spend time on you, and you don't reciprocate? That I send you pics of me and you don't return the favour? Thought you liked me?

I do like you. I just don't send pics like those. I'm not Molly Cooper.

I can see that.

I felt myself grow angry. *What* could he see? That I wasn't half naked and posing for a webcam?

Meaning?

Meaning you're like a nun, Lily. At least girls like Molly know how to have fun.

So message her instead.

I was fuming now – really hot and wound up. If he'd been sitting next to me, I would have screamed at him.

I already have.

What?

Well – did you think I'd sit around waiting for you? I'm not some asshole needs to be treated that way.

Why are you being so mean?

Me? I'm not mean. You're the mean one.

Is that all you wanted – some slutty pics?

The thought made me feel ill. It upset me too. Was that all I meant to him?

I wanted to be your man. I could have any girl in the world, Lily. I chose you though. Big mistake, I reckon. Molly wouldn't have treated me this way. She knows how to enjoy herself.

The anger came back and my grip grew tighter around my phone. Who did he think he was? He knew I was insecure and he knew that his words would bother me. He *had* to know. All the things I'd told him about – like my self-confidence issues, and how I felt about my looks and even my dad . . .

I had trusted him and he was a dickhead. He had told me I was special, nearly convinced me, and now, with a few words, he'd taken it all away. I wanted to cry but I forced myself to be stern. I forced myself to be more like Tilly.

Love yourself much?

See? You are mean. I was just being honest. I'm a teenage boy, Lily. What's with the old-timer attitude?

My friend just died?

I know – all the more reason to let off steam.

I can't.

Well, I'm not sitting around waiting. You wanna play – wanna live your life – let me know. Otherwise, I'm done with this crap. I'm not being ignored by no girl.

* * *

Mum sensed my mood immediately. I hadn't even stepped inside. Part of me was gutted by Benedict's words – the way he'd just reinforced so many insecurities. Yet I had a sense of relief too. Like I was getting away from something. I can't even explain what or why. It was just how I felt.

'What's up?' asked Mum.

I shrugged. 'Just thinking about Max,' I told her.

Mum shook her head. 'There's more, Lily – I can see you've been crying.'

I had. Only my tears had been about Benedict, and not my dead friend. And knowing that brought on guilt, which led to more tears. I was angry with myself for caring what Benedict thought. For wasting my tears over him. He was just some anonymous boy online. He wasn't real, not like Kane. He wasn't Max.

'Nothing, honestly,' I insisted.

'I don't believe you,' she said, 'but I'll let it go. For now.'

'Great,' I replied. 'Nothing like the third degree when I get home – cheers me up no end.'

Mum glared at me. 'Dave's here,' she told me, 'so lose the attitude.'

'*Yeah.*'

Mum shook her head. I could see that she was annoyed with me. I was being spiky and I knew it.

'Just come and say hello to Dave. He's staying for dinner.'

'Did I hear my name?' asked Dave from the living-room door. He looked tired and his face was pasty. The dark green Leicester Tigers top he wore didn't help.

'Hey, Dave,' I said, trying to sound cheerful.

'Lily,' he replied. 'I'm ever so sorry about Max – I know you were close.'

I ran upstairs before any more tears came.

22

Over the next two days, school brought back images and memories of Max. Every room, every corridor held his spore. Even saying it sounds stupid, but it felt that way.

I tried to bury my emotions. Like, if anyone mentioned his name, I'd change the subject. Or when people discussed his death around me, I'd find something urgent to do elsewhere. Tilly got me – she understood my reactions – even if we weren't getting on so well, but I wondered whether everyone else just thought I was a heartless, cold bitch. Not that I cared. I knew what Max had meant to me.

By Friday afternoon form time, things got too much for Tilly. She'd been cracking jokes all week, pretending to the world, but I could see the anguish in her eyes. It was something more too – maybe the strain of keeping her secret hidden.

As we came in from lunch, she burst into tears with no warning. When I tried to comfort her, Jamie Walker started taking the piss and Manisha joined in.

'What's she crying for?' asked Jamie. 'Was she shagging him?'

'Shut up!' I yelled.

'She fancied him, for sure,' Manisha added.

'Crying over some dirty wanker,' said Jamie. 'Man was a nonce.'

'JAMIE!' yelled Mr Warren from the door.

Manisha crawled back under a rock, like the cockroach that she was, as Jamie went red. I wondered what DC Evans had done with the names I'd given her after Amy died. Looking at the two idiots in my class, the answer was obvious. *Nothing*. So much for taking the bullying seriously, I thought.

'I suggest you shut the hell up!' continued Mr Warren. He was livid – actually shaking with rage.

'You can't talk to me like that,' said Jamie, looking around at his friends for support. 'I'll tell my old man – get you done.'

Mr Warren shook his head slowly. 'I don't care who you tell,' he said in a calmer tone. 'I'm sure your father will be delighted to hear that you're besmirching the name of a dead pupil. Shall we call him now?'

Jamie went quiet and lost his bravado.

'Any more of that,' said Mr Warren, 'and you're in *serious* trouble, do you understand?'

'Sir,' Jamie replied sulkily.

'That goes for anyone else,' our form teacher added, looking directly at Manisha.

She scowled and turned away.

'Tilly,' said Mr Warren. 'You come with me – OK?'

Tilly nodded and I stood up too.

'No – just Tilly,' Mr Warren told me.

They walked out, and across the corridor to Mr Dhindsa's office.

'Stupid bitch!' whispered Manisha.

I turned round.

'Yeah – *you*,' she said.

I said nothing, but then Mr Warren came back. 'Is Tilly OK, sir?' I asked.

'Yes,' he told me. 'Just upset. I think recent events have shocked us all. Tilly's calming down in Mr Dhindsa's room.' He sat, flipped open his laptop and took the register.

Tilly went home early, so Kane and I walked back together after school. We cut down past the local supermarket but didn't stop for coffee. The car park was packed with Friday shoppers and lots of pupils from school.

'Why shop on a Friday?' Kane asked.

'Huh?'

'It's always so busy,' he explained. 'Like, why not shop when it's quiet.'

'You think about some random stuff, Kane.' I looked at my reflection in a parked car, just to make sure my hair was OK. After my last spat with Benedict, I'd lost the confusion I'd had over him and Kane. Even if nothing came of it, I knew now that Kane was real. Benedict was just weird and I was still angry with him, and with myself for caring what he thought of me.

Kane stopped to watch a black sports car fly past on the A6. 'Audi R8,' he said softly. 'Max loved his cars.'

'I know,' I told him. 'He had all those posters on his wall.'

Just thinking about it made me tearful. Max would never sleep in his bed again, or read his favourite books. He'd never get the chance to live out his dreams. If I had been his mum, I think I might have died of grief.

'It doesn't feel real,' continued Kane. 'Like – him being gone and that.'

'I know that too.'

'Can't get my head sorted, y'know?'

I nodded. 'It's like a nightmare,' I said.

Kane paused before continuing. 'I keep thinking about that woman, Charlotte,' he added. 'The one he was chatting to online. Like, maybe I should have listened to him more?'

'What do you mean?' I asked.

'Just that it was weird,' he said. 'He was proper into her, but he didn't even know what she looked like.'

'Really?'

'Well – he did,' Kane replied. 'But only 'cos she sent him photos and stuff. I don't think they ever met. I keep wondering if she made him – y'know . . .'

'I can't see it,' I replied. 'What could she have done?'

'Max wouldn't kill himself,' said Kane. 'He just wouldn't.'

I shrugged. 'Maybe not in normal circumstances,' I said, 'but after that video and all the shame – who knows?'

'That's just stupid, though,' Kane replied. 'People would have forgotten about it – eventually.'

'Yeah, but imagine the shit Max would've taken.'

Kane shook his head again. 'I'd rather be

embarrassed and alive than dead,' he told me. 'I just can't understand how people can kill themselves. Doesn't make sense.'

It made no sense to me either. Was getting caught like Max really the worst thing that could happen to a boy? Like, really? Kane's words made complete sense. Surely it was better to be alive?

'You think the newspapers are right?' he added.

'About what?'

'Amy and Max – in some suicide pact?'

I shook my head. It felt like a stupid theory. 'No way,' I told him. 'It's ridiculous . . .'

'You know,' he said, 'I keep getting this feeling like there's more . . .'

'More to what?' I asked, intrigued by what he meant.

'More to Max's death.'

'What makes you think that?'

'I don't know,' he said. 'It's just a feeling . . .'

I realized then that Kane had his own coping strategy. It was different to mine, but that didn't make it better or worse. He was just trying to make sense of Max's death. We didn't say much else, and at my house he kissed me on the cheek. He'd never done that before. The feel of his lips against my skin made me light-headed. I started to think those silly thoughts again – that he really did like me, that I was his type of girl . . .

'Kane?' I said.

'Huh?'

I smiled. 'Nothing,' I replied. 'Just – call me later – if you like.'

He smiled back. 'OK,' he said, before walking off.

In my head, my emotions rocked back and forth between sadness and excitement, and that *tweenie* version of me squealed again.

23

I started my Saturday eating peanut butter on toast, and watching crap telly in my PJs. When the latest idiot boy band appeared, I swore and flicked channels. As each channel flashed by, BBC News 24 caught my eye. They were showing a photograph of Max . . .

'*New details have emerged in the case of Leicester teenager Max Jones. Max, who was fifteen, was found dead just over a week ago, in what appeared to be a suicide. However, Leicestershire Police confirmed this morning that they are widening the scope of their enquiry, and cannot rule out the possibility of foul play. We can cross to Maya Khan, in Leicester . . .*'

Putting my plate down, I turned up the volume. My head was spinning. Were they saying that Max had been *murdered*? I grabbed my phone and called

Kane. He answered at the first tone.

'Are you watching—?' I began, but Kane cut me off.

'Yeah. It's on every news channel,' he said.

'I guess you were right, then,' I told him.

'I *knew* something was wrong,' he replied.

'Call you back in a mo,' I said.

'Or come round?' he suggested.

'OK.'

The BBC reporter was standing by the main gates to school.

'*Teachers described Max as a model pupil, and a huge loss for the school. The sense of shock here is palpable. That shock is bound to increase now that investigators believe Max may have been the victim of foul play and are widening their enquiries. The Hi-Tech Crimes Unit has been called in, a specialist group experienced in cyber-crime, and a fresh appeal has gone out for information.*

'*DI Meadows, who leads the investigation, told reporters this morning that nothing will be ruled out. But he also refuted claims, in some of this morning's daily newspapers, of links between this case and that of fellow pupil Amy Wiggins, who died just over a month before Max Jones disappeared. DI Meadows urged media outlets to steer clear of fanciful theories and to concentrate on the facts.*

'*However, the BBC has learned that in Amy Wiggins's case, enquiries are still ongoing. That her death has not yet been* declared a suicide, nor a death certificate issued, will only lead to more speculation about possible links between the two cases.'

Foul play *had* to mean murder. The idea made me feel nauseous. Who would want to kill Max, and why? And if Amy *had* committed suicide, why were the police still investigating? It had been weeks since she died – surely that was long enough to decide? It just didn't make sense.

I ran upstairs to shower and get dressed. Were the deaths of Amy and Max really linked? How was that even possible? As soon as I was ready, I did some digging on the Internet. My PC was playing up, so I used Mum's laptop. She had blocked Facebook and a couple of other social media sites so I didn't have to face any more of Benedict's messages either, for which I was grateful. I wasn't ready to deal with him again – not after the selfie and the hurtful comment about other girls being more fun than me. An hour later, I'd printed off a stack of information. I left the house and headed for Kane's. It was a fifteen-minute walk – long enough to think things through.

Kane lived in a terrace with his family. The house had a little courtyard front garden filled with plants and brightly coloured flowers. Kane opened the door, and half smiled. He was wearing a white

T-shirt that strained against his arms and chest, grey jersey shorts that fell just below his knees and blue flip-flops. His hair was un-braided again and stood tall.

'Hey,' he said.

'Is it OK to be here?' I asked, feeling self-conscious all of a sudden.

He shook his head. 'Nah – my mum is going to kill and cook you,' he joked. 'Course it's OK, you nutter.'

I smiled and followed him down a narrow hall-way, to the right of the stairs, and into the kitchen at the rear. The room smelled of spicy chicken.

'Jerk,' he said, nodding at the oven. 'Mum always makes it on a Saturday.'

'Smells great,' I told him. 'I might have to steal some.'

'You won't even make the kitchen door,' he replied. 'Alfie will get you first. Man *nyams* chicken like vampires suck blood.'

An open Apple Macbook Pro sat on the wooden kitchen table. 'This is lovely,' I said, running my fingers across the smooth metal case.

'It's my brother's,' Kane told me. 'He's got four computers.'

'What does he do?' I asked.

I'd known Kane since Year Six, but didn't really

know his brother. He was a lot older than us and always busy. His sister, Carmen, was Year Eight, so I saw lots of her, and Kane's parents knew my mum.

'Alfie's a systems analyst. Does computer programming and that too.'

'Sounds boring,' I replied.

'Yeah, it is,' said Kane, 'but it pays good and he can do anything with a computer. Gives us his old ones too.'

'Still sounds boring,' I joked.

'See the new Mercedes C250 outside – the red one?'

I shook my head.

'That's his,' said Kane. 'Thirty-five grand, that. He keeps getting pulled over by the coppers, though. They think he's selling crack . . .'

'That's awful,' I replied.

'How tings run for a wealthy black man,' Kane told me. 'Kinda fucked, you ask me.'

'How come he lives at home, then?' I asked, looking around the kitchen. 'Like, if he's so rich?'

'Dunno,' he replied. 'Mum's cooking? It's cool having him around, though.'

Having eaten Mrs Williams's food before, I could understand that. She was good.

'So what we gonna do?' Kane asked, his expression growing serious. 'About Max?'

I shrugged. 'I don't understand,' I told him. 'What *can* we do?'

'Go to the police?' he suggested. 'Tell them about that Charlotte woman?'

'DC Evans already asked us about that,' I reminded him.

'Yeah,' replied Kane, 'but they thought it was suicide then. Besides there's something I forgot.'

'What?'

'Just about Charlotte – that he'd never actually seen her. It might be important, though.'

Neither of us spoke for a moment, before Kane continued. 'It has to be foul play,' he said. 'It's definitely not a suicide; otherwise they'd close the case.'

I considered Kane's words and realized he might be right. Why would the police mention foul play if they weren't already convinced? But then again, maybe Kane was wrong too. Wouldn't the police have made it clear that it was a murder, if it really was?

'They said that foul play is a *possibility*,' I replied, trying not to get carried away. 'Besides, we don't know the facts.'

'True,' said Kane, 'but we know more than most people.'

'What about Amy?' I added. 'Do you reckon there's a link?'

Kane shook his head again. 'Doesn't look like it,' he told me.

I pulled a wad of paper from my bag. 'I've been doing some research,' I told him. 'After we spoke earlier. There's this thing – the Werther Effect – that leads to copycat suicides . . .'

I gave him a sheet to look at. As we drew closer, I felt the heat from his body. I tried my best not to blush but failed miserably. Thankfully Kane didn't seem to notice.

'See,' I said, pointing at it. 'There's been suicide epidemics all over the world. Psychologists say that the media influences it.'

'How?' he asked.

'Because they report it, and the public become more aware. So people are more likely to copy it,' I explained. 'And if someone you know commits suicide, you're more likely to consider it too – if you're already thinking about ending your life. There are so many examples . . . they call them clusters.'

'And you think Max *copied* Amy?'

'I'm not sure,' I replied. 'Maybe he wanted a way out and he followed Amy's example? Like, even the rope was the same – that's what the reporters said on the news.'

'I guess the police must know this stuff too?' said Kane.

'Hope so,' I replied. 'They're the experts.'

'Who would want to kill Max?' he asked.

I shrugged. It was a good question and I had no idea of the answer.

'That's what I want to know,' I said. 'DC Evans gave me her card. I'm gonna call her.'

The girl is weak. She frets about her weight, and the size of her thighs. She spends her time following her best friend, like some lapdog begging for attention. He's seen the way she is, always uncertain, unsure of her place and worried about what other people think.

Now is the time to change up to another gear. To explain to her some simple truths about the way in which the world works. She is nothing compared to the Spider, and he will not let her escape. Yes, he could move on and leave her be. Maybe even find another to take her place . . .

But where is the fun in that? Where is the game? She is going to take more effort, and perhaps a change of strategy, but the Spider is nothing if not pragmatic. The web is already being spun. He will not let her escape its darkness . . .

24

We met DC Evans at our nearest police station – in a place called Wigston. The walk took us twenty minutes, and as we passed a McDonald's, I saw some Year Nine lads from school. They were hanging around the car park on mountain bikes, doing nothing much. Two girls, probably Year Sevens, were with them – wearing their best clothes and caked in makeup. Each girl was looking at her own phone and not talking to the other.

DC Evans was waiting at reception, and walked us through to an interview room. She sat us at a table and shut the pale wooden door. She wore her uniform – a plain white shirt with dark trousers and flat shoes. Her blonde hair had grown a bit since I last saw her, but was still short and tidy.

'What can I do for you?' she asked, taking the grey plastic chair opposite Kane.

'We have more information,' Kane told her. 'About Max.'

She raised her perfectly shaped left eyebrow. 'Something different to your previous statements?' she asked.

'I dunno,' said Kane. 'Maybe, yeah . . .'

She looked at me. I felt weak under her gaze. She was the most intense woman I'd ever met. Her eyes seemed to burn through me.

'You too, Lily?' she asked.

'No — Kane's got the information,' I told her. 'I just came with him.'

The officer took out a notepad. 'Right,' she said. 'Let's hear what you've got for me. But do remember that this isn't official, so if need be I will have to request formal statements. At that point you'll need to bring in a responsible adult — OK?'

'I don't care about that,' said Kane. 'Max was chatting to this woman — online.'

'I know,' said DC Evans, with a quick smile. 'You told us.'

'Yeah, but she was odd,' he continued. 'Like — Max never saw her face. He told me about the web-cam sessions.'

'You didn't tell us that before,' said DC Evans.

She looked annoyed and intrigued at the same time, and I wondered what was going through her head.

'I forgot,' said Kane. 'My head was all messed up. Only remembered when I discussed stuff with Lily later.'

DC Evans leaned forward in her chair, paying close attention. 'Did Max describe the webcam sessions in detail?' she asked.

'Yeah,' said Kane, looking uncomfortable.

'And?'

'It's a bit seedy,' he said, glancing at me.

I knew that he felt embarrassed talking about what Max had done, but he didn't have a choice. I nodded at him,

'I've heard everything in this job,' said DC Evans. 'Take your time.'

I think she was trying to make it easier for him. Kane definitely relaxed a bit before he replied.

'This woman – Charlotte – she started er . . . *interacting* with him about two or three months back. They met in some chat room.'

DC Evans nodded but didn't say anything this time.

'She was older,' Kane continued. 'Max told me she was like thirty or something. Wanted a toy boy. She got him to do stuff for her . . .'

'Such as?' asked Evans.

'Strip and that, on camera – and other stuff I don't wanna talk about. She sent him sexy text messages too – he showed me a few.'

Again, I couldn't help thinking of Benedict. Was that all he'd wanted from me too? Only there was no comparison. Benedict was just a bit intense and he wasn't that much older than me – a teenager. This woman, Charlotte, if she was involved in what happened to Max, was much worse. She was an adult.

'And did he seem to enjoy this contact?' asked Evans.

Kane nodded. 'Yeah – he was *well* into her. Like, *besotted*.'

DC Evans nodded again. 'Anything else?'

'He never saw her face because her webcam wasn't working. So, when he was online with her, *she* could watch him, but *he* could only see what she was typing. Couldn't see her or hear her voice . . .'

The officer looked up, her dark brown eyes wide. 'Are you saying that all Max ever really knew of this Charlotte was the text she typed?'

'Yeah – *exactly* that,' said Kane. 'She sent a couple of pictures too – just random shots – but that could have been of anyone.'

This time my thoughts about Benedict made me

panic a little. He'd sent me photographs too. I wondered whether I should Google him, just to be sure. Only, I was being stupid. No way were the two connected. That was just too weird . . .

'We've seen those photos,' Evans admitted. 'But there are no traces of their conversations on his PC — at least none we've found yet—' She stopped suddenly — and closed her notebook.

'You're examining his computer?' I asked.

'Yes,' she replied, 'that's part of our enquiry.'

I wondered what else was part of their investigation. Was something else going on? It felt like it. 'So what have you found?' I added.

DC Evans shook her head. 'That isn't your concern,' she told me. 'This is an ongoing case and I cannot divulge sensitive information to the public. I've already said too much.'

Which sort of answered the question in my head. There *was* something else.

'Is there anything more you'd like to add?'

Kane nodded at her and cleared his throat. 'Max would never commit suicide,' he said. 'I've known him my whole life and he wasn't like that. I think someone hurt him.'

'Unfortunately, thinking something isn't evidence,' she replied. 'We need more than that.'

'The woman – *Charlotte*,' said Kane. 'She's your answer.'

'Only she didn't post the video on Max's Facebook page,' DC Evans reminded us. 'Max did that on his own.'

'Nah,' replied Kane. 'She could have hacked him.'

'Which is all speculation and conjecture again,' said Evans. 'If there is something, though, we'll find it.' She looked from me to Kane, and back again. 'Thanks for this,' she added, smiling warmly. 'It *will* help, Kane. You were right to bring it to me. And, remember what I said before. We need you to keep quiet about this woman – Charlotte. I'm trusting you with that – OK?'

'I just want the truth,' he told her. 'Max made a mistake but he didn't deserve to die over it.'

Outside, Kane was upset, so I took his hand without thinking about what it might mean. It felt strong in mine, and his fingers were smooth and warm. He looked at me and gave a slight nod, his honey-brown eyes glistening. In that instant, I felt something click between us. It wasn't ideal – in fact, it was in the worst of circumstances. But when I gave his hand a squeeze, he reacted the same way and the next look he gave me meant something. I was sure of it.

* * *

That evening, I saw that Benedict had messaged me again. I wasn't going to reply, but suddenly I decided that enough was enough; the situation needed to be resolved – one way or another. All I wanted was Kane. If Benedict wanted to be friends, then fine, but if not . . .

He replied immediately after I'd messaged him.

Hey Lily – you in a better mood now?

No – not really.

Still down about your friend – Max?

I shook my head and considered blocking him and logging off. Of course I was still down about Max – he was dead. I began to wonder if Benedict was a complete moron. My reply was harsh but I was past caring.

That's a stupid thing to ask.

Oh – and why is that?

Because Max is dead, Benedict. Of course I'm still upset. I'm not some heartless cow. He was my friend.

If you say so. Seems to me you're ignoring reality. You need to talk about Max and how you feel.

You have no idea about Max.

Yes I do. I know exactly what Max was.

What?

A sad little pervert, Lily – that's the truth. You just can't face it.

His description of Max enraged me. My heart

beat faster and my temples started throb. Benedict
could go to hell.

He wasn't anything like that, you twat!

He posted a sex video on his own Facebook page.
Had webcam sessions with some woman he didn't even
know. He was sleazy.

No he wasn't.

Yeah he was. And when he got caught, he took the
coward's way out. Committed suicide because he
couldn't man up. Hide it all you like, Lily. You know I'm
telling the truth.

I think I've had enough of you, Benedict.

No – I decide when you've had enough.

What does that mean?

It means that people like me can choose, Lily. How
about you – do you have that power?

What did he mean by 'people like him'? What
was going on? I felt a tremor in my lower lip and my
hands grew suddenly cold.

Power? Are you a bit mad?

I'm as sane as anyone else. You've got serious issues,
Lily, and you're taking them out on me. It's not right.

I haven't got issues. I'm fine.

Really?

Well I will be as soon as you fuck off.

I slept badly that night but not because of what

Benedict had said about Max. The nastiness upset me, but wasn't the cause of my insomnia. *That* was the webcam. Hearing the details of Max's online affair with Charlotte had brought it all back to me.

I went back over the details – again and again. I couldn't remember sending my address to him, or asking for anything. Only, I *must* have sent it to him. The proof was there – in our conversation history. But did that mean anything anyway?

Webcams, hacking, suicides and pacts, possible murders – my thoughts were all over the place and it was hard to concentrate. Something didn't add up, and I wanted to know what that was.

The Spider sees that Girl #2 is online again. He types.

Hey?

Hey you!

Guess what babe?

Did they like the photos?

Like? No – they didn't like, babe. They LOVED them!

OMG! OMG! OMG!

They want to see you right away. Down in London . . .

I'm gonna scream or puke or summat. I'm gonna be famous!

I told you, didn't I?

I know but I didn't believe you. Like – not completely. But now I do!

I don't make promises I can't deliver. Said I'd make you famous. Now I'm going to.

Thank you – you're so lovely!

Not half as lovely as you.

When we meet, I'm gonna snog your face off!

No need for that – just remember me when you're swanning around film premieres and on the cover of Hello magazine.

When, when, when???!!!!

Three days. Tuesday evening. I'll sort out travel arrangements and message you where we can meet up. It might be overnight.

OK – I'll pack a bag. OMG – can't wait to tell everyone!

Not yet. The agency demands complete discretion. It's part of the contract. If you tell anyone, they'll cancel.

Why?

The shoot will cost them money. They don't want you running off with a rival agency . . .

You showed the pics to more than one?

To three – they all wanted you. This one offered the most.

How much?

We'll discuss details when I see you. Just remember – keep this a secret. For now . . .

OK – see you on Tuesday.

I look forward to it, Molly.

The Spider signs out. He calls the OTHER.

'Girl #2 is set. Tuesday evening.'

'Do you require my services?'

'Yes – your skills are just what we need,' the Spider replies.

The OTHER chuckles.

'Would your buyers appreciate more videos of this one too?' the Spider asks.

'Yes – the demand for this stuff is high. I'm sure we could raise the price. I told you – it is a seller's market.'

'That's up to you,' the Spider replies. 'Have you recorded any videos that I don't know about – with your little pet project?'

'Yes,' the OTHER replies. 'Is that a problem?'

'Not if you do as I say. I need your recorder and all of your hard drives here. I'm going to remove every trace of these videos before I move on.'

'No problem,' the OTHER tells him. 'They'll be online for ever.'

'As will their star,' replies the Spider.

The Spider wonders if the OTHER has any suspicions. He thinks back through their various conversations and decides that the answer is no. Once again, he is back in that dingy student hovel in Balham, camera in hand.

They've known each other for a very long time. Yet sentimentality isn't the Spider's style. The OTHER has broken the rules. He has endangered the Spider's freedom. He is the only link between them.

There is no alternative. The OTHER must take the fall . . .

25

The Tuesday after speaking to DC Evans, I stood with Kane by the library, chatting to Danny. Molly Cooper walked past, dressed like a Z-list celebrity. She wore tight, glittery, silver shorts which barely covered her bum, a low-cut black top with lace cut-outs across the belly and back, and thick makeup. Her hair, naturally soft and shiny, looked brittle, and on her feet were silver slingback mules with a platform heel.

'Tasty,' Danny bitched. 'No, like, seriously, she's got the wannabe WAG look *down!*'

'Leave her alone,' I told him.

I didn't get on with her, but she wasn't a bad person. Like, I didn't know for sure that she was insecure but I could guess. She seemed to crave attention, and then acted like a cat with the cream when she got it. I couldn't think of another reason why she would act like she did.

'I intend to leave her alone,' replied Danny. 'There's no bargepole long enough and mine isn't interested anyway . . .'

Kane shook his head, his hair back in braids and tight against his scalp. He wore loose-fit jeans with a red zip-up hoodie and brilliant white trainers. His eyes sparkled. Between him and Danny, I felt like a goblin. Was Kane thinking about the other day – the way we'd held hands? I hadn't been able to *stop* thinking about it. For once, however, Danny didn't pick on the vibe between us. His gossip antennae must have been faulty. Besides, he was too interested in Molly.

'She has a huge bag with her too,' Danny told us. 'It barely fits in her locker. Apparently, she's telling everyone that she's got a modelling contract.'

'What?' I asked.

Kane nodded in agreement. 'She told me at registration,' he revealed. 'Said she's gonna be a star.'

I watched Molly totter away on her ridiculous heels, and hoped for her sake that she was telling the truth. She had been the first girl in our year to wear makeup and what Dr Woods would call 'inappropriate' clothing. I wondered if our principal had seen her today. Obviously not, because she was still dressed the same way.

'You can see her arse,' said Danny. 'Like, *seriously?*'

Tilly was absent, and I wanted to text her, but I didn't know how she'd react.

'You OK?' asked Kane.

'Huh?'

'You're staring at nothing,' he added.

'I'm fine,' I replied. 'Just thinking about stuff.'

'Where's Tilly?' asked Danny, like he could read my mind. 'Did you two make up?'

Kane looked right into my eyes, and I felt like a little girl with a crush. I managed to hold his gaze for maybe five seconds.

'Have you spoken to her?' he asked.

I felt my lower lip tremble and took a deep breath. 'I don't want to talk about it,' I told him. 'Not now.'

Kane smiled and took my hand. I felt a surge of desire, and my face coloured. 'You listened to me,' he said, 'about Max and all that. Now I can listen to you. If you want . . .'

Danny's gossip radar was back and on full power. 'Oh my!' he said. 'Is this some karmic-love thing hatching?'

'Shut up, Danny,' ordered Kane, letting my hand fall. Only he didn't look embarrassed or anything.

He looked concerned for me. It was me who fought back awkwardness and looked away, towards the main block. Molly was standing by the doors with a lad called Lakh, her hand on his arm. He leaned in and whispered something in her ear.

'*That* looks more like romance to me,' I said, hoping to deflect Danny's prying.

Kane and Danny turned to see. 'What the *hell*?' Danny said in surprise. 'Molly kept that quiet. Excuse me, you two, but I have an investigation to carry out . . .' He walked off towards Molly and her latest flirt.

'I was being serious, you know,' said Kane.

'About talking?' I asked.

'Yeah – like, any time,' he replied. 'I know how close you and Tilly are.'

'She's forgotten that,' I said, even though it wasn't true.

Kane put his hand on my arm. I grew tense – not because I disliked his touch. I liked it too *much*. 'You wanna come over later?' he asked.

I shrugged and tried to look calm. Only I couldn't escape the feeling that we were going somewhere, Kane and me. Somewhere exciting.

'Well, I'll be home in an hour,' he added. 'Up to you.'

* * *

253

Later, when I got to Kane's, he took me up to his bedroom. It was neat and tidy, and smelled like freshly washed clothes – mine was a festering tip in comparison. A couple of huge posters were pinned to the pale blue walls. One showed an orange Lamborghini, and the other Nelson Mandela as a young man. Kane's desk was piled with books – all of them about politics.

'You studying to become Prime Minister?' I joked.

'I like to know stuff,' he explained. 'But I'm thinking about doing politics at college.'

'I'm worried about this year,' I told him. 'What's happened to Max has seriously affected my revision – I can't concentrate. And I feel bad for saying that too. How can I complain about my exams when Max and Amy are dead?'

'I feel the same way,' he replied. 'We've got to try and focus, though – our GCSEs are too important. It's gonna be difficult with Max gone, but we can't fail. That wouldn't help anyone.' He sat at his desk, and gestured to the bed. I felt reassured in his company – and more confident too. 'Take a seat,' he said.

I sat and looked out of his window while Kane tapped at his laptop – a sleek, silver one.

'You should see my PC,' I told him. 'It's so old it gets a pension.'

'I could sort you a new one,' he replied. 'Alfie's always got a spare lying about. I think he robs geeks in his spare time.'

'That's not nice,' I joked. 'I like geeks.'

He logged into Facebook and scrolled up and down his timeline. 'Usual crap,' he said. 'You still chatting to that American boy?'

I shook my head. It was time to be honest. 'He pissed me off,' I told him. 'I'm done with him.'

'Sent me a friend request last night,' Kane revealed. 'Weird. I ignored it.'

'Why would he do that?'

Kane swivelled to face me, as I wondered what Benedict was playing at. After our bust-up, why contact one of my friends? His behaviour was getting stranger and stranger.

'Dunno, but I never friend strangers,' he explained. 'And I set my privacy on the harshest level. Facebook is full of attachments that carry viruses and that. I know people who download any shit they get sent – *stupid.*'

'I've never even looked at privacy settings,' I admitted, slightly embarrassed and annoyed – I was one of the idiots Kane was talking about.

He shook his head. 'You should,' he told me. 'You can't let the whole world view your page. People out there are weird.'

'Like the nutters on Amy's page?'

'Exactly,' he replied. 'And take a look – Max's memorial page got trolled too.'

I stood and approached him. His shoulders filled the red hoodie, almost to bursting, and I could smell citrus from his skin. The screen showed Max's page, and Kane tapped his perfect fingers against a few comments.

'People are sick,' he said. 'Like, what did Max ever do to them?'

I moved closer still, and leaned in. 'Who set the page up?'

Kane shrugged. 'His family, maybe?' he replied. 'I don't really know.'

'Wouldn't they delete the nasty stuff, though?' I asked.

'Maybe they haven't seen it,' he suggested. 'I know they're upset because they can't bury him yet. The investigation is taking ages. Like with Amy.'

'Have you spoken to them?'

'To his mum,' said Kane. 'She was a mess.'

I read some of the cruel comments and nodded. 'I want to see her, but I can't,' I said. 'I'd get too emotional and that's the last thing Max's parents need. I hope they haven't seen this.'

Kane clicked back to his own page, and I stood up straight. I didn't move, though.

'What happened with American boy, then?' he asked.

I looked at Kane's screen wallpaper – another picture of Nelson Mandela, only he was older here.

'Well?'

'He got a bit weird,' I admitted. 'Like after those messages I showed you?'

'Weird how?'

'Just odd,' I said. 'Like, he wanted me to send him selfies . . .'

'Did you?'

'Just one,' I replied. 'Nothing slutty or anything. But he wanted more and then I started to revise and didn't message him for ages, like I told you. And he wouldn't take the hint. He was messaging me constantly.' I was praying that Kane wouldn't be put off by my admission of the selfie.

'That wind him up – you not replying?'

'Yeah,' I said. 'He told me I was no fun. Said he'd rather chat to Molly Cooper and girls like her. He said some horrible things.'

'His loss.'

I stepped back a touch, aware that my skin was burning. I wondered if he could feel the heat too. It didn't seem like it.

'Then there's the webcam,' I continued. 'I'm still convinced I didn't give him my address.'

'So, how did he find it?' asked Kane.

'That's just it,' I replied. 'He reckons I *did* tell him. Can I show you?'

Kane wheeled back a bit and nodded. 'All yours,' he said with a warm smile.

Opening a new window, I logged into my Facebook. I clicked the icon and scrolled back through my chat with Benedict. 'Here,' I said, pointing at the screen.

'That's your address for real,' said Kane, turning the laptop his way.

'Yeah,' I said, 'but I *swear* I never sent it.'

Kane raised an eyebrow.

'I *know* I sound crazy,' I replied. 'But I would remember, Kane. It's doing my head in.'

Kane thought for a moment. 'Strange,' he said. 'Why the webcam anyway?'

'He wanted to video chat.'

'Ain't your PC got one built in?' he asked.

'My computer was built by the Romans, I told you,' I replied, as Kane returned to my home page. He was about to speak when his jaw dropped open. 'Shit!'

'What?' I asked.

He turned the screen towards me. I'd been tagged in a post with over a hundred others. I saw a video-still of Molly Cooper – half naked and staring back from a webcam. Underneath was a website link.

The only comment asked people to share the video, and to '*name and shame this slut*'.

The comment, the link, and the post came from *me* . . .

PART THREE

PART FIVE

Girl #2 turns into the narrow lane on time. The OTHER watches her walk past a double-glazing factory. She totters and sways on heels too high. She is oblivious to her surroundings. Too busy reading his messages on her phone.

The lane runs behind and beneath Waitrose. It is quiet. Secluded, yet accessible too. His phone buzzes.

'I'm here. Where are you?'

'One minute.'

She passes his car. Doesn't even glance at him. Her overnight bag – tan leather – is heavy. She alternates between hands. Her cheeks are flushed, her brow glistens.

The OTHER gets out – takes a quick look around. No one coming. No one walking a dog or taking a short cut. He approaches her. She turns. Her face is a picture. Confusion – total and utter – creases her pretty features.

'*Sir?* What are you doing here?' she asks.

The OTHER smiles. 'Surprised?'

She does not answer. Not with his hands clamped over her mouth and around her head. She doesn't even struggle. Her eyes hold the scream that her mouth cannot cry.

'The truth is a wonderful thing,' he tells her.

He drags her to the car. Puts her in the boot. Closes it and goes to retrieve her bag. No point in leaving evidence lying around.

'Welcome to celebrity,' he chuckles, as he drives away.

26

'How the hell could I post that?' I asked, panicked and angry at once. 'I'm here with you!'

Kane didn't reply. He was too busy watching the comments rack up. Manisha Patel, Jamie, even Danny got on it . . .

'Twenty-eight likes already,' said Kane. 'What the fuck is happening?'

I felt my stomach turn, and sat down on his bed. Kane grabbed his phone, pointing it at me.

'What are you doing?' I asked.

'If I take your picture, it'll have a time code,' he explained. 'We can prove you were here – if we *need* to.'

'Why do we need to *prove* anything?' I asked. 'I've not done anything wrong.'

Kane shrugged. 'Won't hurt,' he replied.

I let him continue, my head spinning. How had someone hacked my Facebook account whilst Kane and I were accessing it? And why the malicious posts? 'I'm gonna be sick,' I said.

Kane made me sit down with my head between my legs and sat next to me. 'Who else knows your Facebook password?' he asked.

'No one,' I replied through deep breaths.

'Not even Tilly?'

I sat up and gave him a glare. 'Tilly would *never* do this,' I insisted.

I was convinced of it too. Despite all our problems, I knew she loved me. She'd said so. She would never do this to me, no matter what.

'Does she know your password or not?' Kane asked again.

'Yes,' I replied. 'At least I think so – but this isn't her, Kane!'

'What is it?' he asked. 'Your Facebook password?'

'Why?'

Kane looked at my home page. The likes and comments were building up. 'Is it easy to guess?' he said. 'Like, for people who know you?'

I shrugged. 'How do I know?' I replied. 'It's my mum's maiden name with her birth year after it.'

'Your mum's Sikh, right?' he said.

'Punjabi,' I corrected. 'She doesn't do religion.'

'Yeah,' he said, 'but she would have been called *Kaur*, wouldn't she? Like other Punjabi women?'

The surprise must have shown.

'Everyone knows that,' he said. 'At least everyone with Sikh friends does.'

'I guess so.'

'Mother's maiden name is a default security question on loads of sites,' he pointed out. 'If I knew your mum, I could guess at "Kaur", no problem. Then I'd just need her birthday.'

I saw where he was going. 'Yeah,' I countered, 'but you'd have to make the connection. Like, *know* that's how I constructed my password.'

Kane nodded slowly. 'Good point.'

'No one would guess that – it's too random.'

'What about a virus?' he asked.

'How would I know?'

Kane grabbed his laptop and moved next to me. He typed a search into Google. 'Here's a list of suspicious things that infected PCs might do,' he said.

I read through the list and realized a few had happened on mine. My hands felt clammy and my heartbeat raced. I felt almost violated – like someone was rifling through my most private things.

'The screen went blank the other day – like it was dead,' I told him. 'Then it started up again. It does

that a lot and the mouse does its own thing sometimes too. And it's always slow.'

'Have you downloaded anything dodgy?'

I shook my head. 'I don't look at dodgy stuff,' I
told him. 'I'm not a boy.'

Kane smiled, despite this horrible situation. For a
second it made me feel better – but only a second. 'I
ain't talking porn,' he said. 'I mean, like, attachments
or those stupid links people stick on FB.'

I thought hard. Usually, I ignored anything like
that. The only one I remembered came from Amy –
nearly six months earlier now. She had been posting
links to anti-bullying websites, in what I now
realized might have been a plea for help, and I had
viewed them all. One of them had required a
download.

'Amy posted a link,' I told him. 'A video blog
about Internet bullying. Tilly and me looked at it.
Max too. I think we were the only ones she tagged in
it – apart from Molly. Everyone else just took the
piss anyway.'

'You sure there was nothing else?'

'No – just that one.'

'Was the link OK?'

I nodded. 'Yeah,' I said, 'apart from the first bit.'

'Why?'

'It was some unrecognized format – I had to

download a software program to watch it. We all did.'

Kane's eyes lit up. 'A video file that wouldn't open on anything else?'

'It said that,' I revealed. 'But after I downloaded the software, it still played on Windows Media.'

Kane thought a moment. 'Anything else weird or odd?'

'No,' I replied.

'You OK if we get Alfie to check your computer?'

'Check it when?'

Kane grabbed his phone. Seconds later, I heard a reggae ringtone from the landing – Kane hadn't closed his door. 'You home, bro?' he asked.

'Standing at your door,' said Alfonso.

We turned to look at him. He was tall, like Kane, but much bigger. His head was shaved, and his face, although plump, was an older version of Kane's – they had the same pale brown eyes and smooth, caramel skin. Alfonso wore navy jeans, trainers and a blue and white checked shirt,

'Bruv,' said Kane, 'this is Lily.'

'Hey,' I said.

When he smiled, Alfonso's entire face shone. The brothers exchanged glances before Alfie replied.

'Sister,' he said. 'A pleasure to meet you properly.'

'You too, Alfonso.'

He grinned. 'Alfie, please,' he insisted. 'What can I do for you?'

Kane explained what had happened, and showed Alfie the laptop.

'You should change your Facebook password,' Alfie told me. 'Like, right *now*.' He made a few clicks, then gave me the laptop.

I changed the password to my father's name, Dalbir, with his birth year on the end. No one knew my dad's first name except for family and Tilly.

'Where's your PC?' Alfie asked.

The journey to mine was short and fast. Alfie's Mercedes was the nicest car I'd ever been in. The stereo was so loud the bass made my ribs vibrate. And the seats hugged me like a long-lost aunt. When we reached my house, I didn't want to move. I had no idea what would be waiting for me when I booted up my computer.

Inside, I led them straight upstairs, logged on, and Kane and I accessed my Facebook. It asked for my new password and took a while to load. When it did, I quickly wished that it hadn't. My home page was going crazy.

Alfie had taken a briefcase from his boot, and opened it on my bed. 'Various bits I might have to use,' he said. He took out a small laptop, and some flash drives. 'How old is this thing?' he asked, eyeing my PC like it was a turd.

'I dunno – maybe five years?' I replied. 'I hate it.'

He gave me a pitying look then set to work. 'You make tea?' he asked, tapping at my keyboard.

'Sometimes,' I replied.

'Good time, this,' he added. 'Three sugars, strong as you like . . .'

I took Kane downstairs, as Alfie began to mumble to himself. When we got back, five minutes later, he was sitting staring at the screen.

'Did you change your password back at our house?' he asked.

'Yeah – why?'

He pointed to the screen. 'And you didn't access Facebook from your phone – just now?' he added.

'No. I just typed the password in when we got here.'

'Someone's playing games with you, then,' he said. 'I think you've got a RAT infestation.'

'A *what?*' both Kane and I asked together.

'Remote Access Trojan,' Alfie replied.

On the screen, the latest comment on my bogus post was from me too. My blood froze as I read it:

If you think Molly's a slag – make sure to tell her. If I was that desperate, I would kill myself – hint, hint, Molly . . . LMFAO. LOL.

27

I said nothing for nearly ten minutes – just sat and stared at the screen. The brothers saw that I was upset and gave me some space. Alfie drank his tea and Kane read the comments on my bogus post. My phone, lying on my bed, buzzed continuously, but I couldn't look at it. I didn't dare. When, eventually, Alfie broke the silence, I was in tears.

He sat back in my chair. 'Do you know what a Remote Access Trojan does?' he asked.

I didn't, nor did Kane.

'You download an attachment or software,' Alfie explained. 'It can be anything, but you have to click to accept it. Once you do, you let the virus in – like through an unlocked back door.'

'Into your computer?' asked Kane.

'Yeah,' said Alfie. 'Once it's in, the RAT sits in the background. It can access anything on your hard drive, even shut it down . . .'

'That's insane,' I replied, wiping my eyes. Had someone been watching everything I did on my PC? The thought made me shudder.

Kane noticed my discomfort, put his hand on my arm and smiled warmly.

'It happens,' Alfie told me, giving his brother an odd look. 'You know how many people download free music and video torrents? Like all those file-share sites? People never think about infections. They just want free stuff.'

I shook my head again. 'But I've never done that,' I protested. 'I don't download anything that way. It's as bad as stealing from a shop.'

Kane nudged my memory. 'The video from Amy,' he said. 'The one you mentioned round mine?'

My thoughts were so jumbled. I couldn't stop thinking about being watched online. It was creepy. I told Alfie about the video attachment and software download.

'That'll be it,' said Alfie. 'Or something like that, anyway.'

Behind me, my phone continued to vibrate. I wondered if Tilly had seen the post on Facebook but I was too scared to check my messages. I wanted to believe that she would know it wasn't me. Only who could blame her if she did? She wasn't with me, so she didn't know what was happening, I desperately wanted to tell her. But that meant looking at my phone, and I just couldn't bring myself to pick it up. I felt like I was caught in a whirlwind. Things were spiralling out of control and I didn't know what to do. My head throbbed.

'If your PC has a RAT, then the hacker can access it anytime they want. Cyber-criminals use RATs to steal passwords and bank account details. They can capture your keystrokes, or buy things on your eBay account – anything they like. And they're really tough to remove. The hackers make them hard to spot.'

I thought about Alfie's words for a moment. Something was niggling me, but I didn't know what. 'Hang on,' I said. 'Are you saying that some hacker – like an *actual* person – can *control* my computer – from *elsewhere*?'

Alfie nodded. 'That's impossible,' I replied. 'I'd know, wouldn't I?'

'No,' said Alfie. 'You wouldn't have any idea. Maybe if you saw the webcam light come on – something like that . . .'

Kane and I glanced at each other.

'They can control your *webcam*?' Kane asked, his eyes wide.

'Turn it on, record – anything,' said Alfie. 'Depends on how good the hacker is. But with the right R.A.T. – they can take over your PC—'

'Shit!' I shouted. The nagging in my head grew stronger – clearer.

'What?' Alfie asked.

'I don't have a webcam,' I explained. 'But someone posted me one.'

'Posted you a webcam?'

'Yeah,' I said. 'This lad, Benedict, that I've been messaging – from New York . . .'

My phone buzzed several times more. The most recent message was from Danny, so I looked at it.

Why did you do that? What's Molly ever done to you? Thought you were better than this!

I groaned and held it out for Kane to see. He screwed up his face. 'What does Danny care about Molly?' he asked. 'We ain't exactly too nice about her, are we?'

'He doesn't know the truth, Kane,' I replied. 'He's just defending her, that's all.'

'I don't know her,' he said. 'Although I seen plenty of her online . . .'

That was when it clicked.

'*Max!*' I said excitedly.

'Huh?' both brothers replied.

I tried to get my thoughts in order. 'Just give me

a second,' I said. There was a link – I was sure of it. Between Max, Amy and what was happening to me . . .

'Max had that woman friend online, right?' I began.

'Yeah,' said Kane. 'Charlotte.'

Alfie scratched his head. 'Who's Charlotte?' he asked. 'And what are you talking about?'

'Wait!' I ordered.

Alfie scowled and looked into his empty mug. Then he pulled a Snickers bar from his briefcase and began to chomp on it. 'What?' he asked, when Kane shook his head. 'Man gets hungry, bruv, even when things are serious . . .'

'Please,' I said, 'let me finish. It's important.'

Alfie tried to chew quietly.

'Max had this woman,' I continued, 'but he never saw her – *right?*'

'Just chatted online,' agreed Kane. 'She said her webcam was bust.'

'But someone recorded Max's webcam sessions . . .'

Kane began to chew his bottom lip slightly, nodding as he did so. 'We never believed Max would have posted that video,' he said.

'Exactly. Max must have been *hacked*, because he wouldn't have recorded the webcam sessions. Not doing *that*. And Charlotte wasn't on the video – it only showed Max . . .'

'Because Charlotte wasn't *real*,' Kane replied, catching on. 'Charlotte was a fake – *she* must be the hacker . . .'

'Exactly what I'm thinking,' I told him. 'And now someone has hacked my computer too.'

'That video link from Amy – you said Tilly and Max saw it too?' said Kane.

'Yeah – all three of us. I think Molly might have commented too.'

'So you all must have downloaded the software thing,' he added. 'To open the file . . .'

My memory flashed up a mental image from my Facebook page. A throwaway line. The thought of being right scared the hell out of me . . .

'What if it's *not* a coincidence?' asked Kane.

'It can't be,' I replied. 'So the question is – who's my hacker?'

Kane shrugged as I began to feel nauseous again. Could I be right? I thought hard but there was no other explanation. The realization left me cold . . .

'It's Benedict,' I revealed. 'The lad from New York . . .'

Kane's expression started to change. The same awful comprehension dawned. 'Of course!' he shouted. 'The webcam he sent.'

'There's something else too,' I said. I grabbed my mouse, entering my Facebook messages. I scrolled back, finally resting on the line in question. 'I told you Benedict got angry when I didn't reply,' I said. 'You know – after Max died? Anyway, we had an argument and he slated Max . . .' I pointed at the screen and Kane leaned across me to read.

'There,' I said.

Kane studied the line. '*Had webcam sessions with some woman he didn't even know.*'

I tapped on the word '*woman*'.

'How did he know about *Charlotte?*' I asked.

'Because he read about her?' offered Kane. I could see that he was trying to work it all out.

I shook my head. 'That's just it,' I said. 'No one reported Charlotte because the police haven't revealed her existence. They asked us not to mention her – *remember?*'

The light that dawned in Kane's eyes could have illuminated the entire universe. 'The only people who know about Charlotte,' I added, 'are you, me, Tilly and the police.'

'And the hacker!' said Kane.

'*Exactly,*' I agreed. '*We* didn't tell Benedict, the *police* didn't tell him so . . .'

'*Benedict is the hacker!*' Kane said, completing my train of thought.

'I can't see any other way,' I told him, feeling bile climb up my food pipe.

'You OK?' asked Kane. 'You've gone pale.'

I ran to the bathroom and puked my guts out . . .

The OTHER wears a clown mask. He carries the drugged girl through a deserted spinney. The Spider films his every step. They are south of Leicester, next to the Grand Union Canal. The spinney stretches along the southern edge of the waterway. It is perhaps two hundred metres wide and half as deep. Secluded enough to provide cover. Accessible enough for the girl to be found. Eventually . . .

The Spider's mind works quickly. It sorts through tactics, creating new threads and strengthening his web. The Spider is planning for every eventuality. He leaves no mental stone unturned. He cannot be caught. He is a survivor and nothing can stop him.

They find the pre-selected tree, marked with blue

chalk. The Spider waits, as the OTHER finishes his task. The girl is petite, borderline skinny. She has dark hair and olive skin. Her beauty lies hidden beneath a layer of makeup. The Spider wonders what she might have become. The OTHER places climbing rope round her pretty neck and knots the noose. He throws the excess over the thickest, lowest branch.

'Are you ready?' the Spider asks. The camera remains in his hands, silently recording every second.

'Yes,' the OTHER replies.

'Are you excited?'

The OTHER nods, the adrenalin rush visible in his features. 'I never dreamed it could be so easy,' he replies. 'The jump from fantasy to reality.'

'I told you,' the Spider says. 'I said I would guide you. I have . . .'

'We should hurry.'

'Yes, we should,' the Spider replies. He longs to smile but maintains his discipline.

The OTHER takes hold of the slack. Using his weight, he pulls the rope tight. The girl is raised sky-wards, her body tensing. She awakens. Just long enough to realize her fate. To choke on her own screams. The OTHER wraps the rope around the trunk. Ties it off.

The girl's legs wriggle a while. Then she is gone.

As they leave, the Spider drops something.

The OTHER walks on ahead, towards his BMW.

As the ring nestles amongst the weeds, the Spider allows himself a surreptitious grin . . .

28

It wasn't me.

    I wasn't even on Facebook when it was posted.

    No – Kane was with me – ask him!

    I told you – I didn't do it.

    Why would I do that???

Those were just some of the replies I grew sick of sending over the next six hours. They only stopped when I turned my phone off – upset, tearful and tired. I wondered if Max had felt the same way. If the endless comments and texts had pushed him too far. Only, I couldn't imagine that they had. Even with all the messages bombarding me, I wasn't remotely suicidal – just angry and troubled.

    I sat on my bed, praying that my mum wouldn't

hassle me. I'd been quiet during dinner, using a headache as my excuse. Mum had seemed un-convinced, but she didn't push it, thank God. I didn't want to talk to anyone, not even Mum – not yet. I just wanted to sit and stare, and wonder why my world had turned to utter shit.

The brothers left soon after I puked. I thought about Alfie's offer to rid my computer of the RAT, and how I'd told him not to.

'If you remove the virus, we won't know what Benedict does next,' I had replied, causing Alfie to raise an eyebrow.

'Lily's right, bro,' Kane had said. 'We need to see what else he will do.'

'And if the virus is still there,' I added, 'then we can show the police too.'

Alfie went out to the car but Kane stayed behind for a moment. He put his arms around me and told me that I was brave.

'How?' I asked, staring into his beautiful face.

'If we're right, this person – whatever he's called – is dangerous. You're standing up to him.'

'I'm just thinking about what comes next,' I replied. 'I'm about as brave as a mouse hiding under a floorboard.'

Kane shook his head. 'No,' he replied. 'I used to

think you were a mouse, but you're not. You're much more than that.'

He wanted to stay, but I felt like I needed to be alone for a while. I said I'd see him in the morning. He smiled and reassured me with a big hug. As he let go, I leaned in to him, and my lips almost brushed against his. Then, panicking, I pulled back.

'Er . . . sorry about that,' I said.

'Don't be,' he said. 'I'll see you tomorrow.'

We had no concrete proof that Benedict had done anything. Was Benedict even his real name? Don't get me wrong – I knew he was the hacker – it made perfect sense in my head. But could we go to DC Evans with it? We were accusing some lad I'd only ever talked to online of being a hacker, a troll, and of having a hand in Max's death. Thing is, we didn't have a choice. We would have to talk to the police eventually. It was the right thing to do.

I'd have to tell Mum too, and the thought made me nervous. I knew she would freak out and demand to know why I hadn't spoken up sooner. I didn't know how to tell her, either. If we could get out of it without telling my mum, I'd rather we did that. It was going to be unlikely, though. No, that's not the right word. It was going to be *impossible*.

Once I heard Mum go to bed, I logged into

Facebook. I don't know exactly why I did, but the frustration and anger were eating at me. I also had Kane's words ringing in my head – how I was brave and not the girl he'd thought I was – and that made me feel stronger inside. Strong enough to confront things.

'My' bogus post had over one hundred shares, and the comment count was in treble figures too. I searched, but there was nothing from Tilly. In the top left corner, I had messages. I clicked the icon, saw the names Manisha, Danny and Benedict, and ignored all but the last.

Benedict's message brought back the taste of bile.

Hey pretty lady – you chilled out yet?

I stared at it for ages, rubbing at my face and trying not to shake. I was more relieved than ever that I hadn't connected the webcam. He was the worst kind of stalker – one who masqueraded as something else and got under my skin. A stalker I didn't know about, and could not have spotted. My paranoia increased as the night wore on. I was a troll now, harassing Molly Cooper. A sick bitch urging people to kill themselves. Why would anyone believe me? How would I face everyone at school? How could I look Molly in the eye? Or anyone else, for that matter . . .

No reply . . . guess you're sleeping. Maybe we could start afresh???

When the second message flashed up, I wanted to scream. I should have stayed calm. I should have thought through my reaction. Only I didn't. I wanted to wind him up. Get him to admit what he was, and what he had done.

I'm wide awake Benedict or whatever your name is . . .

Even though I was terrified, I wasn't going to let him sense it. I was going to protect my feelings.

She lives . . .

Aren't you going to ask me?

About what, Lily?

The webcam? More slutty pictures?

Oh.

Is that it, you prick?

I'm not sure I like your tone.

I don't care what you think.

Explain?

I took a deep breath and fought back the shakes. No way was he making me cower in fear.

I know about you, Benedict – God – why am I using that name! You're not called that, are you?

Really? So who am I?

I dunno – try Charlotte maybe?

I was messing with a lunatic, I knew. But I sensed a change in myself. Kane had been right – something was making me braver, more determined. It wasn't a surprise either — not after everything that had happened. I had been pushed too far, I guess. When nothing came back for about five minutes I tired of waiting, and gave him a nudge.

That scare you, did it, Benny?

It seems the pretence is at an end.

You admitting to it?

I don't know what you're on about.

Who are you?

Whatever you want me to be. To you I'm Benedict — the charming New Yorker — who is inexplicably attracted to an overweight, distinctly average British girl from some no-hope town. Sound about right?

I shuddered at his reply. He'd just stuck a knife into all of my insecurities and twisted it until I screamed inside.

But I'd let him in. I'd shown him all of my deepest fears, and that was the worst feeling of all. I felt like captured prey. Like I was trapped inside a web of darkness that he had spun all around me.

I swallowed hard and tried to hold my nerve.

And what about Max — what were you to him?

Max who?

Don't play games with me!!!

Oh — and what will you do?

I'll go to the police.

Really? What will you say?

I'll show them these messages . . .

But how will you log back in?

I winced. What did he mean?

What?

To Facebook, Lily? How will you access your account?

I don't understand.

I'll just change the password.

You can't do that. I'll change it back!

Not if you can't log in.

I've already changed it.

Yes, I know – DALBIR_1975 – what a very silly name. Whose is it – darling dead daddy?

I felt sick when I read my dad's name. It wasn't just that he knew it. It was that he had used my dad's death to reel me in when we'd first become friends. So much bullshit, so many lies . . .

Once again, I struggled to stay in control.

None of your business.

It doesn't matter anyway. I changed the password again. During that little hiatus . . .

I don't believe you?

No? Try logging off then – see where you get.

I sat back and took some deep breaths. My eyes were aching and my mouth dry. A sudden shiver

worked its way down my spine. Benedict, or whoever he was, might as well have been sitting next to
me. He knew everything . . .

Why did you pick on me and Max? Amy, even?

Who's Max?

You know Max – my friend – the one who died?

No – can't recall – describe him to me. And this Amy
– sounds like a fat girl's name. Not that I'd know her, of
course.

You're sick! Twisted in the head!

I'm whatever I choose to be. And right now, I choose
to be bored by you. Have you lost any weight yet?

Fuck off.

Seriously – like, baby orca is such a bad look, babe.
Benedict wouldn't want all that blubber rubbing against
his six-pack, now would he?

This had gone too far. My arms itched for no
reason – the edges of my scalp too. But I had to keep
my bravado up – at least on screen.

What if I'm round the corner, Lily? Watching from
underneath the streetlight down the road? Staring at you
undressing from the garden opposite? Behind you as
you walk to school? So many what ifs, Lily . . . What if I
live in the street behind yours – next door to Tilly,
maybe?

My heart began to thud in my chest . . .

How do you know where she lives?

The same way I know your address. The same way I know about all of you.

The shiver returned, and brought more for the ride. My palms were damp and my heart felt like it was being kicked. My tongue felt like a dried-out sponge in my mouth. He was telling me that he *knew* me – that he *knew* my friends . . .

Are you watching Tilly too?

What a ridiculous question, Lily. How else would I know her address? You really are a winning combination: dumb and fat . . .

The police will catch you.

They might – but not before . . .

What? – before what?

What was he going to do? Had I made a mistake by winding him up like this? If he hurt someone else because I'd pushed him into it, I wouldn't be able to live with myself.

Wait and see. It's been a real pleasure. Lily. Time to say goodbye. Benedict is heading for the great trash can in the cyber-sky.

Wait!

Do you like to sleep, Lily?

What?

Sleep, Lily – do you like it?

Yes.

How does it feel then?

How does what feel?

Knowing that after tonight, you'll never sleep again?

You don't have that power over me.

Not online. But I will out there. Oh, by the way, I'm looking forward to meeting your mum.

The knife twisted a last time and cut through to my heart. I started to shake and my vision blurred. He didn't mean it, did he? He was just playing a game – surely?

Not my mum . . .

You leave her out of this!

Why would I do that? She's quite attractive and, like your friend, I do enjoy a nice MILF . . .

I thought you didn't know Max?

Who's Max?

You shit!

Goodnight Lily. See you very soon . . .

The Spider wonders how many people truly understand the Dark Web. The place *beneath* the shiny thing that most people access via Google or some other money-spinning machine.

What most people see is only the beginning. What the masses think of as the never-ending, World Wide Web is just the start. The bit that peeks out. Underneath sits the rest. The other ninety per cent.

Like the sea floor, it's dark down there. And just like the sea floor, it is a wilderness left uncharted. All kinds of monsters lurk in the depths – from terrorists to paedophiles and secret organizations. Want to buy illegal porn, snuff movies, a live grenade or a kilo of heroin? Just jump in and all will be revealed . . .

Much of it is wasteland – abandoned websites and

billions of bytes of searches carried out in the Internet's infancy. That's what makes it such a great place to hide. It is lawless – a brave new frontier full of derelict cities and towns. A Wild West, if you like.

But you have to know how to breathe down there. You have to know the rules and have a map. The unwary, the untrained and the tourists are prey for the experts. And the Spider is certainly an expert.

And once this foray above water is complete, he will dive back in and head for the bottom. Hide out until he is ready to start again . . .

29

'My head's hurting again.'

Mum gave me a funny look – half concerned, half sceptical. She was ready for work, standing in the living room, a mug of coffee in her hand. 'Have you taken paracetamol?' she asked.

'Not this morning,' I told her. 'Took two last night but they didn't help. Feel a bit sick too.'

Mum put down her mug and felt my forehead. 'Feels OK,' she said, 'but you look terrible.'

'Couldn't sleep,' I replied.

'I know it's been a horrendous few weeks, but is there something you're not telling me?'

I fought back the urge to climb onto her knee and tell her everything like I would have done as a kid.

'I haven't seen Tilly for a while,' she added, looking right into my eyes.

'She's busy, Mum – *exams?*' I replied.

I didn't know what to do. I wanted to tell her everything about Benedict – to get her advice – but something was stopping me. It wasn't shame or anything – I was just scared. What if she didn't understand and got angry with me? That was the last thing I wanted. My relationship with Tilly was already in trouble. I didn't want to upset Mum too. I couldn't handle that.

'I'll call the office,' she said after a moment. 'Try and go in after lunch time, if you're feeling better. You can't keep missing school, Lily.'

'I'll try,' I replied.

When Dr Woods saw the post about Molly, I would be in deep shit. My mum might discover what I'd been doing before I'd worked up the courage to tell her. I went to make tea, when something caught my eye. The red failed-delivery card for the webcam still sat on a pile of letters, staring back at me, as it waited to be recycled.

I walked over and studied it. I'd found it after Mr Samuels had given me the package – it had been lost under a pile of my mum's letters. There was a date on it, and my address. Under the reason for non-delivery were several tick boxes describing what kind of parcel it had been. The one for international delivery *hadn't* been crossed. A barcode and delivery number were stuck to the bottom.

I already knew that Benedict wasn't from New York – he'd pretty much admitted it. But the card might prove where the webcam was posted. The delivery number might pinpoint exactly where *he* was. I wondered whether I could ring Royal Mail and ask them.

There was only one way to find out.

The number connected quickly, and I selected the option to speak to an operator. The woman who picked up was Scottish.

'How may I help you?'

'Er . . .' I began. 'I've got this card about a delivery and—'

'Would you like to rearrange a time and date?' the woman asked me. Her tone was plastic and pleasant at the same time. Practised, I guess.

'No – I've got the parcel. I just wanted to know where it came from. Can I do that?'

'Don't you know where?' the woman asked.

'No,' I replied.

'I don't *know* if that's possible,' she told me. 'Hold please . . .'

I waited for two minutes, staring at the card in my hand and hoping.

'Hello there, Miss . . . ?'

'Basra,' I replied. 'Lily Basra.'

'I've spoken to my supervisor, Miss Basra, and we can't divulge any private address because we wouldn't know it.'

'But I need to send it back,' I replied, thinking on my feet.

'I see,' she said, her tone now guarded. 'You didn't order it?'

I thought fast. 'No,' I replied. 'It's worth lots of money and I think it was sent by mistake. I can't keep it – that would be wrong.'

She didn't go for it. 'Then, Miss Basra, you've got a lovely little surprise,' she told me. 'Enjoy it. The sender can always ask for it, if they're concerned. After all, they have your address.'

'Can you at least tell me which city?'

The woman coughed. 'Can't see why not,' she told me.

I gave her the barcode number when asked, and waited.

'That particular parcel was sorted at our Centurion Way office, in Leicester . . .'

My ears started to buzz, and my forehead creased. 'Sorry – did you just say *Leicester*?'

'Yes – that's correct.'

I dropped the card as my heart started to beat

faster. My skin prickled and a felt a wave of panic. 'Can you tell me *which* post office?'

'I'm afraid not – but it will be in Leicester somewhere.'

'OK,' I replied, my right leg shaking.

'Is there anything else, hen?'

'Er . . . no,' I managed. 'Thanks for your help.'

'You're very welcome. Have a *fantastic* morning.'

I rang off and sat at the kitchen table. My phone vibrated several times but I ignored it. My mouth had dried up and my leg continued to tremble. I tried to stop it with my hand, but nothing happened. I was so afraid that I wanted to cry. Whoever he was, he was *in* Leicester . . .

I spent the next few hours pacing the house, unable to settle down to anything. The doorbell sounded just after midday. After checking carefully, I opened up. It was Kane.

'Good job you didn't come to school,' he told me. 'Things are crazy.'

'I'm in serious trouble, aren't I?' A sense of impending doom overcame me as I waited for Kane to reply.

'Dr Woods asked everyone where you were. Warren and Dhindsa too.'

'What did you say?'

Kane shrugged. 'Nothing,' he replied. 'Mr Thomas said you should call him.'

'Dave?'

'Yeah,' said Kane. 'He was with Dr Woods.'

'Great – that means Mum will find out.'

The thought of that brought more panic. Kane half smiled and calmed me down.

'You can't hide, Lily,' he pointed out. 'Best just be honest. I'll back you up – Alfie too.'

I smiled back weakly. I wasn't totally convinced. 'Was Tilly at school?'

'Nope,' he said.

'Shit!'

I wondered where she was – I still hadn't heard from her. What was she thinking about all the stuff on Facebook? She wouldn't really think I'd do something like that, would she?

'I tried calling Tilly but she didn't pick up,' he added. 'Danny tried too.'

'Go into the kitchen,' I said. 'Be there in a mo.'

I went up to my room. My PC was sleeping. I roused it and checked my Facebook page. Benedict hadn't lied – he'd logged me out, and I couldn't get back in. I tried again but the screen froze, then died. I tried to restart it but nothing happened. It was dead. I grabbed a thin hooded top and went downstairs.

'I had a chat with Benedict last night.'

Kane looked expectant.

'I told him I knew,' I said. 'He didn't seem too bothered.'

'Why did you do that?' he asked, concern all over his face.

'I was angry, Kane — I wanted to show him that he can't push me around,' I replied, feeling a little foolish.

'I get that,' he told me, 'but I don't want you hurt and he's dangerous, Lily. You should have done it when I was with you, like we said. I can protect you.'

I wanted to smile but it would have been ill-timed. Instead, I just nodded. 'He threatened my mum,' I admitted.

'What?'

'Yeah — said he was looking forward to meeting her. It was horrible.'

'You shouldn't have confronted him,' said Kane. 'If I ever get my hands on him, I swear he'll be sorry.'

'He's locked me out of Facebook too,' I continued. 'Changed my password. I was gonna call you but it was late.'

'Shall I take a look?' he offered.

'No point,' I said. 'My PC is dead.' I saw the delivery card, back on the waste-paper pile, waiting to be recycled. 'Oh, I checked on the webcam – with Royal Mail.'

'How do you mean?' he asked.

'I wanted to find out where it came from,' I explained. 'Like, where in the UK. It was posted in Leicester.'

Kane gasped. 'Nah?'

I nodded. Neither of us spoke for a little while. Then Kane suggested we go back to his.

'Is Alfie around?' I asked.

'Don't think so,' said Kane. 'I'll call him on the way – see where he is.'

Suddenly I got cold feet. What if the hacker was out there, waiting for me? What if he was watching the house? But then I looked at Kane. I'd be fine if he was with me. It would be different when I was alone, though.

'We need to stop at Tilly's house on the way,' I said, after calming myself. I was thinking about Benedict's admission that he was watching her too. I had to warn her.

'Why?'

'To tell her what's going on,' I replied. 'Benedict said he knew about all of us – that must mean he's hacked into Tilly's computer too. I need to warn her.'

'Really?' asked Kane.

'Makes sense,' I said, 'if we all downloaded the virus from Amy's video.'

The walk only took a minute. Tilly's house was like mine – semi-detached with a little porthole window for the box room. Weeds grew through cracks in the faded grey tarmac, and her mum's hanging baskets were rusting. Despite the warm weather, every window I could see was closed. I rang the bell and we waited.

'She's not in,' said Kane after a minute.

'Or not answering,' I replied.

I tried again, twice more, with the same result. I thumped my hand against the glass. 'Tilly!'

'Sshhh!' said Kane. 'You'll piss the neighbours off.'

'Stuff 'em,' I told him. 'TILLY!!'

I stood back and watched the windows for movement. Nothing.

'Come on,' said Kane. 'We ain't getting anywhere standing here.'

'Let me call her,' I said.

When she didn't answer, I sent Tilly a text – urging her to reply. 'We have to warn her,' I repeated. I was getting panicky now.

'I know,' replied Kane. 'But if she's not around, how can we?'

We took the main road and headed towards

Oadby's centre. The traffic was heavy due to road-works, and I prayed that someone from school wouldn't spot us.

'This was a stupid idea,' I said. 'Should have gone the back way. We'll get seen.'

'Who cares now?' asked Kane. 'Things are already messed up enough.'

He was wearing grey combats with white trainers and a yellow zipped top by Adidas. Every now and then, I caught a waft of his aftershave. He was right. Everything we knew – what good was any of it? How could *we* stop Benedict or whoever he was? We needed help.

'We should call DC Evans or her boss,' I said as we passed Waitrose.

'I thought that last night,' he replied. 'That we should tell her everything.'

'She'll probably think we're nuts,' I told him. 'Like, what evidence have we actually got?'

'I guess,' he replied. 'Thing is, Lily – what else can we do?'

Before I could reply my phone vibrated against my leg. It was Danny again.

Have you gone mental????

I gulped down air and felt my insides grow cold.

'What?' Kane asked, reacting to the change in my expression.

I showed him my phone.

'You think he's done something else – on Facebook?'

I nodded, my heart sinking.

Kane got out his Samsung phone and checked. 'It's bad,' he said when I tried to look.

'How bad?'

He showed me reluctantly:

How NOT To Be a Slut – A Step by Step Guide for dim bitches like Molly Cooper . . .

Step 1 – Keep your fucking clothes on, you stupid, desperate slag.

Step 2 – Don't post selfies to random strangers.

Step 3 – Don't video yourself naked, you retard.

Step 4 – Get some self-respect.

Step 5 – If you can't manage any of the above, see
   Step 6 . . .

Step 6 – Kill yourself and do the world a favour, bitch!

My hand shook as I gave Kane his phone back. I wanted to run and hide, to close my eyes until the danger had gone. Only that wasn't an option. I thought about my mum again, and was tempted to call her. She'd understand, wouldn't she?

But what about Benedict's threat? I couldn't place Mum in danger too – not unless I had no other choice.

'I wonder if he's here,' I said.

Kane looked confused. 'Huh?'

'The hacker,' I explained. 'What if he's watching us right now . . .'

Alfie was away on some work thing so Kane made tea as he flicked TV channels. I wasn't concentrating on anything, not really. It was just something to do. I felt trapped and unsure of where to go, and I really wanted to tell my mum, but the same fears as earlier stopped me. I glanced at Kane, glad he was on my side.

'What do you think?' I asked.

'About?'

'Telling my mum?'

Kane handed me a mug, and sat down. 'You've got no choice,' he said. 'Tell her, face the teachers at school and stand your ground. Like I keep saying – I'm with you.'

I nodded and looked out into the courtyard garden. Every part was crammed full – pots overflowing with brightly coloured flowers, lush green plants, garden lanterns on spiked poles, a trellis lined with climbers. On any another day, the sight would have cheered me up – childhood memories of my dad and his love for gardening. But not now.

'No one will believe me,' I told him.

'Why?' he asked. 'Everyone knows you ain't no troll.'

'Who listened to *Max*?' I replied. '*We* bloody didn't . . .'

Kane grew gloomy at that. He shook his head slowly. 'We never got the chance,' he said. 'He was gone before we could talk.'

I sipped tea and watched a sparrow flit from fence to plant pot. 'It's my name on those posts, and my account,' I said.

'Yeah,' he replied, 'but we know it's been hacked.'

'Only we've got no proof,' I said.

'The fact you can't log in?' asked Kane. 'Surely that would prove—'

'It would only be my word,' I said.

'So that makes me your ace, then,' he replied. 'With that photo I took when your Facebook was hacked.'

'What makes you my what?'

Kane's smile was a little warmer. 'Ace in the hole?' he asked. 'Well-known saying?'

'Never heard it.'

'And there was me thinking you read books.'

I punched him on the arm.

'I'm here for you, Lily,' he told me. 'Anything you need.'

I looked into his honey eyes and felt my face take

on colour. I was so tempted to kiss him. My thighs felt too big, and my shoulders too wide. He'd have to be blind to be—

Kane leaned in, put his hand against my cheek and kissed me softly.

'Kane . . .?'

He pulled away, embarrassed. 'I'm sorry,' he mumbled. 'I just . . . I . . .'

I smiled and pulled him close again. 'I wasn't angry,' I told him. 'Just shocked.'

He smiled and kissed me again.

30

I walked home in a daze. A poet might have said my heart was singing and my footsteps were so light that they kissed the pavement like butterflies dancing amongst rose petals. That I was even *thinking* such thoughts showed just how weird my mood was. Kane's kiss had rocked me – like, seriously. I was overwhelmed by it. Struggling to believe it had actually happened. I felt happy and alive – in my heart.

Only, my head wasn't playing along – not completely. I was still in trouble – *still* facing exclusion and accusations of bullying – and I knew it. My phone kept buzzing me, and my Facebook account had been hacked by a lunatic. A lunatic who had made me feel a little like I felt with Kane, but then ripped it all away.

And Max and Amy were still dead. And Tilly wasn't talking to me.

There was no reason to be cheerful. The thought of school terrified me too. How could I get people to believe me? How was Molly going to react when I saw her? Where was Tilly and what was she thinking? The same questions swam around in my mind, over and over.

As I reached my street, the two opposing moods were still clashing. I could feel Kane's hands holding me – the touch and taste of his lips. I wanted to run back to him, to make sure it hadn't been a mistake. To ask if he really wanted someone as ordinary as me. It was crazy.

Then Benedict came into my head – or at least the person he claimed to be. He was hiding in the shadows, watching me, smirking. His eyes were pitch-black with no pupils, and they were sucking me in. I had to shake my head to get rid of the image.

I saw that my mum's car wasn't on the drive. School had finished an hour earlier, so I assumed she was working late. An elderly neighbour – Mrs Bennett – approached me, walking her dog.

'Who's a lucky girl, then?' she beamed.

'*Lucky?*' I asked.

She nodded towards the house. 'You've got flowers, Lily!'

'Oh . . .' I was puzzled. 'Thanks for letting me know.'

'I used to get flowers,' she told me. Then Mrs Bennett and Lulu, her Chihuahua, continued on their way.

'*Flowers?*' I said out loud.

They were lying against the door, wrapped in scarlet foil. Twelve pink and white carnations, with an envelope taped to them. I glanced around before picking them up. My hands trembled. The paranoia crept slowly back into my head. Even as I opened the envelope, I knew. My stomach clenched.

The white card was cheap, the message printed:

MAYBE IN LOVE FOREVER

The first letter of each word was red, the rest black. MILF. The hacker's idea of a joke. My mum's beautiful face came to mind. He was playing games and they were working.

I hurried inside and dumped the bouquet in the sink. My blood felt like acid – burning its way around my body at speed. Sweat broke on my forehead, and my palms grew damp. The delivery had been made by hand. It was a message – a warning that he could get to me – to my *mum*. I was *truly* frightened – like never before. I wanted to scream.

I grabbed my phone and sent Mum a text.

You OK? When you coming home?

When she replied almost immediately, my heart-beat slowed.

At work. I'll be back in an hour or so. You OK?

Yeah – just miss you.

Miss you too, baby.

Her reply meant that she didn't know about the Facebook post – yet. Relief washed over me, but it was only momentary, and replaced almost instantly by fury. So powerful that my head began to ache. I grabbed the flowers and a box of matches, and stormed into the garden. I threw the bouquet on a patch of bare soil. In the shed, I found white spirit. I doused the carnations and the card, and then dropped a match. I hoped he was watching, from whichever hole he called home.

'You BASTARD!!!!' I shrieked.

Tilly finally responded about an hour afterwards. I was sitting, not really watching the telly, my thoughts elsewhere. I answered quickly.

'Where've you been?' I was so relieved to hear her voice – to know that she was safe. Knowing that she and Mum were fine meant more than anything.

'Well, that's *nice*,' she replied at my impatient tone.

'I've been *trying* to contact you since yesterday,' I told her.

'I wonder why?'

'Meaning?'

'I've seen Facebook,' she told me. 'What the *actual* fuck?'

'It wasn't me,' I told her. 'You *have* to believe me!' My tone was pleading but I didn't care. I *was* pleading with her. 'I got hacked.'

'By who?' she asked.

'That's the point,' I replied. 'It's why I've been calling you. I even came round earlier.'

'School.'

Why was she lying to me? Now more than ever we had to stick together. 'You weren't at school,' I replied. 'Kane told me.'

'Oh, yeah. I . . . had a dentist appointment,' she told me. 'Went in after lunch . . . didn't see Kane. Danny was there, though.'

I remembered Danny's text messages.

'He's fuming,' Tilly added.

'I know.'

'Him and everyone else,' she added. 'Dr Woods is on the war path. It's a good job you skipped school.'

'What else was I supposed to do?' I asked her.

The truth was that I'd been too scared to face it. It hurt that I was hiding that from Tilly – that wasn't what our relationship had been built on.

'Everyone knows,' she revealed. 'Mr Warren asked all about it – Dhindsa too. I think they've called the police in.'

'I'm dead.'

'But if *you* say you didn't do it . . .'

'*What?*' I snapped. 'You don't *believe* me?'

Tilly left a slight pause. 'I *believe* you,' she replied. 'I back *you* completely.'

'You might be hacked too,' I said. 'Seriously – Kane and me, we worked it out . . .'

'You were with Kane?'

'Yes – will you listen?' I was getting impatient. 'That boy – Benedict – he's a fake . . .'

I heard the front door open, and two voices – my mum and Dave.

'Shit!'

'What?' Lily asked.

'Mum's back,' I told her. 'Dave's with her . . .'

'Dave?'

'Yeah – means she must know . . . Dave will have been told at school.'

'Don't worry – Dave is lovely. He'll sort it out.'

'Never mind him!' I said hurriedly. 'Is your PC playing up?'

'I don't know,' she replied. 'I'm not a computer nerd. It *works* fine . . .'

My mum entered the living room, her expression stony. 'Call back,' she ordered.

'But I just need to—'

'NOW!' she yelled.

I felt a surge of panic. 'Gotta go,' I told Tilly. 'Check your PC – please!'

'What for?' she asked.

'Just do it!'

Suddenly the phone had been snatched from me. My mum ended the call and threw the phone on the sofa.

'*MUM!*'

'Shut up!' she demanded, as Dave walked in.

'Calm down, Laila,' he said to Mum. 'Shouting won't help.'

My lower lip quivered and I started to shake. 'It wasn't me,' I whispered.

My mum shook her head. She wore an expression that was half anger, half disappointment. Dave took a seat opposite me, his huge shoulders encased in a white Leicester Tigers polo shirt. He wore faded blue jeans and running trainers. A pink rash spread from just below his left cheek to his Adam's Apple.

'Are you OK?' he asked me.

I couldn't even work out where to start.

'Lily?'

'Course I'm not *OK*, Dave,' I eventually replied.

My mum sat next to him, her eyes filled with anger. The sofa was a two-seater so they were virtually on top of each other. They seemed very comfortable together. 'Don't give him lip!' she told me. 'Dave's here to help you.'

'I haven't done anything,' I told her. 'I got *hacked*.'

Mum and Dave exchanged glances, as though they couldn't trust my word. It made me feel terrible. Didn't they *know* me? Everyone I thought I could trust doubted me.

'Hacked?' he asked.

'Yeah,' I replied. 'It wasn't me – you can ask Kane.'

'Why Kane?'

I sighed. 'I made friends with some lad,' I told them. 'On Facebook. He said he was from New York – Benedict . . .'

'But how does *that* lead to *this*?' asked Mum.

I wanted to scream at her – to say *Shut up and listen*. Only, I would never have spoken to her that way. I adored her. I buried my frustration and continued to explain.

'Benedict is a hacker,' I said. 'He duped me into being friends and then got all weird.'

My mum's eyes widened. She glanced at Dave. 'Weird in what way?' she asked, the obvious concern in her tone making me feel a bit better.

'He wanted pics,' I told her. 'Like, selfies . . .'

My mum gasped.

'Selfies as in nude photographs?' asked Dave.

'They're not *all* nasty,' I replied. 'Most selfies are just people having a laugh or showing off.'

'But this Benedict,' said Mum. 'He wanted more?' She looked close to tears.

'Yes,' I said. 'He kept asking me to have video chats with him. He even sent me a webcam.'

'But how did he get this address?' asked Mum.

'That's the point,' I replied. I stopped and collected my thoughts. It was like trying to catch waves with a sieve.

'What *point*?' asked Dave, sitting forward now, his steel-blue eyes locked on mine.

'Benedict isn't his real name,' I replied. 'I don't know who he is. I think he's the person Max was talking to, though. The person who recorded that awful video clip.'

'Max — as in Max *Jones*?'

I nodded.

'I didn't know he was talking to anyone,' said Dave.

'DC Evans,' I said. 'She knew . . .'

Mum and Dave exchanged another look. I wasn't getting my point across, and I started to get hot. My hands grew clammy and my cheeks burned. Being forced into telling Mum was a huge relief, but things were complicated and I wanted her to understand. I wanted her to be on my side.

'Max was interacting with some woman called Charlotte, only she wasn't real,' I explained. 'She was like Benedict – a fake – because they're the same person, I'm sure of it. *That* person hacked my Facebook and wrote all that nasty stuff about Molly. Kane is a witness – he'll back me up. His brother too.'

'His brother?' asked Mum. 'What's Alfie's connection to this?'

'He checked my computer yesterday,' I revealed. 'He's the one that told me I had a RAT.'

'A rat?' said Dave. Both of them looked confused.

'Remote Access Trojan,' I replied. 'It's a type of virus – hackers use them to take over computers.'

'I'm just baffled now,' said Mum. 'More than when Dave rang to tell me.'

'When did you find out?'

'Maybe an hour ago,' she replied. 'Not that it matters. Why did you lie this morning?'

At least I understood how she knew. Kane had been right – she was always going to find out. It made hiding things from her a pointless decision.

'I didn't lie, Mum.'

'You claimed to be ill,' she reminded me.

'I *was* unwell,' I protested. 'I was scared too.'

'Because of the Facebook post?' asked Dave.

'Yes!' The soft cream seat cushion beneath me was slipping. I stood and shoved it back into place.

Dave still looked puzzled. 'Hang on,' he said. 'Lily – you're saying that this person – this *Benedict* – had something to do with Max's problems?'

'*Yes*,' I replied. 'I'm sure of it.'

The doorbell chimed and Mum went to answer.

Dave came and sat by my side. He put his arm round me. 'Look – I might not understand this,' he told me, 'but I believe you. This is completely out of character.'

His confidence and belief meant the world at that moment. It was all that I needed. I could have hugged him for ever.

'I think we should call the police – speak to DC Evans,' I said.

'You're in luck,' Mum replied from the door. 'She's here to see you.'

DC Evans looked weary. Her face was lined, and dark circles sat under her eyes. The light grey business suit she wore was crumpled and her hair was limp and tired, making it look a shade darker.

'It's about Molly Cooper,' she said. 'I need to ask you some questions.'

'We've just been talking about that,' Dave told

her. 'Lily has something very interesting to tell you.'

DC Evans looked at my mum. 'We *could* talk here,' she told her, 'but we're probably better off going to the station.'

Mum looked horrified. 'Are you *arresting* my daughter?' she asked. 'She's done nothing wrong. She's been hacked.'

'No,' said the police officer. 'But we do need to question her. You'll need to come along, as her parent. You may also call a solicitor, if you wish.'

'Can I ask *why*, Officer?' said Dave.

DC Evans nodded. 'Molly Cooper has been missing since last night,' she revealed. 'Given the recent incidents at your school, we're very concerned. Lily is central to our investigation.'

I knew immediately that Molly was dead too — like an instinct. Benedict had been cryptic — *the police won't catch me*, he'd said, *not before* . . . He'd meant Molly — I was sure of it. When I tried to stand up and walk, I felt queasy. I couldn't get rid of the images in my mind.

Benedict was in there again. I was hanging from a web, the lower half of my body cocooned in silk. He sat above, watching me with soulless eyes . . .

31

DC Evans introduced her boss, DI Meadows, even though I knew who he was. His hair was even shorter than before, grey speckled with white, and his lips so thin, they looked cruel. When he spoke, I saw that his teeth were discoloured and uneven. Patches of eczema, flaky and sore, covered his hands and neck.

The interview room was small and airless. I sat between Mum and Dave, with the officers across a basic wooden table from us. To our right, a tape recorder sat against the grey-painted wall. In the corner, above the door, was a camera. The rest of the room was empty.

'This isn't official,' he told us. 'But you can ask for a solicitor, if you wish. We aren't taping this interview.'

Mum nodded. 'Your colleague mentioned that,' she said. 'If you're not arresting my daughter, I don't see the need. I'm sure that between us, we can manage.' She glanced at Dave and he reassured her with a smile.

DI Meadows looked at me, his eyes a shade darker blue than Dave's but just as intense. 'We're under a great deal of pressure,' he told me. 'So I need you to be honest and tell us everything. Molly disappeared last night. Ordinarily, we'd wait a while longer and see if she turns up, but with the events of late . . .'

He let his sentence trail off and fiddled with a notebook. DC Evans consulted hers and asked the first question.

'Did you see Molly yesterday – that would be *Tuesday*?'

I nodded. It didn't feel so recent to me, however. It felt like days since I'd last seen her, tottering away on her high heels. So much had happened since then.

'At school,' I told her.

'Was she acting strangely or distressed at all?'

Again, I nodded. 'She was acting weird – sort of excited, even,' I said. 'She had this huge tote bag.'

'What colour was the bag?'

'Sort of tan brown – leather too. I saw it in the sales a couple of weeks ago.'

'You said it was huge?'

'Maybe not that big,' I told her. 'But it was packed full. Like almost bursting.'

'Did she say why?'

I shook my head. 'Not to me – we're not exactly best mates or anything. But she did tell people she had a modelling contract.'

DC Evans gave her boss a quick look, and he jotted something in his notebook.

'You said not *you*,' Evans continued. 'Who did she tell?'

'A few people. Danny Sangha, some others . . .'

'Lily – you need to be sure,' said DI Meadows.

'She told Kane Williams and Danny,' I replied. 'I don't know who else.'

Meadows gave DC Evans a little nod, so quick I nearly missed it. She glanced at her notes and took over again.

'Did you see her after school?'

'No.'

'What did you do?'

'After school?' I asked. 'I was in the library, then I went home. No, actually, I went to Kane's house.'

'Which was it?' she asked, arching her eyebrows.

'Kane's first, then home.'

'Why did you go to Kane's house?'

My mum cleared her throat. 'Why is that

important?' she asked the officers. 'Teenagers do that all the time.'

'We just need a clear timeline,' DI Meadows told her.

'Lily?' asked DC Evans.

'I was upset,' I admitted. 'I'd fallen out with my best friend, Tilly, and Kane was there for me . . .'

'Tilly Anderson?' asked Evans, looking at her notes again.

'Yes.'

'Why did you fall out?'

I paused to think. 'She's got a new man,' I said. 'I haven't seen her much and we had an argument about it.'

'You were upset that she's spending time with someone else?'

I saw what Evans was doing and shook my head. 'No – I'm happy for her,' I replied. 'We just had a girl-argument. It was nothing serious.'

'You're sure?'

'Yeah,' I said. 'I was on the phone to her this evening, when Mum came home. Ask her.'

My mum nodded, but didn't speak.

'So,' said the WPC, 'you saw Molly once but didn't speak to her – is that correct?'

'Yes.'

'And you didn't see her after school?'

'Well, yeah, I saw her,' I replied.

When Meadows's face lit up, I explained myself quickly. 'Everyone sees everyone else,' I said. 'Like, *after* school?'

'Who was she with – *after* school?' asked DC Evans. 'Now that you've *remembered* seeing her.'

'A lad called Lakh Singh. I don't know him well.'

'And where were they going?'

'I don't know.'

The officers exchanged another look, then DI Meadows wrote down a load more notes, his ball-point noisy against the pad – like he was pressing too hard. 'You saw Lakh Singh and Molly Cooper walk away from school?' Evans said. 'Together?'

'Yes.'

'Which way did they go?'

'Back towards the A6 – maybe towards the town centre?'

DC Evans nodded. 'Anything else – about Molly and what might have happened yesterday?'

I shook my head. The two officers left the room briefly – just long enough for Mum to pat my arm.

'You'll be fine,' she told me.

'*If* they believe me,' I replied. 'They haven't even *mentioned* Facebook yet.'

DC Evans re-entered alone. 'DI Meadows sends

his apologies,' she told us. 'He's been called away urgently.'

'Nothing serious, I hope,' said Dave, a concerned look on his face.

'No, Mr Thomas,' said Evans. 'It's not that. Shall we continue? I'd like for you all to get home as soon as possible.'

The three of us nodded.

'So,' said DC Evans, retaking her seat. 'Tell me about the Facebook posts, Lily.'

I looked away, my cheeks burning. Whatever I said, I had to make her believe me. I thought of Kane and the photo he'd taken.

'It wasn't me,' I replied. 'I didn't post those.'

Evans made a few more notes before speaking again. 'The posts came from *your* account,' she told me. 'You tagged over a *hundred* fellow pupils. Why should I believe you didn't post them?'

I paused again, gathered my thoughts, and cleared my throat. 'I've been hacked,' I replied.

'Hacked?'

'Yes,' I said.

'Go on . . .'

I looked at Mum, who nodded.

'Tell the officer what you told us,' added Dave, looking at his watch. 'Oh – I need to go too.'

Mum looked disappointed.

'I said I'd speak to Dr Woods,' he told us. 'She wants to know what's going on. There's a meeting of senior staff and governors this evening. I can't miss it.'

'But how will you get back?' asked Mum.

'Don't worry about me, Laila,' he said. 'I'll get a cab.'

I was gutted that Dave had to go – he was on my side and I needed him. I just hoped that Mum was as convinced by my innocence. She seemed to be. Once Dave had gone, DC Evans repeated her question.

I took a deep breath. 'I made friends with a lad called Benedict Pablo,' I said. 'He claimed to be from New York.'

'This is on Facebook?'

'Yeah.'

'Why *claimed*?' she asked. 'You said he *claimed* to be from New York.'

'That's what he told me,' I replied. 'We chatted online for a while – like, a few weeks, but then he got weird. He wanted me to send him photographs.'

'What kind of photographs?'

'Rude ones, I think – like *selfies*?'

'You *think*?'

'I sent him one,' I admitted. 'Nothing slutty –

just a pic of myself, lying on my bed, I had my clothes on.'

I watched Mum's face grow stony again, and knew she'd go mental when we left. It still felt good, though – getting it off my chest.

'Carry on,' said DC Evans, scribbling in her notebook and not looking up.

'He liked the photo, but he wanted more, and I started to get annoyed. Then, after Max died, he sent me a nude picture.'

'Of whom?' Evans asked.

'Himself,' I replied. 'Of his . . . er . . . lower half.'

Mum looked frightened now – she put her hand on mine. Her show of support made me feel safer. '*Lily?*' she said, her eyes searching my face.

'I'm sorry, Mum,' I replied. 'I was going to tell you.'

DC Evans looked up. 'Let me get this straight,' she said. 'The photograph he sent was of his own genitalia?'

'Yes.'

I felt Mum squeeze my hand gently.

'What did you do?'

'I didn't do anything,' I replied. 'I left him to it.'

'You didn't reply or send any of your own?'

'*No!*' I insisted. 'I'm not like that.'

'Not like Molly?' said Evans.

'I don't mean that!' I protested.

'You made two posts about Molly on Facebook,' said Evans. 'They seemed like that's what you meant.'

'I didn't post those, I told you.'

'Not even the second one?'

'*No!*'

DC Evans wrote down a few more lines. I looked at Mum, and saw a tear welling in her right eye. She squeezed my hand again.

'So who made the posts?' Evans asked.

'Benedict, I think . . .'

'This boy from New York?'

'Yes.'

'How do you know that?'

'Because he sent me a webcam – only it was posted in Leicester . . .'

'A *webcam*?' she said.

I nodded.

'He's also the same person that Max Jones was interacting with . . . the *woman*?'

'Charlotte?' said DC Evans, her eyes suddenly more alert.

'Yes.'

'How can you *possibly* know this?'

I cleared my throat again. 'Because I caught him out,' I replied. 'Charlotte and Benedict are the same person – a hacker. And this hacker is connected to me, to Max, to Molly. He's connected to Amy Wiggins too – I'm sure of it.'

The officer's face went so red that I thought she might pass out. She sat back in her chair, exhaled deeply and shook her head.

'You need to find Kane,' I added. 'He was with me – he has proof that it wasn't me who made those horrible posts. He took a photograph at the same time that we saw the post. It's time-coded. You can check it and see that I'm telling the truth.'

'Kane Williams?'

I nodded.

'I need to make a call,' she told us. 'I'll have the desk sergeant bring you refreshments.'

'Can't we leave?' asked Mum. 'I want to take my daughter home. She's been through a lot, Officer.'

Evans shrugged. 'You're free to leave anytime,' she said. 'But I'd rather you stayed. What's happened here is unexpected and I need to speak to my boss. I think we're going to be here for a while . . .'

'Do we need a solicitor?' asked Mum.

'That's up to you, Mrs Basra.'

'You know already, don't you?' I said to DC Evans.

'Know what, Lily?'

'About the link,' I said. 'That's why you're still investigating Max's death, isn't it.' I was guessing.

'I can't comment on that,' she replied.

Something changed in her eyes, though – and I realized my guess had been correct.

The Spider answers immediately.

'I've just had a very interesting conversation,' the OTHER tells him.

'About?'

'The friend – Lily?'

'Yes?'

'She's been talking to the police.'

'Oh . . .'

'This isn't my fault,' the OTHER insists. 'Not this time.'

The Spider listens to his accomplice whine and shakes his head. *No*, he thinks, *it is my fault. I should cut and run. Go back into my lair and wait for the next opportunity.*

Yet something irks him. The girl – Lily – is not

hurting sufficiently. She does not feel his presence keenly enough. No one has ever fought against him like this – and he will not accept it. He has a few days to change the situation. And change it he will . . .

He replies carefully. 'Your task is clear,' he tells the OTHER.

'Yes?'

'You need to tie up your loose end.'

'If that's what you want.'

'Arrange it for this coming weekend,' the Spider tells him.

'Are you sure?' the OTHER asks. 'I think we should wait – so soon after Molly . . .'

The Spider sighs. 'Thinking is my domain,' he replies. 'Let me worry about the trails. You remove the girl.'

'And bring her to you?'

'No – there is another location. I will send you the details.'

'OK.'

'Tell me the moment your task is complete . . .'

'What about the videos? My buyers are—'

'I don't care about your paedophile friends!' the Spider hisses. 'We must protect ourselves first. The videos can wait.'

'But you said they would be wiped—'

'From *your* laptop – yes. I have other, more secret

places to store them. When this is over, I will let you have them.'

'They are offering a great deal of money.'

'Then consider what you will buy with your share,' the Spider replies.

'Have you finished with my computer?'

'Yes – I will bring it with me when you have the girl.'

'I need it sooner – can we meet?'

'No,' the Spider tells him. 'The risks are too great.'

'OK.'

Later, the Spider unpacks another new phone. He inserts the sim card and, when ready, enters just a single number. In the corner of the room, he sees the tan leather tote bag. He smiles, before running through his plan once more. He must cover every angle – tie every knot securely. When this web falls, no one must be allowed to see which shadow he crawls into . . .

32

Dr Woods's office was huge, with windows on two sides and a view across the rear of the school, out into open countryside. One wall was lined with shelves that groaned under the weight of hundreds of books. The wall behind her had framed photographs and certificates mounted on it. In the biggest, she was standing with the Prime Minster – both of them grinning like old friends. The room was divided between an office area and a small seated section, complete with sink, coffee machine, kettle and fridge. Mum and I sat on a boxy black sofa, waiting.

We'd left the police station at two in the morning, and I was tired enough to fall asleep right where I was. DC Evans had called DI Meadows, and on his return, I'd given a formal statement about everything I knew.

I'd told them about Kane and Alfie, and the infected video link that Amy had sent so many months earlier. Dave had come back around ten p.m., after we'd been allowed a break to eat. Then two police officers had taken Mum to ours, and they'd returned with my computer as evidence. Kane had sent me a text around the same time, to say that the police were at his house. He told me not to worry and that he was happier now that DC Evans knew what we did.

Now, first thing on a Thursday, I was thinking about Kane when Dr Woods, Mr Dhindsa and Mr Warren entered the office. Each wore a grave expression, but only Mr Warren asked how I was.

'Not great,' I said honestly.

'We'll get to the bottom of this,' he replied. 'Don't you worry, Lily.'

My principal sat opposite us, and the other two stood at the small worktop that housed the sink.

'Can I get anyone coffee or tea?' asked Dr Woods. She wore a narrow black skirt, a light blue blouse and sensible flat shoes. Her skin had a grey tinge.

Mum shook her head. 'Can we just get on?' she asked politely.

Dr Woods nodded. 'There is very little room for

manoeuvre,' she explained. 'Until this investigation is complete, I'm afraid Lily cannot attend school.'

'So you're excluding her?' said Mum, as my heart sank.

'Not permanently,' said Mr Dhindsa. 'You could call it a temporary leave of absence.'

'Obviously, she *would* be excluded permanently, if proven guilty of bullying,' Dr Woods added. 'I've adopted a zero-tolerance policy since Amy Wiggins's unfortunate case.'

'And what about her GCSEs?' asked Mum. 'Say she *is* innocent, and I have no doubt at all – what then?'

I glanced at her and thought that I might cry. Her support meant everything to me.

Mr Dhindsa, his eyes like chocolate beads, re-assured my mum. 'I've thought about that,' he explained. 'Regardless of what happens from this point, we mustn't let Lily's education suffer. If that's possible . . .'

'I see,' said Mum.

'So I've delegated Mr Warren here to collect all the work she needs and to present it to you each week. It's not long until Year Eleven start exam leave anyway. So the disruption should be minimal.'

Mr Warren nodded and gave us a warm smile. 'It will be my pleasure,' he said.

Dr Woods coughed. 'However,' she said, 'until this matter is resolved, Lily must have no contact with the school — is that clear?'

'Not even her friends?' Mum asked.

I felt my heart sink further.

'Outside of school, fine,' said Dr Woods. 'We cannot control that. But during school hours, she must not enter, nor attempt to gain entry to the premises for any reason . . .'

I wanted to shout *like I would*, but I had enough grief already, without being childish too. Even my GCSEs were beginning to feel trivial compared to what was happening.

'Furthermore,' said the principal, 'we feel it important that Lily not talk to the media about this case. I'm sure the police have already voiced similar hopes.'

Mum nodded. 'They have,' she reiterated. 'But then you've spoken to them, so you already *know* that.' The tension between her and Dr Woods lay thick in the room.

'Yes, we have,' Mr Dhindsa interjected. 'But reporters can be very *insistent* . . .'

'And you wouldn't want your school's hard-won reputation tarnished,' said Mum; although I think her reply was rhetorical and sarcastic.

'We've seen what negative public opinion can do

to schools in this city,' replied Dr Woods. 'You, of *all* people, know that.'

'Well,' said Mum, 'two deaths in just over a month can damage any school. Although that loss of reputation means nothing against the tragedy of the pupils who have died . . .'

Dr Woods looked taken aback. 'That's true,' she said unconvincingly.

'The exclusion is effective immediately, I take it?' asked Mum.

'I'm afraid so, Mrs Basra,' said Mr Dhindsa.

'Well, in that case,' said Mum, standing up, 'we'll be going.'

None of the other three adults moved.

'I'll make sure her homework arrives promptly,' Mr Warren said. 'I have your number, Mrs Basra.'

'Thank you,' she said.

Mum dropped me back at home, then had to go to work. But only after apologizing for having to leave me alone, and warning me not to open the door to anyone. I could see that she was having trouble hiding her guilt, but I made things easier for her by promising to be careful, and showing her my phone. The police were just a quick call away, and the neighbours even closer. Finally, she nodded and gave me a hug before leaving.

The house felt weird – like a prison. I couldn't settle – moving from one room to the next, aimlessly. I was worried about being alone in the house, but I didn't have a choice. Mum's meeting couldn't be cancelled, and besides, she couldn't baby-sit me twenty-four hours a day, could she?

I tried to revise but there was no point. I couldn't even look at the words, never mind understand and take them in. In the end, I opted for daytime TV and cooking shows. They were OK, but my concentration ebbed quickly. I started thinking about Kane and Tilly, and the look in DC Evans's eyes when I'd mentioned Max. Wondering whether to update Kane on my exclusion, I checked my phone. I had a few abusive messages on What's App, plus several texts and an email from some company, telling me my account had been suspended. I deleted it, and another email popped up instantly. This one was from a cosmetic surgery clinic in London. It was confirming my consultation appointment. I was interested in breast enhancement, apparently.

'What the . . . ?'

He was at it again – playing more games: it had to be him. I shook my head and put my phone down. His latest attempt was childish but it left me feeling cold too. I started wondering where he was, and

340

then I couldn't get him out of my head. Mum had left a novel by Dennis Lehane on the coffee table. I grabbed that and started to read. The novel was great but I couldn't focus at all. I had to read and re-read sentences, and my eyes started to ache. In the end, I put the book down too.

At some point I fell asleep. When I awoke, it was past six p.m., and I felt awful. My neck muscles were stiff and my stomach grumbled. I got up and went into the kitchen, where there was no sign of Mum. I opened the fridge, looked at a few things I didn't fancy, and then shut the door. At the table, I rechecked my phone. Kane had been calling me.

'You OK?' he asked, concern showing in his voice, when I called back.

'Yeah – fell asleep,' I told him. 'Sorry – I meant to text you. Did the police keep you for long?'

'Yeah,' he said, 'but that's not important.'

'What is then?' He paused and I felt it coming. 'You're gonna tell me to watch the news, aren't you?'

'Yes,' he admitted, his tone full of sorrow. 'They found Molly.'

'*Dead?*'

'Yeah,' he replied softly. 'Hanged just like Max and Amy . . .'

The OTHER smiles.

'I thought you'd be pleased,' the girl tells him.

'You are very clever,' he tells her. 'One of your many charms.'

'I have to be back for Sunday afternoon, though – Mum'll go crazy otherwise.'

'And we wouldn't want that, would we?'

The girl giggles down the line.

'I'll get you back by three – is that OK?'

'Yeah – that's perfect.'

'Much like you . . .' he tells her.

'I wish you were here now,' she says. 'I would snog your face off!'

'Soon,' he tells her. 'Very soon.'

'Dave?'

'Hmmm?'

'Do you love me?'

'Of course I do,' he replies.

'Like, really love me?' she adds. 'Or just, like, fancy me . . .'

'Why would I risk my career for a fling?' he asks her. 'I'm not a weirdo. I don't make a habit of doing this . . .'

'I know,' she sighs. 'What a shame the world is so fucked up.'

'We are the same,' he tells her. 'We're special people who understand each other. The rest of the world doesn't get people like us. They don't deserve us . . .'

'You're so deep,' she replies. 'I love talking to you.'

'You're sure everything is set?'

'Completely,' she tells him. 'You and me, Dave. God – I'm excited!'

The OTHER rings off, before calling the Spider.

'She is ready,' he says.

'Are you sure?'

'Absolutely.'

'Excellent! Let me know the second she is secure . . .'

33

Kane shook his head slowly.

'My mum used to take us near there,' he said
softly. 'Wistow Maze . . .'

The maze was just over a mile from where Molly's
body had been discovered. The details were sketchy
but that hadn't stopped the media from going crazy.
The school was under siege, according to Kane, and
the story was now international. Every news channel
and radio station in the UK was reporting Molly's
death, and a major investigation was underway. I
knew the police would be back soon – they were
bound to question me again. And all I could do was
sit and wait.

Online, people were slagging me off. Facebook
and Twitter were full of nasty comments – posts

that I *made* Kane show me when he came over after our conversation. I didn't want to look at the messages on my own. And even though I was innocent, I still felt guilty. It was crazy, I know, but I couldn't help it.

When we checked, we found that my Facebook account had been suspended, although by whom I didn't know. It didn't matter anyway because I still had no access to it, and to be honest, I was relieved. It meant that I wouldn't have any more contact with Benedict. I was more convinced than ever that he was behind everything. The thought had given me insomnia, just as he'd said it would. *You'll never sleep again* . . .

'You look really tired,' said Kane.

'Yeah,' I replied. 'I can't sleep. I close my eyes and all I see is Max's face, or Molly walking around school . . .'

'Me too,' he said. 'Have you spoken to Tilly?'

I shook my head. 'Not really – just a few quick texts.'

'I saw her at school earlier,' he told me. 'She was talking about going away this weekend.'

'Really – where's she going?'

'She didn't say – just that she was looking forward to it.'

Tilly had an uncle, Henry, who lived in Bristol,

and two aunts in Liverpool, and I wondered if she was going to see them. I used to know where she was all the time. Now, things were so different, so strange between us. It hurt. Things had changed so much in just a few weeks.

We were sitting in the living room. Kane was next to me, and I wanted to snuggle into his chest and arms. My need was as much about comfort as anything else and he must have realized because he leaned in and kissed me.

'So are we, like, a *thing*?' I asked.

'A big thing.' He smiled shyly. 'I really like you, Lily — have done for ages.'

I tried to stop myself smiling back at him — it didn't work. 'Why didn't you say anything?' I said softly.

Kane shrugged. 'I didn't know if you felt the same,' he replied. 'Like — you're so fit and I was a bit shy.'

I shook my head. I was *far* from being fit. I was the girl no one noticed because there were much prettier ones to look at — girls like Tilly.

'I thought that about you,' I admitted. 'But I never dreamed you would want to be with someone like me . . .'

Kane pulled me to him. I felt the strength in his arms and nearly melted. My tummy started to throb.

'You were worried?' he said, so close that I could feel his breath against my lips, and smell the scent of his skin. 'Are you mad?'

'Why?'

'You know how many lads at school fancy you?' he asked.

'No,' I said, genuinely shocked. 'I bet it's not many.'

Kane smiled. 'Man – you've got no idea . . .' he said.

'Well – I'm only interested in you,' I said. 'If, like, you want me?'

The kiss he gave me clarified things perfectly.

When DC Evans turned up again, Kane was having dinner with Mum and me. His plate was piled high with food, and despite the serious situation, Mum looked happy to have him around. When she found out we were dating, she beamed in delight.

'I'm thrilled for you,' she told us. 'Deanna and I said you'd make the perfect couple when you were babies!' She and Kane's mum had been friends *that long* . . .

Behind her smile, though, the worry was still there. Neither of us mentioned Molly or the case, and I was happy about that. Until the bell rang.

Mum answered and brought DC Evans through

to the kitchen. If the policewoman had seemed tired the day before, now she was almost haggard.

'There have been developments,' she told us. 'My boss asked me to speak to you about them.'

'Why?' I asked.

'I can't go into specifics,' she replied, 'but we've reassigned the investigation. It is now a murder enquiry.'

I forced the cottage pie I'd been eating back down. My throat felt tight and my temples throbbed.

'*Murder?*' asked Kane.

'This is just a heads-up,' said DC Evans. 'The media are going to look at every angle – I just wanted to warn you.'

'Lily won't be speaking to them,' said Mum. 'We told you that.'

'I know,' said the officer, 'but it's worth reiterating. I also have some more questions, if that's OK?'

I looked at Mum, who nodded.

'Shall I go?' asked Kane.

DC Evans shook her head. 'They involve you too,' she revealed. 'And if you could contact your brother that would also be a huge help.'

'Why not take them to the station?' asked Mum.

DC Evans sighed. 'We're under siege there from the media,' she explained. 'They're clutching at any straws they can grab. To be honest, we'll have more privacy here. But it is official, so at some point we'd have to take statements again. Let me worry about that, though.'

Kane and I glanced at each other.

'I'll call Alfie now,' he said.

'Great,' replied DC Evans. 'I'll need to speak to him tonight, if I may? And while you're on the phone, can you get your mother to speak to me and confirm if she's OK to let Mrs Basra act as your appropriate adult? Unless she can come round here too?'

After Kane had got hold of Alfie, and his mum had given her permission to DC Evans, Mum made the officer some tea. The detective sat opposite me, eyeing the Dennis Lehane novel I'd tried to read earlier.

'He's good,' she said, smiling weakly.

'I didn't get far,' I told her. 'I can't concentrate.'

For the first time, I saw sympathy in her eyes. She nodded and told me she understood. 'We've never experienced anything like this before,' she added. 'It's . . .'

She left her sentence hanging, and eventually Mum filled the silence.

'Can you tell us who was murdered?'

'No,' said DC Evans. 'But it will be news soon, I'm sure. We're holding a press conference imminently.'

'How *many* murders?' asked Kane, who'd retaken the seat next to mine.

'Sorry,' she replied. 'Can't say . . .'

I nodded and looked away. Did she mean Max or Molly. Or maybe both?

'You told me that you had been hacked,' began DC Evans.

'Yeah – Alfie called it a RAT,' I replied.

'Do you know exactly how you caught this virus?'

'No,' I replied. 'I think it was from a video Amy Wiggins posted on Facebook, though, as I've already told you. But you have my computer so you can check, surely?'

'Yes,' she told me. 'The problem we have, Lily, is that we can't track your IP address – the one unique to your Internet connection.'

My confusion must have shown because Kane felt the need to explain. 'IP stands for Internet Protocol,' he told me. 'It's like your street address – or the same thing. Every computer that connects to the Internet has its own IP. So when I use my laptop, it leaves my IP as a footprint. When you connect, your IP is logged.'

'Oh,' I replied. 'So if I email you, my IP talks to your IP?'

'Summat like that,' said Kane.

'We checked the trail from your computer, but it was too complex.'

'I don't understand . . .'

'Do you know how to hide an IP address?' she asked.

'I didn't even know I had one until just now,' I reminded her.

She read her notes then made some more. 'When the Facebook post about Molly was created,' she replied, 'the trail should have led back to you. Like a straight path to your door.'

'Yeah,' I said, 'but I didn't do it.'

'That's my point,' said DC Evans. 'The trail *did involve* your IP, but it also goes through several hundred other IP addresses, which we haven't yet located. It's like a labyrinth. There is a source but we don't know where – yet . . .'

Again, my confusion was evident.

'What I'm saying,' said the officer, 'is that we believe you, Lily.'

'You *do*?' I felt a huge weight lift from my chest.

Mum grabbed my arm and smiled. 'Thank God!' she said, the relief evident on her expression.

'So I can go back to school?'

'No – not until we're sure,' Evans said. 'But your hard drive had been completely wiped when we checked it. Did you do that?'

I shook my head.

'What about you?' Evans asked Kane. 'Did you or your brother mess about with it?'

'No,' said Kane. 'But Alfie did *look* at it.'

She made more notes. 'One further thing,' she said eventually. 'Did Max ever wear a ring of any sort?'

I nodded. 'Yeah – silver.'

'It came from his granddad,' Kane added. 'It was on a chain around his neck . . .'

I'd always wondered about that ring – and what it had meant to Max. It had obviously been important. Now I knew why and it just added to the sadness.

'Did he give that to either of you, or any other friend?' asked Evans.

'No way,' said Kane. 'He would never do that. The ring was like a memory of his grandfather. Max was gutted when he died. He never took it off.'

'OK,' said DC Evans. 'We may need to ask you more questions, but for now, please don't speak to anyone about any of this.'

Kane and I nodded.

'You said the murder enquiry is being made public?' said Mum.

'Yes – should be about now,' said DC Evans, looking at her watch. 'There's a news conference scheduled.'

Later, as I lay in bed, unable to sleep, my phone vibrated. It was around two a.m., and I panicked. Only, when I saw the unknown number and read it, panic gave way to fear.

Hello, Lily – how's life? I see Molly got the fame she so desperately aspired to?

I tried to stop my hand from shaking but couldn't.

Talking to the police, Lily – very naughty of you. Bad girls get punished. Wondering how you'll get yours?

I didn't reply. Shivers of dread crawled up my spine. He was more than just close by. He was connected to me in some way. How else could he know I'd spoken to the police? My mind started to race. I went through names and faces and back again. But there was no one I could point at. No one to whom I could say – *Yes, that's you, I know who you are.*

Not even curious as to how I got your number?

I sat and stared at the phone, wishing that I could run away and hide somewhere. My legs began to tremble.

Was it Max's phone I retrieved it from? Or was it Molly's . . . ?

I jumped out of bed and ran to my mum's room.

34

DC Evans came back within an hour and checked all of our locks. Then she took a look at my phone, as Mum made some tea.

'Are you going to take it,' I asked. 'As evidence?'

DC Evans shook her head. 'No – I just need to copy the messages,' she said. 'Besides, he might text again, and if he does, I want to read what he says.'

'What if he comes for us?'

She looked thoughtful for a moment. 'I'll speak to DI Meadows,' she told me. 'See what we can do. In the meantime, I'll give you a number to call if you have any concerns – it will get me immediately. I'll give it to Kane too.'

She left soon afterwards and Mum sat with me. I couldn't sleep – my thoughts going round and round. In the end, Mum slipped in beside me, and soon she was snoring gently. I cuddled up to her, like I'd done as a child, the warmth of her body and her familiar scent almost soothing me. Almost.

Next morning, Tilly called and asked me to come round; she had coursework to finish and hadn't gone into school. Not that it mattered – we were already into revision-only lessons and our exams loomed large on the horizon. She was in dress-down mode when I got there, wearing loose jeans, grimy old trainers and a thin hooded top. She asked about the Facebook thing and what the police had said. I told her I'd been cleared. That DC Evans had told me that herself.

'Last night?' she asked.

'Yeah,' I said. 'She came to the house.'

'And everything is OK?'

I nodded and Tilly looked happy for me. Her smile was warm and genuine – like the Tilly I knew.

'That's what she said – sort of.'

'That's great news, isn't it?' she said.

'Yes.'

'So why do you look so miserable still?'

I shrugged. 'Because there's more to it,' I revealed. 'The hacker – the one I mentioned on the phone – he's been watching me and I'm frightened.'

Tilly's eyes widened. 'Watching you?' she asked.

'Yeah,' I replied. 'Only online to begin with.'

When she grew confused, I told her about the flowers and let her read the text messages.

'Have you shown these to the coppers?' she asked.

'Yes – they know everything.'

'So you'll be safe then,' she said. 'What's to be scared of, babe? They'll catch him soon enough.'

'He threatened Mum,' I told her. 'Said he was looking forward to meeting her . . . I'm scared she might get hurt and it would be my fault because I wound him up.'

'That's horrible,' she replied. 'Can't the police protect you?'

I shook my head. 'DC Evans said she'd talk to her boss but he hasn't done anything yet. Not in the real world. We don't even know who he is.'

'Could be anyone,' said Tilly. 'There's so many nutters online.'

I shook my head again. 'He already knows I've been talking to the police,' I revealed.

Tilly's face filled with horror. 'Hang on,' she said. 'How can he know that?'

'I dunno – but he made it clear in his texts last night. He's *got* to be someone connected to me,' I told her.

'Yeah, but who?'

'I have no idea,' I admitted. 'I keep going over it in my head, but I just get frustrated. That it might be someone we know is terrifying. It's driving me nuts.'

Tilly put her hand on my arm and told me not to worry. 'The police are dealing with it,' she said. 'Whoever it is would be an idiot to try anything now.'

I prayed that she was right but I didn't believe she was. He was dangerous and he was unknown, which meant that he could strike at any time. And not knowing when was the scariest thing of all. It was like he was playing with my emotions, pulling invisible strings that made me jump whenever he felt like it.

'I checked my laptop,' Tilly added.

'Hmm?' I said, lost in my own thoughts.

'You asked me to, remember? When your mum cut me off?'

I nodded. 'Did you find anything suspicious?' I asked.

'No – it was fine.'

'You mind if I get Kane's brother to check it,' I added. 'He's an IT expert.'

'If you want,' she said. 'This is all just mental.'

I'd had enough of talking about serious stuff, so we spent the next hour just drinking tea and chatting. It was odd after the tension, but I loved it.

Tilly was like her old self – my best friend, my sister. She was even wearing her Pandora bracelet, the '*Sisters Forever*' charm dangling from it, reminding us of what we meant to each other. Mine was sitting on my bedroom shelf, the clasp broken. I touched my left wrist anyway, and felt calmer and more relaxed.

Only the tension wasn't far from the surface. We still had a big issue to sort out, and eventually I couldn't hold my question in.

'Are you still seeing this man?'

'Yeah,' she told me, her eyes wary.

'It's OK,' I replied. 'I haven't told anyone – and I'll trust you, yeah?'

She beamed at me, her icy eyes sparkly and alive. 'Thank you,' she said. 'I'm still the same girl, babe.'

I told her my news – the thing I'd been dying to tell her. 'I sort of kissed Kane,' I blurted.

'You *what*?'

'You heard me,' I said.

'LILY BASRA!!!' she screamed. 'You little minx!'

'Well,' I added, 'technically, he kissed me. A few times, actually.'

'Wow!'

I nodded. 'Am I stupid or what?' I said.

'You're *what*,' she told me. 'What's stupid about tonsil hockey with Kane?'

'I'm stuck in this nightmare – we all are – and I start something with a boy . . .' I replied.

'Kane's no *boy*,' joked Tilly. 'Wow. *Just*, like, *wow!*'

We chatted some more, and when I left, she gave me a massive hug.

'What was that for?' I asked.

'For being my girl,' she said.

'I'm always your girl,' I told her. 'Nothing's changed that.'

She shook her head, her pale cheeks taking on colour. 'You don't understand,' she said. 'I thought you hated me – because of my boyfriend. I thought we were going to fall out, like, permanently.'

'No way!' I told her, even though I'd believed that too. 'We argued, Tilly – nothing else. I know it felt like something final but I never believed it – not really. I won't lose you. I can't lose you.'

'Remember when I pushed you off that bus?' she said out of the blue.

'In Year Seven.' I nodded. 'How could I forget?'

'You shouted at me for ages and went home crying. I thought you'd never speak to me again then too . . .'

'But I did, didn't I?' I pointed out.

'I know and I'm so glad.'

'Tilly – are you OK?'

'Yeah,' she said. 'Just after these past few weeks –
I wouldn't know what to do without you.'

'Me too,' I told her.

'No – like you're the only true friend I have,' she
said. 'And life without a true friend – it ain't worth
living . . .'

35

At home, I tidied up, ate some toast and watched telly. Outside, evening was drawing in, and the sky was changing from pale blue to slate grey. Mum was late again, and as it was a Friday, I knew we'd have takeaway. I grabbed the pile of menus that we kept in a kitchen drawer, and leafed through them. The garden looked strange – the light tinged with green and the plants much more vividly coloured. A fat raindrop hit the window. Seconds later, the downpour began.

I watched the storm for a while, and then looked at my phone. I couldn't shake off the feeling of being watched. Was he out there right now, standing in the storm, waiting for me? I shivered.

The nasty messages from people at school had

stopped, replaced with texts from Kane, Mum and Tilly. I also had one from Danny:

Hello lovely – why you no talk to me?

I decided to reply.

Sorry – I thought you hated me. Over the Facebook thing with Molly?

I'm sorry about that. I should have known it wasn't you. Can you forgive me babe?

I'm here now, aren't I?

Have you seen the news?

About Molly?

Of course. Murder inquiry now. It's so creepy and so sad. Like being caught up in a nightmare. School is crazy. Thank God we're finishing soon.

Is it really that bad?

You know that day when flying ants hatch? It's like that, except with journalists not insects! They're camped outside.

I can't get my head around it.

Two murders they're saying now. Max AND Molly . . . it's fucking crazy. I feel so guilty too – for giving Molly all that shit. She was self-obsessed but she didn't deserve this. Her poor family.

I know – Max's too. I still can't believe it.

Me neither. It's like the school has been cursed. Anyway – gotta go.

Let's catch up soon, babe. I miss you!

I put the phone down and switched to BBC News 24. The anchor, a smiley brunette woman with shiny teeth, gave the camera a grave look.

'. . . latest on these shocking developments from Rosie Oswald, live in Leicester.'

The journalist stood outside school, exactly where every recent reporter had stood. I wondered if they took turns to have that spot. Her expression matched that of the newsreader. She didn't look much older than me.

'The focus of this enquiry – for so long about suicide and possible suicide pacts – has taken on dreadful dimensions. Officers now believe that the deaths of Molly Cooper and Max Jones are connected, and that both were murders. Sources close to the investigation said this afternoon that a third death, that of Amy Wiggins, may also be linked. All three pupils attended this school, and all were in Year Eleven. Locals I've spoken to, who wish to remain anonymous, have talked of rising disbelief and terror. A killer is on the loose in this area, and as yet police have no suspects and have made no arrests. One resident, a married mother of three, told me that she has banned her children from playing outside, and now takes them to and from school.

'I must stress that incidences of this nature are rare but nonetheless, tonight, in this leafy and well-to-do suburb of south Leicestershire, fear and tension reign . . .'

Sky and ITV were showing similar reports, and then I saw DI Meadows being interviewed back on the BBC. I wanted to switch off, but I couldn't. Only a knock at the door dragged me away.

Walking nervously into the hall, I gripped my phone like it was a weapon. Our front door was solid, so I couldn't see who was on the doorstep. I toyed with the idea of waiting until they'd gone. But what if it was important? Then I remembered that Kane was coming over. I relaxed a little, but still put the security chain on before I opened the door and peeked out.

A skinny man I didn't know stood under a dripping umbrella. He was about fifty, with stringy grey hair, jowly, stubbly cheeks and piggy blue eyes set too far apart. His light grey suit was shiny, the jacket and trousers creased and worn. He didn't look like much of a threat. He looked sleazy.

'Hello,' he said. 'Are you Molly?'

The next breath caught in my throat.

'This *is* the right address,' said the man. 'It's on your email . . .'

'Who are you?' I asked, clenching the phone tighter.

'Mr Davidson,' he replied. 'I booked yesterday? You look different to the photo on your profile. *Younger* . . .'

'*What* photo?'

'The HOOK-UP.com site?'

I was about to slam the door in his face when he smiled again. 'Maybe I'm after your mum?' he said. 'Are you Molly's daughter?'

'Molly who?' I asked.

'Molly Milf,' he told me.

My stomach nearly folded in on itself, and my heart began to thump.

'*No!*' I screamed, hoping to frighten him.

He took out a Nokia phone. 'Look,' he said, 'I've got the confirmation email. Today at six p.m. – only I'm a touch late. Full body massage with—'

'What?' My mind was racing. What did he mean about full body . . . ? And then it sank in. He thought he was visiting a prostitute. 'You've got five seconds to get lost,' I told him. 'Otherwise I'm calling the police.'

Panic spread across the man's face. He looked up and down the street. '*No!*' he said. 'No police.'

'Who sent you?' I snapped, realizing that he wasn't the hacker. He was just some sad old man.

'No one,' he almost whined. 'I booked through the website.'

I shook my head. 'Listen, you nasty little pervert – you've been tricked!'

'But I emailed you and we booked,' he insisted, his confidence increasing. 'And I'm not leaving until I get my services . . .'

I was about to scream through the doorway at him again when Kane appeared at the bottom of the drive. Relief crashed through my body and I whisked off the chain and slung the door wide open.

'Lily?' Kane shouted when he saw the man. 'You OK?' He ran to the door and grabbed the pervert. 'Who the *fuck* are you?'

'*PLEASE!*' moaned the man. 'I don't want any trouble!'

'I think Benedict sent him,' I told Kane. 'He's been tricked. He thinks a prostitute lives here.'

'Do you know who he is?' Kane asked the man, almost lifting him from his feet.

'*NO!*' The man cowered. 'I booked through a *website* . . .'

Kane was about to punch him when I took hold of his bicep.

'Don't,' I said. 'Let's just look at his phone, see if there's anything there.'

The man, glad to be free of Kane's hands, showed us the website he'd used. His entire body was shaking as he held out his phone. 'There,' he said. 'I'm not lying . . .'

The profile page for 'Molly Milf' showed my mum in a red bikini. The photo had been taken on holiday in Gran Canaria. It had been stolen from my Facebook archive.

'Did you meet or speak to the man who set this up?' demanded Kane.

'*No!*' the stranger insisted. 'I told you: all I do is book through the email system. I don't meet any men. I'm *not* a pervert!'

Kane grabbed his jacket. 'If you're lying to me . . .' he said.

'I'm *not* lying!' the man squealed. '*Please!*'

Kane looked at me and I shrugged. 'He's too scared to lie,' I said.

The man was trembling now, his eyes full of panic. I could tell he wanted to run away.

Kane held him with one hand as he answered me. 'You're sure?'

I nodded and saw relief on the stranger's face as Kane let him go.

'Get lost, you sad twat – go on!' Kane yelled at him.

As the man scuttled away, we went inside, and I sat down at the foot of the stairs.

'What the hell was that?' said Kane, crouching before me.

'It's *him*,' I whispered. 'It's *always* him – he won't leave me alone . . .'

My phone vibrated twice. I looked at it and shrieked.

That wasn't very nice, Lily. Why scream at a

customer? He would have paid £200 for something you'll end up giving away for free anyway. Silly you . . .

When Kane saw the message he ran back into the street. Only he didn't see anyone lurking, and no cars with people in them, watching the house. Just the brake lights of one vehicle, at the top of the street.

'He was outside,' I whispered.

'Call DC Evans,' said Kane. 'Your mum too.'

My hands trembled as I found the number and dialled. When I'd spoken to them both, Kane stood me up and I wrapped myself in his thick arms.

'Don't worry,' he said. 'You can count on me, Lily. I *promise*.'

36

After another endless, sleepless night, I'd never been happier to see white cloud, grey morning light and drizzle. Insomnia had made my eyes sore, and my head felt too heavy for my shoulders. I showered, dressed in jeans and a yellow Superdry polo shirt, and went down to find my mum doing housework. She looked worse than I did, and the frown lines across her forehead worried me.

'Can't sleep either,' she told me.

'You heard me last night?'

'Yes,' she said.

Her face was drawn and her milk chocolate eyes, usually bright and wide, were dull. The jeans she wore sagged off her behind, and her white shirt was a size too big. As soon as I saw her, guilt wormed its way around my head. It was my fault that she was under so much strain, and that wasn't a good feeling. She put the kettle on, and sat down with me.

'You and Kane are getting on well,' she said.

'Yeah, he's lovely,' I replied through a massive yawn. 'It's just a bit weird.'

She rose as the kettle came to a boil. 'What's weird?' she asked. 'That you were friends and now you're going out?'

'No,' I told her. 'That's easy. It's the other stuff. Like, I feel I should be mourning Max and Amy and be sad about Molly – and I am – but I'm also happy because I've got Kane. Makes me feel guilty sometimes . . .'

'You can't feel guilty because you're happy,' she said. 'What happened to Max and Molly isn't your doing. It isn't something anyone can control. Sometimes evil just happens.'

'Yeah,' I said, 'but why now and why us?'

'You don't control that either,' she told me, re-taking her seat. 'There's a Buddhist quote I remember my auntie telling me once; it's something like, we *have* to have Evil, in order for Good to prove itself greater. It's like the flipside of goodness, and maybe we can't have one without the other?'

'But it's so *unfair*,' I said. 'Max, Molly – even Amy, they're saying now – what did *they* do to anyone?'

Mum put her hand on mine. The table was covered in crumbs, brittle and flaky beneath my fingers. The wood was aged, and I studied a deep, nut-brown knot, as she spoke. 'When is Evil *ever* fair?' she asked. 'Look around the world, kid. It's the innocent who pay the biggest price – they always have.'

'Yeah,' I said, looking up at her. 'But you're, like, talking about war and stuff. That's different. This is outside our door. It's not about land or money or religion or whatever stupid reason people fight wars over. It's just random and senseless and I feel like I brought it into our lives because the hacker chose me.'

Mum shook her head. 'You didn't bring anyone in,' she said, stroking my hand now. 'This person, this thing, he decided that. You don't control his actions. You are not accountable.'

I wondered if Mum was as scared as I was. It would be just like her to show me a calm front. Underneath, she must have been worried.

'You can never know what people might do,' she added. 'You need to leave blame for the blame-worthy, Lily. You don't deserve it.'

We sat in silence for maybe ten minutes before Mum made me tea and toast.

'What are you doing today?' she asked.

'Absolutely nothing,' I told her.

'Then you can vacuum and mop the floors down-stairs,' she told me. 'All of them.'

'Hasn't Mr Warren dropped off any schoolwork?' I asked, desperate to get out of my chores.

'Oh, yes,' she replied. 'He arrived as I pulled into the drive yesterday. With everything going on I forgot.'

I nodded. 'He didn't come in then?'

'We teachers are busy people,' said Mum. 'We had a chat outside, though. He thinks you'll be OK to go back next week. It seems that witch you call Principal Woods has spoken to the police. The stupid, reactionary . . .' Her words tailed off before she swore, and I smiled at her.

'The work is by the phone,' she said. 'Chores first, though.'

The girl is wearing her pale blonde hair up. Her makeup-free skin is almost translucent, her eyes the colour of pale blue skies. The OTHER admires her graceful posture, the slightly elfish look she has, and the aroma of her perfume – light and floral with a touch of spice. She is dressed demurely – slim, charcoal trousers, a cream top with chiffon sleeves and a light checked coat. On her feet are cream court shoes with just a touch of heel. She has an overnight case, the kind that you can carry onto flights, and a small, square black leather purse. She looks perfect . . .

The OTHER drives them south, along the A6. He glances at the turnoff towards Wistow. Excitement, touched by a minor sense of loss, builds within. Given the choice, he would not want this. He would hold onto this one for a while longer. But he realizes that the Spider is right. If they want to stay free, they must protect themselves and tie up any loose ends. He glances at her. It is a shame.

'Have you ever ridden a horse?' he asks her.

'No,' she replies. 'Why?'

'I have a treat for you.'

'Really?'

'Yes – a friend of mine owns some stables on the way to the hotel. He's given us permission to borrow a horse.'

'You can't just borrow a horse, Dave – that's crazy! Won't it need proper care?'

The OTHER thinks quickly, but his focus slips. Her neck is so pretty. Her lips so flawless.

'I used to be a stable hand,' he tells her. 'Back when I was your age.'

'Really?'

'Yes.'

'I've never even thought about riding horses.'

'You should try everything once, Tilly.'

The Spider receives confirmation twenty minutes later. The girl is secured. He smiles and looks at the desk before him. Two sim cards. Two mobile phones. Two young people to play.

Once again, he runs through each detail of his next step. When he is sure, he is ready.

It's time to step out of the darkness . . .

37

He sent his next text as I finished my chores.

Hello, Lily – time to play?

I was going to ignore him, but anger got the better of me. I wanted to take the mop I'd just used and stick it up his arse. I typed quickly.

Booked in any more perverts lately?

That's very flippant. Aren't you worried about what I'm capable of? I would be, in your shoes . . .

I *was* worried – he was right about that – but I was also determined that he wouldn't know. That was what he wanted – for me to cower. He wanted that power over me. I was sure of it.

I'm not scared of you, you dickhead. You're the one who's anonymous. Don't hide yourself away . . .

Are you trying to psych me out? Wow – that's so, like, last century.

I'd changed so much since that first contact with him. He'd changed me. I'd been mouse-like back then. Now, even though I wasn't exactly a lion, I wasn't going to run and hide either. No matter how much he frightened me.

You're a coward – afraid to show your face.

If only you knew how far away you are from the truth.

I know the truth. If you were a man, you'd show yourself.

What makes you think I won't?

Because you're weak. You can pretend anything on the end of a keyboard. That's why you do it. In the real world, you're just a loser, aren't you?

Is that big lump Kane a real man? Would he have assaulted me if he'd caught me last night?

He would have killed you, you nasty little shit!

He is nothing, Lily. One of hundreds who believe the fist gives them control. I have more power in my fingers. In one finger. I can tap, tap, tap his life away, if I choose.

No you can't – that's the point. You sit there, pretend-ing to be all-powerful, but you can't face real people.

But I see real people every day, Lily. I see you and your friends. I see your teachers. I see . . .

Is that supposed to scare me?

You're already scared, Lily. You cower in your

bedroom, unable to sleep. I bet you dream of poor Max and Molly – swinging in the breeze . . .

That was the reply that did it. My anger gave way to utter terror and I felt my legs begin to quiver. It was just a game to him. Max and Molly had meant nothing. Even as I typed my next reply, trying to keep up my pretence at bravado, my hands were shaking.

Fuck you!

You're not my type, you dumpy bitch. Your mum, on the other hand . . .

I felt the air rush out of my lungs. My heart hammered against my chest cavity.

I could enter your house tonight, Lily. Through the rotten window in the downstairs loo? You know the one . . .

I felt sick. I wanted to run and check the window. What if he was outside right now? My stomach lurched.

After all, who would see me as I saunter down your side passage, through those overgrown shrubs? Or when I vault your fragile back gate and walk past the abandoned rabbit hutch? The one you and Tilly have carved your names on . . . ?

He was describing my garden perfectly. I felt bile rising but held it back. I wanted to scream but instead I typed:

Is there a point to these messages?

I dunno. Let's see what the day brings, shall we?

What does that mean?

Patience, Lily . . .

I grabbed the biggest knife I could find and walked slowly towards the downstairs toilet. The door was shut. I held the knife in front of me and opened it, bracing myself for his attack. I was so petrified I thought my teeth might fall out they chattered so much.

But nothing happened. I sighed with relief and slumped against the wall, trying not to sob.

Later that afternoon, as I sat in the kitchen and thought about my life, my phone buzzed with a call. The incoming number wasn't one I knew. I stared at it, unsure whether to answer it. It would be him . . .

But he hadn't disguised his number earlier. He didn't seem to care if I knew it. What if this call was urgent? What if something had happened to Mum or Tilly? Or Kane . . . ?

The line buzzed and crackled and I couldn't hear much – just a few snippets of a male voice. I ended the call, and studied the number again. As I wondered who it might be, a text came in from the same number:

Lily – it's Kane. My phone is playing up. This is a

spare. Can you meet me outside Costa? Urgent! It's about Tilly. Think she's in trouble . . .

My stomach somersaulted as I replied.

I'm coming now. What's going on?

I'll explain when you get here. Hurry, yeah?

I ran and grabbed a jacket, just as my mum came through the door with bags of shopping.

'I'm going out for a bit – to meet Kane,' I told her. 'Chores are all done.'

'Wait!' she asked. 'It's too dangerous. What if this man tries something? I want you here.'

I felt awful for lying but I had no choice. 'Kane's just up the road,' I said. 'At Tilly's. I'll be fine!'

I didn't give her time to register my words. Instead, I rushed out and hurried to the main road, desperately worried about my best friend . . .

The Spider brings all his pieces into play . . .

First the anonymous tip-off. The Spider – informing on *himself*. A simple phone call to the investigation team, his accent disguised. He even gives his own name. Well, the name he's been using, anyway. A man called Joseph Spinner has been seen with a young girl – several times. Their relationship is illegal. He is an adult and she is a schoolgirl – Tilly Anderson. It's sick. Joseph Spinner's address is . . .

Then the Spider instructed his accomplice for the last time. *Record the girl using the voice recorder function*, he told the OTHER. *Just the snippet of text I've given you. Send it to me and, afterwards, destroy the phone you use. Then wait for my arrival. Make yourself at home.*

Now, he sits in his car, some hundred metres from Lily's home. He watches Mrs Basra drive up the road back to her house. He grabs the phone – makes his call – holds a tape recording of static to the mouthpiece. When Lily hangs up, he sends her a text.

She replies quickly, and he responds in kind.

Within minutes she's hurrying up the street. She barely registers passers-by, never mind his non-descript, silver hire car. He recalls reading somewhere that the Toyota Corolla is the world's bestselling car ever. Bestselling and least memorable, obviously.

As the girl disappears round the corner, he picks up the second phone. He waits five minutes – then repeats his trick. This time he is the girl, texting her new boyfriend.

Kane! It's me – Lily! My phone is broken – using my mum's. I need help – please! I'm at Costa. Come now – he's after me!!!!

The speed of Kane's response causes the Spider to grin. Like lambs to the slaughter – another of his favourite clichés. Only, in this instance, they're running away from the scene . . .

Stay there – me and Alfie are coming now! If he comes near you, call for help!!

I will – please hurry!

Satisfied, the Spider exits his car. He strolls towards the house – checks his surroundings. The road is quiet

– empty save for an old woman walking her ridiculous dog. He reaches the door – knocks – places a clown mask over his face. He waits . . .

Laila Basra opens up, mumbling something about Lily forgetting her keys again. When she sees him, her eyes grow wide and her lips part in shock and fear. He grabs her round the mouth. She has no time to scream . . .

38

The moment I saw Kane, I burst into tears.

'*Where?*' he yelled. 'Where is he?'

I blinked at him through my tears. 'Where's who?' I asked, confused and alarmed at his tone. Around us, people stopped and gawped. Some shook their heads in disgust. Alfie was in his car, parked illegally in a disabled space. He gawped at us too.

'*Him!*' Kane repeated. 'The hacker! You said he was after you – in your text. I'm gonna kill him!'

'Kane,' I replied. 'I didn't send you a text about *him*. You messaged *me*. About Tilly?'

Kane's eyes lost their rage. His fists unclenched. 'But I didn't text you,' he told me. 'Lily – I *didn't*. I came because you said you were in trouble.' He showed me his phone. '*See?*'

'That's not my mum's number,' I whispered. 'I didn't send that.'

'Then who . . . ?'

We stared at each other as my phone vibrated in my pocket. I pulled it out, although in my heart I knew who it was.

Hey, Lily – got your mummy here. She's very pretty. Shall I kill her? Would you like that?

I lost it then – dropping the phone and shrieking to myself. He was at my house. He had my mum. Had got me out of the way so he could take her. Kane picked up my phone as I doubled over. My legs felt empty, my head grew weightless. I saw flashes of light before my pupils and Max's face in my mind. He was going to kill her too. He was going to kill my mum . . .

'Come on!' roared Kane. 'We've got to help her!' He almost lifted me off my feet and dragged me to Alfie's car. 'Don't speak, bro!' he ordered. 'Just drive – Lily's mum is in serious shit. Come on!'

As Alfie screeched away, Kane shouted my address at him and then rang the number DC Evans had given us for any emergencies. In the back, I sat frozen – unable to speak or think anything beyond how much I loved my mum. How I wouldn't be able to cope if she died . . .

When we reached the house, I couldn't leave the

car. I wanted to, but my legs started to shake and I was blubbing. The front door was ajar, the windows thrown wide open. Heavy, dark clouds hung low in the sky, and the rain got heavier.

Kane grabbed my hand. 'Come on – we've got to get inside!'

'C-can't,' I sobbed. 'He's killed her.'

Kane pulled me out. 'No,' he insisted. 'She's fine.'

'Scared!' I wailed. 'What if she's dead?'

'I'm with you, Lily,' he replied. 'Trust me . . .'

Alfie joined us. Kane told him to hold back as he ran for the house. We followed slowly behind. I heard Kane shouting for Mum. As Alfie and I entered, he came out of the living room and went into the kitchen. He moved slowly, just in case someone was waiting. She wasn't there, but the back door lay open, and the rain had soaked the tiles on the floor.

'I'll check upstairs,' he said.

We returned to the hall, and he went up slowly, careful with each step. My legs felt like dead weight – I was dragging them along. My chest was on fire and I could hear my own breath. The first floor was eerily dark for early evening, and Kane edged into the small bathroom. It was empty. Next came my room, the door partly open. Kane pushed it back on the frame, the hinges squeaking. I dreaded what we might discover inside. The contents of my belly frothed and bubbled.

'Careful, bro,' whispered Alfie.

Outside I heard sirens wailing in the distance. The police were coming. I wanted to scream but nothing came. Silent, shivering, I watched Kane enter my bedroom. Nothing . . .

'Shit!' he said.

Mum's room was empty too, and the spare.

Kane turned and looked at Alfie and me. 'She's not here,' he said.

'Garden?' Alfie suggested.

Kane led the way downstairs. Back in the kitchen, the table was a mess – one of the chairs missing. The floor was littered with broken crockery and Mum's shopping bags lay untouched by the fridge. My belly began to cramp and my hands shook.

'Wait here,' ordered Kane, but I found my breath and refused.

'No – I want to come,' I told him.

As the sirens drew nearer, we walked across the soaked lawn, Alfie wielding the large knife I'd used earlier and left by the sink. The shed sat against the rear fence, its door also ajar. Rain pounded its roof.

'She's in there,' I said, as I stared at the open door. The padlock lay on the floor. 'I just know it—'

Kane held out his arm, stopping three metres

from the entrance. 'Me first,' he said. 'No arguments!'

He moved forward, his fists clenched. Alfie had his back, the knife poised. I heard a muffled sound and knocking come from the shed.

'Kane!' I screamed.

He reached the door, and went in. I expected to hear him cry out in pain, as he was attacked. But I was wrong. Instead, he sounded relieved.

'Got her!' he yelled, and I ran to the shed.

Inside, my mum was tied to a chair, her mouth bound with tape. She looked scared witless. Except for her nose, I didn't see any blood or other wounds. Her eyes were wide, her expression pleading. Kane took the knife Alfie was holding and started to cut her free. In the garden, I heard shouts.

'*POLICE!*'

Alfie replied, telling them where we were. Then more voices, and a dog barking.

Kane carefully removed the tape from my mum's mouth. She started to cry, her eyes never leaving mine. As Kane worked on her hands, secured to the chair, he turned to me.

'There's something in her hand,' he said.

Through the sobs, I heard Mum call out my name. Relieved that she wasn't hurt, I felt rage build inside me – more powerful than I'd ever experienced before.

'Here,' said Kane, taking the object from my mum. 'It's silver . . .'

When I saw what it was, my heart nearly stopped. It wasn't *my* name she had called.

'TILLY!!!!' screamed my mum, as a police officer charged in.

Kane held out the bracelet charm – even in the gloom I saw the inscription on it, saw the unbroken clasp. *Sisters Forever* . . .

And I understood.

39

DI Meadows let Alfie go quickly. But Kane and me – he kept us close. He went over and over our stories, like we were the suspects. I could see Kane getting wound up, and when eventually Meadows relented, I reached across and took my boyfriend's hand.

'Thank you,' I whispered.

Kane nodded. We were in the kitchen, police officers searching and fingerprinting the entire house. Mum was opposite me, wrapped in a blanket, having been checked over by paramedics. The blood from her nose had been cleaned off. Bruising began to show around her right eye. DC Evans sat with her, both of them with their hands cupped around steaming mugs of tea. Despite being asked again and again, Mum couldn't give any real description of her attacker. He'd worn a mask and had overpowered her very quickly, knocking her out cold. She'd shaken as she replayed the events in her head, and I wanted to find him and kill him for hurting her. I had never been so angry.

I told them everything about Tilly, including the fact that she was seeing an older man in secret, and showed them all the latest messages from the hacker. DI Meadows rang someone else and they started searching for my best friend immediately.

Meadows contacted Tilly's mum too. I don't know how she'd reacted but I could imagine. I felt like shit – wishing that she would come round and slap me. I had wanted to keep my best friend, so I'd hidden her secret. Now she might be gone for ever and it would be my fault. The thought ate at my insides, but I tried to stay calm. Breaking down wouldn't change things, and I wanted to help.

When the kitchen was clear, and the search had begun, Meadows made himself a cuppa. He sat and eyed me, his skin condition calmer than when I'd last seen him. His fudge-brown suit was creased, his red tie loosened, and he had a fat dark bags under each eye.

'We had a tip-off,' he replied. 'Earlier this evening. Someone reported seeing Tilly with an adult male. He was arrested at his flat about thirty minutes ago.'

'Who is he?' asked Mum.

'I can't say yet,' he told us, 'but he's being questioned at the station.'

'Was Tilly there – when you arrested him?' I said, my hopes rising.

'No,' said Meadows, 'I'm afraid not.'

I looked away, fighting back tears.

'Is it someone we know?' Kane asked.

DC Evans exchanged a glance with Meadows, and he nodded.

'Yes,' said the PC. 'He's someone all the victims knew.'

Something didn't feel right. 'If he's been arrested,' I said, thinking aloud, 'then why wasn't Tilly with him?'

'That's something we're trying to ascertain,' said Meadows.

'Doesn't make sense,' I told him. 'Did they find any evidence in his flat?'

The officers exchanged another look. This time the senior shook his head.

'Can't say,' Meadows replied, but I could see that they hadn't. His downcast expression gave him away.

I felt useless – unable to help and just waiting on news. But that was all we had. Somewhere, *someone* would find Tilly, and then we'd know. Until that point, we were in limbo. Mum gave me a warm smile, but I knew I'd let her down. If I had told her about Tilly's relationship, she would have acted. And even though Tilly would be angry – maybe never speak to me again – at least she'd have been safe. She'd be tucked up in bed, texting crap to Danny Sangha; or down in the kitchen, arguing with her mum over the length of her skirt or what time she came home. She'd be OK.

And she wasn't OK. She wasn't safe. That's why he'd left the charm. It was a message. It was a boast about how clever he'd been – sending us one way, whilst he went the other. He was telling me that he had taken her. Just like he had taken the others. And there was nothing I could do about it . . .

DI Meadows left an hour later, and agreed to drop Kane at home. DC Evans was given baby-sitting duties over Mum and me. She looked less than pleased but had no choice.

'I think we're stretched over this,' she explained, once her boss had gone.

'Still not ideal, is it?' replied Mum. 'I bet it's hard enough being you as it is.'

DC Evans smiled. 'Wrong sort of plumbing never helps in this job,' she said.

Maybe that was why she'd been helping with

family liaison when we'd first met her. Why she had to look after us, whilst her male boss was out doing the interesting work. I felt sorry for her, but was pleased that she was close. She made me feel safe.

I made us scrambled eggs, toast and more tea, before Mum went to bed. She'd been trying to get hold of Dave but he wasn't answering his phone. I hoped that she would get through – his was a face I would have been relieved and happy to see. DC Evans checked the garden again, and every window and door, before she let Mum go upstairs. Then she sat in the living room and answered emails on her phone. I joined her, wondering what a career in the police might be like.

'You look shattered,' Evans said when she caught me staring.

'I am,' I told her. 'But I won't sleep.'

'You and Tilly are really close?'

'That charm?' I said. 'I gave it to her, back when we were kids. I've got one too. She's like my sister . . .'

Evans nodded. 'We're doing all we can,' she said.

'If I hadn't kept her secret,' I replied, 'maybe this wouldn't be happening.'

'Did you keep secrets for Max?' asked the DC. 'Amy? Molly Cooper? This chain of events isn't your fault, Lily. It's a rare, unforeseen occurrence . . .'

'Yeah, but—' I began, only for Evans to stop me.

'No,' she said. 'The only person to blame is the perpetrator. Don't go shouldering responsibility that you haven't earned . . .'

I nodded and looked at the muted pictures on the TV. 'My mum said that too,' I replied.

'Well, we can't both be wrong.'

The Spider sits outside the police station in another hire car, booked using the credit card of a Japanese man from Osaka. The flat they arrested him at is his own. The place where he lurks, however, is rented through a dummy company. Should they discover it, and they will, they won't find his name listed as a director. That name belongs to someone else. Someone who is yet to conclude his role in the game.

The man he calls the OTHER . . .

The Spider believes that the last three hours have been worth it. The police questioned him, and they harassed and cajoled him. Yet they have nothing on him – something he already knew. After all, they are merely the pawns. The Spider orchestrated every stage of this game. Every thread was woven carefully, painstakingly into the others, until the web was complete.

It is his creation and he is God here . . .

The police will never find the Spider. They won't even search for him. They search only for the killer. He will give them their man. The face that they will feed to the media. Like a gift, the Spider will present the police their quarry, cocooned in silk. And when their killer's name rings out from every news website in the world, the Spider will disappear back into the shadows. Ready to start again elsewhere.

The Spider yawns. He sets his alarm. Three hours of sleep are all he can allow. Then it is time to complete this game . . .

40

DC Evans slept on the sofa, and in the morning a uniformed Asian woman called PC Kaur replaced her. Mum slept late, and I did nothing – just watching telly, texting Kane and thinking about Tilly.

PC Kaur was slightly built, with big brown eyes and short black hair. She stayed in the living room with me, trying to chat. I was too tired to respond, however – too overwhelmed by what had happened. School, revision, exams – none of it mattered now. Only Tilly.

At around midday, DC Evans came back and the uniformed officer seemed glad to leave.

'Has anything happened?'

DC Evans shrugged. 'You'll see it on the news anyway,' she told me. 'The man we arrested last night – a man called Joseph Spinner. We had to release him.'

'Why?'

'Because it's not him,' she said. 'We had nothing to hold him on – no evidence, nothing. It was just a prank call. Some idiot wasting our time.'

I didn't know anyone called Joseph Spinner. But I did know I'd been right about DI Meadows's downcast expression the night before.

'You said we knew him,' I reminded her. 'Last night? You said the victims knew the man you'd arrested.'

'They did. He works at your school.'

'But I don't know anyone by that name,' I told her.

DC Evans sighed, grabbed my remote control and switched to Sky News. 'His name got leaked to the press overnight,' she said. 'Joseph Spinner is an IT technician employed at your school.'

'*Him?*'

He didn't look like a killer. He was just some gamer-boy nerd with a job. More importantly, why would someone play such a stupid prank at such an important time? The murder enquiry was national news. Three young people were dead and another one missing. What went through the minds of the idiots who wasted police time like that?

'You do know him, then?'

I nodded, just as Sky News ran the story. 'Never spoken to him, though,' I told her. 'He doesn't teach or anything. Just helps out when IT goes wrong.'

'My boss was going crazy,' she said. 'About the tip-off *and* the leak. Says Mr Spinner could sue us . . .'

'So, nothing new on Tilly?'

DC Evans nodded. 'We've found some stuff,' she told me. 'The Hi-Tech Crime Unit have managed to unravel all the IP trails . . .'

I felt my excitement rising. Hope too. 'Where do they point?'

She shook her head. 'That, I can't say,' she replied. 'Don't worry – the way our department leaks, it'll be on Twitter by tea time.'

My phone buzzed, making the coffee table vibrate. 'Could you pass me that, please?' I asked DC Evans.

She shook her head, smiled warmly, and picked it up. 'I want one of these,' she told me, studying the screen. Then, suddenly, her face changed – the warm smile became a glare.

'What is it?'

She paused before replying. 'It's Tilly,' she said.

An instant wave of nausea hit me.

'She's just sent you a message . . .'

I felt the shock before my expression revealed it. DC Evans handed me the phone.

Please call me. Now!

I shook my head. He wasn't getting me again.

'It's *him*,' I told DC Evans. 'This is another game . . . what do I do?'

Evans thought quickly. 'Call back,' she told me. 'Put it on speaker . . .' She got out her older smartphone and found the memo recorder function. She placed it on the table. 'Put yours next to it,' she said. 'I'll hit record when it's answered. It's not ideal but it's all I've got . . .'

I sat upright and did what she said. Tilly's phone rang a few times before being picked up. DC Evans tapped the screen on hers to begin recording.

'*Hello, Lily – Mummy feeling better, is she?*'

His voice had a metallic, raspy edge. Something hit me. Why would someone I didn't know disguise his voice? There seemed little point.

'*Are you there, Lily? Do speak up!*'

I looked to DC Evans for help. She nodded and mouthed 'Act normal'.

'Where's Tilly, you freak?'

Evans rolled her eyes, then shook her head.

'*Hello, lovely Lily – how are your thunderous thighs this fine morning?*'

'Tell me where she is!' I yelled, causing DC Evans to flinch slightly.

'*Maybe. Depends on how good you are.*'

'I'm not playing your games any more!'

'*That makes two of us then . . .*'

'What?'

'*I'm tired of all of this, Lily. I might leave this place — go on to better things. Bigger things. This world is so mind-numbingly tiresome.*'

'See — I said you were a coward — always hiding.'

'*You see — that's where you go astray, Lily. Always quick to make assumptions. I can go away and stay in the spotlight simultaneously . . .*'

'I don't understand.'

'*Why would you, Lily? You've been raised on a diet of tedious and dreary nonsense masquerading as culture. You're a dunce, Lily — an obtuse poster-girl for a simple-minded, unperceptive generation.*'

'You talk shit, Benedict.'

'*Benedict? Oh, he was erased a while ago, Lily. This is me. The real me . . .*'

DC Evans wrote 'TILLY????' in her notebook and thrust it at me. I nodded.

'Where is Tilly?'

'*Tilly is safe. Do you want to see her?*'

DC Evans nodded vigorously.

'Yes.'

'*Then tell the lovely officer sitting with you that I will call back in forty minutes. Bye!*'

DC Evans's eyes lit up and, like Kane had done, she ran outside to find him. And just like Kane she was too late.

'Bastard!' she yelled, as she trudged through the door.

Mum came downstairs, dressed and with a towel wrapped around her head. 'What's going on?' she asked.

DC Evans shook her head and explained everything.

The OTHER replies immediately. The Spider tells him to get ready.

'Where the fuck have you been?' asks the OTHER.

'Cleaning up your mess,' the Spider replies.

'Well, hurry up – I'm getting pissed off.'

'I will be there in twenty minutes.'

'You'd better be.'

The Spider brakes to a halt. Some things cannot be allowed to stand. There is a hierarchy. There are rules. 'If you wish,' the Spider tells him, 'I could drive elsewhere. Perhaps to the police station? Maybe I might try my skills out on your life. Your credit card, your reputation . . .?'

'I'm just annoyed about being here for so long,' the OTHER whines. 'Nothing personal.'

'That is good to hear,' the Spider replies. 'I'd hate to get *personal* with you.'

'Yeah – sorry.'

'Be ready for me.'

The call ends. The Spider shakes his head. No partners next time . . .

41

He called back on time. Almost to the second. His voice remained disguised.

'*Are you ready?*'

By that point, the house was full of police officers. This time DI Meadows was my guide. He nodded, as the technicians began to record the call.

DC Evans stood on the periphery with Mum, looking pissed off.

'Where is she?'

'*I will text you the location. Where is the police officer – DC Evans?*'

Meadows raised an eyebrow then motioned for Evans to approach. Her mood changed immediately.

'I'm here, Mr . . . ?'

'*Very witty, DC Evans. You won't catch me out.*'

'They all say that.'

'They *are all average. I am special. To be the early bird with me, DC Evans, you would have needed to wake up months ago. You cannot dream up a predator such as me. I am the Alpha*—'

'Just shut up and tell us where she is!'

The last reply was mine. Meadows gave me a death glare, while Evans half smiled and gave me a wink. I felt the blood rush into my face, colouring my cheeks.

'*Thank you for that interjection, Lily. I'm with you — all this waffle when you could be saving your best friend.*'

'What do you want?'

'*DC Evans and Lily must come alone. I will be watching. If I see any sign of other officers, Tilly dies.*'

'I won't bring the girl.'

'*DC Evans — you will do what I say. You and Lily — you have precisely thirty minutes. If you are late, she dies. If you disobey me, she dies. I would think on that, DC Evans. I would think very carefully . . .*'

'I understand. How do we know Tilly is still alive?'

We heard shuffling over the line, then Tilly sobbing into the phone.

I spoke first. 'Tilly!'

'*Help me please! Lily??? Lily???*'

My heart raced and I could feel the blood it pumped around my body. She was alive. My sister was alive! 'We're coming – me and a police officer,' I told her.

'*Please . . . please!!!*'

DC Evans took over. 'Are you OK, Tilly? Has he hurt you?'

'*Now, now, DC Evans – you've had your chat. Time to play.*'

'But I—'

The line went dead.

Around me, DI Meadows was making hand gestures to his colleagues. Mum looked at me and shook her head. I nodded in return. The officers had a quick conference. Within seconds, they had decided a strategy. Mum told them I couldn't go but DC Evans talked her around.

'She'll be with me,' Evans said to her. 'I won't let anything happen. I promise, Laila.'

DI Meadows called Evans over. They stood and whispered to each other in the hallway, their hand gestures animated. Eventually both returned.

'It's not something we'd ordinarily ask,' Meadows said to Mum. 'But DC Evans is right. We have so little time. We'll put your daughter in a protective vest and every step she takes will be covered . . .'

Mum nodded.

'As soon as he confirms the location, I'll have units cordon off the area,' Meadows added. 'The perimeter will be wide – he won't see us.'

'Air Support a go!' shouted another officer from the living-room door.

Meadows acknowledged him and looked at Mum. 'You see?' he said. 'We have everything in hand, Mrs Basra.'

'*Mum?*' I said.

'I can't,' she replied. 'If you get hurt I'll . . .'

'I *have* to go!' I insisted. 'I didn't tell you about Tilly's secret man. It's *my* fault and I want to make it right! If something happens to her, I won't be able to take it. At least this way, I tried to make amends. I tried to put things right!'

Mum gave me a hug and wiped away tears. 'OK,' she said, 'but you *listen* to DC Evans, OK? You do everything she asks . . .'

'I will,' I told her.

A minute later the text arrived. Evans grabbed the phone. 'Sat-nav coordinates,' she said. 'Let's go!'

Fear began to creep into my mind but I fought back with anger. I *wanted* to see this man. I *wanted* to face him. I was going to watch him pay . . .

The girl is beautiful, according to some. Her hair is straight and pale yellow, her face sharp angles and symmetry. Her lips are plump bows, her body lithe and toned.

The Spider moves closer to her, watches her chest rise and fall. Her eyes betray her fear, as does the fetid stench of her breath. She mumbles and sobs, and he realizes that she is pleading with him. He savours her insignificance . . .

The OTHER is already gone. Moments earlier, he watched the Spider try out the noose. The Spider had attached it to the upper section of the platform. Made a show of testing its strength. He'd pulled it and checked it – narrowed and widened the loop. Eventually, he'd asked the OTHER for an opinion.

The man had approached – oblivious to the peril. He'd stood before the Spider, peering at the rope.

'Will it hold?' the Spider had asked.

'Looks fine to me.'

'Just check the boards,' the Spider had urged. 'The building is old. We have to be sure.'

The OTHER had moved closer to the edge, his back to the Spider. One smooth movement was all it took. Loosen the loop. Slip it over his head. Push him out into the air.

The OTHER was gone the moment his neck snapped. No time to reflect, to think beyond his utter shock at the way his life was ending. His legs twitched and twisted, his ultimate death mask a grimace.

Now, only the girl remains. Once she has stopped screaming into her gag, he moves towards her. Her chest rises again and he smiles. She begs with her eyes, her face a patchwork of pale skin and scarlet blotches. There is no saving her. No mercy. She will become the Spider's last message. Lily will understand, he thinks. She will know, each time she fails to sleep, that the Spider is true to his word. That now his power transcends the boundary between real and cyber . . .

The Spider looks at his watch. He runs through every detail one last time. Ticks every box, follows every thread. Satisfied that he can leave without being followed, he relaxes at long last. His work is almost done.

When it is time, he strokes the girl's face. He whispers to her, tells her not to cry.

'Everyone will know your name,' he tells her. 'Your face will grace a thousand websites. Tears are not appropriate.'

Then he positions her beside her lover. She begins to shake her head. Tries to struggle. He whispers one final message.

'Lily's next . . .'

He shoves her with his right leg.

The rope snaps with tension and she is no more . . .

42

We drove south for a few miles, before eventually turning right down a narrow road. DC Evans said nothing as her radio squawked – she was concentrating on the road. A couple of miles along, a track appeared to our left. It seemed to disappear into a dense copse. DC Evans stopped and looked at her sat-nav.

'That must be it,' she said, reversing and taking the turn-off.

'Hurry, please!' I told her. 'We have to get there in time . . .'

The track was tight and rutted. Trees towered on each side, creating a canopy above us and casting long shadows in the gloom. My nerves returned, and my stomach knotted. The going was slow, but after maybe five minutes we emerged in a clearing. A semi-derelict barn stood in the centre. Building materials surrounded it – concrete blocks, bags of sand and bricks – and part of the rear had been renovated.

'This looks like an abandoned project,' said DC Evans. She parked the car and waited a moment. Then she spoke to her boss, describing the scene for him. Turning to me, she set out the rules. 'You wait here,' she said. 'I'll go in, and make sure it's safe.'

'But if he's in there,' I replied, 'you'll be in danger.'

DC Evans smiled. 'That's what I get paid for,' she told me. 'Whatever happens, you don't move, OK?'

'OK.'

'I'm serious, Lily – we're surrounded by backup, and air support is ready. If he's in there, we'll get him, even if he runs. There's no escape for him now.'

'I don't care about *him*,' I told her. 'I just want Tilly.'

Evans radioed in, and spoke to DI Meadows. When he gave her the signal, she exited the car. The doors were fifty metres away, and she walked carefully, a baton in her right hand. I watched the building for signs of movement, and wondered where the other officers were. What if he was watching? I thought. He might see them and then he'd kill Tilly. I started to panic, and the car began to close in. I opened my door, fighting to breathe.

Up ahead, DC Evans was nearing the barn doors. She didn't hear me open the car door – her focus was trained on the barn. She approached the entrance and walked through, tense and ready to strike. I followed her steps, unsure of what I was doing. I only wanted to see Tilly. Nothing else mattered. Not my safety, not *him* – just my best friend.

When DC Evans reappeared quickly, her face pale, her mouth open, I knew something was wrong. She reached for her phone and made a call, taking deep breaths . . .

I ran then, closing the distance quickly. She heard me approaching and shouted for me to stop.

'*NO, LILY!!!*' she screamed.

I avoided her attempts at stopping me, and burst into the barn. In front of me, hanging from a mezzanine level, were two bodies . . .

One was Tilly. She was naked, her expression almost serene. Vomit bubbled in my stomach, erupting towards my mouth.

The second body was that of our form teacher, Mr Warren . . .

Dave Warren . . .

Three months later . . .

I stood watching Tilly's mum being led away by her ex-husband. She was dressed in black and wailing. Her legs started to buckle but Mr Anderson held onto her. I wiped my eyes and wondered where he'd been when Tilly had needed him. Thing is, I was transferring my own guilt and anger.

Tilly's dad hadn't kept her affair a secret.

Tilly's dad hadn't let her face danger.

Tilly's dad hadn't got her killed.

That was down to me . . .

I was standing under an oak tree, the rain getting heavier each minute. The droplets hit the ground with such force that they seemed to bounce. I watched them because I didn't want to look up. I didn't want to see the faces of my ex-schoolmates and their parents. Dr Woods, Mr Dhindsa and Dave were still at the graveside, huddled under a large black umbrella. Apart from Dave, I had no desire to see any of them.

My mum was by the car. She was chatting to Kane's mum, Deanna, probably about how she and Dave were trying again. They'd become closer since Tilly had died, and it was good to have him around the house again.

Kane had his arm around my back. He was explaining why Danny hadn't come. Apparently, he'd been too distraught and his family were still on his back about being gay. We'd hardly communicated at all recently, and I knew he was someone I would lose touch with. On the few occasions we had messaged each other, he'd been sharp and to the point. I suppose he was one of many who would always blame me for what happened to Tilly – just like her mum.

Mr Warren turned out to be the killer. The police linked him to every death – Amy, Max, Molly and Tilly. The shock wave was huge. No one could quite believe it. That one of the most respected and loved teachers at our school could hide such a dark secret was hard to understand.

But the evidence had been conclusive. It was all linked to him – the rope used to hang each of them,

Max's ring, and Molly's tote bag . . . The digital evidence was the same. From Charlotte to Benedict to the Fat Bitch page aimed at Amy – the trails all went back to his IP address.

And when the police checked into his background, they found other cases that aroused their suspicion. There was mounting speculation that he'd done it before, and that he'd committed suicide as a final act – to gain notoriety as a serial murderer.

The media were like sharks at feeding time – thrashing about looking for any advantage. They covered every detail of the investigation and printed story after story. Even now, three months later, with the investigation over, and the funerals finally planned, the coverage went on.

See, no one could understand why. Like, maybe they got that David Warren and Tilly were having an affair, and the teacher was scared of getting caught, but why had he killed the others as well as himself? And then why leave the evidence just lying around? The journalists made up theory after theory, even after the police had revealed his links to other possible victims. From a suicide pact to a religious cult – they even suggested that Tilly and Warren had planned it together. That they'd made some weird death contract with each other. It was all bollocks and it drove me insane with rage.

I no longer cared why he'd done it – only that he had. My heart was filled with grief and guilt and I felt empty inside. I wanted my sister back, and would have done anything to make that dream come true. If he had been standing with me now, telling me to kill myself in order to save Tilly, I would have done it.

He had taken everything. I didn't go back to school, never mind sit my GCSEs – I couldn't. I had long counselling sessions, and my mum took extended leave to look after me. I was given strong medication that knocked me out most days, and left me a trembling mess for the rest . . .

But I pulled through, and slowly I started to get on with things. I was doing it slowly, and needed support from Mum and Kane, but the physical pain was over. My stomach no longer ached, the phantom stabbing pains in my chest disappeared and my head no longer throbbed all day, every day. I was even considering going back to college, to restart my stalled education. But that was still a way off.

Emotionally, I was still at that abandoned barn, looking up at Tilly's body hanging from a rope. It was an image that I would never break free from – I knew that. The counsellor had said that, at best, the vivid colours of it might fade to black and white – but it would always be with me. She compared my case to shell shock, like people got during wars, and said that I was traumatized.

I didn't know what I was. I just knew that I missed Tilly and that my life would never be complete again. Not without her . . .

Kane said he was going to talk to some lads he knew. I nodded and watched him walk over to them. The rain was easing now, and people were starting to leave. Molly's funeral was happening later the same afternoon and I guessed that most of them were planning to attend that too. I looked over at Mum and she gave me a little half-smile. Safe in the knowledge that she and Kane were close by, I decided to walk around the edge of the cemetery. The path that encircled the graveyard was visible at every point; I'd never lose sight of either of them. In fact, I'd not lost sight of them for the past three months – one of them was always around, just to reassure me.

I had reached the furthest point from Tilly's freshly filled grave when the IT technician who'd been wrongly arrested walked through the nearby gates. He was wearing grey combats, a red and white plaid shirt and heavy walking boots. A backpack hung from his left shoulder. I stopped dead in my tracks, wary, even when he smiled at me.

'Lily, isn't it?' he said. 'We've never met but I'm Joe Spinner.'

I nodded. 'I know who you are,' I told him. 'The funeral is over.'

He shook his head. 'Story of my life,' he told me. 'Always late.'

I told him that the other teachers were still around if he wanted to see them, but he shook his head.

'I don't work at your school any more,' he revealed. 'I got offered a post in the Middle East – Oman . . .'

I wondered why he was telling me his business. When he asked how I was feeling, I shrugged.

'What's it to you?' I asked, unconcerned that I sounded rude. I didn't care about much any more.

'It must be hard, that's all,' he told me. 'After all, you're the only one left now.' His voice dropped. 'No more Lily and Tilly Show . . .'

I stood and stared at him, my mouth hanging open. How on earth could he know about that? My legs trembled but I couldn't move. I wanted to call to Mum and Kane but my tongue felt suddenly thick, like it was too big for my mouth. I nearly retched. *Dave Warren* was the killer. *This* was all wrong . . .

Joe Spinner pulled a knife from his pocket and held it by his right side. I could see it clearly but anyone watching from Tilly's graveside wouldn't.

'Just a little insurance in case you decide to scream,' he said. 'I'm glad we can finally meet. I've watched you, but you're never alone. Good job you decided to go for a walk today. I was running out of time.'

The only word that escaped sounded like a desperate gasp for air: 'Why?'

He looked at me and smiled. I saw the cruelty in his eyes, the kick he got from what he was doing. I realized then that I was looking into the face of real evil. He was the man behind it all. He was 'Benedict'; he was 'Charlotte'.

'What can I say?' he replied. '*Why* is such an awkward question to answer. You see, most people only understand murders when they come wrapped in nice, neat boxes, complete with instructions.'

I turned to look at Mum but she was busy chatting, and didn't notice. Now that the police had closed the case, she was no longer too worried about me being in danger. My stomach felt like it had been washed out with acid. I wanted to vomit.

'*Look* at me!' he snapped.

I turned back and saw rage in his eyes. Yet as soon as he smiled it seemed to vanish, as though he could turn it on and off at will.

'There are no nice, neat boxes here,' he continued. 'No instructions. See, if I were a jealous ex-lover, people would understand. If I stabbed my neighbour over a fence dispute, people would get it. They read about criminals who kill each other and it makes sense to them. Murder always has a reason, doesn't it?'

I nodded, still unable or unwilling to move. I didn't know which.

'*Wrong*, Lily!' he said, his voice filled with almost childish delight. 'See, when I showed Amy how to tie the noose, and helped her to place it round her neck, I wasn't angry or jealous, or after her money. I had no motive, not really. And, besides, she wanted to die. I just helped her to achieve her dream.'

I blinked hard and wondered if Kane had seen us yet. In my head, I imagined him running over, tackling Joe Spinner to the ground and taking the knife. But that wasn't going to happen.

'The same with Molly and Max. They were just things that I wanted to destroy. They fell into my web by clicking on the video of Amy's – just as you did.' He paused and looked around the cemetery behind me. Satisfied that no one was coming, he continued. 'Tilly too,' he said. 'I didn't hate her or anything. You *see* – it doesn't always make sense, does it?'

I nodded again. 'Just do what you came to do,' I said, thinking that I was about to die. I thought about Amy and Max and Molly, and most of all, I heard Tilly's laugh echoing around inside my head. Maybe this was what I deserved . . .

Only, he didn't kill me. He just started to laugh.

'I'm not here to *murder* you,' he said. 'I just wanted to *meet* you. To let you know that I'm going to walk away. That I've done all of this and I will never pay . . .'

I felt my throat loosen and more words came tumbling out. 'I could tell the police,' I said.

'Tell them what, you silly little bitch?' Again the rage in his eyes went on and off in a flash. 'You have nothing on me,' he continued. 'And they have everything on Dave Warren. It's all tied up and pretty, just how they like it. They won't change that for *you*. I gave them their killer . . .'

I shook my head. 'I don't understand why you're here. Why not just walk away?'

'I told you. I'm here because I wanted to meet you,' he said. 'I wanted to explain.'

'But you haven't said why,' I replied. 'You're just talking shit, like you did online.'

'Ah – good old Benedict . . . he got you, didn't he?'

I wanted to take his knife and push it through his head. He sensed my anger.

'Wow,' he told me. 'Didn't know you had that in

you, Lily. That's the fight I saw in Tilly's eyes, right before I kicked her off that ledge. Just think of the confidence I've given you. Back in January you were pathetic. Tilly's lapdog. You should be thanking me . . .'

My eyes began to water, as he looked around one last time.

'OK,' he said. 'I'll tell you why. I killed Tilly and the others for one reason alone. I did it because I could.'

'You did it for fun?'

My heart started to tear open. Inside, something was yelling . . .

'For the *game*,' he replied. 'The same reason I'm letting you live too.'

'The game?'

He nodded. 'I'm letting you live because it's worse than killing you. That would be too easy. Just think, tonight when you go to bed, and the whole world is reading about psycho Warren and his serial murders, you'll *know* . . .'

He looked deep into my eyes as the voice in my chest started to get louder.

'You'll *know* that I'm out there. That I did all this and walked away. And you'll never be able to tell, Lily, because no one will believe you. They'll just think you've gone crazy again. It will be our little secret, Lily – yours and mine – to share, for ever . . .'

He turned and walked to the gates, but I still couldn't move. When he stopped and turned back, he was smiling again.

'Have a nice life, Lily Basra. I'll send you a post-card sometime . . .'